THE CHRONICLE OF
BASEBALL

THIS IS A CARLTON BOOK

A CIP catalogue record for this book is available upon request

Note: all statistics correct to the end of the 1999 season

ISBN 1 84222 069 1

Project editor: Chris Hawkes
Editorial assistant: Luke Friend
Project art direction: Fiona MacDuff
Picture research: Debora Fioravanti
Production: Lisa French

Printed in the United States

Carlton Books Limited
20 Mortimer Street
London W1N 7RD

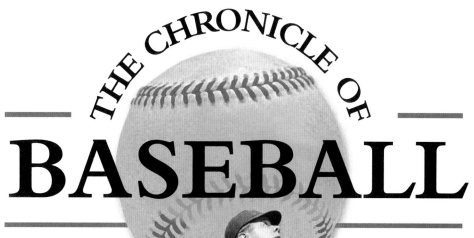

THE CHRONICLE OF
BASEBALL

A CENTURY OF
MAJOR LEAGUE ACTION

J O H N   M E H N O

CARLTON
BOOKS

Contents

1900

1910

1920

1930

1940

1950

1960

1970

1980

1990

Foreword

I was introduced to the game of baseball, like many youngsters in America, by my father and I immediately fell in love with the game. It was something about the feel of a bat hitting a ball and sending that sphere off to far away distances that captured many of my thoughts and continued to do so for almost 50 years. I became one of the fortunate few.

In nearly 130 years of professional baseball slightly less than 16,000 men have reached the pinnacle of Major League Baseball. After making it to the major leagues in 1970 with my home town New York Mets, I played for the next 15 years at baseball's highest level. Following my playing career which was spent with three teams, the Mets, the Montreal Expos, and finally the Baltimore Orioles, I moved to the broadcast booth where I have been working for the past 16 years, first with the Montreal Expos and currently with the Madison Square Garden Network working on New York Yankee telecasts. Combine my playing and broadcast experience and I have spent the last 31 years working in the major leagues and during those years I have seen many changes both in and around the game.

Let's start with the most important aspect of the game of baseball, the players. Almost a quarter of a century ago and after much legal rangling the players gained the right to free agency which raised salaries drastically as teams sought to either obtain or retain those players whose contracts had expired. For example, when I was employed with the Baltimore Orioles, my salary for the 1976 season was somewhere around $80,000 for the season. My contract with the Orioles expired after that season and they decided that I was a player they would like to keep. My next contract called for $250,000 a year for the next five years. Without the threat of free agency that raise in salary would not have happened. Now those numbers pale in comparison to those of players today. The *minimum* salary for a rookie or a first year player is $200,000. The top stars in baseball now earn upwards of $15,000,000 a season with no end in sight to the upward spiral of the growing money tree.

The physical abilities of today's players have changed as well. Players are bigger and stronger than in the past. Much more emphasis is placed on weight training and overall strength. Power is the name of the modern game and there's more home run hitting and offense than ever before. Fans will pay to see the home runs fly out of ballparks and are coming to games in droves. One would get the idea that plenty of money is floating around the business of baseball, and believe me, it is a business. While players salaries are widely published and many fans know exactly what most of the top stars are making, no one knows exactly what the owners are coming away with. I personally don't feel they would pay the players this type of money if they couldn't afford it.

Much of the revenue for the owners of the teams comes from television. This is another area where baseball has changed in recent times. Almost every game is on television, either locally, nationally and now internationally. More and more players are coming from around the world as baseball becomes more and more popular. Asians and Australians are working their way into the major leagues and in the not too distant future I believe we will see players from Europe and Africa playing baseball in ballparks like Yankee Stadium.

The future for the growth of the game on a worldwide basis is unlimited. The only problem might be that baseball can be hard to learn for a novice because of all the rules and strategy. If patient, a person can become a lifelong fan like myself.

Enjoy the game of baseball,

Ken Singleton, July 2000

1900

Professional baseball certainly wasn't new in 1900, but the game was evolving into the structure that would last the rest of the century.

The National League was dominant, but encountered a significant rival when the old Western League was turned into the American League. After a few years of open warfare that was both expensive and destructive, the National League accepted the American League on equal terms, setting up a format that would become familiar to baseball fans for many generations.

The leagues would be separate but equal and did not interact. That added some spice when petty self-interests were finally put aside so that the two champions could meet each fall in a World Series to settle supremacy. The title may have been grandiose, but the Series was clearly baseball's showcase event because of the rooting interest in both leagues.

The biggest star of the decade was Pittsburgh Pirates' shortstop Honus Wagner, an oddly built but skilled player who led his team to four pennants. The volatile John McGraw whipped the New York Giants into a winner.

Ty Cobb made his debut with the Detroit Tigers and ran the bases ferociously in an era when the stolen base was still the leading offensive weapon.

LEADERS

BATTING AVERAGE
Honus Wagner, Pittsburgh, .381

HOME RUNS
Herman Long, Boston Braves, 12

RUNS BATTED IN
Elmer Flick, Philadelphia Phillies, 110

STOLEN BASES
Patsy Donovan, St. Louis Cardinals;
George Van Haltren, NY Giants, 45

PITCHING VICTORIES
Joe McGinnity, Boston Braves, 29

EARNED RUN AVERAGE
Rube Waddell, Pittsburgh, 2.37

STRIKEOUTS
Rube Waddell, Pittsburgh, 130

Pittsburgh's Honus Wagner
was the game's obvious star

It cost the princely sum of 25 cents to get into a baseball game at the turn of the new century.

For that quarter, you were likely to see a game that emphasized stolen bases as the primary way to ignite offensive opportunities. You were also likely to see just two pitchers, since pitchers were generally expected to finish what they started in those days.

You could count yourself lucky if you saw a ball fly over the fence since home runs were something of a rarity in an era when the baseball flew about as efficiently as a well-rounded rock. In 1900, no team would hit more than 48 home runs in the 146-game season and no individual would hit more than Herman Long of the Boston Beaneaters, who had 12.

SHORTS Interest in unionizing baseball players started around the same time that professional baseball got off the ground. Samuel Gompers, president of the American Federation of Labor, announced plans to pursue a players' union in April. By summer, each club sent three delegates to a meeting in New York and the Players Protective Association was formed.

Brooklyn manager Ned Hanlon

True major league baseball was restricted to the National League, which showcased its product in eight cities: Brooklyn, New York, Boston, Pittsburgh, Philadelphia, Chicago, St. Louis and Cincinnati. Those western excursions to St. Louis were the exotic long-distance trips.

The league's biggest star was Honus Wagner, the Pittsburgh outfielder. The squatty Wagner had started his career with Louisville. When that franchise folded as part of the National League's reduction, Wagner was one of many players owner Barney Dreyfuss transferred to his other franchise in Pittsburgh.

Wagner batted .381, hit four home runs and drove in 100 runs. In addition to leading the league in batting average, he also had the top slugging percentage (.573), led the league in doubles (45), triples (22) and total bases (302).

Magnificent as Wagner's season was, Pittsburgh still finished second, 4½ games behind Brooklyn. The Superbas had the league's most dangerous offense, led by Wee Willie Keeler, who finished fourth in the batting race with a .362 average. Keeler led the league in hits with 204 and was famous for a hitting philosophy as simple and pragmatic as it was ungrammatical: "Hit 'em where they ain't."

Keeler had 253 total bases to rank fourth in the league. He was also No. 4 in stolen bases with 41.

Brooklyn's best pitcher was Iron Joe McGinnity, who was 28–8 with a 2.94 earned run average. McGinnity struck out 93 batters while walking 113 in his league-leading 343 innings and completed 32 of his 27 starts. McGinnity's winning percentage of .778 was the league's best.

Pittsburgh boasted a pair of 20-game winners in righthander Deacon Phillippe and lefthander Jesse Tannehill. Phillippe was 20–13 with a 2.84 ERA and Tannehill posted a 20–6 record with a 2.88 ERA. Tannehill was second to McGinnity in winning percentage.

Philadelphia was the only other team in the league to post a winning record. The Phillies were 75–63, which put them eight games behind first-place Brooklyn. The Phillies had the league's best catcher in Ed McFarland, who hit

Hitting 'em where they ain't was Wee Willie Keeler's forte

.305 with 38 RBIs. He did not hit a home run. The Phillies also boasted one of the game's great hitters in Napoleon (Larry) Lajoie. He hit .337 with seven homers and 92 RBIs. Lajoie would turn out to be not long for the Phillies, thanks to the raiding of the upstart American League.

The Phillies also had one of the game's best outfielders in 24-year-old Elmer Flick, who posted a .367 average with 11 home runs and 110 RBIs. Flick was the runner-up to Wagner for the batting title and finished second to Long in home runs. Flick did lead the league in RBIs.

Noodles Hahn of Cincinnati pitched the season's only no-hitter, beating the Phillies on July 12. Hahn led the league with 142 strikeouts. The other highlight for Cincinnati, which finished next to last, was first baseman Jake Beckley's season—he batted .341 with two home runs and 94 RBIs.

St. Louis finished one spot ahead of Cincinnati and was led by third baseman John McGraw and outfielder Jesse Burkett. McGraw hit .344 with two home runs and 33 RBIs while Burkett had a .363 average with seven homers and 68 RBIs.

Bill Dinneen of Boston had a 20–14 record with a 3.12 ERA and 107 strikeouts, which ranked fourth in the league.

Brooklyn and Pittsburgh played a post-season series, which was won by the Superbas, three games to one.

SHORTS

The future of the Detroit franchise was decided in court. The surprise was that the ruling came from the divorce court. The court determined that franchise owner George Von Derbeck had been delinquent in alimony payments. As a result, his ex-wife was awarded the franchise. Von Derbeck soon made the necessary arrangements to regain control and then sold the team a few weeks later.

TIMELINE

April 19: The National League season opened with Philadelphia winning 19–17 at Boston in front of 10,000 fans.

May 6: The Tigers skirted restrictions against Sunday games by playing in a park a few miles outside the city limits.

May 20: Arson was suspected as the Pittsburgh ballpark had its second fire in two weeks.

May 31: Nap Lajoie broke his hand trying to punch a teammate and was suspended without pay for five weeks.

June 19: Clark Griffith of the Cubs and Rube Waddell of the Pirates pitched 13 scoreless innings before Griffith's double in the bottom of the 14th won the game 1–0.

June 21: Brooklyn took over first place for good with an 8–6 win over Philadelphia.

July 5: Cincinnati was stopped on one hit for the second consecutive game.

July 7: Boston's Kid Nichols got his 300th career win.

July 12: Noodles Hahn of Cincinnati pitched a 4–0 no-hitter against Philadelphia.

July 17: Christy Mathewson made his major league debut, allowing six runs with two walks and three hit batsmen against Brooklyn.

July 29: Players demanded a share of the purchase price from the sale of their contracts.

Sept. 11: Nixey Callahan of the Cubs gave up 23 hits in a 14–3 loss to the Giants.

Sept. 12: The Reds made 17 errors in a doubleheader at Brooklyn.

Nov. 14: The National League refused to accept the American League as an equal.

Dec. 12: The National League considered adding four teams to prevent losing cities to the American League.

Dec. 14: The National League decided to adopt a 16-man roster limit after May 1 each season.

Dec. 15: Pitcher Amos Rusie was traded to the Reds for Christy Mathewson.

Americans' pitcher Cy Young (above) led the American League in wins, ERA and strikeouts. Ban Johnson (below) had the vision to challenge the monopoly of the National League

Ban Johnson was a former sportswriter who helped create a major story. Johnson revived the old Western League, renamed it the American League and decided to challenge the National League's baseball monopoly.

In three cities—Boston, Philadelphia and Chicago—Johnson's upstart league went head-to-head with the establishment. When the National League cut back and dropped four cities, the American League was quick to grab three of them. The American League set up shop in Baltimore, Cleveland and Washington, discarding Louisville.

Johnson's vision was sound. He wanted to present an image of stability so that owners were carefully screened and the authority of umpires was backed strongly by the league office. That provided credibility with fans.

Johnson created the league with assistance from Chicago's Charles Comiskey. The Western League had been regional but expanded eastward after Johnson withdrew from the National Agreement.

The 25-year-old National League's supremacy had been challenged just once before— the American Association had taken a run at the National League from 1892–91 but ran out of money.

A war between leagues is always good for players and this was no exception. About 30 players made the jump to the American League, including major stars such as Cy Young, who ended 11 years with St. Louis to move to Boston and promptly won 33 games.

Perhaps the National League was ripe for competition—its relaxed structure allowed ownership of multiple franchises. Baltimore and Brooklyn were under the control of the same group. Pittsburgh and Louisville had been under common ownership. Owners would frequently load talent on one team and use the other as a farm team with major league billing—and major league ticket prices.

SHORTS
Rules changes—a batter was to be charged with a strike on foul balls, unless it was a third strike. Part of the aim was to cut costs as players were deliberately fouling off pitches and using too many baseballs. Rules were also passed that required the catcher to play within ten feet of the batter.

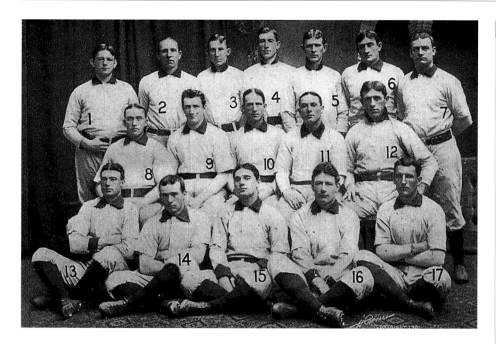

TIMELINE

Jan. 4: Baltimore joined the American League with John McGraw as a part-owner, player and manager.

Jan. 29: The American League rejected a proposal to ban bunting.

Feb. 8: Philadelphia Phillies star Nap Lajoie was one of three players to jump to the American League's Philadelphia Athletics.

March 11: Baltimore manager John McGraw attempted to sign a Cherokee Indian named Tokohoma. The player was really a Negro named Charlie Black and McGraw's move was disallowed.

April 24: The Chicago White Stockings beat the Cleveland Blues 8–2 in the first American League game.

April 25: Cleveland's Erve Beck hit the first home run in American League history.

May 21: New York Giants owner Andrew Freedman ordered umpire Billy Nash to be removed from the park for incompetence. Players from both teams umpired the rest of the game.

May 23: The White Stockings walked Nap Lajoie of the Athletics intentionally with the bases loaded.

June 18: The National League's Boston Somersets reduced ticket prices from 50 cents to 25 cents to match the price being charged by the American League's Boston Beaneaters.

July 15: The Giants' Christy Mathewson pitched a 5–0 no-hitter against St. Louis.

Aug. 20: When umpire Bob Emslie became ill before a Brooklyn-Philadelphia doubleheader, players from both teams made the calls.

Sept. 3: Joe McGinnity of Baltimore pitched complete games in both ends of a doubleheader against Milwaukee, winning one and losing one.

Sept. 19: All games were canceled in memory of President William McKinley, who died five days earlier from an assassin's bullets.

Oct. 20: The St. Louis Cardinals roster was devastated when seven players jumped to the American League's new St. Louis franchise.

Dec. 3: The American League officially approved the transfer of the Milwaukee franchise to St. Louis. The nickname changes from the Brewers to the Browns.

SHORTS Rowdiness was still a problem in all aspects of the game. In July, Cubs' first baseman Jack Doyle ran into the stands to fight with a fan who had been heckling him. Later in the month, St. Louis fans attacked umpire Hank O'Day after a controversial call. Players and security officers were able to rescue O'Day, but he suffered minor injuries in the scuffle.

On the field, the Pittsburgh Pirates were the class of the National League. They moved into first place to stay on June 16 and finished 6½ games ahead of Philadelphia. Manager Fred Clarke, who also played left field, batted .316. Honus Wagner batted .353 even though he didn't have a regular position. Wagner appeared in 61 games at shortstop, 54 as an outfielder and 24 others as a third baseman.

Pittsburgh's pitching staff was led by Deacon Phillippe, Jack Chesbro and Jesse Tannehill. Phillippe went 22–12, Chesbro posted a 21–10 record and lefthander Tannehill went 18–12.

The Phillies were hurt by the defection of Nap Lajoie to the American League. Outfielder-first baseman Ed Delahanty batted .357 with 108 RBIs and outfielder Elmer Flick hit .336 with 88 RBIs.

Philadelphia's pitching was almost as good as Pittsburgh's. Red Donahue was 21–13 and Al Orth was 20–12. Bill Duggleby won 19 games. Brooklyn was devastated by the loss of workhorse pitcher Joe McGinnity to the American League.

Moving across town the Philadelphia

The dominant Pittsburgh Pirates remained the class of the National League

Athletics didn't affect Lajoie's production. He won the Triple Crown with a .422 average, 14 home runs and 125 RBIs.

Still, the Chicago White Sox took the title, finishing four games in front of Boston, which saw its pitching fall apart at the end.

There was an ominous sign for the established National League—the American League franchises in Boston and Chicago had the better attendance in those two-team cities.

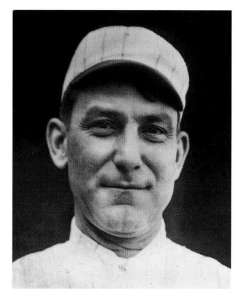

Nap Lajoie joined the American League—and excelled

LEADERS

BATTING AVERAGE
AL: Ed Delahanty, Washington, .376
NL: Ginger Beaumont, Pittsburgh, .357

HOME RUNS
AL: Socks Seybold, Philadelphia A's, 16
NL: Tommy Leach, Pittsburgh 6

RUNS BATTED IN
AL: Buck Freeman, Pilgrims, 121
NL: Honus Wagner, Pittsburgh, 91

STOLEN BASES
AL: Topsy Hartsel, Philadelphia A's, 47
NL: Honus Wagner, Pittsburgh, 42

PITCHING VICTORIES
AL: Cy Young, Boston Pilgrims, 32
NL: Jack Chesbro, Pittsburgh, 28

EARNED RUN AVERAGE
AL: Ed Siever, Detroit, 1.91
NL: Jack Taylor, Chicago Cubs, 1.33

STRIKEOUTS
AL: Rube Waddell, Philadelphia A's, 210
NL: Vic Willis, Beaneaters, 225

Nap Lajoie joined his third team in as many years

Pitcher Rube Waddell made an immediate impact with the A's

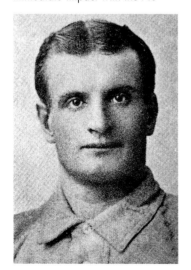

The most serious challenge to the American League's quest for equal status came from within.

Fiery Baltimore player-manager John McGraw found himself at odds with the American League throughout the season. The American League's solution was to hit McGraw with an indefinite suspension in July.

McGraw cooked up a complex plot to get his revenge. He arranged for the Baltimore Orioles to be sold to John Brush, the chairman of the National League Executive Committee. Once Brush had infiltrated the enemy camp, he was able to do some serious damage.

He arranged for the releases of several play-

SHORTS It didn't take the National League long to realize that the war with the American League was costly. The National League teams were losing both players and fans. The last straw may have come when the American League moved to put a franchise in New York to run in opposition to the Giants, who were having problems themselves in drawing the city's fans.

ers—McGraw, Joe McGinnity, Roger Bresnahan, Dan McGann, Joe Kelley, Jack Cronin and Cy Seymour. Freed from their contracts, they were able to sign with National League teams.

The situation was so dire that on July 17 Baltimore didn't have enough players to field a team for its game against St. Louis. The league took swift action. It allowed the Orioles to restock

Pittsburgh's Ginger Beaumont captured the National League batting title

their roster by taking players from other teams. Wilbert Robinson was sent in to manage Baltimore and stabilize the situation.

Meanwhile, the Pennsylvania Supreme Court also had a hand in this baseball season. The court decreed that three players who had left the National League's Philadelphia Phillies to jump to the Philadelphia Athletics of the American League could only play for the Phillies while they were in Pennsylvania. The three were Nap Lajoie and pitchers Chick Fraser and Bill Bernhard. The American League skirted the problem by assigning the contracts of Lajoie and Bernhard to the Cleveland franchise. Fraser was sent back to the Phillies. When the Cleveland Bronchos visited Philadelphia to play the Athletics, Lajoie and Bernhard did not accompany the team. According to some reports, they treated those games as a

SHORTS Both Philadelphia teams had home dates on September 9. A doubleheader between the Athletics and Baltimore drew a crowd of 17,291 fans. The Phillies' game against Pittsburgh attracted only 172 fans. The Athletics outdrew the Phillies during the season by a margin of nearly 4-to-1. It was another reason for the leagues to try to settle their differences.

paid vacation and visited Atlantic City.

Because other states didn't recognize baseball's reserve clause, the Pennsylvania ruling had no effect throughout the rest of the American League circuit.

In stepping up the war with the National League, the American League shifted its Milwaukee franchise to St. Louis to go head-to-head with the established Cardinals. It was a bloody battle as the new St. Louis Browns raided the Cardinals for pitchers Jack Harper and Jack Powell, infielders Bobby Wallace and Dick Padden and outfielders Jesse Burkett and Snags Heidrick. St. Louis became the fourth city with a franchise from each league.

Connie Mack won his first pennant with the Athletics. He had six .300 hitters, headed by third baseman Lave Cross (.339, 106 RBIs) and outfielder Socks Seybold, who batted .317 with 97 runs batted in and a league-leading 16 home runs.

The Athletics compensated for Bernhard's loss by purchasing Rube Waddell from the minor league franchise in Los Angeles. Waddell joined the team in May and went 24–7 with a league-leading 210 strikeouts. Ed Plank was 20–15 for the Athletics.

In the National League, the Pittsburgh Pirates avoided the American League's raids and won a record 103 games. They finished a whopping 27½ games in front of Brooklyn.

Ginger Beaumont batted .357, Fred Clarke hit .321 and Honus Wagner batted .329. Jack Chesbro led the staff with a 28–6 record, Jesse Tannehill was 20–6 and Deacon Phillippe went 20–9.

TIMELINE

Jan. 4: Pitcher Bill Dinneen jumped from the National League to the American League in Boston, leaving the Beaneaters for the Somersets.

April 21: The Pennsylvania Supreme Court granted a permanent injunction that prevented Nap Lajoie and two others from playing for any team other than the Philadelphia Phillies in Pennsylvania.

April 23: St. Louis Cardinals' owner staked $10,000 that the Pirates would not repeat as National League champions. The Pirates won the pennant by 27½ games.

April 26: Addie Joss made his major league debut with Cleveland by throwing a one-hitter against St. Louis.

June 3: Cardinals' pitcher Mike O'Neill got the first pinch hit grand slam.

June 11: Connie Mack of the Athletics signed Rube Waddell from the Pacific Coast League and was rewarded with a 24-win season.

June 30: Giants' left fielder Jim Jones cut down three runners at the plate in an 8–0 loss to Boston.

June 8: John McGraw got his release from Baltimore of the American League and signed to manage the National League's Giants. McGraw helped influence the sale of the Orioles to National League owners and also got the releases of six players, which depleted Baltimore's roster.

Aug. 13: Honus Wagner of the Pirates stole second, third and home in the same inning.

Aug. 16: The Athletics took over first place in the American League for the rest of the season.

Aug. 25: The American League promised to place a franchise in New York in 1903.

Sept. 13: Joe Tinker, Johnny Evers and Frank Chance played their first game as a double-play combination for the Cubs. Tinker was at shortstop, Evers at second and Chance at first.

Sept. 20: Nixey Callahan of the White Stockings pitched a 3–0 no-hitter against Detroit.

Honus Wagner remained a model of consistency

BATTING AVERAGE
AL: Nap Lajoie, Bronchos, .355
NL: Honus Wagner, Pittsburgh, .355

HOME RUNS
AL: Buck Freeman, Pilgrims, 13
NL: Jimmy Sheckard, Superbas, 9

RUNS BATTED IN
AL: Buck Freeman, Pilgrims, 104
NL: Sam Mertes, NY Giants, 104

STOLEN BASES
AL: Harry Bay, Bronchos, 45
NL: Frank Chance, Chicago Cubs;
Jimmy Sheckard, Superbas, 67

PITCHING VICTORIES
AL: Cy Young, Boston Pilgrims, 28
NL: Joe McGinnity, NY Giants, 31

EARNED RUN AVERAGE
AL: Earl Moore, Bronchos, 1.77
NL: Sam Leever, Pittsburgh, 2.06

STRIKEOUTS
AL: Rube Waddell, Philadelphia A's, 302
NL: Christy Mathewson, NY Giants, 267

On January 9, baseball decided to restrict competition to the field. The National and American leagues completed a long series of negotiations and came away with an agreement to co-exist as major leagues.

It was a major victory for the American League, which had rejected an invitation to merge. The American League was allowed to keep nearly all of the players it had raided from National League teams. Its contracts would continue to be honored.

The peace treaty wasn't bad for the National League, either. It was able to concentrate on showcasing its product instead of becoming bogged down in off-the-field matters. In some cases, the entry of American League teams had hurt established National League franchises in two-team cities.

The last blast of the war came in another series of player signings following the 1902 season. Wee Willie Keeler, an annual contender for the batting title, left Brooklyn for the New York Highlanders. Brooklyn lost pitchers Wild Bill Donovan and Frank Kitson to Detroit. The Tigers also got outfielder Sam Crawford from Cincinnati. The Highlanders lured away two of Pittsburgh's best pitchers, Jack Chesbro and Jesse Tannehill.

Despite the losses of those two stalwarts, the Pirates were able to win their third consecutive National League pennant. They topped the New York Giants by 6½ games, taking over first place on June 19 and controlling a three-team race that also involved the Chicago Cubs.

Honus Wagner hit .355 for the Pirates to win the batting title and was supported by Fred Clarke and Ginger Beaumont.

The Giants leaped from sixth to second under John McGraw's first full year as manager. Roger Bresnahan batted .350 to lead the Giants. Joe McGinnity was 31–20

Ban Johnson—American League president for another term

and Christy Mathewson had a 30–13 record.

In the American League the Boston Pilgrims coasted to their total, outdistancing the Philadelphia Athletics by 14½ games. Cy Young won 28 games and led the league for the third consecutive year. Connie Mack's Athletics suffered from a lack of offense.

On September 16, a historic handshake between Pittsburgh owner Barney Dreyfuss and his Boston counterpart, Henry Killilea, sealed an agreement for a postseason series between the two pennant winners. It would become the first inter-league showdown since the first-place teams of the National League and American Association had met after the 1890 season.

The season was filled with tragic incidents. In January, Detroit pitcher Win Mercer, 28, committed suicide by inhaling gas. He had played nine seasons and was about to manage the Tigers.

On August 8, a bleacher overhang at the Philadelphia National League park collapsed. Twelve people were killed and 282 others were injured.

The gossip magazines fixated on the mysterious death of Washington outfielder Ed Delahanty. He had left the team in Detroit and boarded a train back to New York City.

The Pilgrim's Cy Young led the American League in wins

SHORTS The peace settlement between the American and National League was accomplished with the resolution of several thorny issues. The American League agreed to stay out of Pittsburgh as one term of the agreement. The status of star outfielder Sam Crawford was a particularly contentious issue. He had signed with both Detroit and Cincinnati and was awarded to the Tigers.

Delahanty's body was discovered two days later. The circumstances of his death were never clear. It wasn't definitively known if he had fallen, if he had jumped or if he had been pushed. One popular theory held that Delahanty had been ejected from the train for drunken behavior and then died as he tried to walk across a railroad bridge. Delahanty was 35.

SHORTS The World Series was a new concept and it didn't catch on immediately. Owners of the Boston and Pittsburgh franchises agreed to play a best-of-nine series between the two pennant winners. The series was also billed as "The Championship of the United States." The deciding game drew only 7,455 fans, the smallest crowd of the series.

POSTSEASON

The World Series was a natural once the American League became partners with the established National League, but it took the initiative of the owners of the two pennant-winning clubs to make it happen.

In the first game, Deacon Phillippe of the Pittsburgh Pirates beat the Pilgrims' Cy Young 7–3. The first Series homer was hit by Pirates' outfielder Jimmy Sebring. Boston evened the Series on Bill Dinneen's 3–0 three-hitter in Game Two. Patsy Dougherty hit a pair of home runs.

Phillippe was back in Game Three and beat the Pilgrims 4–2. Phillippe returned for Game Four and pitched the Pirates to a 5–4 home win to give Pittsburgh a 3–1 lead in games.

Boston won its second game when Young beat the Pirates 11–2 and also drove in three runs. Honus Wagner made two costly errors to help the Pilgrims rally from a 4–2 deficit. Dinneen was back in Game Six to tie the Series with a 6–3 win over 25-game winner Sam Leever. Phillippe failed for the first time in Game Seven, losing 2–0 and setting the stage for Dinneen's Series-winning 3–0 victory in Game Eight. The losing pitcher was Phillippe, who worked 44 innings and figured in five decisions.

Boston's Huntington Avenue Grounds

GAME 1	
Pittsburgh Pirates 7	Boston Pilgrims 3
GAME 2	
Boston Pilgrims 3	Pittsburgh Pirates 0
GAME 3	
Pittsburgh Pirates 4	Boston Pilgrims 2
GAME 4	
Pittsburgh Pirates 5	Boston Pilgrims 4
GAME 5	
Boston Pilgrims 11	Pittsburgh Pirates 2
GAME 6	
Boston Pilgrims 6	Pittsburgh Pirates 3
GAME 7	
Boston Pilgrims 7	Pittsburgh Pirates 3
GAME 8	
Boston Pilgrims 3	Pittsburgh Pirates 0

Baseball's inaugural World Series

TIMELINE

Jan. 9: The National and American Leagues agreed to co-exist as major leagues.

April 14: Ed Delahanty rejoined the Washington Nationals of the American League after his three-year contract with the National League Giants was canceled.

May 17: Cleveland and the New York Highlanders played a game in Columbus, Ohio, because Sunday games were banned in Cleveland.

June 23: The Boston Pilgrims take over first place for good in the American League.

June 25: Boston Beaneaters' pitcher Wiley Piatt pitched two complete games against Pittsburgh and lost both of them.

July 2: Ed Delahanty of Washington died in a fall from a railroad bridge over Niagara Falls.

July 2: Jack Doscher became the major leagues' first second-generation player. His father, Herm, played for three teams before 1900.

July 17: The Athletics' Rube Waddell was charged with assaulting a heckling fan.

Aug. 8: Joe McGinnity pitched the first of the three doubleheaders he would win during the month. His durability earned him the nickname "Iron Joe."

Aug. 20: The Pirates made six errors in the first inning during a loss to the Giants.

Sept. 3: Jesse Stovall made his major league debut with Cleveland by winning an 11-inning, 1–0 shutout.

Sept. 17: Chick Fraser of the Cubs pitched a no-hitter against the Phillies.

Sept. 18: An informal agreement between the pennant-winning teams called for a best-of-nine postseason championship series between the two titlists.

Sept. 24: Bill Bradley of Cleveland had 12 total bases as he hit for the cycle and also had a double.

Nov. 11: Jimmy Collins signed to manage Boston for three years.

Dec. 18: Ban Johnson was elected to another term as American League president with his salary set at $10,000.

LEADERS

BATTING AVERAGE
AL: Nap Lajoie, Bronchos, .381
NL: Honus Wagner, Pittsburgh, .349

HOME RUNS
AL: Harry Davis, Philadelphia A's, 10
NL: Harry Lumley, Superbas, 9

RUNS BATTED IN
AL: Nap Lajoie, Bronchos, 102
NL: Bill Dahlen, NY Giants, 80

STOLEN BASES
AL: Elmer Rick, Bronchos, 42
NL: Honus Wagner, Pittsburgh, 53

PITCHING VICTORIES
AL: Jack Chesbro, NY Highlanders, 41
NL: Joe McGinnity, NY Giants, 35

EARNED RUN AVERAGE
AL: Addie Joss, Bronchos, 1.59
NL: Joe McGinnity, NY Giants, 1.61

STRIKEOUTS
AL: Rube Waddell, Philadelphia A's, 349
NL: Christy Mathewson, NY Giants, 212

The Highlanders' Jack Chesbro set a modern-day record for wins

When a pitcher wins 20 games he's had a special season. When he wins 30 he's had an exceptional season. So what superlative applies to the season Jack Chesbro had for the 1904 New York Highlanders in compiling over 40 wins?

Chesbro, 30, went 41–12 for New York, making 51 starts and completing 48 of them. He pitched 455 innings. Chesbro had been a reliable winner with both the Pittsburgh Pirates and Highlanders, but nothing in his past suggested that he was on the verge of a 41-victory season.

The Highlanders needed the help because pitcher-manager Clark Griffith was wearing down and Al Orth was ill for part of the season.

Ironically, even though Chesbro won 41 games, this American League season turned on one game that he didn't win. The Highlanders were part of a season-long, five-way fight for the pennant. Boston, Chicago, Cleveland and Philadelphia were all factors in the race at various times.

The race came down to a five-game series between New York and Boston that ended the season. The Highlanders won on October 7 and

SHORTS Both the New York Highlanders and Boston Pilgrims expressed an interest in playing the National League winner in another World Series. The New York Giants rejected the idea, apparently believing that playing the American League would add legitimacy. It was later learned that the decision was stubbornly pushed by Giants' manager John McGraw, who left the American League with bad feelings.

Joe McGinnity won both the ERA and victories titles in the National League

took a half-game lead over Boston. The Pilgrims swept a doubleheader the following day and went ahead by a game and a half.

That left a doubleheader the Highlanders had to sweep in order to overtake Boston.

Chesbro pitched the first game against Bill Dinneen, Boston's 23-game winner. The game was scoreless through four innings until New York took a 2–0 lead. Highlanders' second baseman Jimmy Williams then made a throwing error to tie the game.

In the ninth, Boston's Lou Criger singled, went to second on a sacrifice and advanced to third on a wild pitch. He scored the eventual winning run on Chesbro's wild pitch and the Pilgrims won the pennant.

Boston had an efficient offense, but there were no overwhelming performances. The Pilgrims didn't have a .300 hitter. Cy Young anchored the pitching staff with 26 wins, including a perfect game. Jesse Tannehill was 21–11 and Norwood Gibson 17–14. The Pilgrims used only five pitchers during the entire season. George Winter was the other.

Philadelphia's Rube Waddell set a strikeout record with 349 and Addie Joss of Cleveland won the earned run average title at 1.59.

The New York Giants continued their steady progress in the National League under the iron rule of manager John McGraw. From last place in 1902 to second the next year, the Giants won the 1904 pennant. They won 106 games to top Pittsburgh's 1902 record by three. The Giants finished 13 games ahead of Chicago. They made some sharp acquisitions—shortstop Babe Dahlen came over from Brooklyn and batted .268 with 80 RBIs and 476 stolen bases, while rookie third baseman Art Devlin hit .281, drove in 88 runs and stole 33 bases.

The Giants also featured the best pitching in the league with a pair of 30-game winners. Joe McGinnity was 35–8 with a 1.61 ERA and Christy Mathewson went 33–12 with a 2.03 ERA. They were so good that Dummy Taylor's 21–15 season was barely noticed.

TIMELINE

May 5: Cy Young of the Boston Pilgrims pitched a perfect game against the Philadelphia Athletics, the second no-hitter of his career.

June 11: Bob Wicker of the Cubs pitched 9 1/3 hitless innings before losing 1–0 to the Giants in 12 innings.

June 16: Christy Mathewson's win over the Cardinals started a streak of 24 consecutive victories over St. Louis.

July 4: Jack Chesbro of the New York Highlanders extended his personal winning streak to 14 games.

Aug. 10: Jack Chesbro's streak of 30 complete games ended when he was knocked out by the White Sox.

Aug. 17: Jesse Tannehill pitched a no-hitter for Boston over the White Sox.

Aug. 24: Wee Willie Keeler of New York hit two inside-the-park home runs against St. Louis.

Aug. 30: Doc White of the White Sox pitched his sixth shutout of the month.

Oct. 3: The Giants' Christy Mathewson struck out 16 Cardinals batters.

Oct. 6: Jack Taylor of the Cardinals pitched his 39th consecutive complete game.

Oct. 7: Jack Chesbro of the Highlanders beat Boston 3–2 for his 41st win. He became the first pitcher to lead both leagues in winning percentage.

Oct. 7: For the first time in major league history, a batter hit a home run off his brother. George Stovall of Cleveland hit the homer off his older brother Jesse.

Oct. 10: George Winter went the route in a 1–0 win over New York for Boston's 148th complete game of the season.

Oct. 10: Bill Dinneen of Boston pitched his 37th consecutive complete game.

Oct. 28: Cleveland fired Bill Armour as manager and hired Nap Lajoie to replace him. Armour moved on to manage Detroit.

The Giants' formidable Christy Mathewson

That the annual awards for pitching excellence bear his name, defines Cy Young's impact on the game.

The winningest pitcher of all time

Quite simply, he was the winningest pitcher in the history of baseball and is likely to hold that distinction for a while longer. Young won 511 games in his 22-year career. His nearest competitor, Walter Johnson, trailed him by 95 victories.

Denton True Young came from a farm in eastern Ohio and immediately picked up the nickname "Cy," because someone said his fastball reembled the speed and force of a cyclone.

He was pitching for a minor league team in Canton, which was offering his contract to major league teams for the sum of $500. The Cleveland franchise signed off on the deal and wound up with a pitcher who could work every other day and be counted on to win most of the time. The team moved to St. Louis in 1899 and paid Young the National League's maximum salary of $2,400. The upstart American League came calling and Young made the jump to the Boston Red Sox, which promised to raise his salary to $3,000 per year.

Young pitched 751 complete games and worked 7,356 innings. He won at least 20 games in 16 seasons and had five seasons with at least 30 victories. He pitched three no-hitters and one perfect game. He was so absorbed in his work during the perfect game that accounts claim he had no idea that he hadn't allowed a base runner. The stories hold that Young didn't realize he'd retired 27 men in order until his teammates rushed to the mound to congratulate him.

Young believed he developed his body by doing routine farm chores like chopping wood. He was fond of saying, "I had a good arm and legs."

His baseball training routine was equally unconventional. Upon reporting to spring training, Young would not do any throwing for the first three weeks of the get-together. He was adamant that he wouldn't even pick up a base-

ball in the early stages of camp. He would instead devote himself to running and walking to condition his legs and to build up his overall fitness levels.

Why no pitching at the opening of spring camp?

"I never did any unnecessary throwing," Young said. "I figured the old arm had just so many throws in it and there wasn't any use in wasting them."

Young was serious about that policy. If he was going to be used in relief, he would not warm up in the bullpen before entering the game. He'd get ready with the handful of practice pitches a pitcher is allowed to take from the mound upon entering the game.

Young would warm up before the start of a game, but he had his own way of handling that duty, too. While most pitchers would spend at least ten minutes warming up (and 15 minutes would probably be closer to the norm), Young would take no more than five minutes in the bullpen until he declared himself ready to compete in the game. Often his warm-up time was as short as two or three minutes.

He took that same minimalist approach into the game. Young didn't care about strikeouts, believing that it was an inefficient way to dispose of a hitter. Better to get the batter to pop out or ground out on the first pitch. Why make three pitches when the same goal could be accomplished with one?

"I aimed to make the batter hit the ball and I threw as few pitches as possible," Young said. "That's why I was able to throw every other day." Young issued the fewest walks in 16 seasons. He lasted, too, pitching until he was 44 years old. He threw the last of his three no-hitters when he was 41.

He may have pitched longer but his reflexes weren't willing, even though his remarkable arm was. Young had added weight and didn't move well. Players took advantage of that and bunted on him because a successful bunt virtually guaranteed a base hit. Finally fed up, he retired after the 1911 season with a 511–313 record and a 2.63 earned run average.

He was one of the five members of the Hall of Fame's inaugural class of 1937. Young died in 1955 at 88.

LEADERS

BATTING AVERAGE
AL: Elmer Flick, Bronchos, .306
NL: Cy Seymour, Cincinnati, .377

HOME RUNS
AL: Harry Davis, Philadelphia A's, 8
NL: Fred Odwell, Cincinnati, 9

RUNS BATTED IN
AL: Harry Davis, Philadelphia A's, 83
NL: Cy Seymour, Cincinnati, 121

STOLEN BASES
AL: Danny Hoffman, Philadelphia A's, 46
NL: Art Devlin, NY Giants; Billy Maloney, Chicago Cubs, 59

PITCHING VICTORIES
AL: Rube Waddell, Philadelphia A's, 26
NL: Christy Mathewson, NY Giants, 31

EARNED RUN AVERAGE
AL: Rube Waddell, Philadelphia A's, 1.48
NL: Christy Mathewson, NY Giants, 1.27

STRIKEOUTS
AL: Rube Waddell, Philadelphia A's, 287
NL: Christy Mathewson, NY Giants, 206

In a pitcher-friendly climate, the A's Rube Waddell (l) and Chief Bender (r) reigned

It was a year of absent offense in the American League, which worked in the Philadelphia Athletics' favor.

During a season dominated by pitching, the Athletics had the best staff and won the pennant by two games over the Chicago White Sox.

Two lefthanders led the way for Connie Mack's club—Rube Waddell was 26–11 with a 1.48 earned run average and Eddie Plank was 25–12 with a 2.26 ERA. Two righthanders balanced the staff—Chief Bender was 20–7 with a 2.83 ERA and Andy Coakley was 16–11 with an impressive 1.84 ERA.

For the first three months of the season, the main contenders were the Chicago White Sox and Cleveland Bronchos. The Athletics consistently hung in third place while Chicago and Cleveland slugged it out.

The Indians were jolted in July by the loss of their best player, Nap Lajoie, to blood poisoning. On August 2, the Athletics, having already passed Cleveland, were able to overtake the White Sox for first place.

On September 28, the Athletics' lead over Chicago was limited to percentage points in advance of a three-game series between the clubs in Philadelphia. The Athletics took two of the three games to send the White Sox reeling out of town. But Chicago wasn't officially knocked out

of the race until it lost two games to the lowly St. Louis Browns in the season's last week.

The Detroit Tigers showed a major improvement, rising to third place from seventh. They were led by pitchers George Mullin, who went 22–18, and Ed Killian with a 22–15 record. Wild Bill Donovan was 18–14.

Maybe the biggest development for the Tigers was the major league debut of an 18-year-old outfielder on August 30. Ty Cobb batted .240 in his first 41 games with Detroit.

The Boston Pilgrims were doomed by a shortage of pitching. Bill Dinneen, a 23-game winner in 1904, was just 14–14. Cy Young, 38, had the worst record of his career, 18–19, which didn't seem compatible with his 1.82 ERA.

In New York, Highlanders' pitcher Jack Chesbro won 21 fewer games and still had a good season. Chesbro was 20–15, well off the pace of his record-setting 41 wins a year earlier.

The New York Giants moved into first place in the National League on April 23 and stayed there for the rest of the season. Pittsburgh made

GEORGE EDWARD WADDELL
ATHLETIC BASE BALL TEAM

CHARLES A. BENDER
ATHLETIC BASE BALL TEAM

Mike Donlin led the Giants' offense in 1905

SHORTS Never on Sunday. Playing games on Sunday was problematic because so many cities had blue laws restricting commerce on Sundays. The Brooklyn Superbas were one of the teams that tried to dance around local ordinances. They admitted 30,000 people to the ballpark for an April game against the Giants, but requested that each fan make a "contribution" upon entering the gates.

a run in August, but the Pirates fell short and John McGraw managed New York to another title.

The Giants had a balance of offense and pitching. Outfielder Mike Donlin batted .356 and catcher Roger Bresnahan hit .302. Christy Mathewson had another exceptional season on the mound going 32–6 with a 1.27 ERA. Red Ames and Joe McGinnity each won 20 games for the Giants.

Pittsburgh's Honus Wagner hit .363, but didn't win the batting title. That honor went to Cy Seymour of Cincinnati. Deacon Phillippe returned from a leg injury and led the pitching staff with a 20–13 record and a 2.19 earned run average. Sam Leever helped with a 20–5 record and 2.70 ERA. The Pirates still finished nine games behind the Giants.

POSTSEASON

The New York Giants posted a staff earned run average of 0.00 in the World Series, which begs a simple question—how did the Philadelphia Athletics manage to win a game?

The A's scored three unearned runs in Game Two, otherwise Connie Mack's team was shut out in its other 44 innings. Christy Mathewson dominated the Series, pitching three shutouts in six days and holding the A's to just 14 hits in his 27 innings. Mathewson walked one and struck out 18 as every game saw the losing team shut out.

Mathewson won the opener 3–0 with a four-hitter and he started the winning rally with a single. After the Athletics won Game Two with

three unearned runs, Mathewson won 9–0 on a four-hitter. Joe McGinnity pitched a five-hitter to win Game Four, 1–0, and Mathewson ended the Series with a six-hit, 2–0 win.

Philadelphia had a 0.84 ERA for the Series, allowing just four earned runs as the Giants scored 11 unearned runs. McGinnity was just behind Mathewson, allowing no earned runs in 17 innings. The Giants' top two pitchers worked all but one inning of the Series.

GAME 1	
NY Giants 3	Philadelphia A's 0

GAME 1	
Philadelphia A's 3	NY Giants 0

GAME 1	
NY Giants 9	Philadelphia A's 0

GAME 1	
NY Giants 1	Philadelphia A's 0

GAME 1	
NY Giants 2	Philadelphia A's 0

TIMELINE

May 3: Washington was in first place in the American League for the first time since 1893. The stay lasted only three days.

June 8: Giants' pitcher Red Ames' personal nine-game winning streak was ended by the Pirates.

June 13: It was a double no-hitter through eight innings for Christy Mathewson of the Giants and Chicago's Mordecai Brown. Mathewson completed the no-hitter as the Giants got two hits in the ninth and won 1–0.

June 30: Cleveland's pennant hopes suffered a serious blow when Nap Lajoie was knocked out of the lineup by blood poisoning from a spike wound. Lajoie appeared in only 65 games.

July 4: Rube Waddell of Philadelphia beat Boston's Cy Young in a 20-inning game.

Aug. 1: The Giants beat Cincinnati 10–5 for their 12th consecutive win.

Aug. 8: Dave Brain of the Pirates had three triples in a game for the second time in the season.

Aug. 10: Boston Beaneaters' catcher Pat Moran hit three triples in a game against the Pirates.

Aug. 30: Ty Cobb made his major league debut for the Tigers. Cobb hit a double off Jack Chesbro for his first hit.

Sept. 5: Rube Waddell's streak of 44 shutout innings ended when Boston scored twice and won 3–2 in 13 innings.

Sept. 16: The New York Highlanders used lefthanded-throwing Wee Willie Keeler at second base because of a shortage of infielders.

Sept. 23: Ty Cobb hit his first major league home run, an inside-the-park shot.

Sept. 26: Chicago swept a doubleheader from Boston as Ed Walsh pitched two complete games.

Sept. 27: Boston's Bill Dinneen pitched the season's fourth no-hitter.

Oct. 5: Philadelphia's Chief Bender got two wins, six hits and eight RBIs as the Athletics swept a doubleheader from Washington.

Christy Mathewson (l) and John McGraw (r) masterminded the Giants' World Series win

Chicago was the baseball capital of the United States in 1906. The Cubs and White Sox won their respective pennants, confining many of the season's thrills to one city.

The White Sox had won the American League pennant in 1901, but the Cubs hadn't finished first in the National League since 1886. The excitement helped both teams to lead their leagues in attendance.

The New York Giants stayed with the Cubs until June, when Chicago pulled away en route to 116 wins, breaking the record of 106 the Giants had set just two years earlier.

The Cubs added third baseman Harry Steinfeldt, who proved to be a great help to the middle of their batting order. Steinfeldt batted .327 and drove in 87 runs. Manager-first baseman Frank Chance hit .319, marking his fourth year with a batting average over .310.

As often happens in championship seasons, some players reach unexpected levels of production. That was the case with catcher Johnny Kling, who raised his average from .218 to .312. The famous double play combination of Joe Tinker, Johnny Evers and Chance provided good defense which aided a talented pitching staff.

The Cubs allowed the fewest runs in the National League. Mordecai Brown had a 26–6 record and a 1.04 earned run average. He threw nine shutouts.

Rookie lefthander Jack Pfeister was 20–8, Ed Reulbach was 19–4 and Carl Lundgren had a 17–6 mark. The Cubs made a smart acquisition in midseason when they got Orval Overall for Cincinnati. He went 12–3 with Chicago.

The White Sox came to be known as the "Hitless Wonders" for obvious reasons. Their offensive attack didn't scare many opponents. They hit just .230 as a team.

In early August, the White Sox found themselves in fourth place, trailing the Philadelphia Athletics, New York and Cleveland. They then went on a 19-game winning streak and needed

Joe Tinker, one third of the Cubs' notorious double-play combo

only ten days to move from fourth to first. The Athletics faded and the White Sox edged out both New York and Cleveland in the last week of the season. They had a three-game edge over New York and finished five ahead of Cleveland.

A team dubbed "Hitless Wonders" obviously relied on pitching and defense. Only two White Sox hitters had averages over .260. Frank Owen led the pitching staff with a 22–13 record and Nick Altrock was 20–13. Doc White, a practicing dentist, was 16–6 and his 1.52 ERA led the league.

Spitball specialist Ed Walsh went 17–13 and

Cubs' player-manager Frank Chance led his club to the pennant

Roy Patterson rounded out the staff with a 10–7 record.

New York's big winner was Al Orth at 27–17 and Jack Chesbro wound up 24–16.

Bob Rhoades led Cleveland with a 22–10 record. Addie Joss was 21–9, Otto Hess had a 20–17 mark and the hitting star was Nap Lajoie with a .355 average.

Back in the National League, the Giants got fine work from the two mainstays of their pitching staff. Joe McGinnity won 27 games and Christy Mathewson was 22–12.

It was the first time that the two first-place teams were from the same city in the year that the two last-place teams also shared a city. The two Boston franchises wound up at the bottom of their respective leagues.

POSTSEASON

The baseball "World" for this Series was confined to opposite sides of Chicago.

The Chicago Cubs had destroyed the National League, posting a 116–36 record and winning the pennant by 20 games over the second-place New York Giants. On the other side of town, the White Sox had a modest 93–58 record and finished a slim three games in front of their New York Yankees opponent.

As often happens in these kinds of seeming mismatches, the White Sox had a fairly easy time taking the Series in six games from the Cubs.

Nick Altrock outpitched Mordecai Brown for a 2–1 win in the opener. The Cubs came back to take Game Two, 7–1.

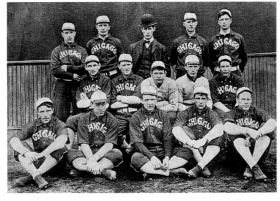

In the battle of Chicago, the White Sox emerged victorious

Big Ed Walsh gave up two hits in the first inning then held the Cubs hitless, as the White Sox won 3–0. Brown threw a two-hitter as the Cubs won Game Four, 1–0.

In Game Five, the White Sox got 12 hits, including Frank Isbell's four doubles and won 8–6. Brown was knocked out in the second inning of Game Six and the White Sox won 8–3 to end the Series.

Walsh won two games for the White Sox and had a 1.80 ERA while George Rohe hit .333 and drove in four runs.

GAME 1	
Chicago White Sox 2	Chicago Cubs 1
GAME 2	
Chicago Cubs 7	Chicago White Sox 1
GAME 3	
Chicago White Sox 3	Chicago Cubs 0
GAME 4	
Chicago Cubs 1	Chicago White Sox 0
GAME 5	
Chicago White Sox 8	Chicago Cubs 6
GAME 6	
Chicago White Sox 8	Chicago Cubs 3

BATTING AVERAGE
AL: Ty Cobb, Detroit, .350
NL: Honus Wagner, Pittsburgh, .350

HOME RUNS
AL: Harry Davis, Philadelphia A's, 8
NL: Dave Brain, Boston Braves, 10

RUNS BATTED IN
AL: Ty Cobb, Detroit, 116
NL: Sherry Magee, Philadelphia Phillies, 85

STOLEN BASES
AL: Ty Cobb, Detroit, 49
NL: Honus Wagner, Pittsburgh, 61

PITCHING VICTORIES
AL: Addie Joss, Cleveland; Doc White,
Chicago White Sox, 27
NL: Christy Mathewson, NY Giants, 24

EARNED RUN AVERAGE
AL: Ed Walsh, Chicago White Sox, 1.60
NL: Jack Pfiester, Chicago Cubs, 1.15

STRIKEOUTS
AL: Rube Waddell, Philadelphia A's, 232
NL: Christy Mathewson, N.Y. Giants, 178

The Chicago Cubs won nine fewer games in the regular season, but wound up with two more wins in the postseason to take the World Series. Considering their disappointment in losing the 1906 Series, it was an exchange they were more than willing to make.

The Cubs had another dominating year, finishing 107–45. Chicago was 17 games ahead of second-place Pittsburgh. The American League race was far closer as Detroit went down to the wire with the Philadelphia Athletics before clinching the pennant.

Hughie Jennings, who had spent his career in the National League, was a winner in his first season as Tigers manager. He led the team to

the pennant one year after it had finished sixth.

The Cubs were led by an infield that boasted the famous double-play combination of Joe Tinker, Johnny Evers and Frank Chance—along with third baseman Harry Steinfeldt, who led the team with 70 RBIs.

Chicago also had a solid starting staff which boasted five pitchers with double-figure victory totals. Orval Overall went 23–7 and Mordecai (Three Finger) Brown was 20–6.

Home runs continued to be scarce as the majors' leader was Boston's Dave Brain with 10.

The key to Detroit's success was the fiercely competitive Ty Cobb and a four-man starting staff responsible for all but four of the Tigers' 92 wins.

The finish between the Tigers and Athletics was controversial. Harry Davis of the Athletics appeared to have hit a tie-breaking home run in extra innings. However, one of the umpires disallowed the apparent homer, ruling that a fan had interfered with center fielder Sam Crawford's ability to catch the ball. Instead of circling the bases, Davis was ruled out.

The game was stopped after 17 innings with the score still tied. It ended that way since there were no provisions for rescheduled or suspended games. With the tie, Philadelphia lost its final chance to overtake the Tigers for first place.

Cobb's dominance of the American League was profound. He led the league in batting average, hits, total bases, slugging percentage, RBIs and stolen bases.

The Pirates were led by shortstop Honus Wagner, who led the National League in both batting average and stolen bases. Vic Willis was a 22-game winner for the Pirates.

Third-place Philadelphia got a 22–8 record from righthander Tully Sparks. Christy Mathewson anchored the New York Giants' staff with 24 wins.

Mordecai (Three Finger) Brown went 20–6 as part of the Cubs' solid pitching staff

The most amazing statistic in the American League was the total of innings pitched by Chicago White Sox's Ed Walsh—he worked 422 innings and led the League in complete games with 37. It was quantity as well as quality for Walsh—he had the League's best ERA at 1.60.

The season was marred by tragedy when Boston Red Sox manager Chick Stahl committed suicide by swallowing large amounts of poison. His death occurred just before the start of the season.

Baseball was anything but a genteel game. There were several incidents during the season of fan rowdiness directed at umpires or opposing players.

Pittsburgh's Honus Wagner

POSTSEASON

L osing a World Series was bad enough; losing to the other team in town added a sting that wouldn't go away easily.

That's what happened to the Chicago Cubs in 1906 when they were defeated by the White Sox. It gave them added motivation in the 1907 season and they repeated easily as National League champions, winning the pennant by 17 games over Pittsburgh.

The White Sox dropped to fourth place and the Detroit Tigers won their first American League pennant, outlasting the Philadelphia Athletics to take first place by a game and a half.

It was the Tigers' misfortune to run into a Cubs team determined not to allow a repeat of their postseason embarrassment.

The highlight for the Tigers was a 3–3 tie in Game One that was called because of darkness after 12 innings in Chicago. The Cubs got the tying run in the bottom of the ninth on catcher Charlie Schmidt's passed ball.

The Cubs swept the next four games, with Detroit scoring a total of three runs, matching the total they'd managed in the opener. Chicago had four different winning pitchers since player-manager Frank Chance set up his rotation perfectly.

Harry Steinfeldt led the Cubs with a .471 average and Johnny Evers batted .350 for Chicago in the Series.

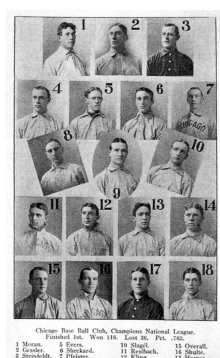

Chicago Base Ball Club, Champions National League.
Finished 1st. Won 116. Lost 36. Pct. .763.

1 Moran.	5 Evers.	10 Slagel.	15 Overall.
2 Gessler.	6 Sheckard.	11 Reulbach.	16 Shulte.
3 Steinfeldt.	7 Pfeister.	12 Kling.	17 Harper.
4 Taylor.	8 Hoffman.	13 Tinker.	18 Lundgren.
	9 Chance (Mgr.)	14 Brown.	

WORLD SERIES

GAME 1	
Detroit 3	Chicago Cubs 3
GAME 2	
Chicago Cubs 3	Detroit 1
GAME 3	
Chicago Cubs 5	Detroit 1
GAME 4	
Chicago Cubs 6	Detroit 1
GAME 5	
Chicago Cubs 2	Detroit 0

TIMELINE

March 28: Boston manager Chick Stahl committed suicide at the end of spring training. Cy Young took over as manager.

May 14: Talk about omens—the flagpole at White Sox Park broke during a ceremony to raise the 1906 championship pennant. This edition of the White Sox finished third, 5½ games behind Detroit.

May 20: The Cardinals won 6–4 at New York, ending the Giants' winning streak at 20 games.

May 26: Ed Walsh of the White Sox pitched a five-inning no-hitter against the Yankees.

May 31: Kid Elberfield of the Highlanders stole home twice in a game against Boston.

June 13: The Red Sox played an exhibition game to benefit the widow of Chick Stahl.

June 19: Miller Huggins of the Reds led off the game by hitting a home run against the Giants' Christy Mathewson.

June 28: New York catcher Branch Rickey was the victim as the Nationals steal 13 bases in one game.

July 30: Reds' manager Ned Hanlon announced his retirement, to become effective at the end of the season. He won five pennants, four in Baltimore and one in Brooklyn, during a career that started in 1889.

Aug. 2: Walter Johnson made his major league debut with a 3–2 loss to Detroit.

Aug. 7: Walter Johnson got his first major league win, a 7–2 decision over Cleveland.

Sept. 20: Only one player got a hit in the game between Pittsburgh and Brooklyn. Pirates' player-manager Fred Clarke had his team's two hits as rookie Nick Maddox pitched a no-hitter for Pittsburgh.

Sept. 25: Pittsburgh's Honus Wagner stole for the cycle, stealing second, third and home in the second inning against the Giants.

Oct. 2: Ty Cobb picked up a $500 bonus by getting his 200th hit of the season.

The Cubs made amends for their 1906 Series defeat

LEADERS

BATTING AVERAGE
AL: Ty Cobb, Detroit, .324
NL: Honus Wagner, Pittsburgh, .354

HOME RUNS
AL: Sam Crawford, Detroit, 7
NL: Tim Jordan, Brooklyn, 12

RUNS BATTED IN
AL: Ty Cobb, Detroit, 108
NL: Honus Wagner, Pittsburgh, 109

STOLEN BASES
AL: Patsy Dougherty, Chicago Cubs, 47
NL: Honus Wagner, Pittsburgh, 53

PITCHING VICTORIES
AL: Ed Walsh, Chicago White Sox, 40
NL: Christy Mathewson, NY Giants, 37

EARNED RUN AVERAGE
AL: Addie Joss, Cleveland, 1.16
NL: Christy Mathewson, NY Giants, 1.43

STRIKEOUTS
AL: Ed Walsh, Chicago White Sox, 269
NL: Christy Mathewson, NY Giants, 259

Fred Merkle became a household name overnight in a way he wished he hadn't. Merkle was a 19-year-old infielder with the New York Giants who was pressed into service when regular first baseman Fred Tenney was felled by an attack of lumbago.

Fred Merkle's legendary blunder cost New York dearly

Merkle was not only playing under the pressure of major league competition, he was playing for one of the most demanding managers in the game. John McGraw had a low tolerance for mistakes and wasn't a bit shy about making his feelings known when something displeased him.

McGraw had run into trouble with umpires and league officials over the years because of his volcanic temper. When the leagues were at war and he felt he had been wronged by the American League, McGraw did everything in his power to undermine the Baltimore franchise that had employed him.

In that context, one can only imagine the agony awaiting Merkle as he made a costly blunder in a pivotal game against the Chicago Cubs on September 23 at the Polo Grounds. The Cubs led the Giants by percentage points in the National League pennant race and the game was tied 1–1 with New York at bat in the bottom of the ninth.

There were two outs in the inning. Mike McCormick was on third and Merkle was at first after delivering a single. Al Bridwell hit a single to center and McCormick scored. Merkle, believing the game was over once McCormick touched the plate, veered toward the clubhouse without ever touching second base.

From that point, reports vary widely on what happened. The Cubs argued that they tagged

Cleveland's Addie Joss achieved
pitching perfection

second base with the ball and that Merkle
should be called out on a force play, negating
the run. Umpire Hank O'Day eventually ruled
in the Cubs' favor and his call was upheld
through a series of appeals. The game was
officially a 1–1 tie.

The makeup was on October 8 and the Cubs
came from behind to win 4–2 behind Mordecai
Brown, who outpitched Christy Mathewson.

The Cubs took their third straight pennant—
none of which would have happened had
Merkle covered those last 15 feet to second
base in September.

The Cubs had a strong infield and got a
29–9 record from Brown. The Pirates were eliminated on the last day, even though Honus
Wagner won his sixth batting championship.

In the American League, the Detroit Tigers
beat the Chicago White Sox on the last day of
the season. Cleveland finished a half game out
of first. Detroit had a game rained out that was-
n't made up, giving the Tigers one less game.

The White Sox were led by Ed Walsh's
incredible season. He was 40–15 and pitched
464 innings. He completed 42 of his 49 games
and walked only 49 while striking out 269.
Walsh valiantly pitched a key game against
Cleveland on two days' rest and wound up
being the losing pitcher in Addie Joss' perfect
game. Walsh allowed only four hits and struck
out 15, but still wound up being a 1–0 loser.

POSTSEASON

Bizarre circumstances helped send the Chicago Cubs to the World
Series and they took full advantage of them.

The Cubs edged out the New York Giants for
the National League title after Fred Merkle cost
the Giants a game by failing to touch second
base while scoring on an apparent game-winning hit. The game was declared a tie and
replayed with the Cubs winning and finishing
one game ahead of the Giants.

The Detroit Tigers had won the American
League pennant by an even thinner margin, finishing half a game in front of Cleveland.

Detroit blew a 6–5 lead in the ninth inning of
the Series opener and lost 10–6, a disaster from
which the Tigers never seemed to recover. They
lost game two 6–1 before Detroit took Game
Three 8–3 behind George Mullin.

Mordecai "Three Finger" Brown steered the

Series back in the Cubs' favor with a 3–0 four-
hitter in Game Four. The Tigers did worse in
Game Five, collecting just three hits off Orval
Overall and losing 3–0, dropping their second
straight Series to the Cubs in five games.

Overall was 2–0 with a 0.98 earned run
average. Frank Chance batted .421 for the
Cubs. Ty Cobb led the Tigers with a .368 average and four RBIs.

GAME 1	
Chicago Cubs 10	Detroit 6
GAME 2	
Chicago Cubs 6	Detroit 1
GAME 3	
Detroit 8	Chicago Cubs 3
GAME 4	
Chicago Cubs 3	Detroit 0
GAME 5	
Chicago Cubs 2	Detroit 0

TIMELINE

March 21: Ty Cobb signed with the
Tigers for a $4,000 salary and an incentive
club that offered an additional $800 if he hit
above .300.

May 12: Orval Overall of the Cubs
had his 14-game winning streak ended by
the Phillies.

June 7: The Tigers pulled a triple play for
the second consecutive game.

June 22: Pittsburgh's Honus Wagner
got his 2,000th career hit.

June 24: Clark Griffith resigned as
manager of the New York Highlanders.

June 30: Cy Young pitched the third no-
hitter of his career.

July 4: Hooks Wiltse of the Giants pitched
a ten-inning no-hitter against the Phillies.

Aug. 4: Christy Mathewson won both
games in the Giants' doubleheader sweep of
the Reds.

Aug. 13: Boston staged a day to honor
Cy Young.

Sept. 5: Brooklyn's Nap Rucker pitched
a no-hitter against Boston.

Sept. 7: Washington's Walter Johnson
pitched his third shutout in four days against
New York.

Sept. 15: Christy Mathewson ran his
winning streak against the Browns to 24
games.

Oct. 2: Cleveland's Addie Joss pitched a
perfect game against the White Sox.

Oct. 7: The regular season
ended with the Giants and Cubs tied with
98–55 records.

Oct. 8: The Cubs beat the Giants in the
playoff for the National League pennant.

Oct. 14: The deciding game of the
World Series drew just 6,210 fans as the Cubs
beat the Tigers.

Dec. 12: The Cardinals acquired Roger
Bresnahan from the Giants. Bresnahan became
the team's player-manager.

Three Finger Brown tossed a four
hit win in Game Four

LEADERS

BATTING AVERAGE
AL: Ty Cobb, Detroit, .377
NL: Honus Wagner, Pittsburgh, .339

HOME RUNS
AL: Ty Cobb, Detroit, 9
NL: Red Murray, NY Giants, 7

RUNS BATTED IN
AL: Ty Cobb, Detroit, 107
NL: Honus Wagner, Pittsburgh, 100

STOLEN BASES
AL: Ty Cobb, Detroit, 76
NL: Bob Bescher, Cincinnati, 54

PITCHING VICTORIES
AL: George Mullin, Detroit, 29
NL: Mordecai Brown, Chicago Cubs, 27

EARNED RUN AVERAGE
AL: Harry Krause, Philadelphia, 1.39
NL: Christy Mathewson, NY Giants, 1.14

STRIKEOUTS
AL: Frank Smith, Chicago White Sox, 177
NL: Orval Overall, Chicago Cubs, 205

Ty Cobb was a fearless competitor—and a fearless opponent

It may not have happened as easily as they anticipated, but the Detroit Tigers won their third consecutive American League pennant. The Tigers hit a midseason slump and some unexpected competition from the rebuilt Philadelphia Athletics before they were able to wrap up the title by 3½ games.

With Sam Crawford and Ty Cobb in the middle of the batting order, the Tigers had one of the most dangerous lineups in the league. Cobb had come into his own at the age of 22 with a .377 average, nine home runs and 107 RBIs to win the Triple Crown. Cobb also led the league with 76 stolen bases.

His value to the Tigers couldn't be measured in numbers alone. Cobb was one of the game's greatest competitors. He set a standard for his teammates and he intimidated his opponents—it was a role he relished. Accounts differ on how much of Cobb's dislike for other players was genuine, but there's no question that he was convincing. He was one of the most unpopular players in the game—and he didn't mind that title a bit.

The Tigers had a strong pitching staff as well. George Mullin was 22–9 with a 2.22 earned run average. Ed Willett was 22–9 with a 2.33 ERA and Ed Summers had a 19–9 record.

There were just three 20-game winners in the American League and the Tigers had two of them. The other was Frank Smith, who pitched for the fourth-place Chicago White Sox.

The new look of the Athletics was testimony to Connie Mack's savvy as a baseball man. His new infield featured Frank Baker at third base, Jack Barry at shortstop and Eddie Collins at second base. Collins was a smash, hitting .346. Baker batted .305. Only Barry disappointed with a .215 average.

The Athletics got good pitching from Eddie Plank (19–8), Chief Bender and Harry Krause, who both had an 18–8 record.

In the National League, the Chicago Cubs were poised to take their fourth consecutive pennant. Instead, the title went to the surprising Pittsburgh Pirates while the Cubs finished 6½ games behind them in second place.

Things went badly for the Cubs from the start. Catcher Johnny Kling had an extended contract holdout and infield mainstay Johnny Evers suffered a nervous breakdown. The Cubs had a bad first month and it wound up costing them the pennant. The Pirates were strong from the start of the season and maintained that pace.

Chicago still won 104 games, but it wasn't enough in a season when the Pirates had a major league-best 110 victories.

The Pirates' player-manager, Fred Clarke

The newly-opened Forbes Field provided the ideal backdrop for the pennant-winning Pirates

Shortstop Honus Wagner led the Pirates with a .329 average and his fourth consecutive batting title. Player-manager Fred Clarke batted .287. Howie Camnitz led the Pirates pitching staff with a 25–6 mark and Vic Willis was 22–11. Lefty Leifeld also won 19 games.

Only the Cubs and third-place New York Giants finished within 30 games of the Pirates, who had a new home in 1909 as Forbes Field opened. Another new National League park debuted on the other side of Pennsylvania as the Phillies moved into Shibe Park.

POSTSEASON

It wasn't easy to keep the Chicago Cubs out of the World Series, as the Pittsburgh Pirates discovered.

The Pirates won 110 games and needed all of them to end the three-year pennant run of the Cubs, who won 104 games. It was the Pirates' first appearance since they represented the National League in the first Series.

The Detroit Tigers were back for the third consecutive year, having lost the previous two Series to the Cubs.

Rookie Babe Adams made the difference for the Pirates, winning three times in the seven-game Series. Adams won the opener 4–1 before the Tigers beat Howie Camnitz 7–2 in Game Two to even the Series.

Pittsburgh scored six runs in the first two innings of Game Three and held on for an 8–6 win behind Nick Maddox. Detroit's George Mullin pitched a 5–0 shutout in Game Four

to again tie the Series.

Adams won Game Five 8–4 before the Tigers to even the Series for a third time with Mullin's 5–4 win.

In Game Seven, Adams threw a six-hit 8–0 shutout, giving him a 1.33 ERA. Batting champion Honus Wagner batted .333 with seven home runs for the Pirates. American League batting leader Ty Cobb hit just .231 for the Tigers, although he drove in six runs.

GAME 1	
Pittsburgh 4	Detroit 1
GAME 2	
Detroit 7	Pittsburgh 2
GAME 3	
Pittsburgh 8	Detroit 6
GAME 4	
Detroit 5	Pittsburgh 0
GAME 5	
Pittsburgh 8	Detroit 4
GAME 6	
Detroit 5	Pittsburgh 4
GAME 7	
Pittsburgh 8	Detroit 0

Pittsburgh's World Series hero, Babe Adams

Feb. 17: A rules change was adopted: relief pitchers are required to retire at least one batter.

Feb. 18: Boston traded Cy Young to Cleveland.

April 8: The Highlanders are quarantined after Hal Chase contracts chicken pox.

April 12: Billy Sullivan became White Sox manager, replacing Fielder Jones.

April 12: Philadelphia's Shibe Park opened with the Athletics beating Boston.

May 2: Pittsburgh's Honus Wagner stole second, third and home in the same inning against the Cubs.

May 5: The Pirates moved into first place and remained there for the rest of the season.

May 25: Detroit's George Mullin won his ninth consecutive decision.

June 15: George Mullin's winning streak ended at 11 games with a 2–1 loss to New York.

June 19: Walter Johnson beat the Highlanders on three hits but walked seven, hit a batter and threw four wild pitches.

June 9: Forbes Field opened in Pittsburgh with the Pirates losing 3–2 to the Cubs.

July 19: Shortstop Neal Ball of Cleveland pulled an unassisted triple play against the Red Sox.

July 29: National League president Harry Pulliam committed suicide.

Aug. 17: Nap Lajoie stepped down as Cleveland's manager but remained as a player.

Sept. 13: Ty Cobb hit his ninth inside-the-park home run of the season.

Sept. 27: The Pirates won their 16th consecutive game to set a National League record. Their streak ended in the second game of that day's doubleheader.

Nov. 26: The Phillies were sold for $350,000.

WAGNER

TEAMS

Teams: Louisville Colonels 1897–99;
Pittsburgh Pirates 1900–17

Games:	2,792
At-Bats:	10,430
Runs:	1,736
RBI:	1,732
Home runs:	101
Hits:	3,415
Doubles:	643
Triples:	252
Stolen Bases:	723
Average:	327
Slugging percentage:	466

At 5'11" and 200 pounds, with bowed legs and abnormally long arms, Honus Wagner didn't look like he was built for either speed or grace.

But Wagner was a superior fielder who covered plenty of ground at shortstop and was one of the finest base stealers of his era, too. He had an easygoing personaility, which belied his competitiveness as well.

John Peter Wagner was one of baseball's biggest stars at the start of the century. His nickname morphed from a family nickname. His parents were Bavarian immigrants who had settled in Pennsylvania so that his father could work in the coal mines. His mother called him "Johannes", which became "Hans" and ultimately "Honus".

His ability on the sandlots caught the attention of scouts, who were impressed with his smooth defensive style and his ability to make consistent contact at the plate. The Louisville National League club paid $2,100 for Wagner, who joined the team in time for the second half of the 1897 season. Wagner was an immediate hit, batting .344 in his first 61 major league games.

A .300 average would become the norm for Wagner. He hit .300 in 17 consecutive seasons. He took eight batting titles, which stood as a record until Tony Gwynn caught him at the end of the century.

Wagner's pleasant demeanor was in sharp contrast to his American League counterpart, Ty Cobb. When Wagner's Pittsburgh Pirates met Cobb and the Detroit Tigers in the World Series, a story was concocted about a confrontation between the two. Cobb was known as a dirty player who used to sharpen his spikes with a steel file in full view of the opposing team.

The story held that Cobb reached first base and shouted down to second that he was not only going to steal the base, he was going to do harm to Wagner. Cobb, legend has it, took off on his stolen base and was tagged out by Wagner. The end of the story holds that Wagner slapped his glove into Cobb's face, cutting the latter on the lip.

The oft-repeated tale probably isn't factual, but it stood for years because it was a believeable premise based on the players' contrasting personalities. Wagner may have been mildmannered, but he was a fierce competitor, too. Baseball players of that era didn't succeed without a certain inner fire. The difference was Wagner kept his hidden, much as his tremendous athletic ability was disguised by his unconventional build.

Yankees' pitcher Lefty Gomez once sized up Wagner and is supposed to have said, "He could tie his shoes standing up."

Mostly, though, Wagner commanded respect because of his ability and the consistency of his production.

Asked the best way to pitch to Wagner, New York Giants' manager John McGraw said, "Just throw the ball ... and then duck." Wagner consistently produced line drives and used the entire field, an important consideration in the deadball era.

Wagner came to Pittsburgh in 1900, after the Louisville franchise folded. Owner Barney Dreyfuss brought many of his Louisville players with him and Wagner's name was at the top of the list. The trust between the men was such that Wagner didn't negotiate a contract—he simply played for whatever amount Dreyfuss judged to be fair.

Wagner played both infield and outfield before he settled in as Pittsburgh's regular shortstop in 1903. He was prepared to retire in 1909 when arthritis in his legs became an issue. Manager Fred Clarke persuaded him to stay and Wagner played until 1917, retiring at age 43.

He served as Pirates' manager for five games, but decided that his personality wasn't suited for that job. Wagner did some coaching at Pittsburgh's Carnegie Tech and had business interests in the area, including a sporting goods store that traded on his famous name.

Wagner collected 3,430 hits in his career and was the second player to reach 3,000 hits, following Cap Anson. He led the league in stolen bases six times, had at least 100 RBIs nine times and hit better than .350 in five seasons.

In 1933, he rejoined the Pirates as an all-purpose coach and the team reaped the benefits of having him associated with the franchise. A statue of Wagner was dedicated and has stood outside every Pirates ballpark for more than 40 years.

Wagner remained a Pirates coach until his death in 1955 at the age of 81.

Wagner's appearance belied his amazing athletic ability

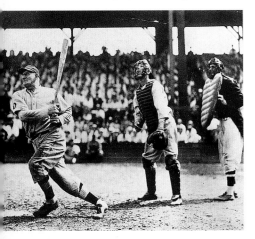

1910

It was a decade of great growth and great shame for baseball. The popularity of the sport was on the increase, but baseball's standing with the public took a severe blow when the decade ended with a game-fixing scandal surrounding the World Series.

Some Chicago White Sox players confessed to conspiring with gamblers to fix the outcome of 1919 World Series games. The notion that players would throw games in a championship round was devastating.

It was a significant problem for baseball, which relied on the trust of the public. The "Black Sox Scandal" came after baseball's popularity had grown in a decade still dominated by pitching and base stealing rather than power.

John McGraw built the New York Giants into a power-house, winning four pennants. McGraw's exact opposite, gentlemanly Connie Mack, had done the same thing with the Philadelphia Athletics in the American League. Mack's building efforts were ultimately undermined by the emergence of a new league prepared to start a price war with the existing leagues.

There was bitter irony attached to the 1919 World Series scandal—baseball had survived World War I and the challenge of the Federal League only to have its biggest threat come from within.

BATTING AVERAGE
AL: Ty Cobb, Detroit, .385
NL: Sherry Magee, Philadelphia Phillies, .331

HOME RUNS
AL: Jake Stahl, Boston Red Sox, 10
NL: Fred Beck, Braves; Wildfire Schulte, Cubs, 10

RUNS BATTED IN
AL: Sam Crawford, Detroit, 120
NL: Sherry Magee, Philadelphia Phillies, 123

STOLEN BASES
AL: Eddie Collins, Philadelphia A's, 81
NL: Bob Bescher, Cincinnati, 70

PITCHING VICTORIES
AL: Jack Coombs, Philadelphia A's, 31
NL: Christy Mathewson, NY Giants, 27

EARNED RUN AVERAGE
AL: Ed Walsh, Chicago White Sox, 1.27
NL: George McQuillan, Philadelphia Phillies, 1.60

STRIKEOUTS
AL: Walter Johnson, Washington, 313
NL: Earle Moore, Philadelphia Phillies, 185

Excitement. Drama. Intrigue. The 1910 pennant races had none of those qualities. Both races were pretty much decided in the middle of the summer and the other teams jockeyed to order the positions behind first place.

Solid batting from Philadelphia's Eddie Collins helped his side to the pennant

The Philadelphia Athletics pulled away from the pack in the American League in June and July and wound up 14½ games ahead of the second-place New York Yankees.

The other New York team was the runner-up in the National League. The Giants only got within 13 games of the pennant-winning Chicago Cubs.

The Athletics boasted a solid everyday lineup. Second baseman Eddie Collins batted .322. Outfielder Danny Murphy hit .300 and another outfielder, Rube Goldberg, had a .306 average.

The strength of the Athletics, though, was an exceptional pitching staff. Righthander Jack Coombs was 31–9 with 13 shutouts. At one point during the season, Coombs threw 46 consecutive innings without allowing a run. Chief Bender was second on the staff with a 23–5 record. Cy Morgan went 18–12 and Eddie

Plank was 16–10.

The defending league champion Detroit Tigers saw their pitching staff fall apart and they finished third, behind the Yankees. Ty Cobb hit .362 for the Tigers and drove in 91 runs while scoring a league-leading 106. Sam Crawford's average fell to .289, but he led the league with 120 RBIs.

Jack Knight was the Yankees' only .300 hitter at .312 and Russ Ford led the pitching staff with a 26–6 record.

After falling short to the Pittsburgh Pirates in 1909 despite winning 104 games, the Cubs won their fourth pennant in five years. Chicago was never out of first place after May. They still had the legendary infield of Joe Tinker, Johnny Evers and Frank Chance, along with third baseman Harry Steinfeldt. Outfielder Solly Hofman batted .325 and Wildfire Schulte hit .301 and led the team with ten home runs.

Mordecai Brown paced the pitching staff with a 25–13 record. He was aided by 24-year-old righthander King Cole, who broke into the major leagues with a bang, posting a 20–4 record in his first season.

The Giants were a streak team throughout the entire season. Their consistency was the pitching of No. 1 starter Christy Mathewson, who was 27–9.

Pittsburgh failed to repeat when its pitching staff collapsed. After leading the Pirates with 24 wins in the championship season, Howie Camnitz fell to a 12–13 record. The Pirates lost 23 wins when Vic Willis left for St. Louis. World Series hero Babe Adams was 18–9.

Baseball introduced

Philadelphia ace Jack Coombs led the league in wins posting an impressive total of 31

something called the Jackrabbit ball, which was supposed to aid the offense. The test didn't last long.

The American League had a new showcase as Comiskey Park opened on Chicago's South Side and became the White Sox's new home. Cy Young celebrated his 500th career win with Cleveland.

One of the great individual performances belonged to Sherry Magee of the Phillies. He batted .331, scored 110 runs, drove in 123 and had a slugging percentage of .507.

The season opened with a flourish as President William Taft watched Walter Johnson pitch the Washington Senators to a one-hit victory over Philadelphia.

Cy Young (r) achieved a unique milestone with Cleveland

POSTSEASON

The Philadelphia Athletics needed only two pitchers to win four games against the Chicago Cubs.

GAME 1	
Philadelphia A's 4	Chicago Cubs 1
GAME 2	
Philadelphia A's 9	Chicago Cubs 3
GAME 3	
Philadelphia A's 12	Chicago Cubs 5
GAME 4	
Chicago Cubs 4	Philadelphia A's 3
GAME 5	
Philadelphia A's 7	Chicago Cubs 2

Connie Mack's Athletics came away with their first title, winning the Series 4–1 with Chief Bender and Jack Coombs pitching all 45⅔ innings in the Series.

Bender, who had gone 23–5 in the regular season, pitched brilliantly in the opener, holding the Cubs to three hits in a 4–1 win. Orval Overall was the losing pitcher.

In Game Two, Coombs, a 31-game winner in the regular season, won 9–3 despite allowing eight hits and nine walks. The Athletics scored six runs in the seventh inning against Mordecai Brown – an inning highlighted by Danny Murphy's two-run double.

Coombs was much better on one day's rest and got the victory in Philadelphia's 12–5 win in Game Three. The Cubs avoided the sweep by scoring a run in the bottom of the tenth against Bender to win Game Four, 4–3. Jimmy Sheckard delivered a two-out, game-winning single for the Cubs.

Coombs was able to wrap it up in Game Five, winning 7–2 against Brown.

Eddie Collins batted .429 for the Cubs and Murphy drove in eight runs while hitting .350. Frank Baker also hit .409 for Philadelphia.

Connie Mack's baseball moxie was the backbone of the A's

The New York Giants certainly proved they were adaptable.

When fire damaged their home field, the Polo Grounds, they moved to Highlander Park across town without missing a beat.

And when the lineup required some personnel changes, manager John McGraw didn't hesitate to act decisively and effectively, switching two members of his starting infield en route to another National League pennant.

The Giants stayed close to the Chicago Cubs for four months, then rocketed past them in August. New York passed the Cubs on August 24 and remained in first place the rest of the way. Winning 20 of the last 24 games helped them increase their final margin to 7½ games over Chicago.

Christy Mathewson had his customary outstanding season for the Giants. He was 26–13 and led the league with a 1.99 earned run average. The Giants also got a major contribution from Rube Marquard, who was 24–7 and led the league with 237 strikeouts.

McGraw sensed that something was lacking in his everyday lineup and he attempted to correct the problem by making changes at two infield spots. Utilityman Art Fletcher was promoted to a starting role at shortstop, replacing Al Bridwell. McGraw was able to get Buck Herzog back from Boston and installed him at third base over Art Devlin.

Fletcher hit .319 and second baseman Larry Doyle batted .310 and led the team with 13 home runs. Catcher Chief Meyers hit .332 and first baseman Fred Merkle hit .283 and drove in a team-leading 84 runs.

Elsewhere in the National League, Pittsburgh's Honus Wagner took his eighth batting title with a .334 average. It was also his last batting championship. Cubs' outfielder Wildfire Schulte lived up to his nickname by hitting 21 home runs, the most the league had seen since 1899.

Pitcher Grover Cleveland had a strong debut with Philadelphia, setting the pace for the League with 28 victories.

In the American League, the Philadelphia Athletics started slowly but kicked into gear by May and won the pennant by 13½ games over Detroit. The race was between the Athletics and Tigers for most of the season.

The Athletics overtook the Tigers on August 4 and stayed in first place. Philadelphia had a balance that most teams couldn't duplicate. Their .296 team average led the league and their pitching staff was experienced and deep.

Philadelphia debuted the "$100,000 Infield" consisting of first baseman Stuffy McInnis, second baseman Eddie Collins, shortstop Jack Barry and third baseman Frank "Home Run" Baker. Speaking of people who lived up to their nickname, Baker led the league with 11 homers.

Philadelphia's Jack Coombs went 28–12 and Eddie Plank had a 22–8 record.

Detroit had a potent one-two combination in outfielders Sam Crawford and Ty Cobb, who occupied the third and fourth spots in their line-

Detoit's Ty Cobb finished the season with an incredible .420 average

SHORTS Ty Cobb had a reputation as one of the game's nastiest competitors and he reinforced that in an incident before a game against Cleveland. He and Joe Jackson were competing for the batting title. Cobb had been something of a hero to Jackson and the rookie approached his idol. Cobb ignored him and Jackson, perhaps upset by the episode, hit poorly in the series.

Joe Jackson's batted .408 but it wasn't enough to help Cleveland to the pennant

up. Cobb led the league with a .420 average and 127 RBIs. Crawford hit .378 and drove in 115 runs. Cobb claimed his fifth batting title.

That was a tough break for Cleveland's Joe Jackson, who batted .408 and still finished 12 points behind the leader. Things were looking up in Cleveland, where rookie Vean Gregg won 23 games and posted a League-best 1.81 ERA.

POSTSEASON

The Philadelphia Athletics repeated as World Series champions and did it in almost the same style.

GAME 1	
NY Giants 2	Philadelphia A's 1
GAME 2	
Philadelphia A's 3	NY Giants 1
GAME 3	
Philadelphia A's 3	NY Giants 2
GAME 4	
Philadelphia A's 4	NY Giants 2
GAME 5	
NY Giants 4	Philadelphia A's 3
GAME 6	
Philadelphia A's 13	NY Giants 2

The Athletics rolled to the American League title by winning 101 games (one less than they had won in 1910) and then went on to handle their National League opponent in the Series – this time it was the New York Giants, who had beaten the Athletics in 1905.

New York won the opening game 2–1 as Christy Mathewson outdueled Chief Bender. The Athletics evened the Series with a 3–1 win in Game Two when Frank Baker hit a tiebreaking two-run homer off Rube Marquard in the sixth inning.

Game Three saw the Athletics score two runs in the top of the 11th to beat Mathewson 3–2. If Philadelphia had momentum, the elements interrupted it. Six days of rain postponed Game Four for a week. The Athletics moved within a win of clinching the series when Bender beat Mathewson 4–2.

The Giants overcame a 3–0 deficit to win 4–3 in Game Five. The Athletics made it easy for Bender with a 13–2 win in Game Six. Philadelphia became the second team to win consecutive championships.

Baker hit .375 with a pair of runs and Jack Barry batted .368.

Philadelphia's Frank "Home Run" Baker

TY COBB

TEAMS
Detroit 1905–26; Philadelphia A's 1927–28

Games:	3,034
At-Bats:	11,434
Runs:	2,245
RBI:	1,933
Home runs:	117
Hits:	4,190
Doubles:	658
Triples:	161
Stolen Bases:	892
Average:	.366
Slugging percentage:	.512

Ty Cobb was better than almost everyone in baseball and he wasn't shy about pointing out that fact.

That cantankerous personality is as much a part of the game's history as Cobb's superiority on the field.

"He was a holy terror," teammate Charlie Gehringer said.

Baseball in Cobb's era was a rough and tumble game. Those who played it for a living were often crude people who hadn't had the benefit of much formal education.

Cobb was an exception to that rule. He came from a prominent family in the south and his father had held elected office. The Cobb family wanted Ty to attend college with the intention of becoming either a doctor or lawyer. Instead, he gravitated to baseball. What he lacked in natural athletic ability was more than adequately replaced with an incredible competitive zeal.

Legend has it that Cobb was in the habit of taking a conspicuous spot in the dugout and sharpening his spikes with a steel file in plain view of the opposing team. When Babe Ruth started to garner headlines for his home run prowess and colorful personality, Cobb expressed his disdain. More to the point, he wanted to demonstrate that hitting home runs wasn't as impressive as the reporters seemed to think it was.

Cobb ordinarily used a grip that gave him bat control, but not much power. To show he could hit home runs if he wanted to, he moved his hands down to the bottom of the bat and swung for the fences. He proved his point by hitting five home runs in two games.

Cobb came to the Detroit Tigers as an 18-year-old in 1905. Two years later, he became their first player to win a batting title. He led the American League in hitting 12 times and won nine batting titles in a row at one point in his career.

He was so disliked that opponents did what they could to sway the 1910 batting championship to Cleveland's Nap Lajoie. Cobb made

enemies of the Philadelphia Athletics in an August series in 1909 when he used his spikes to cut Frank Baker with a slide. Cobb needed a police escort to and from the ballpark and extra protection had to be provided for him each day.

On May 15, 1912, Cobb climbed into the stands to confront a heckler. He was suspended indefinitely as a result and his teammates announced they would refuse to play if Cobb wasn't permitted to play. Commissioner Kenesaw Landis threatened to fine the Tigers $5,000 if they didn't field a team, so ownership scrambled to find amateurs to wear the team's uniforms. The amateurs lost 23–2.

In 1911, Cobb hit safely in 41 consecutive games. He frustrated Joe Jackson, who hit .408 that year and lost the title to Cobb, who had a .420 average. In 1912, Jackson would bat .395 and Cobb would again beat him out with a .410 average.

Cobb's streak of batting titles ended in 1916, when he was edged by Cleveland's Tris Speaker, .386 to .378. That was just a one-year interruption, though, as Cobb would win the next three crowns.

In 1921, he found out how frustrating it was to lose a batting title with a .400 average. Cobb hit .401 but George Sisler led the League at .420.

Cobb managed the Tigers beginning in 1921, but abruptly resigned after the 1926 season. It turned out that he and Speaker, then Cleveland's manager, had been accused by former player Dutch Leonard of fixing the outcome of a game. Still scarred by the 1919 World Series scandal, baseball quietly forced both men to resign. They were cleared by Landis when the accusing player declined to testify against them.

Cobb moved onto the Philadelphia Athletics for two seasons and retired after he had a .328 average in 1928. He was the leader in the first Hall of Fame balloting, falling just four votes short of unanimous selection. Cobb compiled a .367 lifetime average and owned 90 records at the time of his retirement.

Thanks to a wise investment in Coca Cola stock, Cobb lived well in his post-playing career. His net worth was estimated at $11 million in 1960.

Cobb died at 74 on July 17, 1961.

Cobb's .367 lifetime average is a record that still stands today

LEADERS

BATTING AVERAGE
AL: Ty Cobb, Detroit, .409
NL: Heinie Zimmerman, Chicago Cubs, .372

HOME RUNS
AL: Frank Baker, Philadelphia A's;
Tris Speaker, Boston Red Sox, 10
NL: Heine Zimmerman, Chicago Cubs, 14

RUNS BATTED IN
AL: Frank Baker, Philadelphia A's, 130
NL: Heine Zimmerman, Chicago Cubs, 103

STOLEN BASES
AL: Clyde Milan, Washington, 88
NL: Bob Bescher, Cincinnati, 67

PITCHING VICTORIES
AL: Joe Wood, Boston Red Sox, 34
NL: Larry Cheney, Chicago Cubs; Rube Marquard, NY Giants, 26

EARNED RUN AVERAGE
AL: Walter Johnson, Washington, 1.39
NL: Jeff Tesreau, Brooklyn, 1.96

STRIKEOUTS
AL: Walter Johnson, Washington, 303
NL: Grover Alexander, Philadelphia Phillies, 195

Jake Stahl could have been elected Mayor of Boston. He was too busy managing the Red Sox, though, leading the team to an American League pennant with a record-setting 105 wins and a 14-game advantage over second-place Washington. It was the third pennant in Red Sox's history.

The Red Sox made the unlikely rise from fifth to first under Stahl, who was in his first year as manager.

The offense was led by outfielder Tris Speaker, who batted .383 with ten home runs, 90 RBIs and 52 stolen bases. Duffy Lewis was another major contributor. His .264 average wasn't terribly impressive, but his 109 RBIs were.

The sensation for the Red Sox was 22-year-old Smokey Joe Wood, a hard-throwing rookie pitcher. Wood fashioned a flashy 34–5 record with a 1.91 earned run average. Wood completed 35 of his 38 games and struck out 258 in 344 innings. There were no accurate measurements for a pitcher's velocity, so it was up to the players to make the pronouncements about the speed of pitches.

Walter Johnson watched the rookie work a game and proclaimed, "No man alive throws faster than Smokey Joe Wood."

SHORTS

An effort to start a rival major league lasted just one month. The United States League opened play on May 1 and was out of business by the end of the month. There was nothing remotely major league about the quality of play or the facilities and fans were not interested in the product. The same organizers would resurface with the Federal League.

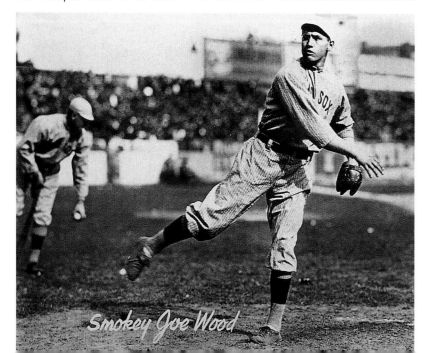

Hard-throwing rookie Smokey Joe Wood helped himself to 34 wins

Smokey Joe Wood

The Giants' Rube Marquard compiled a 19-game win streak

The Detroit Tigers were on the opposite track of the Red Sox. They tumbled to sixth place, undermined by distractions of their own making. On May 15, Ty Cobb had his fill of a heckler's insults and charged into the stands at New York to confront the spectator. As a result, the American League suspended him. The Tigers insisted they wouldn't take the field if Cobb couldn't, but the league stuck by its decisions.

On May 18, the Detroit front office had to scramble to find players because its regular players had essentially called a strike. A pickup team wearing Tigers uniforms lost to the Philadelphia Athletics 23–2. It was such a travesty that Athletics' manager Connie Mack agreed to postpone a game rather than go through with the charade of replacement players.

The Tigers came back on May 21 and Cobb was reinstated on May 26, but things were never quite right in Detroit.

In Washington, the Senators rode ten and 17-game winning streaks to second place. Walter Johnson had another exceptional season, posting a 32–12 record with a 1.39 ERA and 303 strikeouts. First-year manager Clark Griffith also got 88 stolen bases from Clyde Milan.

The New York Giants took an early lead and maintained it, finishing ten games ahead of the Pittsburgh Pirates to win the National League.

Rube Marquard won 19 consecutive decisions on his way to a final record of 26–11 with a 2.57 ERA. Christy Mathewson was 23–12 with a 2.12 ERA.

The Giants also welcomed spitball specialist Jeff Tesreau, who won 17 games. New York had the league's best offense—Merkle led the way with a .309 average, 11 home runs and 84 RBIs with 37 stolen bases. Infielder Larry Doyle had similar numbers, batting .330 with 10 homers, 70 RBIs and 36 steals.

The Pittsburgh Pirates claimed second place on the strength of their pitching. Claude Hendrix was 24–9 and Howie Camnitz went 22–12.

POSTSEASON

The New York Giants let the 1912 World Series slip through their hands. The Giants made a couple of devastating errors in the deciding game of the Series and watched the Boston Red Sox take their second title and first since the inaugural Series in 1903.

The Red Sox won Game One, 4–3, before the second game ended in a 6–6 tie when darkness intruded.

The Giants came back with a 2–1 win in Game Three to tie the Series at one game each. Boston won Game Four, 3–1, and also took Game Five, 2–1, for a 3–1 edge in games. The Giants avoided elimination with a 5–2 win in Game Six and New York forced a deciding game by winning Game Seven, 11–4.

New York took a 2–1 lead into the bottom of the tenth in the deciding game, thanks to Fred Merkle's RBI single. Giants' center fielder Fred Snodgrass dropped a routine fly ball to start the inning and Clyde Engle wound up on second base. After an out and a walk, Merkle failed to catch a foul pop and Tris Speaker, given a second chance, singled in the tying run. The Red Sox won the game and Series on Larry Gardner's sacrifice fly.

GAME 1	
Boston Red Sox 4	NY Giants 3
GAME 2	
Boston Red Sox 6	NY Giants 6 (tie)
GAME 3	
NY Giants 2	Boston Red Sox 1
GAME 4	
Boston Red Sox 3	NY Giants 1
GAME 5	
Boston Red Sox 2	NY Giants 1
GAME 6	
NY Giants 5	Boston Red Sox 2
GAME 7	
NY Giants 11	Boston Red Sox 4
GAME 8	
Boston Red Sox 3	NY Giants 2

The Red Sox's Tris Speaker

Feb. 1: Cubs' second baseman Jim Doyle died after appendicitis surgery.

April 12: The Cubs' famous double-play combination of Joe Tinker, Johnny Evers and Frank Chance played its last game together.

April 20: Fenway Park opened with the Red Sox beating the New York Highlanders 7–6 in 11 innings.

May 3: Philadelphia Athletics pitchers allow ten runs in the ninth inning, but hold on for an 18–15 win over New York.

May 4: The Giants stole nine bases and beat the Phillies 4–3.

May 15: Ty Cobb of the Giants ran into the stands to fight with a heckler in New York.

May 18: Tigers' players voted to strike in protest of the indefinite suspension the American League gave Ty Cobb for entering the stands and fighting with a fan.

May 29: Boton got 59 hits in a doubleheader sweep of Washington and scored 33 runs.

June 10: The Red Sox moved into first place to stay.

June 13: Christy Mathewson got his 300th career win.

June 20: The Giants and Braves combined to score 17 runs in the ninth inning of a 21–12 New York win.

July 3: Rube Marquard of the Giants extended his personal winning streak to 19 games by beating Brooklyn 2–1.

July 6: Construction began on Ebbets Field in Brooklyn.

Aug. 11: Joe Jackson stole home twice in the same game for Cleveland.

Aug. 20: Jay Cashion of Washington pitched a no-hitter against Cleveland.

Aug. 27: The National League made earned run average an official statistic.

Aug. 30: Earl Hamilton of the Browns pitched a no-hitter against Ty Cobb and the Tigers.

Sept. 6: Rookie Jeff Tesreau of Brooklyn pitched a no-hitter against Philadelphia.

LEADERS

BATTING AVERAGE
AL: Ty Cobb, Detroit, .390
NL: Jake Daubert, Brooklyn, .350

HOME RUNS
AL: Frank Baker, Philadelphia A's, 12
NL: Gavvy Cravath, Philadelphia Phillies, 19

RUNS BATTED IN
AL: Frank Baker, Philadelphia A's, 126
NL: Gavvy Cravath, Philadelphia Phillies, 128

STOLEN BASES
AL: Clyde Milan, Washington, 75
NL: Max Carey, Pittsburgh, 61

PITCHING VICTORIES
AL: Walter Johnson, Washington, 36
NL: Tom Seaton, Philadelphia Phillies, 27

EARNED RUN AVERAGE
AL: Walter Johnson, Washington, 1.09
NL: Christy Mathewson, NY Giants, 2.06

STRIKEOUTS
AL: Walter Johnson, NY Giants, 243
NL: Tom Seaton, Philadelphia Phillies, 168

20-game winner
Christy Mathewson

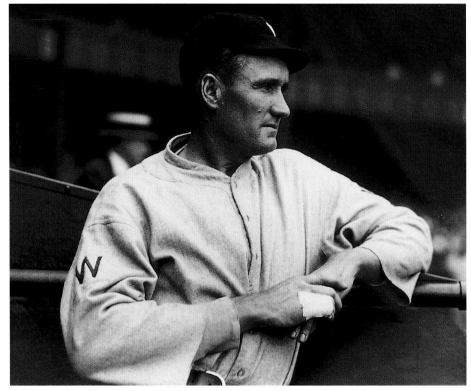

Washington's Walter Johnson was the American League's outstanding pitcher

What happened to Jake Stahl was another reminder of how fleeting baseball success can be.

Stahl was the toast of Boston in 1912 when he led the Red Sox from sixth place to a pennant n his first year as manager. When the team reversed that direction in 1913, the management decided that the best course of action was one without Stahl. He resigned during the season amid the sagging fortunes of the team.

It was a season full of interesting individual performances, but the pennant races were runaways. The Philadelphia Athletics and New York Giants had plenty of time to prepare for their meeting in the World Series because it was obvious they were going to win their respective league titles.

The Athletics moved into first place in late April and never relinquished their position. They survived the loss of 21-game winner Jack Coombs, who was ill and missed the season. Chief Bender was 21–10. He was the only 20-game winner, but the Athletics had five pitchers with a double-figure win total.

Two young pitchers chipped in with 14–6 records—21-year-old Duke Houck and 20-year-old Bullet Joe Bush.

Philadelphia had always succeeded because of its pitching. This time, the offense stepped up and took on a greater share of the responsibility. First baseman Stuffy McInnis batted .326 and drove in 90 runs. Second baseman Eddie Collins hit .345 and led the league by scoring 125 runs. Third baseman Frank Baker had a .336 average and led the league with 12 home runs and 117 RBIs. It was his third consecutive home run title.

Good pitching helped Washington to finish second. Walter Johnson had a huge year – 36–7 with a 1.14 ERA and 243 strikeouts to lead the league in all three categories.

As is usually the case, Boston's fall probably wasn't the manager's fault. The hitters slumped and promising prospect Smokey Joe Wood broke his hand and won just 11 games.

The highlight in Detroit was another batting

SHORTS The Federal League opened in May with six teams – Chicago, Cleveland, Pittsburgh, Indianapolis, St. Louis, Kansas City and Covington, Kentucky. In four of the six cities, the new league went head-to-head with the established major leagues. Cy Young managed the Cleveland franchise. Indianapolis won the league championship. The league would get more ambitious in its second year of existence.

title for Ty Cobb, who hit .390.

The Giants overcame a sluggish start for their third consecutive National League title. Their top three starters accounted for 70 of the team's 101 wins – Christy Mathewson was 25–11, Rube Marquard went 23–10 and Jeff Tesreau had a 22–13 record. The New York staff allowed the fewest runs in the league.

Larry Doyle batted .280 for the Giants and drove in 73 runs while Art Fletcher hit .297 with 71 RBIs.

Even though they were a distant 12½ games off the pace, the Philadelphia Phillies surprised everyone by finishing second. Tom Seaton won 27 games in his first season and led the league with 268 strikeouts. Grover Alexander went 22–6 for the Phillies and Gavvy Gravath hit

.341 and took the home run title with 19.

The Cubs faced the inevitability of change after their successful run. Manager Frank Chance was gone before the season started, pitcher Ed Reulbach was traded to Brooklyn and long-time Cubs' fixtures Joe Tinker and Mordecai Brown were traded to Cincinnati.

SHORTS

Even the baseball was an issue in the early days of the major leagues. A box was placed near home plate in 1912 so that umpires could choose a new baseball to put in play without having to accept one offered by the home team. Standards for the condition of a game-quality ball were still being defined. In June, the Reds and Cubs played a complete game with one baseball.

POSTSEASON

The Philadelphia Athletics were back in the World Series and that was bad news for the New York Giants. The Athletics had dominated the Giants in the 1911 Series and did it again in 1913, winning in five games.

GAME 1	
Philadelphia A's 6	NY Giants 4
GAME 2	
NY Giants 3	Philadelphia A's 0
GAME 3	
Philadelphia A's 8	NY Giants 2
GAME 4	
Philadelphia A's 6	NY Giants 5
GAME 5	
Philadelphia A's 3	NY Giants 1

Philadelphia won the first game 6–4 as the Athletics pounded Rube Marquard for eight hits and five runs in five innings. Christy Mathewson and Eddie Plank hooked up for nine scoreless innings in Game Two, before the Giants scored three in the tenth and won 3–0. Mathewson's single drove in the first run.

Joe Bush and Chief Bender pitched consecutive complete games for the Athletics, allowing Philadelphia to get within one game of ending the Series. Bush won Game Three, 8–2, and Bender took Game Four, 6–5, holding off the Giants in the late innings.

Game Five was in New York and home fans saw Mathewson pitch another good game, but this time Plank pitched better. Plank held the Giants to two hits in the 2–1 win that gave the Athletics the championship.

Frank Baker had another big Series for Philadelphia, driving in seven runs while batting .450. Collins hit .421. Mathewson was just 1–1 despite his 0.95 ERA.

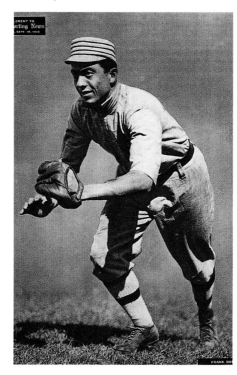

Philadelphia's Home Run Baker

TIMELINE

Jan. 8: Frank Chance, former player-manager with the Cubs, signed to manage the Yankees.

Jan. 10: Cincinnati purchased the contract of former Cubs' star Mordecai Brown.

Feb. 1: The Giants signed Jim Thorpe.

Feb. 8: The Federal League formed with six franchises and a 120-game schedule.

April 5: Brooklyn's Ebbets Field opened with an exhibition game against the Yankees. Casey Stengel hit the first home run.

April 9: Ebbets Field officially opened with a 1–0 loss for Brooklyn to the Phillies.

April 25: Ty Cobb ended his holdout by signing with the Tigers.

May 6: The Federal League opened its first season.

May 30: The Giants' John McGraw won his 1,000th game.

June 6: The Yankees' losing streak extended to 13 games.

June 11: The Philadelphia Athletics' winning streak ended at 15 games with a loss to the Browns.

June 16: Grover Alexander lost his first game after ten wins when the Cubs beat him.

June 30: The Giants moved into first place and stayed there for the rest of the season with an 11–1 win over the Phillies.

Aug. 2: Washington staged Walter Johnson Day.

Aug. 28: Walter Johnson's personal 14-game winning streak ended with 1–0, 11-inning loss to Boston.

Sept. 6: Eddie Collins of the Athletics stole home twice in a game against the Red Sox.

Sept. 14: Larry Cheney of the Cubs shut out the Giants despite allowing 14 hits.

Sept. 22: The Athletics clinched the American League pennant as Herb Pennock and Eddie Plank combined on a 1–0 shutout of the Tigers.

Sept. 27: The Giants won the National League pennant because the second-place Phillies lost.

Sept. 29: Walter Johnson posted his 34th win with a 1–0 win over Philadelphia. It was also his 12th shutout of the season.

LEADERS

BATTING AVERAGE
AL: Ty Cobb, Detroit, .368
NL: Jake Daubert, Brooklyn, .329

HOME RUNS
AL: Frank Baker, Philadelphia A's, 9
NL: Gavvy Cravath, Philadelphia Phillies, 19

RUNS BATTED IN
AL: Sam Crawford, Detroit, 104
NL: Sherry Magee, Philadelphia Phillies, 103

STOLEN BASES
AL: Fritz Maisel, NY Yankees, 74
NL: George Burns, NY Giants, 62

PITCHING VICTORIES
AL: Walter Johnson, Washington Senators, 28
NL: Grover Alexander, Philadelphia Phillies;
Dick Rudolph, Boston Red Sox, 27

EARNED RUN AVERAGE
AL: Dutch Leonard, Boston Red Sox, 1.01
NL: Bill Doak, St. Louis Cardinals, 1.72

STRIKEOUTS
AL: Walter Johnson, Washington, 225
NL: Pete Alexander, Philadelphia Phillies, 214

The first-place Boston Braves? To the complete surprise of the rest of the National League, that's exactly what happened. The Braves, who had finished fifth a year earlier? The Braves, who had been in last place on June 18 during the 1914 season?

Maybe the Braves were in the best position. They had no expectations so they played without pressure and shocked the league by advancing eight spots in the standings within two months.

The New York Giants led the league by a comfortable margin in June, but the Giants weren't the same dominating team they had been. Pitcher Rube Marquard didn't have a good season (he wound up 12–22) but Christy Mathewson and Jeff Tesreau were fine. Hitters Red Murray and Larry Doyle both struggled.

The Braves' rise was steady and started in the middle of July. They were in fourth place by July 21 and moved into second place on August 12. The Braves were an interesting collection of players who had been unwanted by other teams.

They got reliable pitching from Bill James, who was 26–7, and Dick Rudolph, who had a 27–10 record. Lefty Tyler was 16–14. Outfielder Joe Connolly hit .306, veteran Johnny Evers batted .279 and Rabbit Maranville helped steady the middle infield defense.

The Braves passed the Giants on September 8. How could they handle a close race and all the pressure involved? That was never an issue. The Braves won 34 of their last 44 games and put 10½ games between themselves and the Giants.

The Philadelphia Athletics didn't have that comfortable a time, but they still won the American League title fairly easily. The Athletics scored 749 runs, the top figure in the league. Stuffy McInnis batted .314, Eddie Collins hit .344 and Frank Baker had a .319 average and again led the league in home runs with nine.

Philadelphia survived the loss of pitcher Jack

Braves' manager George Stallings achieved the impossible, winning it all

Coombs for a second consecutive year. Coombs was able to pitch only two games because of illness. The Athletics compensated for his absence with a balanced pitching staff and had seven pitchers with double-figure win totals.

The Red Sox continued to be disappointed by Smokey Joe Wood, who encountered injury problems and won only nine games. Boston got another big season from Tris Speaker, who batted .338 with 90 RBIs and 42 stolen bases.

Ray Collins went 20–13 for the Red Sox and Dutch Leonard was just a step behind at 19–5.

The most significant development of the season for the Red Sox may have came when they purchased Babe Ruth from a minor league team in Providence. Ruth was a pitcher who also had a reputation for being able to swing the bat capably.

SHORTS The players gained some significant rights after taking their case to the governing National Commission. After presenting demands, they got written notification of any reassignment of their contracts, travel expenses to spring training, uniforms provided by the clubs, a blank green hitter's background at every ballpark and — most surprising — free agency after ten years in the major leagues.

SHORTS

The Federal League was unable to lure stars Ty Cobb, Tris Speaker or Walter Johnson away from their clubs. The league did succeed in attracting some name players and driving up the costs of player salaries. The Federal League threat caused the budget-conscious Philadelphia Athletics to start disbanding their championship-caliber club. Indianapolis edged Chicago for the title.

Two veterans reached the 3,000-hit plateau – Nap Lajoie and Honus Wagner.

The big story off the field was the formation of the Federal League, which stood ready to raid the rosters of the existing clubs for familiar names. Indianapolis won the first Federal League championship led by Bill McKechnie and Edd Roush.

Honus Wagner became the first player to reach the 3,000 career hits milestone

POSTSEASON

After four consecutive years in the National League cellar, the Boston Braves jumped up to fifth place in 1913.

It was definitely an improvement for the Braves, but they still finished 31½ games out of first place. No one expected their next step, which was to win the 1914 National League pennant by 10½ games over the defending champion New York Giants.

And no one could have accurately predicted that the Braves would sweep the powerful Philadelphia Athletics in four games. Yet that's what happened in one of baseball's most improbable World Series.

Boston jumped on ace Chief Bender for a 7–1 win in Game One, then got a run in the ninth inning of Game Two for a 1–0 victory. The duel between Boston's Bill James and Eddie Plank of the Athletics was settled on Les Mann's ninth-inning single.

The Braves went home for Game Three and won 5–4 in the bottom of the 12th. Hank Gowdy, who had helped save the Braves with a tenth-inning home run, led off with a double and the run eventually scored on an error.

Boston ended the Series with a 3–1 victory in Game Four behind starter Dick Rudolph, who was 2–0 with a 0.50 ERA. Gowdy, a .243 hitter in the regular season, batted .545 in the Series.

GAME 1	
Boston Braves 7	Philadelphia A's 1
GAME 2	
Boston Braves 1	Philadelphia A's 0
GAME 3	
Boston Braves 5	Philadelphia A's 4
GAME 4	
Boston Braves 3	Philadelphia A's 1

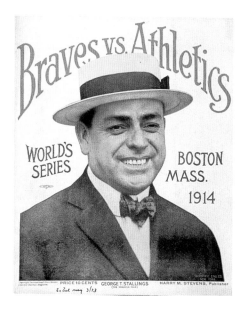

The advertising poster for the 1914 World Series

TIMELINE

April 1: Rube Waddell died of tuberculosis at the age of 37.

April 25: The Browns turned a double play on a double steal, getting Ty Cobb out at the plate.

May 16: Pittsburgh's Joe Kelly got a hit with two outs in the ninth to break up a no-hit bid by Jeff Tesreau of Brooklyn.

May 26: Rube Foster of the Red Sox had his streak of scoreless innings ended at 48 by Cleveland.

May 31: Joe Benz of the White Sox pitched a no-hitter against Cleveland.

July 7: Connie Mack of the Athletics turned down a chance to purchase the contract of minor leaguer Babe Ruth because he could not meet the asking price of $10,000.

July 11: Babe Ruth made his major league debut with Boston as a pitcher.

July 19: The Braves escaped last place with a 3–2 win over the Reds and will shock the National League by going on to win the pennant.

Aug. 11: Ty Cobb rejected an offer from the upstart Federal League and signed a three-year contract with the Tigers.

Sept. 12: Roger Peckinpaugh signed to manage the Yankees and became the major leagues' youngest manager at 23. He replaced Frank Chance.

Sept. 22: Ray Collins of the Red Sox beat the Tigers twice in a doubleheader, throwing two complete games.

Sept. 23: The Reds win at Boston to end their losing streak at 19 games.

Sept. 23: Rube Marquard's personal losing streak was extended to 12 games.

Sept. 27: The Philadelphia Athletics clinched the American League pennant.

Sept. 27: Nap Lajoie of Cleveland got his 3,000th career hit.

Sept. 29: The Boston Braves clinched the National League pennant.

Oct. 1: Gavvy Cravath of the Phillies hit his League-leading 19th home run.

NAP LAJOIE

TEAMS
Philadelphia Phillies 1896–1900; Philadelphia Athletics 1901–02; Cleveland Bronchos 1902; Cleveland Naps 1903–14; Philadelphia Athletics 1915–16

Games:	2,707
At-Bats:	9589
Runs:	1504
RBI:	1599
Home runs:	82
Hits:	3242
Doubles:	658
Triples:	161
Stolen Bases:	380
Average:	.338
Slugging percentage:	.466

Lajoie's popularity resulted in the Naps—named in his honor

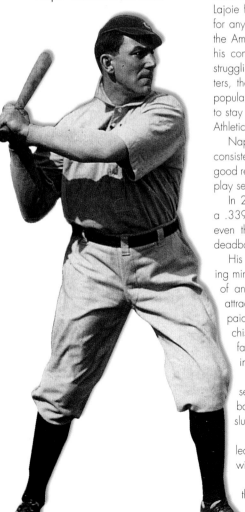

Nap Lajoie didn't just fashion a Hall of Fame career over his 21 major league seasons—he also pioneered the concept of free agency.

Lajoie was an established regular with the Philadelphia Phillies in 1901 when he decided to jump cross-town to the Athletics of the upstart American League. Who could blame him? Lajoie was reportedly making the National League's maximum salary of $2,400 with the Phillies while Connie Mack's Athletics, under no such restraints, were prepared to boost that to $4,000.

Lajoie made the move and a prolonged court case followed. The resulting injunction barred Lajoie from playing any games in Pennsylvania for any team other than the Phillies. As a result, the American League stepped in and awarded his contract to a Cleveland franchise that was struggling. Handed one of the game's best hitters, the Cleveland team saw a huge surge in popularity and success, even though Lajoie had to stay behind when the club played against the Athletics in Philadelphia.

Napoleon Lajoie, known as "Larry," was a consistent right handed hitter who was gifted with good reflexes and sure hands that allowed him to play several positions in the infield.

In 2,475 career games, he wound up with a .339 average and a whopping 1,599 RBIs, even though he hit just 82 home runs in the deadball era.

His career had a dubious start. He was playing minor league baseball and was a teammate of an outfielder named Phil Geier, who had attracted the interest of the Phillies. The Phillies paid $1,500 for Geier's contract. The franchise operator was so pleased with the windfall that he voluntarily threw Lajoie's contract into the deal at no extra charge.

Lajoie became a regular in his second season with the Phillies, playing at first base. He batted .363 and led the league in slugging percentage with a mark of .578.

In 1898, he moved to second base and led the league in RBIs with 127 and doubles with 40.

His career blossomed after he jumped to the Athletics in 1901. In his first American League season Lajoie had a .426 average, which was still a league record at the end of the century.

He also led the league in runs (145), hits (232), total bases (350) and RBIs (125).

During the 1902 season, American League president Ban Johnson ruled that Lajoie should go to Cleveland. Splitting the season between two clubs didn't prevent him from winning a batting title with a .378 average.

In his first full season with Cleveland, he again led the league with a .344 average. His average shot back up to .376 in 1904 as he took his last batting title.

Lajoie was a key figure in an interesting story that developed around the race for the 1910 batting title. League leadership was being contested between Lajoie and Ty Cobb of the Detroit Tigers. Lajoie was generally well-liked around the league and Cobb was one of the most disliked players of the era, because of his abrasive personality and ruthless competitiveness.

A Chalmers automobile was going to be presented to the batting champion. Cobb was the favorite, having won three consecutive titles.

On the last day of the season, Lajoie collected eight hits in a doubleheader against St. Louis. Seven of the hits were bunt singles. Legend has it that St. Louis' third baseman Red Corriden had been ordered by his team to play deep to enhance Lajoie's chances of taking the crown. The league investigated and found no evidence of a conspiracy. The argument was made that Lajoie was such a dangerous hitter that any infielder who played in to guard against a bunt was placing his personal safety in jeopardy because of the possibility Lajoie would take a full swing. Lajoie appeared to win the title, but a week later the American League made an adjustment in Cobb's average that put him a point ahead of Lajoie.

Lajoie managed Cleveland from 1905–09 and the team was nicknamed the "Naps" in his honor. He gave up managing because he thought the extra duties were interfering with his ability to be an effective player.

In his 21-year career, Lajoie won a Triple Crown and four batting titles. He was elected to the Hall of Fame in 1936 and worked in the minor leagues after his retirement. Lajoie died in 1959 at the age of 83.

LEADERS

BATTING AVERAGE
AL: Ty Cobb, Detroit, .369
NL: Larry Doyle, NY Giants, .320

HOME RUNS
AL: Braggo Roth,
Chicago White Sox/Cleveland Indians, 7
NL: Gavvy Cravath, Philadelphia Phillies, 24

RUNS BATTED IN
AL: Sam Crawford, Bobby Veach, Detroit, 112
NL: Gavvy Cravath, Philadelphia Phillies, 115

STOLEN BASES
AL: Ty Cobb, Detroit, 96
NL: Max Carey, Pittsburgh, 36

PITCHING VICTORIES
AL: Walter Johnson, Washington, 27
NL: Grover Alexander, Philadelphia Phillies, 31

EARNED RUN AVERAGE
AL: Joe Wood, Boston Red Sox, 1.49
NL: Grover Alexander, Philadelphia Phillies, 1.22

STRIKEOUTS
AL: Walter Johnson, Washington, 203
NL: Grover Alexander, Philadelphia Phillies, 241

Ty Cobb won his ninth batting title in Detroit

Babe Ruth's versatility for the Red Sox resulted in 18 wins and a .315 average

The Federal League did what the American League couldn't do— it defeated the Philadelphia Athletics.

The challenge of the upstart league hit the Athletics hard and Connie Mack had no choice but tear his championship-caliber club apart because he couldn't match the salary offers the Federal League was making to his players. Mack was loyal to the American League; he tried to place his players with rival clubs rather than have them jump to the Federal League and help the assault on the established major leagues.

Eddie Plank and Chief Bender both went to the Federal League, which blew a huge hole in the Athletics' starting staff. Mack moved second baseman Eddie Collins and outfielder Eddie Murray to the Chicago White Sox.

Pitcher Jack Coombs was released after two years of inactivity due to illness and signed with Brooklyn. Another pitcher, Bob Shawkey, went to the Yankees. Shortstop Jack Barry and pitcher Herb Pennock were shipped to the Boston Red Sox.

Frank "Home Run" Baker must have known what was coming because he said he was retiring at the age of 28 to go home to his farm.

The Athletics had the worst season in their 15-year history, losing 109 games, but things were decidedly happier elsewhere in Philadelphia, where the Phillies rebounded from a fifth-place finish in 1914 to win the National League pennant. Under first-year manager Pat Moran, the Phillies won their first eight games

to build some early confidence.

The Chicago Cubs were challenging for the first two months but started to fade away in June.

Grover Alexander was 31–10 with a 1.22 earned run average. Righthander Erskine Mayer was the No. 2 man on the staff with a 21–15 record. Outfielder Gavvy Gravath had another big year with a .285 average and league-leading totals in home runs (24) and RBIs (115). First baseman Fred Luderus batted .315, hit seven home runs and drove in 62 runs. Dave Bancroft settled down the shortstop position.

Boston couldn't overcome injuries to pitcher Bill James and infielder Johnny Evers. James went 5–4 and Evers was available for only 83 games.

Aside from the Phillies' turnaround, the biggest surprise in the National League was the freefall of the New York Giants. The Giants were perennial contenders, which made it shocking when they skidded to last place.

SHORTS The best pennant race of the season was the one nobody was watching. In its third and final season, the Federal League had an amazing three-way race for first place. Chicago won the title with an 86–66 record, finishing .001 ahead of St. Louis, which was 87–67. Pittsburgh was just a half game back in third place with an 86–67 mark. The league officially disbanded in December.

SHORTS

Home runs were still scarce so players used their legs to generate runs. The steal of home was fairly commonplace as a strategy — it would all but disappear by the end of the century. Ty Cobb was the master of the stolen base and set a record by stealing 96 in 1915. He stole home twice in one game against Washington in June.

Christy Mathewson was 8–14 and Rube Marquard was only 9–8.

The Athletics' decline cleared a path for the Red Sox to win the American League pennant, edging out Detroit. Tris Speaker batted .322 with 69 RBIs and Duffy Lewis had a .291 average.

Boston's deep pitching staff got a boost from the addition of Babe Ruth. Ruth went 18–6 and contributed at the plate, too. Despite getting only 92 at-bats, he led the team with four home runs. Ruth also hit .315 and drove in 21 runs. Rube Foster was 20–8 with a 2.12 ERA for the Red Sox and Smokey Joe Wood rebounded from a couple of sub par years to go 14–5.

The Tigers finished 2½ games behind and Ty Cobb won his ninth consecutive batting title with a .369 average. Cobb also led the league with 96 stolen bases. Teammates Sam Crawford and Bobby Veach tied for the RBI lead with 112.

POSTSEASON

For the second straight year, Boston beat Philadelphia in the World Series. The difference this time was that it was the Red Sox over the Phillies rather than the Braves over the Athletics.

The Red Sox needed only five games to win their third World Series. Grover Cleveland Alexander posted a 3–1 win in the opener for the Phillies. Babe Ruth grounded out as a pinch hitter in the ninth, his only appearance in the Series.

From there the Red Sox took over. Rube Foster held the Phillies to three hits and singled in the winning run in the ninth inning for a 2–1 Boston win. Dutch Leonard got the last 20 batters in order in Game Three and beat Alexander 2–1. Duffy Lewis' RBI single won the game in the ninth.

Boston won again by the 2–1 score in Game Four. Ernie Shore held the Phillies to seven hits.

Philadelphia led Game Five, 4–2, after seven innings, but saw the Red Sox score the

GAME 1	
Philadelphia Phillies 3	Boston Red Sox 1
GAME 2	
Boston Red Sox 2	Philadelphia Phillies 1
GAME 3	
Boston Red Sox 2	Philadelphia Phillies 1
GAME 4	
Boston Red Sox 2	Philadelphia Phillies 1
GAME 5	
Boston Red Sox 5	Philadelphia Phillies 4

tying runs in the eighth, and then win both the game and Series when Harry Hooper homered off Eppa Rixley in the ninth.

Foster won two games for the Red Sox and Lewis batted .444. Fred Luderus led the Phillies with a .438 average.

TIMELINE

Jan. 5: With Nap Lajoie's departure from Cleveland, the team would no longer be known as the Naps. A newspaper launched a contest to find a new nickname, which would turn out to be the Indians.

Feb. 15: Frank (Home Run) Baker told the Athletics he was retiring at 28 to tend to his farm. Baker sat out the 1915 season, but returned to baseball.

April 14: Harry Hooper's single with two outs in the ninth ended Herb Pennock's bid to pitch the first opening day no-hitter.

April 15: Rube Marquard pitched a no-hitter against Brooklyn in the Giants' second game of the season.

May 6: Babe Ruth hit the first of his 714 major league home runs. It came in the third inning off Jack Warhop of the Yankees at the Polo Grounds.

May 29: Herb Pennock went to the Red Sox on waivers.

June 5: Another potential no-hitter was ruined by a two-out hit in the ninth inning. This time the Cardinals' Arthur Butler was the hitter and Grover Alexander was on the mound.

June 11: Ray Caldwell of the Yankees pinch hits his second home run in as many games.

June 13: Bruno Haas debuted for the Athletics against New York and walked 16 batters in nine innings.

June 23: Ty Cobb of the Tigers stole home for the fifth time in the month.

July 2: The Athletics continued to sell players, sending Jack Barry to Boston and Bob Shawkey to the Yankees. The two transactions raised $26,000.

July 17: Grover Alexander's nine-game winning streak ended with a 4–0 loss to the Cubs.

July 29: Honus Wagner hit an inside-the-park, grand slam home run at age 41.

Aug. 18: Braves Field opened in Boston.

The World Champion Boston Red Sox

LEADERS

BATTING AVERAGE
AL: Tris Speaker, Cleveland, .386
NL: Hal Chase, Cincinnati, .339

HOME RUNS
AL: Wally Pipp, NY Yankees, 12
NL: Dave Robertson, NY Giants;
Cy Williams, Chicago Cubs, 12

RUNS BATTED IN
AL: Del Pratt, St. Louis Browns, 103
NL: Heinie Zimmerman,
Chicago Cubs/NY Giants, 83

STOLEN BASES
AL: Ty Cobb, Detroit, 68
NL: Max Carey, Pittsburgh, 63

PITCHING VICTORIES
AL: Walter Johnson, Washington, 25
NL: Grover Alexander, Philadelphia Phillies, 33

EARNED RUN AVERAGE
AL: Babe Ruth, Boston Red Sox, 1.75
NL: Grover Alexander, Philadelphia Phillies, 1.55

STRIKEOUTS
AL: Walter Johnson, Washington, 228
NL: Grover Alexander, Philadelphia Phillies, 167

The Boston Red Sox got rid of their best everyday player and one of their most promising pitchers. It didn't appear to be the framework for success, yet the Red Sox still won their second consecutive American League pennant.

When the Red Sox found themselves in a contract dispute with Tris Speaker, they resolved the issue by sending him to Cleveland. When Smokey Joe Wood held out all year, he, too, was traded to Cleveland.

The Red Sox welcomed an outfielder named Tilly Walker, to take Speaker's place, but didn't come close to matching his production. On the mound, Babe Ruth more than made up for the absence of Wood. Ruth was 23–12 and led the league with a 1.75 earned run average. He struck out 175 batters. On August 13, he out-dueled Walter Johnson 1–0 in a game that went 13 innings.

Ruth batted a respectable .272, tied for the team lead with three home runs and knocked in 15 runs.

The Red Sox finished two games in front of the Chicago White Sox. The Detroit Tigers were third led, as usual, by Ty Cobb, who batted .371 and stole 68 bases. For once, though, Cobb didn't win the batting title. That honor went to Speaker, who compiled a .386 average with Cleveland.

Brooklyn took the National League title, beating out the Philadelphia Phillies by 2½ games and finish four ahead of Boston. Philadelphia and Boston beat each other up in a series of late-season doubleheaders to expedite the pennant for the Dodgers.

The Phillies didn't have enough pitching to support Grover Alexander, who was 33–12 with a 1.55 earned run average. Alexander posted 16 shutouts.

Zack Wheat was Brooklyn's offensive star with a .312 average, nine home runs and 73 RBIs.

A pair of righthanders led the starting staff. Jeff Pfeffer was 25–11 with a 1.91 ERA and Larry Cheney went 18–12 with a 1.92 ERA.

The Boston Braves had too many injury issues to make a stronger run at the Dodgers. They lost

Triple Crown winner, Grover Alexander

center fielder Sherry Magee, pitcher Tom Hughes and second baseman Johnny Evers.

The St. Louis Cardinals finished last, but welcomed Rogers Hornsby, who batted .313.

New York Giants' manager John McGraw was known as a fiery man who wasn't shy about venting his wrath on umpires or players. It stood to reason then that McGraw wouldn't stand passively by and let the Giants continue to finish in the second division. After a shocking last-place finish in 1915, McGraw decided to tear things apart and start over. Out

SHORTS It was a season marked by some unusual streaks. The Washington Senators won 16 straight road games. The Philadelphia Athletics won 20 consecutive games and the St. Louis Browns won 14 in a row. Zack Wheat of Brooklyn had a 29-game hitting streak. Left fielder Sherry Magee of the Braves handled 170 consecutive chances without making an error.

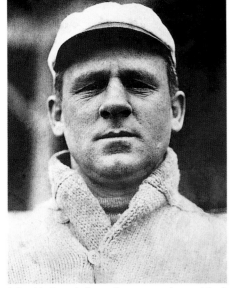

John McGraw's fire sale prompted a spririted finish in New York

went Bill McKechnie, Fred Merkle and Larry Doyle. After years of brilliant service, Christy Mathewson moved on to Cincinnati to become the Reds' manager. McGraw tried to

SHORTS

Was the National League filled with cheaters or people who just couldn't read a tape measure? The league put out a bulletin in March which apparently served as a warning to teams that may have been fudging certain standard measurements. In 1902, the Cubs lost an apparent victory when it was discovered they had shortened the distance from the pitching rubber to home plate.

help the offense by acquiring Heinie Zimmerman from the Chicago Cubs.

McGraw's changes at least pointed the Giants in the right direction. Late in the season they had a streak of 26 consecutive home wins and were able to push their way into fourth place while posting a winning record.

POSTSEASON

The Boston Red Sox had made some changes from their 1915 championship club, but didn't tamper with their pitching staff.

GAME 1	
Boston Red Sox 6	Brooklyn 5
GAME 2	
Boston Red Sox 2	Brooklyn 1
GAME 3	
Brooklyn 4	Boston Red Sox 3
GAME 4	
Boston Red Sox 6	Brooklyn 2
GAME 5	
Boston Red Sox 4	Brooklyn 1

Smart move. The Red Sox staff posted a 1.47 earned run average and that keyed the five-game World Series victory over the Brooklyn Dodgers.

The Red Sox won the opener 6–5. The Dodgers would enjoy their biggest offensive output of the Series. In their other three losses, they would score only four runs.

Brooklyn's Sherry Smith and Babe Ruth of the Red Sox were locked in a 1–1 game in the 14th inning when Smith issued a walk to start his half of the 14th. After a bunt and Del Gainor's pinch single off Smith, the Red Sox had a 2–1 win and were halfway to a World Series victory.

Brooklyn won Game Three, 4–3, behind Jack Coombs.

The Red Sox reclaimed control in Game Four with a 6–2 win keyed by both Larry Gardner's three-run homer and solid

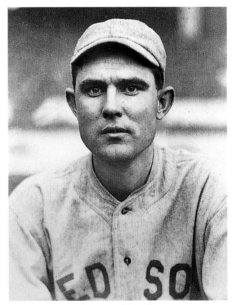

Boston's Series hero, Eddie Shore

pitching from Dutch Leonard.

Boston ended the Series with Ernie Shore's three-hit, 4–1 win.

Shore was 2–0 with a 1.53 ERA and Duffy Lewis batted .353 for his second consecutive outstanding Series. Casey Stengel was the standout for Brooklyn as he batted .364 for a team that managed just a .200 composite average.

CHRISTY MATHEWSON

TEAMS

New York Giants 1900–16;
Cincinnati Reds 1916

Games:	.635
Games started:	.551
Complete games:	.434
Win–Loss:	.373–188
Inning pitched:	.4,780.2
Runs:	.1,616
ERA:	.2.13
Strikeouts:	.2,502
Bases on balls:	.844
Batting average:	.215

When professional baseball was at its rowdiest, a gentleman named Christy Mathewson was the game's best pitcher.

While many players of the era hadn't finished high school, Mathewson had attended Bucknell, where he was a member of the school's glee club and literary society.

Mathewson left school to pursue a career in baseball and spent two seasons toiling for minor league teams. When his second season produced a 20–2 record, the major leagues were interested.

The New York Giants paid $1,500 for his contract, but soon came to regret the transaction. Mathewson lost his first three decisions in 1900, which sent the Giants screaming for a reversal of the deal and a return of their money. Mathewson was subsequently drafted by the Cincinnati Reds for just $100, but was traded back to the Giants without ever pitching for the Reds.

He had his first full season in 1901 and won 20 games, posting a 2.41 earned run average. The Giants still weren't convinced that Mathewson had enough talent to win in the major leagues. Between starts, the Giants had him work out at first base, shortstop and the outfield to prepare for a possible position change.

John McGraw took over the Giants in 1902 and decided that the tall, lean Mathewson would pitch for his club. It was one of the sharpest decisions he made in a Hall of Fame career.

Mathewson led the National League in wins four times, had the best ERA in five seasons, won the strikeout total five times and wound up with a career record of 372–187 with an ERA of 2.13. He threw 78 shutouts in his career.

Mathewson, 6 feet and 190 pounds, featured a pitch he called the "fadeaway." In modern baseball, it's known as the screwball. The pitch is a reverse curveball which is thrown with an unnatural snap of the wrist. The ball would break in to righthanded batters. It was an effective weapon because very few pitchers could master it. Batters didn't have a chance to get accustomed to seeing it. Legend says that Mathewson would often throw it as few as 12 times a game, but the threat of the pitch often fooled with hitters' minds.

He was considered a master of efficiency who could get through a nine-inning game on 80 pitches because of his ability to consistently throw strikes. Mathewson averaged just 1.6 walks per nine innings.

The tough situations he called "pitching in a pinch," which also became the name of his book. Mathewson had one of the most dominating performances in World Series history in 1905 when he shut out the Philadelphia Athletics three times.

Both McGraw and Connie Mack called him the best pitcher they had ever seen. Said Mack, "It was a pleasure to watch him pitch when he wasn't pitching against you."

Because of his reputation for clean living, Mathewson was often held up as a role model for youngsters. It's difficult to separate fact from fiction in that regard but most accounts say Mathewson was intelligent and gentlemanly in most of his dealings. He was one of the players leading the fight to unionize in 1912 and one of the first to suggest that the 1919 Chicago White Sox were throwing games in the World Series.

His best year was in 1908 when he led the league in wins (37), ERA (1.43), strikeouts (259) and shutouts (12). He had 13 seasons with 20 or more wins and had at least 30 in four other seasons.

His last great year was 1914, when he went 24–13. He won just eight games in 1915 and was traded to Cincinnati the following season after winning three games for the Giants. He appeared in just one game for Cincinnati before becoming the Reds manager through the 1918 seasons. He did not equal the success he had as a player, posting a losing record (164–176, .482 winning percentage) as Reds manager.

Mathewson went back to the Giants as a coach for two seasons and held a front office position with a minor league team. He sustained lung damage in a military exercise and died of tuberculosis in 1925 at the age of 47.

Mathewson was among the first five inductees when the Hall of Fame was founded.

A gentleman, a scholar—and a Hall of Fame pitcher

The White Sox's "Shoeless" Joe Jackson

Some teams succeed as long as they have a particular group of players together. The mark of a superior organization is one that manages to win while changing its personnel. It shows that the team has enough savvy to develop a core group that is capable of winning, then can repeat the process.

By that standard, count John McGraw's New York Giants as one of the premier organizations of its time.

Two years after finishing last and just one season after a major personnel overhaul, the Giants were back on top in the National League standings and they won the pennant easily. New York moved into first place on June 27 and had a ten-game advantage on the Philadelphia Phillies when the season ended.

McGraw's reconstruction project affected three-quarters of the infield. His new first baseman was Walter Hocke. He had Buck Herzog at second and ex-Cub Heinie Zimmerman at third. The only holdover was shortstop Art Fletcher. Former Federal League standout Benny Kauff played in the Giants' outfield.

After years of shaping a rotation around Christy Mathewson, McGraw came up with an entirely different starting staff. Lefthander Ferdie Schupp took over the No. 1 spot and responded with a 21–7 record, 1.95 earned run average and six shutouts. Pol Perritt, Rube Benton and Slim Sallee combined for 50 wins.

Grover Alexander had his third 30-win season for the Phillies, but his good work wasn't enough to overcome an overall drop in hitting. The Phillies acquired veteran Johnny Evers from Boston, but he was at the end of his career and batted just .224.

The St. Louis Cardinals had the worst pitching staff in the league, but had a budding star in 21-year-old shortstop Rogers Hornsby, who hit .321 in his second season.

Rube Benton aided the Giants' return to form as part of a 50-win combination

Edd Roush came from the defunct Federal League to Cincinnati and won the batting title with a .344 average. The defending champion Brooklyn Dodgers fell to seventh place and their pitching failed. Zack Wheat failed to provide power, which helped hasten the Dodgers' decline.

In the American League, the Chicago White Sox capped a three-year rise with a pennant under the direction of manager Pants Rowland. The White Sox finished nine games ahead of the Boston Red Sox. The lead seesawed through the middle of August when the White Sox took command.

Outfielder Happy Felsch batted .308 and drove in 102 runs while Joe Jackson had a .301 average and 75 RBIs.

Rookie shortstop Swede Risberg didn't hit much, but he stabilized the position defensively and let the White Sox move Buck Weaver to third base. Eddie Cicotte established himself as one of the league's best young pitchers with a 28–12 record and 1.53 ERA, both of which were league bests.

Boston's strength was its two-man pitching punch—Babe Ruth was 24–13 with a 2.02 ERA and Carl Mays was 22–9, 1.74.

Ty Cobb batted .383 to nail down his tenth batting championship in 11 years. The Tigers had a difficult time finding enough talent to surround Cobb and finished fourth.

SHORTS

It was the end of the line for some of the game's biggest stars. Sam Crawford, who teamed with Ty Cobb to make the middle of the Tigers' order dangerous, called it quits after the season. Eddie Plank retired after winning 325 games. Johnny Evers also decided to end his playing days. The biggest name to finish his career was Pirates' shortstop Honus Wagner, who quit at the age of 43 with eight batting titles.

SHORTS Smokey Joe Wood never fulfilled the promise he had as a pitcher, but he managed to stick around in the major leagues anyway. Wood won 34 games for the pennant-winning Red Sox in 1912, but he developed arm problems which affected his ability to pitch. Wood decided to switch to the outfield in 1917 and stuck around for five more seasons.

Ty Cobb won his tenth batting crown, but his Tigers faltered

POSTSEASON

The Chicago White Sox beat the New York Giants in the World Series, but they had plenty of help.

The Giants seemed intent on beating themselves, making a number of critical mistakes that helped the White Sox to win in six games.

Both teams made it to the postseason with relative ease—Chicago won the American League by nine games over Boston and the Giants finished ten games ahead of Philadelphia in the National League.

Chicago took the opening game 2–1 when Happy Felsch hit a home run to back pitcher Eddie Cicotte. Chicago won Game Two, 7–2, behind Red Faber.

The Giants got their first win in Game Three as Rube Benton beat Cicotte 2–0 with a five-hitter. New York tied the Series by winning Game Four, 5–0, on Benny Kauff's two homers.

The White Sox scored six runs in the last three innings to win Game Five, 8–5, setting up the deciding game.

Third baseman Heinie Zimmerman and right

GAME 1	
Chicago White Sox 7	NY Giants 1
GAME 2	
Chicago White Sox 7	NY Giants 2
GAME 3	
NY Giants 2	Chicago White Sox 0
GAME 4	
NY Giants 5	Chicago White Sox 0
GAME 5	
Chicago White Sox 8	NY Giants 5
GAME 6	
Chicago White Sox 4	NY Giants 2

fielder Dave Robertson made errors to put runners at first and third in a scoreless game. The Giants appeared to have an easy out at the plate on Felsch's grounder, but no one covered home. The run scored and White Sox went on to score three in the inning and record a 4–2 win.

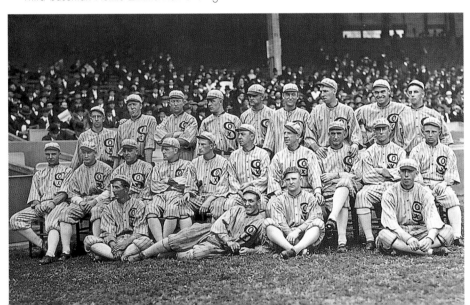

The White Sox won the Series in six games—with a little help from the Giants

Major league teams had to worry about player raids again, but this time they weren't about to resist.

With the country engaged in World War I, many players were called into military service on short notice. In fact, baseball needed a special waiver just to continue its season. The government had ordered a shutdown of non-essential businesses and baseball games weren't contributing anything to the nation's war effort.

The philosophy would change in World War II, but baseball was under orders to end its season early.

The military obligations had some teams scrambling to get enough able-bodied men to fill out rosters. Some teams were hit harder than others and the war-related absences were reflected in the won-lost records of the teams.

Boston Red Sox player-manager Jack Baker was among the first to be called into military service. Left fielder Duffy Lewis also left the club to serve his country. Those departures didn't prevent the Red Sox from winning the American League pennant by 2½ games over Cleveland.

The Red Sox finally began to get the idea that a pitcher with a bat as potent as Babe Ruth's should be in the lineup more often than it was on

Red Faber (l) was one of the many White Sox players to leave for the war effort

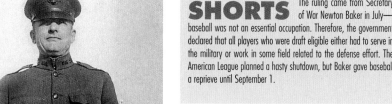

SHORTS The ruling came from Secretary of War Newton Baker in July— baseball was not an essential occupation. Therefore, the government declared that all players who were draft eligible either had to serve in the military or work in some field related to the defense effort. The American League planned a hasty shutdown, but Baker gave baseball a reprieve until September 1.

a starting pitcher's schedule. The Red Sox used Ruth in the outfield for 59 games and played him at first base in 13 others. He responded with a .300 average and league-leading totals in both home runs (11) and RBIs (66). On the mound, Ruth continued his excellent work. He was 13–7 with a 2.22 earned run average.

The Red Sox got some important reinforcements from the Philadelphia Athletics. They added first baseman Stuffy McInnis, outfielder Amos Strunk and catcher Wally Schang.

The Indians may have mounted a more serious challenge had they not lost Tris Speaker to a suspension at the end of August. Speaker, a .318 hitter, was banned by the league after he made contact with an umpire. Smokey Joe Wood, whose pitching career had been affected by injuries, moved to the outfield. He batted .296 and his 66 RBIs were tied for third in the league.

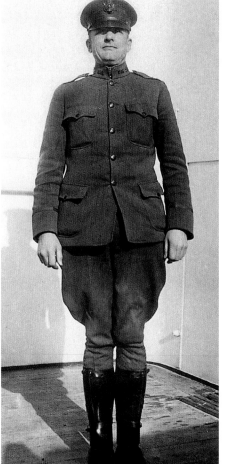

The New York Giants' Christy Mathewson joins the war effort

The Chicago White Sox were hit hard by players leaving for the war effort—Red Faber, Swede Risberg, Joe Jackson, Happy Felsch and Lefty Williams all left the team.

The Detroit Tigers didn't have a good year, but Ty Cobb did. He won his 11th batting championship with a .382 average.

In Washington, Walter Johnson had another quality season, posting a 23–13 record with a 1.27 ERA.

The Chicago Cubs ran away with the National League pennant, beating the New York Giants by 10½ games. The Cubs purchased

The Senators' Walter Johnson remained as awesome as ever

Grover Alexander, but he was drafted into the service after making just three appearances.

Rookie shortstop Charlie Hollocher batted .316 and Fred Merkle had a .297 season.

The pitching staff was led by Hippo Vaughn, who was 22–10 with a 1.74 ERA. Lefty Tyler was 19–8 and Claude Hendrix had a 20–7 record.

The New York Giants were among the clubs affected by the sudden call to arms. Outfielder Benny Kauff was batting .315 when he was drafted.

SHORTS

The tradition of preceding base-ball games with the national anthem began during the 1918 World Series. A military band played "The Star Spangled Banner" during the seventh-inning stretch of the Series games. The practice was revived during World War II and then became a baseball tradition, facilitated by recorded music and public address systems.

POSTSEASON

The Boston Red Sox didn't get to the World Series every year, but they made the trip pay when they did make it. Boston went 5-for-5 in Series play by knocking off the Chicago Cubs in six games.

The government ordered the season to shut down just after Labor Day because of World War I. The Series, an October tradition, instead ran from September 5–11.

The Cubs opted to play across town at Comiskey Park because it had a larger seating capacity than their home park. Boston won Game One, 1–0, as Babe Ruth beat Hippo Vaughn. Lefty Tyler evened the Series the next day with a 3–1 win for the Cubs.

Carl Mays won 2–1 in Game Three as Vaughn took another one-run loss for the Cubs.

Ruth pitched Boston to a 3–2 win in Game Four to put the Red Sox within a game of clinching the Series.

Vaughn won 3–0 in Game Five. Mays beat Tyler 2–1 in the deciding game to give Boston its fifth title.

Mays and Ruth each had two wins. Mays had an ERA of 1.00 while Ruth's was 1.06 in a Series thoroughly dominated by pitching. Boston batted only .186 while the Cubs were slightly better at .210. There were no home runs in the Series.

GAME 1	
Boston Red Sox 1	Chicago Cubs 0
GAME 2	
Chicago Cubs 3	Boston Red Sox 1
GAME 3	
Boston Red Sox 2	Chicago Cubs 1
GAME 4	
Boston Red Sox 3	Chicago Cubs 2
GAME 5	
Chicago Cubs 3	Boston Red Sox 0
GAME 6	
Boston Red Sox 2	Chicago Cubs 1

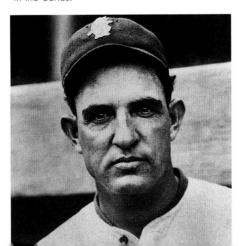

The Cubs' Hippo Vaughn suffered mixed fortunes in the Series

LEADERS

BATTING AVERAGE
AL: Ty Cobb, Detroit, .384
NL: Edd Roush, Cincinnati, .321

HOME RUNS
AL: Babe Ruth, Boston Red Sox, 29
NL: Gavvy Cravath, Philadelphia Phillies, 12

RUNS BATTED IN
AL: Babe Ruth, Boston Red Sox, 114
NL: Hi Myers, Brooklyn, 73

STOLEN BASES
AL: Eddie Collins, Chicago White Sox, 33
NL: George Burns, NY Giants, 40

PITCHING VICTORIES
AL: Eddie Cicotte, Chicago White Sox, 29
NL: Jesse Barnes, NY Giants, 25

EARNED RUN AVERAGE
AL: Walter Johnson, Washington, 1.49
NL: Grover Alexander, Chicago Cubs, 1.72

STRIKEOUTS
AL: Walter Johnson, Washington, 147
NL: Hippo Vaughn, Chicago Cubs, 141

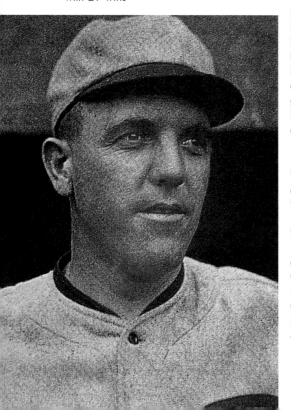

Chicago's Eddie Cicotte finished with 29 wins

How different the history of baseball might well have been if the Cleveland Indians had won the 1919 American League pennant?

They didn't, though, finishing 3½ games behind the Chicago White Sox. The White Sox moved onto the World Series against the Cincinnati Reds and became involved in a gambling scandal that tainted the integrity of baseball and the participants who were allegedly involved in conspiring to deliberately lose World Series games.

The details of what came to be known as the "Black Sox Scandal" would be examined and debated for the rest of the century. Long after all the key parties were dead, their involvement would still be discussed and examined in both books and movies.

It should have been a glorious baseball season on Chicago's South Side. The White Sox had a magnificent team. Joe Jackson batted .357 and drove in 96 runs. Happy Felsch hit .275 with 86 RBIs and Eddie Collins had a .319 average and 80 RBIs. Pitcher Eddie Cicotte was 29–7 with a 1.82 earned run average. Lefty Williams was 23–11.

The White Sox were challenged by both the Indians and New York Yankees, but pulled away from both of those teams.

The other big story in the American League was the emergence of a good-hitting pitcher with the Boston Red Sox. Babe Ruth had somehow managed to hit 29 home runs in an era when the league leader often barely got into double figures. Ruth pitched in 17 games and was showing that he belonged in the everyday lineup, not on the pitcher's mound.

He was one of the few bright spots in a bad season for the Red Sox, who fell from first to sixth. Pitcher Carl Mays jumped the club at one point in the season, which was instrumental in the decision to sell his contract to the Yankees.

In the National League, the Reds caught up with the leading New York Giants in August, then beat New York in two late series to earn the top spot. Cincinnati wound up winning fairly handily, ending up nine games in front of the Giants.

Edd Roush batted .321 and drove

The Babe's propensity for the long ball saw him given reduced time on the mound

SHORTS Pitcher Carl Mays had a volatile temper, which explained why he moved so often during his career. He essentially quit the Boston club on July 13, accusing his teammates of not supporting him well enough. Although league president Ban Johnson ordered no action to be taken until he could rule, Boston traded Mays to the Yankees for two players and $40,000.

Just two games into the World Series, rumors abounded that the White Sox weren't giving an honest effort. Sox owner Charles Comiskey told confidants that Chicago manager Kid Gleason had suspicions that something was amiss. Sportswriter Ring Lardner was also one of the first to suspect that the Series was tainted. The issue was untouched until a grand jury returned an indictment the following September.

in 71 runs. Third baseman Heinie Groh had a .310 average and 63 RBIs.

Slim Sallee led an underrated pitching staff with a 21–7 record and a 2.05 earned run average. Hod Eller was 20–9 and Dutch Reuther finished 19–6.

The Giants got pitcher Jesse Barnes back from military service. He picked up where he left off, posting a 25–9 record, but it wasn't enough.

The Chicago Cubs made a strong run, thanks to some excellent pitching from their top two starters. Grover Alexander was 16–11 but had an exceptional ERA of 1.72, which led the National League. Alexander did exactly what the Cubs thought he would do when they acquired him from the Phillies a year earlier. The Cubs had watched that deal turn sour when Alexander was drafted into military service after making just three appearances for them. Hippo Vaughn was 21–14 for the Cubs with a 1.79 ERA.

POSTSEASON

The Chicago White Sox lost the World Series, which raised the bigger question: was that exactly what they intended to do?

Eight members of the White Sox were charged with conspiring to fix the outcome of the Series. The eight, who were banned from baseball, became known as the Black Sox.

The eight were acquitted in the courts, but the questions were never adequately answered—did they throw the Series? When

Eddie Cicotte hit Morrie Rath with the first pitch of the Series, was it a signal to gamblers that the fix was in? When Cicotte made two errors in one inning of Game Four, was it to make sure that the Reds won?

If the White Sox players intended to throw investigators with inconsistency, they did a great job. Joe Jackson, one of the players implicated, hit .375 in the Series. Yet there were accusations that he let some balls drop in for hits in the outfield.

Starter Lefty Williams lost three games in the Series after winning 23 in the regular season. Since he was one of the players charged, did he deliberately pitch badly?

It turned into one of the most memorable World Series—sadly, for all the wrong reasons.

Despite his performance, Joe Jackson was implicated for his role in the suspected fix

GAME 1	
Cincinnati 9	Chicago White Sox 1
GAME 2	
Cincinnati 4	Chicago White Sox 2
GAME 3	
Chicago White Sox 3	Cincinnati 0
GAME 4	
Cincinnati 2	Chicago White Sox 0
GAME 5	
Cincinnati 5	Chicago White Sox 0
GAME 6	
Chicago White Sox 5	Cincinnati 4
GAME 7	
Chicago White Sox 4	Cincinnati 1
GAME 8	
Cincinnati 10	Chicago White Sox 5

April 19: Sunday baseball became legal in the state of New York. Major league teams had been battling for the right to play on Sundays for several years and ran afoul of the law by trying to find loopholes in the laws governing Sunday activities.

May 4: Sunday baseball was a hit with fans. The New York Giants played their first legal Sunday game and drew more than 35,000 fans.

May 11: The Yankees and Washington played 27 innings over two days and decided nothing. Their games ended in 0–0 and 4–4 ties before they were called because of darkness.

May 11: Hod Eller of the Reds pitched a no-hitter against the Cardinals.

May 21: Jim Thorpe went from the Giants to Boston on a waiver transaction.

June 9: Rube Marquard of the Dodgers broke his leg in a base-running mishap.

July 8: Former pitcher Jack Coombs resigned as manager of the Phillies and was replaced by Gavvy Cravath.

Aug. 14: A doubleheader between the Cubs and Dodgers was completed in less than two hours and 20 minutes.

Aug. 24: Cleveland pitcher Ray Caldwell was struck by lightning. He was still able to complete the game.

Sept. 8: Babe Ruth hit his 26th home run to set a single-season record. Buck Freeman had hit 25 in 1899.

Sept. 24: The White Sox beat St. Louis and clinched the American League pennant.

Sept. 27: Babe Ruth's 27th home run of the season came at Washington. He became the first player to hit a home run in every park.

Nov. 10: Former pitcher Clark Griffith became a part owner of the Washington Senators.

Dec. 26: Boston sold Babe Ruth to the Yankees.

"SHOELESS" JOE JACKSON

JACKSON

"Say it ain't so, Joe."

It's one of baseball's most famous quotes, supposedly uttered by a small boy and directed to Shoeless Joe Jackson after the player emerged from a courtroom dealing with the 1919 Chicago Black Sox scandal.

Jackson had admitted to taking money in the scheme to fix the results of World Series games on behalf of gambling interests. The young fan, with tears in his eyes, supposedly looked up to his baseball hero for an assurance that wasn't forthcoming.

It makes a compelling story, but it probably isn't a truthful one. Most reports suggest the boy and his questions were inventions of a writer who fabricated the scene to make his story more interesting. Delve into the baseball life of Joe Jackson and it's difficult to separate fact from fiction in a number of areas.

If Jackson was supposed to be throwing games in the 1919 World Series, why did he bat .345 in the seven games? Why did he handle 30 fielding chances flawlessly? Why did he go to White Sox owner Charles Comiskey and manager Kid Gleason and ask both men to bench him in the Series because he'd heard of the fixing plot and didn't want to be part of tainted games? Why did he turn down a verified offer of $10,000, then reject another proposal that would have paid $20,000 to negatively influence the outcome of the games for the White Sox? All these years later, questions still outnumber answers by a wide margin.

In 1949, nearly 30 years after his lifetime banishment, Jackson told *Sport* magazine, "I can say that my conscience is clear and I'll stand on my record in that World Series."

There is a school of thought that holds that Jackson was a convenient scapegoat for what happened in the 1919 World Series. For all his baseball skills, Jackson was ill-equipped to deal with real-life

situations. He was a farm boy who had never learned to read or write. He broke in with the Philadelphia Athletics, where owner-manager Connie Mack wound up giving him away because Jackson couldn't handle the cruel taunts of his teammates.

Jackson went to Cleveland and became one of the game's best players. In his first five seasons, his lowest batting average was .338. The Cleveland franchise ran into money problems and had to trade Jackson to the White Sox, where both his life and career would change dramatically.

He helped to get Chicago to the World Series by batting .351 with 96 RBIs. He was even better in 1920, hitting .392 with 12 home runs and 121 RBIs.

But that was also his last season. Even though the eight defendants in the Black Sox scandal were acquitted, Commissioner Kenesaw Landis banned all eight for life.

Landis rejected arguments that Jackson had been used by others and permanently threw out one of the game's best players. Part of the problem may have been that Jackson was aware of the plot, but didn't report it. That was countered with evidence that lives had been threatened, but the argument carried no weight with Landis, who stood by his inflexible ruling.

Jackson was out of baseball despite hitting above .300 in ten different seasons. "Black Betsy," the 36-inch, 48-ounce bat he used was seen only at scattered sandlot games.

Jackson should have realized how hard a label was to shed in baseball. He was tagged with the name "Shoeless Joe" because he once discarded a pair of spikes that were hurting him and played in his socks. From that single episode came a nickname that outlived him.

Despite his lack of formal education, Jackson prospered outside of baseball. He went back to his native South Carolina and was involved in a number of businesses, including dry cleaning. He did well and didn't force the issue of getting back into baseball.

He told an interviewer, "I gave baseball my best and if the game didn't care enough to see me get a square deal, then I wouldn't go out of my way to get back in it."

Jackson died of a heart attack in 1951. Efforts to clear his name and present him as a Hall of Fame candidate have gained momentum, but still haven't been successful.

Joe Jackson—few names in baseball could trigger such an array of opinion

1920

Even people who didn't follow baseball knew who Babe Ruth was.

The New York Yankees' slugger had a powerful personality to go along with the home run excitement he generated on the field. Ruth lived all aspects of his life to the full and was a public figure made for the Roaring '20s.

He helped to establish the New York Yankees as one of the premier franchises in sports and he increased baseball's popularity with his record-shattering power shows. The Yankees had plenty of talent, but Ruth was the name that came to mind when most people thought of either baseball or the Yankees.

Ruth was the right person at the right time. The sport had just switched to a livelier baseball and Ruth was the perfect person to make the transition from a speed game to one that valued home runs. Even more important, he was able to start a completely new storyline in the wake of the 1919 World Series game-fixing scandal involving the Chicago White Sox.

Ruth was brash and outrageous, traits best demonstrated when a reporter mentioned that Ruth's new contract provided him with a larger salary than the President of the United States.

Said Ruth, "I had a better year than he did."

BATTING AVERAGE
AL: George Sisler, St. Louis Browns, .407
NL: Rogers Hornsby, St. Louis Cardinals, .370

HOME RUNS
AL: Babe Ruth, NY Yankees, 54
NL: Cy Williams, Philadelphia Phillies, 15

RUNS BATTED IN
AL: Babe Ruth, NY Yankees, 137
NL: Rogers Hornsby, St. Louis Cardinals, 94

STOLEN BASES
AL: Sam Rice, Washington Senators, 63
NL: Max Carey, Pittsburgh Pirates, 52

PITCHING VICTORIES
AL: Jim Bagby, Cleveland Indians, 31
NL: Grover Alexander, Chicago Cubs, 27

EARNED RUN AVERAGE
AL: Bob Shawkey, NY Yankees, 2.45
NL: Grover Alexander, Philadelphia Phillies, 1.91

STRIKEOUTS
AL: Stan Coveleski, Cleveland, 133
NL: Grover Alexander, Chicago Cubs, 173

For the second straight year, real life intruded rudely on the fun and games of baseball.

In 1919, it was the Black Sox Scandal, the allegations that members of the Chicago White Sox had conspired with gamblers to throw games in the World Series.

That was a character issue. In 1920, the game was visited by genuine tragedy. During a game on August 16 at New York's Polo Grounds, Cleveland Indians' infielder Ray Chapman was struck in the head by a fastball from Yankees' pitcher Carl Mays.

Chapman died in a New York hospital the next day as baseball had its first and only on-field fatality.

Mays was known as a brushback pitcher, but the beaning was accidental. Nonetheless, the shocking episode took a severe emotional toll on the Indians and affected their ability to compete in the pennant race.

Many observers credited Cleveland manager Tris Speaker with pulling his team together and steering it to the American League pennant. In September, the Indians added two key players—shortstop Joe Sewell and pitcher Walter Mails. Sewell batted .329 in 22 games and Mails was

SHORTS The worst scandal of baseball's existence was threatening the sport's future. Fans had to be able to believe they were watching legitimate competition. To restore the image of the game, the owners hired federal Judge Kenesaw Landis (below). Landis agreed in principle on a seven-year contract in November.

The Browns' George Sisler ended Ty Cobb's reign as the AL batting champion

7–0 in nine starts. They helped push the Indians to first place.

Because of the Black Sox episode, the competition got a bit easier for Cleveland. The White Sox threw the players off the team who had been accused in the incident. That left the roster depleted and the White Sox stumbled, finishing two games behind Cleveland.

The New York Yankees finished third, but they made a move that would affect competition in the American League for more than a decade. At the end of the 1919 season the cash-strapped Boston Red Sox, anxious to raise money, were willing to sell pitcher-outfielder Babe Ruth. The Red Sox had also gotten rid of Mays after he had left the team without authorization.

The Red Sox got the money they needed in the two transactions—$177,500. But the

Yankees got the No. 1 pitcher they needed in Mays and a power hitter in Ruth, who was destined to break all the existing home run records. Mays went 26–11 for the Yankees and Ruth slugged 54 home runs, which was an astonishing total for the times. Most teams of that era didn't hit 54 home runs. The feat established the Yankees as a power and set up Ruth as one of the game's great drawing cards.

Ty Cobb's stranglehold on the American League batting title was broken by George Sisler of the St. Louis Browns. Sisler hit .407 to Cobb's .334.

In the National League, the Brooklyn Dodgers took the crown, finishing seven games ahead of the New York Giants. The Dodgers were boosted by the addition of righthander Burleigh

SHORTS

The evolution of rules and policies continued. In February, the owners made a major decision by banning the spitball and any other pitches that were delivered by applying a foreign substance or somehow altering the surface of the baseball. Under the new policy, an automatic ten-game suspension was to be given to any violator. Pitchers were allowed to use illegal substances for one more season in the American League, two more in the National.

Grimes, who went 23–11. Outfielder Zack Wheat batted .328 and drove in 78 runs.

The Giants fell short despite having three 20-game winners on their pitching staff.

The defending champion Reds finished in third place, 10½ games off the pace. Cincinnati's pitching staff had an off year, but Edd Roush's offense was consistent. Roush batted .339, drove in 90 runs and stole 36 bases.

TIMELINE

Jan. 5: The December 26, 1919 purchase of Babe Ruth from Boston was officially announced.

Feb. 10: Ticket prices went up. Grandstand prices increased to one dollar, with bleacher tickets going at half that cost.

May 1: Detroit's 0–13 start equalled the record set by Washington in 1904.

May 14: Walter Johnson (right) won his 300th game.

May 20: An undercover gambling raid in the bleachers at Wrigley Field resulted in 24 arrests.

June 20: Grover Cleveland suffered his first defeat of the season after winning 11 consecutive decisions.

June 8: The Giants made an important acquisition by getting shortstop Dave Bancroft from the Phillies for two players and cash.

July 1: Walter Johnson pitched the first no-hitter of his career, beating the White Sox. The only runner reached on Bucky Harris' error.

July 6: The Yankees scored 14 runs in the fifth inning on the way to a 17–0 win over Washington.

July 17: Babe Ruth hit his 30th home run to break the single season record he'd set a year earlier.

Aug. 20: Baseball's first on-field fatality occurred when Cleveland shortstop Ray Chapman was hit in the head by a fastball from the Yankees' Carl Mays. Chapman died the following day as a result of the skull fracture.

Sept. 17: Two players hit for the cycle—George Burns of the Giants and Bobby Veach of the Tigers.

Sept. 20: Reds' second baseman Maurice Rath hit two inside-the-park home runs against the Giants.

Sept. 28: Eight White Sox players were indicted by a grand jury on charges that they consorted with gamblers and conspired to throw games in the 1919 World Series.

Sept. 29: Babe Ruth hit his 54th home run. He hit more home runs than every team except the Phillies.

POSTSEASON

The Cleveland Indians triumphed over tragedy to take the 1920 World Series.

The Indians were devastated in mid-August when shortstop Ray Chapman died a day after being struck in the head by a pitch.

Cleveland was able to acquire shortstop Joe Sewell from the minor leagues and he batted .329 in 22 games after he replaced Chapman. It was another important late-season acquisition for the Indians, who had also added pitcher Walter (Duster) Mails, who had spent most of the season in the minor leagues.

Mails went 7–0 down the stretch and helped the Indians to outlast the Chicago White Sox and New York Yankees in a three-team race for the American League pennant.

Brooklyn finished seven games ahead of the New York Giants to claim the National League flag.

Their series turned with Cleveland's 5–1 win in Game Four, which led to a history-making Game Five in the best-of-nine Series. Cleveland's Elmer Smith hit the first Series grand slam, Jim Bagby became the first pitcher to homer in a Series and Bill Wambsganss turned an unassisted triple play. The Indians wrapped up the Series with shutouts in the final two games and held the Dodgers to two runs over the last four games.

GAME 1	
Cleveland 3	Brooklyn 1
GAME 2	
Brooklyn 3	Cleveland 0
GAME 3	
Brooklyn 2	Cleveland 1
GAME 4	
Cleveland 5	Brooklyn 1
GAME 5	
Cleveland 8	Brooklyn 1
GAME 6	
Cleveland 1	Brooklyn 0
GAME 7	
Cleveland 3	Brooklyn 0

Cleveland's Jim Bagby

LEADERS

BATTING AVERAGE
AL: Harry Heilmann, Detroit, .394
NL: Rogers Hornsby, St. Louis Cardinals, .397

HOME RUNS
AL: Babe Ruth, NY Yankees, 59
NL: George Kelly, NY Giants, 23

RUNS BATTED IN
AL: Babe Ruth, NY Yankees, 171
NL: Rogers Hornsby, St. Louis Cardinals, 126

STOLEN BASES
AL: George Sisler, St. Louis Browns, 35
NL: Frankie Frisch, NY Giants, 49

PITCHING VICTORIES
AL: Urban Shocker, St. Louis Browns, 27
NL: Burleigh Grimes, Brooklyn; Wilbur
Cooper, Pittsburgh, 22

EARNED RUN AVERAGE
AL: Red Faber, Chicago White Sox, 2.48
NL: Bill Doak, St. Louis Cardinals, 2.59

STRIKEOUTS
AL: Walter Johnson, Washington, 143
NL: Burleigh Grimes, Brooklyn, 136

Babe Ruth had broad shoulders, which was a good thing. It seemed as though he was carrying baseball.

Ruth was the biggest player in the biggest city and his amazing work on the field helped draw some attention away from the seamy story that was being played out away from the ballpark.

Ruth didn't make the Black Sox Scandal go away, but he provided a tremendous distraction for baseball fans.

His 54 home runs stunned the baseball world in 1920. What would he do for an encore? He hit five more. Ruth had 59 homers in 1921, part of a monster year that also saw him bat .378 and drive in 170 runs. He didn't win the Triple Crown because, amazingly, his average was only the third best in the American League.

Because of Ruth, the Yankees were the team everyone wanted to see as it traveled to the other seven American League cities. Ruth was a bigger-than-life character with an outgoing personality, a ready smile and a memorable name.

SHORTS The relationship between baseball and broadcasting began on August 5 when announcer Harold Arlin described a game between the Phillies and Pirates live on KDKA Radio in Pittsburgh. As radio became more prominent, some owners worried that live coverage would hurt their gate. Instead, broadcast rights became an important source of revenue and daily coverage of games served to promote the team.

Babe Ruth's incomparable talents took the game to new heights

The Yankees relied heavily on him, but he wasn't the team's only weapon. His partner was outfielder Bob Meusel, who was the runner up for the home run title with 24. It says something about Ruth's power that he more than doubled the total of his nearest competitor. Meusel was also third in RBIs with 135.

The Yankees also had solid pitching. Carl Mays was 27–9 and Waite Hoyt posted a 19–13 record. Bob Shawkey went 18–12 as the Yankees pulled away from the Cleveland Indians to win their first pennant.

Cleveland's chances of competing were diminished by injuries to player-manager Tris Speaker and outfielder Steve O'Neill. Lacking those players, the Indians didn't have enough offensive power to seriously challenge the Yankees. The Indians finished 4½ games back.

The St. Louis Browns slipped into third place, led by offensive stars George Sisler and Ken Williams. First baseman Sisler hit .371 with 12 home runs and 104 RBIs. He also stole 35 bases. Williams hit .347 with 24 home runs and 117 RBIs. Urban Shocker led the pitching staff with 27 wins.

The Chicago White Sox were a non-factor, finishing seventh as they still battled the fallout from the 1919 World Series scandal.

The National League title went to the New York Giants, who won their seventh pennant under manager John McGraw. They finished four

New York's Bob Meusel provided the Yanks with some impressive numbers

The Giants' Art Nehf recorded 20 wins as New York captured the pennant

games ahead of Pittsburgh and helped themselves by sweeping a five-game series from the Pirates at the end of August.

First baseman George (High Pockets) Kelly hit 23 home runs and had 122 RBIs. Shortstop

Frankie Frisch had a .341 average, 100 RBIs and a league-leading 49 stolen bases.

Outfielder Ross Youngs batted .327 and drove in 101 runs. Dave Bancroft gave the Giants exceptional defense at shortstop and had a .318 average. Emil Meusel was a key mid-season acquisition from Philadelphia. He hit .329 for the Giants and helped them overtake the Pirates.

Art Nehf led the New York pitching staff with a 20–10 record.

SHORTS Umpiring became a dirty business in 1921. Umpires in both leagues began the process of rubbing mud into the daily supply of baseballs. The mud made the ball easier to grip by taking away the slickness of the natural hide cover. Former major league player Lena Blackburne supplied the special mud for many years after discovering it on the banks of the Delaware River.

POSTSEASON

The World Series was a brand new experience for the New York Yankees in 1921.

GAME 1	
NY Yankees 3	NY Giants 0
GAME 2	
NY Yankees 3	NY Giants 0
GAME 3	
NY Giants 13	NY Yankees 5
GAME 4	
NY Giants 4	NY Yankees 2
GAME 5	
NY Yankees 3	NY Giants 1
GAME 6	
NY Giants 8	NY Yankees 5
GAME 7	
NY Giants 2	NY Yankees 1
GAME 8	
NY Giants 1	NY Yankees 0

The Yankees held off defending champion Cleveland to win their first American League pennant and earned the right to meet the New York Giants, for whom they were a tenant at the Polo Grounds.

Yankees' ace Waite Hoyt pitched 27 innings without allowing an earned run, Carl Mays had a 1.73 earned run average in 26 innings and Babe Ruth batted .313 with a homer and four RBIs. Despite those impressive stats, the Yankees still lost the best-of-nine Series in eight games.

Jesse Barnes was 2–0 for the Giants with a 1.65 ERA, Frank Snyder hit .364 and Irish Meusel hit .345 and drove in seven runs.

The Giants lost the first two games by the same score (3–0) and were down 4–0 in the third inning of Game Three. They scored eight runs in the seventh to win 13–5. That helped spur them to five wins in the next six games.

Ruth had his only at-bat after Game Five because of knee and arm injuries. Art Nehf pitched a 1–0 four-hitter in Game Eight to give John McGraw's Giants their first title since 1905.

TIMELINE

Jan. 21: Judge Kenesaw Mountain Landis began his term as baseball's first Commissioner.

Jan. 22: The Reds acquired pitcher Eppa Rixey from Philadelphia.

Feb. 23: The Pirates traded three players and cash to Boston for shortstop Rabbit Maranville.

May 4: Brooklyn's 11-game winning streak ended with a loss to the Giants.

May 7: The Yankees' Bob Meusel hit for the cycle against Washington.

June 4: Wilbur Cooper of the Pirates had his personal eight-game winning streak ended by the Giants.

June 6: Babe Ruth hit his 120th career home run, which made him baseball's all-time leader.

July 1: The Giants acquired Casey Stengel from the Phillies.

July 18: The "Black Sox" trial began in Chicago.

July 29: Cy Young pitched two innings of an old-timers' game in Cleveland at the age of 54.

July 29: The Giants purchased outfielder Emil Meusel from the Phillies, who had suspended him for indifferent play.

Aug. 2: The "Black Sox" were acquitted but remained under a lifetime ban from baseball imposed by Commissioner Landis.

Aug. 5: The live play-by-play of a baseball game is heard on radio for the first time. Announcer Harold Arlin called the action of a game between the Phillies and Pirates in Pittsburgh over station KDKA.

Aug. 15: George Sisler's streak of ten consecutive hits ended.

Aug. 19: Ty Cobb got his 3,000th career hit.

Sept. 5: Walter Johnson became baseball's all-time strikeout leader. He raised his total to 2,287 to pass Cy Young.

Sept. 15: Babe Ruth his his 55th home run of the season.

Sept. 26: Babe Ruth hit two more home runs and raised his season total to 58.

Oct. 2: Babe Ruth hit his 59th home run in the Yankees' final game.

Waite Hoyt's heroics couldn't prevent defeat for the Yanks

A .331 season for the Giants' Emil Meusel

The baseball was livelier and that made for livelier baseball.

The powers-that-be finally determined that fans wanted to see offense, so they commissioned a redesigned baseball that would travel farther when hit.

That simple adjustment changed the game. Strategy was different. Instead of relying on stolen bases, teams tried to get power hitters who could let runners trot home after a ball was blasted over the fence.

Offense, particularly home runs, captivated fans. Thanks to Babe Ruth they scrambled for the morning newspaper to read about the power feats of the New York Yankees' No. 1 star. Gradually other power hitters entered the game and found that the Dead Ball Era was indeed over. It may not have been a pleasing development for pitchers, whose blood pressure was presumably rising as rapidly as their earned run averages were.

Baseball had made another major tactical adjustment by banning the spitball and other pitches that compromised the surface of the ball. No longer could a pitcher use a nail file to rough up one side of the ball and cause it to dip erratically away from the batter.

Some of the pitchers who specialized in gimmick pitches like the spitball were run out of the game by the new rules. That was a small price to pay for having baseballs flying over the fences and bringing ticket-buying fans out to the ballparks.

It changed the way teams scouted and it also altered the approach of hitters. Fame and fortune clearly belonged to those who could hit the ball a long way. So hitters loaded up to swing for the fences, often sacrificing contact in the process. The beleaguered pitchers didn't mind padding their strikeout totals at the expense of home-run-happy hitters. There was only one Babe, but there were a lot of players who wanted to be like him.

Ruth had run afoul of baseball Commissioner Kenesaw Mountain Landis by going on an unauthorized barnstorming tour after the 1921 World Series. In addition to handing Ruth and team-

No one exemplified the death of the dead ball era with more clarity than Babe Ruth

mate Bob Meusel stiff fines, Landis also suspended them until May 20. That helped clear the way for the St. Louis Browns to make a race of it. The Yankees won the pennant, but only by one game.

The Browns had a balanced attack that featured four 100-RBI players. Ken Williams led the league with 155 RBIs, Marty McManus had 109, batting champion George Sisler drove in 105 runs and Baby Doll Jacobson knocked in 102. All four also hit over .300.

The New York Giants led the National League throughout the season and won the pennant by seven games. They had a superb offense, posting a team batting average of .308.

Emil Meusel batted .331 and drove in 132 runs. George (High Pockets) Kelly hit .328 with 107 RBIs. Sparkplug Frankie Frisch batted .327 and Casey Stengel joined the team in the middle of the season and batted .327.

Art Nehf again led the pitching staff with a 19–13 mark and Rosie Ryan was 17–12.

SHORTS In a costly lapse of judgment, Giants' pitcher Phil Douglas wrote a letter to a friend on the Cardinals, suggesting he would be willing to harm the Giants to get revenge on manager John McGraw. Commissioner Landis barred Douglas from baseball. The Giants replaced him with free agent Jack Scott, who won eight games and helped New York to win the pennant.

Geo. L. Kelly
INFIELDER, NEW YORK, N. L.

The Giants' George Kelly was just one of New York's .300 hitters

POSTSEASON

Same teams, same result. The World Series stayed in New York with another match-up between the Yankees and Giants. The National League team won again, this time accomplishing the task in five games, one of which didn't have a winner.

The Giants took the opener 3–2 with three runs in the eighth inning. Game Two was a 3–3 tie when the umpires made a controversial decision and called the game after ten innings because of darkness. Reports suggested that there was at least another half hour of daylight remaining. The stats went into the record book, though, and Commissioner Landis tried to minimize the public relations damage by donating the gate receipts to charity.

Jack Scott pitched the Giants to a 3–0 win in Game Three. The Giants got a two-run single from Dave Bancroft to win Game Four, 4–3. For the second consecutive year, Art Nehf was on the mound for the deciding game, winning 5–3.

Babe Ruth was hitless in nine at bats over the last three games of the Series and was just 2-for-17 (.118) with one RBI.

Heinie Groh led the Giants with a .474 average, Frankie Frisch batted .471 and Irish Meusel had seven RBIs for the second straight year.

GAME 1	
NY Giants 3	NY Yankees 2
GAME 2	
NY Giants 3	NY Yankees 3 (tie)
GAME 3	
NY Giants 3	NY Yankees 0
GAME 4	
NY Giants 4	NY Yankees 3
GAME 5	
NY Giants 5	NY Yankees 3

Dave Bancroft's base hit clinched Game Four for the Giants

LEADERS

BATTING AVERAGE
AL: Harry Heilmann, Detroit, .403
NL: Rogers Hornsby, St. Louis Cardinals, .384

HOME RUNS
AL: Babe Ruth, NY Yankees, 41
NL: Cy Williams, Philadelphia Phillies, 41

RUNS BATTED IN
AL: Babe Ruth, NY Yankees, 131
NL: Emil Meusel, NY Giants, 125

STOLEN BASES
AL: Eddie Collins, Chicago White Sox, 47
NL: Max Carey, Pittsburgh, 51

PITCHING VICTORIES
AL: George Uhle, Cleveland, 26
NL: Dolf Luque, Cincinnati, 27

EARNED RUN AVERAGE
AL: Stan Coveleski, Cleveland, 2.76
NL: Dolf Luque, Cincinnati, 1.93

STRIKEOUTS
AL: Walter Johnson, Washington, 130
NL: Dazzy Vance, Brooklyn, 197

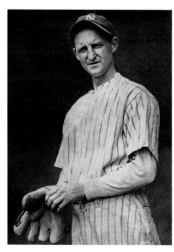

Traded from the rival Red Sox, Herb Pennock won 19 games for the Yankees

Babe Ruth was one of the few players who could bat .315 and have it considered a bad year. That's what happened in 1922. Ruth hit .315 with 35 home runs and 99 RBIs—a year most players would happily accept without condition.

But it wasn't a Babe Ruth-type of year, especially since Ruth was limited to 110 games largely because of his own misbehavior. He had defied Commissioner Kenesaw Mountain Landis and undertaken a lucrative barnstorming tour after the 1921 World Series. Landis slapped him with a hefty fine that Ruth could handle, but he also ruled that Ruth could not play in a game with the Yankees prior to May 20.

When Ruth did report he lost another five games, the result of a suspension for a confrontation with an umpire. Ruth was never really in good baseball shape throughout the season and he hit a woeful .118 in the World Series that the Yankees lost to the Giants. Even New York Mayor Jimmy Walker got into the act, criticizing Ruth for falling down as a role model to the city's children.

Ruth came back 20 pounds lighter in 1923 and came back with a purpose. He was anxious to erase the memories of the 1922 season—and he did. As usual, his timing was impeccable.

After being a tenant of the Giants at the Polo Grounds, the Yankees were ready to move across the East River into their own stadium. The new facility was considered baseball's finest showplace. The novelty of a new stadium and the rejuvenated Ruth kept the turnstiles spinning all season.

Ruth improved his average to .393, hit 41 home runs and drove in 131 runs, leading the American League in the latter two categories. The Yankees ran away with the pennant, outdistancing the Detroit Tigers by 16 games.

As good as Ruth was, the Yankees were not a one-man show. They had Ruth's power, but they also had pitching and defense. Sad Sam Jones led the staff with a 21–9 mark. Herb Pennock, who came over from the Boston Red Sox in a trade, was 19–6. Bullet Joe Bush was 19–5 and Waite Hoyt was 17–9.

SHORTS Number, please? The St. Louis Cardinals introduced the concept of numbers on uniforms, although it bore little resemblance to the modern practice. The Cardinals affixed small numbers to the sleeves of players' jerseys. The backs of the shirts remained blank. The numbering system was simple—players wore the number of the spot they occupied in the batting order.

The Phillies' Cy Williams led the league in homers with 41

Detroit outfielder Harry Heilmann won the batting title with a .403 average. At the age of 36, player-manager Ty Cobb batted .348 with 88 RBIs. The Tigers got a lift from 21-year-old rookie Heinie Manush, who batted .334.

Cleveland had weak pitching and the St. Louis Browns were unable to compete when first baseman George Sisler missed the entire season because of an eye problem.

The New York Giants won their third consecutive National League pennant, nipping the Cincinnati Reds in a close race.

Emil Meusel led the league with 125 RBIs. Frankie Frisch batted .348, drove in 111 runs and stole 29 bases.

Cincinnati had an excellent pitching staff led

SHORTS

Babe Ruth's lefthanded swing was famous, but there's evidence that Ruth toyed with the idea of switch hitting. On August 4 he stepped into the righthanded batter's box for a pitch against Cleveland's Sherrod Smith. Four days later, he again batted righthanded during an intentional walk that was issued by one of the Browns' pitchers. Was it a plan or just a way for the Babe to amuse himself?

by Dolf Luque (27–8), Eppa Rixey (20–15) and Pete Donahue (21–15). The Reds didn't have enough hitters like outfielder Edd Roush (.351).

Rogers Hornsby of the St. Louis Cardinals won his fourth consecutive batting title with a .384 average. Cy Williams of the Philadelphia Phillies led the league with 41 home runs.

POSTSEASON

The New York Yankees won the Series four games to two. The Yankees were no longer the second-class citizens in New York baseball—they had their own park and their first World Series title.

GAME 1	
NY Giants 5	NY Yankees 4
GAME 2	
NY Yankees 4	NY Giants 2
GAME 3	
NY Giants 1	NY Yankees 0
GAME 4	
NY Yankees 8	NY Giants 4
GAME 5	
NY Yankees 8	NY Giants 1
GAME 6	
NY Yankees 6	NY Giants 4

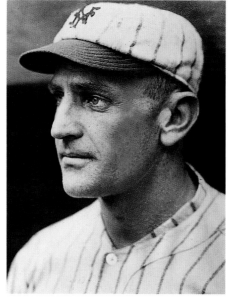

Casey Stengel's two homers were both game-winners—but they weren't enough

The third consecutive all-New York Series between the Giants and the Yankees had a decidedly different finish.

Babe Ruth bounced back from a poor Series in 1922 to bat .368 with three home runs for the Yankees.

The Series started in Yankee Stadium, which had opened to rave reviews in 1923. The Yankees had christened the new facility by making a shambles of the pennant race and finishing 16 games ahead of second-place Detroit.

Casey Stengel's ninth-inning, inside-the-park home run provided the margin in the Giants' 5–4 win in Game One. Ruth homered twice in Game Two, a 4–2 Yankees win behind Herb Pennock.

Stengel's home run won Game Three for the Giants and Art Nehf, 1–0. The Yankees' offense dominated in the next two games as they won 8–4 and 8–1, collecting 27 hits in the two games. Joe Dugan had four hits and three RBIs in Game Five, the Yankees' first Series win in their stadium.

Ruth had a homer in Game Six and Bob Meusel hit a two-run single in the Yankees' 6–4 victory.

TIMELINE

Jan. 30: The Yankees acquired pitcher Herb Pennock from the Red Sox for three players and $50,000.

Feb. 20: Christy Mathewson became part owner of the Boston Braves when he was a member of a group that purchased the franchise for $300,000. Mathewson was named club president.

March 6: The Cardinals announced plans to have players wear numbers on their uniforms. The numbers would be assigned according to position in the batting order.

March 8: In a surprising decision, Commissioner Landis allowed pitcher Rube Benton to come back to baseball. Benton had admitted to prior knowledge of the plan to fix the 1919 World Series.

April 18: Yankee Stadium opened. A crowd of 74,217 saw Babe Ruth hit a home run in the 4–1 win over the Red Sox.

May 2: Walter Johnson pitched his 100th shutout.

May 11: The Phillies and Cardinals combined for ten home runs in Philadelphia.

May 25: Ty Cobb took over the career lead in runs scored with 1,741. He broke Honus Wagner's record.

July 10: Rookie pitcher Johnny Stuart pitched two complete games and beat Boston in a doubleheader.

Aug. 17: Dazzy Vance's personal ten-game winning streak ended with a loss to the Cardinals.

Sept. 4: Sam Jones pitched a 2–0 no-hitter for the Yankees over the Athletics.

Sept. 14: Red Sox first baseman George Burns turned an unassisted triple play on a line drive.

Sept. 17: George (High Pockets) Kelly of the Giants hit home runs in three consecutive innings against the Cubs.

Sept. 27: Lou Gehrig hit his first home run in the major leagues.

Sept. 28: The Yankees collected 30 hits to beat the Red Sox 24–4.

Oct. 19: American League owners agreed to league president Ban Johnson's suggestion that they should not make their parks available for boxing matches.

Just when it looked like the New York Yankees were settling in for a long run atop the American League, they were hit by a Big Train.

Walter "Big Train" Johnson, the leader of the Washington pitching staff, helped lead the Senators to their first pennant. Washington finished two games ahead of the Yankees.

Johnson had been toiling with distinction for the Senators since 1907. Although Washington came close, the Senators hadn't won anything in Johnson's long tenure with the team. Their contending years were outweighed by some gloomy seasons. In seven of Johnson's years with the Senators, Washington either finished in the American League cellar or next-to-last.

Johnson was an unusual pitcher in that he succeeded with a limited repertoire. His main pitch was a sidearm fastball. Everyone knew what he was likely to throw, but doing something with the pitch was another issue.

At the age of 36, Johnson probably wasn't throwing as hard as he once did. He was a workhorse for the Senators, taking the ball often and usually piling up 300 innings. But he knew how to pitch and posted a 23–7 record for the Senators with a 2.72 earned run average. His win total led the league and his ERA was certainly a respectable number in an era of rapidly increasing offense.

Lefthander Tom Zachary was 15–9 for the Senators and George Mogridge had a 16–11 record.

Outfielder Leon (Goose) Goslin batted .344 and led the league with 129 RBIs. Outfielder Sam Rice hit .334 and drove in 76 runs. First baseman Joe Judge had a .324 average and 79 RBIs.

The New York Yankees finished second, two games behind the Senators. The Yankees pitching staff disappointed and the abrasive Carl Mays was released during the season. Herb Pennock was one of the few Yankees pitchers to have a good year. He was 21–9.

The Detroit Tigers finished third, six games off the pace. Player-manager Ty Cobb hit .338 and outfielder Johnny Weaver posted a .346 average.

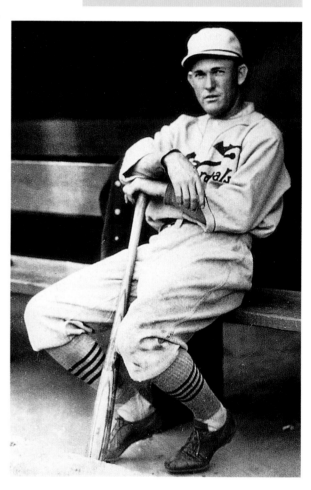

The Cardinals' Mr Consistency, Rogers Hornsby

The Tigers had five regulars who hit better than .300. In addition to Cobb and Weaver, first baseman Lu Blue hit .311, second baseman Del Pratt batted .303 and outfielder Harry Heilmann led the team at .346.

The Yankees may not have been able to win their fourth consecutive pennant, but the New York Giants turned the trick in the National League. They won a close race, finishing 1½

Brooklyn's Dazzy Vance compiled some impressive numbers

games in front of Brooklyn and three games ahead of Pittsburgh.

Pitcher Dazzy Vance had a brilliant season that kept the Dodgers in contention. Vance was 28–6 and posted a 2.16 ERA, both of which led the League.

The Chicago Cubs dropped out of the race

in August when their best pitcher, Grover Alexander, broke his wrist. Cincinnati had too many injuries to challenge for the pennant.

Wilbur Cooper led Pittsburgh's pitching staff with a 20–14 record. Outfielder Kiki Cuyler hit .354 with 85 RBIs and 32 stolen bases.

It was business as usual for the St. Louis Cardinals—the team wasn't a factor in the race, but Rogers Hornsby won his fifth consecutive batting title. Hornsby's average of .424 was the best of the century.

SHORTS The World Series finally got a format, thanks to Dodgers' President Charles Ebbets' suggestion. Owners approved a plan that would have the first two games in one park, the next three on the other team's home field and the last two in the park where the Series started. The extra game was to alternate each year between leagues.

POSTSEASON

It took 18 seasons, but the game's best pitcher finally got to the World Series. Walter Johnson made the most of his chance, pitching four innings of scoreless relief in Game Seven to help the Washington Senators beat the New York Giants.

It was the Senators' first trip to the postseason as they edged past the defending champion New York Yankees by two games. John McGraw's New York Giants represented the National League for the fourth consecutive year and the eighth time in 14 years.

Johnson, 38, may have been the sentimental favorite, but he wasn't the pitching star for the Senators. Johnson lost both of his starts before

securing the Series-winning game in relief. Tom Zachary was 2–0 with a 2.04 ERA for the Senators as he won both Games Two and Six.

Washington needed some good fortune to win. Muddy Ruel of the Senators appeared to foul out, but catcher Hank Gowdy stumbled over his discarded mask and dropped the ball. Given a second chance, Ruel doubled. Johnson reached on an error and the Series-winning run scored when Earl McNeely's grounder hit a pebble and took a wild bounce over third baseman Fred Lindstrom.

It was a case of better late than never for Washington's Walter Johnson

GAME 1	
NY Giants 4	Washington 3
GAME 2	
Washington 4	NY Giants 3
GAME 3	
NY Giants 6	Washington 4
GAME 4	
Washington 7	NY Giants 4
GAME 5	
NY Giants 6	Washington 2
GAME 6	
Washington 2	NY Giants 1
GAME 7	
Washington 4	NY Giants 3

An easy delivery didn't prevent Johnson from throwing pure heat

Walter Johnson didn't drive a hard bargain when professional teams came calling for his services.

From the Washington Senators, he demanded and got $350 a month in salary, a $100 signing bonus and the train fare from Idaho to Washington, D.C. There was one other provision —Johnson made the Senators promise to provide return train fare in case he didn't make it as a major league pitcher. He never needed that return ticket.

Johnson spent 21 seasons whipping his patented sidearm fastball past American League hitters, winning 417 games and proving to be one of the game's most durable pitchers.

Calculating the velocity of pitchers was guesswork in that era since no reliable system existed to measure the speed of a pitch. However, word-of-mouth favors Johnson as one of the hardest throwers of that era. He had long limbs and an easy throwing motion from the more natural sidearm angle. Hitters claimed that his fastball seemed to explode on them as it crossed the plate and popped into the catcher's mitt.

He had 110 career shutouts, won at least 20 games in 12 different seasons, including seven consecutive years in which he had at least 25 victories. He completed all but one of his 37 starts in 1911 and finished 531 of the 666 games he started as a major leaguer.

In nine of ten seasons, his earned run average was below 2.00 and he struck out 3,508 batters.

Fittingly, he was the winning pitcher when the Senators took their only World Series with a 4–3 win over the New York Giants in 1924.

His nickname was "Big Train," a tag hung on him by sportswriter Grantland Rice for the power his pitches had as they sped to the plate. Teammates generally called him "Barney" after a race car driver of the day, a nod to Johnson's devil-may-care style behind the wheel.

Johnson was pitching semi-pro ball in Idaho as a 19 year-old when a scout was intrigued by his potential. He signed with the Senators and made his debut that summer, losing to the Detroit Tigers on August 2, 1907. Johnson was not an immediate sensation, posting records of 5–9, 14–14 and 13–25 in his first three full major league seasons.

In 1908, he won five games in eight days, testimony to his ability to pitch both often and well. He had a breakthrough season in 1910, going 25–17 and completing 38 of his 42 starts. In 1913 and '14, he was a combined 69–19 in the two seasons.

It was in 1914 that the Chicago franchise of the Federal League made an offer to lure Johnson. He was ready to jump until Senators' owner Clark Griffith made an emergency trip to improve Johnson's existing contract.

Keeping him was one of the smartest investments the Senators ever made. Over the next five seasons his record was 118–76, even though Washington rarely contended for the American League pennant.

The next four seasons showed Johnson's career in decline. He posted an ordinary 57–52 record from 1920–23. He rebounded at age 36 in 1924 and won the Most Valuable Player award with a 23–7 record and a 2.72 ERA. The Senators also won the pennant.

Johnson was 20–7 in 1925 and although the Senators repeated as American League champions, they lost the World Series to Pittsburgh. Johnson pitched a complete game in the seventh game, but came away with a 9–7 loss.

His record took a tumble in 1926 as he finished the season 15–16 and the Senators fell back to fourth place. He sustained a broken leg during 1927's spring training and had a 5–6 record before the injury caused him to announce his retirement at the age of 40.

In 1929 Johnson was installed as Washington's manager, a position he would hold for four seasons. The Senators won at least 90 games in three of his four years as manager, but consistently finished behind the Philadelphia Athletics and New York Yankees.

Johnson continued his managerial career with Cleveland from 1933 to 1935. Although the Indians had winning seasons under his leadership, they did not contend for the American League pennant. He had a winning record as a manager. The case against him was that the easygoing personality that made him so popular as a player was a drawback as a manager because his players took advantage of his good nature.

Johnson was one of the five charter members of the Hall of Fame when the shrine was created in 1936. He died ten years later.

LEADERS

BATTING AVERAGE
AL: Harry Heilmann, Detroit, .393
NL: Rogers Hornsby, St. Louis Cardinals, .403

HOME RUNS
AL: Bob Meusel, NY Yankees, 33
NL: Rogers Hornsby, St. Louis Cardinals, 39

RUNS BATTED IN
AL: Bob Meusel, NY Yankees, 138
NL: Rogers Hornsby, St. Louis Cardinals, 143

STOLEN BASES
AL: Johnny Mostil, Chicago White Sox, 43
NL: Max Carey, Pittsburgh, 46

PITCHING VICTORIES
AL: Ted Lyons, Chicago White Sox, 21
NL: Dazzy Vance, Brooklyn, 22

EARNED RUN AVERAGE
AL: Stan Coveleski, Washington; Eddie Rommel, Philadelphia A's, 2.84
NL: Dolf Luque, Cincinnati, 2.63

STRIKEOUTS
AL: Lefty Grove, Philadelphia A's, 116
NL: Dazzy Vance, Brooklyn, 221

It was beginning to seem as though the World Series was part of the schedule for the New York Giants.

For four consecutive years the Giants finished first in the National League. Their run came to a halt in 1925, though, as the Pittsburgh Pirates took the title.

The Pirates had been one of baseball's powers in the early part of the century, thanks to shortstop Honus Wagner. He was the game's premier player from 1900–09 and the Pirates won the pennant four times in that decade. Times were tougher after Wagner's retirement and the Pirates were more likely to be found in the second division.

By the early 1920s, though, Pittsburgh had begun to assemble some formidable talent, a group that included Pie Traynor, Kiki Cuyler, Rabbit Maranville and Max Carey. The Pirates weren't built for home run power, but were better suited to finding players who could run and stretch line drives into extra-base hits.

After three consecutive third-place finishes, the Pirates won the pennant in 1925 as they were 8½ games better than the defending champion Giants.

Carey batted .343, scored 109 runs and stole 46 bases to lead the league. Cuyler had a .357 average with 18 home runs and 102 RBIs. He scored 144 runs, tops in the National League. Traynor hit .320 and drove in 106 runs

Kiki Cuyler typified the versatility of the Pittsburgh Pirates

and outfielder Clyde Barnhart batted .325 with 124 RBIs.

The Pirates had five starting pitchers who won at least 15 games, led by Lee Meadows with a 19–10 mark.

The other big story in the National League was Rogers Hornsby's Triple Crown. He hit .403 with 39 home runs and 143 RBIs. What else could he do for the St. Louis Cardinals? He took over as player-manager, succeeding Branch Rickey.

The Washington Senators waited so long to get into first place, they decided to stay a while.

The Senators took their second consecutive American League pennant by finishing a comfortable 9½ games in front of the Philadelphia Athletics. The New York Yankees stumbled into seventh place and were not a factor in the race. The Yankees wound up 28½ games out of first place as Babe Ruth appeared in only 98 games, batting .290 with 25 home runs and 66 RBIs. It was his worst season since joining the Yankees.

SHORTS Few took note on June 1 when Lou Gehrig pinch hit for the Yankees. It was huge news the next time his name wasn't in the box score. With the pinch-hitting appearance (he batted for Pee Wee Wanninger), Gehrig started a streak of 2,130 games that lasted until failing health made it impossible.

Triple Crown winner, the Cardinals' Rogers Hornsby

The Senators' 20-game winner,
Stan Coveleski

The race was basically between the Senators and Athletics and Philadelphia dropped out with a 12-game losing streak in August.

Walter Johnson was 20–7 for the Senators and Stan Coveleski had a 20–5 record. The Senators made a smart move by claiming Dutch

SHORTS The ongoing battle between Babe Ruth and Yankees' manager Miller Huggins became full-scale war in August when Ruth skipped batting practice after a late night. Huggins fined his star $5,000, a penalty that was backed by owner Jacob Ruppert. Ruth was allowed to rejoin the Yankees nine days later, but not until he apologized to both Huggins and the team.

Reuther on waivers—he was 18–7. Washington survived a bad season from lefthander Tom Zachary. After making a significant contribution to the first pennant, Zachary was just 12–15. Washington used Firpo Marberry effectively in relief as he appeared in 55 games.

Goose Goslin had another big year, batting .334 with 18 home runs and 113 RBIs. He also stole 26 bases. Sam Rice hit .350 with 87 RBIs and 26 steals.

TIMELINE

April 5: Babe Ruth collapsed and required surgery for an ulcer.

April 18: Dodgers' president Charles Ebbets died on the morning of his team's scheduled home opener in the stadium that bore his name.

April 22: The Cardinals got 12 hits in the first inning of their home opener.

May 1: Jimmie Foxx made his major league debut at age 17 for the Philadelphia Athletics. Foxx appeared as a pinch hitter and singled.

May 5: Ty Cobb went 6-for-6 against Boston and half of the hits were home runs.

May 7: Pirates' shortstop Glenn Wright turned an unassisted triple play.

May 17: Tris Speaker got his 3,000th career hit.

May 20: George Sisler's hitting streak ended at 34 games.

May 30: Perennial batting champion Rogers Hornsby took over as manager of the Cardinals, succeeding Branch Rickey. Rickey concentrated solely on his duties as general manager.

June 1: Lou Gehrig began a consecutive game streak that would eventually cover 2,130 games.

June 3: Eddie Collins got his 3,000th career hit.

June 12: The Giants turn a bizarre triple play against the Pirates. In the scorebook, it was 6-2-5-9-4-3. Translation: shortstop to catcher to third baseman to right fielder to second baseman to first baseman.

June 15: The Athletics scored 13 runs in the eighth inning and came back from a 15–4 deficit to beat the Indians 17–15.

June 30: Walter Johnson beat Philadelphia 7–0 to knock the Athletics out of first place.

July 4: Milt Stock of the Dodgers had his fourth consecutive four-hit game.

July 20: Dazzy Vance struck out 17 against the Cubs.

Sept. 30: Dazzy Vance pitched a no-hitter against the Phillies after throwing a one-hitter against them in his previous start.

POSTSEASON

For the second consecutive year, Walter Johnson was on the mound for Game Seven of the World Series. This time, though, the Pittsburgh Pirates would rewrite the storybook ending.

GAME 1	
Washington 4	Pittsburgh 1
GAME 2	
Pittsburgh 3	Washington 2
GAME 3	
Washington 4	Pittsburgh 3
GAME 4	
Washington 4	Pittsburgh 0
GAME 5	
Pittsburgh 6	Washington 3
GAME 6	
Pittsburgh 3	Washington 2
GAME 7	
Pittsburgh 9	Washington 7

The Pirates became the first team to come back from a 3–1 deficit in games and win a Series, capping their comeback by beating Johnson 9–7 in Game Seven.

Johnson won the opener 4–1 before Vic Aldridge tied the Series with a 3–2 win for the Pirates. The Senators scored two runs in the seventh to win Game Three, 4–3, and Johnson pitched a 4–0 shutout in Game Four.

Faced with elimination, the Pirates won the last three games. Aldridge won Game Five, 6–3, and Pittsburgh took Game Six when second baseman Eddie Moore hit a tiebreaking

home run and Ray Kremer won 3–2.

Johnson had a 7–6 lead in the eighth thanks to Roger Peckinpaugh's home run. He had two out in the bottom of the inning when the Pirates rallied for three runs, highlighted by Kiki Cuyler's tiebreaking double.

The offensive star of the Series was Washington's Goose Goslin, who hit three home runs for the second consecutive postseason. Max Carey hit .458 for the Pirates and Aldridge and Kremer accounted for all four wins.

Ray Kremer's Game Six victory tied the Series

BATTING AVERAGE
AL: Heinie Manush, Detroit, .378
NL: Bubbles Hargrave, Cincinnati, .353 (below)

HOME RUNS
AL: Babe Ruth, NY Yankees, 47
NL: Hack Wilson, Chicago Cubs, 21

RUNS BATTED IN
AL: Babe Ruth, NY Yankees, 145
NL: Jim Bottomley, St. Louis Cardinals, 120

STOLEN BASES
AL: Johnny Mostil, Chicago White Sox, 35
NL: Kiki Cuyler, Pittsburgh, 35

PITCHING VICTORIES
AL: George Uhle, Cleveland, 27
NL: Pete Donahue, Cincinnati; Flint Rehm, St. Louis Cardinals; Ray Kremer and Lee Meadows, Pittsburgh, 20

EARNED RUN AVERAGE
AL: Lefty Grove, Philadelphia Athletics, 2.51
NL: Ray Kremer, Pittsburgh , 2.61

STRIKEOUTS
AL: Lefty Grove, Philadelphia Athletics, 194
NL: Dazzy Vance, Brooklyn, 140

"What a difference a year makes" might be one way to sum up the 1926 New York Yankees. But perhaps the more appropriate phrase might be, "What a difference a healthy Babe Ruth makes."

Sidelined for nearly 60 games in 1925 with what writers referred to as "the stomachache heard 'round the world," Ruth's absence from the Yankee lineup was one of many reasons they skidded into seventh place.

But 1926 was an entirely different story. Ruth was back, belting a league-leading 47 home runs, driving in 145 runs and scoring 139 runs to lead the league in three departments. His .372 batting average didn't lead the league, but was impressive nonetheless.

No doubt the run support was weclomed by Yankees' ace Herb Pennock as well, as he finished with a 23–11 record to lead a fine pitching staff.

The Yankees jumped out to a strong start, leading by as many as ten games in August. But challenges by the Cleveland Indians, Philadelphia Athletics and Washington Senators threatened the New York stronghold in early September.

Cleveland, in particular, made a serious run at the Yankees. Led by pitcher George Uhle's 27–11 mark and solid hitting throughout their lineup, the Indians pulled to within four games of New York. First baseman George Burns was their leader at the plate with a .358 batting average.

But the Yankees, behind Ruth, Lou Gehrig, Bob Meusel and others, including solid hitting and defense from rookie second baseman Tony Lazzeri, shored up their lead and went to the World Series.

In the National League, the St. Louis Cardinals were treated to their first National League flag as player-manager Rogers Hornsby led his club to the championship. Hornsby posted a .317 batting mark and first baseman Jim Bottomley had a league-leading 120 runs batted in. Third baseman Les Bell led St. Louis in home runs (17) as well as batting average (.325), while pitcher Flint Rehm anchored the

SHORTS You could say that Pittsburgh Pirates' owner Barney Dreyfuss was a hands-on executive. In mid-August when Pirate players complained about Dreyfuss' crony Fred Clarke's constant presence on the bench with them, Dreyfuss responded by releasing Babe Adams and Carson Bigbee and suspending Max Carey, who was eventually waived to Brooklyn. It would come as no surprise to say that the protests stopped—publicly, at least.

The Yankees' rookie sensation, Tony Lazzeri

Cardinal staff with a 20–7 record.

The Cardinals and Cincinnati Reds engaged in a tight race for the pennant, but a head-to-head series between the two in September decided the race in St. Louis' favor.

Another key to the Cardinal's success was the pitching of 39-year-old Grover Cleveland Alexander, who rejoined his old club late in mid-

The Cubs' slugger Hack Wilson belted a league-leading 21 homers

season and posted a 9–7 record, including two shutouts.

Reds' catcher Bubbles Hargrave led the league with a .353 batting average and Pete Donahue was their leading pitcher with a 20–14 record as the Cincinnati club finished two games behind St. Louis. Left fielder Walter "Cuckoo" Christensen was not far behind Hargrave with a .350 mark.

The Pittsburgh Pirates finished a close third and could boast two 20-game winners in Ray Kremer (20–6) and Lee Meadows (20–9). Kiki Cuyler's .321 batting mark and 35 stolen bases sparked the Pittsburgh offensive attack as the Pirates finished just 4½ games out of first place.

Chicago Cubs' centerfielder Hack Wilson was the National League's home run king with 21 as the Cubs finished fourth, seven games behind the Cardinals.

POSTSEASON

The Cardinals and the Yankees combined on a Series that was packed with compelling drama and which came to a peak in Game Seven.

GAME 1	
NY Yankees 2	St. Louis Cardinals 1

GAME 2	
St. Louis Cardinals 6	NY Yankees 2

GAME 3	
St. Louis Cardinals 4	NY Yankees 0

GAME 4	
NY Yankees 10	St. Louis Cardinals 5

GAME 5	
NY Yankees 3	St. Louis Cardinals 2

GAME 6	
St. Louis Cardinals 10	NY Yankees 2

GAME 7	
St. Louis Cardinals 3	NY Yankees 2

The teams traded victories through the first six games, with the Cardinals tying the Series on Grover Cleveland Alexander's 10–2 win in Game Six. After pitching a complete game, who knew that Alexander would also be a key figure in Game Seven?

Cardinals' manager Rogers Hornsby called on Alexander in a critical relief situation in the seventh inning with the Cardinals holding a 3–2 lead. Alexander came in with the bases loaded and struck out rookie Tony Lazzeri.

Alexander was perfect in the eighth and quickly got two outs in the ninth to set up the

showdown with Babe Ruth, who had already hit four home runs in the Series. Alexander walked Ruth on a 3–2 pitch and had to face Bob Meusel. That match-up was scuttled when Ruth tried to steal second and was thrown out by catcher Bob O'Farrell to end the Series.

Jesse Haines, the Game Seven winner, and Alexander were both 2–0 and Cardinals' shortstop Tommy Thevenow batted .417.

Grover Alexander faced the heat of the Yankees' lineup—and came out on top

BATTING AVERAGE
AL: Harry Heilmann, Detroit, .398
NL: Paul Waner, Pittsburgh, .380

HOME RUNS
AL: Babe Ruth, NY Yankees, 60
NL: Cy Williams, Philadelphia Phillies, 30

RUNS BATTED IN
AL: Lou Gehrig, NY Yankees, 175
NL: Paul Waner, Pittsburgh; Hack Wilson, Chicago Cubs, 131

STOLEN BASES
AL: George Sisler, St. Louis Browns, 27
NL: Frankie Frisch, St. Louis Cardinals, 48

PITCHING VICTORIES
AL: Waite Hoyt, NY Yankees; Ted Lyons, Chicago White Sox, 22
NL: Charlie Root, Chicago Cubs, 26 (below)

EARNED RUN AVERAGE
AL: Wilcy Moore, NY Yankees, 2.28
NL: Ray Kremer, Pittsburgh, 2.47

STRIKEOUTS
AL: Lefty Grove, Philadelphia Athletics, 174
NL: Dazzy Vance, Brooklyn, 184

When George Herman (Babe) Ruth was a pitcher in the Boston Red Sox organization, home runs were so rare that season totals in the teens were thought to be high.

By 1927, however, Ruth had already taken home run hitting to a different level for several seasons. Ruth's size and strength, and the distance of his shots, made him the biggest drawing card in the game.

His 60 home runs have certainly become part of baseball history. This feat is so special it even impressed New York fans who had become accustomed to seeing Ruth do things that no other hitter could do. His total of 60 doubled the total of National League leader Chuck Klein.

Ruth was part of a Yankee lineup that was known as "Murderer's Row." His 60 home runs and first baseman Lou Gehrig's league leading 175 RBIs and .373 batting average (along with 47 home runs of his own) topped a team that many proclaim was the best in the history of the game.

It's hard to argue, since the 1927 Yankees didn't have a weakness. Waite Hoyt's 22–7 record, the best in the American League, led a solid pitching staff and helped New York to finish 19 games ahead of its closest rival, the Philadelphia Athletics.

Athletics' pitching star Lefty Grove was the league's strikeout leader with 174, complementing his own 20–13 record. Center fielder Al Simmons narrowly missed the coveted .400 mark with a .392 batting average

while driving in 108 runs and hitting 17 home runs for Philadelphia.

Goose Goslin's .334 batting mark and 120 runs batted in led the offense of the third-place Washington Senators.

While the Yankees shredded their competition in the American League, the National League race was a hotly-contested, four-way struggle that lasted most of the season.

The Pittsburgh Pirates jumped to an early lead, but by August Joe McCarthy's Chicago Cubs were on top. Pittsburgh regained the lead in September, but the Pirates were challenged by the Chicago Cubs, the St. Louis Cardinals and New York Giants. The Pirates clinched the flag on the very last day of the season.

The Pirates' offense was led by Paul Waner, whose .380 batting average and 131 runs batted in led the league. Carmen Hill's 22–11 record topped the pitching staff and Ray

The Pirates' Paul Waner led the league in both average and RBI

Kremer's 2.47 earned run average led the league. Kremer was 19–8. Lee Meadows, at 19–10, led the league in starts (38) and complete games (25).

The Cardinals, behind Jesse Haines with a 24–10 mark and an offense sparked by Frankie Frisch's .337 average and league-leading 48 stolen bases, finished 1½ games behind the Pirates.

Rogers Hornsby, now playing second base for the New York Giants, batted .361, hit 26 home runs and drove in 131 runs to lead them to a close third-place finish, two games out of first. Hornsby was one of six Giants regulars to bat over .300.

The Cubs once again had the league's top home run hitter in Hack Wilson with 30. Wilson also led his club in RBIs (129) and batting average (.318). But Charlie Root's pitching (26–15) shared the spotlight with Wilson's offensive numbers.

The New York Giants' Rogers Hornsby (left)

POSTSEASON

Woe was the National League team that had to encounter the New York Yankees in the World Series.

That team was the Pittsburgh Pirates and they needed only four games to discover what the American League had learned that summer—the Yankees didn't have a weakness.

New York swept the Series in four games

GAME 1	
NY Yankees 5	Pittsburgh 4
GAME 2	
NY Yankees 6	Pittsburgh 2
GAME 3	
NY Yankees 8	Pittsburgh 1
GAME 4	
NY Yankees 4	Pittsburgh 3

and cemented its reputation as one of the best teams in the history of the game. The Yankees had won the pennant by a margin of 19 games, thanks to a 110–44 record that was best in American League history.

Babe Ruth and Lou Gehrig combined for 107 regular-season home runs and 337 runs batted in. Ruth set the home run record with 60.

Ruth hit .400 in the Series with two homers and seven RBIs. Gehrig hit a respectable .308, but that was only sixth on the Yankees' list. Shortstop Mark Koenig batted .500.

Despite New York's power, only one game was a blowout—their 8–4 victory in Game Three. The Yankees hit .279 as a team and Ruth had both of their homers.

The ending was frustrating for Pittsburgh as John Miljus threw a wild pitch that allowed Earle Combs to score the Series-winning run.

Two reasons why the 1927 Yankees were remembered as the best—Ruth (l) and Gehrig (r)

TIMELINE

Jan. 15: The Chicago White Sox traded pitchers Sloppy Thurston and Leo Mangum to the Washington Senators for shortstop Roger Peckinpaugh.

Feb. 9: Cincinnati traded outfielder Edd Roush to the New York Giants for George Kelly and an undisclosed amount of cash. Roush had been a contract holdout.

April 1: Travis Jackson, shortstop for the New York Giants, had his appendix removed. The surgery would keep him on the sidelines for six weeks.

May 21: The Chicago Cubs swept a doubleheader from the Brooklyn Dodgers and took over first place in the National League from the Giants, who lost to Pittsburgh. Chicago scored nine runs in the ninth inning to take the second game 11–6.

June 16: Pittsburgh pitcher Lee Meadows won his ninth game of the season, shutting out the Braves 6–0. Pirates' outfielder Paul Waner also extended his hitting streak to 19 games and drove in a run for the 12th consecutive game.

June 18: St. Louis native Charles Lindbergh was given a day in his honor at Sportsman's Park. The aviator helped to raise the 1926 National League flag before the game against the Giants, which the Cardinals won 6–4.

July 7: Charlie Root threw a one-hitter for the Chicago Cubs, putting them in first place ahead of Pittsburgh.

July 18: The legendary Ty Cobb, now playing for the Philadelphia Athletics, got his 4,000th career hit against the Tigers, a double off Sam Gibson.

Aug. 22: Babe Ruth hit his 40th home run of the season, but the Yankees lost to Cleveland 9–4.

Aug. 29: The Yankees beat the St. Louis Browns for the 18th consecutive time.

Sept. 27: Babe Ruth hit his second grand slam home run in three days. It was also his 57th home run of the season.

BABE RUTH

TEAMS

Teams: Boston Red Sox 1914–19, New York Yankees 1920–34, Boston Braves, 1935.

Games:	2,503
At bats:	8,399
Hits:	2,873
Doubles:	506
Triples:	136
Home runs:	714
Runs:	2,174
RBI:	2,204
Stolen bases:	123
Average:	.342
Slugging percentage:	.690

Ruth's legend has transcended the game he changed irrevocably

Babe Ruth's records may have fallen, but his place in baseball history is stronger than ever.

Even though others have topped his accomplishments, the numbers 714 and 60 are inextricably linked to Ruth. He hit 714 home runs over his career, a standard that stood until it was broken by Hank Aaron in 1974. His single-season record of 60 homers lasted until 1961, when another Yankee, Roger Maris, hit 61.

Born in 1895 and raised in a Baltimore orphanage, George Herman Ruth played for the hometown minor league Baltimore Orioles until that cash-strapped franchise sold the 19 year-old to the Boston Red Sox. Ruth broke into the major leagues with Boston in 1914 as a pitcher and won 89 games over six seasons. That lasted until someone realized his bat was being wasted and the spindly-legged, barrel-chested Ruth was converted to the outfield.

Ruth was involved in one of baseball's most notorious transactions. In 1920, the Red Sox sold him to Yankees for $120,000 and he promptly hit 54 home runs that season to lead the American League in a particularly conspicuous way—Ruth hit more home runs than any American League team did.

Ruth and New York were a perfect match. He was a flamboyant figure who needed the enormity of the New York stage. Because media coverage was fairly benign and protective during his career, a lot of Ruth's off-field escapades weren't reported until decades later—they only added to the legend of a player who would have been well known only for what he accomplished on the field.

Ruth's greatest accomplishment may have been in deflecting attention away from the 1919 Black Sox scandal and allowing baseball to again draw fans. People who may have been driven away from the game by the gambling controversy stayed because of the daily exploits of the Yankees' slugger.

Ruth won 12 home run titles, including one during the 1927 season when he hit 60, a record that stood until 1961. He had 15 more homers in seven World Series and helped the Yankees to win four titles. Ruth finished with 714 home runs, hitting his last homers while a member of the Boston Braves.

Ruth never achieved his secret goal of managing the Yankees. The belief is that his colorful life off the field was at odds with what the staid

club perceived as its image. Ruth died of throat cancer on August 14, 1948, at the age of 53.

He was a member of the Hall of Fame's inaugural class of 1936. In fact, Ruth's storied career was one reason the Hall was established. He, Cobb, Honus Wagner, Walter Johnson and Christy Mathewson were the first inductees.

Ruth's career average of .342 is still tied for eighth in major league history. Although he's known almost exclusively for his home runs, Ruth compiled a .370 batting average over five years from 1920–24. That is still 11th all-time for average over a five-year span.

Ruth remains third in major league history with 2,174 career runs scored and led his league eight times in runs scored, which still stands as a record. He is second in career home runs, but is the American League's career leader with 708. His 659 home runs with the Yankees are second only to Aaron's 733 with the Braves for homers with one club.

He is still the top lefthanded home run hitter, leading Reggie Jackson by 51. Ruth is the all-time leader for home runs by an outfielder with 692. Aaron hit 661 when he was in the lineup as an outfielder—the rest came when he played first base. Ruth's .690 career slugging percentage has never been topped. He is third in career extra base hits with 1,356 and is second only to Aaron in career runs batted in with 2,213. He is the all-time RBI leader among lefthanded hitters and he's tied for the lead in most 100-RBI seasons. He, Jimmie Foxx and teammate Lou Gehrig each had 13 seasons of driving in at least 100 runs. Ruth walked 2,056 times, which is a major league record, and speaks of opponents' desire to avoid him, particularly with the game on the line. He had 13 seasons with at least 100 walks, which is a record.

Ruth has been dead for more than 50 years, yet his name is still magic among baseball fans. The Yankees remembered Ruth with a monument placed in center field of Yankee Stadium. Ruth was the fourth long-time Yankees personality honored in that way. The monument was dedicated in 1949, a year after Ruth's death. The inscription reads: George Herman "Babe" Ruth, 1895–1948, A Great Ballplayer, A Great Man, A Great American, Erected by the Yankees and the New York Baseball Writers, April 19, 1949.

The New York Yankee dynasty continued to roll in 1928, though not as strongly as it had in the previous season.

Babe Ruth continued to dominate the power categories with 54 home runs and his 142 runs batted in tied teammate Lou Gehrig in that department. Gehrig's .374 batting average led the team. George Pipgras was the ace of the Yankee staff with a 24–13 mark.

But a third consecutive Yankee pennant was not that easy to achieve. Although they jumped to an early season lead, the Yankees had to hold off a serious challenge by Connie Mack's Philadelphia Athletics, led once again by pitcher Lefty Grove with a 24–8 record. Al Simmons led Philadelphia's offense with a .351 batting average, 15 home runs and 107 RBIs.

The Athletics posted a phenomenal 25–8 record for the month of July and stayed close to the Yankees throughout August. In early September they moved into first place for one day, but lost a doubleheader to New York. The Yankees took over first and held it to the end of the season.

The St. Louis Browns were a distant third, but got impressive numbers from Heinie Manush with a .378 batting average, along with 13 home runs and 108 RBIs. Pitcher General Crowder's 21–5 record gave him the league's best winning

Babe Ruth (l) and Lou Gehrig (r) were again the stars for the Yankees

percentage at .808. The league's leading hitter, however, was Washington's Goose Goslin with a .379 batting average. Goslin also drove in 102 runs and belted 17 home runs.

In the National League, the St. Louis Cardinals, now managed by Bill McKechnie, survived a strong September effort by John McGraw's New York Giants to win the flag by two games. "Sunny" Jim Bottomley, the Cardinals' popular first baseman, led the league in runs batted in with 136 and tied with Chicago's Hack Wilson for the home run crown with 31. The St. Louis pitching staff was led by Bill Sherdel with a 21–10 record.

The Giants, meanwhile, were helped by the presence of a 19-year-old slugger named Mel

The 1928 World Series was a sweep for the Yankees

Ott. In his first year as a regular, he hit a team-leading 18 home runs and posted a .322 batting average. Third baseman Fred Lindstrom led the club in most of the other offensive categories, however, including RBIs (107), batting average (.358) and stolen bases (15). Larry Benton's 25–9 record and "Fat" Freddie Fitzsimmons' 20–9 mark were tops on the Giants' pitching staff.

Along with Hack Wilson's league-tying 31 home runs and 120 runs batted in, the Chicago Cubs could also claim the stolen base leader in Kiki Cuyler with 37.

The Pittsburgh Pirates tumbled to fourth place and never came very close to repeating their championship. Pitcher Burleigh Grimes

SHORTS New York Yankees fans were shocked and saddened by the death of pitcher Urban Shocker. Shocker, 18–6 in 1927, had appeared in only one game in 1928, but had left the team for Denver. He had an enlarged heart and had been unable to sleep in a prone position for nearly two years. He contracted pneumonia and died at age 38. Shocker had never posted a losing record in his career.

posted an impressive 25–14 mark and Paul Waner continued to put up solid numbers with a .370 batting average, one of six Pirates (including brother Lloyd) to top the .300 mark. But the team, while solid throughout, just didn't have the power to compete with the front-runners.

POSTSEASON

The New York Yankees were battered by injuries heading into the World Series. That didn't even slow them down.

GAME 1	
NY Yankees 4	St. Louis Cardinals 1

GAME 2	
NY Yankees 9	St. Louis Cardinals 3

GAME 3	
NY Yankees 7	St. Louis Cardinals 3

GAME 4	
NY Yankees 7	St. Louis Cardinals 3

The pitching star for New York was Waite Hoyt, who won two games and had a 1.50 ERA.

Despite struggling to win the American League pennant after taking the 1927 title by 19 games, the Yankees were again the class of baseball. Even though 17-game winner Herb Pennock was unavailable because of a sore arm and center fielder Earle Combs was limited to pinch hitting because of a broken finger, the Yankees still needed only four games to eliminate the St. Louis Cardinals.

Babe Ruth had a bad ankle but no one noticed, particularly in Game Four, when he hit three of the Yankees' five home runs. Unlike the 1927 Series against the Pirates, these games weren't close. The Yankees outscored the Cardinals 27–10 and won each game by at least three runs.

Ruth hit .625 in the Series and six of his ten hits were for extra bases. Lou Gehrig hit .545 and actually hit one more homer than Ruth did as the Yankees got nine home runs in four games. Together Ruth and Gehrig hit .593 from the third and fourth spots in the Yankees' order.

New York Yankees' Waite Hoyt

87

TIMELINE

Feb. 14: The Major League Advisory Council donated $50,000 to the American Legion baseball program to fund a national championship tournament.

April 19: St. Louis Browns and Detroit Tigers pitchers combined for 18 walks as the Tigers won 9–8.

May 14: Giants' manager John McGraw was struck down by an automobile as he tried to cross a street outside Chicago's Wrigley Field, sentencing him to six weeks on the sideline while Roger Bresnahan called the shots.

May 23: Cleveland executed a triple play against the White Sox.

May 28: Pitcher George Earnshaw was acquired by the Athletics from Baltimore for two players and $50,000 cash.

June 2: The Phillies set a record by hitting three pinch hit home runs against St. Louis.

July 10: Senators pitcher Milt Gaston shut out Cleveland 9–0, scattering 14 hits.

July 23: Pitcher Tom Zachary, waived by the Senators, was signed by the New York Yankees.

Sept. 3: Ty Cobb got the last hit of his career. Hit No. 4,191 was a pinch hit double off Senators' pitcher Bump Hadley.

Sept. 7: The Philadelphia Athletics swept a doubleheader from the Red Sox and moved into a first place tie with New York, who lost a twinbill to Washington.

Sept. 29: The St. Louis Cardinals clinched the National League pennant, beating the Braves 3–1.

Sept 30: Ty Cobb retires after his 24th major league season.

Nov. 3: The Chicago Cubs traded five players and $200,000 cash to the Boston Braves for Rogers Hornsby.

Dec. 13: An interesting proposal by National League president John Heydler to adopt a rule placing a tenth player in the lineups to hit for the pitcher was voted down at the major league meeting in Chicago.

LEADERS

BATTING AVERAGE
AL: Lew Fonseca, Cleveland, .369
NL: Lefty O'Doul, Philadelphia Phillies, .398

HOME RUNS
AL: Babe Ruth, NY Yankees, 46
NL: Chuck Klein, Philadelphia Phillies, 43

RUNS BATTED IN
AL: Al Simmons, Philadelphia Athletics, 157
NL: Hack Wilson, Chicago Cubs, 159

STOLEN BASES
AL: Charlie Gehringer, Detroit, 28
NL: Kiki Cuyler, Chicago Cubs, 43

PITCHING VICTORIES
AL: George Earnshaw, Philadelphia Athletics, 24
NL: Pat Malone, Chicago Cubs, 22

EARNED RUN AVERAGE
AL: Lefty Grove, Philadelphia Athletics, 2.81
NL: Bill Walker, NY Giants, 3.09

STRIKEOUTS
AL: Lefty Grove, Philadelphia Athletics, 170
NL: Pat Malone, Chicago Cubs, 166

Throughout his lengthy managerial career, the courtly Connie Mack always commanded respect.

The legendary A's manager Connie Mack (center) with Mule Haag (l) and George Earnshaw (r)

Players knew not to call him by his first name, or the even more informal "Skip," which most managers accepted. It was always "Mr. Mack."

And in 1929 Mr. Mack took his Philadelphia Athletics to the top of the major leagues—19 games ahead of the seemingly invincible New York Yankees.

Behind the power of outfielder Al Simmons (34 home runs and a league-leading 157 runs batted in) and first baseman Jimmie Foxx (33 home runs, 117 RBIs), along with the sensational pitching of George Earnshaw (24–8) and Lefty Grove (20–6), with a league-leading 170 strikeouts and 2.81 earned run average), the Athletics rolled to the American League pennant in a year the Yankees expected to dominate.

Babe Ruth again led the league in home runs with 46 and drove in 154 runs as well. Ruth also hit for a .345 batting average, tying him with teammate Earle Combs. Both were just behind second baseman Tony Lazzeri, who hit .354. Catcher Bill Dickey, in his first full season in Yankee pinstripes, batted .324. But the Philadelphia lead was insurmountable and the "Bronx Bombers" were forced to settle for a second-place finish.

The Yankees' season turned from disappointing to tragedy in September when manager Miller Huggins took ill and died with 11 games remaining in the season. Art Fletcher finished the season in charge.

Cleveland Indians' first baseman Lew Fonseca took the American League batting crown with a .369 average. Wes Farrell's 21–10 mark topped the Cleveland pitching staff.

The Chicago Cubs completely dominated the National League, finishing 19½ games ahead of Pittsburgh. They had their most potent lineup ever, with Hack Wilson belting 39 home runs and driving in a league-leading 159 runs.

Second baseman Rogers Hornsby also hit 39 homers and led the club with a .380 batting mark. Kiki Cuyler's league-topping 43 stolen bases and .360 batting average also contributed to the Chicago offense.

The Cubs' pitching staff was led by Pat Malone with a 22–10 record. Malone also led the league in strikeouts with 166. Charlie Root's 19–6 record gave him the league's best winning percentage.

SHORTS When the New York Yankees became the first team to assign uniform numbers to their players, they initially did so on the basis of a player's spot in the batting order. That's how Babe Ruth and Lou Gehrig came to be associated with the Nos. 3 and 4, which would be among the first numbers retired by the Yankees.

Philadelphia A's Al Simmons led the league in RBI with 157

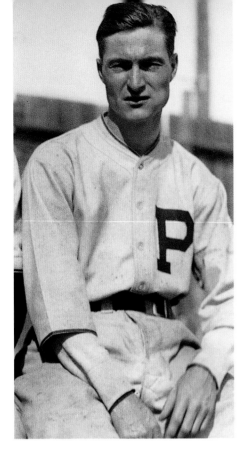

The Pirates finished a distant second, but their lineup contained six regulars with averages of .300 or better. Tops among them was third baseman Pie Traynor with a .353 mark. Traynor also led the Pirates in RBIs with 108. Paul Waner continued to be a standout at the plate as well. He had a club-leading 15 home runs, along with 100 RBIs and a .336 average. His brother Lloyd posted a .353 mark.

The New York Giants weren't far behind the Pirates and boasted a potent offense of their own, led by Mel Ott with 42 home runs, 151 runs batted in and a .328 batting average. First baseman Bill Terry's .372 average led the team.

Jim Bottomley and Chick Hafey each hit 29 home runs for the fourth place St. Louis Cardinals.

The Pittsburgh Pirates' Lloyd Waner posted a .353 batting average

TIMELINE

April 16: Cleveland Indians' outfielder Earl Averill hit a home run in his first major league at bat, becoming the first American League player to do so. Earl Whitehill was the Detroit Tigers' pitcher.

May 7: Pitching in relief against the St. Louis Browns, Tom Zachary won his first game of the season for New York. He would finish the season with a 12–0 record.

May 8: New York Giants' hurler Carl Hubbell threw a no-hitter against Pittsburgh. He walked one Pirate in the 11–0 victory. Hubbell was the first lefthander since Hub Leonard in 1918 to toss a no-hitter.

May 11: Cleveland and New York played the first major league game between two teams with numbers on their uniforms.

May 18: The Dodgers and Phillies scored a combined 50 runs in a doubleheader at Philadelphia's Baker Bowl. Brooklyn won the first game 20–16 and Philadelphia took the second 8–6.

July 5: A public address system was used for the first time in a major league ballpark as the New York Giants met the Pittsburgh Pirates at the Polo Grounds.

Aug. 14: Second baseman Charlie Gehringer was honored in Detroit before the Tigers' game with New York. Gehringer responded with four hits, including a home run, and a steal of home to help his team beat the Yankees 17–13.

Sept. 24: New York Giants' slugger Mel Ott hit his 41st and 42nd home runs of the season in a doubleheader sweep of the Boston Braves. New York won both games.

Oct. 5: Philadelphia outfielder Chuck Klein took the National League home run crown by one over Mel Ott, hitting his 43rd against the Giants. After hitting a single in his first time at bat in the second game of their double header, Ott was walked intentionally five times—including once with the bases loaded.

POSTSEASON

R unners–up in three of the previous four seasons, the Philadelphia Athletics finally broke through in the regular season.

GAME 1	
Philadelphia A's 3	Chicago Cubs 1
GAME 2	
Philadelphia A's 9	Chicago Cubs 3
GAME 3	
Chicago Cubs 3	Philadelphia A's 1
GAME 4	
Philadelphia A's 10	Chicago Cubs 8
GAME 5	
Philadelphia A's 3	Chicago Cubs 2

three-run ninth inning for a 3–2 win in Game Five. Mule Haas' three-run, inside-the-park home run was the big blow in the ten-run inning. Bing Miller's double was the winning hit in Game Five.

The Athletics had gotten a lift in Game One when Howard Ehmke, an unexpected starter, struck out 13.

They won 104 games and took the American League pennant by a margin of 18 games over the two-time defending champion New York Yankees. The surprise National League winner was the Chicago Cubs, who hadn't seriously competed since winning in 1918. The Cubs finished 10½ games in front of Pittsburgh.

Just when it appeared that the Cubs might make it a competitive Series by winning Game Three, the Athletics had one of the biggest innings in postseason history to devastate the Cubs. Chicago had a 8–0 lead in the seventh inning of Game Four and appeared to be on the verge of tying the Series with the prospect of playing the last two games at Wrigley Field.

Philadelphia rallied for ten runs, won the game 10–8, then ended the Series with a

The A's Howard Ehmke was Game One's surprise victor

1930

The 1930s began with America in the throes of the Depression. It ended with America getting closer to being involved in World War II.

Through it all, baseball persevered. The decade began with Babe Ruth and Lou Gehrig dominating the game. By the end of the decade, Ruth and Gehrig were both retired while new stars, such as Joe DiMaggio and Ted Williams, had emerged as the game's next heroes.

Other players who graced the game included Jimmie Foxx, Hank Greenberg, Lefty Grove, Dizzy Dean, Mel Ott, Bob Feller, Carl Hubbell and Mickey Cochrane.

Some of their individual achievements still stand today. In 1930, Hack Wilson of the Chicago Cubs drove in 191 runs, a mark that hasn't been matched. Gehrig drove in 184 the following season, a record that still stands today. Bill Terry of the New York Giants batted .401 in 1930 and is the last National League player to reach the .400 mark.

The 1930s also featured great teams. The Philadelphia A's won back-to-back American League titles in 1930 and 1931. The New York Yankees won the World Series in 1932 before winning four championships in a row from 1936–39.

Baseball's first All-Star Game was played in 1933 and the Baseball Hall of Fame in Cooperstown, New York, opened its doors in 1939.

The 1930s provided some of the most memorable moments in the history of the game.

LEADERS

BATTING AVERAGE
AL: Al Simmons, Philadelphia, .381
NL: Bill Terry, NY Giants, .401

HOME RUNS
AL: Babe Ruth, NY Yankees, 49
NL: Hack Wilson, Chicago Cubs, 56

RUNS BATTED IN
AL: Lou Gehrig, NY Yankees, 174
NL: Hack Wilson, Chicago Cubs, 190

STOLEN BASES
AL: Marty McManus, Detroit, 23
NL: Kiki Cuyler, Chicago Cubs, 37

PITCHING VICTORIES
AL: Lefty Grove, Philadelphia, 28
NL: Pat Malone, Chicago Cubs; Ray Kremer, Pittsburgh, 20

EARNED RUN AVERAGE
AL: Lefty Grove, Philadelphia, 2.54
NL: Dazzy Vance, Brooklyn, 2.61

STRIKEOUTS
AL: Lefty Grove, Philadelphia, 209
NL: Bill Hallahan, St. Louis Cardinals, 177

SAVES
AL: Lefty Grove, Philadelphia, 9
NL: Hi Bell, St. Louis, 8

The 1930 season will go down as the "Year of the Hitter." After the stock market crashed on October 29, 1929, baseball owners feared economic worries would keep fans away from the games. The owners' solution was to add more action to the game, which meant more offense.

National League owners juiced up the baseball, and owners from both leagues lowered the height of the stitches on the ball. The change made it tough for the pitchers to get a good grip on the ball to throw their breaking pitches.

The changes gave the owners what they wanted. Offense took off and the pitchers ran for cover.

The National League's team batting average totaled .303 while the American League batted .288. The New York Giants set a modern record with a .319 team average. The Philadelphia Phillies batted .315, but their pitching was so bad (a 6.70 team ERA), that the Phils finished last.

The St. Louis Cardinals, who featured an all .300-hitting lineup, won the National League pennant, but their .314 team average was only third in the league.

There were plenty of individual accomplishments. The best season belonged to the Chicago

The Dodgers' Dazzy Vance

Cubs' Hack Wilson, whose record 190 RBIs still stands today. He also hit 56 home runs and batted .356.

Wilson did it all in 1930. He hit his 50th home run on September 15. Three days later he drove in his 176th run, passing Gehrig's record of 175 that was set in 1927. Wilson hit his 56th home run on September 27.

Bill Terry of the New York Giants finished the season at .401, and is the last NL player to hit over .400.

The baseballs were also flying around in the American League. Al Simmons of the Philadelphia A's led the league with a .381 average. As usual, the New York Yankees were well represented. Babe Ruth led the league with 49 homers, while Lou Gehrig was on top with 174 RBIs.

The powerful A's rolled to a 102–52 record for their second straight AL pennant. The A's clinched the pennant by defeating the Chicago

SHORTS The last bounced home run in Major League history was hit on September 12. Brooklyn catcher Al Lopez hit a long drive over the head of Cincinnati left fielder Bob Meusel, and the ball bounced into the bleachers at Ebbets Field. The National League rules were changed after the season and from then on balls that bounced into the stands were ruled a double. The American League changed the rule after the 1929 season.

The Giants' Bill Terry achieved every hitter's dream in 1930 when he posted a season's batting average of .401

White Sox 14–10 on September 18, finishing eight games ahead of Washington. Philadelphia featured a well-balanced team with pitcher Lefty Grove winning 24 games and saving nine others and Jimmie Foxx hitting 37 homers and driving in 156 runs.

The Cardinals moved into a tie for first place on September 16 when Bill Hallahan out-dueled Dazzy Vance 1–0 in ten innings. The Cards finished a three-game sweep at Ebbets Field two days later and clinched the pennant on September 26 with a 10–5 win over Pittsburgh. The A's won the World Series in six games.

Ruth also made news off the field. Before the season, he signed a two-year deal for $160,000 making him the highest-paid player of all time.

The season also featured the end of pitcher Grover Cleveland Alexander's career. He was released by the Phillies on June 3 after posting an 0–3 record. Alexander ended his career thinking he had the National League record for most wins at 373, one more than Christy Mathewson. In 1946, a win disallowed in 1902 was restored to Mathewson's record, to leave the two future Hall of Fame pitchers at a tie.

POSTSEASON

The high-powered Philadelphia A's, featuring stars Mickey Cochrane, Lefty Grove, Al Simmons and Jimmie Foxx, defeated the St. Louis Cardinals in six games for their second straight title.

The Series opened with a game at Philadelphia's Shibe Park. Spitballer Burleigh Grimes held the defending world champs to five hits, but they all went for extra bases to key the A's win. Cochrane and Simmons both homered, and the A's had two triples and a double. Lefty Grove held the Cards to five hits and the A's won 5–2.

The A's pounded out a 6–1 win in Game Two, highlighted by a Cochrane homer. George Earnshaw stopped the Cardinals on six hits.

The Series went to St. Louis for Game Three. Cardinal's starter Bill Hallahan came through by blanking the A's 5–0. St. Louis tied the Series in Game Four with a 3–1 win.

Game Five featured a scoreless pitching duel, which was broken up by Foxx's two-run homer in the ninth.

The A's wrapped up the Series in Game Six.

Earnshaw, going on one day's rest, pitched shutout ball until the ninth in a 7–1 win. Simmons and Jimmy Dykes homered. Earnshaw went seven innings and Grove pitched the final two innings for the win.

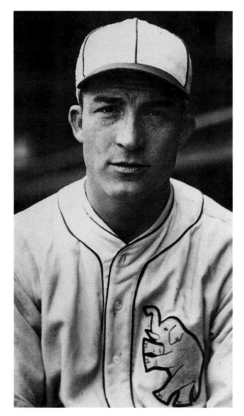

The A's Al Simmons swung a hot bat throughout the Series

WORLD SERIES

GAME 1	
Philadelphia 5	St. Louis Cardinals 2
GAME 2	
Philadelphia 6	St. Louis Cardinals 1
GAME 3	
St. Louis Cardinals 5	Philadelphia 0
GAME 4	
St. Louis Cardinals 3	Philadelphia 1
GAME 5	
Philadelphia 2	St. Louis Cardinals 0
GAME 6	
Philadelphia 7	St. Louis Cardinals 1

TIMELINE

April 29: In seven major league games 123 runs were scored.

May 21: At 35 years old, Babe Ruth had his first three-homer performance in a regular-season game. The Yankees lost 15–7 to the Philadelphia A's at Shibe Park.

July 21: It was a great day for pinch-hitters. George Puccinelli and Jim Bottomley of the St. Louis Cardinals and Hal Lee and Harvey Henrick of the Brooklyn Dodgers all homered, appearing as pinch-hitters in one game.

July 23: Pittsburgh's Pie Traynor hit game-winning homers in both ends of a doubleheader. His ninth-inning home run won the opener and he ended the nightcap when he connected in the 13th.

Sept. 15: Newspapers carried the story of the disappearance of Cardinals' pitcher Flint Rhem on the eve of a crucial series in Brooklyn. Rhem returned to the Cardinals with a story that he was kidnapped by gamblers and forced to drink bootleg whiskey.

Sept. 17: With three consecutive home runs, Cleveland's Earl Averill drove in eight runs in a 13–7 victory over the Senators in the doubleheader opener. He narrowly missed a fourth when the umpire ruled a long drive foul. He then added another homer in the second game to set an American League record with 11 RBIs in the twin bill.

Sept. 20: Joe Hauser of the Baltimore Orioles, playing in the International League at the time, set a new minor league record by hitting his 63rd home run.

Sept. 25: Joe McCarthy, not receiving the support of Cubs' owner William Wrigley, resigned as manager. Rogers Hornsby was named to finish the season.

Sept. 28: Dizzy Dean scattered three hits for a 3–1 victory in his Major League debut. The 19-year-old rookie, called up from the Texas League, pitched the final game of the season for the pennant-winning Cardinals.

MOST VALUABLE PLAYER
AL: Lefty Grove, Philadelphia
NL: Frankie Frisch, St. Louis Cardinals

BATTING AVERAGE
AL: Al Simmons, Philadelphia, .390
NL: Chick Hafey, St. Louis Cardinals; Bill Terry, NY Giants .349

HOME RUNS
AL: Babe Ruth and Lou Gehrig, NY Yankees, 46
NL: Chuck Klein, Philadelphia, 31

RUNS BATTED IN
AL: Lou Gehrig, NY Yankees, 184
NL: Chuck Klein, Philadelphia, 121

STOLEN BASES
AL: Ben Chapman, NY Yankees, 61
NL: Frankie Frisch, St. Louis Cardinals, 28

PITCHING VICTORIES
AL: Lefty Grove, Philadelphia, 31
NL: Bill Hallahan, St. Louis Cardinals, Heinie Meine, Pittsburgh, Jumbo Elliott, Philadelphia,19

EARNED RUN AVERAGE
AL: Lefty Grove, Philadelphia, 2.06
NL: Bill Walker, NY Giants, 2.26

STRIKEOUTS
AL: Lefty Grove, Philadelphia, 175
NL: Bill Hallahan, St. Louis Cardinals, 159

SAVES
AL: Wilcy Moore, Boston Red Sox, 10
NL: Jack Quinn, Brooklyn, 15

The 1931 Philadelphia A's will go down as one of the greatest teams in Major League baseball history.

The A's of Connie Mack had won the World Series in 1929 and 1930. They featured five future Hall of Famers: catcher Mickey Cochrane; left fielder Al Simmons; first baseman Jimmie Foxx; and pitchers Lefty Grove and Waite Hoyt. The A's also had three 20-game winners (Grove, George Earnshaw and Rube Wallberg). Grove finished the season with a 31–4 record, won 16 in a row at one point and earned the American League's first Most Valuable Player Award. He led the league in wins, winning percentage, shutouts, complete games, strikeouts and ERA.

Philadelphia also put together two remarkable winning streaks. The A's won 17 straight in May and 13 in a row in July.

The A's were so good they made a mockery of the American League pennant race, even though the New York Yankees finished the regular season with a 94–59 record. All the Yankees could do was finish second, 13½ games behind

SHORTS
The race for the National League batting title went into the final day of the season. St. Louis' Chick Hafey (below) got one hit in eight at-bats in a doubleheader, but New York's Bill Terry had one hit in four at-bats. The title went to Hafey, who batted .3488 to Terry's .3486. Jim Bottomley, Hafey's St. Louis Cardinals teammate, finished at .3481.

Double X proved an integral member of the A's dominant line-up

the A's, who went 107–45. The A's clinched the pennant on September 15 with a win at home over Cleveland.

The following day, the St. Louis Cardinals clinched the National League pennant by beating Philadelphia. That, however, was the end of the A's storybook season. In a rematch of the 1930 Series, the Cardinals upset Philadelphia in seven games.

And that would be the end of the A's dynasty. After the loss, Mack dismantled his team by slowly trading away his stars and by 1934 his team had fallen into the second division of the American League.

The Cardinals rolled to the National League pennant with a 101–53 record, which was good enough for a 13-game finish over the New York Giants. Centerfielder Pepper Martin had a particularly dominant season, Chick Hafey won the batting title with a .349 average and 38-year-old spitballer Burleigh Grimes won 17 games.

The Yankees' Lou Gehrig added another mark to his storied career. He drove in 184 runs, a league record that still stands today. Gehrig broke his own record of 175, set in 1927.

Gehrig and teammate Babe Ruth also engaged in a home-run duel. Both finished with 46 and tied for the league lead. Ironically, Gehrig's last homer of the season denied Grove his 32nd victory.

Ruth and Gehrig had outstanding seasons. On July 2, Ruth homered to drive in a run for the 11th consecutive game. He had 18 RBIs in that stretch. On August 21, Ruth became the first major leaguer to hit 600 career homers. On September 1, Gehrig hit his third grand slam in four days and his sixth homer in consecutive games.

Earl Webb of the Boston Red Sox set a record that still stands today. Webb finished the season with 67 doubles. He would have had 68, but on August 4 the league corrected a May 1 box score, turning what had been credited as a double into a single.

POSTSEASON

The Series was a rematch between the Philadelphia A's and the St. Louis Cardinals. This time the Cardinals got their revenge by winning in seven games.

The Series started in St. Louis as the A's rolled to a 6–2 win. Lefty Grove scattered 12 hits while Al Simmons hit a two-run homer in the seventh.

The Cardinals evened the Series in Game Two as Wild Bill Hallahan shut out the A's 2–0. Hallahan walked seven, but shut out the hard-hitting A's on three hits. Cards' second baseman Pepper Martin, who had three hits in Game One, scored two runs and stole two bases.

The now-illegal spitball was Burleigh Grimes' most effective weapon as he led the Cardinals to victory

WORLD SERIES

GAME 1	
Philadelphia A's 6	St. Louis Cardinals 2
GAME 2	
St. Louis Cardinals 2	Philadelphia A's 0
GAME 3	
St. Louis Cardinals 5	Philadelphia A's 2
GAME 4	
Philadelphia A's 3	St. Louis Cardinals 0
GAME 5	
St. Louis Cardinals 5	Philadelphia A's 1
GAME 6	
Philadelphia A's 8	St. Louis Cardinals 1
GAME 7	
St. Louis Cardinals 4	Philadelphia A's 2

As the Series moved to Philadelphia for Game Three, Lefty Grove was outpitched by Burleigh Grimes, who had a no-hitter until the eighth. Catcher Jimmie Wilson had three hits and Martin continued to dazzle with two more hits in the Cardinals' 5–2 win.

Philly's George Earnshaw won Game Four with a 3–0 shutout as Jimmie Foxx homered to even the Series, but the Cards won Game Five as Martin homered and drove in four runs.

One loss from elimination in St. Louis, the A's kept their hopes for three straight Series wins alive as Grove won 8–1 in Game Six, but their dreams ended the next day. Grimes threw eight shutout innings and Hallahan worked out of trouble in the ninth for a 4–2 win. Martin batted .500 for the Series.

TIMELINE

Feb 5: The Chicago Cubs' Hack Wilson, who set National League records for homers and RBIs the previous season, signed for $35,000. Wilson's RBI records still stand today. He drove in 191 runs in 1930.

April 12: Joe McCarthy made his debut as Yankee manager.

April 29: Indians' pitcher Wes Ferrell no-hit the St. Louis Browns. Cleveland won the game 9–0.

May 4: Due to an injury, Babe Ruth played first with Lou Gehrig moving to right field. Gehrig commited an error helping the Red Sox to beat the Yankees.

May 18: The Dodgers' Babe Herman hit for the cycle for the first of three times, which became a major league record.

July 7: The Browns and the White Sox played a 12-inning game in which not a single strikeout was recorded. It was the longest whiffless game in Major League history. Chicago won 10–9.

Aug. 5: Detroit's Tommy Bridges retired the first 26 batters in a game against the Washington Senators. Bridges was denied immortality on a bloop single by pinch-hitter Dave Harris. The Tigers crushed the Senators, 13–0.

Aug: 23: A misplayed ball by A's outfielder Jim Moore led to a 1–0 defeat to the St. Louis Browns. The loss ended a 16-game winning streak for Lefty Grove.

Sept. 13: Guy Bush of the Cubs pitched his second one-hitter of the season, against the Braves. His first was against the Cards on August 9.

Sept. 18: Cardinals' spitballer Burleigh Grimes hit Mel Ott in the head with a pitch in a game at St. Louis. Ott was hospitalized with a concussion and was out for the season.

Oct. 20: Mickey Mantle was born in Spavinaw, Oklahoma. His dad, Mutt, named him after major league catcher Mickey Cochrane. Mutt Mantle didn't realize Cochrane's first name was Gordon, not Mickey.

The season saw the return to glory of the New York Yankees. After winning six American League pennants and three World Series titles in the 1920s, the Yankees hadn't finished first since 1928.

That changed in 1932. Finishing 107–47, the Yankees easily beat out the Philadelphia A's by 13 games to win the pennant.

Although Philadelphia's Jimmie Foxx dominated play during the regular season by leading the league with 58 home runs (becoming only the third player to hit 50 homers), 169 RBIs and

winning the Most Valuable Player Award, the Yankees had the better team.

Babe Ruth blasted 41 homers and drove in 137 runs while Lou Gehrig hit 34 home runs with 151 RBIs. Pitcher Lefty Gomez finished with 24 wins while Red Ruffing (18), Johnny Allen (17) and George Pipgras (16) completed the rotation.

The Yankees clinched the pennant on September 11 with a 9–3 win at Cleveland. The Chicago Cubs had a tougher road to the National League pennant. They didn't clinch until a 5–2 win over Pittsburgh on September 20. The Cubs finished 90–64 and four games ahead of the Pirates. No Chicago player reached the 100 RBI mark. Riggs Stephenson led the team with 85 RBIs while Johnny Moore hit a team-high 13 homers.

The Cubs were built on pitching. Lon Warneke finished 22–6 while Guy Bush won 19 and Pat Malone and Charlie Root won 15 apiece.

The Cubs overcame a managerial change to win the pennant. On August 2, Rogers Hornsby was fired as manager and first baseman Charlie Grimm took over, but the story didn't end there. After Hornsby was fired, reports surfaced that he had obtained money from his players, either loaned to him to bet on horse races, or to share in joint ventures. The players wanted refunds and Hornsby wanted a payoff from the Cubs, who refused. Commissioner Kenesaw Mountain Landis investigated the case, but didn't discipline anyone.

The Yankees swept the World Series, but their season did have some rough moments. On July 4, catcher Bill Dickey broke the jaw of Washington outfielder Carl Reynolds with a punch. Reynolds was sidelined indefinitely. Dickey was suspended for 30 days and handed a $1,000 fine.

Dickey returned to the Yankees' lineup on August 4 with a grand slam and three singles, as New York beat Chicago, 15–3. Dickey batted

Jimmie Foxx's MVP season still wasn't enough to lead the A's past the Yankees

SHORTS The A's beat the Indians 18–17 in 18 innings in Cleveland on July 10. The Indians' Johnny Burnett had nine hits in 11 at-bats. To save train fare, A's manager Connie Mack brought only two pitchers. The starter was knocked out after one inning, leaving Eddie Rommel to pitch the final 17 innings. He gave up a record 33 hits, but got the win.

The A's Jimmie Dykes ended the season as a victim of Connie Mack's cost-cutting exercise

.310 with 15 homers and 84 RBIs.

The season also saw the end of the career of one of baseball's top managers. On June 3, citing poor health, the Giants announced the resignation of long-time skipper, John McGraw. In his 32-year tenure, the fiery manager won three World Series and nine National League flags, including a record four consecutive pennants. McGraw, who came to New York in 1902, was replaced by Bill Terry, the team's star first baseman.

The season also marked the beginning of the end of the Philadelphia A's dynasty, which had won three straight pennants and two World Series from 1929–31. Even though the A's finished second, manager Connie Mack sold Al Simmons, Jimmie Dykes and Mule Haas to the White Sox for $100,000 in a move to cut costs.

POSTSEASON

The 1932 World Series will go down as one the most memorable of all time. Not only did it feature the return of the New York Yankees, it had perhaps the most-talked-about moment in Series history.

The Yankees won the first two games over the Chicago Cubs in easy fashion at Yankee Stadium. Lou Gehrig homered to key a 12–6 win in Game One. Gehrig added three hits and Lefty Gomez pitched New York to a 5–2 win in Game Two.

Then came Game Three in Chicago and the moment fans are still talking about. The first two games featured a running battle between Babe Ruth and the Cubs players. Emotions reached their peak in the fifth inning with the score tied 4–4. Ruth, who hit a three-run homer off Charlie Root in the first, stepped to the plate with one out. Ruth took two strikes and acknowledged both with a raised hand.

As legend has it, Ruth then gestured toward the center field stands. Whether he was calling his shot or gesturing at Root is still a matter of debate, but he hit the next pitch into the bleach-

ers to put the Yankees ahead and they won 7–5. The Cubs were finished. The Yankees wrapped up the sweep of the Series with a 13–6 win in Game Four.

The Babe's called shot was the highlight of New York's Series sweep

WORLD SERIES

GAME 1	
NY Yankees 12	Chicago Cubs 6
GAME 2	
NY Yankees 5	Chicago Cubs 2
GAME 3	
NY Yankees 7	Chicago Cubs 5
GAME 4	
NY Yankees 13	Chicago Cubs 6

TIMELINE

April 6: Holdout Chick Hafey, last year's batting champ, was traded by the Cardinals to the Reds.

May 30: After losing a doubleheader in Cleveland, furious Chicago players blamed umpire George Moriarty and fought with him under the stands. Moriarty broke his fist knocking down Milt Gaston, but was pummeled by manager Lew Fonseca and catchers Charlie Berry and Frank Grube.

June 3: In Philadelphia, Lou Gehrig became the first player in the 20th century to hit four home runs in one game and barely missed a fifth. New York's Tony Lazzeri hit for the cycle. The Yankees hammered out a major league record for total bases with 50 against the A's.

June 22: The National League, at a meeting of club presidents, finally approved players wearing numbers. The American League had started in 1929.

July 6: Cubs' shortstop Bill Jurges was shot in the shoulder and hand in his Chicago hotel room by a spurned girlfriend. Jurges, who didn't press charges, returned to the lineup on July 22. The woman who shot him, Violet Popovich Valli, capitalized on the incident, signing a contract to sing in local nightclubs and theaters.

July 31: Cleveland played its first game in the new Municipal Stadium before a crowd in excess of 80,000 (paid attendance of 76,979), but Mel Harder lost to the A's Lefty Grove 1–0.

Aug. 21: Cleveland's Wes Ferrell became the first 20th-century pitcher to win 20 or more games in each of his first four seasons, beating Washington 11–5. Nine days later, Ferrell was suspended by the Indians for insubordination.

Sept. 11: The Dodgers' John Quinn, 49, became the oldest pitcher to win a Major League game. It was the 247th and final win of his career.

Sept. 11: The Cardinals signed Branch Rickey to a five-year contract as general manager and director of the farm system.

97

MOST VALUABLE PLAYER
AL: Jimmie Foxx, Philadelphia A's
NL: Carl Hubbell, NY Giants

LEADERS
BATTING AVERAGE
AL: Jimmie Foxx, Philadelphia A's, .356
NL: Chuck Klein, Philadelphia Phillies, .368

HOME RUNS
AL: Jimmie Foxx, Philadelphia A's, 48
NL: Chuck Klein, Philadelphia Phillies, 28

RUNS BATTED IN
AL: Jimmie Foxx, Philadelphia A's, 163
NL: Chuck Klein, Philadelphia Phillies, 120

STOLEN BASES
AL: Ben Chapman, NY Yankees, 27
NL: Pepper Martin, St. Louis Cardinals, 26

PITCHING VICTORIES
AL: Lefty Grove, Philadelphia A's, General
Crowder, Washington, 24
NL: Carl Hubbell, NY Giants, 23

EARNED RUN AVERAGE
AL: Monte Pearson, Cleveland, 2.33
NL: Carl Hubbell, NY Giants, 1.66

STRIKEOUTS
AL: Lefty Gomez, NY Yankees, 163
NL: Dizzy Dean, St. Louis Cardinals, 199

SAVES
AL: Jack Russell, Washington, 13
NL: Phil Collins, Philadelphia Phillies, 6

Rookie managers sometimes have a rough first year. That wasn't the case with Joe Cronin when he took over as player-manager of the Washington Senators in 1933. Not only did Cronin bat .309 with 118 RBIs, he guided Washington to the American League pennant. Finishing 99–53, the Senators beat out the mighty New York Yankees by seven games.

The difference in the race came in August when the Senators won 13 straight games. They clinched the pennant on September 21 by beating the St. Louis Browns.

A lot went right for the Senators. Outfielder Heine Manush had a 33-game hitting streak and batted .336 with 95 RBIs. First baseman Joe Kuhel hit .322 with 107 RBIs and second baseman Buddy Myer batted .302. Pitcher General Crowder tied Lefty Grove for the league lead with 24 wins while Earl Whitehill won 22.

Meanwhile, the New York Giants finished first in the National League with a 91–61 record, five games ahead of Pittsburgh. They clinched the pennant on September 19, despite a defeat to St. Louis, because Pittsburgh lost to Philadelphia the same day.

The Giants were paced by pitcher Carl Hubbell, who led the league in wins (23), shutouts (10) and ERA (1.66). On August 1, Carl Hubbell set a National League record for consecutive scoreless innings with 45⅓, breaking the 1908 mark of Ed Ruelbach.

Hal Schumacher added 19 wins and Freddie Fitzsimmons won 16. First baseman/manager Bill Terry batted .332 while outfielder Met Ott drove in 103 runs. Terry had one setback during the season—on April 24 he broke his wrist when he was hit by a pitch in a game with the Dodgers. He missed three weeks, which ended

General Crowder's 24 wins helped the Senators to the pennant

his consecutive-game streak at 468.

Another more famous streak nearly came to an end. The Yankees' Lou Gehrig had his consecutive-games-played streak threatened on two occasions. On April 23, he was knocked unconscious by a Whitehill pitch in a game against Washington. However, Gehrig recovered and finished the game. On June 14, Gehrig and Yankees' manager Joe McCarthy were ejected for arguing with an umpire. McCarthy was suspended for three games, but Gehrig wasn't. He had played in 1,249 games at that point. He broke Everett

Scott's consecutive-games-played record of 1,307 on August 17.

Philadelphia's Lefty Grove shut out the Yankees 7–0 on August 3. It was the first time the Bronx Bombers were shut out in 309 games, dating back to August 2, 1931.

Another Yankees' star stole the show at the first-ever All-Star game, played at Chicago's Comiskey Park on July 6. Babe Ruth hit two home runs as the American League defeated the National League, 4–2.

The dismantling of the once-mighty Philadelphia A's continued. Manager Connie Mack had already unloaded several stars to cut the team's payroll. The A's, who had won three straight pennants from 1929–31, fell to third place with a 79–72 record. On December 12, the A's swapped Grove, their star pitcher, along with Rube Wallberg and Max Bishop, to the Red Sox for Bob Kline, Rabbit Warstler and $125,000.

POSTSEASON

Behind strong pitching, the New York Giants beat the Washington Senators in five games.

WORLD SERIES

GAME 1	
NY Giants 4	Washington 2
GAME 2	
NY Giants 6	Washington 1
GAME 3	
Washington 4	NY Giants 0
GAME 4	
NY Giants 2	Washington 1
GAME 5	
NY Giants 4	Washington 3

New York Giants' screwballer Carl Hubbell

New York ace Carl Hubbell pitched the New York Giants to a 4–2 win in Game One at the Polo Grounds. He didn't give up an earned run and struck out ten while the Senators fell apart as Buddy Myer made a record-tying three errors. Mel Ott tied a Series record by going 4-for-4.

New York kept rolling in Game Two, a 6–1 win. The Giants scored all their runs in the sixth inning and Hal Schumacher held the Senators to five hits.

The Series moved to Washington for Game Three and Earl Whitehill blanked the Giants 4–0 on five hits, but that was it for the Senators.

The Giants took a commanding 3–1 lead by

winning Game Four, 2–1 in 11 innings. Blondy Ryan's RBI single gave New York the win. The Giants wrapped up the Series on Ott's tenth-inning home run for a 4–3 win. New York won the final two games with extra-inning victories to wrap up its first title since 1922.

The Giants' pitching staff was definitely the star of the Series. New York held the Senators, who hit .287 during the season, to just a .214 average.

MOST VALUABLE PLAYER

AL: Mickey Cochrane, Detroit
NL: Dizzy Dean, St. Louis Cardinals

LEADERS

BATTING AVERAGE

AL: Lou Gehrig, NY Yankees, .363
NL: Paul Waner, Pittsburgh, .362

HOME RUNS

AL: Lou Gehrig, NY Yankees, 49
NL: Mel Ott, NY Giants; Ripper Collins, St. Louis Cardinals, 35

RUNS BATTED IN

AL: Lou Gehrig, NY Yankees, 165
NL: Mel Ott, NY Giants, 135

STOLEN BASES

AL: Bill Werber, Boston Red Sox, 40
NL: Pepper Martin, St. Louis Cardinals, 23

PITCHING VICTORIES

AL: Lefty Gomez, NY Yankees, 26
NL: Dizzy Dean, St. Louis Cardinals, 30

EARNED RUN AVERAGE

AL: Lefty Gomez, NY Yankees, 2.33
NL: Carl Hubbell, NY Giants, 2.30

STRIKEOUTS

AL: Lefty Gomez, NY Yankees, 158
NL: Dizzy Dean, St. Louis Cardinals, 195

SAVES

AL: Jack Russell, Washington, 7
NL: Carl Hubbell, NY Giants, 8

The Brothers Dean—(l to r) Paul and Dizzy

The 1934 season will be remembered for one of the tightest pennant races in history and for Babe Ruth's last moment in a New York Yankees uniform.

The pennant race occurred in the National League, where the St. Louis Cardinals trailed the New York Giants by six games on Labor Day, but caught them down the stretch to win by two games.

The Dean brothers, Dizzy and Paul, sparked the Cardinals' comeback. Dizzy won 30 games while Paul, a rookie, added 19 wins. The Cardinals, known as a team filled with colorful characters, were nicknamed "The Gashouse Gang."

Dizzy won his 25th game on September 10, beating the Phillies 4–1. It was the fifth straight win for the Cardinals, who trailed the Giants by four games. On September 16, the Cards gained two games by sweeping a doubleheader at the Polo Grounds as the Deans picked up both wins.

The Deans continued to spark the Cardinals, who swept a doubleheader from the Dodgers on

September 21. Dizzy allowed one hit in a 13–0 win in Game One, but Paul topped him by throwing a no-hitter in Game Two, a 3–0 win.

On September 24, the Cardinals beat the Cubs 3–1 and moved two games behind the Giants. Dizzy won his 28th game of the season the following day, beating the Pirates, 3–2. That cut the lead to just one game when the Phillies rallied in the ninth for a 5–4 win over the Giants.

With the Giants idle for two straight days, the Cardinals moved into a tie with a 13–7 win over Cincinnati on September 27 and a 4–0 win the following day, which featured Dizzy, pitching on two days' rest, earning his 29th win.

The Cardinals took over sole possession of first on September 29. Brooklyn's Van Lingle Mungo beat the Giants at the Polo Grounds, 5–1, while Paul Dean stopped the Reds in St. Louis, 6–1.

Dizzy Dean clinched the pennant the following day. He blanked the Reds 9–0 for his 30th win while the Dodgers again beat the Giants, 8–5.

Meanwhile, the Detroit Tigers had an easier path to the American League pennant, beating out the Yankees by seven games.

The Tigers wrapped up the pennant on

SHORTS The All-Star Game on July 10 produced Carl Hubbell's amazing feat of striking out five future Hall of Famers in a row. Hubbell had a shaky start with two runners on base in the first inning, but used his screwball to fan Babe Ruth, Lou Gehrig, and Jimmie Foxx. Al Simmons and Joe Cronin struck out to start the second.

September 24 when the Red Sox beat the Yankees, 5–0, in the final game of the season at Yankee Stadium. The Tigers were led by player-manager Mickey Cochrane. First baseman Hank Greenberg batted .339 with 26 homers and 139 RBIs while second baseman Charlie Gehringer hit .356 and drove in 127 runs. Schoolboy Rowe (24–8) and Tommy Bridges (22–11) paced the pitching staff.

But the Yankees' elimination wasn't the biggest news. The day saw the last game of Ruth's career at Yankee Stadium. Ruth walked in the first inning, but limped to first and left for a pinch runner in his last home game.

On September 29, Ruth hit his last homer as a Yankee. He was hitless in his last game in a Yankee uniform the following day.

Ruth had announced on August 10 that the 1934 season would be his last as a regular player. He said he wanted a manager's job and would continue playing as a pinch-hitter. Ruth hit his 700th career home run on July 14. He batted .288 with 22 homers and 84 RBIs.

The Cardinals' momentum carried over into their seven-game win over the Tigers in the World Series.

The Tigers' Hank Greenberg and Schoolboy Rowe

POSTSEASON

The hard-fought Series between St. Louis and Detroit went right down to the wire, with the Cardinals finally winning in seven games.

The Series started in Detroit, but Game One went to the Cardinals in an easy 8–3 decision. St. Louis' ace Dizzy Dean picked up the win and Joe Medwick went 4-for-4 with a home run. The jittery Tigers made five errors, all in the first three innings.

The Tigers bounced back in Game Two with a 3–2 win in 12 innings. Detroit pitcher Schoolboy Rowe didn't allow a run after the third and Goose Goslin's single scored the winning run.

The Series moved back to St. Louis and Paul Dean, Dizzy's brother, pitched the Cardinals to a 4–1 win. Dean pitched shutout ball until the ninth and Pepper Martin doubled, tripled and scored twice.

Poor defense did in St. Louis in Game Four. The Cardinals made five errors as the Tigers, behind Hank Greenberg's record-tying four hits, rolled to a 10–4 win.

The Tigers took the Series lead with a 3–1 win in Game Five, but the Cardinals won Game Six in Detroit, 4–3, behind Paul Dean. Game Seven was anti-climactic. Behind Dizzy Dean, the Tigers rolled to an 11–0 win. The Dean brothers won all four games for the Cardinals.

WORLD SERIES

GAME 1	
St. Louis Cardinals 8	Detroit 3
GAME 2	
Detroit 3	St. Louis Cardinals 2
GAME 3	
St. Louis Cardinals 4	Detroit 1
GAME 4	
Detroit 10	St. Louis Cardinals 4
GAME 5	
Detroit 3	St. Louis Cardinals 1
GAME 6	
St. Louis Cardinals 4	Detroit 3
GAME 7	
St. Louis Cardinals 11	Detroit 0

TIMELINE

Feb. 5: Future all-time home run leader Hank Aaron was born in Mobile, Alabama.

Feb. 25: At the age of 60, legendary manager John McGraw died in his home in New Rochelle, NY. His last public appearance was at the 1933 All-Star game.

April 4: The Red Sox discovered that Lefty Grove, bought from the A's, had a sore arm. He won only eight games in 1934, but returned to good form in 1935.

April 5: Babe Ruth, sponsored by Quaker Oats, agreed to do weekly NBC broadcasts. His 13-week radio salary was $4,000 more than his Yankee contract.

June 1: The Dean brothers claimed to have "sore arms" that only pay raises could heal. Diz was getting $7,500 and Paul, a rookie, $3,000. The brothers backed down.

June 29: Lou Gehrig was beaned in an exhibition game played in Norfolk, Virginia. He played the next day and had three triples, but the game was rained out after 4½ innings, depriving him of a record.

July 13: Lou Gehrig left in the first inning with a severe case of lumbago, almost ending his consecutive-game streak. The streak was extended the next day when he batted leadoff and was listed in the lineup at shortstop. He singled and left the game. Gehrig returned to first base on July 15.

Aug. 26: Tigers' pitcher Schoolboy Rowe won his record-tying 16th straight game. He lost his next start going for 17 straight.

Sept. 25: Lou Gehrig played in his 1,500th consecutive game.

Oct. 9: Commissioner Kenesaw Mountain Landis ordered the Cardinals' Joe Medwick to leave Game Seven of the World Series for his own safety. Detroit fans were upset with his aggressive slide into third and the angry mob began hurling fruit at the St. Louis outfielder during the Cards' 11–0 series-clinching win.

JAY HANNA "DIZZY"  DEAN

TEAMS

St. Louis Cardinals 1930–37; Chicago Cubs 1938–41; St. Louis Browns 1947

Games:	.317
Games started:	.230
Complete games:	.154
Win–Loss:	.150–83
Inning pitched:	.1,967.1
Runs:	.774
ERA:	.3.02
Strikeouts:	.1,163
Bases on balls:	.453
Batting average:	..225

The colorful Dean was a firm favorite with the press

Other pitchers may have won more games than Dizzy Dean, but it's safe to guess that no pitcher had as much fun as Dean did.

Dean was one of the best pitchers of his era and one of the game's most colorful characters during the century. His given name was either Jay Hanna Dean or Jerome Herman Dean. It depended on Dean's mood, because he gave both versions to writers who were looking into his background. He would often provide conflicting versions of the same stories, probably to keep himself interested while repeating familiar material.

When he provided different versions of the same story, he would dismiss it by saying, "Them ain't lies, them are scoops."

By most accounts, Dean quit school before he reached the sixth grade. At 16, he enlisted in the Army and earned his nickname from one of his commanding officers. Dean played baseball for an Army team and first started to sharpen his skills against that competition.

Once out of the military he played for a semi-pro team in San Antonio and caught the attention of some scouts when he attended a professional try-out camp. Dean headed to the minor leagues and had a combined 25–10 record with two teams.

The St. Louis Cardinals called him up late in the 1930 season and he made his major league debut on the last day of the season by throwing a three-hitter against Pittsburgh.

That strong performance still didn't win him a spot on the major league staff. Dean was back in Houston for the 1931 season. He won 26 games and struck out 303 batters to force his way onto a Cardinals club that was the defending World Series champion.

As a 21 year-old in 1932, he won 18 games and led the National League in innings pitched, strikeouts and shutouts. He helped himself by batting .258, better than some regular players.

From 1933–36, Dean won 102 games and regularly led the League in complete games. He averaged more than 300 innings per season. In one 1933 game he struck out 17 Cubs batters.

Dean was a great pitcher and an even better interviewee. He kept baseball in the headlines by providing writers with stories that were either interesting or outrageous. Dean reveled in the attention and didn't mind putting the pressure on himself to perform.

Before the 1934 season, for example, he

predicted that he and his younger brother, Paul, would combine to win 45 games for the Cardinals. Paul Dean was instantly nicknamed "Daffy" so the Cardinals could have a matched set of Deans.

His prediction missed the mark. He and Paul actually combined for 49 wins to help the Cardinals to the National League pennant and then to the World Series—Dizzy won 30 games and Paul won 19. Dizzy led the League in wins, strikeouts, shutouts and complete games. He finished second to Carl Hubbell of the Giants in earned run average.

The Deans were almost as good in 1935, combining for 47 wins. Dizzy had 27 of them.

His career changed dramatically in 1937 when he was pressured into appearing in the All-Star game. Dean had wanted to skip the game to rest his arm and take a brief vacation away from baseball. He wound up pitching in the game and took an Earl Averill line drive off his foot. The force of the blow broke a toe which kept Dean out of the Cardinals' lineup.

Even when he returned, the injury forced him to alter his delivery. That led to bursitis in his shoulder. The Cardinals suspected Dean would never be the same pitcher and traded him to the Cubs before the 1938 season. He could still command a high price in a trade—the Cubs gave up three players and $185,000 to get Dean.

He went 7–1 with a 1.81 ERA in 13 games to help the Cubs win the pennant, but over the next three years, Dean would win just 30 games, a one-year total in his prime years.

At the age of 30 he became a broadcaster for the St. Louis Browns, delighting audiences with his fractured English, including liberal use of the word "ain't." His work drew protests from educational groups who were worried that children would begin to adopt Dean's speech.

To those who would question his command of English, Dean had a typically Dizzy reply: "There are a lot of people in the United States who say isn't ... and they ain't eatin'."

Dean did national broadcasting on the Game of the Week and often treated audiences to his version of "The Wabash Cannonball." He was elected to the Hall of Fame in 1953 and died in 1974.

MOST VALUABLE PLAYER
AL: Hank Greenberg, Detroit
NL: Gabby Hartnett, Chicago Cubs

MOST VALUABLE PLAYER
AL: Hank Greenberg, Detroit
NL: Gabby Hartnett, Chicago Cubs

LEADERS

BATTING AVERAGE
AL: Buddy Myer, Washington, .349
NL: Arky Vaughan, Pittsburgh, .385

HOME RUNS
AL: Jimmie Foxx, Philadelphia A's and Hank Greenberg, Detroit, 36
NL: Wally Berger, Boston Braves, 34 (below)

RUNS BATTED IN
AL: Hank Greenberg, Detroit, 170
NL: Wally Berger, Boston Braves, 130

STOLEN BASES
AL: Bill Werber, Boston Red Sox, 29
NL: Augie Galan, Chicago Cubs, 22

PITCHING VICTORIES
AL: Wes Ferrell, Boston Red Sox, 25
NL: Dizzy Dean, St. Louis Cardinals, 28

EARNED RUN AVERAGE
AL: Lefty Grove, Boston Red Sox, 2.70
NL: Cy Blanton, Pittsburgh, 2.58

STRIKEOUTS
AL: Tommy Bridges, Detroit, 163
NL: Dizzy Dean, St. Louis Cardinals, 182

SAVES
AL: Jack Knott, St. Louis Browns, 7
NL: Dutch Leonard, Brooklyn, 8

The biggest news of the 1935 season actually happened before play had gotten under way.

On February 26, the New York Yankees released Babe Ruth, who had announced the previous season that he no longer would be an everyday player. Ruth signed with the Boston Braves, meaning Ruth had gone from one of the most dominant teams in baseball to one that traditionally finished in the middle of the pack in the National League. Ruth signed with the Braves for $20,000 and a profit-sharing plan.

Ruth's National League debut on April 16 was a memorable one. The Babe's presence drew 25,000 fans, the largest Opening Day crowd in Braves' history. As he usually did when he was in the spotlight, Ruth responded. He had two hits, including a 430-foot home run off Giants' ace Carl Hubbell, as Boston beat New York, 4–2.

However, it was obvious Ruth was no longer a productive player and he wasn't seeing much action with the Braves. His final big moment came on May 25 in Pittsburgh when he hit three home runs. The final one—the 714th of his career—was the first to clear the right-field grandstand at Forbes Field and traveled 600 feet.

On May 30, Ruth played the first inning of the opener of a doubleheader between Boston and Philadelphia at the Baker Bowl. It was his final appearance. He retired on June 2 at the age of 40. Ruth batted .181 with six homers and 12 RBIs with the Braves.

Ruth's brief tenure with the Braves didn't help much. Boston finished with a 38–115 record, a mark that stood for the most losses in a season until the New York Mets lost 120 in 1962. Amazingly enough, the Braves did have something to boast about. Boston's Wally Berger led the National League with 34 homers and 130

Babe Ruth's career came to an end as the incomparable slugger signed with the Braves before retiring in June

The Cubs' catcher Gabby Hartnett posted numbers that won him National League MVP honors

April 21: Cleveland set a new American League record, playing a total of 41 innings in their third-straight extra-inning game—14 innings against St. Louis (win 2–1), 24 innings against Detroit (win 2–1), and 13 innings against Detroit (lose 3–2).

May 8: Reds' catcher Ernie Lombardi equaled the Major League record with four doubles in consecutive innings, each off a different pitcher.

June 9: The Cardinals became the tenth team in history to score in every inning, beating the Cubs 13–2 at St. Louis.

June 16: Senators' outfielder John Stone had eight hits—two triples, two doubles and four singles—in a doubleheader split with the Browns. Stone scored five runs in the opener. He also had four hits the previous day.

June 18: All seven scheduled Major League games are rained out.

July 5: Tony Cuccinello, with Brooklyn, and brother Al, with New York, both homered in a game at the Polo Grounds. The next time brothers homer in a game against each other will be on June 30, 1950, when Joe and Dom DiMaggio did it.

July 26: Jesse Hill's line drive bounced off the head of pitcher Ed Linke and back to catcher Jack Redmond on the fly, who threw to second, doubling off Ben Chapman. Linke was hospitalized for two days.

Aug. 4: Walter Johnson resigned as Cleveland manager and was replaced by Steve O'Neill.

Sept. 7: Boston's Joe Cronin lined a drive off the head of Cleveland third baseman Odell Hale. The ball caromed to shortstop Bill Knickerbocker, who started a triple play that ended the game.

Sept. 17: Len Koenecke, released by the Dodgers, hired a private plane. During the flight he got into a fight with the pilot and died when he was hit over the head with a fire extinguisher.

RBIs. On August 11, Berger hit a homer, two doubles, and a triple, to tie the modern record for extra-base hits in a game.

Meanwhile, the Yankees were still one of the most powerful teams in baseball, even without Ruth. Behind Lou Gehrig, now the undisputed leader of the team, the Yankees finished with an 89–60 record, but it was only good enough for a second-place finish behind Detroit, which won its second-straight pennant with a 93–58 record.

The Tigers clinched the pennant on September 21 by sweeping a doubleheader from St. Louis. Slugger Hank Greenberg was named the AL's Most Valuable Player after tying Philadelphia's Jimmie Foxx for the league lead with 36 homers and leading the league with 170 RBIs. Rightfielder Pete Fox, who batted .321, had a 29-game hitting streak. Tommy Bridges paced the Tigers' pitching staff

with a 21–10 record while Schoolboy Rowe added 19 wins.

While the Tigers edged the Yankees by three games in the American League, the National League race was another tight one. Thanks to a 21-game winning streak in September, the Chicago Cubs beat out the St. Louis Cardinals, who had won the previous season's World Series, by four games. The battle was a three-way race for most of the season between the Cubs, Cardinals and the New York Giants, who led by nine games midway through the season.

The Cubs defeated the Dodgers on September 14 for their 11th straight win and went into first place. Five days later, the Cubs completed a four-game sweep of the Giants for their 16th straight win.

The Cubs clinched the pennant on September 27 by beating the Cardinals in the first game of a doubleheader as pitcher Bill Lee won his 20th game. The Cubs extended their streak to 21 by winning the second game. It was the league's longest winning streak since the Dodgers won 15 straight in 1924.

Cubs' catcher Gabby Hartnett was named the National League's MVP. In addition to doing a solid job behind the plate and in handling the pitching staff, Hartnett batted .344 with 13

SHORTS The dismantling of the A's dynasty continued. After the A's finished last in the AL with a 58–91 record, Connie Mack, who had already unloaded most of his stars from the team that won pennants from 1929–31, traded Jimmie Foxx and Johnny Marcum to the Red Sox for Gordon Rhodes, prospect George Savino and $150,000.

The Senators' Buddy Myer had to wait until the final day to secure his batting crown

part, by a rainout of the next day's game and an open date.

Gehrig, who signed a contract with the Yankees before the season for $30,000, had another close call on August 5. In a rain-soaked game between the Yankees and the Red Sox, he left in the fourth inning with another lumbago attack.

Ironically, Ruth's replacement in right field, George Selkirk, batted .312 with 11 homers and 94 RBIs. On August 10, Selkirk drove in eight runs, one short of Jimmie Foxx's AL record, with two home runs and a single.

The first-ever scheduled major league night game was rained out in Cincinnati on May 23. The following night at Crosley Field, 20,000 fans watched the Reds beat the Phillies 2–1. During the pre-game ceremonies, President Franklin Roosevelt pushed a button at the White House to illuminate the field. The Reds scheduled night games, one each against the other NL teams.

A night game later in the season led to some controversy. The Reds oversold the game and 30,000 fans jammed into Crosley Field for the contest against the defending World Series champion Cardinals. Kitty Burke, a female fan, slipped under the ropes around the infield and grabbed a bat. Paul Dean lobbed a pitch to Burke, who grounded out. St. Louis manager Frankie Frisch demanded it count as an at-bat, but lost the argument.

Cardinals' pitcher Dizzy Dean, who had won 30 games in 1934, announced on February 6 he that wanted a yearly salary of $25,000 and would hold out until he got it. Dean signed for $19,500 the following day and won 28 games.

On August 31, Chicago's Vern Kennedy pitched the first American League no-hitter since 1931, and the first ever in Comiskey Park, by blanking Cleveland, 5–0. Kennedy also was the batting star with a bases-loaded triple.

The season featured a tight batting race in the American League between Washington's Buddy Myer and Cleveland's Joe Vosmik. Myer went 4-for-5 on the final day of the season to edge Vosmik, .349 to .348. Pittsburgh's Arky Vaughan won the National League batting title with a .385 average.

The American League continued its mastery of the All-Star Game, which was held in Cleveland's Municipal Stadium on July 8. Behind Jimmie Foxx, who homered and drove in three runs, the AL won for the third straight time with a 4–1 decision.

homers and 91 RBIs. Leadoff man Augie Galan led the league with 133 runs scored and 22 stolen bases.

The Tigers won the World Series in six games for their first ever championship.

Gehrig's consecutive-games-played streak continued, but not without some close calls, as had been the case during the past several years. He had to leave the June 8 game after a collision at first base, which resulted in arm and shoulder injuries. The streak was preserved, in

The 1935 World Series featured a battle between two franchises looking for a championship after several past failures. The Detroit Tigers lost the Series in 1907, 1908, 1909 and 1934. The Chicago Cubs lost the Series in 1910, 1918, 1929 and 1932. The frustration ended for the Tigers, who won their first title by beating the Cubs in six games.

The Series started in Detroit, but Cubs' ace Lon Warneke shut out the Tigers and Schoolboy Rowe 3–0. The Tigers evened the Series in Game Two with an 8–3 win. Tommy Bridges pitched a six-hitter and slugger Hank Greenberg hit a two-run homer. However, the Tigers lost Greenberg (who drove in 170 runs and batted .338 during the regular season) for the rest of the Series with a broken wrist. He was injured trying to score from first on a single.

The Series moved to Chicago and Game Three featured controversy. American League umpire George Moriarty ejected Chicago manager Charlie Grimm and shortstop Billy Jurges in the third inning. The Cubs tied the game in the bottom of the ninth, but Detroit scored an unearned run to win in the 11th.

The Tigers won their third straight in Game Four, a 2–1 victory. The winning run scored on a sixth-inning error.

One loss from elimination, the Cubs rebounded in Game Five. Chuck Klein hit a two-run homer and Lon Warneke pitched six shutout innings for his second win of the Series. Warneke left the game with a sore arm, but Bill Lee finished up in relief in the 3–1 win.

However, that was it for the Cubs. The Series returned to Detroit and the Tigers wrapped it up in front of their hometown fans with a dramatic 4–3 win. Goslin's single with two outs in the ninth scored Mickey Cochrane

Tom Bridges threw two complete games in the Tigers' Series triumph

with the game-winner. Bridges pitched his second complete game, but had to pitch out of a major jam in the top of the ninth. The Cubs' Stan Hack tripled to start the inning, but Bridges, the Tigers' ace all season in winning 21 games, retired the next three hitters to get out of the jam.

The victory finally ended years of frustration for Detroit fans as the Tigers won the World Series for the first time.

WORLD SERIES	
GAME 1	
Chicago Cubs 3	Detroit 0
GAME 2	
Detroit 8	Chicago Cubs 3
GAME 3	
Detroit 6	Chicago Cubs 5
GAME 4	
Detroit 2	Chicago Cubs 1
GAME 5	
Chicago Cubs 3	Detroit 1
GAME 6	
Detroit 4	Chicago Cubs 3

The remaining years of the 1930s would not be pleasant times for fans who didn't like the New York Yankees.

The Yankees became one of baseball's most powerful teams in the 1920s. New York won six American League pennants and three World Series titles between 1921 and 1928, but Yankee haters actually enjoyed the early part of the 1930s. New York won the pennant and World Series only once—in 1932—in the first five years of the decade.

All that changed, beginning in 1936, when the Yankee dynasty returned. The remaining years of the decade saw New York win four straight pennants and four more World Series titles.

The American League race was strictly no contest in 1936. The Yankees took over early and never looked back. New York moved into first place on May 10 and remained there for the rest of the season. They clinched the pennant on September 9—the earliest date ever—with an 11–3 and 12–9 doubleheader sweep of the Cleveland Indians. The Yankees finished the regular season with a 102–51 record, 19½ games ahead of second-place Detroit.

Since Babe Ruth left New York after the 1934 season, the Yankees had officially become Lou Gehrig's team. Gehrig responded with a big year in 1936. He led the league with 49 home runs and 167 runs scored while winning the American League's Most Valuable Player Award. Gehrig also played in his 1,700th consecutive game on June 5.

National League MVP, the Giants' Carl Hubbell

The Giants' Mel Ott led the National League with 33 home runs

The 1936 season also featured the debut of center fielder Joe DiMaggio, who played his first regular-season game with the Yankees on May 3. DiMaggio had three hits, including a triple, as New York routed St. Louis, 14–5. DiMaggio put together an outstanding rookie season. He hit .323 with 29 homers and 125 RBIs while leading the league with 22 outfield assists.

On June 24, DiMaggio hit two homers in the fifth inning in an 18–4 rout of the Browns. He also tied three records on June 24 in New York's ten-run fifth inning against the White Sox. DiMaggio hit two homers for eight total bases. He also hit two doubles, which equaled the modern record of four extra-base hits in a game on June 24.

The Yankees' biggest day came on May 24 when they hammered Philadelphia, 25–2. Second baseman Tony Lazzeri hit three home runs, including two grand slams, and a triple for 15 total bases. He also set a new AL mark

of 11 RBIs in one game. The big day gave Lazzeri seven homers in four games and six in three games.

Five Yankees topped the 100-RBI mark. Gehrig led the way with 152, followed by DiMaggio (125), Lazzeri (109) and right fielder George Selkirk and catcher Bill Dickey (both with 107). Selkirk, in his second season as Ruth's replacement, had another solid year, batting .308 with 18 home runs.

The Yankees' pitching staff was just as impressive as the hitters. Six pitchers hit double figures, with ace Red Ruffing leading the way with a 20–12 record. Monte Pearson (19–7), Johnny Broaca (12–7), Lefty Gomez (13–7), Bump Hadley (14–4) and Pat Malone (12–4) rounded out the staff's top winners. Malone led the league with nine saves.

While the Yankees rolled in the American League, the story was very different in the National League. In a hard-fought race that went into the final week of the season, the New York Giants emerged out of a three-team battle with the Chicago Cubs and St. Louis Cardinals to win the pennant. The Giants finished with a 92–62 record while the Cubs and Giants tied for second at 87–67. New York didn't clinch the pennant until September 24 with a 2–1 win over the Boston Bees (formerly known as the Braves) in the first game of a doubleheader.

The Giants were paced by ace left-hander Carl Hubbell, who was named the league's Most Valuable Player for going 26–6 with a 2.31 ERA. The Giants relied heavily on Hubbell down the stretch. At one point, he appeared in ten straight games. His final win of the season came on September 23. It was also his 16th straight win, a streak that would reach 24 the next season. Hubbell's last defeat came on July 13 when he lost a 1–0 duel with the Cubs' Bill Lee. The streak began on July 17 when he beat Pittsburgh, 6–0.

A 15-game winning streak keyed the Giants' race to the pennant. They took over first place on August 25 with their 13th straight win. The 15th came on August 28 in a 7–4 victory over Pittsburgh in 14 innings. Manager Bill Terry, the last National Leaguer to bat over .400, inserted himself as a pinch-hitter and delivered a bases-loaded single to break the 1–1 tie in the 14th.

Giants' right fielder Mel Ott led the league with 33 home runs. He also hit .328 with 135 RBIs.

The Cubs stayed in the race thanks primarily to winning 15 games in a row in June. The race for the American League's batting title was

An impressive year for Pittsburgh's Paul Waner (left) who finished with a .373 average

a hot one for most of the season. Chicago's Luke Appling wrapped it up on September 24 when he went 4-for-4 in the second game of a doubleheader with Cleveland. Runner-up Earl Averill of the Indians was held hitless, leaving Appling as the champ with a ten-point margin at .388.

The Indians' Hal Trosky led the American League with 162 RBIs. Detroit's Tommy Bridges led the league with 23 wins while Boston's Lefty Grove, bouncing back from a sore arm in 1935, had the league's lowest ERA (2.81).

Pittsburgh's Paul Waner led the National League with a .373 batting average while St. Louis' Joe Medwick was the top RBI man with 138. Medwick also set an NL record with 64 doubles

Cleveland right-hander Bob Feller made his debut at 17 years old on July 19. Feller

pitched one inning in relief against Washington. He didn't allow a hit and struck out one. Feller made his first start on August 23. He struck out 15, one less than the league record, in a 4–1 win over St. Louis. On September 13, he broke the AL record and tied the Major League mark with 17 strikeouts and defeated the A's, 5–2.

It was a short season for Detroit first baseman Hank Greenberg, the American League's MVP in 1935. Greenberg broke his wrist in a baseline collision with Washington Senator's Jake Powell on April 29 and missed the rest of the season. Detroit Tigers' player-manager Mickey Cochrane, the American League MVP in 1934, also missed most of the season after breaking a finger on April 30. He also was hospitalized for emotional problems during parts of the season.

The 1936 World Series was a landmark for the New York Yankees. It was their first Series without Babe Ruth and their first with Joe DiMaggio.

The key name might have been different, but the results didn't change. The Yankees defeated the New York Giants in six games.

Giants' ace Carl Hubbell started Game One. He won his last 16 decisions during the regular season and finished with a 26–6 record and a 2.31 ERA. Hubbell showed the Yankees why he put up such good numbers by holding them to seven hits and one run—a solo homer by George Selkirk, who, ironically, replaced Ruth in right field—for a 6–1 win. Hubbell struck out eight.

That was about the last shining moment for the Giants, however. The Yankees won four of the next five games to wrap up another Series title.

In Game Two, which was delayed a day by rain, the Yankees hammered the Giants, 18–4. New York had 17 hits, including a grand slam by Tony Lazzeri. Every member of the Yankees' lineup had a hit. Lefty Gomez pitched a six-hitter.

The Series moved to Yankee Stadium for Game Three. The Giants' pitching was much better, but the Yankees still won 2–1. Frank Crosetti's infield hit in the eighth scored the winning run. Lou Gehrig and Jimmy Ripple exchanged home runs earlier in the game.

Game Four also went to the Yankees, who won 5–2. Gehrig homered for the second straight day and Monte Pearson was the winning pitcher.

Facing elimination in Game Five, the Giants squeezed out a 5–4 win. Giants' player-manager Bill Terry drove in the winning run with a ten-inning sacrifice fly as Hal Schumacher got the victory.

The Yankees wrapped it up in Game Six at the Polo Grounds. The Yankees' big bats struck again and rolled to a 13–5 win. Jake Powell homered and drove in four runs while DiMaggio, Lazzeri and Red Rolfe had three hits apiece. The Yankees put the game away with seven runs in the ninth and Gomez picked up another win.

There's no doubt the Yankees' offense was the star of the Series. They pounded out 65 hits in six games. Powell batted .455, Rolfe hit .400, DiMaggio had a .346 average and Gehrig drove in seven runs.

WORLD SERIES

GAME 1	
NY Giants 6	NY Yankees 1
GAME 2	
NY Yankees 18	NY Giants 4
GAME 3	
NY Yankees 2	NY Giants 1
GAME 4	
NY Yankees 5	NY Giants 2
GAME 5	
NY Giants 5	NY Yankees 4
GAME 6	
NY Yankees 13	NY Giants 5

Yankees' star Jake Powell led the way in the battle of New York with a Series average of .455

MOST VALUABLE PLAYER

AL: Charlie Gehringer, Detroit
NL: Joe Medwick, St. Louis Cardinals

LEADERS

BATTING AVERAGE

AL: Charlie Gehringer, Detroit, .371
NL: Joe Medwick, St. Louis Cardinals, .374

HOME RUNS

AL: Joe DiMaggio, NY Yankees, 46
NL: Mel Ott, NY Giants and Joe Medwick, St. Louis Cardinals, 31

RUNS BATTED IN

AL: Hank Greenberg, Detroit, 183
NL: Joe Medwick, St. Louis Cardinals, 154

STOLEN BASES

AL: Bill Werber, Philadelphia; Ben Chapman, Boston/Washington, 35
NL: Augie Galan, Chicago Cubs, 23

PITCHING VICTORIES

AL: Lefty Gomez, NY Yankees, 21
NL: Carl Hubbell, NY Giants, 22

EARNED RUN AVERAGE

AL: Lefty Gomez, NY Yankees, 2.33
NL: Jim Turner, Boston Bees, 2.38

STRIKEOUTS

AL: Lefty Gomez, NY Yankees, 194
NL: Carl Hubbell, NY Giants, 159

SAVES

AL: Clint Brown, Chicago White Sox, 18
NL: Mace Brown, Pittsburgh; Cliff Melton, NY Giants, 7

The pennant finishes in the 1937 season were almost identical to the results of the previous season.

In the American League, thanks to the New York Yankees, there was no race for the second year in a row. In the National League, the New York Giants won in an even tighter battle than they had the year before.

The Yankees rolled to the pennant with a 102–52 record—the same number of wins they had in 1936—and finished 13 games ahead of the Detroit Tigers. New York's hitters in the middle of the order put on an awesome display of production.

Center fielder Joe DiMaggio, following up on a strong rookie season, hit .346, led the league with 46 homers and drove in 167 runs. First baseman Lou Gehrig batted .351, blasted 37 homers and knocked in 159 runs. Catcher Bill Dickey hit .332, belted 29 homers and drove in 133 runs. The three combined to drive in 459 runs. George Selkirk, the right fielder who replaced Babe Ruth in 1935, missed half of the season because of injuries, but still hit 18 homers and drove in 68 runs in only 78 games.

As was usually the case, the Yankees had a strong team overall and won with more than just hitting. New York also had an excellent pitching staff, paced by starters Lefty Gomez and Red Ruffing. Gomez led the league with 21 wins, while losing only 11, and a 2.33 ERA. Ruffing finished 20–7 with a 2.98 ERA. Bump Hadley had an 11–8 record while Johnny Murphy finished 13–4 with ten saves.

Gehrig played in his 1,900th straight game on August 3. The Yankees clinched the pennant on September 23 when the Tigers lost to Boston.

Despite big seasons from several Yankees, the Most Valuable Player Award didn't go to a New York player. That award went to Detroit second baseman Charlie Gehringer, who led the league with a .371 batting average. First baseman Hank Greenberg, who missed most of the 1936 season with an injury, led the league with 183 RBIs. On September 19, Greenberg became the first player to hit a ball into the center field stands at Yankee Stadium.

SHORTS In a ten-inning game between the Indians and Yankees on August 6, Cleveland outfielders had no chances. In the tenth, Joe DiMaggio hit a drive which third baseman Odell Hale deflected into foul territory. One umpire called it foul and no fielder chased after the ball. However, another overruled the call and the winning run scored. Cleveland's protest of the game was upheld.

The Tigers' Mickey Cochrane renounced his playing duties due to injury

The Tigers also got a big season from rookie catcher Rudy York, who batted .307 with 35 homers and 105 RBIs in only 375 at-bats. On August 31, York set a new record for homers in a month by hitting his 17th and 18th to surpass Babe Ruth's mark set in September 1927. York set a record for the league's highest slugging percentage for a rookie with a .651 mark and the highest home run percentage for a rookie with a homer every 9.3 at-bat.

The Tigers finished the regular season with an 89–65 record, but that wasn't enough to catch the mighty Yankees.

The Yankees and Tigers had quite a rivalry. After hitting a home run against the Yankees on April 25, Tigers' player-manager Mickey Cochrane suffered a fractured skull on a pitch from Hadley. Cochrane was hospitalized and never returned to active play. Coach Del Baker ran the team in his absence. Cochrane returned as manager on July 26.

The Giants, meanwhile, had a much tougher

Carl Hubbell winds up during his winning streak of 24 games

TIMELINE

Feb. 17: The Red Sox sold first baseman Babe Dahlgren to the Yankees. Dahlgren replaced Lou Gehrig two years later.

March 20: In one of the biggest trades in Negro League history, Josh Gibson and Judy Johnson were traded to the Homestead Grays for $25,000 and two journeymen.

June 25: Cubs' switch-hitter Augie Galan became the first National Leaguer to hit a homer from each side of the plate in the same game.

April 22: Satchel Paige and Josh Gibson were among 18 black players who jumped to the Dominican Republic League. Negro League owners regarded this as desertion and planned to ban the players from the league. In May, Paige was banned for life.

June 1: White Sox's pitcher Bill Dietrich threw an 8–0 no-hitter against the Browns. It was the third no-hitter caught by Luke Sewell. He was previously behind the plate for no-hitters thrown by Wes Ferrell in 1931 and Vern Kennedy in 1935.

Aug. 17: The Cardinals beat the Reds in Cincinnati with the final out being recorded at 12:02 a.m., making it the first major league game ever completed after midnight.

Aug. 27: The Dodgers' Fred Frankhouse lost his chance to pitch a full no-hitter against the Reds when rain stopped the game with two out in the eighth.

Sept. 25: Cleveland's Bob Feller struck out 16 Red Sox hitters, one less than his own AL record in an 8-1 victory.

Oct. 2: 34-year-old rookie Jim Turner of the Boston Bees won his 20th game.

Oct. 2: The Pirates beat the Reds in a doubleheader on the final day of the season. The sweep extended Pittsburgh's winning streak to ten and the Reds' losing streak to 14. The Pirates beat the Reds 21 of 22 games, tying the record set by the Cubs over the Braves in 1909.

path to their second straight National League pennant. New York finished with a 95–57 record and beat out the Chicago Cubs by three games. The Giants featured two 20-game winners. Carl Hubbell finished 22–8 and reached the 20-win mark for the fifth straight season. Rookie Cliff Melton went 20–9 and tied for the league lead in saves with seven. In addition to leading the league in wins, Hubbell was the top strikeout pitcher with 159.

Hubbell continued his amazing pitching.

He finished the 1936 season with 16 straight wins, a streak that started July 17. His 17th straight win came on April 23 when he pitched a three-hitter against the Boston Bees. He extended the streak to 24 on May 27 when he pitched two innings in relief. Hubbell's win streak stayed alive, thanks to a ninth-inning home run by Mel Ott that gave the Giants a 3–2 win over the Reds. Hubbell's streak finally came to an end on May 31 in a 10–3 loss to Brooklyn.

Melton struck out 13 in his first game on April 25, but lost to the Bees, 3–1. Melton won his 20th game in the opener of a doubleheader against the Phillies on September 29, but the Giants couldn't clinch the pennant because they lost the second game. The clincher came the next day when Hubbell won his 22nd game.

The Cardinals' Joe Medwick became the last National Leaguer to win the Triple Crown

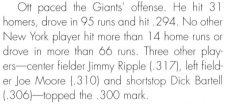

SHORTS In an August 14 doubleheader against the St. Louis Browns, the Tigers set a Major League record by scoring 36 runs in the two games. The Tigers won by 16–1 and 20–7 scores. Detroit's Pete Fox had the busiest day as he scored eight times in the doubleheader. Tigers' pitcher Eldon Auker recorded a win and also hit two home runs.

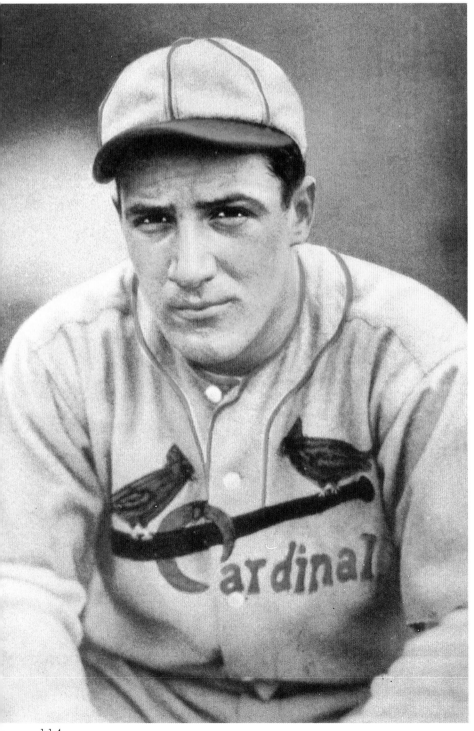

Ott paced the Giants' offense. He hit 31 homers, drove in 95 runs and hit .294. No other New York player hit more than 14 home runs or drove in more than 66 runs. Three other players—center fielder Jimmy Ripple (.317), left fielder Joe Moore (.310) and shortstop Dick Bartell (.306)—topped the .300 mark.

Cardinals' left fielder Joe Medwick had an outstanding season, even though St. Louis finished in fourth place, 15 games out of first with an 81–73 record. Medwick led the league in batting average (.374), runs scored (111) and RBIs (154) and tied Ott for the lead in home runs (31).

Pittsburgh right fielder Paul Waner established a 20th-century National League record with his eighth season of 200 or more hits.

In the July 7 All-Star Game in Washington, Gehrig homered, doubled and drove in four runs in the American League's 8–3 win, but that wasn't the biggest news. Cardinals' pitcher Dizzy Dean had a toe fractured by a drive off the bat of the Indians' Earl Averill. Dean changed his delivery after the injury and his new motion led to an arm injury from which he never regained his previous from. He finished the season with a 13–10 record.

Dean was at the center of controversy for most of the season. Dean, his brother, Paul, and Medwick were involved in a fight with two sportswriters in a Tampa hotel lobby on April 2. On May 19, a knockdown pitch from Dean in a game against the Giants triggered a bench-clearing brawl that had to be broken up by policemen. On June 2, National League President Ford Frick suspended Dean for comments he made following the brawl. Dean denied the statements and his suspension was lifted a few days later.

Cleveland pitcher Johnny Allen, who missed eight weeks because of an appendectomy, finished the season with a 15–1 record. He won his 12th straight without a loss on September 17, equaling Tom Zachary's American League record of 12–0 set in 1929. Allen's effort to tie the record of 16 straight wins ended on October 3 when he lost a 1–0 decision to Detroit's Jake Wade on the final day of the season.

WORLD SERIES	
GAME 1	
NY Giants 6	NY Yankees 1
GAME 2	
NY Yankees 18	NY Giants 4
GAME 3	
NY Yankees 2	NY Giants 1
GAME 4	
NY Yankees 5	NY Giants 2
GAME 5	
NY Giants 5	NY Yankees 4
GAME 6	
NY Yankees 13	NY Giants 5

Lefty Gomez was the Game Six hero as the Yankees clinched another World Championship

The 1937 World Series was a rematch of the 1936 Fall Classic as the New York Yankees and New York Giants battled again. The only difference in the results was the Yankees won in five games, instead of six, as they had done the previous season.

The Series opened in Yankee Stadium and the home team rolled to an 8–1 win. Giants' starter Carl Hubbell took a 1–0 lead into the sixth when the Yankees exploded for seven runs on five singles, three walks and two errors. Joe DiMaggio and George Selkirk had bases-loaded singles and Yankees' pitcher Lefty Gomez, known as a weak hitter, drew two walks in the inning. Tony Lazzeri homered in the eighth.

Game Two, another 8–1 Yankee win, was almost an instant replay. Behind Cliff Melton, the Giants held a 1–0 lead in the fifth, but the Yankees scored twice. Pitcher Red Ruffing drove in the go-ahead run with a single and capped a four-run sixth with a double that scored two.

Ruffing wasn't bad on the mound, either, holding the Giants to seven hits. Selkirk added three RBIs for the Yankees.

By Game Three, it was apparent that the Giants were falling apart, even though they were returning to the Polo Grounds. They made four errors and lost 5–1. Monte Pearson and Johnny Murphy combined to pitch a five-hitter.

Staring at a sweep, the Giants put together their own big inning by scoring six times in the second in Game Four to spark a 7–3 win. Hank Leiber started the rally with a single and later drove in two with another single. Hubbell pitched a six-hitter for the win. The ninth inning featured a historic matchup when Lou Gehrig homered off Hubbell. It turned out to be the last Series home run for Gehrig and the last inning Hubbell would pitch in the World Series.

The Giants' euphoria lasted one day. The Yankees clinched the Series with a 4–2 win in Game Five. Myril Hoag and DiMaggio homered for the Yankees, but Mel Ott tied it in the third with a two-run homer. Yankees' starter Lefty Gomez drove in the winning run in the fifth after Lazzeri doubled. Gomez then scored on Lou Gehrig's double. The victory for Gomez was his fifth without a loss, a Series record. The Yankees set another record with no errors in the Series.

MOST VALUABLE PLAYER
AL: Jimmie Foxx, Boston Red Sox
NL: Ernie Lombardi, Cincinnati

LEADERS
BATTING AVERAGE
AL: Jimmie Foxx, Boston Red Sox, .349
NL: Ernie Lombardi, Cincinnati, .342

HOME RUNS
AL: Hank Greenberg, Detroit, 58
NL: Mel Ott, NY Giants, 36

RUNS BATTED IN
AL: Jimmie Foxx, Philadelphia, 175
NL: Joe Medwick, St. Louis Cardinals, 122

STOLEN BASES
AL: Frank Crosetti, NY Yankees, 27
NL: Stan Hack, Chicago Cubs, 16

PITCHING VICTORIES
AL: Red Ruffing, NY Yankees, 21
NL: Bill Lee, Chicago Cubs, 22

EARNED RUN AVERAGE
AL: Lefty Grove, Boston Red Sox, 3.08
NL: Bill Lee, Chicago Cubs, 2.66

STRIKEOUTS
AL: Bob Feller, Cleveland, 240
NL: Clay Bryant, Chicago Cubs, 135

SAVES
AL: Jonny Murphy, NY Yankees, 11
NL: Dick Coffman, NY Giants, 12

The 1938 season was a memorable one for many reasons. It featured the third straight World Series title for the mighty New York Yankees. The Yanks rolled to the American League pennant with a 99–53 record, which was good for a 9½ game finish over the Boston Red Sox. New York went on to sweep the Chicago Cubs to become the first team to win three straight World Series championships.

Unknowingly, this was to be Lou Gehrig's last full season in baseball

Once again, the Yankees' success was a total team effort. Center fielder Joe DiMaggio led the way with another outstanding season in his third big-league year. DiMaggio batted .324 with 32 homers and 140 RBIs. Catcher Bill Dickey also had another big year, hitting .313 with 27 homers and 115 RBIs.

For first baseman Lou Gehrig, it was the final productive year of his career. He batted .295 with 29 home runs and 114 RBIs. The numbers were solid, but a drop-off from his production throughout his career. On August 20, Gehrig hit a first-inning grand slam, the 23rd and last of his career for a still-standing record. His consecutive-games-played streak also continued. Gehrig played in his 2,000th straight game on May 31 and in his 2,100th consecutive game on September 9. Little did anyone know the streak would end early the next season. No one knew it at the time, but Gehrig was suffering from a condition that would end his career the following season and claim his life in 1941.

Rookie second baseman Joe Gordon stepped into the lineup and made a big contribution by blasting 25 homers and driving in 97 runs. Right fielder Tommy Henrich added 22 homers and 91 RBIs while batting .270. Shortstop Frank Crosetti stole a league-leading 27 bases.

Pitching was another Yankees' strength as four hurlers won at least 14 games. Red Ruffing led the staff with a 21–7 record and a 3.31 ERA. His 21 wins led the league. Lefty Gomez finished with an 18–12 mark, Monte Pearson went 16–7 and Spud Chandler ended with a 14–5 record. Bullpen ace Johnny Murphy finished 8–2 and saved a league-high 11 games. Pearson had a ten-game winning streak and pitched a no-hitter against Cleveland on August 27. A doubleheader sweep that day gave the Yankees a 12-game lead and ended any hopes teams had for making it a race.

The Yankees clinched the pennant on September 18, even though they lost a doubleheader to the St. Louis Browns.

Despite several outstanding seasons from individual players, the league's Most Valuable Player

SHORTS In a June 7 game against the Red Sox, Indians' pitcher Johnny Allen stormed off the mound when ordered by umpire Bill McGowan to cut off his sweatshirt sleeve that was dangling from his uniform and distracting hitters. Allen refused to return to the game and was fined $250. The controversial shirt ended up in the Hall of Fame.

Award did not go to one of the Yankees. That honor went to Boston first baseman Jimmie Foxx, who led the league with a .349 batting average and 175 RBIs. Foxx also hit 50 home runs, but Detroit first baseman Hank Greenberg led the league in that department with 58. Greenberg hit two home runs in the same game a record-setting 11 times during the season.

The Cubs overcame controversy to win the National League pennant by two games over Pittsburgh. New York finished five games out and in third-place while fourth-place Cincinnati was six games out.

The Cubs won the pennant despite a managerial change that saw catcher Gabby Hartnett take over for Charlie Grimm on July 20. The Cubs were 45–36 and in third place when Hartnett took over. They finished 44–27 after the change.

It looked like the Pirates, led by the Waner brothers, Lloyd and Paul, would take the pennant. They held a seven-game lead on Labor Day, but the Cubs won seven straight and trailed the Pirates by 1½ games on September 27 when the teams opened a series at Wrigley Field.

The Cubs, who had been getting help from an unexpected source all season, turned to that player again in the first game of the series. Dizzy Dean, whose career hadn't been the same since breaking a toe after being hit by a line drive in the 1937 All-Star Game, was acquired from St. Louis on April 16. The broken toe forced Dean to change his delivery, which led to a sore arm, and the Cardinals thought he was finished.

Dean proved them wrong. He went 7–1 with a 1.81 ERA for the Cubs. Dean held the Pirates to one run in 8⅔ innings and got relief help from Bill Lee, who pitched four straight shutouts in September to get the win and cut Pittsburgh's lead to a half-game.

One of the most famous moments in baseball history came the following day. The teams were tied 5–5 after eight innings. Even though it was getting dark at Wrigley Field, the umpires decided to play one more inning. The Pirates didn't score in the top of the ninth. Hartnett came to bat with two outs in the bottom of the ninth and homered on an 0–2 pitch to win the game.

TIMELINE

April 19: In the top of the first inning at Philadelphia, Dodger Ernie Koy homered in his first Major League at-bat. In the bottom of the inning, !eadoff man Emmett Mueller also hit a home run in his first time up in the Majors.

April 20: Bob Feller pitched the first of 12 career one-hitters, beating the Browns, 9–0.

May 5: Harold Kelleher of the Phillies faced 16 batters in the sixth inning, as the Cubs scored 12 runs. Both marks were NL records off one hurler in a single inning.

June 10: Red Sox rookie pitcher Bill Lefebvre homered in his first Major League at-bat and only plate appearance for the season. However, Lefebvre was hammered by the White Sox in a 15–2 loss. He was the first AL player to homer in his only at-bat.

June 18: Babe Ruth was signed as a Dodgers coach for the rest of the season.

June 21: Red Sox third baseman Pinky Higgins extended his consecutive-hit string to 12, with eight hits in a doubleheader with Detroit. He struck out in his first at-bat the following day.

June 26: Carl Hubbell won his 200th game, as the Giants beat the Cubs. Hubbell had elbow surgery in August and missed the rest of the season.

July 6: The National League won the All-Star Game, 4–1. NL starter Johnny Vander Meer got the win and the AL made four errors.

Aug. 5: 40-year-old Browns pitcher Fred "Cactus" Johnson won his first Major League game since 1923. He won 252 minor leagues games in his career.

Aug. 6: Mickey Cochrane was fired as Detroit manager.

Aug. 25: St. Louis Browns' George McQuinn's 34-game hitting string was stopped.

Sept. 3: Rudy York of the Tigers hit his fourth grand slam, tying the record for one season.

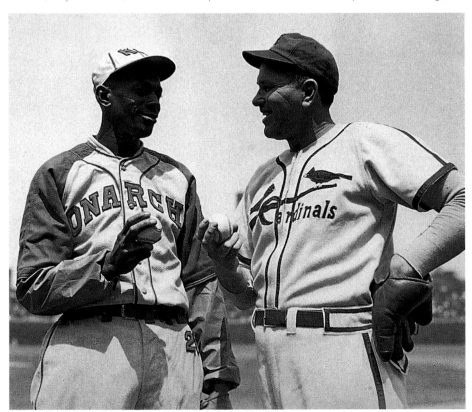

Dizzie Dean (seen here with Satchel Paige) silenced his doubters as he helped the Cubs to the World Series

Lefty Johnny Vander Meer hurled his way into history with consecutive no-hitters for the Reds

Since the umpires planned to call the game because of darkness after Hartnett's at-bat, the blast was remembered as the "homer in the gloamin'."

The Cubs clinched the pennant on October 1 when they beat the Cardinals in the second game of a doubleheader while the Reds beat the Pirates. Hartnett hit ten homers and drove in 59 runs while first baseman Rip Collins hit 13 homers with 61 RBIs. The Cubs, who finished 89–63, featured two .300 hitters—third baseman Stan Hack (.320) and left fielder Carl Reynolds (.302). Lee finished with a 22–9 record—a league-high in wins—and a league-leading 2.66 ERA. Clay Bryant was 19–11 while Tex Carleton finished with a 10–9 record and Charlie Root, who gave up Babe Ruth's "called shot" home run in the 1932 World Series, won eight games and saved eight others.

Cincinnati left-hander Johnny Vander Meer made history when he became the only pitcher in history to throw back-to-back no-hitters. The first came on June 11 in a 3–0 win over Brooklyn. The second no-hitter came on June 15 when Vander Meer beat Brooklyn, 6–0, in the

SHORTS NL President Ford Frick ordered the May 14 game between the Reds and Cardinals to be replayed. Cincinnati protested the 7–6 loss after one umpire ruled a drive hit by the Reds' Dusty Cooke a home run, but another umpire ruled the hit a triple. Cooke, thinking he had a homer, slowed down while running the bases, and was tagged out.

first night game ever at Ebbets Field. He walked the bases loaded after retiring the first hitter in the ninth. Vander Meer, who walked eight and struck out seven, got Ernie Koy to ground into a force out at home and retired Leo Durocher on a fly ball to wrap up the no-hitter. Vander Meer extended his hitless streak to 21⅔ innings in his next start on June 19 against Boston. He finished the season with a 15–10 record and a 3.12 ERA.

Reds' catcher Ernie Lombardi hit .342 with 19 homers and 95 RBIs to win the National League's MVP award. St. Louis right fielder Joe Medwick led the league in RBIs for the second straight year with 122 while Giants' right fielder Mel Ott hit 36 homers to lead the league. Ott and Medwick had tied for the league lead in homers in 1937.

As was the case in 1937, the New York Yankees were looking at a rematch in the 1938 World Series. This time, the Yankees were facing the Chicago Cubs, the team they swept in 1932.

Once again, the Yankees were up to the rematch. And once again, they swept the Cubs.

The Series opened at Wrigley Field, but the home field didn't help the Cubs. Yankees' catcher Bill Dickey tied a World Series record with four hits. He scored a run and drove in another as Red Ruffing pitched the Yankees to a 3–1 win.

Game Two featured former St. Louis legend Dizzy Dean pitching for the Cubs. Dean was obtained from the Cardinals in April and won seven of eight decisions. For most of the game, Dean looked like "The Diz" of old. Through seven innings he held the Yankees to three hits and led 3–2. George Selkirk opened the eighth with a single, but two force outs left Dean one batter away from getting out of the inning. At that point, Frank Crosetti hit a two-run homer to put the Yankees ahead 4–3. Joe DiMaggio added a two-run homer in the ninth. Lefty Gomez raised his career mark to 6–0 in the World Series and the Yankees won 6–3.

The win would be the last Series victory of Gomez's career.

As the Series moved to New York, the stunned Cubs were finished. Dickey and rookie second baseman Joe Gordon homered for the Yankees. Gordon added a two-run single and Monte Pearson pitched the Yanks to a 5–2 win.

That was all for Chicago. The Yankees rolled to an 8–3 win in Game Four to become the first team to win three straight World Championships. Crosetti drove in four runs with a double and a triple as Ruffing won his second game of the Series.

While the Series once again showed the Yankees' dominance, there was also a sign that things in New York were about to change. Lou Gehrig managed four singles and didn't drive in a run in 14 at-bats. No one knew it at the time, but Gehrig was in declining health. Not only would he have to retire the next season, he would die in 1941.

WORLD SERIES	
GAME 1	
NY Yankees 3	Chicago Cubs 1
GAME 2	
NY Yankees 6	Chicago Cubs 3
GAME 3	
NY Yankees 5	Chicago Cubs 2
GAME 4	
NY Yankees 8	Chicago Cubs 3

Yankees' manager Joe McCarthy looks on from the dugout

MOST VALUABLE PLAYER
AL: Joe DiMaggio, NY Yankees
NL: Bucky Walters, Cincinnati

LEADERS
BATTING AVERAGE
AL: Joe DiMaggio, NY Yankees, .381
NL: Johnny Mize, St. Louis Cardinals, .349

HOME RUNS
AL: Jimmie Foxx, Boston Red Sox, 35
NL: Johnny Mize, St. Louis Cardinals, 28

RUNS BATTED IN
AL: Ted Williams, Boston Red Sox, 145
NL: Frank McCormick, Cincinnati, 128

STOLEN BASES
AL: George Case, Washington, 51
NL: Lee Handley, Pittsburgh; Stan Hack, Chicago Cubs, 17

PITCHING VICTORIES
AL: Bob Feller, Cleveland, 24
NL: Bucky Walters, Cincinnati, 27

EARNED RUN AVERAGE
AL: Lefty Grove, Boston Red Sox, 2.54
NL: Bucky Walters, Cincinnati, 2.29

STRIKEOUTS
AL: Bob Feller, Cleveland, 246
NI: Claude Passeau, Chicago/Philadelphia, 137

SAVES
AL: Jonny Murphy, NY Yankees, 19
NL: Bob Bowman, St. Louis Cardinals; Clyde Shoun, St. Louis Cardinals, 9

BETTING PROHIBITED

As the career of one legend ended during the 1939 season, the career of another was just beginning. While New York Yankees' first baseman Lou Gehrig retired because of illness, the Boston Red Sox introduced an outfielder who would dominate the game—Ted Williams.

Many baseball fans thought Gehrig, the Yankees' powerful first baseman, would go on forever. His consecutive-games-played streak stood at 2,122 going into the season, but those close to the team knew that Gehrig's physical condition was declining rapidly. Not only was he struggling on the field, he was having trouble with simple tasks, like keeping his balance and tying his shoes.

Any hopes Gehrig would find his old form once the season started were dashed quickly. Through the first eight games of the season, he was batting .143 with no extra-base hits and one RBI, and covering first base on routine plays had become a chore. Prior to the May 2 game in Detroit, the Yankees announced Gehrig's streak would end at 2,130 straight games. Babe Dahlgren, acquired during the 1937 season,

replaced Gehrig at first base, and homered and doubled in New York's 22–2 win. The Yankees moved into first place on May 11 and remained there the rest of the season.

Doctors later discovered Gehrig had amyotrophic lateral sclerosis, an illness that affects the central nervous system. On June 21, the Yankees announced Gehrig was retiring, but would remain with the team as a captain. On July 4, the Yankees held "Lou Gehrig Day" at Yankee Stadium. A tearful Gehrig told fans, "I consider myself the luckiest man on the face of the earth." The Yankees retired Gehrig's No. 4, the first time a Major League player had his number retired. He was elected into the Baseball Hall of Fame in December as the normal five-year waiting rule was waived. Gehrig died in 1941.

Lou Gehrig says goodbye

In addition to Gehrig's retirement, the Yankees lost star center fielder Joe DiMaggio in the seventh game of the season with torn muscles in his foot. The injury occurred on April 29 while DiMaggio was fielding a line drive and he missed the next 35 games.

However, nothing stopped the Yankees from winning their fourth straight pennant. New York rolled to a 106–45 record—an astounding .702 winning percentage—and finished 17 games ahead of the Red Sox. The Yankees clinched the pennant on September 16 by beating Detroit.

DiMaggio, despite the missed time, was named the league's Most Valuable Player. He batted .381 with 30 home runs and 126 RBIs. Three other Yankees topped the 100-RBI mark. Second baseman Joe Gordon drove in 111 runs while batting .284 and hitting 28 homers. Left fielder George Selkirk knocked in 105 runs and batted .306 with 21 home runs. Catcher Bill Dickey had 105 RBIs and hit 24 homers.

Dahlgren, in replacing Gehrig, hit .235, but drove in 89 runs and hit 15 home runs.

The Yankees' biggest moment during the regular season came in a June 28 doubleheader against Philadelphia. The Yankees hit eight home runs in the first game and five more in the second while recording 53 total bases for the doubleheader. Both were Major League records. DiMaggio (who returned to the lineup on June 7), Dahlgren and Gordon each hit three home runs. The Yankees won the opener, 23–2, and the second game 10–0. The Yankees beat up on the A's again on August 13 with a 21–0 win, which equaled the record for lopsided shutouts.

Seven New York pitchers reached double figures in wins. Red Ruffing led the staff with a 21–7 record and a 2.93 ERA. Rookie Atley Donald won 13 games, including 12 straight at one point, Lefty Gomez, Bump Hadley and Monte Pearson each won 12, Steve Sundra won 11 and Oral Hildebrand won ten. Johnny Murphy saved a league-high 19 games.

The Red Sox had a solid season and finished with an 89–62 record, but they couldn't stay with the Yankees. Williams had a big impact in his rookie season. He began his career with a double off New York's Red Ruffing on April 20. Gehrig went hitless in the only game that featured the two great sluggers. The game also featured DiMaggio, Dickey, Jimmie Foxx, Joe Cronin, Bobby Doerr and Lefty Grove—all future Hall of Famers.

Williams led the American League with 145 RBIs, a rookie record for runs batted in for one season. He also batted .327 and hit 31 homers, while setting an AL record for walks by a rookie with 107. On May 4, in his first-ever at-bat in Detroit, Williams became the first player to totally clear right field at Briggs Stadium.

Williams wasn't the only Boston player to have a big season. Jimmie Foxx led the league with 35 homers while Lefty Grove had the league's lowest ERA (2.54). Foxx won the title despite missing most of the last month with appendicitis. He had season-ending surgery on September 9. The ERA title was the ninth of Grove's career. Cleveland's Bob Feller, still only 20 years old, became the youngest 20th century pitcher to win 20 games when he defeated

SHORTS
On August 26, the first Major League baseball game was telecast from Ebbets Field in Brooklyn, N.Y., as the Reds played the Dodgers in a doubleheader. Red Barber did the play-by-play of the broadcast, which was shown in New York City, over experimental station W2XBS.

TIMELINE

May 28: Robert Joyce, who gave up two home runs to the Yankees' George Selkirk the previous day, relieved for the A's. Selkirk hit two more homers off Joyce, which gave him four homers in four at-bats against the same pitcher in successive games.

July 3: Johnny Mize equaled a National League record with four extra-base hits, a double, triple, and two homers in the Cards' 5–3 win over the Cubs. Johnny Mize led the league with a .349 batting average and 28 home runs.

July 4: Jim Tabor of the Red Sox hit four homers as Boston swept Philadelphia, 17–7 and 18–12. Three of his homers, including a record-tying two grand slams, came in the nightcap. He totaled 19 bases and 11 RBIs in the doubleheader.

July 11: With another Yankee-dominated lineup, the AL defeated the NL, 3–1, in the seventh All-Star Game at Yankee Stadium.

July 15: A disputed call on a fly ball down the left-field foul line at the Polo Grounds touched off an argument in which the Giants' Billy Jurges and umpire George Magerkurth spat at each other. Both were fined $150 and suspended for ten days.

July 22: A Boston Bees fan, outraged when Al Lopez dropped a pop foul, his second and the team's seventh of the game, jumped from the stands to punch the Boston catcher.

Aug. 16: The Giants suspended second baseman Burgess Whitehead, who showed up the next day in full uniform at Yankee Stadium and asked to work out. Yankee manager Joe McCarthy refused. Whitehead rejoined the Giants a few days later, but he was suspended again in mid-September after leaving the team.

Aug. 28: Cleveland outfielder Jeff Heath punched a taunting fan leaning over the railing, but the umpires missed the incident and he went unpunished.

Hall of Famers: back row (l to r) Honus Wagner, Grover Alexander, Tris Speaker, Nap Lajoie, George Sisler and Walter Johnson; front row (l to r) Eddie Collins, Babe Ruth, Connie Mack, Cy Young

Red Barber was the voice that accompanied baseball's first telecast

St. Louis on September 8. Feller led the league with 24 wins and 246 strikeouts while losing nine games all season.

The Cincinnati Reds finished first in the National League with a 97–57 record. Although the Reds moved into first place for good on May 26, they didn't clinch the pennant until September 28 when pitcher Paul Derringer beat second-place St. Louis, 5–3. The Reds beat out the Cardinals by 4½ games. It was quite a turnaround for a team that finished last in 1937 with a 56–98 record.

Cincinnati was paced by pitcher Bucky Walters, who was named the National League's MVP. Walters led the league with 27 wins, while losing only 11, and ERA (2.29). He also tied Claude Passeau for the lead in strikeouts (137). Derringer finished with a 25–7 record while Whitey Moore and Junior Thompson won 13 apiece.

First baseman Frank McCormick paced the Reds' offense with a .332 batting average,

18 home runs and 128 RBIs, a league high. Right fielder Ival Goodman batted .323 with 84 RBIs while reliable catcher Ernie Lombardi hit 20 homers, drove in 85 runs and hit .287.

The dedication of the museum containing the Baseball Hall of Fame took place on June 12 in Cooperstown, New York. A six-inning game at Doubleday Field featured lineups filled with players who would be elected in the Hall in the future. Babe Ruth, Ty Cobb, Honus Wagner, Walter Johnson, Grover Alexander, Nap Lajoie, George Sisler, Eddie Collins, Tris Speaker, Cy Young and Connie Mack accepted their plaques.

SHORTS
In the second game of a July 2 doubleheader at the Polo Grounds, Dodgers player-manager Leo Durocher grounded into a double play and spiked Giants' first baseman Zeke Bonura as he crossed the bag. Bonura chased Durocher down the right-field line, threw his glove at him and wrestled him to the ground. Both players were ejected.

For the fifth straight season the New York Yankees reached the World Series. And for the fifth straight season their National League opponents failed to stop them. This time, the Yankees rolled to a four-game sweep of the Cincinnati Reds.

The Series began in New York where strong pitching and timely hitting led the Yankees to a 2–1 win. Red Ruffing held the Reds to four hits. Paul Derringer, who won 25 games in the regular season for Cincinnati, matched Ruffing until the ninth. Charlie "King Kong" Keller started the rally with a one-out triple. The Reds intentionally walked Joe DiMaggio, but Bill Dickey's single proved to be enough for the Yankees to win the game.

Game Two featured more good pitching by the Yankees in a 4–0 win. Monte Pearson pitched no-hit ball until catcher Ernie Lombardi singled with one out in the eighth. Pearson ended up with a two-hitter. Meanwhile, the Yankees got enough offense to win. First baseman Babe Dahlgren, who took over when Lou Gehrig was forced out of the game by declining health earlier in the season, doubled and homered.

The Series resumed at Crosley Field, but that didn't help the Reds. The Yankees homered four times and won 7–3. Keller hit two-run homers in the first and fifth, Joe DiMaggio hit a two-run homer in the third and Dickey added a solo shot in the fifth. That was enough for the Yankees' pitchers. Lefty Gomez and Bump Hadley combined for the win that gave the Yankees a 3–0 Series lead.

Game Four featured another memorable Series moment. The game was scoreless until the seventh inning when Keller and Dickey both homered. The Reds weren't done, though. They scored three unearned runs in the bottom of the inning and added another in the eighth for a 4–2 lead.

The Reds were three outs away from their first win, but the Yankees tied it in the ninth. Shortstop Billy Myers' error on a potential double-play ball helped one run score and the Yankees tied it when DiMaggio beat a throw to the plate on an infield hit.

DiMaggio's single put the Yankees ahead in the tenth. Right fielder Ival Goodman misplayed the ball and Keller, who was also on

Bill Dickey was one of several Yankees to get hot during the Series

base, headed home. Lombardi couldn't handle the throw and was knocked down by Keller. Lombardi was too stunned to retrieve the ball and DiMaggio raced all the way home to score. The Yankees won 7–4 to wrap up the Series.

WORLD SERIES		
GAME 1		
NY Yankees 2		Cincinnati 1
GAME 2		
NY Yankees 4		Cincinnati 0
GAME 3		
NY Yankees 7		Cincinnati 3
GAME 4		
NY Yankees 7		Cincinnati 4

LOU GEHRIG

TEAMS
New York Yankees 1923–39

Games:	2,164
At-Bats:	8,001
Runs:	1,888
RBI:	1,995
Home runs:	493
Hits:	2,721
Doubles:	535
Triples:	162
Stolen Bases:	102
Average:	.340
Slugging percentage:	.632

Had Lou Gehrig played for a team other than the New York Yankees, perhaps he would have been more readily noticed.

But the shy, soft-spoken Gehrig spent his entire career with the Yankees, being overshadowed first by the flamboyant Babe Ruth and later by the stylish Joe DiMaggio.

Gehrig's claim to fame is the streak of 2,130 consecutive games he played from 1925 to 1939. It was a record long thought to be unbreakable until Cal Ripken Jr. of the Baltimore Orioles finally surpassed it near the end of the twentieth century.

Ripken's streak turned into a national celebration. The day he voluntarily ended the streak was also a media event.

The star-crossed Gehrig saw his streak end because of the debilitating illness that would claim his life and bear his name.

Gehrig was the New York-born son of German immigrants. He was the only child of four to survive and his mother doted on her only son. Gehrig stayed in New York to attend Columbia University, where he batted .444 as a sophomore with a slugging percentage of .937. Gehrig had also set a school record by striking out 17 batters in a game he pitched for Columbia.

The Yankees were headquartered a few subway stops from Columbia's campus and were well aware of Gehrig's accomplishments in college. They wanted him to eschew college for a professional contract and there were rumors that Columbia coach Andy Coakley, a former major league player, was secretly paid $500 to try and influence Gehrig's decision.

He signed with the Yankees and left New York for the first time in his life. He didn't go far, though, spending two seasons with Hartford in the Eastern League. He debuted with the Yankees two days short of his 20th birthday and then spent brief parts of both the 1923 and '24 seasons with the Yankees.

He appeared in just 34 major league games before his streak started. The first of the 2,130 games was on May 31, 1925, when Gehrig was sent to pinch hit for Pee Wee Wanninger.

The next day regular first baseman Wally Pipp begged out of the starting lineup with a headache and Gehrig replaced him for the second game of the streak. Although legend has it that Gehrig won the job quickly, some circumstances should be noted.

The Yankees were having a miserable season and were seventh in the eight-team American League at the time Gehrig replaced Pipp. A team in that position is more likely to experiment with younger players to see if it can find a winning mix. The Yankees would finish the 1925 season in seventh place, 28½ games behind the pennant-winning Washington Senators.

Gehrig had established himself as a major league player by 1927. The Yankees installed him in the cleanup spot behind Ruth and Gehrig led the American League with 175 RBIs. His .373 batting average was second to Harry Heilman of Detroit.

The Yankees rolled on and so did Gehrig. For 13 consecutive seasons he scored at least 100 runs and drove in 100. In 1931, he set an American League record with 184 RBIs.

He took the Triple Crown in 1934 with a .363 average, 49 home runs and 165 RBIs. His streak continued despite a broken thumb, broken toe, back spasms and lumbago.

For the first time since he'd become a regular, Gehrig failed to finish with an average above .300 in 1938.

His streak ended the following year when it became obvious he was in physical distress. On May 2 he took himself out of the lineup and never played again. As team captain he would continue to take the lineup card to home plate, but even that had become a physical challenge.

The doctors gave Gehrig the grim news—he had an incurable condition known as arterial lateral sclerosis. It would come to commonly be known as "Lou Gehrig's disease," a devastating illness that gradually robbed its victims of their muscular function.

The Yankees staged Lou Gehrig Day on July 4, 1939. Gehrig made the famous speech in which he proclaimed himself the luckiest man on the face of the earth. The speech was recreated to great effect by actor Gary Cooper in the movie, *Pride of the Yankees*.

Gehrig was inducted into the Hall of Fame in a special election in 1939. He spent his last days working for New York mayor Fiorello LaGuardia.

Gehrig died on June 2, 1941, a few weeks short of his 38th birthday.

Lou Gehrig let his bat do the talking throughout his career

1940

Some of the game's biggest stars were wearing drab military uniforms instead of colorful baseball uniforms in the 1940s.

Night games became part of the routine, starting a trend that would eventually make most players nocturnal creatures.

Television became a factor, expanding the popularity of the game while also making teams wealthier with rights fees.

There were many significant developments in the 1940s, but none as significant as Jackie Robinson's breaking of the color line in the 1947 season.

Brooklyn Dodgers' general manager Branch Rickey enjoyed a reputation as an innovator, so it was no surprise that he would be the one to end the major league's voluntary boycott of black players. It was also no surprise that he chose the strong-willed Robinson as the player to endure the scrutiny of the pioneering effort.

Rickey's bold step changed baseball and changed attitudes. It also hastened the end of the Negro Leagues, whose best stars would be snapped up by major league teams in short order.

Attendance grew and short-sighted franchise operators came to realize that television was a promotional tool to be exploited rather than a rival to be feared.

Women played baseball to keep the game alive while men were at war and the available talent pool for the majors even included a one-armed outfielder, Pete Gray.

Change always comes with risk and the Detroit Tigers were taking on a considerable amount of risk. Detroit manager Del Baker had an idea and the Tigers' front office had some monetary incentives to back it up and make it more palatable to the parties involved.

The Tigers convinced first baseman Hank Greenberg to move to left field so they could get Rudy York's bat into the lineup on an everyday basis. Baker knew he was taking a gamble. If the moves worked, he'd look like a genius. If they flopped, the Tigers might have a disaster on their hands.

Fortunately for Baker, this move worked in a big way. York had hit 20 home runs in 1939 in a secondary role, backing up Greenberg at first base and also subbing for Birdie Tebbetts behind the plate. With Tebbetts entrenched in the catching position, a move was at least worth a try.

Greenberg's league-leading 41 home runs and 150 RBIs and York's 33 homers and 134 RBIs (second in the league) helped lead Baker's Tigers to the 1940 flag as they finished with a 90–64 record.

Also contributing to Detroit's success was a pitching staff anchored by Bobo Newsom, who posted a 21–5 record with a 2.63 ERA and Schoolboy Rowe with a flashy 16–3 record. Al Benton's 17 saves also helped.

The crown didn't come easily for the Tigers. The Cleveland Indians mounted a challenge that took the pennant race down to the wire.

Fireballing ace Bob Feller set the tone for the season by no-hitting the Chicago White Sox on Opening Day, April 16th. The fans who braved 47 degree temperatures and windy conditions in Comiskey Park saw history as their team lost 1–0 and every White Sox headed into the second game with the same .000 batting average he'd taken into the opener.

Feller went on to lead the league in strikeouts with 261, well ahead of Newsom's second place 164. He posted a record of 27–11 and an ERA of 2.61. Hal Trosky's 25 homeruns led Cleveland in that department and shortstop Lou Boudreau, in his first full major league season, drove in 101 runs and batted a respectable .295.

Despite their success on the field the Cleveland clubhouse was far from a happy one. Manager Ossie Vitt was overtly insulting to his players when they didn't perform well. Even Feller did not escape Vitt's barbs. If "Rapid Robert" had a rare off day, Vitt would disparage him not only in front of his teammates but within earshot of fans in attendance as well.

Things became so bad that on June 16th the Cleveland players presented a petition to Indian's owner Alva Bradley calling for him to

Hank Greenberg's impressive numbers helped Detroit to the Fall Classic

The Reds' Frank McCormick

Frank Crosetti and Bill Dickey saw their home run totals drop to single digits.

In 1939, five of the regulars hit better than .300. In 1940 only one player, Joe DiMaggio, repeated—and he did it impressively. He coasted to his second consecutive batting title with a .352 average.

In mid-September the Tigers dislodged the Indians from the top spot and expanded their lead to two games on Sept. 21 with a crucial shutout by Schoolboy Rowe over Cleveland. On the 27th, the Indians sent their ace, Feller, against the Tigers, who needed a victory to clinch the pennant. In one of those classic storybook moves, Baker called upon rookie pitcher Floyd Giebell to pitch the critical game. Feller allowed only three Tiger hits, but it was Giebell who got the shutout and clinched the flag for Detroit with a 2–0 win to give the Tigers their first pennant since 1935.

The Boston Red Sox and Chicago White Sox tied for fourth place with identical 82–72 records. Jimmie Foxx's 36 home runs and Ted Williams' .344 batting average, third in the League, topped the Red Sox offense. White Sox shortstop Luke Appling finished second in the league with a .348 average.

The fifth-place St. Louis Browns boasted five players with homers in double figures, topped by center fielder Walt Judnich's 24. Bucky Harris' Washington Senators finished sixth as Sid Hudson was their only pitcher with a winning record, posting a 17–16 mark. Connie Mack's Philadelphia Athletics finished in the cellar, despite "Bullet" Bob Johnson's 31 home runs and 103 RBIs.

The National League race wasn't nearly as dramatic, however.

The Brooklyn Dodgers reeled off nine consecutive wins at the start of the season, tying a League record set by the 1918 New York Giants. The streak was capped with a no-hitter by Tex Carleton against the Cincinnati Reds. The 33-year-old righthander had not pitched in the majors since 1938. Brooklyn signed him in the off-season as a free agent after he was dropped by the minor league Milwaukee Millers. Carleton allowed only four Reds base runners, two on walks and two on errors.

Following that defeat, the Reds began their pennant drive and were in first place by mid-July, thanks in part to the efforts of their catcher Ernie Lombardi, whose .319 average was second in the league, even though Lombardi suffered several injuries during the season. Their pitching staff was anchored by Bucky Walters, who sported a 22–10 record with a 2.48 ERA and

dismiss Vitt. Bradley chose to ignore the petition and some followers of the game branded the players "Crybabies". But by the end of the month, the Indians were in first place and held on to the lead until mid-September when the defending champion New York Yankees took over for one game by defeating the Indians in the first game of a doubleheader. Cleveland regained first place by winning the nightcap.

The Yankees were in the hunt despite a horrible start that saw them in the cellar at one point in May. They gradually started a charge that put them into contention and kept them there until the end of the season when they finished with an 88–66 record. The reasons for the Yankees' slide are hard to pinpoint, but some comparisons with the 1939 team might provide some answers.

Although the pitching staff and starting eight were virtually the same, the 1939 starters all produced home runs in double figures. In 1940

SHORTS Washington Senators' pitcher Sid Hudson learned firsthand that baseball can be a rollercoaster ride. He went from Class D in 1939 to a 17–16 major league record in 1940, capping his season with a one-hitter against Connie Mack's Athletics. Hudson would go on to pitch for 12 years in the majors.

Willard Hershberger's suicide was the obvious low-point of the Reds otherwise great season

Paul Derringer, who went 20–12. First baseman Frank McCormick, who won the Most Valuable Player award, drove in 127 runs, second in the league to Johnny Mize's 137.

The Dodgers remained in the chase until mid-August when their speedy shortstop Pee Wee Reese broke his foot, leaving player-manager Leo Durocher and utility infielder Johnny Hudson to share duties at short for the remainder of the season. At about the same time, they also lost third baseman Cookie Lavagetto to appendicitis and Pete Reiser filled in for him.

The season's only managerial casualty occurred when Cardinal owner Sam Breadon fired Ray Blades after a dismal 14–24 start. Interim skipper Mike Gonzalez managed only one win in six games before the Redbirds hired Billy Southworth from the Rochester minor league team to manage the team for the remainder of the season. Southworth turned the team around with an impressive 69–40 record for the rest of the season. The Cardinals' bright spot was first baseman Johnny Mize, who slugged a League-leading 43 home runs to set a club mark that would stand until 1998 when Mark McGwire shattered all records with 70.

Bill McKechnie's Reds clinched the National League flag on September 18, finishing the season 12 games ahead of Brooklyn with 100 wins. But their season was not without tragedy. On August 3, second-string catcher Willard Hershberger returned to his room at the Copley Plaza Hotel in Boston and took his own life by slashing his throat. He had been hitting a respectable .309 as Lombardi's backup, but was reportedly despondent over what he perceived as his role in a recent loss to the Giants.

Cincinnati's catching woes were further compounded when Lombardi suffered a sprained ankle in September and 39-year-old player-coach Jimmie Wilson had to take over behind the plate. Fortunately for the Reds, Wilson did an outstanding job and was a major contributor to the team's World Series victory over Detroit.

The Pittsburgh Pirates finished fourth behind Cincinnati, Brooklyn and St. Louis. But they had the league's leading hitter in the unlikely person of third baseman Debs Garms, who had joined the team on May 3 after being purchased from the Boston Braves. Garms, playing a secondary role, accumulated just 358 at bats, but it was enough to let him to win the batting title with a .355 average.

The fifth-place Chicago Cubs had a 20-game winner in Claude Passeau (20–13) and the legendary Dizzy Dean started nine games for them, compiling a 3–3 record before being sent down to Tulsa in an attempt to revive his sore arm.

The Cubs' ace Claude Passeau

Veteran Mel Ott's 19 homers and Dale Young's 101 RBIs were tops for Bill Terry's sixth place New York Giants. Casey Stengel's Boston Braves finished seventh, but boasted the National League's All-Star Game hero as Max West's three-run shot in the first sparked the National League's 4–0 win, the first shutout in the short history of the All-Star Game.

Doc Prothro's last-place Philadelphia Phillies got a charge from left fielder Johnny Rizzo, acquired at the trade deadline from Cincinnati for Morie Arnovich. Rizzo's 20 home runs were tops for the Phils.

SHORTS Debs Garms of the Pittsburgh Pirates may be a relatively obscure name among batting champions because he barely had enough times at bat to qualify for the crown. But consider this: In his previous two seasons with the Boston Braves, he batted 941 times and got 288 hits for a .306 average. His career average was a respectable .293.

GAME 1	
Detroit 7	Cincinnati 2
GAME 2	
Cincinnati 5	Detroit 3
GAME 3	
Detroit 7	Cincinnati 4
GAME 4	
Cincinnati 5	Detroit 2
GAME 5	
Detroit 8	Cincinnati 0
GAME 6	
Cincinnati 4	Detroit 0
GAME 7	
Cincinnati 2	Detroit 1

This time the Cincinnati Reds had a World Series championship that was free of any suspicion. They earned their seven-game win over the Detroit Tigers.

The Reds may have earned the 1919 Series win over the Chicago White Sox as well. But eight White Sox players were accused of conspiring to fix the Series by throwing games to earn a payoff from gamblers.

There were conflicting stories over the years and evidence began to mount that the outcomes of the 1919 games were legitimate. Still, the Reds' victory in eight games always carried the taint of what came to be known as the "Black Sox Scandal."

This time the Reds had a fairly easy path to the postseason. They clinched the pennant on September 18, holding off both the Brooklyn Dodgers and the St. Louis Cardinals, who made a late rush at first place.

The key to success for the Reds was an airtight defense. Cincinnati made only 117 errors, which set a record for the fewest errors in a major league season. The Reds had 18 fewer miscues than the previous record holder. Their .981 fielding percentage also set a record.

Aided by the Reds' amazing defense, Bucky Walters went 22–10

The fielding efficiency made a good pitching staff even better. Bucky Walters was 22–10 and Paul Derringer was 20–12. Just behind them was Junior Thompson with a 16–9 mark.

The Reds were back in the Series for a second consecutive year. Their 1939 season ended with disappointment when the New York Yankees swept them in four games, but they rebounded from that to win 100 games and finish 12 games ahead of the pack.

The Detroit Tigers had a tighter race, finishing just one game in front of both Cleveland and New York.

In Game One, it was a familiar story. The Tigers won 7–2 in Cincinnati, stretching the American League's winning streak to ten games. Detroit got five runs in the second off Derringer. Bruce Campbell hit a two-run homer later for the Tigers and Bobo Newsom protected the lead.

The streak of American League dominance ended the next day as Walters won 5–3. Jimmy Ripple hit a two-run homer in the second inning to make the difference. It was the first National League win in a Series game since Carl Hubbell of the Giants beat the Yankees in 1937.

The Tigers staged a late-inning comeback against Jim Turner to win Game Three, 7–4, in Detroit. Tommy Bridges pitched a complete game for the win.

Derringer ended a personal streak of four Series starts without a win in Game Four. He allowed five hits in a complete game 5–2 win. Ripple hit a third-inning double to knock out starter Dizzy Trout.

Detroit took the lead again in Game Five with Newson's 8–0 complete game. Newsom allowed only three hits, walked two and struck out seven. Hank Greenberg drove in four runs, three of them with a homer.

Facing elimination, the Reds called on Walters and he pitched as well as Newsom had in the previous game for the Tigers. Walters had a five-hitter and the Reds won 4–0 to even the Series. It was a big day all the way around for Walters, who became the first pitcher to hit a home run in the Series for 14 years.

With the Series on the line, the Tigers called on Newsom to start with one day's rest. He held the Reds scoreless through the first six innings and had a 1–0 lead because of an unearned run in the third inning off Derringer.

Newsom tired in the seventh and the Reds took advantage. Frank McCormick and Ripple hit back-to-back doubles to tie the score at 1–1. Jimmy Wilson moved McCormick to third with a bunt and Billy Myers' sacrifice fly put the Reds ahead.

Derringer was perfect over the last three

innings and the Reds claimed the title.

One of the unsung heroes of the Series was Wilson, a 40 year-old who had started the season as one of the Reds' coaches. He wound up starting six of the seven games in the Series.

The Reds had a catching crisis during the season as first-stringer Ernie Lombardi was bothered by recurring injuries throughout the season. The last came on September 15 and affected his availability for the Series. Cincinnati was short in catching following the midseason suicide of backup Willard Hershberger, who took his own life while the club was on a trip to Boston. Wilson was activated and hit .353 in the Series after appearing in only 16 games during the regular season.

Series stars Paul Derringer and Billy Myers

JIMMIE FOXX

TEAMS:
Philadelphia Athletics 1925–35; Boston Red Sox 1936–42; Chicago Cubs 1942, 1944; Philadelphia Phillies 1945.

Games:	2,317
At-Bats:	8,134
Runs:	1,751
RBI:	1,921
Home runs:	534
Hits:	2,646
Doubles:	458
Triples:	125
Stolen Bases:	87
Average:	325
Slugging percentage:	609

A three-time MVP, Foxx also played in nine All-Star games

Jimmie Foxx hit home runs two ways— deep and often.

Foxx earned the nickname "The Righthanded Babe Ruth" for the power shows that he provided during his 20-year career with three teams.

Foxx more than held his own as a home run hitter, leading the League four times. That he did so while competing against the likes of Ruth and Lou Gehrig and then Hank Greenberg and Joe DiMaggio speaks both to his ability and consistency.

It is ironic that Foxx was discovered by former major leaguer Frank "Home Run" Baker, who was impressed with the Maryland schoolboy's raw ability. Baker owed a favor to longtime Philadelphia Athletics owner Connie Mack, so he steered Foxx to Mack.

Foxx signed with the Athletics as a catcher but didn't play much at any position. He joined the team as a 17-year-old, but spent most of the first three years of his career on the bench. In his first three seasons, 1925–27, Foxx got only 171 at-bats.

The Athletics didn't have a need at catcher so Foxx was converted to first base and became a regular at that position in 1928. His first season was a success as he hit .328 with 13 home runs and an impressive 79 RBIs. By the next year, he had established himself as one of the game's premier players at age 22—he batted .354 with 33 home runs and 117 RBIs.

Foxx would combine power and average throughout his career. He won the Triple Crown in 1933 with a .356 average, 48 home runs and 163 RBIs. He just missed another Triple Crown in 1938 when Greenberg hit 58 home runs to beat him in that category. Foxx drove in 175 runs in 1938.

Despite a pleasant disposition and a rather normal physique (6 feet, 195 pounds), Foxx was tagged with the name "The Beast" because of his power.

In addition to the statistics he was amassing, Foxx was leaving his mark on parks throughout the American League. In Chicago's Comiskey Park, they talked about the blast he hit that cleared the left-field roof and was estimated to have traveled 600 feet.

In Yankee Stadium, a Foxx home run reached the upper deck with such force that it shattered a wooden seat. He won Game Five of the 1930 World Series with a home run that was considered the longest blast ever in Sportsman's Park.

Foxx made the first All-Star team in 1933 and was a member of every one through 1941. He was the American League's Most Valuable Player in 1932, '33 and '38. He led the League in batting average twice, topped the League in home runs four times and took four RBI titles.

He had at least 100 RBIs in 13 consecutive seasons, which matched the record set by Ruth and Gehrig. He had a chance to match or break Ruth's single-season home run record in 1932, but two factors conspired against him—Foxx injured his wrist in August and he ran into a right-field screen in St. Louis that had been installed after Ruth hit 60 home runs in 1927. Historian Fred Lieb claimed that Foxx hit the screen five times in 1932 and settled for doubles that would have been home runs without the barrier.

Foxx hit 30 or more home runs for 12 consecutive seasons. He stayed with Philadelphia through 1935 before he moved to the Boston Red Sox for some productive seasons. He became an unofficial mentor for Ted Williams who said of Foxx, "I never saw anyone hit a baseball harder."

Foxx spent the waning days of his career in the National League, but his best days were clearly in the past. In 1942 he batted just .205 for the Chicago Cubs and followed that up with a .050 average in very limited play.

His last season was back in Philadelphia, this time with the Phillies, and he finished with a respectable .268 mark. Foxx even pitched in a few games at the end of his career.

Post-baseball, Foxx managed in the minor leagues and also spent a season announcing Red Sox games. He was elected to the Hall of Fame in 1951.

Foxx met a tragic end, choking to death on a piece of meat while eating dinner with his brother in 1967. He was just 59 when he died.

Foxx's towering home runs became legendary around the league

MOST VALUABLE PLAYER
AL: Joe DiMaggio, NY Yankees
NL: Dolph Camilli, Brooklyn

LEADERS
BATTING AVERAGE
AL: Ted Williams, Boston Red Sox, .406
NL: Pete Reiser, Brooklyn, .343

HOME RUNS
AL: Ted Williams, Boston Red Sox, 37
NL: Dolph Camilli, Brooklyn, 34

RUNS BATTED IN
AL: Joe DiMaggio, NY Yankees, 125
NL: Dolph Camilli, Brooklyn, 120

STOLEN BASES
AL: George Case, Washington, 33
NL: Danny Murtaugh, Philadelphia Phillies, 18

PITCHING VICTORIES
AL: Bob Feller, Cleveland, 25
NL: Whitlow Wyatt; Kirby Higbe, Brooklyn, 22

EARNED RUN AVERAGE
AL: Thornton Lee, Chicago White Sox, 2.37
NL: Elmer Riddle, Cincinnati, 2.24

STRIKEOUTS
AL: Bob Feller, Cleveland, 260
NL: Johnny Vander Meer, Cincinnati, 202

"The Splendid Splinter" warms up

It was considered by many to be baseball's dream season. There's no question it was for Joe DiMaggio and Ted Williams. Arguably the game's best two players, they were united in pursuit of statistical achievements that would stand for the rest of the century.

DiMaggio's 56-game hitting streak and Williams' .406 batting average loom even larger when you realize that the most serious challenges to them have fallen considerably short of the mark.

Fittingly, the teams of these two immortals, the New York Yankees and Boston Red Sox, finished first and second respectively. The Yankees rebounded from their third-place finish in 1940, thanks not only to DiMaggio's hitting (he finished with a .357 average, making six consecutive seasons that he hit better than .300. though he failed to surpass Williams to take his third straight batting title), but to 30-plus home run seasons from DiMaggio (31) and fellow outfielders Charlie Keller (33) and Tommy Heinrich (31). Lefty Gomez's 15–5 record was tops on a staff that saw no standouts but got the job done.

Nearly overshadowed by his .406 batting average were Williams' league-leading 37 home runs and 120 RBIs, placing him fourth in that category behind DiMaggio, Cleveland's Jeff Heath and the Yankees' Charlie Keller, denying Williams the Triple Crown in what was otherwise a stellar season for the man known as "The Splendid Splinter". Pitcher Dick Newsome's 19–10 record topped Boston's pitching staff, but the Yankees finished 17 games in front of the Red Sox.

The Chicago White Sox were a distant third, finishing at the .500 mark, but they could boast one of the league's two 20 game winners. Left hander Thornton Lee's 22–11 record was accented by a 2.37 ERA.

The other 20-game winner was Cleveland's Bob Feller, with a 25–13 record. Cleveland players finally got their wish in the off-season when owner Alva Bradley fired manager Ossie Vitt on December 12. But new skipper Roger

Peckinpaugh was unable to get the Tribe over the .500 mark and the loss of first baseman Hal Trosky to a broken finger for much of the season didn't help. Right fielder Jeff Heath (.340 batting average, 120 RBIs and 18 stolen bases) was a bright spot in an otherwise disappointing season.

Del Baker's defending champion Detroit Tigers ended up in a fourth place tie with their rival Indians. The escalation of the war in Europe and the imminent involvement of the United States military affected the Tigers profoundly when, after 19 games, Hank Greenberg, 1940's Most Valuable Player, reported for duty in the United States Army. Rudy York's 27 home runs and Barney McCoskey's .324 average took up the slack somewhat.

Tigers staff ace Bobo Newsom went from a 21 game winning season in 1940 to a league-leading 20 losses in 1941.

The St. Louis Browns had the only managerial casualty of the season as Fred Haney's 15–29 start resulted in his dismissal. Luke Sewell took over and was able to muster them to an even

TIMELINE

Feb. 15: Babe Dahlgren, who succeeded Lou Gehrig as the Yankees' first baseman, was sold to the Boston Braves.

March 19: Paul "Daffy" Dean, brother of the legendary Dizzy Dean, was signed by the New York Giants.

April 14: The Sporting News, in its Opening Day edition, picked the Cincinnati Reds to repeat in the National League but predicted the Cleveland Indians would take the American League title.

April 26: Wrigley Field became the first major league park to employ an organist. Roy Nelson played better than the Cubs, who lost to the Cardinals, 6–2.

May 15: Joe DiMaggio began his record-setting 56-game hitting streak with a single off Ed Smith of the White Sox.

May 17: "Connie Mack Day" was declared a Pennsylvania state holiday and the Athletics manager was honored at Shibe Park.

June 1: The Dodgers won their ninth consecutive game.

June 2: Lou Gehrig died at age 37.

July 17: Joe DiMaggio's streak was stopped, thanks primarily to two outstanding fielding plays by Indians' third baseman Ken Keltner, who robbed DiMaggio of sure hits both times.

Aug. 1: Yankee pitcher Lefty Gomez set a new major league record, walking 11 St. Louis Browns in his 9–0 shutout.

Sept. 1: Rudy York, continuing to fill the void left by the departure of Hank Greenberg to military service, hit 3 home runs for the Detroit Tigers.

Sept. 10: Johnny Schmitz threw only one pitch in his major league debut for the Chicago Cubs, but was credited with the win over Brooklyn.

Sept. 29: The National League champion Brooklyn Dodgers were honored with a tickertape parade attended by over a million jubilant fans.

Nov. 25: Cleveland shortstop Lou Boudreau, after only his second full season in the big leagues, was named player manager of the Indians at age 24.

Bobo Newsom—from the sublime to the ridiculous

Largely overshadowed by Joe DiMaggio's streak is the fact that up until early May, he had been in a terrible slump. Held hitless on May 5th by Bobo Newsom and the Tigers, he had hit only .162 over the span of 12 games.

55–55 record for the rest of the season, tying them with the Washington Senators for fifth place.

Dutch Leonard, just 22 years old, was tops on the Washington Senators staff with an 18–13 record. Connie Mack's Philadelphia A's finished in the cellar again, but got continued power from Bob Johnson (22 home runs and 107 RBIs) and Ben Chapman (25 home runs and 106 RBIs).

DiMaggio's amazing streak began on May 15 and ended on July 17 against the Indians when he failed to get a hit off either Al Smith or Jim Bagby. However, two sparkling defensive plays by third baseman Ken Keltner probably kept him from extending the streak. In his very next game, DiMaggio began a new hitting streak of 16 games.

On the saddest development of the season, former Yankee first baseman Lou Gehrig, whose "Iron Horse" record of 2,130 consecutive games

was thought to be unbreakable at the time, succumbed to the form of lateral sclerosis that forced him out of baseball and would eventually bear his name.

The All-Star Game, played on July 8 at Detroit's Briggs Stadium, had its most dramatic finish to date when Ted Williams stepped to the plate to face the Cubs' Claude Passeau, who had loaded the bases by walking the Senators' Cecil Travis, then yielded a run-scoring grounder by DiMaggio. Williams hit a three-run shot into the upper right field stands to win the game for the American League.

In the National League, a third straight flag for Bill McKechnie's Cincinnati club was not to be. The Reds never recovered from a slow start. Frank McCormick, 1940's Most Valuable Player, dropped 40 points in batting average and his RBI total declined by 30. Elmer Riddle and Bucky Walters managed 19 wins each, but Paul Derringer's numbers dropped from 20–12 the previous season to 12–14 in 1941.

The pennant race belonged to the Brooklyn Dodgers and St. Louis Cardinals, who battled for the crown until late September. Among the many keys to the Dodgers' success was their early May

The Cardinals' Jack Hallett, John Rigney and Thornton Lee

acquisition of Cubs' second baseman Billy Herman in exchange for Johnny Hudson, Charlie Gilbert and $65,000 cash. Brooklyn owner Larry MacPhail believed that if his team was going to contend seriously, it needed a more productive bat at the second base position than Pete Coscarart. Herman, in New York with the Cubs for a game against the Giants at the Polo Grounds, took a subway, got off near Ebbets Field and walked in, donned a Dodger uniform for the first time and belted four hits in four at-bats for his Brooklyn debut.

The next day the Cardinals, in first place by a half game, came to Brooklyn for a two-game set which the Dodgers swept to take over the top spot by a game and a half. Three weeks later, the two clubs were tied for first.

By the All-Star break, the Dodgers had a three-game lead over St. Louis, who again came in for a two-game series which they swept. By July 31, the Redbirds held a two-game lead over Brooklyn. On August 30, after again falling behind the Dodgers, the Cardinals got a lift from Lon Warneke, who tossed a no-hitter against Cincinnati for his 15th win of the season, giving them first place by two percentage points.

The Dodgers got hot again and within a week after Labor Day had taken a three-game lead over the Cardinals. But they dropped a doubleheader to the Cubs while the Cardinals swept Philadelphia in a twinbill to move within one game of Brooklyn. The Dodgers came to St. Louis for a critical four-game series, which they split.

After sweeping the New York Giants and pulling to within 1½ games of the Dodgers, the Cardinals called three players up from the minors. One of them was a first baseman from Donora, Pennsylvania named Stan Musial, who had gone home after his Rochester Red Wings were eliminated from the International League playoffs.

Musial had started the season for Class C Springfield, Illinois of the Western Association where he hit an impressive .379 with 27 home runs and 94 RBIs in just 87 games before advancing to the Rochester club and hitting .326 in 54 games. Musial made his major league debut on September 17 against Boston and had two hits in four at bats.

Despite Musial's sensational .426 batting

The Pirates' Vince DiMaggio

average in September, the Cardinals finished the race 2½ games behind Brooklyn. With four regulars hitting better than .300 and a solid pitching staff with six pitchers posting wins in double figures (including a phenomenal 10–0 record by Howie Krist), St. Louis remained in the chase throughout.

Contributing to Brooklyn's success were Most Valuable Player Dolph Camilli, who belted a league-leading 34 home runs with 120 RBIs, and center fielder Pete Reiser, whose .343 batting average was tops in the circuit. Kirby Higbe and Whitlow Wyatt each posted 22 wins and Wyatt went on to pitch two impressive complete games in the Dodgers' World Series loss to the Yankees, winning one and losing one.

Vince DiMaggio, Joe's older brother, hit 21 home runs and drove in 100 runs for Frankie Frisch's fourth-place Pittsburgh Pirates and Mel Ott continued his stellar career for the New York Giants with 27 roundtrippers. He had hit his 400th career home run, and driven in his 1500th run, on June 1.

Jimmie Wilson, after that great clutch performance for Cincinnati in the 1940 World Series, took over the helm in Chicago from Gabby Hartnett, but the Cubs dropped from fifth in 1940 to sixth place in 1941. The previous year's All-Star hero, Max West, topped the Boston Braves with only 12 home runs, but the Braves made other news when they were sold by the Charles Adams estate to 12 Boston businessmen for $350,000. Danny Lithweiler, with a .305 batting average and 18 homers was the standout for Doc Prothro's Philadelphia Phillies, who finished in the basement again.

SHORTS Pirates' manager Frankie Frisch unwittingly inspired a classic Norman Rockwell oil painting when he stepped onto Ebbets Field carrying an umbrella, cursing the playing conditions, and taunting umpire Jocko Conlan to toss him from the second game of their doubleheader on August 19. The ever-compliant Conlan was more than willing to oblige the Pirates skipper.

GAME 1	
NY Yankees 3	Brooklyn 2
GAME 2	
Brooklyn 3	NY Yankees 2
GAME 3	
NY Yankees 2	Brooklyn 1
GAME 4	
Brooklyn 7	NY Yankees 4
GAME 5	
NY Yankees 3	Brooklyn 1

Strike three ... You're out. Only the first part of that was true and therein lies the tale of the 1940 World Series, because striking out Tommy Henrich turned out to be the worst thing to happen to the Brooklyn Dodgers.

The Dodgers were already trailing 2–1 in games in the Series when Henrich came to bat in the ninth inning of Game Four. Brooklyn led the game 4–3 in the ninth inning and seemed to be on its way to closing out the game and bringing the Series even at two games apiece on their home field.

Brooklyn had fallen behind 3–0, but overcame that deficit as Jimmy Wasdell pinch hit a double in the fourth, followed by Pete Reiser's two-run homer an inning later.

The ninth opened quietly against reliever Hugh Casey, who had pitched out of a bases loaded jam in the fifth inning. Johnny Sturm grounded out to open the Yankees' ninth and Red Rolfe was retired the same way.

It appeared the game was over when Henrich swung and missed at Hugh Casey's two-strike pitch. But catcher Mickey Owen couldn't handle the ball and Henrich was able to reach first safely. The Yankees turned that small break into a stunning turnaround that won Game Four and sent them on their way to taking the Series a day later.

After Owen reached first, Joe DiMaggio singled. Charlie Keller lined a double into the gap that scored two runs and put New York ahead 5–4. Bill Dickey drew a walk and Joe Gordon doubled to score two more runs and make the score 7–4.

Johnny Murphy retired the Dodgers in order in the bottom of the ninth and the Yankees won to take a commanding 3–1 lead in games—all because of a mishandled third strike.

"The ball was a low curve that broke down," Owen said. "It hit the edge of my glove and glanced off, but I should have had it."

The Yankees needed the break because their offense hadn't kicked into gear.

New York won the opener 3–2 as Gordon hit a home run and drove in a pair of runs to support Red Ruffing. Brooklyn came back to win Game Two on the same score with Whitlow Wyatt on the mound.

The Yankees got an odd break to win Game Three. Freddie Fitzsimmons of the Dodgers and the Yankees' Marius Russo were in a scoreless game in the seventh inning.

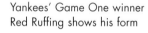

Yankees' Game One winner
Red Ruffing shows his form

Russo lined a ball off the leg of Fitzsimmons, that knocked the Dodgers' starter out with a broken kneecap.

Brooklyn manager Leo Durocher switched to Casey, who didn't pitch well. He allowed four hits and two runs in the eighth inning and the Dodgers went on to lose the game 2–1.

That set up the improbable scenario that led to the Yankees' comeback in Game Four. Henrich, who batted just .167 in the Series, helped to spark a victory by swinging and missing.

"I'll bet Mickey feels like a nickel's worth of dog meat," Henrich said afterward. "That was a tough break for him."

Henrich had a home run in Game Five as the Yankees won 3–1 behind the four-hit pitching of Tiny Bonham.

While Owen's gaffe obviously turned the Series, it wasn't the only reason the Dodgers lost. Brooklyn compiled a team batting average of just .182 with one home run in five games.

Among the everyday players, Joe Medwick had the highest Series batting average and he hit only .235. Right fielder Dixie Walker batted .222 while Reiser and shortstop Pee Wee Reese each hit .200. Dolph Camilli and Owen each batted .167.

The powerful Yankees didn't do much better with the bats after running away with the American League pennant by a margin of 19 games. New York hit .247 as a team during the Series and had only two home runs.

Gordon had seven hits in 14 at bats to lead the Yankees with a .500 average. Keller hit .389 and Rolfe batted .300. While the rest of the players were well below their regular season averages, including DiMaggio, who batted .263 in the Series.

The Yankees' staff compiled a 1.80 ERA. Murphy, New York's top reliever, didn't allow a run in his six innings over two games and Ruffing and Bonham were each charged with a single earned run in their starts.

Brooklyn's manager Leo Durocher lets out his frustrations

AWARDS

MOST VALUABLE PLAYER
AL: Joe Gordon, NY Yankees
NL: Mort Cooper, St. Louis Cardinals

LEADERS

BATTING AVERAGE
AL: Ted Williams, Boston Red Sox .356
NL: Ernie Lombardi, Boston Braves .330

HOME RUNS
AL: Ted Williams, Boston Red Sox, 36
NL: Mel Ott, NY Giants, 30

RUNS BATTED IN
AL: Ted Williams, Boston Red Sox, 137
NL: Johnny Mize, NY Giants, 110

STOLEN BASES
AL: George Case, Washington, 44
NL: Pete Reiser, Brooklyn, 20

PITCHING VICTORIES
AL: Tex Hughson, Boston Red Sox, 22
NL: Mort Cooper, St. Louis Cardinals, 22

EARNED RUN AVERAGE
AL: Ted Lyons, Chicago White Sox, 2.10
NL Mort Cooper, St. Louis Cardinals, 1.78

STRIKEOUTS
AL: Bobo Newsom, Washington;
    Tex Hughson, Boston Red Sox 113
NL: Johnny Vander Meer, Cincinnati 186

In a climate of World War II and a loss of life already too enormous for many Americans to fathom, it isn't surprising that baseball must have seemed insignificant to many.

Bob Feller was one of many major league stars whose career were halted by the war

Whether it was this sentiment or just an insincere gesture on the part of Commissioner Kenesaw Mountain Landis, his letter to President Franklin D. Roosevelt asking what he should do about baseball while the war was on prompted a response that struck a popular chord with Americans at home and abroad.

"I honestly feel that it would be best for the country to keep baseball going," wrote the President.

A longtime friend of Washington Senators' owner Calvin Griffith and a frequent visitor to Senators' home games, Roosevelt knew military service had already claimed some key players—

most notably Hank Greenberg. Many more would follow. But he also knew the importance of morale both on the home front and with the troops abroad at a time when uncertainty was breeding fear in American hearts.

So the 1942 season began with most of the game's stars still in tow. A notable exception was Indians' hurler Bob Feller, who had posted 76 wins in the past three seasons for Cleveland and led the league in strikeouts for the past four.

Cleveland also made news with another off-season move when the Indians announced that 24-year-old Lou Boudreau would manage the club. Boudreau had just completed only his second full season as a major league player. He would continue to play, of course, but would also pilot the club from his shortstop position.

Although the President had alluded to the increased use of "older players" in his letter to Landis, the fact is that at the start of the 1942 season a record number of rookies—100 to be exact—were on major league rosters.

SHORTS Cleveland pitcher Jim Tobin's pinch-hit home run on May 12 and his three consecutive shots the next day were part of a bizarre season for the Indians righthander. He hit six home runs altogether in the season, led the league in pitching losses with 21, complete games with 28 and innings pitched with 288.

The World Champion New York Yankees, sparked by the continued production of Joe DiMaggio (21 home runs, 114 runs batted in) and Charlie Keller (26 home runs, 108 RBIs) and the outstanding pitching of Ernie "Tiny" Bonham (21–5 with a 2.27 earned run average) ran away with their second straight pennant, finishing nine games ahead of the Boston Red Sox. Yankee second baseman Joe Gordon's 18 home runs, 103 RBIs and .322 batting average earned him Most Valuable Player honors.

Presenting a strong challenge to Gordon's MVP selection was Boston's Ted Williams, who captured the Triple Crown with a .356 batting average, 36 home runs and 137 RBIs. Some sportswriters cited Gordon's defensive play, despite the fact that he committed 28 errors at second base, the most in that position. More than likely, it was Gordon's offensive presence on a championship club that swayed the voting, coupled with Williams' sometimes-stormy relationship with the writers.

The other standouts for the Boston club were pitcher Tex Hughson, who topped the league with 22 wins, and shortstop Johnny Pesky in his rookie year. The aptly named Pesky belted a league leading 205 hits.

Williams enlisted in the Navy in June, but asked to finish out the season in order to make sure his mother was financially secure before he reported for overseas duty. The request didn't set well with many patriotic Americans, who didn't fully understand Williams' reasons for waiting.

The surprise team of the season, however, was the third place St. Louis Browns who finished above the .500 mark for the first time since 1929. At one point the Browns reeled off an eight-game winning streak. Veteran right fielder Chet Laabs sparked the St. Louis offense with 27 home runs and 99 RBIs.

Despite an early season streak of 13 consecutive wins, the Cleveland Indians, hurt by the loss of Feller and the retirement of first baseman Hal Trosky due to untreatable migraine headaches, finished fourth, four games under .500.

The Detroit Tigers continued to get power from first baseman Rudy York, who slugged 21 home runs. The Tigers also got an encouraging performance from rookie pitcher Virgil Trucks, who sported an impressive 14–8 record and 2.73 ERA.

Forty-one-year-old Ted Lyons achieved his 250th career victory and anchored the Chicago White Sox pitching staff with a 14–6 record, but the entire Sox team could only muster a total of 24 home runs, 12 less than league leader Williams had hit himself.

The Washington Senators, finishing seventh, could boast league leaders in triples (Stan Spence with 15), stolen bases (George Case with 44), and strikeouts (Bobo Newsom, who was purchased from Detroit prior to the start of the season, had 113 to tie with Boston's Tex Hughson in that department). Newsom would finish the season in the other league as the Dodgers purchased his contract on August 31.

T I M E L I N E

Feb. 7: The Cincinnati Reds sold catcher Ernie Lombardi to the Boston Braves.

April 14: Ted Williams had three hits, including a home run, and five RBIs in Boston's opener against the Philadelphia Athletics.

May 13: Boston Braves' pitcher Jim Tobin hit three consecutive home runs against the Chicago Cubs one day after hitting a homer as a pinch hitter.

July 6: The All-Star Game, originally scheduled to be played at Ebbets Field, was played at the Polo Grounds to accommodate a larger gate for charity. The American League, thanks to home runs by Lou Boudreau, Rudy York and Mickey Owen, won 3–1.

July 15: Commissioner Landis, responding to an editorial in the *Communist Daily Worker*, declared the major leagues had no policy against the hiring of black players.

July 19: Mike Ryba, normally a pitcher, caught both games of a doubleheader for the Boston Red Sox.

July 21: In a Negro League game at Forbes Field in Pittsburgh, Satchel Paige struck out Josh Gibson on three straight fastballs, fulfilling a prediction he had made to Gibson several years before.

Aug. 6: *The Sporting News* published an editorial declaring that whites and blacks "prefer to draw their talents from their own ranks", thereby endorsing baseball's current segregation practice.

Aug. 9: The St. Louis Cardinals won their 7th consecutive game as rookie pitcher Johnny Beazley defeated the Pirates 7–2.

Aug. 25: Brooklyn pitcher Whitlow Wyatt and the Cardinals' Mort Cooper each work 13 scoreless innings. The Cardinals finally won the game 2–1 in the 14th.

Aug. 28: Brooklyn outfielder Pete Reiser was admitted to hospital with a torn thigh ligament.

Aug. 31: The Dodgers purchased pitcher Bobo Newsom from the Washington Senators. In his debut for Brooklyn, Newsom blanked Cincinnati 2–0.

It was a disappointing year for the White Sox pitching staff

The Dodgers' Dolph Camilli

paying fans as the proceeds were designated for various war relief charities. A second exhibition game was scheduled for the next night in Cleveland between the winner of the first game (the American League, led by a Rudy York home run) and a "service" team composed of major leaguers already in the military.

For much of the season, the drive for the National League flag didn't look like much of a race either. The defending champion Brooklyn Dodgers, still led by the volatile Leo Durocher, seemed certain to take the title again.

Pete Reiser's .310 batting average and league-leading 20 stolen bases were complemented by another great year from first baseman Dolph Camilli, who belted 26 home runs and drove in 100 runs. Whitlow Wyatt was the ace of the pitching staff again with a 19–7 record.

Reiser had been hitting a phenomenal .379 before colliding with a wall chasing an Enos Slaughter fly ball in a game against the St. Louis Cardinals in early July. He suffered a concussion and was sidelined for several games before coming back, only to be taken out of action again with a torn thigh ligament.

As the old expression goes, somebody forgot to tell the Cardinals the race was over. In second place for most of the season, and 10½ games out when play began on August 4, the Cardinals began one of the most incredible runs in baseball history. They swept a doubleheader from Brooklyn and went on to win 43 of their last 52 games. By mid-September, after sweeping another two-game set from the Dodgers, the Cardinals were in a tie for first place. When it was all over, Brooklyn amassed a record of 104–50, bettering their win total of last season by four games. But the Cardinals clinched the pennant on September 27 and finished at 106–48.

Much of the Cardinals' success can be attributed to the vision of the legendary Branch Rickey. Rickey's basic organizational concept was that a minor league system should be a "farm" system designed to "grow" players for the parent team. It was revolutionary at the time but would prove to be the prototype for organizations of the future. One such graduate of the Cardinals' system was Stan Musial. After coming up in September of 1941 and enjoying a phenomenal month, Musial played his first full year in the St. Louis outfield and hit .315. Pitcher Mort Cooper led the pitching staff with a 22–7 record that earned him Most Valuable Player honors in the National League.

Mel Ott had taken over as player-manager of the New York Giants, who finished in third place

Once again, Connie Mack's Philadelphia Athletics, despite good pitching from Phil Marchildon (17–4), finished in the American League cellar.

The All-Star game did not escape the effects of World War II either. Originally scheduled at Ebbets Field in Brooklyn, the game was moved to the Polo Grounds to accommodate more

behind St. Louis and Brooklyn. Ott's 30 home runs led the league and he also picked up his 2,500th career hit during the season. Not far behind in the home run count was first baseman Johnny Mize with 26. Mize, acquired in the off-season from the Cardinals, also posted a .305 batting average.

The Cincinnati Reds, behind solid pitching from Johnny Vander Meer with an 18–12 record and 2.43 ERA, finished fourth at the .500 mark.

Thirty-five-year-old veteran Rip Sewell was 17–15 for the fifth place Pittsburgh Pirates, who got some power from Vince DiMaggio with 15 home runs.

Claude Passeau continued to post good numbers on the mound for the Chicago Cubs with a 19–14 record and a 2.69 ERA. Right fielder Bill Nicholson provided the only power for Chicago with 21 home runs while third baseman Stan Hack and left fielder Lou Novikoff both hit the .300 mark. Jimmie Foxx, picked up

on waivers from the Boston Red Sox, provided a couple of home run heroics before he was sidelined in June with a broken rib.

Ernie Lombardi, purchased in the off season from Cincinnati, hit a league-leading .330 for Casey Stengel's Boston Braves, while also providing some power with 11 home runs. Max West, however, was the club leader in that department with 16.

The Philadelphia Phillies' woes continued, despite the presence of a new manager, Hans Lobert.

SHORTS The war effort affected baseball in many ways. The most obvious was the loss of players to military obligations. The owners decided in March that players on furlough or stationed near a game site could not rejoin their teams. Charity games were staged to raise funds for the war effort. Late in the season, several clubs had scrap metal drives, providing admission to anyone who contributed metal for the defense effort.

The Cardinals' Enos Slaughter was part of a team that won 43 of their last 52 games to clinch the pennant

GAME 1	
NY Yankees 7	St. Louis Cardinals 4
GAME 2	
St. Louis Cardinals 4	NY Yankees 3
GAME 3	
St. Louis Cardinals 2	NY Yankees 0
GAME 4	
St. Louis Cardinals 9	NY Yankees 6
GAME 5	
St. Louis Cardinals 4	NY Yankees 2

The Redbirds' Whitey Kurowski

The New York Yankees should have been forewarned—the St. Louis Cardinals were no strangers to comebacks.

If the Cardinals hadn't been a resilient team, they never would have been in the World Series. At the beginning of August, they were ten games behind the first-place Brooklyn Dodgers in the National League and seemingly finished. Instead, the Cardinals staged a two-month rally and wound up taking the pennant, finishing two games ahead of the Dodgers. St. Louis went on a 43–8 stretch run to shock the Dodgers and win the title.

So when the Cardinals went into Game One of the Series trailing 7–0, they viewed it as just another challenge to be met and overcome.

Through eight innings the Cardinals had been overmatched by veteran Red Ruffing, who had limited them to one hit while his teammates battered Mort Cooper, who was undermined by some poor defense. Ruffing had pitched 7⅔ hitless innings until Terry Moore singled.

With one out in the ninth, Walker Cooper singled. After a second out, it looked like a quiet ending for the Cardinals, but pinch hitter Ray Sanders drew a walk and the Cardinals

followed with five straight hits to score four runs and load the bases. Stan Musial, who had opened the inning with a pop foul, then grounded out to end the inning in the Yankees' 7–4 win.

The rally fell short, but it let the Cardinals know they could play with the Yankees. That was important, considering that St. Louis was making its first trip to the Series since 1934 while New York was appearing in postseason play for the sixth time in seven years.

As it turned out, from the ninth inning of Game One, the Series belonged to the Cardinals.

Johnny Beazley, who had won 21 games as a rookie for the Cardinals, was sailing through Game Two with a 3–0 lead in the eighth inning. He left with a tie game after Joe DiMaggio's RBI single and a two-run homer from Charlie Keller.

The Cardinals still wound up winning the game with a rally in the ninth. Enos Slaughter hit a double and scored on Musial's single. Slaughter preserved the win with an exceptional defensive play in the bottom of the inning. He made a strong throw from right field to cut down a runner at third base and helped to quell a Yankees rally.

The Yankees had still gotten the requisite road split in the first two games and headed back to New York feeling good about their chances. That feeling didn't last long.

In Game Three, Ernie White pitched a six-hitter and shut out the Yankees 2–0. After the sloppy fielding in Game One, the Cardinals were brilliant defensively. Moore made a run-saving catch in the sixth inning and Musial and Slaughter each made a grab to prevent a home run an inning later.

Mort Cooper, a 22-game winner in the regular season, couldn't find that same groove in the Series. He was knocked out in the sixth inning of Game Four, as New York scored five runs in the inning. Three of them came on Keller's three-run homer.

Yankees' starter Hank Borowy wasn't much better—he pitched into the fourth. The Cardinals scored six times in that inning with Whitey Kurowski and Cooper providing two-run singles.

Walker Cooper hit a tie-breaking single in the seventh and Marty Marion had a sacrifice fly. Pitcher Max Lanier worked three innings of scoreless relief and also contributed a run-scoring single as the Cardinals won 9–6.

Phil Rizzuto gave the Yankees a lead in Game Five when he hit a solo homer off Beazley in the first. Slaughter's home run in the fourth tied the game.

DiMaggio's single in the bottom of the fourth put the Yankees ahead 2–1 before the Cardinals tied it in the sixth on Walker Cooper's sacrifice fly.

Cooper singled in the ninth and advanced on a bunt. Kurowski then hit Ruffing's pitch into the left field stands and Beazley nailed down the Series-winning 4–2 victory.

The Cardinals didn't have a big offensive Series, posting a team average of just .239, but

they had a knack of getting timely hits and, aside from regular season ace Cooper, their staff provided quality innings. The Yankees scored 13 earned runs and eight were off Cooper. The other five came off Beazley as the Yankees didn't touch the other four pitchers St. Louis used for 14 innings.

The Yankees lost a Series for the first time since 1926. They had won eight consecutive appearances.

Phil Rizzuto's Game Five homer couldn't prevent a Yankees defeat

President Roosevelt's resolve to "keep baseball going" was becoming more problematic as each day passed in 1943. More than 60 regular major league players, ranging from superstars like Ted Williams and Joe DiMaggio to veterans like 39-year-old Yankee pitcher Red Ruffing, were either enlisting or being drafted for military service. Front office personnel, coaches, prospects and players of all abilities were setting baseball aside for their country's service.

Sensing that the depletion of talent and the dissatisfaction of fans with the current product might eventually shut baseball down for the duration of World War II, Chicago Cubs' owner Phillip Wrigley and Branch Rickey, then the general manager of the Brooklyn Dodgers, proposed an alternative.

Basing their teams in cities around Chicago like Rockford, Illinois and Racine, Wisconsin, Wrigley and Rickey formed the All-American Girls Professional Softball League, hoping the novelty would draw some interest, especially if the major leagues did suspend operations for awhile. But once they saw just how many talented athletes there were among the women, it wasn't long before the game was changed from softball to full-scale baseball. The league used former major leaguers as managers and coaches and did, in fact, attract some significant attention from the fans.

Although there were some significant residual effects from the war, major league baseball did not close down. In addition to the absence of many players, there were rulings from the Commissioner's office that reflected the climate of fear in the country. For instance, teams were directed not to train south of the Mason-Dixon line but to stay "closer to home". Towns like Cape Girardeau, Missouri, whose closest connection to major league baseball had been radio broadcasts of the games, were now hosting their heroes—at least for the spring.

As for the season itself, to no one's surprise Joe McCarthy's New York Yankees repeated as winners of the American League pennant. What was surprising was the early challenge, and eventual second-place finish, of the Washington Senators.

Although Yankees success was considered almost automatic, this lineup was very different with DiMaggio, Phil Rizzuto, Tommy Henrich and Buddy Hassett wearing military uniforms instead of the familiar pinstripes. One thing that had not changed was the power production of left fielder Charlie Keller, whose 31 home runs

were second only to Detroit first baseman Rudy York's 34.

Tiny Bonham, 1942's Yankees ace, finished with a respectable 15–8 record, but it was 35-year-old Spud Chandler who led the staff at 20–4, making him one of only two 20-game winners in the league. Detroit's Dizzy Trout was the other.

Even more impressive was Chandler's 1.64 ERA, the lowest in the league since the legendary Walter Johnson posted a 1.49 mark in 1919.

While their challenge to the Yankees was never really serious, the Senators' rise from seventh place to second was certainly a moral victory. They were a team with no big stars, but George Case's 61 stolen bases and 23-year-old Early Wynn's 18–12 record were certainly standout performances.

The Cleveland Indians finished a close third. Allie Reynolds led the American League with 151 strikeouts, and Al Smith and Jim Babgy each won 17 games. Jeff Heath hit 18 home runs for the Indians.

The fourth-place Chicago White Sox still

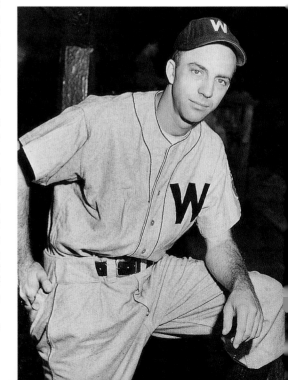

Washington's George Case

The White Sox's Luke Appling led the league with a .328 average

TIMELINE

Jan. 4: Yankees' pitcher Red Ruffing was drafted for military service at age 37.

Feb. 9: The Philadelphia Phillies were put up for sale by the National League when owner Gerry Nugent defaulted on his loans.

Feb. 17: Joe DiMaggio joined the United States Army.

Feb. 26: Bucky Harris was hired to manage the Philadelphia Phillies.

April 22: Player-manager Mel Ott went 4 for 4 for the New York Giants in a game against the Brooklyn Dodgers at Ebbets Field.

July 10: Under the leadership of shortstop Arky Vaughn, Dodger players threatened to strike before their game against the Pittsburgh Pirates. Irate over manager Leo Durocher's three-game suspension of pitcher Bobo Newsom, Vaughn and his teammates were persuaded to play by general manager Branch Rickey.

July 12: A team of Armed Forces All-Stars, managed by Babe Ruth, defeated the Boston Braves in a charity game 9–8. Ted Williams homered, Ruth appeared as a pinch hitter and Joe DiMaggio also played.

July 31: The Brooklyn Dodgers traded first baseman Dolph Camilli to the New York Giants, but Camilli refused to report and chose to sit out the rest of the season.

September 6: Carl Scheib, age 16, became the youngest player in American League history to appear in a game.

Sep. 20: The Washington Senators won their 10th consecutive game as they swept a doubleheader from the League-leading Yankees.

Sep. 24: Just 314 fans, the smallest crowd in the history of Wrigley Field, saw Andy Pafko drive in four runs in a rain-shortened game against Philadelphia. The Cubs won 7–4 in five innings.

Nov. 23: Less than a year after he purchased the Philadelphia Phillies, William Cox was barred from baseball for betting on his own team and Commissioner Landis put the team up for sale again.

lacked power, but their lineup featured two of league's top five hitters: Luke Appling led the league at .328 and Ralph Hodgin was third at .314. More than anything, the White Sox had speed with three of the league's top four base stealers. Wally Moses' 56 steals were a formidable challenge to the league lead and teammates Thurman Tucker (29) and Appling (27) were threats on the basepaths as well.

The White Sox staff also had a good bullpen with Gordon Maltzberger credited with 14 unofficial saves.

The Detroit Tigers finished two games above .500, sparked by York's league-leading 34 home runs and 118 RBIs and Dizzy Trout's 20–12 record.

The St. Louis Browns dropped to sixth, but got

SHORTS It must have seemed strange for fans of the Philadelphia Athletics to look at their scorecards and not see "Bullet Bob" Johnson in the lineup. Since his debut in 1933, Johnson had hit home runs in double figures in every year until his trade to the Washington Senators prior to the 1943 season. He hit just seven for Washington.

The Tigers' Rudy York

although Estalella did lead the team in home runs with just 11.

The World Champion St. Louis Cardinals, despite the off-season loss of Enos Slaughter, Terry Moore and Johnny Beazley to the war effort, continued to validate Branch Rickey's belief in the "farm" system. Stan Musial continued to shine, leading the National League in four offensive categories: batting average (.357), hits (220), doubles (48) and triples (20). These numbers and his 13 home runs earned the 22-year-old Musial the Most Valuable Player award.

Mort Cooper, the National League's MVP in 1942, posted his second straight 20-plus victory season with a 21–8 mark while fellow pitchers Harry Breechen and Al Brazle came up from the system along with second baseman Lou Klein to contribute to another flag for the Cardinals.

Howie Pollet pitched in only 16 games before reporting for Army duty, but posted enough innings to capture the National League's ERA title with an impressive 1.75 mark. The Cardinals clinched the pennant on September 13.

Cincinnati rebounded from its slide in 1942, finishing a distant second behind St. Louis. Right hander Elmer Riddle got back on the winning track, posting 21 wins to tie for the league lead. Durable first baseman Frank McCormick's power numbers fell somewhat as he only played in 120 games, but he did manage a .303 batting average.

Leo Durocher's Brooklyn Dodgers, torn with dissension over Durocher's suspension of veteran pitcher Bobo Newsom and the trade of stalwart first baseman Dolph Camilli (who refused to report to the New York Giants and sat out the remainder of the season), still managed a third-place finish 11 games above the .500 mark. Whitlow Wyatt, 35 years old and nursing a sore arm, was still able to anchor the Brooklyn pitching staff with a 14–5 record and a 2.49 ERA, while Les Webber saved 10 games out of the bullpen.

The Dodgers also had the league's leading base stealer in Arky Vaughn who swiped 20 bases and led a threatened player's strike against Durocher before their July 10 game against the Pittsburgh Pirates. Durocher had suspended Wyatt after a strong verbal confrontation and Vaughn, uniform in hand, told Durocher he would not play. Several players followed him.

General manager Branch Rickey, who had come over from the Cardinals after Larry MacPhail's resignation, was called in to calm the situation. Rickey convinced Vaughn and the others

good production from shortstop Vern Stephens with 22 home runs and a 15–11 record from pitcher Steve Sundra.

The loss of Ted Williams' bat and the decline of pitcher Tex Hughson (12–15) were obstacles the Boston Red Sox couldn't overcome, but second baseman Bobby Doerr's club-leading 16 home runs continued his rise as a major league star.

The pre-season trade of veteran power hitter "Bullet Bob" Johnson by the Philadelphia Athletics for Bob Estalella and Johnny Pofahl did nothing to help Connie Mack's club out of the cellar,

The Dodgers' Arky Vaughn (with bat) led a player revolt against manager Leo Durocher (second left)

to play and the game went on as was scheduled.

Ten days later, Newsom was traded to the St. Louis Browns.

Veteran Pittsburgh pitcher Rip Sewell debuted a new pitch called the "dew drop" (later renamed the "blooper" or "eeephus" pitch) which apparently confused National League batters enough to help take Sewell to a league tying 21 wins against only four losses. Vince DiMaggio continued to be the offensive spark for the Pirates with 15 home runs. He also had the distinction of nearly hitting for the cycle in the All-Star Game, falling a double short of completing the feat.

The game, the first All-Star contest to be played under lights, was won by the American League on Bobby Doerr's three-run home run off Mort Cooper in the second inning of the game. The final score was 5–3.

Chicago Cubs' right fielder Bill "Swish" Nicholson, one of the few players in the league to play the full complement of 154 games, led the circuit with 29 home runs and 128 RBIs. Interestingly, Nicholson didn't hit his first home run until May 30 against the Boston Braves. It was the team's first home run of the year. Nicholson was the only Cub to reach double figures in that department.

Boston Braves' manager Casey Stengel's broken leg, suffered at the hands of an errant taxicab in April, provided the bulk of the team's excitement.

Stengel's flippant remarks about the Braves' hapless performance did not sit well with at least one Boston sportswriter—he named the cabdriver "Sportsman of the Year".

The Philadelphia Phillies, thanks in large part to veteran pitcher Schoolboy Rowe's 14–8 record and outfielder Ron Northey's 16 home runs, managed to get themselves out of the cellar for the first time since 1937. Mel Ott's New York Giants had the honor of replacing the Phillies in that dubious spot. It was the Giants' first last-place finish since 1915. Ott continued to provide power, however, with 18 home runs (all at his home ballpark) and veteran catcher Ernie Lombardi, playing in a secondary role, slugged 10 for New York. The aptly named "Ace" Adams was the leading pitcher on the staff with an 11–7 record.

SHORTS The new cork/balata baseball was supposed to be livelier, but players complained profusely. A representative of A.G. Spalding, who manufactured the baseball, blamed cold, wet conditions for the ball's lack of life. Sure enough, the home runs started multiplying after awhile. But by this time Spalding had admitted that the ball was inferior and began working on a new and improved one.

GAME 1	
NY Yankees 4	St. Louis Cardinals 2
GAME 2	
St. Louis Cardinals 4	NY Yankees 3
GAME 3	
NY Yankees 6	St. Louis Cardinals 2
GAME 4	
NY Yankees 2	St. Louis Cardinals 1
GAME 5	
NY Yankees 2	St. Louis Cardinals 0

New York Yankee Joe Gordon tags the runner

The St. Louis Cardinals proved they were no fluke, working their way back to the World Series for a second consecutive year.

Boosted by their 4–1 win in the 1942 World Series, the Cardinals breezed to their second straight National League pennant, finishing 18 games ahead of the Cincinnati Reds. St. Louis won 105 games, which was actually one off the pace they'd set the year before with a frantic stretch run that allowed them to overtake the Brooklyn Dodgers.

Mort Cooper had a second-straight strong season, posting a 21–6 record with a 2.30 earned run average. Stan Musial batted .357, scored 108 runs and drove in 87 in his second season as a regular in the major leagues.

Like all major league teams, the Cardinals had to contend with players lost to military service in World War II. St. Louis lost outfielders Enos Slaughter and Terry Moore, pitchers Johnny Beazley and Howie Pollet and second baseman Jimmy Brown.

As much as those losses hurt, the Cardinals

were able to come up with adequate replacements. Lou Klein filled in at second base and the pitching staff was boosted when Al Brazle and Harry Brecheen came aboard.

The Yankees had also sacrificed some significant players to the war effort. The list was headed by Joe DiMaggio and Phil Rizzuto and also included Red Ruffing, the team's No. 1 starting pitcher. In Ruffing's absence, Spud Chandler became the leading pitcher, posting a 20–4 record with a 1.64 earned run average. Nick Etten helped the offense with 107 RBIs after he was acquired from the Philadelphia Athletics.

The Yankees wound up winning the American League pennant by 13½ games over the Washington Senators.

Chandler won Game One of the Series 4–2. The game was tied 2–2 in the sixth inning when the Yankees got singles from Frank Crosetti, Billy Johnson and Bill Dickey, plus a wild pitch by Max Lanier.

Mort Cooper started Game Two with a heavy heart. He and battery-mate brother Walker had lost their father a day earlier. Cooper pitched well, holding the Yankees to a single run over eight innings and taking a 4–1 lead into the ninth inning. Cooper held on and completed the game, even though the Yankees scored two in the bottom of the ninth to make the score 4–3.

In Game Three, shortstop Marty Marion hit a solo home run in the third for the Cardinals and Ray Sanders added a two-run homer in the fourth.

Brazle had proven to be a key addition for the Cardinals, posting an 8–2 record with a 1.53 earned run average. He carried that work over to his first Series appearance, holding the Yankees to a single run over seven innings. He took a 2–1 lead into the eighth when New York staged the rally that would forever change the momentum of the Series.

Johnny Lindell opened the eighth with a single and took second when center fielder Harry Walker mishandled the ball for an error. The Cardinals tried to get Lindell at third on George Stirnweiss' bunt. The throw was good, but Lindell collided into third baseman Whitey Kurowski and was safe when the ball came loose. Stirnweiss moved to second on a fly ball and Frank Crosetti was

intentionally walked to load the bases setting up a confrontation with rookie Billy Johnson.

Johnson tripled to put the Yankees ahead 4–2. Joe Gordon and Etten added RBI singles and Johnny Murphy retired the Cardinals in order in the ninth.

The Yankees won Game Four behind the arm and bat of pitcher Marius Russo. Russo had labored through an undistinguished regular season, but rose to the occasion in his only Series appearance. He threw a seven-hitter and the only run against him was unearned. Russo hit an RBI double in the eighth and came in to score the winning run as the Yankees won the game 2–1 for a 3–1 edge in the Series.

The Series came to a frustrating end for the Cardinals. They collected ten hits off Chandler, but couldn't score. St. Louis stranded 11 runners. Mort Cooper pitched well but made one big mistake. Bill Dickey hit a two-run homer in the sixth inning and the Yankees won 2–0 to take their ninth title in ten Series.

It was Yankees manager Joe McCarthy's seventh World Championship and it also proved to be his last.

Johnson led the Yankees with a .300 average in the Series. Dickey hit .278 with four RBIs. New York had a staff ERA of 1.50 and held the Cardinals to a .224 team average. Marion led the Cardinals at .357.

Joe McCarthy addresses his World Champion Yankees

What a year to be a baseball fan in St. Louis. World War II continued to rage in Europe, Japan and the Pacific, but for a few weeks in the Fall of 1944 St. Louis newspapers had reason to give the conflict a secondary role on their front pages.

Baseball took center stage in the city known as the "Gateway to the West" when, for the first time in major league history, both of its teams captured the flag in their respective leagues.

For most of the season it was a four-team race in the American League as the St. Louis Browns, Detroit Tigers, New York Yankees and Boston Red Sox battled. But the Red Sox lost two more key players to the military—second baseman Bobby Doerr and pitching ace Tex Hughson. Hughson still managed to post an 18–5 record in 23 starts before his departure, but the Red Sox were unable to keep up the pace after the personnel losses.

The Browns opened with nine consecutive wins to set an American League record. Most baseball experts dismissed the fast start as one of those quirky streaks that can happen to any team, but the Browns would prove them wrong.

At the beginning of the season, Detroit looked like the most serious challenger to the defending World Champion Yankees as Hal Newhouser reeled off a league-leading 29 wins against nine losses, two more than teammate Dizzy Trout, who posted a 27–14 mark. Newhouser's performance earned him Most Valuable Player honors in the league. Trout's league-leading 40 starts fueled his reputation as one of baseball's most durable pitchers.

The Tigers' Dizzy Trout continued to provide Detroit with both innings and wins

The Tigers also continued to get punch from Rudy York with 18 home runs and 98 RBIs. Left fielder Dick Wakefield also hit 18 home runs and carried a .355 batting average before reporting for military duty.

As for the Yankees, their ace, Spud Chandler, pitched only one game before leaving for the service. Hank Borowy anchored the staff with a 17–12 record. The Yankee lineup suffered another huge loss, however, when Charlie Keller signed on with the Merchant Marines. First baseman Nick Etten helped to fill the void with a league-leading 22 home runs while center fielder Johnny Lindell contributed 16 triples while driving in 103 runs.

Another big hole in the Yankee infield developed when second baseman Joe Gordon entered military service before the start of the season. But Stuffy Stirnweiss, who had primarily been a utility infielder, filled in more than adequately, hitting .319, tying teammate Lindell's 16 triples and wresting the stolen base crown from Washington's George Case by stealing 55.

Still, the Yankees fell short of their fourth consecutive league championship. It remained a tight race in the final week of the season when Detroit took a one-game lead over the Browns while New York trailed by three. But when St. Louis swept a doubleheader from the Yankees

TIMELINE

Feb. 18: Pitcher Joe Nuxhall was signed by the Cincinnati Reds at age 15.

April 16: The Associated Press announced its picks in the American League. The New York Yankees were the favorites with the St. Louis Browns chosen to finish in the cellar.

April 18: The Philadelphia Athletics opened the season with a rookie third baseman, George Kell, who was the minor leagues' leading hitter with a .396 average in 1943.

April 19: Mel Ott hit the first home run in the National League against the Boston Braves, the 464th homer of his career.

May 1: Chicago Cubs' manager Jimmie Wilson resigned. Roy Johnson was appointed as the interim replacement.

June 2: The Detroit Tigers won their seventh consecutive game as they defeated the Boston Red Sox 4–1.

June 16: Philadelphia Phillies' hurler Bill Lee had a one-hitter against Brooklyn and Whitlow Wyatt, but two errors gave the Dodgers a 4–3 win. It was Wyatt's first victory of the season.

July 16: Brooklyn ended a 16-game losing streak, defeating the Boston Braves on eight unearned runs.

Aug. 9: The St. Louis Browns capped another nine-game winning streak with a victory over the New York Yankees.

Aug. 29: Boston Braves' third baseman Damon Phillips tied a major league record for assists in a game with 11.

Sept. 5: The New York Yankees moved into first place for one day in the American League.

Sept. 27: The Boston Red Sox broke a ten-game losing streak by defeating the St. Louis Browns and temporarily knocking them out of first place. The Detroit Tigers briefly took over the League lead.

Nov. 25: Baseball Commissioner Kenesaw Mountain Landis died at the age of 78. Judge Landis had been the iron-willed leader of major league baseball since 1920.

Top: MVP Hal Newhouser

Left: Commissioner for 24 years, Kensaw M. Landis died in November

and Detroit split a twinbill with the Senators, the Yankees were all but eliminated. Both St. Louis and Detroit won on September 30, keeping them in a dead heat for first. On the very last day of the season, the Washington Senators handed the Tigers a 4–1 defeat and the Browns, on come-from-behind home runs by Chet Laabs and Vern Stephens, defeated the Yankees and took the pennant.

The Browns got standout performances from several players, notably shortstop Vern Stephens with a league-leading 109 RBIs and pitcher Nels Potter, whose 19–7 mark was tops on the Brownies' starting corp. Left fielder Mike Kreevich posted a .301 batting average and pitcher Jack Kramer sported a club-leading 124 strikeouts while winning 17 games. Another interesting story for St. Louis was pitcher Sig Jakucki. Retired from baseball since 1938 with a 0–3 career record, Jakucki won several key games in the stretch, ending the season with a 13–9 record (including four shutouts).

The Cleveland Indians finished fourth, but their player-manager Lou Boudreau won the batting title with a .327 average. Connie Mack's Philadelphia Athletics moved out of the American League cellar for the first time since 1939.

Hal Trosky, retired for three years after suffering migraine headaches while playing for Cleveland, resurfaced as the first baseman for the Chicago White Sox and clouted ten home runs for Jimmie Dykes' club.

The Senators fell to last place, but center fielder Stan Spence continued to provide offensive punch with 18 home runs and 100 RBIs while George Case continued to be a threat on the bases with 49 steals.

The Browns' St. Louis counterparts, the Cardinals, skated to their third consecutive National League pennant, spending only four days of the season out of the top spot. The Redbirds jumped to a 73–27 start in their first 100 games and their 105–49 record at season's end made them the first National League team to win over 100 games in three consecutive seasons. The Cardinals had a solid offensive attack throughout their lineup, sparked by Stan Musial's .347 batting average, Whitey Kurowski's 20 home runs and Ray Sander's 102 RBIs.

Mort Cooper continued to pace the pitching staff with a 22–7 record. Cooper also got plenty of support from the other Cardinal starters as Ted Wilks (17–4), Max Lanier (17–12) and Harry Breechen (16–5) posted solid seasons. George Munger was also on his way to a fine season with an 11–3 record before military duty called. But it was the all-around play of shortstop Marty

Marion that caused him to be chosen the National League's Most Valuable Player, making him the third different Cardinal in as many years to capture the award.

Although they never posed a threat to the Cardinals, the Pittsburgh Pirates made a significant move to the runner-up spot. Rip Sewell's 21–12 record continued to solidify his role as ace of the Bucs' pitching staff. Sewell's dew drop, or "eephus" pitch as it was now called, continued to befuddle not only National League hitters but the American League All-Stars as well as he helped his teammates take a 7–1 victory before the home crowd at Pittsburgh's Forbes Field. Sewell's nearly perfect three innings in the middle of the game didn't give him the victory, however. That went to Ken Raffensberger of the Philadelphia Phillies.

Cincinnati pitcher Clyde Shoun had passed his physical for the United States Navy and waited for his call up while his team was in spring training. Told he could go ahead and play, Shoun reported to manager Bill McKechnie in late April and was assigned to the bullpen. But on May 15th, Shoun was given the nod to start against the Boston Braves and responded by tossing a 1–0 no-hitter. Third baseman Chuck Aleno's home run was all the Reds needed, thanks to Shoun's gem.

Shoun's teammate Bucky Walters finished the season with a league-leading 23 wins against eight losses and Frank McCormick's 20 home runs, 102 RBIs and .305 batting mark topped the Cincinnati offense. Another Reds pitcher, 35-year-old Ed Heusser, topped the league in earned run average with 2.38 while posting a 13–11 record.

Bill "Swish" Nicholson's 33 home runs and 122 RBIs led the league and made him a close second in the MVP voting. Two of Nicholson's Chicago Cub teammates posted averages over the .300 mark—first baseman Phil Caveretta at .321 and left fielder Dom Dellessandro with a .305 mark. Charlie Grimm took over from Jimmie Wilson as manager of the Cubs just 11 games into the season.

Player-manager Mel Ott belted 26 home runs for his New York Giants and Bill Voiselle topped

the New York pitchers with a 21–16 record. Ace Adams' 13 saves and 65 appearances also led the league.

Bob Coleman had taken over from Casey Stengel as manager of the Boston Braves. Coleman came to the Braves' helm with 23 years of professional managing experience in the minor leagues, but could only muster a sixth-place finish in his debut season in the majors. The Braves did make headlines, however, when pitcher Jim Tobin pitched the second no-hitter of his career and also homered against the Brooklyn Dodgers, giving Boston a 2–0 win.

As for the Dodgers, their one bright spot was Dixie Walker's league-leading .357 average. Walker punctuated his season by hitting for the cycle on September 2 against the New York Giants.

The 1944 season ended with the Cardinals taking the World Series from their hometown rivals, four games to two. But baseball was to make headlines one more time before the calendar year ended. On November 25, the only commissioner major league baseball had ever known, Judge Kenesaw Mountain Landis, passed away at the age of 78. While his conservative political bent and firm stand against integration in baseball were unpopular in many circles (but supported in many others), Landis' death left a void in the game's leadership. Many felt the absence of a strong czar-like figure at the top could result in an even more serious decline for the sport.

Cards' Marty Marion clinched MVP honors in the National League

SHORTS How important is fielding to the success of a team? The 1944 St. Louis Cardinals set a major league record for fewest errors in a season (112) and best fielding percentage (.982). The record was previously held by another championship team, the 1940 Cincinnati Reds. Except for catching duties, shared by Walker Cooper and Ken O'Dea, all of the Cardinal regulars played in at least 136 games.

1944 POSTSEASON

GAME 1	
St. Louis Browns 2	St. Louis Cardinals 1
GAME 2	
St. Louis Cardinals 3	St. Louis Browns 2
GAME 3	
St. Louis Browns 6	St. Louis Cardinals 2
GAME 4	
St. Louis Cardinals 5	St. Louis Browns 1
GAME 5	
St. Louis Cardinals 2	St. Louis Browns 0
GAME 6	
St. Louis Cardinals 3	St. Louis Browns 1

A Game Five homer from Ray Sanders helped the Cards on their way

It was no surprise to have the World Series in St. Louis. The Cardinals had developed into a National League powerhouse and were appearing in the Series for the third consecutive year.

The shock was that the Cardinals didn't have to leave the city limits for the postseason. After two years of meeting the New York Yankees—and splitting the meetings—the Cardinals were staying home to face the most unlikely American League champion, the St. Louis Browns.

From their formation in 1902 until 1953, when they would transfer to Baltimore and emerge as the Orioles, the Browns won only one pennant. It was the 1944 flag.

The sad fact is that their championship probably should have come with an asterisk or some other consumer warning device. The United States was in the midst of World War II and the call for able-bodied men included plenty of draft-age baseball players. Most teams were devastated by their losses to military service.

The Yankees were without Joe DiMaggio and Phil Rizzuto and could finish no better than third, six games behind Luke Sewell's Browns. In a year when anything was possible, the Detroit Tigers jumped up to second place, making a ten-game improvement to finish a single game behind the Browns.

Nels Potter was the Browns' big winner with a 19–7 record. Jack Kramer had a staff-leading earned run average of 2.49 with a 17–13 record. Outfielder Vern Stephens batted .293 with 20 home runs and 109 RBIs.

While the American League pennant was up for grabs, it became apparent that no one was going to stop the Cardinals from winning their third consecutive pennant. The Cardinals won 105 games, making it the third straight season that they'd established that as their minimum total for victories.

Billy Southworth's club had endured military losses, too, but the Cardinals had a group of talent that was clearly the class on the National League.

Stan Musial, only 23 years old, batted .347 in his third season. He scored 112 runs and drove in 94. Third baseman Whitey Kurowski hit .270 with 20 home runs. Catcher Mort Cooper had a .317 average with 13 home runs and 72 RBIs.

Cooper's brother Walker led the pitching staff with his third consecutive 20-win season. He was 22–7 with a .246 earned run average. Max Lanier was 17–12.

Anything can happen in a short series and the Browns were buoyed after a 2–1 win in the opener.

Denny Gatehouse, who was 9–10 with a 3.12 ERA in the regular season, won the pitching duel against Cooper in Game One. First baseman George McQuinn hit a two-run homer in the fourth and Gatehouse made it stand up by holding the Cardinals to a run on seven hits. That turned out to be the Browns' only home run in a Series that would see their offense struggle with a .183 average.

The Cardinals took over in Game Two, winning 3–2 with a run in the 11th inning.

Ken O'Dea got the game-winning hit, a pinch single off reliever Bob Muncrief. Blix Donnelly picked up the win in relief of Lanier. Donnelly worked four innings, surrendering two

Walker Cooper contributed
to the Cardinals Series
victory with a .318 average

hits and a walk while striking out seven.

The Browns shook off the tough loss and won Game Three, 6–2. McQuinn was 3-for-3 with two RBIs and Kramer pitched a seven-hitter.

Sig Jakucki had been one of the regular season's great stories, a 34-year-old pitcher who came back after spending five years out of baseball. He was 13–9 for the Browns, but his bubble burst in Game Four. He was knocked out after three innings, allowing four runs as the Cardinals won 5–1. Musial hit a two-run homer to support Brecheen.

Cooper was the story of Game Five as he held the Browns to seven hits and won 2–0. Cooper walked two and struck out 12 to beat Gatehouse. The Cardinals' runs came on homers by Ray Sanders and Danny Litwhiler.

The Browns' dream season ended with a 3–1 loss in Game Six. Lanier and Ted Wilks combined on a three-hitter to wrap up the Cardinals' second Series win in three years. Wilks, who had been roughed up as the Game Three starter, was perfect against the 11 batters he faced. Emil Verban and Lanier delivered RBI singles in a three-run fourth inning that was prolonged by Stephens' throwing error from shortstop.

Second baseman Verban was the Cardinals' leading hitter with a .412 average. Walker Cooper batted .318 and Musial had a .304 average. Mort Cooper split two decisions, but his ERA was 1.13.

McQuinn, a .250 hitter in the regular season, led the Browns with a .438 average and five RBIs. Aside from him, the rest of the team batted a paltry .160.

MOST VALUABLE PLAYER
AL: Hal Newhouser, Detroit
NL: Phil Cavaretta, Chicago Cubs

LEADERS

BATTING AVERAGE
AL: Stuffy Stirnweiss, NY Yankees, .309
NL: Phil Cavarretta, Chicago Cubs, .355

HOME RUNS
AL: Vern Stephens, St. Louis Browns, 24
NL: Tommy Holmes, Boston Braves, 28

RUNS BATTED IN
AL: Nick Etten, NY Yankees, 111
NL: Dixie Walker, Brooklyn, 124

STOLEN BASES
AL: Stuffy Stirnweiss, NY Yankees, 33
NL: Red Schoendienst, St. Louis Cardinals, 26

PITCHING VICTORIES
AL: Hal Newhouser, Detroit, 25
NL: Red Barrett, Boston Braves/St. Louis Cardinals, 23

EARNED RUN AVERAGE
AL: Hal Newhouser, Detroit, 1.81
NL: Hank Borowy, Chicago Cubs, 2.13

STRIKEOUTS
AL: Hal Newhouser, Detroit, 212
NL: Preacher Roe, Pittsburgh, 148

For years, they occupied their own world, one where good pay, good working conditions and respect were often difficult to find. But in 1947 the dreams of a handful of black baseball players gradually began to come true.

Hank Greenberg celebrated his return to the majors with a homer against the A's

It was a year that saw the continued departure of some of the game's heroes and the gradual return of some others; a year of new blood and new thinking at the very top of baseball's hierarchy; a year in which fans' curiosity was transformed into amazement, along with a warming of their hearts, as they witnessed an outfielder playing with only one arm. And it was a year that saw the pennant dreams of fans in two cities finally become reality again.

Detroit baseball fans had plenty to cheer about in 1945. Their Tigers survived another grueling pennant race, finishing at the top of the American League for the first time since 1940. Their ace pitcher, Hal Newhouser, had another stellar season, posting a 25–9 record and leading the league in five categories—wins (25), winning percentage (.735), shutouts (8), strikeouts (212) and earned run average (1.81). Newhouser's performance earned him

Most Valuable Player honors for the second year in a row, making him the first player to accomplish that feat since Jimmie Foxx in 1931 and 1932.

First baseman Rudy York had another great year with 18 home runs. An early-season trade with Cleveland, involving utility player Don Ross, brought outfielder Roy Cullenbine to the Motor City. Both Ross and Cullenbine became everyday players for their new teams, but it was Cullenbine's 18 home runs and 93 runs batted in that appeared to give the Tigers the better end of the deal.

July 1 saw the most significant event of the Detroit season, however. One day after his release from the United States Army, Hank Greenberg donned a Tigers uniform for the first time in four years and entered a major league game.

In true storybook fashion, Greenberg thrilled the 47,700 fans in attendance by homering off the Philadelphia Athletics Charlie Gassaway. Greenberg would go on to belt 13 home runs and 60 RBIs in just 72 games for Detroit and bat .311 in the process.

Detroit finished the season 1½ games ahead of the Washington Senators, whose speed and pitching kept them in contention to the very last week of the season. Paced by a corps of knuckleball pitchers in their starting rotation, the Senators' staff posted impressive records, led by Roger Wolff, who had a 20–10 record with a 2.12 ERA. Perennial base-stealing threat George Case had competition in second baseman George Myatt as each stole 30 bases for the season.

The defending league champion St. Louis Browns finished third, just six games out of first place. Shortstop Vern Stephens continued to be the hitting star of the team with a league-leading 24 home runs. The pitching staff was led by Nels Potter with a 15–11 record and an ERA of 2.47.

But the story of interest on the St. Louis Browns was that of outfielder Pete Gray. Gray was a fast runner, a decent fielder and a fair hitter. He also had only one arm. In his debut on April 18, Gray got one hit in four at bats, but had no outfield chances. Besides hitting with only one arm, Gray's fielding technique was something to behold. He would catch the baseball in his glove and in a fluid motion toss the ball out of his glove, tuck the glove under the stump of his right arm, then catch the ball in his bare hand before throwing it to the proper base.

Gray's shining moment came on May 20 when, in a doubleheader against the New York Yankees, he got three hits in the opening game

The St. Louis Browns' inspirational Pete Gray who defied his disability

including two RBIs. He also caught seven flies in the outfield, with three of them described as sensational catches.

As for the fourth place Yankees, first baseman Nick Etten and second baseman Stuffy Stirnweiss continued to stand out on a team still devoid of most of its regulars. Etten hit 18 home runs and led the league with 111 runs batted in. Stirnweiss could boast the league lead in three offensive categories—batting average (.309), stolen bases (33) and triples (22). The Yankees' pitching staff was in sad shape, with Bill Bevens' 13–9 record topping the team. Jim Turner did manage to lead the league with ten saves. Hank Borowy, the ace of 1944, had posted a 10–5 record before being sold to the Chicago Cubs on a waiver deal gone awry.

Lou Boudreau missed nearly 60 games with a broken ankle, but managed to bat .307 for his Cleveland Indians. Left fielder Jeff Heath topped the Tribe in home runs with 15 and Steve Gromek and Allie Reynolds posted 19–9 and 18–12 records respectively. But the big news on the Cleveland pitching staff was the return of Bob Feller. His return drew 46,777 fans to see "Rapid Robert" strike out 12 Detroit Tigers and win a 4–2 game over the League's leading pitcher, Hal Newhouser.

Feller ended the year with a 5–3 record in nine starts, including a one-hitter and a pair of four-hitters.

Thornton Lee led the Chicago White Sox

SHORTS Kentucky Senator Albert "Happy" Chandler wasn't even on the original list of candidates for Commissioner of Baseball, but Larry MacPhail suggested his name. The first ballot vote was 11–5, a simple majority, but a 75 percent majority was required. After some heated discussion a second ballot was taken and the election was unanimous for Chandler.

Yankees' first baseman Nick
Etten

pitching staff with a 15–12 record and third
baseman Tony Cuccinello was the team's
leading hitter with a .308 mark.

The league's top rookie was David "Boo"
Ferris, who topped the Boston Red Sox staff
with a 21–10 record. Ferris won his first eight
starts of the season, setting a major league
record by pitching 22 consecutive scoreless
innings at the outset.

The Philadelphia Athletics finished last again
as pitcher Russ Christopher was the only A's
pitcher who did not post a losing record,
finishing at 13–13.

The National League pennant chase was not
quite as dramatic as the Chicago Cubs finished
three games ahead of the defending World
Champion St. Louis Cardinals.

The Cubs were paced by first baseman Phil
Cavarretta who posted a .355 average and
pitcher Hany Wyse with a 22–10 record. Bill
Nicholson continued to be the main power
source for the Chicago club with 13 home runs,
but center fielder Andy Pafko contributed 12 of

his own while driving in 110 runs.

Hank Borowy, purchased from the New York
Yankees for $97,500 in July, posted an
impressive 11–2 record after joining the team
and his 2.12 ERA led the league.

The Cardinals' bid for a fourth consecutive
National League flag suffered a hard blow
when Stan Musial left for Army duty before the
start of the season. But Whitey Kurowski's 21
home runs and 102 RBIs helped to keep them
in contention. The acquisition of outfielder
Buster Adams from the Phillies also helped as
Adams found a home in the St. Louis outfield
and belted 20 home runs with 101 runs batted
in. Another bright spot for the Redbirds was the
showing of a 22-year-old rookie named Albert
"Red" Schoendienst.

Schoendienst, primarily an infielder in the
minor leagues, could do it all, it seemed. With
Musial gone, he was given a place in left field
and he made the most of it, stealing a league-
leading 26 bases.

Pitcher Red Barrett, brought over from the

Boston Braves in a controversial trade for Mort Cooper, led the league in victories with a 21–9 record with St. Louis combined with his 2–3 record with Boston. Cooper's salary demands were deemed unreasonable by St. Louis owner Sam Breadon. The Cardinals received $60,000 cash from Boston along with Barrett.

The Brooklyn Dodgers rebounded from seventh place to third, thanks to a lineup that had four .300 hitters, topped by Goody Rosen at .325. Dixie Walker drove in 124 runs to lead the league and pitcher Hal Gregg managed an 18–13 mark to lead the Brooklyn staff.

Johnny Barrett's 15 home runs and 25 stolen bases were tops on the Pittsburgh Pirates. Preacher Roe's 148 strikeouts led the National League and his 14–13 record was second only to Nick Strincevich's 16–10 mark for the team lead.

New York Giants' player-manager Mel Ott not only led his team with 21 home runs and a .308 batting average, but he also made history by hitting his 500th career home run on August 1. He ended the season third on the all-time list behind Babe Ruth and Jimmie Foxx.

The Boston Braves had the League's leading home run hitter in Tommy Holmes with 28. Holmes also drove in 117 runs.

Bill McKechnie's Cincinnati Reds finished seventh. Shortstop Eddie Miller led the club with 13 home runs, despite missing 42 games with a broken kneecap.

Vince DiMaggio became the Philadelphia Phillies' new left fielder in an off-season trade and provided the only offensive excitement for the last-place Phillies with 19 home runs and 12 stolen bases.

With the death of Commissioner Kenesaw Mountain Landis, a meeting of the owners in Cleveland resulted in the second ballot election of Senator Albert "Happy" Chandler to the post. Chandler eventually resigned his Senate seat in October. His first year on the job was met with mixed reviews as he did not possess the strong personality or iron fist of Judge Landis.

The Braves' Tommy Holmes led the league in both homers and RBIs

GAME 1	
Chicago Cubs 9	Detroit 0
GAME 2	
Detroit 4	Chicago Cubs 1
GAME 3	
Chicago Cubs 3	Detroit 0
GAME 4	
Detroit 4	Chicago Cubs 1
GAME 5	
Detroit 8	Chicago Cubs 4
GAME 6	
Chicago Cubs 8	Detroit 7
GAME 7	
Detroit 9	Chicago Cubs 3

It was the last baseball season that was distinguished by who was absent. President Franklin Roosevelt had decreed that baseball would continue through World War II to provide a morale boost for American citizens through trying times. But when it came to taking able-bodied men to serve in the military, the government didn't make special exemptions for major league players. Some of the game's best-known players were serving their country while their teams continued to scramble to field teams.

The depletion of rosters made the pennant races unpredictable. The successful teams were the ones that did an adequate job of replacing the players who were serving in the armed forces. The pennant races were wide open, as was demonstrated in 1944 when the St. Louis Browns rose from sixth to first to claim the American League pennant.

The players on military duty represented a couple of All-Star teams worth of talent. In the American League, those serving in 1945 included Joe DiMaggio, Phil Rizzuto, Joe Gordon, Bill Dickey and Tommy Henrich (Yankees) along with Ted Williams, Dom DiMaggio and Johnny Pesky from the Red Sox.

In the National League, the defending champion St. Louis Cardinals lost Stan Musial, Terry Moore, Enos Slaughter, Harry Walker, Johnny Beazley, Al Brazle and Howie Pollet to military service in 1945. It was probably an accomplishment for the Cardinals to finish within three games of the first-place Chicago Cubs, who took the title with 98 wins. The Cardinals won 95 games, ten fewer than they'd won in 1944 when Musial was still in their lineup.

The Tigers wound up 1½ games in front of the Washington Senators and six ahead of the Browns.

The Cubs cast most of their hopes with pitcher Hank Borowy, who started three times in seven days and also made a four-inning relief appearance. Borowy had been 10–5 with the Yankees when the Cubs picked him up on waivers at the end of July. He went 11–2 for the Cubs, winning the confidence of

manager Charlie Grimm, who started him in Game One of the Series.

That strategy worked as Borowy pitched Chicago to a six-hit, 9–0 victory. The Cubs scored their first seven runs off Hal Newhouser, a 25-game winner in the regular season. Bill Nicholson had three RBIs while Phil Cavarretta and Mickey Livingston each drove in two runs.

Virgil Trucks got the Tigers even with a 4–1 in Game Two. Trucks, who was freshly discharged from the Navy, had pitched just one game in the regular season for Detroit, working 5⅓ innings. The offense was provided by Hank Greenberg, who hit a three-run homer off Hank Wyse.

Pitching continued to dominate in Game Three as Claude Passeau of the Cubs pitched a one-hitter to win 3–0. The only Detroit hit was Rudy York's two-out single in the second inning. Passeau walked one and had just one strikeout as Nicholson drove in the game's only run.

It was the Tigers' turn for an exceptional pitching performance in Game Four and Dizzy Trout didn't disappoint. He held the Cubs to four hits and an unearned run in the 4–1 victory. Roy Cullenbine had a double in the Tigers' four-run fourth.

The Series became a best-of-three proposition and offense played a bigger role in the final three games. The Tigers won two of them and Borowy figured in the decision in all three games.

Detroit tagged Borowy for five runs in an 8–4 win in Game Five behind Newhouser. Greenberg hit three doubles for the Tigers, who opened the sixth with four consecutive hits off Borowy en route to a four-run inning.

In Game Six, the Cubs avoided elimination thanks to Borowy's four scoreless innings of relief in a 12-inning, 8–7 win. Stan Hack's double was the game-winning hit.

Despite having pitched in two previous games, Grimm called on Borowy for Game Seven on one day's rest since his relief appearance. He didn't make it out of the first

Chicago Cubs'
Phil Cavarretta

Stan Hack's game-winning double in Game Six kept the Cubs hopes alive—but not for long

inning, yielding singles to Skeeter Webb, Eddie Mayo and Doc Cramer. The Tigers went on to score five runs in the first and ride the early lead to a 9–3 win. Newhouser, pitching on two days' rest, pitched a complete game and struck out ten, matching the number of hits he allowed.

The Tigers wrapped up the second World Series title in their history. The other had come in 1935, when, ironically, they beat the Cubs in six games.

It would turn out to be the Cubs' last trip to the postseason in the century.

BOB FELLER

TEAMS:
Cleveland Indians 1936–56

Games:	.570
Games started:	.484
Complete games:	.279
Win–Loss:	.266–162
Innings pitched:	.3,827
Runs:	.1,557
ERA:	.3.25
Strikeouts:	.2,581
Bases on balls:	.1,764
Batting average:	.151

How fast was the man nicknamed "Rapid Robert?"

People were forever trying to rig up tests, but none had the reliability of the modern radar gun. Consensus is, however, that Feller in his prime must have thrown somewhere around 100 miles per hour and did indeed deserve the nickname that followed him throughout his career.

Feller developed his pitching arm in Van Meter, Iowa, under the watchful eye of his father. Legend has it that the Indians secretly signed

Feller overpowered hitters with one of the game's greatest fastballs

Feller when he was 16 years old, offering one dollar, an autographed baseball and a chance to play in the major leagues.

When his career ended after the 1956 season, Feller had 266 victories and was the winningest pitcher in Indians' history, even though he sacrificed almost four years of his career to serve in the US Navy during World War II.

Feller led the AL in wins six times. He was the strikeout leader seven times, claimed one ERA title and was on eight All-Star teams. He was the first Indians player to have his number retired and the first pitcher to be elected to the Hall of Fame on the first ballot since Walter Johnson.

Despite his legendary fastball, Feller maintained that many of his strikeouts came on either curveballs or sliders. The fear of Feller's fastball was as important as the pitch itself. Said Billy Johnson of the New York Yankees, "He was so deceptive when he cranked up before releasing the ball. You'd expect the 100 mile per hour fastball but he'd give you an outstanding curveball."

Feller had a reputation before he got to the major leagues. He worked three innings of an

exhibition game against the Cardinals and eight of the nine outs came on strikeouts. He came up at the end of the 1936 season as a 17 year-old and struck out 15 St. Louis Browns in his major league debut. Shortly thereafter, he had a 17-strikeout game against the Philadelphia Athletics.

Hitters couldn't handle a lot of his pitches and neither could catchers. Feller's early years were plagued by wildness—just as his fastball was a little better than most, his wildness was a little more profound than the usual case.

In 1938, Feller won 17 games and led the league with 240 strikeouts. He also set a major league record by walking 208 batters. His control improved with more experience. Feller had become such a big name that his games would frequently draw as many as 10,000 extra fans on the road. Fans like power, whether it comes from home run hitters or strikeout pitchers and Feller didn't disappoint. In 1940, he opened the season with a no-hitter against the Chicago White Sox, the first of 27 wins, which represented a personal best.

When he enlisted in the Navy, Feller was just 23, but had already won 107 major league games. By the time he emerged from his military obligation, the Indians were assembling one of the most formidable starting staffs in major league history. It was Feller with Early Wynn, Bob Lemon and Mike Garcia.

Feller won 26 games in 1946 and broke the strikeout record with 348. He pitched the second of his three no-hitters (he also had 12 career one-hitters).

He led the league in strikeouts for the final time in 1948. He contributed six wins down the stretch to help the Indians win their first American League title in 28 years. He was a 1–0 loser in his only World Series start.

Feller had two substandard years before he rebounded to go 22–8 in 1951. He led the league in wins for the fifth time and had the best winning percentage for the only time in his career.

He was an important figure off the field as well, being one of the first to lead the fight for a players' pension fund.

Longtime AL first baseman Vic Power recalled the experience of batting against Feller in the waning days of the pitcher's career. Power fouled off several pitches and realized he still couldn't get around on a fastball from a pitcher who was supposedly at the end of the line.

"I had to laugh thinking how tough he must have been when he was younger," Power said.

Bob Feller

Despite the end of World War II and the return of players to their teams, baseball was in a state of turmoil. Many players responded to promises offered them by wealthy Mexican businessman Jorge Pasquel who formed the Mexican League with his brothers. Their mission—to rival the majors.

Mickey Owen was one of several players to receive a five-year ban for plying his trade in the new Mexican League

Several players made the move to the new league, most notably power-hitting shortstop Vern Stephens of the St. Louis Browns. Stephens' defection was short-lived, however, as he heeded the threat of Commissioner Happy Chandler. Chandler promised a five-year ban for any players who jumped once the major league season had started.

Several players tested Chandler's edict and were not allowed to return once the season began. As for the major leagues themselves, several teams were strengthened by the return of more key players from military service once the war had ended.

The greatest beneficiaries were the Boston Red Sox. Their returning superstar, Ted Williams, helped take them to the American League pennant. Williams' 38 home runs, 123 runs batted in and .342 batting average were second in the league in all three categories, but the overall performance was enough to earn Most Valuable Player honors for the man known as "The Splendid Splinter."

The Red Sox clinched the American League flag on September 11, when they were 12 games in front of second-place Detroit Tigers. Not to be overlooked in Boston's success were the performances of another returnee, second baseman Bobby Doerr, and first baseman Rudy York, who was acquired in an off-season trade from the Tigers. Doerr hit 18 home runs and drove in 116 runs. York, a consistent power hitter throughout his career in Detroit, hit 17 home runs and drove in 119.

No team wins without pitching and the Boston pitching staff was also outstanding. They got 20-win seasons from Boo Ferris (25–6) and

SHORTS Early in the season, Washington shortstop Cecil Travis put together a string of six consecutive hits, a remarkable feat considering the damage Travis had suffered to his feet in Europe during the war. Both feet were frozen and Travis never completely recovered. Despite incredible pain, he continued to play—spending hours on the training table before each game.

Tex Hughson (20–11) and solid relief work from Bob Klinger, who saved a league-leading nine games. With the trade of York, Hank Greenberg returned to his original first base position for Detroit. His 44 home runs and 127 RBIs led the league. Hal Newhouser continued to be among the league's dominators, tying Cleveland's Bob Feller with 26 wins and posting a circuit leading 1.94 ERA. But the Tigers still finished second to the Red Sox.

Several stars also rejoined the New York Yankees. But while Joe DiMaggio may have received most of the press as a returning hero, it was left fielder Charlie Keller who posted the superior power numbers after rejoining his club. Keller belted a team-leading 30 home runs and 101 runs batted in. Spud Chandler regained his spot as the ace of the Yankee staff with a 20–8 record.

Another event of note in the Yankee season was the resignation of Joe McCarthy as manager of the club. McCarthy had piloted the team since 1931 and had a 22–13 record in 1946 before stepping down. His replacement was popular catcher Bill Dickey, still an active player. Dickey led the team to a 57–48 record before handing the reins over to Johnny Neun for the last 14 games.

The player who beat out Ted Williams for the American League batting title was Mickey Vernon, first baseman for the fourth-place Washington Senators. Vernon's .353 batting mark and Stan Spence's 16 home runs topped the Senators offensively.

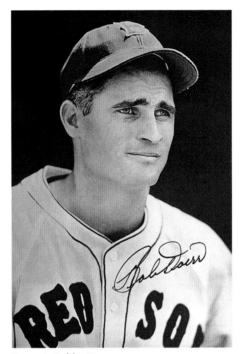

Boston's Bobby Doerr

After 30 games, Chicago White Sox manager Jimmie Dykes was replaced by 45-year-old pitcher Ted Lyons. Lyons, still an active pitcher, led the Sox to a 64–60 record for the remainder of the season.

Lou Boudreau's Cleveland Indians could boast one of the league's premier pitchers in Bob Feller, whose 26 victories tied Detroit's Hal Newhouser for the league lead. But Feller had sole possession of the lead in the following categories—strikeouts (348), games (48), starts (42), complete games (38), innings pitched (371) and shutouts (10).

They also had the league's leading base stealer in George Case, obtained from the Senators for Jeff Heath. Case swiped 28 sacks for his new club. Vern Stephens' decision to return from Mexico was a good one for the St. Louis Browns as his .307 batting mark led the team. He also belted 14 home runs. Browns' manager Luke Sewell joined the ranks of departing skippers on August 31 when he stepped down. Zack Taylor replaced him for the remainder of the season.

Sam Chapman's 20 home runs weren't enough to help the Philadelphia Athletics out of the cellar. Connie Mack's club finished 55 games out of first place.

The Boston Red Sox's 20-game winner, Tex Hughson

Most experts felt that the National League race would be between the St. Louis Cardinals and the Brooklyn Dodgers, because they were the teams with the best crop of returning players from the service.

The defending champion Chicago Cubs had almost the same cast as in 1945, while the Cardinals and Dodgers were vastly improved. With Stan Musial back playing primarily at first base and Red Schoendienst moving to second from the outfield, the Cardinals had a different look. Catcher Walker Cooper, considered by many to be the best receiver in the game, had been sold to the Giants in January. St. Louis native Joe Garagiola and Del Rice shared the catching duties.

As they prepared to play their last games of the regular season, the Cardinals and Dodgers were tied for first place with identical records. Since the Cubs were already eliminated, the outcome would determine the league champion. But Chicago played the "spoiler" role to perfection as they defeated the Redbirds 8–5.

Former Cardinal Mort Cooper, pitching for the Boston Braves, shut out the Dodgers 4–0. The losses set the stage for the first league playoff series in the history of major league baseball. The best-of-three series began in St. Louis with Brooklyn at a decided disadvantage, having suffered the loss of their top home run hitter and base stealer Pete Reiser, who had fractured his ankle early in September.

Cardinals' ace Howie Pollet, who had posted a 21–10 record to lead the National League in pitching victories, gave up only three Dodger hits and notched the win for the Cardinals 4–2. Game Two, played in Brooklyn, was a 2–0 victory for the Cardinals, who then prepared to face the Boston Red Sox in the World Series.

Musial's league-leading .365 batting average, complemented by additional league-topping numbers in doubles (50) and triples (20) continued to fuel his reputation as one of the best pure hitters in the game and led him to the league's Most Valuable Player award. Right fielder Enos (Country) Slaughter was the league's leading RBI man with 130 and led St. Louis in

home runs with 18. Pollet not only led the National League in wins, but in ERA as well with a 2.10 mark.

Leo Durocher's Brooklyn club, in the running to the very end, got fine pitching from a staff headed by Kirby Higbe with a 17–8 record. Despite an injury-shortened season, returning outfielder Reiser still led the league with 34 stolen bases and belted a team leading 11 home runs. Dixie Walker had an impressive .319 average with 116 runs batted in. But catcher Mickey Owen, lost for much of the 1945 season to military service, decided to sign on with the upstart Mexican League. When he attempted to rejoin the Brooklyn team in August of 1946, he found out that Commissioner Chandler was not bluffing.

Chandler denied Owen's request for reinstatement. The defending champion Cubs were plagued with injuries to several of their regulars. Second baseman Don Johnson, third baseman Stan Hack and outfielder Andy Pafko suffered fractures that kept them out of action for a significant number of games. Bill Nicholson, perennially a power hitter in the Chicago lineup, had an off year and was relegated to a secondary role. The Cubs' pitching staff posted mediocre records, but Johnny Schmitz struck out a league-leading 135 hitters.

Billy Southworth's Boston Braves had a 20-game winner in Johnny Sain (20–14). Tommy Holmes' power numbers were down as he hit just six home runs, tying him with first baseman Ray Sanders (purchased at the start of the season from the Cardinals). But Holmes did manage a respectable .310 average. Sanders was expected to provide some extra punch in the Boston lineup, but was sidelined for more than half the season with a broken arm.

Del Ennis sparkled in the Philadelphia Phillies' lineup with a .313 batting average and 17 home runs. The fifth place Phils also got good pitching from veteran Schoolboy Rowe, who posted a 17–4 mark, and Ken Raffensberger who saved a League-leading six games.

The Cincinnati Reds finished sixth, 30 games behind St. Louis. The Pittsburgh Pirates were seventh, despite a league-leading 23 home runs from Ralph Kiner.

The last-place New York Giants, still piloted by Mel Ott who hit the last home run of his career on Opening Day (his 511th), got home run production from Johnny Mize, who belted 22 despite missing 54 games with a broken hand.

SHORTS Baseball Commissioner Happy Chandler originally imposed a lifetime suspension on players defecting to the Mexican League, but reduced it to five years as more players tried to return. Mickey Owen, Max Lanier, Fred Martin and Lou Klein were all handed the five-year ban. One positive result of the Mexican situation was increased discussion between players and management regarding players' rights.

Brooklyn's Dixie Walker

GAME 1	
Boston Red Sox 3	St. Louis Cardinals 2
GAME 2	
St. Louis Cardinals 3	Boston Red Sox 0
GAME 3	
Boston Red Sox 4	St. Louis Cardinals 0
GAME 4	
St. Louis Cardinals 12	Boston Red Sox 3
GAME 5	
Boston Red Sox 6	St. Louis Cardinals 3
GAME 6	
St. Louis Cardinals 4	Boston Red Sox 1
GAME 7	
St. Louis Cardinals 4	Boston Red Sox 3

It was Enos Slaughter's mad dash, but it carried all of the St. Louis Cardinals to a World Series championship. Slaughter's aggressive base running at a critical juncture of a close Game Seven against the Boston Red Sox helped the Cardinals to win their second Series in five years.

Series hero Enos Slaughter

Both Slaughter and pitcher Harry Brecheen contributed clutch performances that allowed the Cardinals to win the final two games of the Series.

The Cardinals had the more difficult time reaching their fourth Series in five years. They tied the Brooklyn Dodgers and had to win two games in a playoff to get to the Series. It was the first time two teams finished deadlocked and

needed to have a tie-breaking playoff. Boston, on the other hand, breezed to the American League title, winning 104 games and finishing 12 games ahead of the Detroit Tigers.

The Red Sox took Game One, 3–2, on Rudy York's tenth-inning home run. The Cardinals got even in Game Two by winning 3–0 behind Brecheen, who allowed four hits, all singles, in the complete game shutout.

Boston returned the shutout in Game Three, winning 4–0 behind Boo Ferriss, a 25-game winner in the regular season. York hit his second homer for the Red Sox.

Game Four broke the cycle of tautly-pitched games as the Cardinals pounded 20 hits en route to a 12–3 victory. Slaughter, Whitey Kurowski and rookie catcher Joe Garagiola, who occupied the middle three spots in the St. Louis batting order, each had four hits. The three players were a combined 12-for-16 with seven runs and five RBIs. Tex Hughson, a 20-game winner, was the Red Sox starter who was knocked out in the third inning.

The Red Sox bounced back with a 6–3 win in Game Five behind Joe Dobson. Dobson allowed four hits and the three runs he gave up were unearned.

The Cardinals were desperate for a win in Game Six and Brecheen delivered. He gave up seven hits in the 4–1 complete game victory. That set up one of the most memorable deciding games in Series history.

The Cardinals took a 3–1 lead into the seventh behind the solid pitching of Murry Dickson. The game's first two batters, Wally Moses and Johnny Pesky, got singles off Dickson, but he held the Red Sox to just one hit over the next six innings.

Dickson helped spark the tie-breaking rally for the Cardinals in the fifth. His double scored Harry Walker to make it 2–1 and Dickson scored the third run when Red Schoendienst singled.

It appeared that Dickson was beginning to tire in the eighth inning. Pinch hitter Rip Russell led off the inning with a single. Another pinch hitter, George Metkovich, doubled, moving Russell to third.

Manager Eddie Dyer called on Brecheen to face Moses and Pesky, both lefthanded batters. Moses struck out. Pesky lined out to left and Slaughter's throw kept the runners at third and second.

Righthander Dom DiMaggio tied the game with a double off the right-center field wall. Brecheen stranded DiMaggio at second by getting Ted Williams to pop out.

In the bottom of the inning, Red Sox reliever Bob Klinger faced Slaughter, who singled for his eighth hit of the Series. Kurowski failed on a bunt attempt and Del Rice hit a fly ball for the inning's second out.

Harry Walker lined a ball to left-center and Slaughter was off with the crack of the bat. Pesky, the Red Sox shortstop and relay man on the play, may have been surprised to

see that Slaughter hadn't stopped at third. When Pesky made his throw, it was too late to catch Slaughter.

Even then, the Red Sox weren't through. Brecheen started the ninth by surrendering two singles. He got a force out that put the tying run at third with one out. Roy Partee was retired on a foul pop. Brecheen nailed down the win by getting pinch hitter Tom McBride on an infield grounder.

Brecheen was 3–0 with a 0.45 ERA, Slaughter batted .320 and Walker hit .412 with six RBIs.

Rudy York crosses home after his game-winning dinger in the Series opener

AWARDS

MOST VALUABLE PLAYER

AL: Joe DiMaggio, NY Yankees

NL: Bob Elliott, Boston Braves

ROOKIE OF THE YEAR

AL, NL: Jackie Robinson, Brooklyn

LEADERS

BATTING AVERAGE

AL: Ted Williams, Boston Red Sox, .343

NL: Harry Walker, St. Louis
Cardinals/Philadelphia, .363

HOME RUNS

AL: Ted Williams, Boston Red Sox, 32

NL: Ralph Kiner, Pittsburgh; Johnny Mize,
NY Giants, 51

RUNS BATTED IN

AL: Ted Williams, Boston Red Sox, 114

NL: Johnny Mize, NY Giants, 138

STOLEN BASES

AL: Bob Dillinger, St. Louis Browns, 34

NL: Jackie Robinson, Brooklyn, 29

PITCHING VICTORIES

AL: Bob Feller, Cleveland, 20

NL: Ewell Blackwell, Cincinnati, 22

EARNED RUN AVERAGE

AL: Joe Haynes, Chicago White Sox, 2.42

NL: Warren Spahn, Boston Braves, 2.33

STRIKEOUTS

AL: Bob Feller, Cleveland, 196

NL: Ewell Blackwell, Cincinnati, 193

For years they occupied their own world, one where good pay, good working conditions and respect were often difficult to find. But in 1947 the dreams of a handful of black baseball players gradually began to come true.

Because major league baseball had always been a white man's world, it took the efforts of a white man, Branch Rickey, to pry open its doors and allow blacks to enter. And it took the courage of 28-year-old Jackie Robinson to begin the process.

Robinson was one of several black players who had attempted to work out with major league teams, despite a general lack of interest or encouragement by major league baseball. But Branch Rickey was anything but shortsighted. He had observed the performance of black players in the Negro Leagues for years. He knew the legend surrounding players like Josh Gibson, Cool Papa Bell, Buck O'Neill, Oscar Charleston and Satchel Paige.

So when Rickey signed Robinson and pitcher John Wright to contracts with Montreal of the International League, he was confident it was the beginning of a new era for baseball. When Robinson won the International League batting title in 1946 with a .349 average, Rickey's beliefs in his ability were validated.

The 1947 season began with controversy of a different sort, however. Larry MacPhail, former Brooklyn Dodger executive and now part owner of the New York Yankees, had coaxed Charlie Dressen and Red Commiden away from coaching positions at Brooklyn. Dodger manager Leo Durocher, never one to mince words, countered by accusing MacPhail of consorting with gamblers during an exhibition game between the Yankees and Dodgers in Cuba. MacPhail responded by filing libel charges against Durocher with the Commissioner's office.

Happy Chandler, in the greatest test of his authority to date, weighed the evidence and suspended Durocher for the season. He also imposed fines on most of the parties from both sides.

With the situation resolved, the Yankees set about to regain superiority in the American League. Joe DiMaggio failed to lead the league in any of the categories, but his .315 batting average, 20 home runs and 97 RBIs earned him Most Valuable Player honors. The pitching staff was led by Allie Reynolds, acquired from Cleveland in an off-season trade for Joe Gordon and Eddie Backman. Reynolds posted a 19–8 record for the Yanks. Spud Chandler continued to be a dependable pitcher, leading

A determined, yet dignified, Jackie Robinson excelled in the face of adversity

Former Yankees' pitcher Ralph Branca went to the Dodgers and posted a 21–12 record

the league in ERA with a 2.46 mark.

Joe Page, along with Cleveland's Eddie Klieman, topped the circuit with 17 saves for New York.

In a surprising off-season move, the Detroit Tigers sold their defending home run champion, Hank Greenberg, to the Pittsburgh Pirates. Greenberg's successor at first base, Roy Cullenbine, led the Tigers with 24 home runs and Fred Hutchinson's 18–10 record was best on the staff, but the Tigers finished 12 games behind the Yankees.

The third-place Boston Red Sox installed lights in Fenway Park before the season started, enabling more fans to see Ted Williams win the second Triple Crown of his career. Williams hit 32 home runs, drove in 114 runs and posted a .343 average. Joe Dobson's 18–8 record led a pitching staff troubled by injuries and sore arms. Boo Ferris and Tex Hughson were particularly bothered as they each finished with undistinguished 12–11 records.

Joe Gordon wasted no time acclimatizing himself to his new surroundings in Cleveland as he led the team with 29 home runs. But it was Bob Feller who continued to grab most of the headlines for the Tribe, leading the league with another 20-win season against 11 losses. He also took the honors in strikeouts with 196. Don Black, acquired from the Philadelphia Athletics on waivers, tossed a no-hitter against his old team on July 10. Eddie Klieman, besides tying New York's Joe Page for the league lead in saves, also posted the most appearances with 58.

The other big story in Cleveland was Larry

Doby, the first black player to appear in an American League game. Doby's first at-bat came as a pinch hitter on July 5 against the White Sox. He would go on to bat 32 times in 29 games, but his best years were still to come.

Rudy York came to the Chicago White Sox in June from Boston and hit 15 home runs to lead his new club. Stan Spence continued to power the Washington Senators with 16 home runs and Jeff Heath belted 27 home runs for Muddy Ruel's St. Louis Browns, who also made history by playing Hank Thompson and Willard Brown in the lineup at the same time. It was the first time two black players appeared simultaneously for one club.

Robinson's emergence for the Brooklyn Dodgers was instrumental in taking them to the 1947 National League pennant. He and Pee Wee Reese both went deep 12 times during the season for their club, but it was Robinson's 29 stolen bases and .297 batting average that made him baseball's first Rookie of the Year.

Clyde Sukeforth managed the club for the first two games before handing the reins over to Burt Shotton. Robinson's presence was certainly explosive in every city in which he appeared and several teams, including the defending National League champion St. Louis Cardinals, staged protests against sharing the field with him.

But Robinson had been warned by Branch Rickey not to respond to the taunts and insults—whether they came from the stands or from the opposing dugout. His mental strength and dignity, coupled with his ability on the field, saw him through.

Meanwhile, the Dodgers were on their way to a pennant. Besides the performances of Robinson and Reese, Dixie Walker and Pete Reiser both topped the .300 mark again, hitting .308 and .309 respectively. Ralph Branca's 21–12 record led their pitching staff, backed by Joe Hatten's 17–8 record.

Stan Musial's team-leading .312 average for the St. Louis Cardinals was impressive enough, especially considering he was hitting just .140 in mid-May. But the real offensive clout for the

SHORTS The Dodgers used three pitchers to hold the Yankees to just one hit in their exhibition game in Cuba. Pete Reiser doubled home Carl Furillo for Brooklyn's only tally and infielder Stuffy Stirnweiss got the Yankees' only hit. The new Havana stadium was called Stadium del Cerro. But it was the aftermath of the game that grabbed headlines as the verbal fireworks between Leo Durocher and Larry MacPhail heated up.

Ewell Blackwell's no-hitter proved the high-point of an awesome season

Giants' rookie pitcher Larry Jansen's remarkable 21–5 record gave him an .808 winning percentage, best in the National League. Jansen's last ten wins were consecutive and were all complete games.

The Cincinnati Reds also had one of the league's best arms in Ewell Blackwell, who posted 22 wins and 193 strikeouts to lead the League in both of those categories. Blackwell also threw a no-hitter against the Boston Braves on June 18. In his next start he almost duplicated the feat against Brooklyn, but Eddie Stanky spoiled the bid with a one-out single in the ninth inning. Blackwell's unusual sidearm motion, coupled with his tremendous velocity, earned him the nickname "The Whip."

Bill Nicholson regained his power stroke for the Chicago Cubs, belting 26 home runs. Charlie Grimm's club had little else to brag about, however, as they finished the season 16 games under .500, 25 out of first place.

Harry Walker, traded to Philadelphia by the St. Louis Cardinals in May for Ron Northey, hit .371 for his new team which, combined with his .200 mark in St. Louis, was enough to capture the National League batting title.

Even though they finished in the cellar, the Pittsburgh Pirates had Kiner's 51 home runs and 127 RBIs. With the acquisition of long-time American League slugger Greenberg, Kiner had a partner and a mentor. Greenberg hit 25 home runs for his new team.

The All-Star Game, played on July 8 at Wrigley Field in Chicago, was primarily a pitcher's showcase as Frank "Spec" Shea of the Yankees picked up the win. Giants' slugger Mize accounted for the only National League run with a solo home run in the fourth inning.

The season's most emotional scene occurred at Yankee Stadium on April 27 when the legendary home run king came back for "Babe Ruth Day" ceremonies. The Stadium was packed with 58,339 fans, who cheered and wept as Ruth, his voice weakened by the throat cancer that would take his life, told the crowd that "the only real game in the world" was baseball.

Cardinals came from third baseman Whitey Kurowski, who hit 27 home runs and drove in 104 runs for the second-place Redbirds. George Munger led the Cardinal pitchers with a 16–9 mark, followed by Harry "The Cat" Brecheen's 16–11 record.

Finishing a close third were Billy Southworth's Boston Braves, whose pitching tandem of Warren Spahn and Johnny Sain inspired one of baseball's most enduring expressions: "Spahn and Sain and pray for rain." Southworth's resolve to go primarily with his two aces for the stretch drive drew criticism from fans and sportswriters alike, but Spahn's 21–10 record and league-leading 2.33 ERA and Sain's 21–12 mark could not be denied. Third baseman Bob Elliott's 22 home runs, 113 RBIs and .313 batting mark made him one of the league's most dangerous hitters.

Mel Ott's New York Giants finished above the .500 mark in fourth place, but their line-up contained one of the most potent threats in baseball as first baseman Johnny Mize knocked a phenomenal 51 home runs and a league-leading 138 RBIs. But Mize shared the home run crown with another slugger—Pittsburgh's Ralph Kiner.

The Babe's final farewell

SHORTS Various stories have circulated about the meeting St. Louis Cardinals players had to discuss a protest against sharing the field with Jackie Robinson. The most popular version has owner Sam Breadon persuading them to go ahead and play. National League president Ford Frick reported Breadon's actions to the press, but Breadon denied that version of the story.

GAME 1	
NY Yankees 5	Brooklyn 3
GAME 2	
NY Yankees 10	Brooklyn 3
GAME 3	
Brooklyn 9	NY Yankees 8
GAME 4	
Brooklyn 3	NY Yankees 2
GAME 5	
NY Yankees 2	Brooklyn 1
GAME 6	
Brooklyn 8	NY Yankees 6
GAME 7	
NY Yankees 5	Brooklyn 2

The Brooklyn Dodgers thwarted Bill Bevens' no-hitter and made a catch that caused Joe DiMaggio to make a rare show of emotion on the baseball field. Those moments didn't add up to a Series victory, though, as the Dodgers fell to the New York Yankees in seven games of an intra-city World Series.

The mighty Yankees were back on top of the American League standings after a three-year absence from the postseason. They sailed to the American League pennant, finishing 12 games ahead of the Detroit Tigers with 97 victories. Near the end of June, the Yankees started a 19-game winning streak that would propel them past the rest of the league.

The Dodgers outlasted the St. Louis Cardinals and Boston Braves to claim the National League pennant. It had been an eventful year for the Dodgers, who broke baseball's color line by signing Jackie Robinson and installing him as a regular in the lineup.

The hidden strength of the Yankees was a good starting staff, headed by Allie Reynolds and Spec Shea, and those two pitchers got New York off to a 2–0 start at Yankee Stadium.

Ralph Branca, the Dodgers' 21-game winner, ran into trouble in the fifth inning of Game One and gave up five runs. Shea and reliever Joe Page combined on a six-hitter as the Yankees won 5–3. Tommy Henrich and Johnny Lindell both drove in a pair of runs.

In Game Two, Reynolds pitched a complete game and won 10–3. New York collected 15 hits off four Brooklyn pitchers and Lindell had two RBIs for the second consecutive game.

The Series shifted to Brooklyn and the Dodgers came to life in front of their rabid home fans. They started with a wild 9–8 win in Game

Al Gionfriddo's glove denied DiMaggio—and the Yankees— a crucial home run in Game Six

Three. The Dodgers scored six runs in the second inning, but had to hold on to win by a single run.

The Dodgers built their lead on two-run doubles by Eddie Stanky and Carl Furillo. The latter pinch hit for Pete Reiser in the second inning. The Yankees' comeback started with a two-run homer by DiMaggio in the fifth inning. Tommy Henrich's RBI double an inning later got the Yankees within one at 9–7. Yogi Berra, batting for Sherman Lollar, got the first pinch hit homer in Series history for the Yankees' last run in the seventh.

It looked as though Bevens was headed for history in Game Four. Instead, he wound up with a loss. He had allowed a run in the fifth inning on a pair of walks, a bunt and an infield grounder, but hadn't allowed a hit through the first eight innings. He took a 2–1 lead into the ninth.

Catcher Bruce Edwards hit a fly ball for the first out of the ninth. Furillo walked—the ninth issued by Bevens in the game—but Spider Jorgensen was retired on a foul ball.

Brooklyn's Hugh Casey proved almost unhittable in the Series

Pinch runner Al Gionfriddo stole second and pinch hitter Reiser was walked intentionally. Cookie Lavagetto batted for Stanky and drove a double to right field that ended the no-hitter and gave the Dodgers a 3–2 win that tied the Series after four games.

DiMaggio homered in Game Five and Shea pitched a four hitter for a 2–1 Yankees win.

Back in Yankee Stadium for Game Six, the Dodgers couldn't hold a 4–0 lead through three innings. The Yankees briefly went ahead 5–4 before Brooklyn responded with a four-run rally and an 8–5 lead.

It looked as though DiMaggio had tied the game in the sixth when he drove a pitch toward the left field wall with two men on base. Gionfriddo, who had come in as a defensive replacement, reached out and made a difficult catch, which caused the usually serene DiMaggio to kick the dirt near second base in frustration. The Dodgers held on and won 8–6.

Brooklyn jumped out to an early 2–0 lead in Game Seven, knocking Shea out of the game. The Yankees came back and got a strong relief outing from Joe Page to win the game 5–2 and take the Series.

Despite the short outing in Game Seven, Shea was 2–0 with a 2.35 ERA. Lindell hit .500 for the Yankees and drove in seven runs.

The Dodgers' Hugh Casey was 2–0 with a 0.87 ERA and Furillo hit .353.

JACKIE ROBINSON

TEAMS:
Brooklyn Dodgers 1947–56

Games:	1,382
At-Bats:	4,877
Runs:	947
RBI:	734
Home runs:	137
Hits:	1518
Doubles:	273
Triples:	54
Stolen Bases:	197
Average:	0.311
Slugging percentage:	0.474

Brooklyn Dodgers' general manager Branch Rickey chose the fiercest competitor he could find for a special assignment.

Then Rickey asked that player to do the impossible—he wasn't allowed to fight back. Jackie Robinson followed those orders in the remarkable 1947 season that saw him change more than baseball.

Robinson was the multi-sport athlete chosen by Rickey to break baseball's unofficial, but very

Robinson's talent was as impressive as his bravery

real, color line—Robinson would be playing for a race of people, and Rickey knew it was a tough job. He also knew that the whole experiment might fail if the player couldn't shoulder the enormous burden. Robinson met that challenge and managed to more than hold his own against major league competition.

"Not everybody could have handled it. Jackie did. The Dodgers were the right club to be with and Jackie Robinson was the right person to achieve the goal," said Hank Aaron years later.

Robinson was 28 years old when he played his first major league game. He had been an athletic legend at UCLA, the school's first four-sport letterman.

Robinson was playing shortstop for the Kansas City Monarchs in the Negro Leagues when Brooklyn scout Clyde Sukeforth was dispatched to file reports on him. Rickey was feigning interest in backing a Dodgers' team in the Negro Leagues to keep his real plan a secret. Rickey's true desire was to integrate the existing major

leagues. Rickey was a smart enough baseball man to know that teams like his were turning their backs on an amazing pool of talent.

He signed Robinson on October 23, 1945 and sent him to the Dodgers' Class AAA team in Montreal. Rickey again had done his homework. He knew that Montreal had a more casual attitude toward race than most cities in the United States and knew it would be a favorable setting for Robinson to break in. Robinson helped the Montreal Royals win a championship and Rickey brought him to the majors the following year. He selected Robinson because he sensed he had "the guts not to fight back."

There were rumors that some of the Dodgers players were prepared to strike rather than welcome Robinson as a teammate. Manager Leo Durocher put down that controversy. Robinson frequently wasn't allowed to stay in the hotels the Dodgers used. Their spring training complex at Vero Beach, Florida, "Dodgertown", was an outgrowth of the segregated conditions that existed in the south at the time.

But it was nasty just about everywhere. Some of the St. Louis Cardinals were supposedly ready to refuse to play against the Dodgers if Robinson was in the lineup. Bench jockeying was vicious, especially in Philadelphia.

Robinson changed the way the game was played. He brought speed, stealing 37 bases in 1949, the highest total in 19 years. He stole home 19 times, the most since World War I. He played ably at first base, second, third and the outfield.

Robinson played ten seasons in the major leagues, retiring after 1956. The Dodgers tried to sell his contract to the New York Giants, but Robinson had already decided to leave the game and embark on a career in the business world. He became an executive with a New York company and continued to enjoy a high profile.

He was politically active in his post-baseball years and often championed the cause of black managers. Baseball didn't hire its first black manager until 1974, two years after Robinson's death at 53 in 1972.

In 1987, baseball marked the 40th anniversary of Robinson's debut by naming its annual Rookie of the Year award after him. Ten years later, it mandated that all teams retire No. 42 in honor of Robinson.

AWARDS
MOST VALUABLE PLAYER
AL: Lou Boudreau, Cleveland
NL: Stan Musial, St. Louis Cardinals

ROOKIE OF THE YEAR
Alvin Dark, Boston Braves

LEADERS
BATTING AVERAGE
AL: Ted Williams, Boston Red Sox, .369
NL: Stan Musial, St. Louis Cardinals, .376

HOME RUNS
AL: Joe DiMaggio, NY Yankees, 39
NL: Ralph Kiner, Pittsburgh; Johnny Mize, NY Giants, 40

RUNS BATTED IN
AL: Joe DiMaggio, NY Yankees, 155
NL: Stan Musial, St. Louis Cardinals, 131

STOLEN BASES
AL: Bob Dillinger, St. Louis Browns, 28
NL: Richie Ashburn, Philadelphia Phillies, 32

PITCHING VICTORIES
AL: Hal Newhouser, Detroit, 21
NL: Johnny Sain, Boston Braves, 24

EARNED RUN AVERAGE
AL: Gene Bearden, Cleveland, 2.43
NL: Harry Brecheen, St. Louis Cardinals, 2.24

STRIKEOUTS
AL: Bob Feller, Cleveland, 164
NL: Harry Brecheen, St. Louis Cardinals, 149

It is often said that baseball makes legends and legends make baseball. In 1948, one legend passed on after years of making history in the major leagues. Another legend in the making appeared in a major league game for the first time.

Three weeks after attending the premiere of his biographical—and occasionally fictional—movie life story, George Herman (Babe) Ruth, arguably the most famous name and face in the history of the game, succumbed to the throat cancer that had diminished his voice and ravaged his body. On August 16, 1948, news emerged that, at age 53, baseball's "Sultan of Swat" was gone.

Three days earlier 51,013 fans packed Chicago's Comiskey Park to see another legend. Leroy (Satchel) Paige, at least 42 years old, was signed by Bill Veeck for the Cleveland Indians on July 7 and shut out the White Sox 5–0. After years of hearing all the legends about his pitches, his speed, his ability to literally call his own shots and his pinpoint control, major league fans and players were finally seeing at first-hand what Negro League spectators and players had known all along.

Veeck was already building a reputation as a man who would do anything to draw a crowd, and his signing of the aging pitcher was viewed by some as just another typically Veeck publicity

Satchel Paige finally made it into the Major Leagues in 1948

stunt. But Cleveland happened to be in a pennant race and while Veeck may have been colorful, he was no fool. Down the stretch, quality pitching is what wins pennants.

The Indians had it all. Their lineup could boast six players with home runs in double figures, topped by Joe Gordon's 32 and Ken Keltner's 31. Gordon's 124 RBIs topped the club. Dale Mitchell's .336 average and 13 stolen bases provided good table setting for the team's power hitters. But it was the pitching that ultimately enabled the Indians to keep up with the Boston Red Sox and New York Yankees, forcing a playoff for the American League flag for the first time in the League's history.

Besides the ageless Paige, who still posted a 6–1 record in spite of his late late arrival, the Indians had two 20-game winners—rookie Gene Bearden (20–7) and Bob Lemon (20–14). Lemon punctuated his season with a no-hitter against Detroit on June 30. The Indians' perennial ace, Bob Feller, had somewhat of an off year, if 19–14 could be considered an "off" performance. Nonetheless, Feller again took the league's strikeout title with 194.

Boston fought hard under new manager Joe McCarthy, led by Ted Williams' sensational .369 batting average and 127 RBIs. His 25 home runs were second on the club to Vern Stephens' 29.

The Yankees were in the hunt, too—as usual. Joe DiMaggio's league-leading 39 home runs and 155 RBIs paced the club and kept the race going until October 2 when New York was finally eliminated by Boston. Vic Raschi and Ed Lopat, acquired from the Chicago White Sox in a pre-season trade, led the Yankee pitching staff.

On the last day of the regular season the Indians clinched at least a tie by beating the Detroit Tigers on Feller's shutout while the Red Sox kept pace with another victory over New York. The one-game playoff was scheduled for the following day at Fenway Park.

The playoff game was predictably dramatic as player-manager Lou Boudreau went with his rookie Bearden. McCarthy chose an unlikely starter in Denny Galehouse. Boudreau belted two home runs, but the game-winner was hit by Ken Keltner in the fourth inning—a three-run shot. The Indians went on to win 8–3 and prepared to

The Indians' Ken Keltner provided the heroics in the American League playoff game at Fenway

face the Boston Braves in the World Series.

Connie Mack's Philadelphia Athletics finished fourth, 14 games above the .500 mark. Third baseman Hank Majeski's 12 home runs, 120 RBIs and .310 batting average led the club.

Hal Newhouser's 21–12 record and 143 strikeouts showed he was still the ace of the Detroit Tigers' pitching staff. Center fielder Hoot Evers posted his best offensive marks with a .314 batting average and 103 RBIs while Pat Mullin belted 23 home runs to lead the club.

The St. Louis Browns had some decent numbers among their hitters with Bob Dillinger swiping a league-leading 28 bases and posting a .321 average, just behind Al Zarilla's club-leading .329.

The Washington Senators and Chicago White Sox rounded out the league, finishing in the last two spots. Left fielder Pat Seerey, obtained in a June trade from the Indians for Bob Kennedy, led the White Sox with 18 home runs.

The "Spahn and Sain" legend continued for the Boston Braves, with Johnny Sain putting up the top numbers. Sain posted a 24–15 record and helped the Braves to win the 1948 National League pennant. Third baseman Bob Elliott powered the team with 23 home runs and 100 RBIs. Outfielder Jeff Heath, despite missing 39 games due to injuries, hit 20 homers.

Eddie Dyer's St. Louis Cardinals finished

second, 6½ games behind the Braves, but Stan Musial, now playing left field for the Redbirds, narrowly missed the Triple Crown as he led the league with a .376 batting average and 131 runs batted in, but fell one home run short of Pittsburgh's Ralph Kiner and New York's Johnny Mize. They tied for the home run lead with 40. Musial also posted league-leading marks in doubles (46) and triples (18), all of which helped him to be elected the league's Most Valuable Player.

Harry Brecheen's 20–7 record gave him the league lead in winning percentage (.741). Breechem, nicknamed "The Cat," also led the National League in strikeouts with 149 and earned run average with 2.24. Relief pitcher Ted Wilks suffered his first loss since 1945, having won 12 straight decisions in 77 appearances during the three-year period. Wilks also posted a team-leading 12 saves.

Musial and Brecheen were both holdouts in the early spring, but both signed contracts just before the start of spring training.

Leo Durocher returned as manager of the Brooklyn Dodgers following his one-year suspension, but stepped aside in mid-July to take the skipper's job for the New York Giants, who had just axed long-time player-manager Mel Ott. Last year's substitute manager, Burt Shotton, once again took the reins for Brooklyn after Durocher left.

The Dodgers' drop from first to third place could be attributed not only to an improved Boston club, but to lower numbers from pitcher Ralph Branca (14–9 after a 21–12 mark in 1947) and 1947's rookie sensation Jackie Robinson. Robinson was still an exciting baserunner and hitter, but was not the offensive

SHORTS Chicago Cubs' outfielder Bill Nicholson was called "Swish" because of his consistent home run production. His most dramatic shot came on April 24, 1948, at Wrigley Field when he hit a ball completely out of the park. The ball landed on Sheffield Avenue, took a bounce off a nearby building and hit the hood of a moving car.

Jan. 30: Former Yankee pitcher Herb Pennock and current general manager of the Phillies, collapsed in the lobby of a New York hotel and died in hospital.

Feb. 24: The Chicago White Sox traded pitcher Ed Lopat to the New York Yankees for three players.

March 6: The Brooklyn Dodgers traded infielder Eddie Stanky to the Boston Braves for Bama Rowell and cash.

April 20: Rookie first baseman George Vico hit a home run in his first major league at bat off White Sox hurler Joe Haynes.

April 24: Ted Wilks suffered his first loss as a relief pitcher since 1945. He had won 12 consecutive decisions for the Cardinals.

May 23: Joe DiMaggio leads the Yankees to a 6–5 win over Cleveland in the first game of a doubleheader by hitting three straight home runs, two of them off Bob Feller.

May 27: Hank Greenberg, who retired in the off season from the Pirates, purchased stock in the Cleveland Indians.

June 15: At the trade deadline the Indians and Browns exchanged pitchers, with Sam Zoldak going to Cleveland for Bill Kennedy.

June 30: Bob Lemon tossed a no-hitter for Cleveland against Detroit, thanks in part to spectacular defensive plays by Dale Mitchell and Ken Keltner.

July 31: The Boston Red Sox moved into first place in the American League.

Aug. 31: The Dodgers moved into a tie with the Boston Braves for first place in the National League.

Sept. 23: The Braves clinched the National League pennant with a 3–2 win over the New York Giants.

Oct. 12: Casey Stengel was hired to manage the New York Yankees.

Nov. 30: Indians' player-manager Lou Boudreau was named Most Valuable Player in the American League.

Dec. 2: Cardinal outfielder Stan Musial was named the National League's Most Valuable Player.

force he was in 1947. Dixie Walker, traded to Pittsburgh in the off season, and Pete Reiser, on the disabled list for nearly two-thirds of the season, were both out of the regular lineup.

Gene Hermanski filled his new role as a regular admirably, belting a team-leading 15 home runs, including three in one game in August against Chicago.

Dodgers' pitcher Rex Barney grabbed the headlines in September when he tossed a no-hitter against the Giants, throwing almost strictly fastballs in the process. The game was delayed by rain three different times, including a one-hour interruption. Because Brooklyn was still in the pennant race, it was decided to wait the showers out.

Dixie Walker hit .316 for his new club, the Pirates, and Ralph Kiner continued to post monster home run numbers with his league-tying 40.

In an interesting bit of trivia, 17 of Kiner's homers came on Sunday, including a string of eight consecutive Sundays with at least one home run. The Pirates also got good speed on

The Indians' Bob Lemon was a vital component of Cleveland's success

184

Cleveland's player-manager
Lou Boudreau

the basepaths with shortstop Stan Rojek, who stole 24 bases. But the Pittsburgh offense suffered a major blow in the off-season with the retirement of Hank Greenberg after just one season for the Bucs. Greenberg had been a complementary slugger to Kiner. Later in the year, Greenberg became a part owner of the Cleveland Indians.

After taking over as skipper of the New York Giants, Durocher led the club to a 51–38 record for the remainder of the season. Unfortunately, he inherited a 27–38 mark from Ott, his predecessor. Eight of the nine regulars in the New York lineup posted at least ten

home runs, topped by Johnny Mize's 40.

Outfielders Del Ennis and Richie Ashburn sparkled for the Philadelphia Phillies. Ashburn hit .333 and stole 32 bases in his rookie season and at one point had a 23-game hitting streak. Ennis hit 30 home runs, while shortstop Eddie Miller slugged 14.

Hank Sauer's 35 home runs topped the Cincinnati offense, but the seventh-place Reds couldn't overcome a poor start. On August 6, they fired Johnny Neun as manager and replaced him with Bucky Walters.

Andy Pafko's 26 home runs, 101 RBIs and .312 batting average were the offensive highlights for the last-place Chicago Cubs. Johnny Schmitz posted an 18–13 record to top the Cubs' pitching staff.

Baseball history was also made in Chicago in the pre-season when Jack Brickhouse broadcast an exhibition game between the Cubs and White Sox on WGN-TV—the first televised game ever in Chicago.

SHORTS Babe Ruth's last appearance at Yankee Stadium was June 13 when the team celebrated the 25th anniversary of the ballpark. Ruth's uniform number 3 was retired during the pre-game ceremonies. Fittingly, the Yankees won the game, beating the Indians 5–3. Though he could barely speak or move, Babe was able to acknowledge the cheers of the fans with his familiar smile.

GAME 1	
Boston Braves 1	Cleveland 0
GAME 2	
Cleveland 4	Boston Braves 1
GAME 3	
Cleveland 2	Boston Braves 0
GAME 4	
Cleveland 2	Boston Braves 1
GAME 5	
Boston Braves 11	Cleveland 5
GAME 6	
Cleveland 4	Boston Braves 3

Larry Doby's Game Four homer helped the Indians on their way

The Cleveland Indians broke the heart of every baseball fan in Boston en route to the 1948 World Series championship. If you liked the Boston Red Sox, your disappointment came when the Indians won the one-game playoff to claim the American League pennant. If the Boston Braves were your team, the Indians took care of them, too, winning the World Series in six games.

Indians' player-manager Lou Boudreau had a major role in getting his team to the postseason. Boudreau batted .351 with 16 home runs and 104 runs batted in. The Indians and Red Sox were both 96–58 when the season ended, so they had a one-game showdown at Fenway Park.

Boudreau went 4-for-4 with two home runs and two singles as the Indians won 8–3. Rookie lefthander Gene Bearden got the win, his 20th of the season.

The Braves had an easier time taking the National League pennant. They finished 6½ games ahead of the St. Louis Cardinals, helped by a solid pitching staff that inspired one of the game's greatest verses. Manager Billy Southworth coined the phrase, "Spahn and Sain and pray for rain." Translation: the Braves had sure winners in Warren Spahn and Johnny Sain, but less certain options for the other two spots.

It made for a lasting identity but one that Sain maintained was unfair. The other Braves starters may not have been at the level of Spahn and Sain, but Bill Voiselle won 13 games, only two fewer than Spahn, and Vern Bickford went 11–5 for Boston.

Cleveland's staff was led by two big-game pitchers in Bob Feller and Bob Lemon. Feller allowed just two hits in Game One of the Series, but came out a 1–0 loser to Sain because Tommy Holmes singled home a run in the bottom of the eighth.

Sain had to pitch out of trouble in the ninth when third baseman Bob Elliott made a two-base throwing error, but he held on for the four-hit shutout.

Lemon allowed a first-inning run in Game Two but shut out the Braves the rest of the way and won 4–1. Boudreau and Larry Doby each had two hits and an RBI to help the Indians even the Series.

Gene Bearden gave Cleveland its third consecutive excellent start in Game Three. He allowed five hits and didn't walk a batter in the 2–0 win. He singled, doubled and scored a run to help himself.

Game Four was another tight pitching battle. Cleveland's Steve Gromek bested Sain in a 2–1 decision. Doby hit another home run and so did the Braves' Marv Rickert. Rickert was one of the more obscure figures in the Series. He was a replacement for outfielder Jeff Heath, who was sidelined with a broken ankle. Rickert appeared in only three games during the regular season, but started five of the six games in the Series.

A crowd of 82,288 crammed into Cleveland's Municipal Stadium on the shores of

Lake Erie for Game Five, hoping to see the Indians win the Series on their home field. Instead, the Braves came away with an 11–5 win to force the Series back to Boston.

The Braves scored three runs in the seventh inning. Boston led from the start as Elliott hit a three-run homer in the first inning, then added a solo shot in his next at-bat. That gave the Braves a 4–1 lead through three innings, but the Indians overcame that with four runs in the fourth.

Jim Hegan hit a three-run homer for the Indians, but the lead was temporary because Bill Salkeld tied the score with a homer off Feller in the sixth.

The Indians trotted out five pitchers, including Satchel Paige, but couldn't shut down the Braves until six runs had crossed the plate in the seventh. Spahn got the win for Boston.

Lemon won Game Six, 4–3, to give Cleveland the Series. Bearden let a couple of inherited runners score in the eighth, but stopped the Braves in the ninth.

Lemon was 2–0 with a 1.65 ERA and Doby batted .318 for the Indians. Paige, who was at least 42, became the first black pitcher to appear in a World Series. The Indians won despite a .199 team batting average and Feller's 0–2 mark with a 5.02 ERA.

Elliott was Boston's offensive star with a .333 average, two home runs and five RBIs.

The Indians celebrate their World Series win

It was hard to take Casey Stengel seriously. He was always good for a funny quote, once reporters figured out exactly what he said. But his previous stints as a major league manager were considered laughable at best by many baseball experts. At worst, many sportswriters lacked the patience required to enjoy Stengel's unique sense of humor.

The New York Yankees' Joe DiMaggio was slowed by injury but returned in fine form

So when the New York Yankees hired the colorful Casey to take the reins of their club, some of the jaded New York writers saw lots of good copy in their future—but little success for an ailing Yankee team. Bucky Harris had been viewed by Yankee ownership as too easy while Stengel, despite his comedic nature, was considered more of a traditional, hard-line manager who could control his players.

Problems with the team were evident right from the beginning. Joe DiMaggio, the undisputed hitting star of the club, was plagued with lingering problems with his left heel that dated back to 1947. The pain was unbearable and DiMaggio sat out most of the first three months of the season, returning to action on June 28. Tommy Henrich was moved to first base, a position from which he hit 24 home runs to lead the team. Speedy Phil Rizzuto, entrenched at shortstop, stole 18 bases.

The pitching staff was led by Vic Raschi with a 21–10 record, supported by Allie Reynolds, Tommy Byrne and Ed Lopat. Reynolds, considered by many to be almost as fast as the

Cleveland Indians' Bob Feller, worked on varying his pitches more and his 17–6 record showed that the strategy paid off.

But it was Stengel's use of Joe Page that may have been the biggest component in New York's success. Appearing in a league-leading 60 games with no starts, Page posted a 13–9 record with 27 saves.

The Boston Red Sox, considered the favorites in the American League, made a strong run at the Yankees, who had begun the season well. Boston, with a lineup that could combine both average and power, swept a crucial September series from Stengel's club and entered the final weekend of the season with a one-game lead as they prepared to face the Yankees in New York. But the Yankees took those last two contests and won the American League flag on the last day of the season.

Ted Williams once again gave a performance worthy of Most Valuable Player honors, which he won. He hit for a .343 batting average, led the league in home runs (43) and doubles (39) and tied teammate Vern Stephens for the league RBI lead with 159. Mel Parnell anchored the Boston pitching staff with 25 wins to lead the league while Ellis Kinder posted a 23–6 record.

Lou Boudreau's defending champion Cleveland Indians suffered off years by pitcher Gene Bearden and third baseman Ken Keltner, but Larry Doby continued to produce with 24 home runs. Left fielder Dale Mitchell tied Doby for the team stolen base lead with ten, but his 23 triples easily captured the league lead.

Outfielder Vic Wertz made significant improvement offensively for the Detroit Tigers with 20 home runs, 133 RBIs and a .304 batting mark, but it was teammate George Kell who led the league with a .343 average.

Connie Mack's Philadelphia Athletics finished fifth, as lefthander Alex Kellner went 20–12 and Ben Chapman hit 24 home runs and drove in 108 runs.

The Chicago White Sox boasted two hitters among their regulars with averages above the .300 mark—second baseman Cass Michaels with a .308 average and veteran shortstop Luke Appling who, at age 42 still played in all but 12 games for the season and hit a respectable .301.

The St. Louis Browns continued to get good offensive production from Bob Dillinger, who stole a league-leading 20 bases and hit .324. First baseman Jack Graham provided the power for St. Louis with 24 home runs. Outfielder Roy Sievers captured Rookie of the Year honors in the

Boston's Vern Stephens

American League as he hit 16 home runs and batted .306. It was the first season a separate award was given in each league.

For the last-place Washington Senators, first baseman Eddie Robinson provided the home run production with 18.

Fourteen days after his return to action, Joe DiMaggio helped his American League team to an 11–7 victory over the National League in the All-Star game at Brooklyn's Ebbets Field. DiMaggio doubled, singled and batted in three runs. Originally put on the team as a reserve, DiMaggio started in place of Yankee teammate Tommy Henrich, who was sidelined with an injury to his knee.

The 1949 All-Star Game was also the first game in which black players participated as Jackie Robinson, Roy Campanella and Don Newcombe, all Brooklyn Dodgers, performed in the contest on their home field, while Cleveland's Larry Doby played for the American League squad.

The National League pennant race was just as close as the Yankees–Red Sox battle, with the Dodgers and St. Louis Cardinals fighting for the top spot throughout the season, while the defending National League champion Boston Braves skidded to a disappointing fourth-place finish. Burt Shotton's young Brooklyn club had no regulars over the age of 30.

Jackie Robinson's hitting stroke was right on the money as he won the National League batting title with a .342 mark and also stole a league-leading 37 bases to take him to the Most Valuable Player

The Dodgers' Roy Campanella and Don Newcombe

award. He was the first black player in major league history to capture the honor.

Gil Hodges continued to stand out at first base, while 22-year-old outfielder Duke Snider broke into the Dodgers' everyday lineup and belted 23 home runs to tie Hodges for the team lead. Outfielder Carl Furillo's contribution to the offense was a .322 average. Don Newcombe

SHORTS Yankee Stadium, already steeped in tradition, dedicated a granite monument in center field to Babe Ruth on April 19 during ceremonies prior to the home opener. Lou Gehrig and former manager Miller Huggins were also honored with plaques during the emotional event, which was attended by New York Governor Thomas Dewey, Mayor William O'Dwyer and Ruth's widow, Claire.

was the best on the pitching staff with a 17–8 record, followed by veteran Preacher Roe's 15–6 mark. Newcombe also captured Rookie of the Year honors in the National League.

The St. Louis Cardinals stayed with the Dodgers all season until the last week. The Cardinals lost four in a row and enabled Brooklyn to close the door with a win over the Philadelphia Phillies on the last day of the season.

Stan "The Man" Musial continued to excel in all the hitting categories with a .338 batting average, 36 home runs, 123 runs batted in, a league-leading 41 doubles and 13 triples. He shared that leadership in triples with teammate Enos Slaughter, who also contributed a .336 average as well.

Pacing the St. Louis pitching staff was Howie

Pollet with a 20–9 record and 108 strikeouts and George Munger with a 15–8 mark. Ted Wilks was the league's top reliever with nine saves, 59 appearances and a 10–3 record out of the bullpen.

The Philadelphia Phillies finished a surprising third, eight games over .500 as Del Ennis continued to provide the punch with 25 home runs, 110 RBIs and a .302 batting mark. Catcher Andy Seminick was right behind with 24 home runs. Russ Meyer paced the Phillies' pitching staff with a 17–9 record.

The defending National League champion Braves were unable to come close to repeating their success of the previous season. Johnny Sain, the staff ace in 1948, dropped to a 10–17 record. His partner, Warren Spahn, did post a 21–14 mark, leading the league with 151 strikeouts in the process. Bob Elliott still hit a formidable 17 home runs, but none of the Braves regulars were able to crack the .300 mark. Injuries to outfielder Jeff Heath and first baseman Earl Torgeson lingered. Heath was still bothered by an ankle injury from the previous season and Torgeson suffered a shoulder separation.

Elbie Fletcher, released by the Cleveland Indians after missing the entire 1948 season, did a good job at first for the Braves, hitting 11 home runs.

Leo Durocher's New York Giants got good numbers from Bobby Thomson with 27 home runs, 109 RBIs and a .309 batting average. Third baseman Sid Gordon's 26 homers stood out as well, as did Whitey Lockman's .301 average.

But the undisputed home run king of the National League was Pittsburgh's Ralph Kiner, who hit 54 for the Pittsburgh Pirates and sported a .310 average as well. Kiner also drove in 127 runs to lead the National League.

Cincinnati and Chicago both changed managers before the end of the season, with Luke Sewell taking over for Bucky Walters to pilot the Reds and Frankie Frisch relieving Charlie Grimm for the Cubs. Walker Cooper, obtained by Cincinnati early in the season, belted 16 home runs for his new club. He took over behind the plate for Ray Mueller who went to the Giants in the deal. The Reds and Cubs also engaged in a deal that sent Hank Sauer to Chicago, where he immediately found a home in the Cubs outfield and hit 27 home runs.

Cincinnati's big first baseman Ted Kluszewski led his club with a .309 batting average, while no Chicago hitters were able to hit above the .300 mark.

SHORTS The true story behind the shooting of Philadelphia Phillies' first baseman Eddie Waitkus may never be completely known. Ruth Steinhagen was only 19 when she shot Waitkus at Chicago's Edgewater Beach hotel. She was arrested and then confined to a mental institution. Waitkus was initially in critical condition but recovered well enough to play a full season at first base for the Phillies in 1950.

The Cardinals' Howie Pollet

GAME 1	
NY Yankees 1	Brooklyn 0
GAME 2	
Brooklyn 1	NY Yankees 0
GAME 3	
NY Yankees 4	Brooklyn 3
GAME 4	
NY Yankees 6	Brooklyn 4
GAME 5	
NY Yankees 10	Brooklyn 6

Casey Stengel was known as the baseball player who had once doffed his cap to let a sparrow escape. He was also known as the sardonic manager of the Boston Braves who aimed sharp insults at his unsuccessful club. He had a double-talk act that either delighted or confused and diverted attention from his minimal success as a major league manager in Brooklyn and Boston.

In short, while Stengel may have been an entertaining personality, he didn't seem like the ideal candidate to manage the New York Yankees, baseball's marquee franchise.

But Stengel was hired to replace Bucky Harris, who had made the mistake of finishing in third place in 1948. The Yankees had expectations of a championship every year and Stengel became an appealing candidate because of the success he'd had managing the Oakland franchise in the Class AAA Pacific Coast League. He was fresh from a 1948 championship with Oakland and his minor league work helped erase memories of his time with Brooklyn and Boston.

Stengel's biggest impact on the Yankees was his insistence on platooning at most positions. He was a strict believer in getting as many favorable lefthanded–righthanded match-ups as possible and would juggle his lineup daily to meet that goal. Of the regulars, only shortstop Phil Rizzuto and center fielder Joe DiMaggio could count on being in the lineup every day.

His Yankees didn't have an easy time winning the American League pennant. They were a game behind Boston at the start of a season-ending series at Yankee Stadium. The Yankees swept the two games and finished a game ahead.

The Brooklyn Dodgers had an equally close call, beating the St. Louis Cardinals by a single game to claim the National League title.

Brooklyn's Don Newcombe pitched brilliantly

New York's Allie Reynolds

in Game One, but Allie Reynolds of the Yankees was even better. Reynolds checked the Dodgers on two hits over nine innings and was the winner when the Yankees' Tommy Henrich drilled a homer off Newcombe in the bottom of the inning for the 1–0 win.

Game Two had the same score, but the teams were reversed. This time it was Brooklyn's Preacher Roe getting the best of the pitchers' duel as he limited the Yankees to six hits and didn't issue a walk. Vic Raschi pitched the first eight innings for the Yankees and gave up the game's only run in the second. Jackie Robinson doubled and scored on Gil Hodges' single.

The bats were finally a factor in Game Three, a 4–3 win for New York. The game was tied 1–1 heading into the ninth. Johnny Mize, a late-season acquisition from the New York Giants, drove in a pair of runs with a bases-loaded single to give the Yankees a 3–1 lead. They made it 4–1 when Jerry Coleman hit an RBI single.

The Yankees needed all those runs because Joe Page gave up solo homers to Luis Olmo and Roy Campanella in the bottom of the ninth before closing out the win.

New York solved Newcombe in Game Four,

scoring three runs off him through four innings. Cliff Mapes had a two-run double in the fourth and the Yankees got three more runs off reliever Joe Hatten an inning later. Bobby Brown hit a bases-loaded triple for New York.

Reynolds bailed out starter Ed Lopat with 3⅓ innings of hitless relief to nail down the 6–4 win.

The Yankees' offense overwhelmed the Dodgers in a decisive 10–6 Game Five victory. Coleman drove in three runs while DiMaggio and Brown each had two RBIs. One of DiMaggio's RBIs came on a home run.

Hodges hit a three-run homer for the Dodgers in the seventh before Page came on to save the game for Raschi.

Reynolds pitched 12 scoreless innings for the Yankees and Brown batted .500 with five RBIs. DiMaggio had a disappointing Series, hitting just .111 with two hits in 18 at-bats.

Brooklyn captain Pee Wee Reese led the Dodgers regulars with a .316 average.

It turned out to be the first of four consecutive Series championships that Stengel would claim as Yankees manager. He won a total of seven until he was replaced after the 1960 Series loss to Pittsburgh.

The Yanks' Joe Page won Game One and got the save in Game Five

JOE DiMAGGIO

Babe Ruth was the bigger-than-life New York Yankee, Lou Gehrig was the tragically flawed one. Whitey Ford was street-smart while his running mate, Mickey Mantle, was pure country. Joe DiMaggio?

He was the stylish one, the most mysterious of the high-profile stars the Yankees featured in the century.

Long after both had retired, DiMaggio and Lefty Grove were at a charity event in Las Vegas. A visitor asked Grove how DiMaggio was doing. "Same as always. A man of mystery," Grove said. "A bartender told me he hasn't seen Joe yet, but he's seen Howard Hughes four times."

DiMaggio was intensely private in a public profession, playing for the most famous franchise in the nation's biggest media market. Somehow DiMaggio bent the spotlight's glare to his will and remained reclusive despite his high profile.

DiMaggio and his brothers grew up playing baseball in northern California, where their father made his living as a fisherman. Joe and brothers Vince and Dom would all make it to the major leagues.

He started playing softball on an asphalt surface before he graduated to more conventional baseball. From the ages of 14 to 16, DiMaggio lost interest in the game and didn't play at all. In 1932, he was back on the field and had moved up to a higher level of competition.

The minor league San Francisco Seals already had Vince DiMaggio under contract and were interested in his younger brother. In 1933, Joe joined the Seals for their final three games. They offered him a contract for 1934 and older brother Tom handled the details and collected the bonus—two suits. DiMaggio got $225 a month in salary and a written assurance that he wouldn't be sent to a lower league. The latter was never an issue.

In his first year he batted .340 and had a 61-game hitting streak. He batted .341 the following year and ended his minor league career with a .398 average, helped by an 8-for-10 performance in a doubleheader on the last day of the season.

The Yankees signed him for the following season and DiMaggio debuted at 22. His .323 average was third on the team behind Bill Dickey and Lou Gehrig. He was second in home runs to Gehrig with 29.

DiMaggio settled in for a long run with the Yankees, which coincided with some golden years for the franchise. His 56-game hitting streak started on May 15, 1941. During the streak, there were six times when DiMaggio didn't get a hit until his final at-bat. He surpassed the old streak record of 41, which had been set by George Sisler of the St. Louis Browns.

In 1950, DiMaggio was making $100,000 with the Yankees. But by his calculations, his career peaked in 1948 and started on a downhill slide that was perceptible only to DiMaggio.

He'd always set a high standard for himself. He once told attorney Edward Bennett Williams that he played as hard before 5,000 people as he did in front of 70,000. Williams said, "He told me, 'I have to. There might be a kid out there who will only see me once.'"

DiMaggio said he knew it was time to quit when he felt his bat slowing and he started to hit more balls to right field. Or, as his brother Tom put it, "He quit because he wasn't Joe DiMaggio anymore." He turned down another $100,000 contract offer.

DiMaggio did some broadcasting for the Yankees and became a commercial spokesman for Bowery Bank and Mr. Coffee. He was married briefly to actress Marilyn Monroe, a subject which was declared off-limits to interviewers after their divorce.

DiMaggio spent some time as a coach with the Oakland Athletics in the late 1960s, returning to his native Bay Area to tutor Reggie Jackson among others. Mostly, though, he was Joe DiMaggio, the last player introduced on Old Timers Days at Yankee Stadium. He quit playing in the games because he believed he could only tarnish his reputation by stumbling around the field. He would put on the uniform and acknowledge the cheers.

When the autograph-collecting craze hit, few managed the demand as well as DiMaggio, who made millions selling his signature. He died in 1999 at 84.

The effortless power of Joe DiMaggio

1950

It seemed as though the two constants in the decade were pennants flying over Yankee Stadium and moving vans backing up at other ballparks.

The New York Yankees dominated the decade, winning all but two pennants under Casey Stengel's leadership. Mickey Mantle emerged as the new star, replacing Joe DiMaggio in center field. Whitey Ford succeeded Allie Reynolds as the anchor of the pitching staff. Catcher Yogi Berra was an unspectacular but dependable star.

The other major story was the shifting of franchises, highlighted by the National League's shocking desertion of New York and completely predictable mining of the rich California territory.

Dodgers' owner Walter O'Malley saw a crumbling neighborhood in Brooklyn and a gold mine in Los Angeles. He convinced the Giants to take San Francisco and transfer their rivalry west. The two teams abandoned New York, leaving the National League without a presence in the largest city and media capital.

In earlier years, the St. Louis Browns had become the Baltimore Orioles, the Athletics had left Philadelphia for Kansas City and the Braves shifted from Boston to Milwaukee.

But the shift to California in a sport that had previously gone no further west than St. Louis represented another major change for baseball.

The New York Yankees were winning everything but preseason popularity polls. Every year the experts would sit down to predict the outcome of the pennant races and every year it seemed they'd pick someone other than the Yankees to win the American League title.

The Boston Red Sox were the choice in 1950, even though the Yankees had won the last two World Series. The voters should have caught on to the fact that the mighty Yankees were the safest bet in baseball.

It wasn't easy, but they pulled away from three other teams and won their third consecutive pennant, making Casey Stengel a perfect three-for-three since he had taken over as the club's manager. Was the colorful Stengel born under a lucky star? It was nothing like that.

To some degree Stengel was in the right place at the right time. The Yankees had an impressive collection of proven major league players and a productive farm that was producing some of the best prospects in the game. The

NY Yankees' manager
Casey Stengel

Red Sox's Billy Goodman batted .354 to lead the American League

Yankees could slip one or two younger players onto the roster every year because they had enough experience to cover for the rookies.

The Yankees also had a front office that made trades when necessary. Stengel was not a bystander in all this. A firm believer in the value of platooning, he juggled his personnel on an almost daily basis to get the maximum results from his roster.

The Yankees set a record by claiming their

SHORTS The Brooklyn Dodgers had a disappointing season, which led to a major change. General manager Branch Rickey, considered one of the game's great innovators, resigned under pressure on October 26 and sold his 25 percent stake in the club. The new ownership of the Pittsburgh Pirates hired Rickey as executive vice president and general manager, signing him to a five-year contract on November 6.

17th pennant.

At the end of August, only two games separated the top four teams—the Yankees, Detroit Tigers, Cleveland Indians and Red Sox. The Yankees weren't able to clinch the pennant until September 29, two days before the end of the season.

The Yankees moved into first place in mid-May with a nine-game winning streak. Pitcher Whitey Ford won seven straight en route to a 9–1 final mark. Vic Raschi led the staff with 21 victories.

Phil Rizzuto had a big year, collecting 200 hits for a .324 average and setting several fielding records at shortstop. Rizzuto was also a sparkplug on offense, a catalyst who made things happen on the bases and set the table for the Yankees' power hitters. Johnny Mize, 37 years old, hit 25 home runs and drove in 72 runs after spending some humbling time in the minor leagues. The Yankees were smart enough to bring Mize up from Kansas City and he made solid contributions down the tense stretch drive.

Joe DiMaggio was benched in August when his average fell to an un-DiMaggio-like .279. He bounced back to contribute and finished with a .301 average. DiMaggio was near the end of his career, but taking him out of the lineup was still a bold move on Stengel's part. DiMaggio had become a Yankees legend and a decision to sit him was not one to be taken lightly.

The New York front office was able to make some deals that helped. A trade for Tom Ferrick helped the bullpen when Joe Page struggled in that role. The Yankees were able to mysteriously get Pittsburgh's Johnny Hopp through waivers on September 5. Hopp appeared in 19 games for the Yankees and batted .333.

Whatever went wrong with the Red Sox, offense wasn't the problem. Boston hit .302 as a team and broke 13 team offensive records. Walt Dropo came up from the minors and made

The Braves would regret trading
Alvin Dark to the Giants

an immediate contribution. The Red Sox pitching sagged, however. Mel Parnell dropped from a 25–7 record to 18–10 in 1950. Ellis Kinder had a similar decline, going from 23–6 in 1949 to 14–12. Even though the Red Sox could outslug just about any team—especially in Fenway Park—run prevention was still the top priority and Boston was ill-equipped to handle it with its top two starters struggling.

Boston lost 11 of 13 games in June, which led Joe McCarthy to resign as manager. The Red Sox lost Ted Williams for a time, but survived when replacement Billy Goodman stepped in.

Detroit's hopes of contending took a serious blow on May 19 when arm troubles ended pitcher Virgil Trucks' season.

Cleveland lost four straight games to the lowly St. Louis Browns late in the season to knock themselves out of the race. The season was so disappointing that Cleveland fired manager Lou Boudreau as soon as it was over.

Bucky Harris returned as manager and lifted the Senators from last to fifth.

The Chicago White Sox weren't able to overcome an 8–22 start. Jack Onslow was fired as the White Sox manager and replaced by coach Red Corriden. There was a changing of the guard at shortstop as Luke Appling, a regular since 1931, was replaced by Chico Carrasquel.

Connie Mack marked his 50th season as a manager with another last-place finish for the Philadelphia Athletics.

In the National League, the Philadelphia story was a happier one. Despite staggering at the end, the Phillies won their first pennant since 1915 and the second in the team's history.

The "Whiz Kids" had a dramatic finish, winning the pennant in the tenth inning of the season's last game. The Phillies got two singles, then Dick Sisler blasted a home run to give them a 4–1 win and a trip to the World Series.

The Phillies had a seemingly comfortable seven-game lead with nine days left in the season. They made the finale meaningful by going 2–8 down the stretch.

The St. Louis Cardinals were in first place on

SHORTS Trains were still the preferred method of travel in a sport that had no franchise west or south of St. Louis. That changed in May when a rail strike forced some teams to fly to their next series. The Red Sox, Yankees, Dodgers, Giants and Reds all took to the skies. The Washington Senators found another alternative. They took a bus.

July 25, but the Phillies took a doubleheader from the Chicago Cubs that day as Bubba Church and Robin Roberts won the games. The Phillies moved into first place and stayed there the rest of the way.

The Phillies' success may have been improbable, but it wasn't a complete shock. Philadelphia had risen to third place in 1949. Del Ennis led the team with a .311 average, 31 home runs and 126 runs batted in. Bespectacled reliever Jim Konstanty was one of the big stars, pitching in a record 74 games and going 16–7. Sisler's home run also made Roberts the Phillies' first 20-game winner since Grover Cleveland Alexander in 1917.

The Phillies were tested by injuries. Church was hit in the face by a line drive on September 15 and pitcher Bob Miller hurt his arm late in the year.

The Brooklyn Dodgers' failure could be traced to poor pitching. The Dodgers led the league in most offensive and defensive categories, but didn't get enough pitching. Things were so disappointing that Branch Rickey went public with criticism of his club, accusing the Dodgers of complacency.

The New York Giants had a strong second half, but a pair of seven-game losing streaks undermined their chances.

The Boston Braves had traded their double-play combination, Eddie Stanky and Alvin Dark, to the Giants and lived to regret it. The Braves didn't get enough in return and they didn't adequately replace Stanky and Dark, who had provided a spark.

The Cardinals led the National League in late June but faded.

The Cincinnati Reds didn't give themselves a chance because of a poor first half. The Reds started the season 16–38. Pitcher Ewell Blackwell came back and had a staff-leading 17–15 record. Massive first baseman Ted Kluszewski was the hitter other teams did their best to avoid. Kluszewski hit .307 with 26 home runs and 111 runs batted in.

The Chicago Cubs made some minor progress. They climbed out of the National League cellar and finished seventh.

The bottom spot was inherited by the Pittsburgh Pirates, who proved that having one star was almost as important as having a good team. The Pirates had a season's attendance of 1.1 million, third best in the league, despite putting an awful product on the field. Why did they come? To see if Ralph Kiner could hit a home run. Kiner hit 47 of them, an amazing figure considering most teams would opt to pitch

around Kiner in the weak Pirates lineup.

The Pirates made headlines off the field by paying $100,000 to 18-year-old pitching prospect Paul Pettit of Lomita, California. Some teams claimed that the deal was shady because the Pirates negotiated for Pettit's services with a Hollywood agent. Those teams should have considered the Pirates' record in other matters of judgment and saved themselves the trouble of complaining. Pettit never amounted to much as a major league player and the Pirates would spend most of the rest of the decade in or near last place.

In other off-the-field news, some owners led a movement to oust Happy Chandler as commissioner.

Connie Mack finally ended his long career, retiring as a manager after 50 years. Mack announced his decision at the end of the season. Jimmie Dykes had the distinction of replacing the legendary Mack.

Connie Mack's 50th year as a manager would also be his last

WORLD SERIES	
GAME 1	
NY Yankees 1	Philadelphia Phillies 0
GAME 2	
NY Yankees 2	Philadelphia Phillies 1
GAME 3	
NY Yankees 3	Philadelphia Phillies 2
GAME 4	
NY Yankees 5	Philadelphia Phillies 2

They were the Whiz Kids, the team that had shocked the National League by beating out the Brooklyn Dodgers and New York Giants for the pennant.

Their story didn't have a happy ending, though, because the Philadelphia Phillies' Whiz Kids were no match for a powerful New York Yankees team that had come to be comfortable in the World Series.

The Yankees swept the Series and tabloid headline writers in New York delighted in referring to the upstart Phillies as the "Fizz Kids."

Fact is, though, it wasn't as easy for the Yankees as the four-game sweep might suggest.

"We were in every game until the last out," Phillies' catcher Andy Seminick said.

The Phillies may have been worn out from a difficult stretch drive that saw them hold off the Dodgers and Giants to give the Phillies their first National League pennant in 35 years. They won it on October 1 when Dick Sisler hit a three-run homer in the tenth inning

to beat the Dodgers and clinch the title.

The Phillies got to the Series in some disarray. One of their best pitchers, Curt Simmons, was on military duty. He was prohibited from pitching even though the Army had granted him a furlough. The Phillies had to use ace Robin Roberts to pitch the pennant-clinching game so he was unavailable for the opener of the Series. The ending was so frantic for the Phillies that Roberts had actually worked in three of the team's last five games.

Faced with limited choices, manager Eddie Sawyer reached into the bullpen and used his closer, Jim Konstanty, to start the first game of the Series against the Yankees. It was Konstanty's first start of the season.

Although he wasn't a starter by trade, there's no question Konstanty was one of the Phillies'

Joe DiMaggio broke the 1–1 deadlock with a tenth-inning homer in Game Two

most effective pitchers. He worked in 74 games during the season with a 16–7 record and 2.66 earned run average.

He was solid in the opener, holding the Yankees to four hits and one run in eight innings. It was his misfortune to match up with Vic Raschi, who allowed just two singles and won the game 1–0.

Roberts pitched Game Two and he and Allie Reynolds were tied 1–1 through nine innings. Joe DiMaggio led off the tenth with a home run to break the tie and Reynolds pitched the complete game for the win.

Having lost two on their home field, the Phillies had to try to beat the Yankees in New York.

The Phillies' pitching was still unsettled because of Simmons' absence and injuries to rookies Bob Miller and Bubba Church. Ken Heintzelman got the call in Game Three despite going 3–9 during the regular season. Heintzelman had won 17 games for the Phillies in 1949 and he reverted to that form in Game Three against the Yankees.

He took a 2–1 lead into the eighth inning but tired and walked three consecutive hitters after getting the first two outs on the inning. Konstanty relieved and it appeared he had pitched out of the jam by getting Bobby Brown to ground to short. Granny Hamner misplayed the ball for an error, which allowed the tying run to score.

The Yankees got three hits in the bottom of the ninth off Russ Meyer. Jerry Coleman had the game-winning hit in the 3–2 victory.

Game Four was the only one in Series not decided by a single run. Thanks mostly to Yogi Berra's offensive contributions (RBI single and home run), rookie Whitey Ford had a 5–0 lead with two out in the ninth. The Phillies got a pair of runs when left fielder Gene Woodling dropped Seminick's fly ball for an error that cost two runs.

Reynolds relieved and struck out Stan Lopata for the final out in the 5–2 win.

Despite the error, Woodling was the Yankees' leading hitter with a .429 average. Hamner led the Phillies with the same average and was one of the few Philadelphia hitters to have a good Series at the plate.

The Phillies batted .203 as a team, didn't have a home run and had just three RBIs in the four-game Series. Raschi and Ford did not allow an earned run in their victories.

Rookie Whitey Ford gave up no earned runs in his first World Series

MOST VALUABLE PLAYER
AL: Yogi Berra, NY Yankees
NL: Roy Campanella, Brooklyn

ROOKIE OF THE YEAR
AL: Gil McDougald, NY Yankees
NL: Willie Mays, NY Giants

LEADERS
BATTING AVERAGE
AL: Ferris Fain, Philadelphia A's, .344
NL: Stan Musial, St. Louis Cardinals, .355

HOME RUNS
AL: Gus Zernial, Chicago White Sox/
Philadelphia A's, 33
NL: Ralph Kiner, Pittsburgh, 42

RUNS BATTED IN
AL: Gus Zernial, Chicago White Sox/
Philadelphia A's, 129
NL: Monte Irvin, NY Giants, 121

STOLEN BASES
AL: Minnie Minoso, Cleveland/Chicago
White Sox, 31
NL: Sam Jethroe, Boston Braves, 35

PITCHING VICTORIES
AL: Bob Feller, Cleveland, 22
NL: Larry Jansen, Sal Maglie, NY Giants 23

F or the third consecutive year, the National League pennant was decided in the last inning of the season's last game.

The 1951 version of the drama was a classic, with the New York Giants and Brooklyn Dodgers taking their bitter rivalry into a best-of-three playoff series.

The Dodgers faded down the stretch and the Giants came to life, forcing a playoff when they both finished with 96–58 records. It was a bitter pill for the Dodgers, who had led handily through much of the season. Brooklyn lived to regret the words of peppery manager Chuck Dressen. Asked during the middle of the season about the possibility of being overtaken by the Dodgers' No. 1 rival, Dressen had said, "The Giants is dead."

It was as incorrect as it was ungrammatical. The Giants were still very much alive and there was nothing to energize them like a challenge coming from the Brooklyn camp. Dressen's ill-advised comment became a rallying point for the Giants and baseball-mad New York watched the unlikely scenario unfold as the Dodgers' leisurely summer turned into a very tense September.

Across town in the Bronx, the New York Yankees were taking care of their own business,

getting busy with a third consecutive American League pennant.

The action was across the Hudson in the Giants' home park, the Polo Grounds, and in Brooklyn, where the Dodgers' Flatbush faithful were still waiting for their first World Series championship.

One couldn't blame Dressen for thinking the Giants were dead. They were 13½ games out of first place in August, which is usually a signal to begin preparations for next year. Who could have known they'd pick that precise point to go on a fabulous 37–7 streak that would force the tie at the end of the season?

Early in July, Brooklyn had started distancing itself from the Giants with an eight-game winning streak that opened with three wins against New York. But the Giants would later fashion a 16-game winning streak that included a three-game sweep of the Dodgers.

They were still seven games out of first place when they started a series at the Polo Grounds on September 1. The Giants swept the two games and chipped away at the Dodgers' lead.

It looked as though the magic had finally disappeared on September 8 and 9 when the teams met again and split the two games. A split favors the team on top because it keeps the standings stagnant while knocking two more games off the schedule.

By the end, though, the Dodgers had to scramble just to force the tie. The Giants won their last game to claim at least a share of the pennant. The Dodgers were playing Philadelphia and needed 14 innings to down the Phillies. They got the tie when Jackie Robinson hit a home run off Robin Roberts to win the game.

The Giants took the first game of the playoff 3–1. No one thought it terribly significant that Bobby Thomson hit a home run off Ralph Branca. In the sec-

Bobby Thomson heads for home following his dramatic "shot heard 'round the world"

The Giants' Sal Maglie

T I M E L I N E

Feb. 9: The St. Louis Browns signed Satchel Paige, at least 45, who last pitched in the major leagues in 1949 with Cleveland.

Feb. 10: One day after asking for a $600,000 loan, the St. Louis Browns announced plans to move to Milwaukee.

April 17: Golf great Sam Snead helped the Chicago Cubs to open their season by teeing up at home plate and driving a ball off the scoreboard in center field.

May 1: Mickey Mantle hit his first major league home run off Chicago's Randy Gumpert.

May 6: Pittsburgh's Cliff Chambers walked eight in a 3–0 no-hitter against the Braves in Boston.

May 20: Richie Ashburn of the Phillies got four hits in each game of a doubleheader sweep of the Pirates.

May 28: Willie Mays of the Giants hit his first major league home run off Warren Spahn of the Braves.

June 19: Tommy Holmes replaced Billy Southworth as Boston Braves' manager.

July 1: Bob Feller pitched his third career no-hitter, beating Detroit 2–1.

July 10: Allie Reynolds of the Yankees pitched a 1–0 no-hitter against Cleveland.

July 15: The Yankees optioned Mickey Mantle back to Class AAA Kansas City.

July 29: Willie Mays stole his first base, then was picked off second.

Aug. 20: The Yankees recalled Mickey Mantle from the minor leagues.

Sept. 2: Don Mueller of the Giants hit two home runs against Brooklyn. Mueller hit five home runs in two days.

Oct. 1: The opening playoff game between the Brooklyn Dodgers and New York Giants is the first game broadcast live on a nationwide basis.

Dec. 11: Joe DiMaggio announced his retirement from the Yankees after 13 seasons. DiMaggio hit .325 with 361 home runs and had a 56-game hitting streak in 1941.

ond game, Brooklyn's Clem Labine pitched a six-hitter and won 10–0.

The Dodgers were leading the deciding game 4–2 with one out and two men on in the ninth. Legend has it that Dressen called the bullpen and was told by a coach that Branca was loose and ready to go.

Branca came in and almost instantly his and Thomson's names were inextricably linked in

baseball history. The Giants' comeback was complete when Thomson's homer sailed over the wall for one of the great moments in the history of the game.

Widely circulated photos the next day showed the inconsolable Branca stretched out on the steps leading to the clubhouse, the back of his uniform on display to the camera. Branca wore No. 13.

The Dodgers had stumbled down the stretch as their best hitters, Gil Hodges and Duke Snider, slumped.

The Giants got season-long contributions from their two best pitchers, Larry Jansen and Sal Maglie. Each won 23 games.

The rest of the National League mostly watched the two-team race being slugged out

SHORTS Owner Bill Veeck staged his most outrageous publicity stunt on August 19 when he sent a pinch hitter named Eddie Gaedel to the plate for the St. Louis Browns. Gaedel was 3-foot-7 and wore the number 1/8 on his uniform. He walked on four pitches from Detroit's Bob Cain and was replaced by pinch runner Jim Delsing.

Pirates' slugger Ralph Kiner led the majors with 42 roundtrippers

In the American League, the Yankees won their 18th American League pennant and their third straight with Casey Stengel, who became the fifth manager to win three consecutive titles.

It wasn't easy for the Yankees, though. The Chicago White Sox had a 14-game winning streak in May that allowed them to stay in first place from May 28 to July 1. Cleveland had a three-game lead in late August until a 2–6 streak knocked the Indians out of first place.

New York stormed to the top by winning nine of 12 in September, including two important games against Cleveland. Bob Feller and Bob Lemon both lost for the Indians at Yankee Stadium.

The Yankees finished with a flourish. On September 28, Allie Reynolds pitched his second no-hitter of the season, this time against the Boston Red Sox. In the second game of that doubleheader, Vic Raschi won his 21st game and Eddie Lopat posted his 21st win of the season the next day.

Reynolds' season had gotten off to a rocky start as he had an elbow injury that kept him out until May 3. When he came back he started the year with a 1–3 record, but Reynolds soon found the form that made him one of the game's most dependable pitchers and went 16–5 the rest of the way to lead the Yankees' staff.

Reynolds had thrown his first no-hitter against Cleveland on July 12, beating Feller 1–0 as Gene Woodling homered. Feller himself had pitched a no-hitter ten days earlier against the Detroit Tigers.

The Yankees had an efficient offense, but it wasn't spectacular. Gil McDougald (.306) was the only .300 hitter and no one had 100 RBIs. Yogi Berra led the club with 88.

Mickey Mantle made his debut with the Yankees, but was sent back to the minor leagues after he struggled against major league pitching.

The Yankees had more success with pitcher Tom Morgan. Summoned from the minor leagues, he won eight consecutive decisions. Joe DiMaggio had the poorest season of his career, batting .262 with 12 home runs and 72 RBIs.

Cleveland manager Al Lopez had the league's best pitching staff, but his offense wasn't up to par. Larry Doby and Al Rosen saw their production slip and Luke Easter was troubled throughout the year by a bad knee.

The Boston Red Sox were done in by a shallow pitching staff and too many injuries to key players. At various times during the season, the Red Sox were without Walt Dropo, Bobby Doerr, Lou Boudreau and Vern Stephens.

The Detroit Tigers were one of the game's

in New York. The St. Louis Cardinals were third but finished 15½ games behind the Giants. Everyone else was at least 20 games off the pace.

Stan Musial of the Cardinals won his fifth batting title with a .355 average. The Braves got off to a 10–4 start, but faded fast and wound up fourth. Warren Spahn had his fourth 20-win season for the Braves.

The Phillies declined after winning the pennant in 1950. Only Richie Ashburn and Robin Roberts performed at the same level. The Cincinnati Reds had the worst offensive club in the league. Ted Kluszewski saw his average fall from .307 to .259 while his RBI total declined from 111 to 71.

Deposed Dodgers' leader Branch Rickey took over operations in Pittsburgh, where Ralph Kiner had another big home run season for the Pirates with 42. The Chicago Cubs finished last for the third time in four years.

great disappointments. Hoot Evers failed to follow up on a great season. His average dipped to .224 from .323 and his RBI total dropped from 101 to 46.

Jimmie Dykes replaced Connie Mack as manager of the Philadelphia Athletics, but the change had little impact on the field. The Athletics started the season 3–13. They had an impressive 29–12 run at the end of the season that helped them finish two spots from the bottom.

The Washington Senators finished behind the

SHORTS Baseball owners wanted Happy Chandler out as commissioner and there was no shortage of interesting suggestions for his successor. FBI chief J. Edgar Hoover turned the job down, California governor Earl Warren denied any interest and the Reds supported Gen. Douglas MacArthur. Chandler resigned on July 15 and National League president Ford Frick replaced him on September 20.

Athletics, as did the St. Louis Browns. The biggest development for the Browns was the sale of the franchise to a group headed by Bill Veeck. The Browns weren't going to win any more, but Veeck could be counted on to make the losing more palatable with his endless supply of promotional ideas.

Off the field, owners continued to express dissatisfaction with the leadership of Commissioner Happy Chandler. He sold six years' worth of TV and radio rights to the All-Star game for $6 million. Some owners blasted Chandler for making a shortsighted deal, claiming that the rights would be worth more than $1 million per year before the contract expired.

Chandler lost his fight to stay in office when a March vote went against him, 9–7. The owners rejected a suggestion that the players should have a hand in choosing the new commissioner. Chandler said in mid-June that his resignation would officially take effect on July 15.

Bill Veeck's publicity stunts became increasingly bizarre as he sent 3ft 7in Eddie Gaedel to the plate

GAME 1	
NY Giants 5	NY Yankees 1

GAME 2	
NY Yankees 3	NY Giants 1

GAME 3	
NY Giants 6	NY Yankees 2

GAME 4	
NY Yankees 6	NY Giants 2

GAME 5	
NY Yankees 13	NY Giants 1

GAME 6	
NY Yankees 4	NY Giants 3

"The Giants win the pennant! The Giants win the pennant."

Announcer Russ Hodges' frantically jubilant radio call of the New York Giants' victory over the Los Angeles Dodgers in the National League playoff has been replayed tens of thousands of times since 1951. Bobby Thomson's pennant-clinching home run off Ralph Branca is one of baseball's great moments.

In that context, it's easy to forget that while the Giants did indeed win the pennant over the Dodgers, it was the New York Yankees who won the World Series. Again.

The outcome of the National League playoff was fine with some of the Yankees.

"The Giants weren't as strong a team as the Dodgers," Yankees outfielder Gene Woodling said.

The Giants appeared to be riding the momentum of their playoff win as they won the first game of the Series 5–1 on the day after

The Giants' Alvin Dark blasted a three-run shot in Game One

Thomson's homer had propelled them to the matchup against the Yankees.

Dave Koslo pitched a strong game, holding the powerful Yankees to seven hits. Alvin Dark hit a three-run homer for the Giants. Monte Irvin went 4-for-5 with three singles, a triple and the first Series steal of home since 1928.

The Yankees cooled off the Giants in Game Two with steady veteran Ed Lopat pitching a five-hitter in a 3–1 win. Lopat also contributed a run-scoring single. The win came at a significant cost for the Yankees. Mickey Mantle, their 19-year-old rookie outfielder, was chasing a fly ball when his spikes caught on a drainage cover. Mantle injured his knee on the play, which ended his Series five innings into the second game.

The Giants rode a five-run fifth inning to a 6–2 win in Game Three. Whitey Lockman hit a three-run homer to support starter Jim Hearn. The scrappy Eddie Stanky keyed the inning by kicking the ball out of shortstop Phil Rizutto's glove to avoid being thrown out stealing. Stanky's play prolonged the inning and allowed Lockman to come up with two men on base.

The elements may have helped the Yankees. Game Four was postponed because of rain, and the one-day delay allowed the Yankees to again use Allie Reynolds. Even though Reynolds had lost the first game, he was still the Yankees' best pitcher.

Reynolds beat Sal Maglie 6–2 in Game Four, which also featured the final Series home run of Joe DiMaggio's career.

Game Five was no contest, a 13–1 win for the Yankees. Starter Larry Jansen was tagged for five runs in the third inning and that was more than enough support for Lopat. The righthander pitched a complete game, allowing five hits and an unearned run. Gil McDougald had the big hit, a grand slam off Jansen that keyed the third inning.

The Yankees wrapped up the Series with a third consecutive win in Game Six. Hank Bauer broke out of an extended postseason slump with a bases-loaded triple off Koslo that broke a 1–1 tie in the sixth. To that point, Bauer had hit only .132 in Series play and had driven in just one run.

Bauer wound up saving the 4–3 win on defense. The Giants had the tying run in scoring position when Bauer made an exceptional catch of Sal Yvars' sinking liner to end the game.

The Series was significant because it was the last major league action for DiMaggio. He retired at age 36 and batted .261 in his final Series. He doubled in his final at-bat.

Thomson, the hero who got the Giants to the Series, didn't do as well against the Yankees. He batted .143 and both of his hits were singles. He did not have an RBI.

Lopat was the pitching star for the Yankees, winning two games with a 0.50 earned run average. Bobby Brown hit .357 and the grand slam helped McDougald to a Series-leading seven RBIs.

Irvin led the Giants with a .458 average and Alvin Dark batted .417. They were the only regulars who hit well for the Giants, who managed just a .237 team average with two home runs in the six games. Minus Irvin and Dark, the rest of the Giants batted .164 with one homer.

Monte Irvin's heroics could only carry the Giants so far

MOST VALUABLE PLAYER
AL: Bobby Shantz, Philadelphia A's
NL: Hank Sauer, Chicago Cubs

ROOKIE OF THE YEAR
AL: Harry Byrd, Philadelphia A's
NL: Joe Black, Brooklyn

LEADERS
BATTING AVERAGE
AL: Ferris Fain, Philadelphia A's, .327
NL: Stan Musial, St. Louis Cardinals, .336

HOME RUNS
AL: Larry Doby, Cleveland, 32
NL: Ralph Kiner, Pittsburgh; Hank Sauer, Chicago Cubs, 37

RUNS BATTED IN
AL: Al Rosen, Cleveland, 105
NL: Hank Sauer, Chicago Cubs, 121

STOLEN BASES
AL: Minnie Minoso, Chicago White Sox, 22
NL: Pee Wee Reese, Brooklyn, 30

PITCHING VICTORIES
AL: Bobby Shantz, Philadelphia A's, 24
NL: Robin Roberts, Philadelphia Phillies, 28

EARNED RUN AVERAGE
AL: Allie Reynolds, NY Yankees, 2.06
NL: Hoyt Wilhelm, NY Giants, 2.43

STRIKEOUTS
AL: Allie Reynolds, NY Yankees, 160
NL: Warren Spahn, Boston Braves, 183

The New York Yankees appeared to be vulnerable in 1952. Their resident superstar, Joe DiMaggio, was gone, having retired after a 1951 season that would have pleased any player but the demanding DiMaggio.

Military commitments wreaked havoc with the roster. Jerry Coleman, Bobby Brown and Tom Morgan were all due to spend time in the service, poking some major holes in the Yankees' lineup.

Competition in the American League was better, too. The Cleveland Indians had the best starting staff in the League and plenty of offense from Al Rosen, Larry Doby and Luke Easter.

Even though the Yankees had won three consecutive World Series, they weren't a popular pick to repeat as American League champions. Perhaps some of the voters still weren't sold on Casey Stengel, the manager who had earned a reputation as a clown throughout his baseball career.

The preseason predictions of an Indians summer looked strong when Cleveland opened the season with seven consecutive wins.

But when it was all over, the Yankees had prevailed again. They found ways to patch the holes in their lineup, they won games they absolutely had to win and Stengel had become the third manager in the history of the game to win pennants in four consecutive years. Joe McCarthy had done it with the Yankees from 1936–39 and John McGraw had accomplished the same feat with the New York Giants from 1921–24.

It was a season-long race. At the All-Star break, the Yankees and Indians were being chased by the Boston Red Sox, Philadelphia Athletics and Washington Senators. There were still four teams in the race at the end of August. Only the Senators had dropped out.

Other teams got close, but the Yankees were in charge. They went into first place on June 10 and spent only two days out of the top spot through the rest of the season.

Cleveland put on a strong rush in August, going 18–7. The schedule favored the Indians with an imbalance of home games. The Yankees'

Luke Easter was one of several big bats in the Indians line-up

schedule was weighed heavily toward road games down the stretch.

On September 14, the Yankees visited Cleveland and 73,609 people packed into the giant lakefront stadium. They went away disappointed as the Yankees won 7–1 with Eddie Lopat getting the best of Mike Garcia in a pivotal game.

Lopat had missed six weeks during the season with shoulder problems, but that was another bit of adversity the Yankees confronted and defeated.

SHORTS Did he or didn't he? Detroit's Virgil Trucks pitched his second no-hitter of the season, but a press box debate kept it in doubt for three innings. Official scorer John Drebinger's call of an error on shortstop Johnny Pesky was challenged and changed to a hit. Late in the game Drebinger called the dugout for Pesky's input and was convinced to change the call back to an error, giving Trucks the no-hitter.

Lefty Bobby Shantz proved that size doesn't matter as he posted 24 wins

Allie Reynolds had his best year in the major leagues, posting a 20–8 record with a 2.06 earned run average that led the American League, just as his 160 strikeouts did.

After bouncing between the majors and minors as a rookie, Mickey Mantle became the star everyone expected him to be. Mantle batted .311 with 23 home runs and 87 RBIs. Yogi Berra, the dumpy looking catcher, continued to be one of the game's most reliable run producers, driving in 98 runs and hitting 30 home runs to set a record for catchers.

The top of the Indians' rotation was the envy of baseball. Early Wynn won 22 games while Mike Garcia and Bob Lemon each posted 22 wins. The disappointment of the season was Bob Feller, who had the worst season of his career,

falling from 22 wins to 9–13. The Indians' first-rate pitching was also undermined by substandard defense.

Offensively, Cleveland had the top two RBI men in the league with Rosen and Doby and the top two home run hitters with Doby and Easter. Easter rebounded after a poor first half, but the Indians still came up two games short to the Yankees.

The other six teams were never really a factor in the pennant race. The Chicago White Sox threatened to join the pack with a 24–10 record in June, but they fell back by losing nine of ten.

The big man for the Athletics was the smallest man in the league—lefthander Bobby Shantz, who stood just 5'6" and weighed 139 pounds, led the league in wins with his 24–7 record. Ferris Fain hit .327 to take his second consecutive batting title. It was the second time since 1933 that the Athletics finished in the first division.

The Washington Senators were 78–76, thanks in part to a shrewd trade for outfielder Jackie Jensen.

The Boston Red Sox had to deal with Bobby Doerr's retirement and Ted Williams' return to military service on May 1 and duly fell apart late in the season.

The St. Louis Browns were under Bill Veeck's ownership. He promptly hired Rogers Hornsby as his manager, but his return after a 14-year absence didn't last long. He was fired on June 10 and replaced by former Cardinals hero Marty Marion.

Detroit had the dubious distinction of finishing in last place for the first time in franchise history. The Tigers set a team record by losing 111 games and settled into the cellar for good on

May 2. The season cost manager Red Rolfe his job. Fred Hutchinson took over.

After the heartbreak of their playoff loss to the New York Giants in 1951, the Brooklyn Dodgers eased the stress with a fairly comfortable ride to the National League pennant. They finished 4½ games ahead of the Giants.

The Dodgers took over first place on June 1 and stayed there for the rest of the season. In fact, Brooklyn was out of the top spot for only 15 days and were never lower than second the entire year as they won their third pennant in six years.

An early 16–2 spurt helped the Dodgers establish themselves and a nine-game winning streak after the All-Star break provided a positive start to the second half of the season.

The Dodgers did one of the things a winning team has to do—they beat up on the bad teams. They were 19–3 against Pittsburgh, 18–3 against Boston and held a 17–5 edge against Cincinnati. Their record was far less impressive against the three teams closest to them in the standings—29–37.

Joe Black wasn't expected to make the club, but he had a strong spring training and wound up going 15–4. He was voted the National League Rookie of the Year. Brooklyn's 3.53 earned run average was second-best in the National League and the Dodgers led in home runs with 153.

They had three .300 hitters—Jackie Robinson, George (Shotgun) Shuba and Duke Snider. Gil Hodges hit 32 homers and drove in 102 runs while catcher Roy Campanella hit 22 home runs with 97 RBIs.

The Dodgers even survived the bold words of their manager. Charlie Dressen had given the Giants a rallying cry in 1951 by declaring, "The Giants is dead." He had to eat those words when the Giants beat the Dodgers in the pennant playoff. This time, Dressen's brash prediction was an exclusive for the *Saturday Evening Post*. Its September 13 issue featured an article titled, "The Dodgers Won't Blow It Again."

They didn't, but maybe they had help from the United States Army. Willie Mays was called into military service and the Giants didn't recover. Their offense was already hurting from the broken

Brooklyn's Joe Black won 15 games and Rookie of the Year honors

Hank Sauer led the league in RBIs and tied for home runs, but his Cubs struggled

ankle that Monte Irvin sustained on April 2. Irvin, who had batted .312 with 24 home runs and 121 RBIs in 1951, was limited to just 46 games in 1952. To replace him, the Giants traded for Braves holdout Bob Elliott. But Elliott at 35 hit only .228.

Sal Maglie started the season with a glitzy 11–2 record, but didn't sustain that success. He was 7–6 after that. Larry Jansen was just 11–11 and didn't win a game after July 26. Rookie Hoyt Wilhelm was a bright spot, appearing in a record 71 games and posting a 13–3 record.

The St. Louis Cardinals came to life under first-year manager Eddie Stanky and finished third. Stan Musial won another batting title with a .336 average and Enos Slaughter showed no signs of being 36 as he batted .300 and drove in 101 runs. Red Schoendienst had his finest offensive season, batting .303.

Philadelphia Phillies' manager Eddie Sawyer was a genius when he led the Whiz Kids to the 1950 pennant. In 1952, he was just another manager who got fired when his team didn't win. A stretch of 11 losses in 13 games convinced the Phillies to sack Sawyer and replace him with Steve O'Neill. Philadelphia belied the notion that success starts with solid pitching. The Phillies had the league's best ERA at 3.07 and issued the fewest walks, 373.

A good portion of the positive pitching statistics was a tribute to Robin Roberts. He was 28–7 and finished the season on a 17–1 roll. Roberts lost just two games after June 17.

Hank Sauer of the Chicago Cubs led the league with 121 RBIs and tied Pittsburgh's Ralph Kiner for the lead with 37 homers. Hornsby found work as the Cincinnati Reds' manager after Luke Sewell resigned the job. The Boston Braves fell from fourth to seventh and Charlie Grimm replaced Tommy Holmes as manager.

Pittsburgh set a modern record with 112 losses, even though Kiner had a share of the home run title for the seventh consecutive year.

GAME 1	
Brooklyn 4	NY Yankees 2
GAME 2	
NY Yankees 7	Brooklyn 1
GAME 3	
Brooklyn 5	NY Yankees 3
GAME 4	
NY Yankees 2	Brooklyn 0
GAME 5	
Brooklyn 6	NY Yankees 5
GAME 6	
NY Yankees 3	Brooklyn 2
GAME 7	
NY Yankees 4	Brooklyn 2

For once, it looked like it wasn't going to be the New York Yankees' year. Down 3–2 in games, the Yankees had to go back to Brooklyn to finish the Series against the Dodgers. Given the atmosphere at Ebbets Field, it could have been a daunting task for most teams.

But a situation that might cause a normal team to fold wasn't likely to have that effect on a Yankees team that had three consecutive Series championships to its credit.

The Yankees squeezed out a late-inning win in Game Six to tie the Series, then won the Series with a 4–2 victory in the decisive game.

The Dodgers actually appeared to be on their way to winning Game Six. Duke Snider broke a scoreless tie with a solo home run in the sixth inning off Vic Raschi. The lead didn't last against the unflappable Yankees, though. Yogi Berra got the run back when he led off the next inning with a home run to the same spot that Snider had hit his. The Yankees tagged on a run for a 2–1 lead, thanks to Raschi's run-scoring single.

Mickey Mantle hit his first career Series home run in the eighth to stretch the lead to 3–1.

Snider started bringing the Dodgers back with another home run. Raschi left the game after George (Shotgun) Shuba doubled. Yankees' manager Casey Stengel called on Allie Reynolds to relieve. Like most of his moves, this one worked for Stengel. Reynolds, who led the Yankees staff with 20 wins, struck out Roy Campanella to end the eighth and then retired the Dodgers in the ninth to save the win for Raschi and force a seventh game.

The Yankees took a 4–2 lead in the seventh inning of Game Seven before the Dodgers staged what would be their last rally. Raschi, who had pitched into the eighth inning the day before, was back in the mound to try and get the Yankees through the seventh inning.

He issued walks to Carl Furillo and Pee Wee Reese and gave up a single to Billy Cox to load the bases with one out.

Stengel called on Bob Kuzava to close out the inning. Snider popped out. Jackie Robinson hit an infield pop, too, but there wasn't anything routine about it. First baseman Joe Collins couldn't find the ball and, with two out, the three Dodgers base runners were off with the pitch. Finally, second baseman Billy Martin realized that Collins was in trouble and dashed over to catch the ball just before it hit the ground. Most accounts have Martin making the catch at knee level.

Kuzava was perfect over the final two innings and Martin's alert play saved the game and Series for the Yankees.

Brooklyn won the opening game 4–2 behind a strong effort from Joe Black. Robinson, Reese and Snider all hit home runs to back Black's seven-hit complete game. The Yankees got even in Game Two as Raschi beat Carl Erskine. Martin hit a three-run homer and drove in another run with a single as New York won 7–1.

Preacher Roe won Game Three for the Yankees, 5–3, even though

Allie Reynolds made a seventh game necessary with his crucial Game Six save

he gave up solo home runs to Berra and pinch hitter Johnny Mize. Reynolds drew the Yankees even again with a four-hit 2–0 shutout in Game Four. The Dodgers only allowed four hits but one of them was a home run by Mize.

Brooklyn scored a run in the top of the 11th of Game Five and won 6–5. Erskine had a tough fifth inning, giving the Yankees all five of their runs on four hits. But he was as good after that inning as he had been before it and allowed just one hit over the remaining six innings.

Raschi was the pitching hero for the Yankees, managing a 2–0 record and 1.59 earned run average. Mize batted .400 with three home runs and six RBIs. Mantle made his mark with a .345 average and two homers.

Snider was Brooklyn's offensive star, batting .345 with four home runs and eight RBIs. Reese hit .345 for the Dodgers.

The four consecutive Series victories tied a Yankees club record. They also won four straight championships under manager Joe McCarthy from 1936–39.

The Brooklyn Dodgers' short stop Pee Wee Reese

MOST VALUABLE PLAYER
AL: Al Rosen, Cleveland
NL: Roy Campanella, Brooklyn

ROOKIE OF THE YEAR
AL: Harvey Kuenn, Detroit
NL: Jim Gilliam, Brooklyn

LEADERS

BATTING AVERAGE
AL: Mickey Vernon, Washington, .337
NL: Carl Furillo, Brooklyn, .344

HOME RUNS
AL: Al Rosen, Cleveland, 43
NL: Eddie Mathews, Milwaukee, 47

RUNS BATTED IN
AL: Al Rosen, Cleveland, 145
NL: Roy Campanella, Brooklyn, 142

STOLEN BASES
AL: Minnie Minoso, Chicago White Sox, 25
NL: Bill Bruton, Milwaukee, 26

PITCHING VICTORIES
AL: Bob Porterfield, Washington, 22
NL: Robin Roberts, Philadelphia Phillies;
Warren Spahn, Milwaukee, 23

EARNED RUN AVERAGE
AL: Eddie Lopat, NY Yankees, 2.42
NL: Warren Spahn, Milwaukee, 2.10

STRIKEOUTS
AL: Bill Pierce, Chicago White Sox, 186
NL: Robin Roberts, Philadelphia Phillies, 198

The New York Yankees kept winning and it actually got easier for them. After winning pennants by margins of one, three, five and two games, the Yankees' fifth straight trip to the American League title was the most smooth.

The Yankees went 99–52 to finish 8½ games ahead of the Cleveland Indians. They were in first place 158 of 167 days and their last day out of first place was May 10 when they lost a game to Cleveland.

They lost their season opener, then won nine of their next ten games. On May 27 the Yankees began an 18-game winning streak that would give them a 10½-game lead just two months into the season.

The Yankees didn't have a weakness. They led the American League with a .263 batting average and a 3.20 earned run average.

After two years of military service, Whitey Ford went 18–6 and established himself as one of the league's best pitchers. Eddie Lopat came back from chronic shoulder problems and led the league in winning percentage with a 16–4 record and an earned run average with a 2.43 mark.

The Yankees had the luxury of moving Allie Reynolds to relief and their former No. 1 starter had a 13–7 record.

Mickey Mantle batted .296 with 21 home runs and 92 RBIs and Yogi Berra had his typical season, batting .296 with 27 home runs and 108 RBIs. Berra also had a reputation as one of the game's great money players. He was a tougher out in the late innings when the game was on the line because he could adapt to the situation.

The Indians were a dominant team as long as they were in Cleveland. They had a 53–24 record at home but were a very ordinary 39–38 on the road. It didn't help that they lost their first seven head-to-head match-ups against the Yankees, either.

The Indians led the league with 160 home runs, even though Luke Easter was limited to

SHORTS The Braves went to spring training unsure of where they'd play their home games. After 77 years in Boston, the franchise was granted permission to move to Milwaukee in mid-March. It became the first franchise relocation since 1903. The ripple effect had the minor league Milwaukee franchise moving to Toledo. Major league baseball would prove to be a huge hit in Milwaukee.

Cleveland's Al Rosen just missed out on winning the elusive Triple Crown

Rookie Harvey Kuenn's performance was a bright spot in an otherwise sorry season for the Detroit Tigers

Feb. 19: Ted Williams had a scary moment on combat duty for the U.S. Marine Corps in Korea. He was able to safely crash-land his damaged plane.

March 18: The Braves got permission to move from Boston to Milwaukee.

April 17: Mickey Mantle hit the longest home run in Washington's Griffith Stadium. It was estimated to have traveled 565 feet.

April 29: Joe Adcock of the Braves became the first major league player to hit a ball into the center field bleachers at the Polo Grounds.

May 10: Pirates' infielders Johnny and Eddie O'Brien were the first twins to play for the same team at the same time.

May 25: Veteran Max Surkont of the Braves struck out eight consecutive Cincinnati hitters.

June 4: The Pirates traded their greatest gate attraction, Ralph Kiner, to the Cubs in a nine-player deal that also brought the Pirates $150,000.

July 12: Eddie Mathews hit the Milwaukee Braves' first grand slam home run.

Aug. 11: Brooklyn's Duke Snider hit his second grand slam in three days.

Aug. 12: The Yankees had 28 hits against Washington.

Sept. 20: Ernie Banks of the Cubs hit his first major league home run.

Sept. 22: The Dodgers beat the Pirates and won their 60th home game. Brooklyn's 60–17 home record was one game off the record set by the Cardinals in 1942.

Sept. 26: Billy Hunter hit the last home run in the history of the St. Louis Browns.

Sept. 27: The Browns play their final game in St. Louis.

Oct. 17: Bill Veeck, out as the Browns' owner, became a special adviser to Cubs' owner Philip Wrigley.

Oct. 28: Red Barber resigns his job as a Dodgers broadcaster and takes a similar job across town with the Yankees.

just 68 games because of a broken foot. Al Rosen had a fabulous year, just missing the Triple Crown. Rosen led the league with 43 home runs and 145 RBIs, but his .336 average was a single point behind batting champion Mickey Vernon.

The Indians had been accustomed to having as many as three 20-game winners. This year only one pitcher reached that level. Bob Lemon was 21–15.

The Chicago White Sox were 89–65, which represented their highest win total since 1920. Chicago's offense was too weak, however, to mount a serious challenge to the Yankees and Indians.

Minnie Minoso was the White Sox's biggest threat. The Cuban-born outfielder batted .313 and drove in 104 runs. He also had a knack for getting hit by pitches and would contort himself into the path of the ball when the White Sox needed a base runner.

Two-time batting champion Ferris Fain came over from the Philadelphia Athletics, but his .256 average was a disappointment. A pitching staff that was already good got a lift when Virgil Trucks came over in a trade from the St. Louis Browns and went 20–10.

Ted Williams completed his service obligation and came back to the Boston Red Sox at the end of the season. Williams was only able to play in 37 games, but he batted .407 with 13 home runs and 34 RBIs. The Red Sox lost another veteran when Dom DiMaggio announced his retirement on May 12. Mel Parnell led the Red Sox pitching staff with a 21–8 record.

Washington had two stars—Vernon won the batting title with a .337 average and Bob Porterfield won 22 games. The Senators acquired Gil Coan but he fractured a leg in spring training and didn't have much of a season. Coan hit only .196 in 68 games.

Detroit had a terrible start, losing 60 of their first 87 games. They picked it up from there, though, going 33–34. Rookie Harvey Kuenn hit .307 and Ray Boone came over from Cleveland to hit 26 home runs and drive in 114 runs.

One year after leading the league in wins, Bobby Shantz developed arm problems and was just 5–9 for the Philadelphia Athletics.

The Browns marked their last year in St. Louis by finishing last for the second time in three seasons under Bill Veeck's ownership. At one point the Browns lost 20 consecutive home games, which was undoubtedly a factor in their poor attendance. The Browns had an operating loss of nearly $400,000 and were a decided second-class citizen to the Cardinals in St. Louis.

The A's Gus Zernial hit 42 home runs, but it didn't help his Philadelphia team

The Browns had one of the year's genuinely odd moments. They called pitcher Bobo Holloman up from the minor leagues to fill in for one start. It happened that he pitched a no-hitter in that start on May 6 and the Browns couldn't very well send him back to the minors, which had been the plan. Holloman kept pitching, but won only two more games and was back in the minor leagues on July 23.

In the National League, the Brooklyn Dodgers became the first repeat winners since the 1944 St. Louis Cardinals.

At 105–49, the Dodgers set a team record for wins and finished 13 games ahead of the Milwaukee Braves. They had the most wins and the biggest margin since the 1944 Cardinals.

From the All-Star break to September 1, the Dodgers were 41–9 for a sizzling .820 win-

ning percentage. Carl Erskine beat the Braves on September 12 to clinch the pennant, the earliest that any team had wrapped up a title in the history of the 154-game schedule.

A year after Gil Hodges batted .254 and went 0-for-21 in the World Series, he batted .302 with 31 home runs and 122 runs batted in. From a .247 average, right fielder Carl Furillo led the National League with a .344 average. He also contributed 21 home runs and 92 RBIs and was an expert at playing the tricky right field wall at Ebbets Field. Furillo had a gun for an arm and opposing baserunners knew they were taking a risk on a ball hit in his direction. Furillo's temper cost him a month of the season, though, as he fought with New York Giants' coach Leo Durocher on September 6 and was injured. He didn't play again until the World Series.

The Dodgers had more than enough offensive firepower. Roy Campanella and Duke Snider each had their best year in the majors. Campanella batted .312 with 41 homers and 142 RBIs. The latter two figures were records for catchers. Snider hit .336 with 42 home runs and 126 RBIs.

Jackie Robinson moved a couple of times. He went from second to third to make room for rookie Junior Gilliam, then shifted to left field from third to create a spot for Billy Cox.

The Dodgers had an uncharacteristic year on the mound. Erskine was really the only consistently reliable starter. He was 20–6. Russ Meyer had a 15–5 record, but his ERA was high at 4.57. Billy Loes started the year 8–2, then went 6–6. Joe Black did not repeat his success, but Preacher Roe was 11–3.

The Braves celebrated their move to Milwaukee with a leap from seventh to second. Eddie Mathews, 21, hit .302 with 47 home runs and 135 RBIs in his second major league season. The Braves blasted a team-record 156 home runs. They also had the best staff in the National League with a 3.30 ERA. Warren Spahn was 23–7 with a 2.20 ERA. Lou Burdette was 7–0 out of the bullpen, which forced the Braves to find a spot for him in the rotation. Burdette became a starter at the end of July and finished the year with a 15–5 record.

Red Schoendienst of the St. Louis Cardinals was the runner-up for the batting title with a .342 average. Stan Musial was No. 3 in the league with a .337 average. He hit 30 homers with 113 RBIs. Musial had a 0-for-21 streak early in the season, but also had a stretch that saw him get 24 hits in 43 at-bats, a .558 pace. Rookie lefthander Harvey Haddix won 20 games and led the league with six shutouts.

Robin Roberts of the Philadelphia Phillies looked like he was headed for a 30-win season when he won his 20th on August 12. However, he went 3–8 the rest of the way and settled for a 23–16 record. The Phillies lost Curt Simmons for a month when he seriously mangled his foot in a lawn mower accident.

The Giants were the league's biggest disappointment as they finished fifth. The Reds shortened the right field fence at Crosley Field by 24 feet and topped the team record for home runs by 56. Ted Kluszewski hit 40, a Reds record.

The Chicago Cubs were sunk by a 14–36 start and a hand injury that limited Hank Sauer to 108 games. The Cubs added some power when they acquired Ralph Kiner from the Pittsburgh Pirates on June 4. Manager Fred Haney lost 104 games in his first season with the Pirates, but that actually represented an improvement of eight games.

Carl Erskine's victory against the Braves saw Brooklyn head back to the World Series

WORLD SERIES

GAME 1	
NY Yankees 9	Brooklyn 5
GAME 2	
NY Yankees 4	Brooklyn 2
GAME 3	
Brooklyn 3	NY Yankees 2
GAME 4	
Brooklyn 7	NY Yankees 3
GAME 5	
NY Yankees 11	Brooklyn 7
GAME 6	
NY Yankees 4	Brooklyn 3

Some teams would go through an entire season without winning five in a row. Imagine, then, the magnitude of what the New York Yankees accomplished by winning their fifth consecutive World Series.

For the third consecutive year, the Yankees didn't have to leave the city limits for the Series. They were meeting the Brooklyn Dodgers for the second straight year, having started the intracity streak by playing the New York Giants across the Hudson River. For all the big guns the Yankees had, one of the key players in this Series was a scrawny infielder with more attitude than talent. Billy Martin had grown up in the Bay Area of northern California, scuffling out a career in professional baseball. It was that feisty nature that made Martin a favorite of manager Casey Stengel.

Each team had a rather easy path to the Series. The Yankees finished 8½ games in front of the Cleveland Indians. It was an even smoother ride for the Dodgers, who won 105 games and wound up 13 games better than the second-place Milwaukee Braves. Carl Erskine, a 20-game winner in the regular season, lasted just one inning in Game One of the Series. He gave up two hits, walked three and was charged with four runs, which led manager Chuck Dressen to make a change. The big blow in the first inning was Martin's bases-loaded triple. Yogi Berra and Joe Collins homered for the Yankees. The Dodgers got home runs from Jim Gilliam, Gil Hodges and pinch hitter

George (Shotgun) Shuba, but the offense came too late in 9–5 loss.

Martin was a key figure in Game Two as well, hitting a solo home run off Preacher Roe. Mickey Mantle had a two-run homer an inning after Martin's blast. The Yankees won 4–2 behind Eddie Lopat. Erskine got the Dodgers back on track with a good outing in Game Three. He allowed six hits and two runs but registered 14 strikeouts as he beat Vic Raschi for a 3–2 win. Mantle struck out four times as Erskine set a Series record for strikeouts in a single game.

The difference in the game was an eighth-inning solo homer by Roy Campanella, the National League's Most Valuable Player in the regular season. The Dodgers tied the Series in Game Four with a 7–3 victory. Duke Snider drove in four runs with a pair of doubles and a home run. Gilliam had three doubles out of the leadoff spot to get the Dodgers started. Billy Loes won the game with relief help from Clem Labine. Whitey Ford pitched just one inning, giving up three runs.

The Yankees regained control of the Series in Game Five and did it with their bats. They won 11–7 as Mantle hit a grand slam home run off Russ Meyer in the third inning. Gil McDougald

Billy Martin proved the unlikely hero for New York as he closed out the Series with a ninth-inning home run in Game Six

and Gene Woodling also provided home runs.

Martin was back in the spotlight as the Yankees won the Series in Game Six. The Dodgers had tied the score in the top of the ninth when Furillo hit a two-run homer off Allie Reynolds. But that created another opportunity for Martin to be a hero. He didn't disappoint. Martin singled in the winning run against Labine, who was in his sixth inning of relief. The hit was Martin's 12th, which set a record for a six-game World Series.

The Yankees again enforced the idea that the American League was superior. Brooklyn had constructed an excellent regular season, filled with individual achievements. Campanella was the League's Most Valuable Player and Gilliam was Rookie of the Year. Campanella led the National League with 143 RBIs, Snider was third with 126 and Hodges was fifth with 122. Snider's 42 home runs were second in the National League. Erskine was one of just four 20-game winners in the National League and one of eight in the majors.

The Dodgers' Carl Furillo hit .333 for the Series, including a two-run homer in Game Six, but it wasn't enough to halt the Yankees

The New York Yankees won 103 games, their biggest victory total since 1942. Their win total represented a four-game improvement from the previous season. On the surface, it would appear to have all the makings of another great season for baseball's glamour franchise.

It didn't matter, though, as the Yankees' streak of American League titles ended at five. The odd thing about it was it wasn't even really their fault. As good as the Yankees were, the Cleveland Indians were even better. The Indians went 111–43 and took their first American League pennant since 1948.

How good were the Indians? Even with 103 wins the Yankees finished eight games behind them in the standings. The 111 wins topped by one the total posted by the 1927 Yankees, considered the strongest American League team to that point. After five years of looking up to the Yankees, the Indians decided a different perspective might be refreshing. Of the Indians' 43 losses, 22 were to the Yankees and the third-place Chicago White Sox. The Indians beat up on the rest of the league.

The White Sox and Detroit Tigers started the season 11–5 while after nine games the Indians were stuck in last place with a 3–6 record. They rebounded quickly from that. On August 6, the Indians started a stretch in which they won 13 out of 14 games. The Yankees took two of three in a series at the beginning of September, but Cleveland followed by winning 11 consecutive

American League home run champion Cleveland's Larry Doby

Mike Garcia—part of Cleveland's awesome pitching rotation

games. The Indians celebrated clinching the pennant on September 18.

After falling short to the Yankees for so many years, the Indians overhauled their team. They coaxed Hal Newhouser out of retirement and he went 7–2 in relief. Vic Wertz came over from Baltimore in a trade and was a contributor with a .275 average. Rookies Don Mossi and Ray Narleski stabilized the bullpen. Bobby Avila won the American League batting title with a .341 average. He hit 15 home runs, 13 of which either tied games or gave Cleveland the lead. Al Rosen hit .300 with 24 home runs and 102 RBIs.

The strength of the Indians was again the team's experienced starting staff. Together, Bob Lemon, Early Wynn and Mike Garcia accounted for 70 wins—24 by Lemon and Wynn and 22 for Garcia. Bob Feller was 13–3 in a reduced role.

Said George Kell of the Boston Red Sox, "Feller, Lemon, Garcia, Wynn, Narleski and Mossi all threw bullets. When you went into Cleveland for a four-game weekend series, if you didn't manage your times at bat well, you'd come out there 0-for-15. At that point, Lemon was the toughest righthander in the league. Garcia and Wynn weren't far behind."

The Indians trounced some of the lesser teams, winning 20 of 22 from the Boston Red Sox and beating the Baltimore Orioles 19 times in 22 meetings, which included a streak of 17 consecutive wins.

The Yankees became the fourth team to win at least 100 games and not claim a pennant.

Despite their record, it appeared as though age had finally caught up with some of the Yankees' stars—specifically, Phil Rizzuto, Allie Reynolds, Eddie Lopat and Johnny Sain. Rookie Bob Grim won 20 games and Yogi Berra had 125 RBIs, one behind Doby for the league lead. Mickey Mantle drove in 102 runs, matching

Rosen's total. Berra won the League's Most Valuable Player award and Grim was the American League's top rookie.

The Chicago White Sox won 94 games, their best total since 1920. Manager Paul Richards resigned late in the season to take on a dual role as general manager and field manager with Baltimore, the first sign that the Orioles were getting serious about building a winner. Marty Marion took over the White Sox for the last nine games. Former batting champion Ferris Fain had a second disappointing year, missing half of the season with injuries.

Ted Williams missed six weeks of the season with a broken collarbone he sustained on March 1, which limited Boston's chances of contending. As usual, the Red Sox were short on pitching. Their leader was Frank Sullivan with a 15–12 record.

The highlights for Detroit were Harvey Kuenn's .306 average and Steve Gromek's 18 pitching victories. In Washington, Roy Sievers took advantage of a short left field fence and hit 24 home runs. His average, however, was only .232.

Major league baseball was back in Baltimore after an absence of 51 years. The St. Louis Browns were transplanted to Baltimore and then adopted the traditional name that minor league franchises had used over the years. It was a good thing the Orioles had the novelty of major league baseball to sell, because the product on the field was still the hapless Brownies in new uniforms. Baltimore finished the year 54–100. Bob Turley did lead

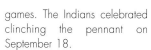 **SHORTS** Chicago Cubs' owner Philip Wrigley sat down with manager Phil Cavarretta near the end of spring training and asked him to honestly assess the team. Cavarretta was blunt and honest and paid with his job. Wrigley fired him for having a negative attitude and the Cubs became the first team to voluntarily change managers in spring training. Stan Hack was named manager.

the league, though, with 185 strikeouts.

The Athletics spent their final season in Philadelphia and finished last for the 18th time.

In the National League, Willie Mays completed his obligation to the Army and returned to the New York Giants, who rose from fifth place to first. Coincidence? Hardly. Mays was a multifaceted weapon, a player who could have a major impact on the game at the plate, in the field or on the bases. He had 31 home runs at the All-Star break, which put him ten days ahead of the pace Babe Ruth set in hitting his record-setting 60 in 1927. Mays hit his 36th homer in his 99th game, then got just one in the following 22 games. That ended his hopes of catching Ruth and Mays wound up not even winning the

National League home run title. No one was about to complain about his 41 home runs or 110 RBIs. Mays batted .345 to lead the league.

In addition to getting Mays back from the Army, the Giants helped themselves with a smart trade. Johnny Antonelli had been just 11–11 in Milwaukee. Once he got to the Giants, he was a different pitcher—a big winner. He went 21–7 to lead the league in winning percentage. He also set the pace in ERA at 2.30 and had a league-leading six shutouts.

Like the Indians' relief combination of Narleski and Mossi, the Giants offered two quality relievers in Marv Grissom and Hoyt Wilhelm.

The Dodgers had a new manager in Walter (Smokey) Alston, whose career in the major

Chicago Cubs' Minnie Minoso

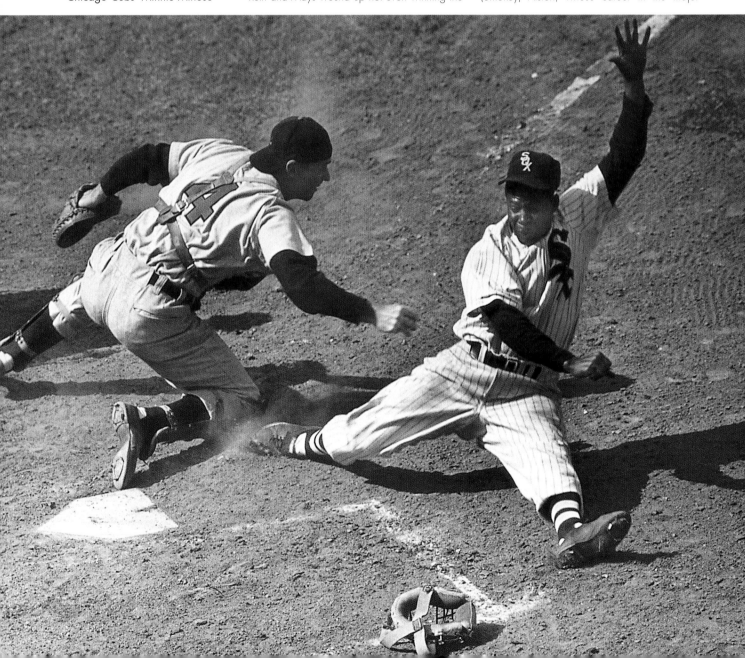

leagues had started and ended with one at-bat. Alston was hired and given the first of many one-year contracts when the bombastic Charley Dressen talked himself out of the job. Apparently at the urging of his wife, Dressen went to the Dodgers and demanded a multi-year contract. He was told the same thing he'd been told before—that the Dodgers preferred to make decisions about their manager on a year-to-year basis. Dressen stuck to his demand, believing he had enough leverage to make the Dodgers eventually relent. They didn't and Dressen chose to stick to his guns, opening the door for Alston to take over.

Not much went right for Alston or the Dodgers. Roy Campanella had a hand injury, missed one-third of the season and batted only .211. Carl Erskine, the Dodgers' No. 1 starter, won 18 games but lost 15. Don Newcombe ended his military obligation but only won nine games. Johnny Podres was sidelined for a month after an appendectomy.

The Milwaukee Braves lost Bobby Thomson for a good portion of the season because of a broken ankle. Warren Spahn was as good as ever, posting a 21–12 record. He became the first lefthander in the century to have six 20-win seasons.

The Philadelphia Phillies made another managerial change, replacing Steve O'Neill with former Cardinals' star Terry Moore. Robin Roberts had his usual fine season for the Phillies, going 23–15.

The Cincinnati Reds moved up one spot in the standings under new manager Birdie Tebbetts. First baseman Ted Kluszewski led the National League with 49 home runs and 141 RBIs. He also batted .326. The problem for the Reds was a shortage of pitching. Cincinnati didn't have a pitcher with more than 12 wins.

The Cardinals fell to sixth, their worst season since 1938 and their first time in the second division since then. They also came up short when it came to pitching—St. Louis had the National League's best team batting average at .281.

The Chicago Cubs spent their eighth consecutive season in the second division. The highlight of their season was the power hitting of Hank

Chicago's Hank Sauer again posted impressive power numbers

Sauer, who blasted 41 home runs.

The Pittsburgh Pirates finished last for the third consecutive season and lost 100 games for the third consecutive year. Pittsburgh couldn't even offer the daily Ralph Kiner home run derby, having traded their slugger to the Cubs during the previous season.

The Pirates dropped into last place on May 4 and stayed there for the rest of the season. Under Branch Rickey's leadership, the Pirates were beginning to develop some younger players to replace the over-the-hill veterans. It would take time, though. For 1954, the Pirates were last in batting average, fielding percentage and earned run average.

SHORTS Following the lead of St. Louis and Boston, Philadelphia became a one-team town when the Athletics transferred to Kansas City after the season. The Browns left St. Louis and became the Baltimore Orioles and the Braves kept the same nickname when they transferred to Milwaukee. Businessman Arnold Johnson bought controlling interest in the Athletics from the Mack family for $3.5 million.

Regular season success often has a short shelf life once the postseason starts. No one understood that cruel lesson better than the 1954 Cleveland Indians.

The Indians had a fabulous regular season, winning 111 games and finishing eight games ahead of the New York Yankees, who had nothing to show for a 103-win season.

Said Cleveland outfielder Al Smith, "The Yankees had won five straight titles so at our training camp we didn't assume we could beat them. But about two weeks into the season, we realized we were good enough."

The Indians were a solid team, led by Bob Lemon and Early Wynn, each of whom won 23 games in the regular season. Larry Doby was the American League RBI leader with 126 and Al Rosen was an excellent all-around player. The Indians had balance but their pitching was the strength of the club.

Said George Kell of the Boston Red Sox, "When you went into Cleveland for a four-game weekend series, if you didn't manage your at-bats well, you'd come out of there 0-for-15."

The New York Giants prevailed in the National League, winning the pennant by five games over the defending champion Brooklyn Dodgers. The Giants didn't have a 20-game winner, but they did have Willie Mays, who was the league's Most Valuable Player.

The series was over in four games as the Giants shocked the Indians with a sweep that ended the National League's seven-year losing streak in the World Series. Mays, who had returned from military duty during the regular season, set the tone in Game One. The game was tied 2–2 and the Indians had two runners on base in the eighth inning when Vic Wertz drove a ball to deep center field. Mays got an excellent break on the ball and was in full retreat in the open acreage of center field at the Polo Grounds. Mays caught the ball over his shoulder, managed to quickly stop, then twirled and fired the ball back to the infield. He killed the rally and kept the score tied.

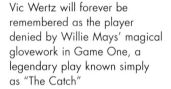

Vic Wertz will forever be remembered as the player denied by Willie Mays' magical glovework in Game One, a legendary play known simply as "The Catch"

That set the stage for an unlikely hero to win the game in the 10th. Dusty Rhodes, a journeyman player, pinch hit a three-run homer off Lemon to end the game. The homer was estimated to have traveled about 200 feet less than Wertz's blast, which Mays had turned into an out.

Cleveland started Game Two on a positive note as Smith hit Johnny Antonelli's first pitch for a home run, a Series first. But Rhodes was a factor for a second consecutive game. He pinch hit a tying single in the fifth inning and stayed in the game. He hit a two-run homer in his next plate appearance against Wynn and provided the margin of victory in a 3–1 win. Antonelli pitched a complete game for the win.

The Series then moved to Cleveland but nothing else changed. The Giants scored a run in the first and Rhodes, pinch hitting for Monte Irvin in the third inning, drove in two runs with a bases-loaded single. The Giants won 6–2 behind Ruben Gomez and Hoyt Wilhelm.

New York had an easier time in the fourth game. The Giants went ahead 7–0 in the fifth and Don Liddle won the game 7–4 with help from relievers Wilhelm and Antonelli.

Mays hit .286 in the Series and drove in three runs. Shortstop Alvin Dark had a good offensive Series, batting .412. But the biggest offensive star was Rhodes, who wound up with a .667 average and seven RBIs. Rhodes had two fewer RBIs than the entire Cleveland team.

None of the Indians starters did well. Lemon had a 6.75 earned run average, Mike Garcia's was 5.40 and Wynn checked in at 3.86. Was the result unexpected? In some respects, yes. "It wasn't a surprise that we won, only that we won in four straight games," Antonelli said. "In the spring, the Indians were in Tucson and the Giants were in Phoenix and we played many times. We even barnstormed together, playing every day. We didn't have any problems with them. We matched up well with them so we were confident."

The Giants' Dusty Rhodes and Johnny Antonelli celebrate their Series triumph. Both men made vital contributions as New York completed the sweep

MOST VALUABLE PLAYER
AL: Yogi Berra, NY Yankees
NL: Roy Campanella, Brooklyn

ROOKIE OF THE YEAR
AL: Herb Score, Cleveland
NL: Bill Virdon, St. Louis Cardinals

LEADERS
BATTING AVERAGE
AL: Al Kaline, Detroit, .340
NL: Richie Ashburn, Philadelphia Phillies, .338

HOME RUNS
AL: Mickey Mantle, NY Yankees, 37
NL: Willie Mays, NY Giants, 51

RUNS BATTED IN
AL: Ray Boone, Detroit; Jackie Jensen,
Boston Red Sox, 116
NL: Duke Snider, Brooklyn, 136

STOLEN BASES
AL: Jim Rivera, Chicago White Sox, 25
NL: Bill Bruton, Milwaukee, 25

PITCHING VICTORIES
AL: Whitey Ford, NY Yankees; Bob Lemon,
Cleveland; Frank Sullivan, Boston Red Sox, 18
NL: Robin Roberts, Philadelphia Phillies, 23

EARNED RUN AVERAGE
AL: Bill Pierce, Chicago White Sox, 1.97
NL: Bob Friend, Pittsburgh Pirates, 2.83

STRIKEOUTS
AL: Herb Score, Cleveland, 245
NL: Sam Jones, Chicago Cubs, 198

The American League pennant race was the equivalent of a heavyweight fight that went the limit. It was as compelling as any of the daily dramas that aired on network radio. A devoted baseball fan checked his morning paper on a daily basis to see how the contenders had reshuffled the order after another day or night of fighting it out.

American League Rookie of the Year—Cleveland's Herb Score

For most of the year, half of the American League's eight teams were in the thick of one of the best races in memory. When it finally ended, the New York Yankees were standing above the others—but the Yankees knew they had been in a fight. So much so that the toll of the race may have been a factor in the Yankees' World Series loss to Brooklyn.

Cleveland entered the season as both the defending American League champion and favorite to take the title again. The Indians spent significant time in first place, part of the revolving quartet that included the Yankees, Chicago White Sox and Boston Red Sox.

The Yankees finally pulled away from the pack by winning 15 of their last 19 games to finish three games ahead of Cleveland. Casey Stengel had to do some of his most significant lineup juggling and the Yankees' record (96–58) was the second-worst mark the team had posted in Stengel's seven seasons as manager.

On September 8, only four games separated three teams (the Red Sox had fallen out earlier). Cleveland had taken over first place on May

1 and settled in for a three-week stay. The Yankees won 15 of 17 and took over at the top on May 21. When the Indians lost seven of eight at home in early June, New York took advantage and built its lead to 5½ games over the second-place White Sox.

By July 1, New York was 6½ games ahead, the largest lead any team would enjoy all season. At the All-Star break the Yankees were five games ahead of Cleveland, six in front of Chicago and had a seven-game edge on Boston.

Just when all seemed under control in the Bronx, the Yankees went 9–16 after the break and threw the race wide open again. From July 22 to September 7, no more than two games separated the top three teams. The Red Sox were never more than five games out of first place in that span. Boston was in fourth place on August 9 but the Red Sox were just 1½ games behind. In eight days in late August, the lead changed hands five times with the Yankees, Indians and White Sox all involved.

The White Sox were first at the end of August. On Labor Day, all three contenders split their doubleheaders. On September 11, the Indians and Yankees split two games before 65,310 fans in New York.

Two days later the Indians swept Washington, but the Yankees started a seven-game winning streak by beating Detroit. The next night Washington beat Cleveland in the only loss reliever Ray Narleski would suffer all year.

Detroit had a major role in deciding the pennant as the Tigers won three straight games against the Indians. The Yankees took a two-game lead and clinched the pennant on September 23 when Don Larsen beat the Red Sox in the second game of a doubleheader.

Stengel had to be a hands-on manager. Only three of his players—Mickey Mantle, Gil McDougald and Yogi Berra—were able to stay in the lineup on a regular basis. Mantle batted .306 and led the league with 37 home runs. Berra's average was just .272, but he led the team with 108 RBIs and hit 28 homers.

Hank Bauer helped down the stretch. He hit half of his 20 home runs from August 11 to the end of the season. Billy Martin got out of the Army in time to help in September.

The pitching staff started to change when Allie Reynolds retired after the 1954 season. Age was beginning to catch up with Eddie Lopat. Bob Grim, a 20-game winner as a rookie, had arm trouble. Still, the Yankees led the league with a 3.23 earned run average and set a record for the fewest hits allowed. Whitey Ford anchored the staff with an 18–7 record and 2.62 ERA, the second-best in the league.

Tommy Byrne made an amazing comeback and went 16–5. The Yankees got help from their 18-player offseason swap with Baltimore. Bob Turley won 17 games and Larsen went 8–1 after spending time in the minor leagues.

The Indians went 13–9 against the Yankees, becoming the first team to take a season series

TIMELINE

April 12: Braves' rookie outfielder Chuck Tanner hit a home run in his first major league at-bat.

April 12: The Athletics played their first game in Kansas City and beat Detroit 6–2.

April 14: Catcher Elston Howard became the first black player to wear a Yankees uniform.

April 22: The Dodgers' season-opening winning streak ended at ten games with a 5–4 loss to Milwaukee.

April 22: The Yankees lost infielder Jerry Coleman for the season after he broke his collarbone in a rundown.

May 5: The Dodgers' Tom Lasorda threw three wild pitches in one inning of his first major league start.

May 12: Sam Jones of the Cubs threw a no-hitter against the Pirates, winning 4–0. He walked the bases full in the ninth, then struck out the last three hitters. The Cubs got 15 hits against Vernon Law and Nellie King.

May 28: Harry Walker replaced Eddie Stanky as Cardinals' manager.

June 3: The Cardinals' Stan Musial hit his 300th career home run.

June 12: Brooklyn's Don Newcombe had a 10–1 record after the Cubs beat him 10–1 to end his personal winning streak.

June 24: Harmon Killebrew of the Senators hit his first major league homer.

July 19: Pittsburgh's Vernon Law pitched 18 innings and beat Milwaukee 4–3.

Sept. 5: Don Newcombe of the Dodgers won his 20th game and hit his seventh home run.

Sept. 14: Cleveland's Herb Score set a rookie record for strikeouts by topping Grover Alexander's mark of 235.

Sept. 24: Leo Durocher resigned as Giants' manager and was replaced by Bill Rigney.

Oct. 6: The Cardinals hired Frank Lane as general manager.

Oct. 25: Branch Rickey, 74, resigned as Pirates' general manager and Joe L. Brown was hired as his replacement.

Willie Mays led the National League in home runs with 51

SHORTS It wasn't a good year to be a pitcher. For the first time in the history of the American League, there wasn't a 20-game winner. The National League had two, Robin Roberts of the Phillies and the Dodgers' Don Newcombe. Home runs were on the increase as the two leagues combined for 2,224. Willie Mays of the Giants became the seventh player in baseball history to hit at least 50.

from New York in Stengel's tenure. But Cleveland gave that edge back by posting an inexplicable 9–13 record against lowly Washington.

Things were never quite right for the Indians. Their big three of Bob Lemon, Early Wynn and Mike Garcia won 19 fewer games than they had in 1954. Al Rosen fought a finger injury and his average fell to .244. The entire club seemed to fall into a late-season hitting slump. First baseman Vic Wertz's season ended on August 26 when he was diagnosed with polio.

The White Sox were third for the fourth consecutive year, but they were closer to the top than they had been since 1920. Their 91–63 record was their best since 1935. Minnie Minoso slumped badly in the first half and had a .254 average and two home runs at the All-Star break. Pitcher Dick Donovan was knocked out for three weeks by an appendectomy. When he came back he lost five straight decisions.

The Red Sox were visited by tragedy when first baseman Harry Agganis died on June 27. Agganis had been hospitalized twice with pneumonia—he died from a blood clot.

Ted Williams didn't report to the team until May 13 and didn't appear for the first time until 15 days later. Williams was away dealing with a divorce. The Red Sox went on a 44–16 streak from June 5 to August 9 and pulled within 1½ games of the lead. They slipped back with a 20–24 slide.

Detroit's Al Kaline won the batting title at the age of 20 with a .340 average. He also hit 27 home runs and drove in 102 runs.

The Athletics had bigger crowds, thanks to their move from Philadelphia to Kansas City. They still weren't successful on the field, though.

Paul Richards had a frustrating time in his first season as Baltimore's field manager and general manager.

Washington manager Charley Dressen was reminded that good players make good managers. Dressen, whose most recent experience was with the pennant-winning Brooklyn

With home runs being hit with greater frequency, the Phillies' Robin Roberts was one of just two 20-game winners

Dodgers in 1953, led a Senators team that was 53–101.

Brooklyn got along quite well without Dressen. The Dodgers went 98–55 and finished 13½ games ahead of Milwaukee (the National League's largest margin since the 1944 St. Louis Cardinals won by 14½ games). They pulled away by opening the season with ten straight wins, part of a 22–2 start. They spent all but two days in first place and would have gone wire-to-wire if it hadn't been for Cincinnati's traditional one-day head start and a rain postponement of their own opener.

The ten consecutive wins to open the season broke a National League record of nine that three teams had shared. By July 4, the Dodgers were 12½ games ahead of the second-place Chicago Cubs, which was within two games of the record for biggest advantage on that date.

Alston coolly handled some clubhouse issues. Jackie Robinson complained about not playing enough and Roy Campanella balked about batting eighth. Alston stood up to both. His biggest test came in early May when Don Newcombe refused Alston's order to pitch batting practice. Alston told his best pitcher to leave the clubhouse and the front office backed the manager by suspending Newcombe. A contrite Newcombe was back the next day and went on to lead the Dodgers' staff with a 20–5 record.

Several pitchers battled injuries, including Carl Erskine, Karl Spooner, Billy Loes and Johnny Podres. Two players from the minor leagues stepped in. Don Bessent came up from St. Paul and was 8–1 while Roger Craig moved up from Montreal and had a 5–3 record.

The Dodgers had a tremendous offensive attack and led the league in batting average (.271) and home runs (201). Campanella hit his way back into the cleanup spot with a .318 average, fourth best in the league. He also hit 32 home runs and had 107 RBIs. Duke Snider batted .309 and tied a team record with 42 home runs. His 136 RBIs led the league. Robinson had his worst season, batting .256, but shortstop Pee Wee Reese hit a solid .282.

Brooklyn played rather ordinary baseball in the second half, but its hot start and lack of serious competition carried the Dodgers to their third pennant in four years.

The Milwaukee Braves lost pitcher Gene Conley and first baseman Joe Adcock to injuries. The New York Giants' pitching staff fell apart and manager Leo Durocher turned in his resignation at the end of the season.

SHORTS The Pirates finished last for a fourth consecutive season in what was the fifth year of Branch Rickey's five-year plan. The Pirates opened the year with eight straight losses and fell into last place for good on May 30. That made pitcher Bob Friend's accomplishment even more amazing—he went 14–8 and led the league with a 2.84 ERA.

Al Kaline shone in Detroit winning the American League batting crown

WORLD SERIES

GAME 1	
NY Yankees 6	Brooklyn 5
GAME 2	
NY Yankees 4	Brooklyn 2
GAME 3	
Brooklyn 6	NY Yankees 3
GAME 4	
Brooklyn 8	NY Yankees 5
GAME 5	
Brooklyn 5	NY Yankees 3
GAME 6	
NY Yankees 5	Dodgers 1
GAME 7	
Brooklyn 2	NY Yankees 0
MVP: Johnny Podres, Brooklyn	

Finally, it was "next year" for the Brooklyn Dodgers. After seven unsuccessful trips to the World Series, the Dodgers and their fans could at last abandon the cry of "Wait 'til next year."

The Dodgers beat the New York Yankees in seven games to raise the first championship flag over Ebbets Field.

Brooklyn had enjoyed something of a dream season. The Dodgers opened the year with ten consecutive wins and a 22–2 record. After enduring the stress of close races and the heartbreak of the 1951 playoff loss to the New York Giants, the Dodgers breezed to the 1955 National League title, finishing 13 ½ games ahead of the Milwaukee Braves.

The Yankees, on the other hand, were confronted with a closer race. New York finished three games ahead of the Cleveland Indians and five in front of the Chicago White Sox. Don Newcombe, a 20-game winner in the regular season, was on his way to establishing a reputation as a pitcher who did not do well in

The Dodgers' Roy Campanella hugs Series MVP Johnny Podres as Brooklyn finally gets it done

the postseason. Newcombe was touched for all the runs in less than six innings of the 6–5 Game One loss to the Yankees and their ace, Whitey Ford.

Newcombe served two home runs to Joe Collins and another to Elston Howard. The Dodgers fell behind 2–0 in games when they couldn't solve veteran Tommy Byrne in Game Two. Byrne held the Dodgers to five hits and won 4–2. Byrne also drove in two runs.

Game Three appeared to be a mismatch as the Yankees sent 17-game winner Bob Turley against Johnny Podres, who had been a game under .500 in the regular season for the Dodgers. Podres celebrated his 23rd birthday with an 8–3 win. Podres limited the Yankees to seven hits, including a home run by Mickey Mantle, whose participation was limited by leg injuries.

The Dodgers used power to tie the Series. Roy Campanella, Gil Hodges and Duke Snider hit home runs in an 8–5 win in Game Four. Starter Carl Erskine was ineffective for Brooklyn but the Dodgers held on to even the Series at two games each.

Another unlikely pitching hero emerged for Brooklyn in Game Five. Rookie Roger Craig held the Yankees to two runs over six innings and won 5–3 with relief from Clem Labine.

The Dodgers tried to wrap up the Series back at Yankee Stadium but lost Game Six 5–1. Brooklyn started Karl Spooner, its sixth different starting pitcher in six games. He lasted just one-third of an inning, allowing all five runs, three of which came on a home run by Bill Skowron. Brooklyn got good relief pitching from Russ Meyer and Ed Roebuck, who shut out the Yankees the rest of the way. It didn't matter as the Brooklyn hitters couldn't do anything with Ford, who allowed just four hits and won for the second time in the Series.

That set up the deciding game and history was not on Brooklyn's side. Dodgers' manager Walter Alston chose Podres to start, making him the only Brooklyn pitcher to start more than one game in the Series. His opponent was Byrne.

The Dodgers broke a scoreless tie in the fourth when Hodges singled to score Campanella, who had doubled. Hodges drove in the second run with a sacrifice fly in the sixth. The Series spotlight often finds obscure players and that was the case in 1955. Sandy Amoros, a defensive replacement in left field, saved the game with a running catch on a slicing liner hit by Berra. Amoros not only tracked down the ball, he alertly got it back to the infield to allow the Dodgers to double Gil McDougald off first

base. His play saved two runs and spared the Dodgers a tied game in the late innings.

Podres worked out of another jam in the eighth inning and got the side in order in the bottom of the ninth to end Brooklyn's frustration. It would turn out to be the Dodgers' only title in Brooklyn as the franchise moved to Los Angeles following the 1957 season. Most Valuable Player honors went to Podres, the only Dodgers pitcher to win two games in the Series—with a big assist from Sandy Amoros.

Brooklyn slugger Duke Snider came up big in Game Five with two homers in a 5–3 win

MOST VALUABLE PLAYER
AL: Mickey Mantle, NY Yankees
NL: Don Newcombe, Brooklyn

CY YOUNG AWARD
AL, NL: Don Newcombe, Brooklyn

ROOKIE OF THE YEAR
AL: Luis Aparacio, Chicago White Sox
NL: Frank Robinson, Cincinnati

LEADERS

BATTING AVERAGE
AL: Mickey Mantle, NY Yankees, .353
NL: Hank Aaron, Milwaukee, .328

HOME RUNS
AL: Mickey Mantle, NY Yankees, 52
NL: Duke Snider, Brooklyn, 43

RUNS BATTED IN
AL: Mickey Mantle, NY Yankees, 130
NL: Stan Musial, St. Louis Cardinals, 109

STOLEN BASES
AL: Luis Aparacio, Chicago White Sox, 21
NL: Willie Mays, NY Giants, 40

PITCHING VICTORIES
AL: Frank Lary, Detroit, 21
NL: Don Newcombe, Brooklyn, 27

EARNED RUN AVERAGE
AL: Whitey Ford, NY Yankees, 2.47
NL: Lew Burdette, Milwaukee, 2.70

STRIKEOUTS
AL: Herb Score, Cleveland, 263
NL: Sam Jones, Chicago Cubs, 176

After an exceptionally stressful race to the pennant in 1955, the New York Yankees cruised to the 1956 American League title. They won their seventh pennant in eight years and took it by the widest margin in Casey Stengel's years as manager.

The Yankees moved in first place to stay on May 16, spent just ten days out of the top position and finished nine games ahead of the Cleveland Indians. In doing so, the Yankees added to their legend by claiming their 22nd American League championship in a streak that didn't begin until 1921.

They clinched the title almost two weeks before the end of the season, which gave them ample time to get ready for the World Series.

Maybe their opening game foretold how the season would go. They beat the Senators in Washington 10–4 as Mickey Mantle hit a pair of long-distance home runs over the center field fence at Griffith Stadium and drove in four runs.

Mantle reached the major leagues in 1951 and performed well, but he found another level in 1956. He won the Triple Crown with a .353 batting average, 52 home runs and 130 RBIs. The heir apparent to Joe DiMaggio had finally elevated his game and rightfully put his name alongside the other Yankees legends.

Like the other Yankees stars, he had an exceptional supporting cast. Gil McDougald hit .311 and could play all over the infield and outfield. First baseman Bill (Moose) Skowron hit .308 with 23 home runs and 90 RBIs. Yogi Berra batted .298 with 30 home runs and 105 RBIs. His totals would have led most clubs—the significant contribution was dwarfed on the Yankees because of Mantle's monster season.

Hank Bauer contributed 26 homers and 84 RBIs even though he only batted .241. The Yankees set a team record for home runs with 190, topping the 182 the 1936 Yankees hit.

Mantle's best friend, Whitey Ford, led the pitching staff with a 19–6 record and the league with a 2.47 ERA. Johnny Kucks was promoted from the bullpen and went 18–9. Don Larsen featured a new no-windup delivery and went 11–5.

Mickey Mantle's tape-measure blasts were among the highlights of his Triple Crown season

Luis Aparicio gave the Sox great defense and was a constant threat on the base paths

Feb. 5: Owners turned down a request from players to raise the minimum salary by $1,000 to $7,000.

Feb. 8: Connie Mack died at 93. He managed the Athletics for 50 years.

Feb. 15: The Pirates and Athletics chose not to play an exhibition game in Birmingham, Alabama because of a city ordinance that prevented white and black players from participating in the same game.

April 28: Frank Robinson of the Reds hit his first major league home run.

May 15: The Dodgers purchased pitcher Sal Maglie from the Cleveland Indians.

May 26: Johnny Klippstein, Hersh Freeman and Joe Black of the Reds pitched 9⅔ hitless innings against the Braves.

May 30: Mickey Mantle hit one of the longest home runs of his career off Washington's Pedro Ramos. It was within two feet of clearing the upper deck facade at Yankee Stadium.

July 8: The Giants hit seven home runs against the Pirates and won 11–1. Willie Mays, Daryl Spencer and Wes Westrum each hit two.

July 14: Mel Parnell pitched the Red Sox's first no-hitter since 1923, beating Chicago 4–0 at Fenway Park.

Aug. 25: The Yankees released shortstop Phil Rizzuto. He would move into the broadcast booth the following season, replacing Jim Woods.

Sept. 18: Mickey Mantle hit his 50th home run, becoming the eighth player in baseball history to reach that level.

Sept. 30: Al Lopez resigned as Indians' manager. In six years, he finished first once and second in the other five seasons.

Oct. 30: To increase pressure for a new stadium, the Dodgers sold Ebbets Field and became a tenant. They signed a contract through 1959, with options to stay another two additional years.

Nov. 14: The Pirates claimed they may have to leave Pittsburgh unless a new stadium is built.

Dec. 13: The Dodgers traded Jackie Robinson to the Giants. Robinson, who had been planning to retire, rejected the trade.

The Yankees were as lucky as they were good. They tried to send pitcher Tom Sturdivant to their minor league team in Denver. The Detroit Tigers claimed the righthander on waivers, forcing the Yankees to keep him on the major league roster. Sturdivant wound up with a 16–8 record for the Yankees.

The opening day win—which also featured a 4-for-4, five-RBI game by Berra—was part of a 7–1 start.

The major threat to the Yankees' status came in June when the Chicago White Sox visited and swept four games to cut New York's lead to just one game. From that point, though, the Yankees won 18 out of 20 and were again comfortably ahead. At the All-Star break, their advantage over the White Sox was 6½ games.

Immediately after the break, the Yankees won three straight from Cleveland. In July, New York had an 11-game winning streak, the best in the majors for the season.

As usual, the Indians had tremendously solid pitching. Herb Score, Early Wynn and Bob Lemon were all 20-game winners. They were second through fourth in the league in ERA.

The Indians didn't have enough hitting. Al Rosen's RBI total fell to 61 and former batting

SHORTS Dale Long wasn't one of the game's great power hitters, but he did something that even Babe Ruth didn't manage: long hit home runs in eight consecutive games for the Pirates from May 19–28. His seventh, an eighth-inning shot off Ben Flowers of the Phillies, broke the record. He hit his eighth off Brooklyn's Carl Erskine before teammate Don Newcombe stopped the streak.

champion Bobby Avila saw his average dip to .224. In 101 games, rookie Rocky Colavito batted .276 and hit 21 home runs, but he also spent six weeks in the minor leagues. First baseman Vic Wertz came back from polio and hit 32 home runs with 106 RBIs.

The White Sox had one excellent pitcher and one offensive star. Lefthander Bill Pierce went 20–9 while Minnie Minoso batted .316 with 21 home runs and 88 RBIs. The White Sox also welcomed Luis Aparicio as the replacement at shortstop for Chico Carrasquel. Aparicio batted a respectable .266 and led the league with 21 stolen bases.

The Boston Red Sox were the opposite of the Indians. The Red Sox always had plenty of offensive power but failed to come up with enough pitching. Ted Williams, Jackie Jensen and

Don Newcombe helped the Dodgers to the World Series with 27 victories

Mickey Vernon all hit over .300 for the Red Sox.

The Tigers finished fifth for the third consecutive year and had the distinction of holding a 12–10 edge in the season series with the Yankees. Harvey Kuenn batted .322 and Charley Maxwell hit .326. Al Kaline had a .314 average with 27 home runs and 128 RBIs. Frank Lary, 21–13, had a well-deserved reputation as a Yankee killer. Billy Hoeft won 20 games for the first time.

Baltimore showed a slight improvement, which at least indicated that the club was headed in the right direction under Paul Richards.

Roy Sievers hit 29 home runs for Washington and teammate Jim Lemon had 27.

The Kansas City Athletics' top winner was Art Ditmar with 12. He also led the league with 22 losses.

The nature of the pennant races was reversed from the previous season. The action

was in the National League in 1956 with a spectacular season-long battle. The defending World Series champion Brooklyn Dodgers spent only 17 days in first place. One of them was the last day of the season as they held off the Milwaukee Braves and Cincinnati Reds to win their second consecutive pennant. The Braves finished just one game behind Brooklyn and Cincinnati was two games off the pace.

After Labor Day, the Braves had a lead of 3½ games over both the Dodgers and Reds. From that point, though, Milwaukee went 11–12 while Brooklyn went 15–7.

Milwaukee still had a one-game lead heading into the season's final series. The Dodgers swept three games from the Pirates just a short time after they'd lost three out of four at Pittsburgh. The Braves lost two out of three at St. Louis. Milwaukee had spent 126 days in first place, but it didn't matter.

In the first half of the season, five of the eight teams were involved in the race. Only the Philadelphia Phillies, New York Giants and Chicago Cubs were excluded.

Pittsburgh was the first to drop out. The Pirates actually had nine days in first place early in the season. That in itself was an accomplishment for a team that had spent four seasons in last place.

The Pirates faded with an eight-game losing streak in mid-June. The Dodgers were six games behind on July 19. By August 2, Milwaukee's lead was one game over the Reds and two over the Dodgers.

The Dodgers tied for the lead on September 11 when Sal Maglie beat Milwaukee's Bob Buhl 4–2. It was Brooklyn's first time in the lead since the second week of the season.

On September 25, Maglie threw a no-hitter against the Phillies. On September 29, Warren Spahn of the Braves held St. Louis to three hits in 11 innings, but lost the game in the 12th. The Dodgers wrapped up the title the next night with an 8–6 win over the Pirates.

Maglie, acquired from Cleveland in mid-May, wound up 13–5 and helped ease the absence of Johnny Podres to military service. Don Newcombe was 27–7 and Clem Labine was a workhorse out of the bullpen, pitching in 62 games.

Duke Snider led the league with 43 home runs and had 101 RBIs. Gil Hodges had 32 home runs and 87 RBIs while Carl Furillo hit 21 homers and drove in 83 runs.

Braves' pitchers Buhl and Lew Burdette faded in the stretch and sluggers Joe Adcock and Eddie Mathews slumped in September. Spahn won 20 games for the seventh time and Hank Aaron took the batting title with a .328 average.

The Reds ended a streak of 11 second-division seasons and hit 221 home runs to tie the Giants' 1943 record. Rookie Frank Robinson batted .290 and hit 38 home runs. He, Wally Post and Gus Bell became the first three outfielders to combine for at least 100 homers. First baseman Ted Kluszewski had 35 home runs, 102 RBIs and a .302 average.

New St. Louis general manager Frank Lane lived up to his nickname of "Trader" by dealing Harvey Haddix, Bill Virdon and Red Schoendienst. Stan Musial had his usual fine season, batting .310 with 109 RBIs and Ken Boyer hit .306 with 98 RBIs.

In Philadelphia, Robin Roberts was 19–18 and saw his streak of 20-win seasons end at seven.

Under first-year manager Bill Rigney, the Giants won eight of their last ten to claim sixth place. New Pirates' manager Bobby Bragan steered the club out of the cellar. Virdon, a .211 hitter when the Cardinals traded him on May 17, thrived with Pittsburgh and wound up .319, second in the league. Roberto Clemente batted .311 in his second year.

The Cubs set a club record by losing 94 games. They never managed to climb any higher than sixth place during the season. Even bad teams have good players—Ernie Banks batted .297 and hit 28 home runs.

National League Rookie of the Year honors for the Reds' Frank Robinson

WORLD SERIES

GAME 1	
Brooklyn 6	NY Yankees 3
GAME 2	
Brooklyn 13	NY Yankees 8
GAME 3	
NY Yankees 5	Brooklyn 3
GAME 4	
NY Yankees 6	Brooklyn 2
GAME 5	
NY Yankees 2	Brooklyn 0
GAME 6	
Brooklyn 1	NY Yankees 0
GAME 7	
NY Yankees 9	Brooklyn 0
MVP: Don Larsen, NY Yankees	

Don Larsen was perfect. The rest of the New York Yankees' starting pitchers were merely outstanding. Thanks to Larsen's historic perfect game and some other excellent work by starters, the Yankees took the World Series from the Brooklyn Dodgers in seven games after dropping the first two.

Larsen's gem was in Game Five, which put the Yankees ahead for the first time in the unusual Series. Long before Larsen made history, it looked as though the Dodgers were going to win handily. Brooklyn won the first two games 6–3 and 13–8, as the Yankees ran through all 11 of their pitchers trying to slow down the Dodgers.

Yankees' ace Whitey Ford was roughed up in Game One as Sal Maglie pitched a complete game for the Dodgers. Jackie Robinson and Gil Hodges hit home runs for the Dodgers.

Neither starter did well in Game Two. Larsen was knocked out in the second inning, although the four runs he allowed were all officially unearned. Staked to a 6–0 lead, Larsen couldn't hold it. The Yankees had scored six runs in the second inning to chase Brooklyn starter Don Newcombe. The Dodgers continued to add on runs, forcing the Yankees to use seven pitchers in the game.

The Yankees were back on home turf for the next three games and won them all with solid work from their starting pitchers. In fact, Game Two was the last time Yankees' manager Casey Stengel called on a relief pitcher in the Series.

Ford rebounded to win 5–3 in Game Three, allowing the Dodgers just two earned runs. Billy Martin and Enos Slaughter hit home runs for the Yankees.

Tom Sturdivant matched Ford's work with a 6–2 win in Game Four. Sturdivant consistently pitched out of trouble as he allowed six hits and walked six other batters. Mickey Mantle and Hank Bauer supported him with home runs.

The Series was even at two games apiece when Larsen and Sal Maglie locked up in Game Five. Larsen, nicknamed "Goony Bird" by his teammates, was in his second year with the Yankees after being part of a 17-player trade with the Baltimore Orioles. Larsen, 27, had a

Don Larsen became the first pitcher to toss a perfect game during World Series play

Larsen's slice of perfection gave the Yanks a 3–2 lead in the Series

reputation as a player whose results didn't match up with his talent. He had managed an awful 3–24 record for the Orioles in 1954.

Larsen was superb and Maglie was pitching well, too. The Brooklyn starter retired the first 11 batters he faced. That streak was broken by Triple Crown winner Mantle, who lined a home run off Maglie with two outs in the fourth inning.

Mantle helped preserve the perfect game with an excellent catch of a liner hit by Gil Hodges in the fifth. In the sixth, Maglie gave up another run. Andy Carey singled, moved up on Larsen's bunt and scored on Bauer's single. In the Dodgers' ninth, Carl Furillo flied to right. Roy Campanella grounded out. Dale Mitchell, the pinch hitter for Maglie, watched a third strike and Larsen finished the only perfect game in Series history and the first in the major leagues in 34 years.

The momentum had a short life as the Yankees lost Game Six to Clem Labine in ten innings.

Labine was a reliever who was called upon to make an emergency start. He responded by holding the Yankees to seven hits, all but one a single. Brooklyn won the game when Robinson delivered an RBI single off Bob Turley.

The Yankees scored two runs each in the first and third innings of Game Seven and cruised to a 9–0 win behind Johnny Kucks. Newcombe gave up home runs to Yogi Berra and Elston Howard and Bill Skowron hit a grand slam off reliever Roger Craig. Kucks allowed just three hits.

In the first two games of the Series, Yankees pitchers allowed 19 runs, 12 of them earned. Over the last five games of the Series, New York pitchers surrendered just six runs, five of them earned.

Larsen was the Series' Most Valuable Player on the strength of his perfect game. Berra was the Yankees' offensive star with a .360 average, three home runs and ten RBIs. Slaughter had a .350 average with a home run and four RBIs.

The Yankees' Yogi Berra provided the hot bat as he finished the Series with a .360 average and ten RBIs

MOST VALUABLE PLAYER
AL: Mickey Mantle, NY Yankees
NL: Hank Aaron, Milwaukee

ROOKIE OF THE YEAR
AL: Tony Kubek, NY Yankees
NL: Jack Sanford, Philadelphia Phillies

LEADERS
BATTING AVERAGE
AL: Ted Williams, Boston Red Sox, .388
NL: Stan Musial, St. Louis Cardinals, .351

HOME RUNS
AL: Roy Sievers, Washington, 42
NL: Hank Aaron, Milwaukee, 44

RUNS BATTED IN
AL: Roy Sievers, Washington, 114
NL: Hank Aaron, Milwaukee, 132

STOLEN BASES
AL: Luis Aparicio, Chicago White Sox, 28
NL: Willie Mays, NY Giants, 38

PITCHING VICTORIES
AL: Jim Bunning, Detroit; Bill Pierce, Chicago White Sox, 20; NL: Warren Spahn, Milwaukee, 21

EARNED RUN AVERAGE
AL: Bobby Shantz, NY Yankees, 2.45
NL: Johnny Podres, Brooklyn, 2.66

STRIKEOUTS
AL: Early Wynn, Cleveland, 184
NL: Jack Sanford, Philadelphia Phillies, 188

Milwaukee was one of the smallest cities in the major leagues, but you wouldn't have known it from the crowds at County Stadium.

Milwaukee was crazy about its Braves—and with good reason. The Braves had developed into one of the National League's premier teams. They had come within a game of winning the pennant in 1956 and returned with a powerful team headed by an exceptional pitching staff.

The romance between the city and its baseball team had started in 1953, when the Braves abandoned Boston to move to bring major league baseball back to Milwaukee in the first franchise shift since 1903.

Anxious to prove it didn't have to take a back seat to New York or Chicago as a major league city, Milwaukee fans packed the park to watch the Braves. The 1957 season saw a major league record season attendance of 2,215,404 in Milwaukee. The Braves went over the two million mark for the fourth consecutive year and broke the single-season record they set in 1954 with 2,131,388 paid admissions.

It was quite a show the Braves gave their fans. They endured in a five-team race that saw the Cincinnati Reds, Philadelphia Phillies, Brooklyn Dodgers and St. Louis Cardinals all take a run at the top spot. In late July, just 2 ½ games separated the top five teams in the National League.

One by one, though, the other contenders fell. The Phillies lost 20 of 27 games in August. The Dodgers started a streak of 11 losses in 18 games in August as well. The Reds dropped 18 of 23, including 10 in a row. On August 6, the Braves moved into first place to stay. They won eight consecutive games down the stretch and clinched the pennant on September 23 when Hank Aaron hit a game-winning home run in the 11th inning off Billy Muffett to beat St. Louis.

It was one of 199 home runs the Braves hit. They had to adjust during the season due to injuries. First baseman Joe Adcock broke a bone in his right leg on June 23 and didn't return until September 2. Center fielder Billy Bruton had a knee injury that ended his season on July 11.

The Braves summoned Bob "Hurricane" Hazle from the minor leagues on July 28 and he was an instant hit. In 41 games with the Braves, Hazle batted .403. The Braves also got good production from outfielder Wes Covington, who was called up from the minors.

Milwaukee's front office made a smart trade in mid-June, acquiring second baseman Red Schoendienst from the New York Giants.

(from l to r) The Braves' Eddie Mathews, Hank Aaron and Frank Torre

Milwaukee's Lew Burdette helped the Braves to the pennant with 17 wins

Hank Aaron had another big season, batting .322 while leading the league in home runs (44) and runs batted in (132). Eddie Mathews contributed 32 home runs and 94 RBIs.

At age 36, Warren Spahn headed the pitching staff with a 21–11 record. Bob Buhl was 18–7 and Lew Burdette had a 17–9 record.

The Cardinals' second-place finish was their best since 1949. Manager Fred Hutchinson improved his team with a pair of moves in late May: he installed rookie Eddie Kasko at third base and shifted Ken Boyer to center field, shoring up two positions. The Cardinals got hot and were able to advance from sixth place to first in less than a month.

Stan Musial claimed his seventh batting title with a .351 average. Musial also drove in 102 runs.

Larry Jackson and Lindy McDaniel had identical 15–9 records. McDaniel's brother Von was a rookie sensation with a 7–5 record at age 18.

The Dodgers marked their last season in Brooklyn with a third-place finish, breaking a streak of eight years in either first or second. Duke Snider slumped to a .267 average but had his fifth consecutive year with at least 40 home runs. Don Drysdale had a 17–9 record and

SHORTS What started as a celebration of Billy Martin's 29th birthday ended up being the end of his career with the Yankees. A fight involving several players at the Copacabana night club embarrassed the Yankees, who traded Martin to Kansas City a month later. Hank Bauer was arraigned for his role but was later cleared. The Yankees also issued more than $5,000 worth of fines to the players involved.

Johnny Podres returned from military service and led the league with a 2.66 ERA. Gil Hodges just missed a couple of round numbers—he batted .299 and drove in 98 runs.

The Cincinnati Reds had two major problems: injuries to Ted Kluszewski and a 4–18 record against the Braves.

Philadelphia got help from five rookies—pitchers Jack Sanford, Dick Farrell and Don Cardwell, first baseman Ed Bouchee and outfielder Harry Anderson. Sanford was 19–8, which helped take some of the sting out of a 10–22 season from Robin Roberts.

The Giants said good bye to New York with their second sixth-place finish in as many years. Willie Mays batted .333 with 35 home runs, 97 RBIs and 38 stolen bases. Ruben Gomez became the league's first ten-game winner on

TIMELINE

Jan. 5: Jackie Robinson announced his retirement.

Feb. 22: Dodgers' owner Walter O'Malley announced the team may play as many as ten exhibition games in California in 1958.

April 22: The Phillies became the last National League team to integrate when John Kennedy appeared in a game for them.

May 7: Indians' pitcher Herb Score was struck in the face by a line drive off the bat of the Yankees' Gil McDougald.

May 28: The National League gave preliminary approval for the Dodgers and Giants to transfer to California for the 1958 season. The approval includes a number of stipulations, including the demand that both teams move at the same time.

June 1: Wally Moon of the Cardinals saw his hitting streak end at 24 games.

June 6: The Brooklyn Dodgers, leading Chicago 1–0 with one out in the second inning, were defeated by Mother Nature, who dropped a foggy shroud over Ebbets Field and forced one of the stranger postponements in baseball history.

June 12: The Cardinals' Stan Musial set a National League record for consecutive games by playing in his 823rd. He broke the record set by Gus Suhr.

June 13: Ted Williams had his second three-homer game of the season.

June 21: Von McDaniel, 18 years old, pitched a two-hit 2–0 win over the Dodgers in his major league debut.

June 28: Cincinnati fans stuffed the ballot box and elected eight Reds players to the starting All-Star team. Commissioner Ford Frick rejected three of their choices—Gus Bell, George Crowe and Wally Post.

July 18: Gil Hodges of the Dodgers hit his 12th career grand slam.

Aug. 19: The Giants' board of directors approved a move to San Francisco for the 1958 season.

Sept. 21: Gail Harris was the last player to hit a home run for the New York Giants.

Sept. 23: Hank Aaron's 11th-inning home run off Billy Muffett of St. Louis gave the Braves the National League pennant.

18-year-old rookie sensation Von McDaniel posted seven wins for the Cards

June 30 but finished 15–13. Johnny Antonelli battled shoulder problems and had a disappointing 12-18 season.

Pittsburgh made a managerial change, replacing Bobby Bragan with Danny Murtaugh in August. The Pirates had three .300 hitters— Dick Groat, Bob Skinner and Dee Fondy.

The Chicago Cubs tied for seventh, their 11th consecutive year in the second division. Dale Long, acquired on May 1 from Pittsburgh, batted .298 while Ernie Banks had 43 home runs and 102 RBIs. Dick Drott, a 21-year-old rookie, was 15–11 to lead the Cubs staff.

It was business as usual in the American League, where the New York Yankees won their eighth pennant in nine years. They finished eight

games ahead of the Chicago White Sox.

The Yankees had a 28–4 streak and took over first place on June 30. Mickey Mantle battled a variety of injuries and didn't duplicate his Triple Crown season. Mantle did bat .365 with 34 homers and 94 RBIs. First baseman Bill Skowron hit .304 and drove in 88 runs. Yogi Berra slumped to a career-low .251 average, but had 24 home runs and 82 RBIs. Berra tried wearing glasses to break out of his slump but the experiment didn't last long.

Tom Sturdivant headed the pitching staff with a 16–6 record. Bobby Shantz was 11–5 and led the league with a 2.45 ERA. Bob Turley won 13 games as Whitey Ford had shoulder problems and won just 11 games.

The White Sox started the season 11–2 under new manager Al Lopez. They lost outfielder Larry Doby and catcher Sherm Lollar to injuries during the season and didn't help themselves with an 8–14 record against the Yankees.

Lopez liked the running game and the White Sox stole 109 bases. Chicago had the league's top three stealers—Luis Aparicio, Minnie Minoso and Jim Rivera. Minoso also hit .310 and drove in 102 runs. Nellie Fox led the team with a .317 average.

Bill Pierce was 20–12 for his second straight 20-win season. Dick Donovan had a 16–6 record and 2.77 ERA while Jim Wilson won 15 games and led the league with five shutouts.

The Boston Red Sox were never a factor, even though 38-year-old Ted Williams became the oldest man to win a batting title with a .388 average. Frank Malzone hit .292 and drove in 103 runs. Mel Parnell was unable to pitch because of injuries, and retired.

Cleveland's season took a chilling turn on May 7 when promising pitcher Herb Score was struck in the face by a line drive off the bat of the Yankees' Gil McDougald. It was a disappointing first season for Kerby Farrell, who had succeeded Lopez as Indians' manager.

Kansas City fired manager Lou Boudreau and replaced him with Harry Craft. The last-place Washington Senators kicked manager Chuck Dressen upstairs to a front office job and named coach Cookie Lavagetto their new manager.

The big news of the season was the end of National League baseball in New York. The Dodgers announced plans to leave Brooklyn for Los Angeles and the Giants abandoned the city for San Francisco.

While the official announcement may have been something of a jolt, there was no doubt both teams were restless and anxious to make major changes. The Dodgers and Giants both maintained they were stuck in outdated stadiums that lacked the parking spaces necessary in an era when people drove to games rather than using public transportation.

More to the point, the owners felt the neigh-borhoods they occupied were deteriorating and that their fan base was increasingly relocating to the suburbs.

California was ripe for the taking. Air travel made coast-to-coast travel viable and any part of the state was considered a growth market. California fans had been loyal to minor league baseball and figured to be even more excited about the prospect of the major leagues.

Fees for broadcast rights were becoming an important source of revenue. In New York, that money was split three ways among the Dodgers, Giants and Yankees. In California, the Dodgers and Giants would have market exclusivity.

The Giants made the first official announcement while O'Malley haggled with Los Angeles officials over a sweetheart real estate deal that would provide the site for what became Dodger Stadium. Despite the delay, it was clear the Dodgers were moving.

In baseball's new climate, other teams were soon positioning themselves to use the threat of a move to New York to get better deals in their home cities.

The end of the road in New York for the Giants as they packed their bags and headed for San Francisco

The World Series may have been old hat to jaded followers of the New York Yankees, but fans of the Milwaukee Braves had no problem mustering enthusiasm for postseason games.

Whitey Ford won Game One for the Yankees, but suffered a crucial loss in Game Five

Milwaukee loved its Braves from the time the franchise transferred from Boston for the 1953 season. The affection was frenzied in 1957, when the Braves erased the heartbreak of two consecutive second-place finishes and won the National League pennant. Baseball-mad Milwaukee set a National League attendance record as 2,215,404 fans went through the turnstiles at County Stadium to see a team that went 95–59.

The Braves combined power with a first-rate pitching staff, which was headed by Warren Spahn, Lew Burdette and Bob Buhl. The Braves finished eight games ahead of the St. Louis Cardinals to get the franchise to its first World Series since 1914.

As usual, the Yankees tore through the American League to finish eight games ahead of the Chicago White Sox. They won the pennant for the third consecutive year and the ninth time in ten years. The Series opened in New York with the Yankees winning Game One 3–1 behind Whitey Ford. He held the Braves to five hits and outpitched Spahn, who left the game in the sixth inning. The Braves got the requisite road split by winning Game Two 4–2 behind Burdette's complete game and a catch by Wes Covington in left field that snuffed a Yankees threat.

The Yankees easily won Game Three, beating the Braves 12–3 as Buhl failed to complete the first inning. Wisconsin native Tony Kubek, the Yankees' 20-year-old shortstop, hit a pair of home runs and drove in four runs. New York starter Bob Turley left the game in the second inning but the Yankees got 7⅓ innings of solid relief from Don Larsen to take a 2–1 lead in the Series.

The Braves got even in Game Four, thanks to Spahn's messy 7–5 win. It wasn't a classic performance by any means—Spahn allowed 11 hits and five runs—but he endured and was still around when Milwaukee won the game in the 10th.

Spahn had a 4–1 lead in the ninth and retired the first two hitters. Down to their last out, the Yankees scored three runs to tie the game. Yogi Berra and Gil McDougald singled before Elston Howard slammed a 3–2 pitch for a home run.

In the top of the 10th, Kubek singled and scored on Hank Bauer's triple for a 5–4 lead. The winning rally came with a controversy when Nippy Jones, pinch hitting for Spahn, claimed that Tommy Byrne's first pitch hit him in the foot. As evidence, he offered a baseball that had a show polish smudge and he was awarded first base. Johnny Logan doubled to tie the game 5–5. Eddie Mathews then hit a two-run game-winning homer off Bob Grim.

The Braves parlayed that momentum into a tense 1–0 win in Game Five. Burdette pitched a seven-hitter to beat Ford. Covington prevented a home run by McDougald by making a leaping catch at the wall in the fourth inning. Milwaukee staged a two-out rally to score in the sixth on singles by Mathews, Hank Aaron and Joe Adcock.

The Series went back to New York and the Yankees won Game Six 3–2 on Bauer's seventh-inning home run. All the runs came on homers: Berra hit a two-run home run for the Yankees and the Braves had gotten solo shots from Frank Torre and Aaron. Turley pitched a complete game for the Yankees, allowing just four hits.

The Braves won the Series by roughing up Larsen early and winning the final game 5–0 behind Burdette. Larsen was knocked out in the third inning as Milwaukee scored four runs. Mathews had a two-run double and Crandall put on the finishing touch with an eighth-inning home run.

Burdette took Series Most Valuable Player honors by going 3–0 with a 0.67 earned run average and throwing three complete games. In 27 innings, he allowed two earned runs, walked four and struck out 13. He used accusations that he threw a spitball to his psychological advantage. The Braves' best offensive player was Aaron, who batted .393 with three home runs and seven RBIs.

Hammerin' Hank Aaron led the Braves' offense with three homers and seven RBIs

MOST VALUABLE PLAYER

MOST VALUABLE PLAYER
AL: Jackie Jensen, Boston Red Sox
NL: Ernie Banks, Chicago Cubs

CY YOUNG AWARD
AL, NL: Bob Turley, NY Yankees

ROOKIE OF THE YEAR
AL: Albie Pearson, Washington
NL: Orlando Cepeda, San Francisco

LEADERS
BATTING AVERAGE
AL: Ted Williams, Boston Red Sox, .328
NL: Richie Ashburn, Philadelphia Phillies, .350

HOME RUNS
AL: Mickey Mantle, NY Yankees, 42
NL: Ernie Banks, Chicago Cubs, 47

RUNS BATTED IN
AL: Jackie Jensen, Boston Red Sox, 122
NL: Ernie Banks, Chicago Cubs, 129

STOLEN BASES
AL: Luis Aparacio, Chicago White Sox, 29
NL: Willie Mays, San Francisco, 31

PITCHING VICTORIES
AL: Bob Turley, NY Yankees, 21; NL: Bob Friend, Pittsburgh; Warren Spahn, Milwaukee, 22

EARNED RUN AVERAGE
AL: Whitey Ford, NY Yankees, 2.01
NL: Stu Miller, San Francisco, 2.47

STRIKEOUTS
AL: Early Wynn, Chicago White Sox, 179
NL: Sam Jones, St. Louis Cardinals, 225

The New York Yankees were the only game in town in 1958. The Giants had abandoned New York for San Francisco and the Dodgers had made the stunning switch from the neighborhood streets of Brooklyn to the fast-moving freeways of Los Angeles.

That left the Yankees to carry the banner of Major League Baseball in the nation's largest city … And who did that better than the Yankees, the game's marquee franchise?

They took the American League pennant by ten games, their largest margin in Casey Stengel's ten years as manager. If Stengel still had his critics, no one was paying any attention to them. His team had won the pennant for nine of the ten years. With that accomplishment, he tied the record Connie Mack had needed 50 years to fashion to get nine winners with the

Bob Turley's early-season form epitomized the Yanks' hot start

Casey Stengel silenced his detractors with another division title

Philadelphia Athletics. The Yankees took their 24th title since 1921 and finished first for the fourth consecutive year.

Yet their record of 92–62 represented the lowest winning percentage among Stengel's pennant-winners. And the Yankees could trace a good deal of 1958's success to a hot start and general mediocrity among the other seven clubs. The Yankees had a losing record over the last two months and not only won the pennant, they took it without a serious challenge.

The Yankees started the season by winning seven out of eight games. At the same time, two of their main competitors stumbled out of the gate. The Boston Red Sox lost seven of their first eight games and the Chicago White Sox managed just two wins in nine games.

From the start of May, the Yankees won 16 of 18 and managed ten consecutive wins as part of that stretch. Bob Turley was nearly unhittable in his first seven starts for the Yankees, completing all seven games, throwing four shutouts and giving up just seven runs and 31 hits in his 63 innings.

At one point the Yankees were so hot that the

Detroit Tigers won seven straight and still couldn't get any closer than 7½ games behind New York. The spurt by the Tigers was unusual, though, as most of the American League clubs stumbled because of injuries or disappointing seasons from important players.

On August 3, every club other than the Yankees had a record below .500. Second-place Cleveland was 51–52. The other clubs would improve, but New York was immune because of the large margin it had built earlier in the season.

The Yankees stumbled through the last two months. Stengel was irked enough to order a full-team workout on August 18. The Yankees went through a streak that saw them lose nine of 12, their worst stretch in five years.

New York was 15–16 in August and got only slightly better in September, splitting the 24 games in the final month. Every aspect of their game declined. The pitching dropped off, the defense became less reliable and the bats cooled off considerably.

Through all the problems at the end, the Yankees still had a championship season. They had a strong five-man starting staff with Turley, Whitey Ford, Don Larsen, Bobby Shantz and Ryne Duren. Turley wound up 21–7 with a 2.98 earned run average. Ford was second on the staff with a 14–7 record, but his 2.01 ERA led the league for the second time in three years. Overall, the Yankees had a team ERA of 3.22, the American League's best.

Mickey Mantle lost time to a shoulder injury yet still had a banner season with a .304 average, 42 home runs and 97 RBIs. His average was down from .365 in the previous year, but he showed increases in homers and RBIs.

Elston Howard hit .314 for the Yankees and Norm Siebern batted .300. Yogi Berra's average was .266 with 22 home runs and 90 RBIs.

The White Sox were sunk by their usual light-weight offensive attack and some uncharacteristically weak pitching. They were in last place

TIMELINE

Jan. 29: Dodgers' catcher Roy Campanella was permanently paralyzed after an auto accident on Long Island.

Jan. 30: After last year's All-Star ballot box stuffing episode, the voting was taken away from fans by Commissioner Ford Frick.

March 11: The American League made batting helmets mandatory.

April 15: The Giants beat the Dodgers in the first major league game at San Francisco's Seals Stadium.

April 18: The Dodgers beat the Giants in their first home game in Los Angeles. Attendance was 78,682.

May 12: Willie Mays hit the first grand slam in San Francisco Giants' history.

May 13: Stan Musial got his 3,000th career hit, a pinch double off Moe Drabowsky of the Cubs at Wrigley Field.

June 10: Bill Norman became manager of the Tigers, replacing Jack Tighe.

June 26: Joe Gordon replaced Bobby Bragan as Indians' manager.

July 7: The National League began to study the possibility of adding two new franchises.

July 20: Detroit's Jim Bunning pitched a no-hitter against the Red Sox.

Aug. 14: Birdie Tebbetts resigned as Reds' manager and was replaced by Jimmie Dykes.

Aug. 23: Gil Hodges of the Dodgers set a National League record with his 14th career grand slam.

Sept. 13: Warren Spahn of the Braves won his 20th game for his ninth season at that level. He set a record for most 20-win seasons by a lefthander.

Sept. 14: The Yankees clinched the American League pennant, their ninth under Casey Stengel. He tied Connie Mack's record for the most titles won by a manager in the American League.

Sept. 20: Hoyt Wilhelm of the Orioles pitched a no-hitter against the Yankees.

Sept. 29: Mayo Smith was hired to manage the Reds.

Dec. 3: American League president Will Harridge retired.

Teddy Ballgame again led Boston—and the league—with a .328 average

runs and a league-leading 122 RBIs. Ike Delock became the No. 1 starter after he was promoted from the bullpen and was 14–8.

Cleveland's chances were doomed when a number of players missed significant time with injuries: Vic Wertz broke his ankle; Herb Score, who was trying to come back from being struck in the face by a line drive, developed elbow trouble; Mike Garcia had a slipped disk in his back; and Bob Lemon needed elbow surgery. The Indians wound up releasing Garcia and Lemon, two mainstays of past Cleveland pitching staffs.

Rocky Colavito batted .303 with 41 homers and 113 RBIs and Cal McLish led the staff with a 16–8 record. Their good work wasn't enough to save manager Bobby Bragan, who was fired on June 26 and replaced by Joe Gordon.

Detroit also made a managerial change, dropping Bill Norman for Jack Tighe. The Tigers still finished in the second division for the seventh time in eight years, thanks largely to a power shortage.

Baltimore had no offense to go with a burgeoning pitching staff.

The Athletics had their best season since moving to Kansas City and their 73 wins exceeded manager Harry Craft's pre-season goal by three. The Washington Senators finished last, despite Roy Sievers' 39 home runs and 108 RBIs.

Baseball was a hit in California, even if the Dodgers and Giants didn't have standout years. The Dodgers' temporary home was the Coliseum, a cavernous football stadium that had to be altered for baseball. A seating capacity of 94,000 allowed the Dodgers to draw in excess of 1.8 million fans. The Giants were stuck temporarily in minor league Seals Stadium, which held fewer than 23,000 people. The Giants, however, were able to nearly double the attendance from the final year in New York by drawing just under 1.3 million.

The Dodgers were struck by tragedy even before the season started when catcher Roy Campanella's career was ended by an auto accident. Campanella was driving home to Long Island late on a January night when his car ran off the road. The accident left Campanella paralyzed.

The Dodgers were never a factor in the race, falling to seventh to end a streak of 13 years without finishing lower than third. The Milwaukee Braves took over first place in early August and won their second consecutive pennant.

Warren Spahn went 22–11, his ninth 20-win season. Lew Burdette, 6–7 at the All-Star break, finished 20–10. Hank Aaron had a big second half to wind up with a

on June 15 and didn't top the .500 mark for good until the beginning of August. Bill Pierce was 17–11 with a 2.68 ERA that was second-best in the league.

Catcher Sherman Lollar hit .273 with 20 homers and 84 RBIs. Nelson Fox batted .300 and keystone partner, Luis Aparicio, stole 29 bases. In fact, the White Sox had the league's top three base stealers with Jim Rivera (21) and Jim Landis (19) following Aparicio. The White Sox relied on speed because they didn't have much power. Their 101 home runs were last in the league. Dick Donovan had a 10–4 second half to finish 15–14.

It was the customary story in Boston—the Red Sox had plenty of hitting and a shortage of pitching. Ted Williams led the league with a .328 average and Pete Runnels was No. 2 at .322. Jackie Jensen had another good all-around year with a .286 average, 35 home

.326 average, 30 home runs and 95 RBIs.

The Braves were able to endure after losing second baseman Red Schoendienst for most of the season with pleurisy and a broken finger. Pitcher Bob Buhl missed a good portion of the season with injuries and was just 5–2. Carlton Willey came up from the minor leagues and won nine games.

The surprise team was the Pittsburgh Pirates, who finished second after occupying one of the bottom two spots for eight consecutive years. Bob Friend was 22–14 for the biggest season by a Pirates pitcher since Burleigh Grimes in 1928.

Frank Thomas hit .281 with 35 home runs and 109 RBIs for the Pirates. Reliever ElRoy Face was 5–2 with 26 saves and a pair of rookies, first baseman Dick Stuart and pitcher George Witt, made big contributions. Shortstop Dick Groat rallied in the second half to finish with a .300 average and Bob Skinner's .321 mark led the club.

The Giants fell out of the race by losing ten out of 11 in early August. Orlando Cepeda, just 20 years old, led an exceptional rookie class by batting .312 with 25 home runs and 96 RBIs. The other outstanding rookies were third baseman Jim Davenport, catcher Bob Schmidt and outfielders Leon Wagner and Willie Kirkland. Willie Mays had his customary exceptional year—a .329 average, 29 home runs and 96 RBIs.

The Cincinnati Reds were such a disappointment that manager Birdie Tebbetts resigned on August 14. Chicago's Ernie Banks was the Most Valuable Player even though the Cubs didn't contend. Banks batted .313 and led the league with 47 homers and 129 RBIs.

The Cardinals dropped manager Fred Hutchinson late in the season and the last-place Philadelphia Phillies fired Mayo Smith and named Eddie Sawyer to replace him. The seventh-place Dodgers traded Don Newcombe after a 0–6 start and a publicized curfew violation.

Roy Campanella's career ended in tragic circumstances

WORLD SERIES	
GAME 1	
Milwaukee 4	NY Yankees 3
GAME 2	
Milwaukee 13	NY Yankees 5
GAME 3	
NY Yankees 4	Milwaukee 0
GAME 4	
Milwaukee 3	NY Yankees 0
GAME 5	
NY Yankees 7	Milwaukee 0
GAME 6	
NY Yankees 4	Milwaukee 3
GAME 7	
NY Yankees 6	Milwaukee 2
MVP: Bob Turley, NY Yankees	

Braves' ace Warren Spahn won two games in the Series, but the Yankees proved too strong

Same teams, same seven-game World Series, but this time a different winner. The New York Yankees and Milwaukee Braves were matched again in the World Series, but this time the Yankees endured by winning the seventh game.

Neither team had been seriously challenged en route to its league championship. The Yankees finished ten games in front of the Chicago White Sox while the Braves were eight games better than the surprising Pittsburgh Pirates in the National League. It wasn't easy for the Yankees, who looked like they were going to fall to the powerful Braves for a second consecutive year.

Warren Spahn won the opening game for the Braves, who rallied for a winning run in the bottom of the 10th against reliever Ryne Duren. Milwaukee bunched singles by Joe Adcock, Del Crandall and Billy Bruton to win Game One.

Lew Burdette was the beneficiary of a blowout 13–5 win in Game Two but Burdette was anything but a bystander. He hit a three-run homer in a seven-run first inning as the Braves jumped on starter Bob Turley. Burdette took a 13–2 lead into the ninth before allowing late home runs to Hank Bauer and Mickey Mantle.

Don Larsen and Duren combined on a six-hit-

ter in Game Three for a 4–0 Yankees win. Bauer was the offensive star with all four RBIs; he had a bases-loaded single and a two-run homer and stretched his World Series hitting streak to 17 games. Bauer, who hit in the leadoff spot, had three of the Yankees' four hits.

Spahn pitched a brilliant two-hitter in Game Four to win 3–0. He surrendered a triple to Mantle in the fourth and a single to Bill Skowron in the seventh. Spahn drove in one of Milwaukee's runs as the Braves came within a game of closing the Series.

Game Five offered a Burdette–Turley rematch but this one followed a different script. Turley held the Braves to five hits, walked three and struck out ten as the Yankees won 7–0, scoring six runs in the sixth against Burdette and Juan Pizarro. Gil McDougald's home run had given the Yankees their first run.

The Yankees tied the Series by winning Game Six 4–3. New York scored two runs in the top of the 10th, then shut down a Milwaukee rally after the Braves had scored one run in the bottom of the inning. McDougald broke the 2–2 tie with a leadoff homer against Spahn in the 10th. The Yankees' second run came when Skowron hit an RBI single off reliever Don McMahon. Desperate to close the win, the Yankees called on Turley to get the final out in the bottom of the 10th.

Burdette was back on two days' rest to start Game Seven against Larsen, who was working

on his fifth day. Larsen was knocked out of the game in the third inning and Yankees' manager Casey Stengel again leaned on Turley at a critical juncture. The Yankees were holding a 2–1 lead at the time and Turley pitched out of a bases-loaded jam in the third to keep the Yankees ahead.

Crandall tied the game in the sixth with a solo home run off Turley. Burdette had two outs and nobody on base in the eighth inning when the Yankees rallied for the winning runs. Yogi Berra doubled and scored on Elston Howard's tie-breaking single. Andy Carey singled and Skowron cleared the bases with his second home run of the Series.

Turley shut down the Braves in the ninth and the Yankees claimed their 18th World Series title. He took Most Valuable Player honors for his ability to appear in four games—two as a starter and the two emergency relief appearances. Turley won the honor despite being pounded for four runs in one-third of an inning in one of the starts. His work in Game Five changed the momentum of the Series and allowed the Yankees to become the second team ever to come back from a 3–1 deficit in games.

Had Turley not won the award, serious consideration would have gone to Bauer. He led both teams in runs (six), hits (ten), home runs (four) and RBIs (eight). His .323 average led the Yankees. Although his hitting streak was stopped at 17 Series games, it stood as a record.

Gil McDougald looks to tag the runner, but it was his tenth-inning, Game Six homer that gave the Yankees the impetus for victory

LEADERS

MOST VALUABLE PLAYER
AL: Nellie Fox, Chicago White Sox
NL: Ernie Banks, Chicago Cubs

CY YOUNG AWARD
AL, NL: Early Wynn, Chicago White Sox

ROOKIE OF THE YEAR
AL: Bob Allison, Minnesota
NL: Willie McCovey, San Francisco

LEADERS

BATTING AVERAGE
AL: Harvey Kuenn, Detroit, .353
NL: Hank Aaron, Milwaukee, .355

HOME RUNS
AL: Rocky Colavito, Cleveland; Harmon Killebrew, Washington, 42
NL: Eddie Mathews, Milwaukee, 46

RUNS BATTED IN
AL: Jackie Jensen, Boston Red Sox, 112
NL: Ernie Banks, Chicago Cubs, 143

STOLEN BASES
AL: Luis Aparicio, Chicago White Sox, 56
NL: Willie Mays, San Francisco, 27

PITCHING VICTORIES
AL: Early Wynn, Chicago White Sox, 22: NL: Lew Burdette, Warren Spahn, Milwaukee; Sam Jones, San Francisco, 21

EARNED RUN AVERAGE
AL: Hoyt Wilhelm, Baltimore, 2.19
NL: Sam Jones, San Francisco, 2.83

STRIKEOUTS
AL: Jim Bunning, Detroit, 201
NL: Don Drysdale, Los Angeles, 242

The Dodgers found themselves with a new address but a familiar position—they were in a do-or-die playoff series to determine the National League pennant winner.

The league had needed a playoff to settle a pennant race three times. The Dodgers were involved in all of them. The process had not been kind to them, either.

In 1946, they lost two playoff games to the St. Louis Cardinals. Five years later, the deciding game ended with Bobby Thomson's famous "Shot Heard 'Round the World" that gave the pennant to the New York Giants. Those disappointments had come in Brooklyn—now the Dodgers were in their second season in Los Angeles. Maybe their luck had changed during the cross-country move.

The Dodgers won the two playoff games to complete a comeback season and deny the Milwaukee Braves a third consecutive National League pennant.

Los Angeles won the first playoff game 3–2 in Milwaukee. The Braves were scrambling to find a starter and had to lean on Carlton Willey, who had pitched just three innings since August 3. He did a creditable job, but John Roseboro's leadoff homer in the sixth inning made the difference. The Dodgers got seven innings of shutout relief from Larry Sherry, who replaced starter Danny McDevitt. It was a prelude to Sherry's exceptional work in the World Series.

The Dodgers took the pennant by winning 6–5 in the 12th inning the following day. Milwaukee's Lew Burdette took a 5–2 lead into

Elroy Face won 17 consecutive decisions on his way to posting an 18–1 record for the Pirates

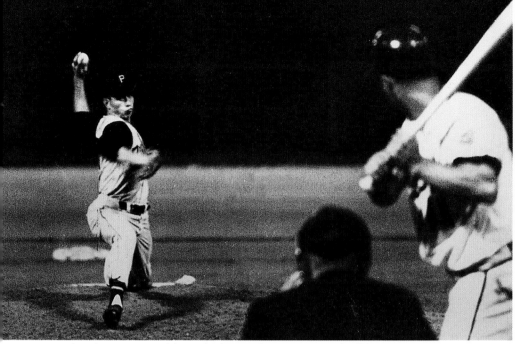

Pittsburgh's Harvey Haddix pitched 12 perfect innings—and still lost

the ninth when Wally Moon, Duke Snider and Gil Hodges all hit singles to load the bases. Don McMahon relieved and gave up a two-run single to Norm Larker. Desperate to nail down the win, the Braves called on Warren Spahn to face Carl Furillo, who delivered a game-tying sacrifice fly.

Bob Rush, the Braves' fifth pitcher, had two outs in the 12th when he walked Hodges. Joe Pignatano singled to move Hodges to second. Furillo hit a ground ball to short that took a high bounce. Felix Mantilla, who had replaced the injured Johnny Logan, fielded the ball but made a wild throw to first that left Hodges to score the winning run.

The Dodgers had managed the kind of stretch run a championship team needs—they won 13 of 18 games before sweeping the playoffs and taking their seventh pennant in 13 years.

The San Francisco Giants had spent two months in first place during the summer before the race became a two-team duel between the Dodgers and Braves.

The Dodgers retooled their team as they gradually said goodbye to the players who had keyed their success in Brooklyn. The front office was active and made a number of pivotal personnel decisions. Starter Roger Craig was summoned from the minor leagues on June 19 and went 11–5 with four shutouts and a 2.06 earned run average. He just missed having enough innings to qualify for the league ERA title.

Sherry was brought up on July 2 and went 7–2 out of the bullpen. Shortstop Maury Wills, who had spent almost ten years in the minors, came up on June 1 and struggled at first. Wills caught fire down the stretch and batted .429 in the Dodgers' last 17 games. He went 7-for-13 in a big series against the Giants.

A couple of holdovers from the Brooklyn days did well. Snider batted .308 with 23 home runs and 88 RBIs while Hodges added 25 home runs

and 88 RBIs. Hodges tied Mel Ott's major league record with his 11th consecutive year with at least 20 homers.

The pitching staff established a major league record by striking out 1,077 batters. Don Drysdale led the way with a 17–13 record and a league-leading 242 strikeouts.

Milwaukee had its share of struggles. Second baseman Red Schoendienst missed the season with tuberculosis and the Braves tried seven different replacements without a great deal of success. Outfielder Wes Covington sat out the last six weeks with a knee injury. The three leading pitchers were up to their usual standards. Warren Spahn and Burdette had identical 21–15 records and Bob Buhl was 15–9, but the three pitchers behind them—Carlton Willey, Joey Jay and Juan Pizzaro—were a combined 17–22.

Hank Aaron won the batting title with a .355 average. He also hit 39 home runs and had 123 RBIs. Eddie Mathews batted .306 with 114 RBIs and a league-leading 46 home runs.

The Giants faded as the season wore on. Four starters—Sam Jones, Johnny Antonelli, Jack Sanford and Mike McCormick—along with reliever Stu Miller, accounted for 85 percent of the Giants' innings.

Jones was 21–15 to tie for the league lead in wins and his 2.82 ERA was the National League's best. On July 30, the Giants called up first baseman Willie McCovey and he blasted his way into their powerful lineup. McCovey batted .354 with 13 home runs and 52 RBIs, winning the National League Rookie of the Year award despite his late start. Both Willie Mays and Orlando Cepeda had big seasons. Cepeda batted .317 with 27 home runs and 105 RBIs. Mays hit .313 with 33 home runs and 104 RBIs.

Too many Pittsburgh players failed to follow

Chicago's Early Wynn won 22 games as part of the league's most dominant staff

up on their 1958 success. Bob Friend went from a 22-win season to an 8–19 record. Bill Mazeroski's average dropped from .275 to .241 and George Witt declined from 9–2 to no wins because of injuries.

Two Pittsburgh pitchers contributed amazing individual performances. Reliever Elroy Face went 18–1 and won his first 17 decisions until the Dodgers beat him on September 11.

Harvey Haddix pitched the greatest game ever lost against the Braves on May 26. Haddix was struggling with a cold, but still managed to retire the first 36 batters in order. No pitcher had ever taken a perfect game beyond nine innings and no one had ever pitched more than 10⅔ hitless innings in one game. The game was still score-less even though the Pirates had gotten 12 hits, all singles, against Burdette.

Mantilla led off the 13th with a grounder to third and was safe on Don Hoak's throwing error. Mathews bunted him to second. Aaron was intentionally walked and Joe Adcock hit Haddix's second pitch over the wall in right center to give the Braves the game. The score wound up being 1–0 because Aaron left the field without completing the path around the bases. That also resulted in Adcock's hit going into the books as a single.

In the American League, the Chicago White Sox proved that home runs weren't a requirement for success. The "Go Go" White Sox scored runs with their legs and depended on a solid pitching staff and good defense.

The White Sox took the pennant by finishing five games ahead of Cleveland. Their 97 home runs were the low figure in the major leagues, but they led the league in ERA (3.29), fielding percentage (.979) and stolen bases (113).

They beat the teams they had to beat—they were 15–7 against Cleveland and 13–9 against the Yankees, marking the first time since 1925 that they had taken the season series from New York.

Early Wynn, at the age of 39, was 22–10 with a 3.16 ERA. Bob Shaw had an 18–6 record with a 2.69 ERA. Gerry Staley and Turk Lown were outstanding out of the bullpen. The 40-year-old Staley set a White Sox record with 67 appearances. He was 8–5 with a 2.20 ERA while Lown was 9–2 in 60 games.

Nellie Fox had a .306 average and captured the American League Most Valuable Player award. Luis Aparicio batted .257 and stole 56 bases. Catcher Sherman Lollar hit 22 homers and drove in 84 runs.

The Indians had power but came up short in pitching. They had four players with at least 20 homers, led by Rocky Colavito's 42. Cal McLish was the leading pitcher with a 19–8 record and ten of his wins came against the White Sox and Yankees.

The Yankees had their worst season since 1925, a carryover from their losing record over the last two months of the previous season. Bob Turley fell from 21 wins to an 8–11 year and Don Larsen started the year 6–1 but didn't win a game after the middle of June.

Mickey Mantle's average and homer total dropped while Bill Skowron's season ended at the end of July because of a broken wrist.

The Tigers' 2–15 start got Bill Norman fired with Jimmie Dykes moving in as manager. Harvey Kuenn (.353) and Al Kaline (.327) had the top two spots in the batting race. New acquisition Don Mossi won 17 games.

Ted Williams had his worst season for the Red Sox and Boston replaced manager Mike Higgins with Bill Jurges after the team fell into last place on July 3.

Hoyt Wilhelm, 35, had a big season at Baltimore, going 15–11 with a league-best 2.19 ERA. It was one of the few highlights for the Orioles, aside from the 15–9 record posted by 20-year-old Milt Pappas.

American League MVP, the White Sox's Nellie Fox

WORLD SERIES	
GAME 1	
Chicago White Sox 9	Los Angeles 0
GAME 2	
Los Angeles 4	Chicago White Sox 3
GAME 3	
Los Angeles 3	Chicago White Sox 1
GAME 4	
Los Angeles 5	Chicago White Sox 4
GAME 5	
Chicago White Sox 1	Los Angeles 0
GAME 6	
Los Angeles 9	Chicago White Sox 3
MVP: Larry Sherry, Los Angeles	

Major league baseball moved west in 1958; it took the World Series a year to catch up. The Dodgers made it to the postseason for the first time since 1956, when they were headquartered at cozy Ebbets Field in Brooklyn. This time, they were playing home games in the cavernous Los Angeles Coliseum, a football field that had been revamped into a baseball park while the Dodgers' new home was being constructed at Chavez Ravine.

The Dodgers' Charlie Neal

The Dodgers had to win a best-of-three playoff series from the Milwaukee Braves to get to the Series. Los Angeles took two games to knock off the Braves after the teams had finished with identical 86–68 records after the 154-game regular season. The Brooklyn Dodgers had twice lost playoffs, including the famous 1951 game decided on Bobby Thomson's home run for the New York Giants.

The Chicago White Sox took advantage of a sub par year by the New York Yankees and won the American League pennant by five games over the Cleveland Indians. The Yankees finished a distant third, 15 games behind.

The "Go-Go" White Sox were built for speed and had an underrated pitching staff that was expertly handled by manager Al Lopez, a former catcher. The Series opened at Comiskey Park for the first postseason games there since the scandal-ridden 1919 Black Sox Series.

Series MVP Larry Sherry

The White Sox belied their running identity by slugging their way to an 11–0 win in the first game. Starter Roger Craig was knocked out in a seven-run third inning as Ted Kluszewski had five RBIs with a pair of two-run homers and a run-scoring single. Early Wynn and Gerry Staley combined to shut out the Dodgers.

The Dodgers used a three-run seventh to win Game Two 4–3. Pinch hitter Chuck Essegian homered to tie the game at 2–2. Jim Gilliam walked and Charlie Neal broke the tie with his second home run of the game. Larry Sherry pitched the last three innings to preserve the win for John Podres.

The Series shifted to California for the first time and the Dodgers won Game Three 3–1. Carl Furillo, one of the few holdovers from the Brooklyn teams, delivered a two-run pinch single in the seventh. Sherry pitched the final two innings to save the win for Don Drysdale.

The Dodgers took a 3–1 lead in games by winning Game Four 5–4 on Gil Hodges' eighth-inning home run. Chicago's Sherm Lollar had tied the game with a three-run homer an inning earlier. Sherry got the win by holding the White Sox scoreless over the last two innings.

The Dodgers came close to wrapping up the Series in five games but Bob Shaw and Dick Donovan outpitched Sandy Koufax for a 1–0 win. The White Sox got only five hits and the game's only run scored when Lollar grounded into a dou-

ble play in the fourth inning. Chicago right fielder Jim Rivera, a defensive replacement, saved two runs with a running catch against Neal in the seventh. The Dodgers failed to score despite collecting nine hits.

The Dodgers ended the Series in Game Six with a 9–3 win. They scored five runs off Wynn and three more off Donovan and had a comfortable 8–0 lead in the fourth. Duke Snider tagged Wynn for a two-run homer in the third and Wally Moon had a two-run homer in the fourth. Essegian set a Series record by pinch hitting a second home run.

Podres ran into trouble and left the game in the fourth. That left Sherry to finish the Series by pitching 5⅔ innings of shutout relief to nail down the win and Series Most Valuable Player honors. In the Series, Sherry appeared in four games, pitched a team-high 12⅔ innings and allowed just eight hits with two walks and five strikeouts. His earned run average was 0.71.

The White Sox's best performer was Kluszewski, who had been acquired in August specifically for the stretch drive and the postseason. He batted .391 with three home runs and ten RBIs, which was a record for a six-game Series. Second baseman Nellie Fox was a close second with a .375 average. In Brooklyn, the Dodgers needed eight World Series to claim their first championship. They did it on the first try in Los Angeles.

1960

Baseball went where it had never gone before as eight expansion teams were added and the game opened its first indoor stadium.

The New York Yankees' dynasty prospered for half of the decade, then abruptly fell apart. The Los Angeles Dodgers won with pitching excellence, much of it provided by the star-crossed Sandy Koufax. The St. Louis Cardinals went to the World Series three times and won twice, thanks to Bob Gibson's arm and Lou Brock's legs.

Jim Bunning was perfect one sunny afternoon and Denny McLain had a season in the sun, winning 31 games. Roger Maris got 61 in 1961 and, like Mickey Mantle, left the game before the decade ended.

Maury Wills stole more than anyone, the Philadelphia Phillies pulled the game's most infamous fold and the New York Mets went from bad joke to good team by winning the last championship of the decade.

Casey Stengel left and Earl Weaver arrived. Franchises in Milwaukee, Washington and Kansas City changed addresses. An increasingly violent society was still shocked when Juan Marichal clubbed John Roseboro with a bat.

Yankee haters everywhere rejoiced when Pittsburgh's Bill Mazeroski lived the backyard wiffle ball dream and ended the 1960 World Series with a home run.

MOST VALUABLE PLAYER
AL: Dick Groat, Pittsburgh
NL: Roger Maris, NY Yankees

CY YOUNG AWARD
AL, NL: Vernon Law, Pittsburgh

ROOKIE OF THE YEAR
AL: Ron Hansen, Baltimore
NL: Frank Howard, Los Angeles

LEADERS
BATTING AVERAGE
AL: Pete Runnells, Boston Red Sox, .320
NL: Dick Groat, Pittsburgh, .325

HOME RUNS
AL: Mickey Mantle, NY Yankees, 40
NL: Ernie Banks, Chicago Cubs, 41

RUNS BATTED IN
AL: Roger Maris, NY Yankees, 112
NL: Hank Aaron, Milwaukee, 126

STOLEN BASES
AL: Luis Aparacio, Chicago White Sox, 51
NL: Maury Wills, Los Angeles, 50

PITCHING VICTORIES
AL: Chuck Estrada, Baltimore; Jim Perry, Cleveland, 18; NL: Ernie Broglio, St. Louis Cardinals; Warren Spahn, Milwaukee, 21

EARNED RUN AVERAGE
AL: Frank Baumann, Chicago White Sox, 2.67
NL: Mike McCormick, NY Giants, 2.70

STRIKEOUTS
AL: Jim Bunning, Detroit, 201
NL: Don Drysdale, Los Angeles 246

The success of the Pittsburgh Pirates validated one of baseball's oldest truths: the game is never over until the last man is out.

The 1960 Pirates, picked to finish fourth, instead won their first National League pennant since 1933. No team had gone longer without a title. The Pirates won 23 games in their last time at bat. Fifteen of those victories came on the road. On 12 occasions, they scored a last at-bat win when they were down to their last out.

They were a model of consistency, never losing more than four games consecutively all season. Every time it appeared a slump was imminent, Vernon Law was there to stop the losing streak.

At 95–59, the Pirates were one game better than their 1927 team that lost to the mighty New York Yankees in the World Series. They wound up seven games ahead of the defending National League champion Milwaukee Braves.

The success was the culmination of a five-year plan that took eight years. Legendary executive Branch Rickey had gone to Pittsburgh in the early 1950s to take over a Pirates team that had become the National League's doormat.

Rickey's concept was right, it's just that his timetable was off. Under his leadership, the Pirates acquired the core of their championship team—pitchers Law, Bob Friend and Elroy Face, infielders Dick Groat, Bill Mazeroski and Dick Stuart and outfielders Roberto Clemente and Bob Skinner.

Rickey's successor, Joe L. Brown, put the finishing touches on the team. Brown traded for pitchers Harvey Haddix and Wilmer (Vinegar Bend) Mizell, catcher Smoky Burgess, third baseman Don Hoak and outfielder Bill Virdon.

The Pirates started the season with an ordinary 3–3 record, but then put together a nine-game winning streak, the team's longest since 1944 and the franchise's hottest start (12–3) since 1938. They acquired a sense of confidence early, winning an Easter Sunday game they'd trailed 5–0 going into the ninth. They were overtaken for 12 days by the San

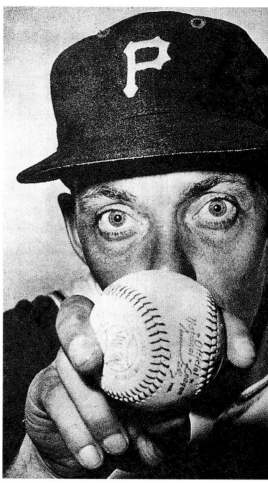

Pirates' reliever Elroy Face tied the club record for appearances

Francisco Giants, but regained first place on May 24 and spent all but one day in first place for the rest of the season.

The Braves made their move in June. They went 16–6 at the start of the month but Pittsburgh was still five games ahead at the All-Star break. Competition heated up after the break, with the Los Angeles Dodgers winning 18 of 23 while the St. Louis Cardinals put together a 17–6 run.

In late August, the Pirates started pulling away by winning 17 of 23 games. They beat the Braves twice in Pittsburgh in early September and actually clinched the pennant while losing to the Braves because the Cardinals had lost to the Chicago Cubs.

Groat led the league with a .325 average. His wrist was broken when he was hit by a Lew Burdette pitch on September 6. Groat came back for the last three games and went 3-for-10 to edge Norm Larker of the Dodgers for the batting title by two points.

Clemente batted .314 and led the team with

SHORTS Odd managerial changes were common in 1960. The Giants fired Bill Rigney with the team in second place and eight games over .500. Eddie Sawyer quit the Phillies after one game. Lou Boudreau came out of the Cubs broadcast booth to replace Charlie Grimm. On August 3, Cleveland traded Joe Gordon to the Tigers for Jimmie Dykes, the only all-manager swap.

Harvey Haddix completed a formidable Pittsburgh rotation

Feb. 23: Three years after the Dodgers' last season in Brooklyn, demolition of Ebbets Field began.

March 13: The White Sox introduced new road uniforms with the players' names on the back.

April 12: The Giants opened San Francisco's Candlestick Park with a 3–1 win over the Cardinals.

May 4: Lou Boudreau moved from the Cubs' broadcast booth to the dugout to replace Charlie Grimm as manager. Grimm, still on the payroll, took over Boudreau's spot on the announcing team.

May 10: Joe Ginsberg of the Orioles tied a record with three passed balls in one inning. The record had been set six days earlier by teammate Gus Triandos. Both catchers were victims of knuckleball specialist Hoyt Wilhelm. The problem would prompt Baltimore general manager Paul Richards to invent an oversized catcher's mitt.

May 15: Don Cardwell, traded from the Phillies, made his Cubs' debut with a 4–0 no-hitter against the Cardinals. It was the first no-hitter against the Cardinals since 1919.

June 17: Ted Williams hit his 500th career home run.

June 18: Tom Sheehan, 66, became the oldest rookie manager in major league history when he replaced Bill Rigney with the Giants.

July 13: Pittsburgh's Vernon Law won the second All-Star game, giving the Pirates a clean sweep. Teammate Bob Friend was the winning pitcher in the first game two days earlier.

Aug. 18: Milwaukee's Lew Burdette pitched a 1–0 no-hitter against the Phillies.

Sept. 16: Warren Spahn got his 20th win with a no-hitter against the Phillies.

Sept. 26: Ted Williams homered off Baltimore's Jack Fisher in his final plate appearance. It was his 521st career homer.

Oct. 26: The Yankees instituted a mandatory retirement age to oust 70-year-old manager Casey Stengel after the World Series loss to Pittsburgh. Stengel made it clear he was being fired. Two days later, coach Ralph Houk was introduced as his replacement.

94 RBIs. Hoak hit .371 in the last 26 games to finish at .282. Danny Murtaugh platooned his catchers effectively—Burgess hit .294 and Hal Smith batted .295. When Groat was out, Dick Schofield stepped in and hit .403 in 21 games.

Law was 20–9 and took the Cy Young award. Friend turned around his fortunes, going 18–12 after an 8–19 season in 1959. Mizell, acquired from the Cardinals on May 27, went 13–5 and gave the Pirates the fourth starter they lacked. Haddix won 11 games and Face tied a club record by appearing in 68 games.

Maybe the Braves simply had the misfortune to run up against a team of destiny. They finished second for the fifth time in eight years.

Warren Spahn, just 4–4 on June 22, finished the season 21–10, his 11th 20-win season. Bob Buhl was 16–9 and Burdette was 19–13.

Hank Aaron hit 40 home runs and led the league with 126 RBIs. Eddie Mathews had 39 homers and drove in 124 runs. Joe Adcock contributed 25 home runs and 91 RBIs. The Braves had disappointments, too. Johnny Logan and Wes Covington fell short of expec-

The Yankees' Mickey Mantle

tations offensively and reliever Don McMahon had a bad year.

The Cardinals were ready to phase out 39-year-old Stan Musial and switch to a youth movement when it looked like they wouldn't contend. That plan changed when the team started to win and Musial was a big part of the success. He was back in the everyday lineup on June 24 and hit .275 with 17 home runs and 63 RBIs. Ken Boyer batted .304 with 32 homers and 97 RBIs.

The strength was the St. Louis pitching staff. Ernie Broglio went 21–9 and posted the Cardinals' first 20-win season since 1953. Curt Simmons, released by the Phillies, was still a useful pitcher and had a 7–4 record. Lindy McDaniel was tremendous out of the bullpen, compiling a 12–4 record and 2.09 ERA in 65 games.

The Dodgers fell from first to fourth. Despite the hitter-friendly dimensions of the Los Angeles Coliseum, the Dodgers managed just 126 home runs, a league low. Frank Howard came up from the minor leagues on May 23 and hit 23 home runs with 77 RBIs. Maury Wills batted .295 and stole 50 bases.

The San Francisco Giants fired their manager with the team in second place and eight games over .500. They dumped Bill Rigney and replaced him with Tom Sheehan. The players didn't like their new home at Candlestick Park because of cold, windy conditions that developed during night games.

The Cincinnati Reds' acqusition of Cal McLish from Cleveland didn't pay off. He was 4–14. Bob Purkey led the staff at 17–11 and Jim Brosnan was a bullpen star, going 7–2 with a 2.36 ERA in 57 games.

A managerial change from Charlie Grimm to Lou Boudreau didn't prevent the Cubs from a 14th straight second-division finish with a record-tying 94 losses. Ernie Banks hit 271 and finished third in the league with 117 RBIs.

In the American League, the Yankees rebounded from a third-place season with their tenth pennant in manager Casey Stengel's 12 seasons.

The Yankees were locked in a tight race with the defending champion Chicago White Sox and the surprising Baltimore Orioles. The Yankees pulled away at the end, winning 19 out of 21 games, including 15 consecutive wins to end the season.

Stengel had to do his best of managing as the Yankees didn't have their usual dominating year. Art Ditmar was the staff's big winner with a 15–9 record. Jim Coates was 13–3 and Whitey Ford slumped to 12–9.

Mickey Mantle batted only .275, but led the league with 40 home runs. He also had 90 RBIs. Roger Maris, an offseason acquisition from Kansas City, claimed the RBI title with 112. He hit .283 and had 39 home runs. Bill Skowron had a good all-around year with a .309 average, 26 home runs and 91 RBIs.

The Orioles had their best year since they moved to Baltimore in 1953. At 89–65, they matched the record they had as the pennant-winning St. Louis Browns in 1944. They worked five rookies into the lineup—first baseman Jim Gentile, second baseman Marv Breeding, shortstop Ron Hansen and pitchers Chuck Estrada and Steve Barber.

The White Sox finished third, the first time a team managed by Al Lopez was below second place. Chicago led the league in hitting, but was 22–23 in one-run games. Early Wynn's victory total dropped from 22 to 13 and Bob Shaw finished as 13–13 after leading the league in winning percentage. Reliever Gerry Staley won 13 games but faded at the end.

The Indians had to overcome injuries and get accustomed to general manager Frank Lane's overhaul of the team. His most controversial trade sent fan favorite Rocky Colavito to Detroit for Harvey Kuenn. Kuenn hit .300, but he wasn't Colavito and Cleveland fans wanted the Rock.

The Indians lost shortstop Woodie Held for six weeks with a broken finger and Gary Bell battled shoulder problems. Bell didn't win a game after July 20.

After three straight seasons in last place, the Washington Senators made some progress. Harmon Killebrew, who had only four home runs through June 7, hit 37 for the year. The Senators might have done better, but finished by losing 15 of 18.

The Tigers had their worst year since 1954

because of poor hitting. Even reliable Al Kaline slipped to a .278 average and 15 home runs. Colavito led his new team with 35 homers and 87 RBIs, but his average was only .249.

The Boston Red Sox were hurt by the retirements of Jackie Jensen and Sammy White. Manager Bill Jurges was fired and his eventual replacement was the man he'd succeeded, Mike Higgings.

Pete Runnels won the batting title with a .320 average and Ted Williams ended his career with a .316 average, 29 home runs and 72 RBIs.

The Kansas City Athletics fell into the basement in July and stayed there. Bud Daley, 12–4 at the All-Star break, reversed that record in the second half and finished 16–16.

Ted Williams bowed out in style with a homer in his very last at-bat—the 521st of his career

GAME 1	
Pittsburgh 6	NY Yankees 4
GAME 2	
NY Yankees 16	Pittsburgh 3
GAME 3	
NY Yankees 10	Pittsburgh 0
GAME 4	
Pittsburgh 3	NY Yankees 2
GAME 5	
Pittsburgh 5	NY Yankees 2
GAME 6	
NY Yankees 12	Pittsburgh 0
GAME 7	
Pittsburgh 10	NY Yankees 9
MVP: Bobby Richardson, NY Yankees	

What do you call a team that loses World Series games by embarrassing scores of 16–3, 10–0 and 12–0? The World Champion Pittsburgh Pirates.

Through the first six games of the Series, the New York Yankees had outscored the Pirates 46–17. Yet even though the Yankees were causing daily revisions in the record books, they still headed into Game 7 even.

When it all ended, the underdog Pirates had achieved the most improbable victory and the greatest ending in World Series history. Pirates outfielder Gino Cimoli summed it up this way: "They broke all the records and we won the Series."

The Yankees were just a season removed from their last Series appearance, having taken a one-year break while the Chicago White Sox scored a rare American League pennant. The Pirates were in the Series for the first time since 1927, when they fell in four games to the mighty Yankees of Babe Ruth and Lou Gehrig.

The 1960 Series appeared to be a mismatch, too. But the Pirates won the first game 6–4 at Forbes Field behind Cy Young award winner, Vernon Law.

The next two games followed the expected script with the Yankees winning 16–3 and 10–0. Amid all the Yankees' stars, the hitting standout was second baseman Bobby

The Pirates' Bill Mazeroski nears home after his dramatic ninth-inning, Series-ending homer against the Yankees in Game Seven

Yankees' manager Casey Stengel saw his team come up just short against the Pirates in the now legendary '60 World Series

Richardson, who had finished the regular season slumping.

Richardson led the 19-hit attack in the second game as the Yankees pounded six different pitchers. Mickey Mantle hit a two-run homer in Game 3, providing ample support for Whitey Ford, who pitched the four-hit shutout.

The Pirates tied the series in Game 4, thanks to another solid performance by Law. He and reliever ElRoy Face combined on a 3–2 win.

Despite the battering they took in the second and third games, the Pirates actually led the Series 3–2 after winning Game 5. Harvey Haddix picked up the win with relief help from Face. The Pirates went home with a chance to win the Series in six games.

But Pirates' starter Bob Friend, who had had a tough postseason, lasted just two innings, allowing five runs. Relievers let the game get out of reach and the Yankees won 12–0 with Ford pitching a seven-hit shutout.

For some reason, manager Casey Stengel elected not to start Ford in the first game. Managers traditionally start their best pitcher in the opening game so that he's available to pitch three times if the Series goes the limit. That's what Pirates' manager Danny Murtaugh did with his ace, Law.

The Yankees started Bob Turley in Game 7 and he was gone in the second inning as the Pirates jumped out to a 4–0 lead. The Yankees got a run in the fifth and then went ahead 5–4 with a sixth-inning rally.

In the eighth inning the Yankees stretched their lead to 7–4, but the Pirates had been a come-from-behind team all season and that trait carried over to the Series. Cimoli led off with a single and Bill Virdon hit a possible double-play ball to shortstop. The ball struck a pebble, bounced sharply and hit Tony Kubek in the throat, sending him to hospital and putting runners at both first and second. Singles by Dick Groat and Roberto Clemente got the Pirates within one. Clemente's hit was the result of a critical mental error by the Yankees' pitcher, Jim Coates, who failed to cover first base on the infield roller.

Catcher Hal Smith drove a pitch over the left field for a three-run homer that put the Pirates ahead 9–7 and left them just three outs from the Series victory.

The Yankees tied the game in the ninth as they continued their success against Friend. The inning featured another odd play—Mickey Mantle was able to dive back into first base on a ground ball to first, which allowed the tying run to score.

The play and the inning allowed Bill Mazeroski to become both a legendary name in baseball history and a folk hero in Pittsburgh. The second baseman was the Pirates' No. 8 hitter, a player known more for exceptional defense than his power. However, he slammed Ralph Terry's 1–0 pitch over the left field wall to give the Pirates the Series and touch off a spontaneous, city-wide party that lasted well into the night.

265

TED WILLIAMS

TEAMS
Boston Red Sox 1939–60

Games	2,292
At-Bats	7,706
Runs	1,798
RBI	1,839
Home runs	521
Hits	2,654
Doubles	525
Triples	71
Stolen Bases	24
Average	.344
Slugging percentage	.634

Ted Williams' goal was as simple as it was lofty. He wrote in his autobiography that he wanted to be able to walk down the street and have people say, "There goes the greatest hitter who ever lived."

Whether Williams was the greatest hitter in baseball can be debated—there is no doubt, however, that he belongs on any short list of nominees.

The major leagues' last .400 hitter, Williams treated hitting as a science and every ballpark was his laboratory. He not only became a great hitter himself, he also developed into one of the foremost authorities on the craft that he often described as the single most difficult feat in sports.

Williams won six batting titles, two of them in Triple Crown seasons. He led the American League in home runs and runs batted in six times, setting the pace in slugging percentage nine times. He won two Most Valuable Player awards and probably would have done better in the polling had he not carried on a cold war with the writers who voted. He was a member of the All-Star team 16 times.

And as impressive as his career statistics are, what might they have been had he not lost five seasons to military service? Williams served in the Navy in World War II when he was between the ages of 24 and 26, prime years in any player's career. He lost two years later when he flew combat missions for the Marines during the Korean War.

Williams was a self-taught hitter who grew up using broomsticks to launch rolls of tape and other materials that might simulate a baseball. The San Diego franchise of the Pacific Coast League signed him and he did well enough to draw the interest of the Boston Red Sox, who gave up $25,000 and four players to acquire him. After one season in the minors, Williams headed to Boston in 1939 to begin a career that would cover parts of four decades.

His finest season was 1941, when he headed into the last game of the season batting .39955. Because averages are rounded up, Williams would have gone in the record books as a .400 hitter. He rejected the easy way and played both games of a doubleheader. He had six hits in eight at-bats and wound up with a .406 average.

A quirk in the rules cost him the 1954 batting title. Williams batted .345, but only had 386 official at-bats because he drew 136 walks. The qualifications for the title were based on at-bats rather than plate appearances, as they are today. Williams lost out to Cleveland's Bobby Avila, who had a .341 average.

Williams was regarded as a solid defensive player whose skills were often overshadowed by his offensive abilities. He knew how to play the tricky left field wall in Boston's Fenway Park and he was fundamentally sound with his throws. But people came to the park to watch Williams hit. So did players.

"He was the only player I remember who had everyone watch him take batting practice," said former teammate Fred Hatfield. "I saw that hand-eye coordination, bat quickness and a little strength were the secret to hitting. When Ted pulled the trigger, the bat exploded."

Williams lasted long enough to hit against two generations of pitchers. He homered off Thornton Lee in 1939, then hit a home run against Lee's son Don in 1960. Williams had a poor season by his standards in 1959 and was angered at suggestions that he should retire.

He came back in 1960 to hit .316 with 29 home runs and 72 RBIs at the age of 42. He homered in his last at-bat and retired to a life of fishing.

Williams surprised everyone by signing on to manage the Senators in 1969. His first club showed improvement and helped him win the Manager of the Year award. The Senators became the Texas Rangers in 1972 and Williams resigned with a career record of 273–364.

Williams went back to fishing and had a rebirth of popularity when memorabilia collecting exploded. He opened a Florida museum that pays tribute to the game's great hitters—most of whom spent their careers trying to live up to the standard that Ted Williams set.

The greatest hitter who ever lived?

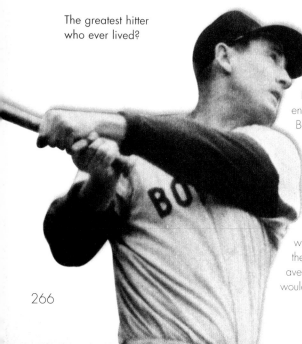

266

Yankee Stadium had its greatest level of home run excitement since Babe Ruth played—and Ruth's ghost seemed to be present at the legendary Bronx ballpark all season.

Roger Maris, a 27-year-old player who had given no previous indication that he would threaten one of the game's most fabled records, wound up beating the Babe—but not without controversy.

Maris hit 61 home runs, topping by one the total that Ruth had hit in 1927, when he beat his own record by one. This was different, though. Thanks to expansion that brought in two new teams, the American League had expanded the schedule, moving from the standard 154 games to 162.

With eight extra games, should a challenge to Ruth's record stand as a new mark? Baseball commissioner Ford Frick, who had ghost-written Ruth's autobiography, didn't think so.

When it appeared in late July that the chase would get serious, Frick issued a statement: Babe Ruth's mark of 60 home runs, made in a schedule of 154 games in 1927, cannot be broken unless some batter hits 61 or more within his club's first 154 games.

Frick's edict didn't diminish interest in Maris'

pursuit of 60. In fact, Maris, a shy man who didn't like a lot of attention, battled the media as often as he did opposing pitchers. Perhaps that makes his feat even more surprising. He held up under the pressure and hit his 61st off Boston's Tracy Stallard on the last day of the season.

Maris got a late start on the chase for the record. He hit only one home run in April but made up for lost time with a steady surge throughout the summer. No doubt Maris benefited from a pitching pool that had been diluted by the two-team expansion that had created 20 more pitching jobs.

Maris' pursuit of the record was so unlikely that some media outlets sent baseballs to research laboratories to determine if they were livelier. The conclusion: there was no change. Maris may have taken advantage of weaker pitching and Yankee Stadium's short right field porch, but he did the rest on his own.

It was a two-man battle for a good part of the season. Maris' teammate and close friend Mickey Mantle wound up with 54 homers.

Roger Maris hits his 61st home run of the season to surpass Babe Ruth's old mark set in 1927. Maris' record would stand some 37 years.

Mantle faded a bit down the stretch. Maris tired, too, from the grind of the season and the off-field pressures but he managed to belt the record-setting home run off Stallard, which provided the Yankees with a season-ending 1–0 win.

The home run show overshadowed an excellent season for the Yankees, who had a smooth transition to a new manager. Casey Stengel had been fired after the 1960 World Series loss and replaced by Ralph Houk, a member of his coaching staff. Houk figured out a way to get Whitey Ford on the mound more often and the veteran lefthander responded with a 25–4 season. Houk moved Yogi Berra to the outfield to let Elston Howard take over as the regular catcher. Pitcher Roland Sheldon was a find; promoted from Class D, he went 11–5.

The Yankees had also made a change at general manager, hiring Roy Hamey to take over for George Weiss. The new ideas helped but the Yankees were still coasting on their

T I M E L I N E

April 8: Vedie Himsl became the first of the Cubs' "College of Coaches" to take the title of Head Coach.

April 26: Roger Maris hit the first of his 61 home runs at Detroit off Paul Foytack. It came in the Yankees' 11th game.

April 30: San Francisco's Willie Mays became the ninth player in major league history to hit four home runs in a game. Mays drove in eight runs in a 14–4 win at Milwaukee.

June 16: Kansas City righthander Lew Krausse pitched a three-hit shutout against the Angels in his major league debut. Krausse, 18, also got two hits in the game, which came two weeks after his high school graduation.

June 18: Midget Eddie Gaedel, who pinch hit for the St. Louis Browns ten years earlier, died in St. Louis at the age of 35.

July 17: Hall of Famer Ty Cobb died in Atlanta, aged 74.

July 17: Commissioner Ford Frick issued his ruling that anyone breaking Babe Ruth's record of 61 home runs would have to do it in 154 games, the length of the 1927 season in which Ruth set the mark.

Aug. 11: Braves' lefthander Warren Spahn beat the Cubs 2–1 for his 300th career victory.

Aug. 28: The Phillies ended a 23-game losing streak with a 7–4 win over the Braves. The streak established a modern-era record.

Sept. 22: Baltimore's Jim Gentile tied a major league record by hitting his fifth grand slam homer of the season.

Sept. 26: Maris ties Ruth's record with his 60th home run against Baltimore's Jack Fisher in the Yankees' 159th game.

Oct. 1: Maris makes history by connecting off Boston righthander Tracy Stallard for his 61st home run.

Oct. 10: The New York Mets and Houston Colt .45s combine to select 45 players in the National League's first expansion draft.

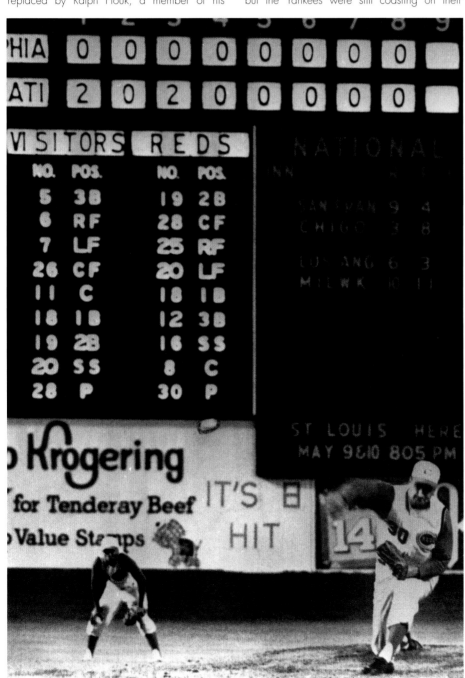

The scoreboard tells the tale as the Reds' Joey Jay completes his one-hitter against the Phillies

Veteran Braves' lefty Warren Spahn celebrates after his 300th career win. The victory came against the Cubs on August 11

superior talent base that had been amassed under the old regime.

The Detroit Tigers took a run at the Yankees and were in first place in July. New York swept a doubleheader against the Chicago White Sox on July 25 and moved into first place where they stayed. The Tigers' last chance came in a three-game series at the beginning of September. The Yankees swept the series and the Tigers, who had an impressive offense led by batting champion Norm Cash, Al Kaline and Rocky Colavito, were sunk by their lack of pitching depth.

The expansion teams were placed in Los Angeles and Washington, D.C., although the latter was part of a confusing situation. The existing Washington Senators franchise was transferred to Minnesota and renamed the Twins. Long-suffering Washington fans got stuck with a ragtag expansion team.

SHORTS Maris' chase of Ruth's record helped obscure a monstrous offensive season in the National League. San Francisco first baseman Orlando Cepeda led the league with 46 home runs and matched Maris' RBI total of 142. Cepeda wasn't the only one whose good work was overshadowed by Maris' historic accomplishment. The Yankees' Mickey Mantle hit 56 home runs and didn't even lead his own team. Orioles' first baseman Jim Gentile hit 46 home runs and drove in 141 runs. Rocky Colavito of the Tigers had 140 RBIs.

The Los Angeles Angels were better than expected, winning 70 games. The Angels managed to play .500 over their last 90 games and boasted five hitters with at least 20 home runs.

The Senators lost 44 of 58 games after August 1. Baseball fans in the nation's capital continued to suffer; they just did it with a new cast of characters.

Bill Veeck sold his interest in the Chicago White Sox because of health problems, bringing to an end his reign as the game's most outlandish promoter. The White Sox were his third franchise, following stints with the St. Louis Browns and Cleveland Indians. Veeck's partners also sold out, which ended the Comiskey family's long association with the team.

A new owner, Charles O. Finley, offered a preview of his bold, hands-on style when he purchased the woeful Kansas City Athletics. Finley fired manager Joe Gordon in June and replaced him with Hank Bauer. In August, Finley also fired general manager Frank Lane.

In the National League, the Cincinnati Reds shocked the baseball world by winning the pennant handily. In The Sporting News' pre-season poll of 232 experts, the Reds didn't get a single first-place vote. They won 93 games, posting a 26-game improvement over their 1960 record. An off-season trade helped the Reds vault past the rest of the contenders. They acquired pitcher Joey Jay from the Milwaukee Braves and picked up third baseman Gene Freese from the White Sox in the same three-way deal. Both were big contributors. Jay led the staff with a 21–10 record after failing to win more than nine games in any previous major league season. He had been famous as the first graduate of a Little League baseball program to reach the majors. Freese hit 26 home runs and, with first baseman Gordy Coleman, gave the Reds a second tier of offense behind stars Frank Robinson and Vada Pinson.

Robinson was named the National League's Most Valuable Player, batting .323 with 37 home runs, 124 runs batted in and 22 stolen bases. Pinson didn't have Robinson's power but he batted .343 and scored 101 runs.

The Reds were led by the fiery Fred Hutchinson, who was runner-up to Houk in *The Sporting News'* polling for top manager.

The defending champion Pirates fell to sixth place. Too many players were unable to duplicate the career-best years they'd had in 1960 and staff ace Vernon Law struggled with a sore arm. It was quite literally the price of success—Law had sustained a twisted ankle in the 1960 pennant celebration. He hurt his arm by overcompensating for the ankle injury.

The powerful Milwaukee Braves continued to slip after winning pennants in 1957 and '58 and made a managerial change in September, hiring Birdie Tebbetts to replace Charley Dressen. Catcher Del Crandall developed a sore arm and the Braves were robbed of one of their key players.

The St. Louis Cardinals' pitching collapsed while the Los Angeles Dodgers and San Francisco Giants fell short.

The strangest approach belonged to the Chicago Cubs, where ownership decided to abandon the traditional manager's role and instead hired a rotating "college of coaches." Four men took turns filling the role of head coach, none with any great success. The Cubs finished seventh in the eight-team league.

They probably would have finished eighth had the Philadelphia Phillies not had a record 23-game losing streak. The Phillies also lost 28 of 29 games in a midsummer stretch.

Milwaukee lefthander Warren Spahn won his 300th game and did it in typical style. Spahn, 40, made the historic victory in one of the league-leading 21 complete games he posted in 1961. Willie Mays had a four-homer game for the Giants, who had plenty of power and not enough pitching.

Two players were voted into the Hall of

Fame: Cleveland's Bob Feller got strong support while Jackie Robinson was elected narrowly. The Veterans Committee approved Edd Roush, a former center fielder with the Reds and Giants, and Bill McKechnie, who managed three different National League clubs to pennants.

Baseball lost one of its biggest names on July 17 when Ty Cobb died in Atlanta at 74. The game also lost Hall of Fame pitcher Dazzy Vance and Eddie Gaedel, the midget who pinch hit in a 1951 game for the St. Louis Browns in one of Veeck's most famous stunts.

For all the excitement on the field, and despite the addition of two new teams, overall attendance declined by five percent.

The National League won the first All-Star Game, which was played in San Francisco's Candlestick Park. The nation got a good look at how powerful the tricky winds by the Bay could be. Giants pitcher Stu Miller was actually blown off the mound in the late innings. The bizarre episode led to his being charged with a balk.

The other All-Star Game, in Boston, ended in a 1–1 tie that was called because of rain.

The Reds' Frank Robinson led Cincinnati to its first pennant since 1940, thanks to his MVP season

GAME 1	
NY Yankees 2	Cincinnati 0

GAME 2	
Cincinnati 6	NY Yankees 2

GAME 3	
NY Yankees 3	Cincinnati 2

GAME 4	
NY Yankees 7	Cincinnati 0

GAME 5	
NY Yankees 13	Cincinnati 5
MVP: Whitey Ford, NY Yankees	

Manager Ralph Houk greets his triumphant Yankees team as they clinch the World Series in Game Five over the Reds

The Cincinnati Reds had waited a long time to get into a World Series, but they picked the wrong year to get there.

The Reds ran into a Yankees team that was still stinging from its unexpected Series loss to the Pirates the year before. The Yankees spent most of the regular season beating up pitching that had been watered down by expansion. They staged a two-man race to beat Babe Ruth's single-season home run record and Roger Maris accomplished the feat, hitting his 61st home run on the last day of the season. Mickey Mantle hit 54, but had to settle for runner-up status.

Legendary Yankees manager, Casey Stengel, was gone, after some questionable strategy in the 1960 Series. His replacement was Ralph Houk, who pushed all the right buttons with his talented team.

The Yankees' offense was so overwhelming it was easy to overlook their pitching. Whitey Ford led the staff with a 25–4 record in the regular season and won the Series opener handily. He held the Reds to two hits—singles by Eddie Kasko and Wally Post—and rolled to a 2–0 win over Jim O'Toole. O'Toole didn't pitch badly, but Ford's work left him no room for error. Elston Howard and Bill Skowron hit home runs for the Yankees.

The Reds got their only win of the Series in Game Two thanks to starter Joey Jay, who had led the Cincinnati staff in the regular season. Jay pitched a complete game, holding the Yankees to six hits in a 6–2 win. Gordy Coleman hit a two-run homer for the Reds.

The Series turned in Game Three. The Reds

took a 2–1 lead into the eighth inning and the Yankees quickly made two outs against starter Bob Purkey. Johnny Blanchard pinch hit for pitcher Bud Daley and hit a game-tying home run.

Maris, who had been 0-for-10 in the Series, led off the ninth with a home run off Purkey that gave the Yankees a 3–2 lead. The Reds got the tying run in scoring position in the ninth when Leo Cardenas hit a one-out double, but reliever Luis Arroyo retired pinch hitters Dick Gernert and Gus Bell to preserve the 3–2 lead and put the Yankees ahead 2–1 in games.

Ford was back in Game Four, working on a streak of 27 consecutive scoreless innings in the World Series. He broke Babe Ruth's record of 29 innings by pitching the first five innings without allowing a run. Ford had to leave the game in the sixth inning because of an ankle injury, but it didn't make a difference. The Yankees scored two runs off O'Toole and blew the game open with five more off reliever Jim Brosnan over three innings.

Clete Boyer doubled in two runs for the Yankees and Hector Lopez had a two-run single. Reliever Jim Coates was as good as Ford had been, allowing just one hit over the last four innings.

Right from the start of Game Five, the Yankees made it clear that the Series would end there and then, meaning that the return trip to New York would be for a victory parade rather than another game. Blanchard hit a two-run homer in the first inning as the Yankees scored five times against Jay and Jim Maloney. New York added five more runs in the fourth, and it was just a matter of time until the Yankees closed out both the game and Series.

Ralph Terry had a tough start, allowing six hits and three runs in less than three innings; Daley finished the 13–5 victory and pitched solidly to earn the win.

The Yankees' dominance was thorough: they won handily even though Mantle was limited to six at-bats because of a hip injury. Maris was just 2-for-19 in the Series, but Blanchard hit .400 with two home runs and Bobby Richardson, the MVP of the previous Series, batted .391. Skowron had five RBIs to go with a .353 average.

The big story was the Yankees' pitching: Ford, Coates and Daley worked a total of 25 innings and didn't allow a run. Frank Robinson only hit .200 for the Reds and Vada Pinson batted just .091.

After winning 109 games in the regular season, anything less than a World Series win would have been a disappointment for the Yankees. They accomplished their goal in Houk's first season as a major league manager.

For the first time since 1947, the Yankees had won a World Series with a manager other than Stengel.

ROGER MARIS

Roger Maris had a dream season in 1961, but getting there was something of a nightmare. Maris hit 61 home runs to break Babe Ruth's record set in 1927 and helped the Yankees to win another American League pennant, and he became a household name. It was the latter that bothered him.

"I never wanted all the hoopla," Maris would say later. "All I wanted is to be a good ballplayer—hit 25 to 30 home runs, drive in around 100 runs and help my club win pennants."

The home run chase was an unexpected event in Maris' life. He had power, but there was nothing to indicate that he'd be the one to break Ruth's record. His previous high for home runs had been 39 in 1960, when he finished one behind teammate Mickey Mantle for the American League lead. He would never hit more than 33 in any season after 1961.

Not only were there people who didn't think he could do it, there were many who didn't want him to. There was a romance about Ruth's record that some didn't want to see obliterated. There were those who wanted Mantle to break the record. The two had a season-long, in-house home run derby and had to deal with fabricated stories about their supposed rivalry.

Critics argued that pitching talent had been diluted by the addition of expansion teams in Washington and Los Angeles. Maris didn't have to face the Yankees' staff, the most talented group of pitchers in the American League. Even the baseball establishment seemed to line up against Maris.

Commissioner Ford Frick announced that unless Maris broke Ruth's record in 154 games, it would be listed separately. The American League had stretched the schedule to 162 games in 1961 to account for the two extra teams. It was widely misreported that Maris' record would carry an asterisk, but the intention was the same —leave Ruth's hallowed mark unblemished.

The spotlight bothered Maris, but his release came on the field. The rest of the time he was either answering redundant questions or avoiding interviewers. Maris was a shy, midwestern type who didn't enjoy talking about himself and wasn't at ease with all the attention.

"No one in this world can understand the pressure he had," teammate Tom Tresh said.

The season started modestly enough for Maris. He had only one home run in April. He obviously made up for lost time, and hitting ahead of the feared Mantle in the lineup helped, too. Maris had come to the Yankees in advance of the 1960 season, another in a long line of lopsided trades New York made with the Kansas City Athletics.

Maris turned down coach Bud Wilkinson's offer of a football scholarship to the University of Oklahoma to accept a bonus contract from the Cleveland Indians. He spent four years in the minors before joining the Indians, then was traded to Kansas City in his second major league season.

His Yankees debut in 1960 was a smash: he hit two home runs, a double and a single. That season, he led the league in RBIs with 112, despite missing 17 games with injuries.

After his record-setting season, he hit 33 home runs and drove in 100 runs. It was a good season by any measure, but well off the pace of 1961. It was also his last big season with the Yankees.

Maris was then slowed by injuries over the next several years, and was traded to the St. Louis Cardinals for the 1967 season. He fitted in well with the Cardinals and helped the team reach the World Series in both of his seasons there. In fact, Maris participated in more World Series (six) in the 1960s than any other player.

The Cardinals' connection also helped set up his post-baseball career: he and his brother ran an Anheuser-Busch distributorship. And although Maris never got much serious consideration for the Hall of Fame, the Yankees retired his No. 9 and honored him with a plaque in their center-field memorial park.

Maris died of lymphoma on December 14, 1985 at the age of 51.

Not just a home run hitter, Roger Maris appeared in more World Series than any other player in the 1960s

Maury Wills almost stole the 1962 National League pennant for the Los Angeles Dodgers. Wills couldn't run the Dodgers to the title but he set a major league record with 104 stolen bases, and he changed the way baseball treated the running game. One year after home runs dominated, Wills turned the stolen base into an important part of offensive strategy.

Wills was an overachiever who endured after being buried in the Dodgers' fruitful minor league system. Other players had more talent but Wills succeeded by studying the game and seizing opportunities. He took a scientific approach, keeping notes on the pickoff moves of opposing pitchers. No edge was too small to ignore. Wills eschewed a batting helmet on the bases and wore just one pair of white sanitary socks with his uniform (most players wore two pairs of the thin socks). He believed shedding those extra ounces would give him an aerodynamic advantage in running the bases.

How dominating was Wills' performance? Consider that the American League leader, Luis Aparicio of the White Sox, stole just 31 bases. Wills' Dodgers wilted down the stretch and wound up losing a best-of-three playoff to the San Francisco Giants for the National League pennant. The Giants had their first measure of success since their move west and it came under the guidance of one of the team's former players, Alvin Dark.

Pittsburgh and Cincinnati made token runs at first place during the season but the race was essentially between the Dodgers and Giants, who had transferred their New York City rivalry to California after the 1958 season.

The National League's first 162-game schedule was actually expanded by another three games so the Dodgers and Giants could settle their intrastate race.

The Giants came from behind in the deciding playoff game, becoming the fifth National

A spectacular aerial shot of the newly-opened Dodger Stadium in Los Angeles

The Dodgers' Maury Wills stole a Major League record 104 bases during the regular season

April 9: Washington beat Detroit 4–1 in the first game at D.C. Stadium.

April 10: Cincinnati beat Los Angeles 6–3 to open Dodger Stadium.

April 13: National League baseball returned to New York as the Mets lost their home opener to Tom Sturdivant and the Pirates, 4–3.

April 23: The Mets ended a nine-game losing streak with the franchise's first win. Jay Hook pitched a five-hitter to beat the Pirates at Forbes Field.

April 24: Sandy Koufax struck out 18 Cubs hitters in a 10–2 Dodgers win.

May 18: The American League tabled owner Charles Finley's request to move the Kansas City Athletics to Dallas-Fort Worth.

June 26: Boston's Earl Wilson pitched a no-hitter against the Angels.

June 28: Hall of Fame catcher Mickey Cochrane died in Illinois at 59.

June 30: Sandy Koufax pitched the National League's only no-hitter, beating the Mets.

July 2: Johnny Podres of the Dodgers tied a major league record by striking out eight consecutive hitters against the Phillies.

July 19: The Minnesota Twins hit two grand slams in the first inning of a 14–3 rout of the Indians. Bob Allison and Harmon Killebrew each homered with the bases loaded.

Aug. 1: Bill Monbouquette of the Red Sox pitched a no-hitter against the White Sox.

Aug. 26: Jack Kralick of the Twins came within two outs of a perfect game before settling for a no-hitter against Kansas City. Kralick walked George Alusik with one out in the ninth.

Sept. 12: Washington's Tom Cheney struck out 21 batters in a 16-inning 2–1 win over Baltimore.

Oct. 3: The Giants win the deciding game of a best-of-three playoff to take the National League pennant.

Oct. 29: Branch Rickey, 80, is hired as a consultant by the St. Louis Cardinals.

League team in as many seasons to win the coveted pennant.

It was business as usual in the American League, though, where the New York Yankees won for the 12th time in 14 years. Only one team other than the Yankees held first place for more than two days. That distinction belonged to Cleveland and the Indians started to tumble with a mid-July losing streak.

Things were far more interesting in the National League, thanks to what was happening in California and what was happening in the city the Giants and Dodgers abandoned. The New York Mets were created from a pool of castoffs selected in an expansion draft. Their fortunes were supervised by the former Yankees' brain trust: general manager George Weiss and manager Casey Stengel. Both men had been deposed after the Yankees lost the 1960 World Series.

SHORTS The year's most interesting no-hitter was turned in by Los Angeles Angels' rookie Bo Belinsky. The streetwise Belinsky was the Angels' first star. He made all the important Hollywood parties, often with a starlet conspicuously by his side. Belinsky, who had been a pool hustler, wasn't intimidated by the major leagues. He proved that on May 5 when he threw the no-hitter against the Baltimore Orioles in his fifth major league start. Belinsky also won the start after the no-hitter but finished the year with a 10–11 record, a disappointment that would typify his brief career.

Fans were so grateful to have the National League back in New York, they didn't care that the Mets were bad. In fact, the Mets were so bad that it became a status symbol to be a fan of theirs. The Mets tried to recapture some of the magic by bringing back familiar names but too many players were at the end of the line or rookies who had been rushed to the major leagues.

The Mets were so inept that their inaugural season spawned half a dozen books. The title of one came from Stengel's plaintive plea after watching his team: "Can't anybody here play this game?" The Mets went 40–120 and offered a preview of what was to come when they lost their first nine games.

The more futile the player, the more likely he was to become a hero. Journeyman first baseman Marv Throneberry was nicknamed "Marvelous Marv" and reporters delighted in the trivial note that his initials were M.E.T.

Stengel, a consistent winner with the Yankees, knew he had a bad team and did his best to shift the focus away from what was happening on the field. It was Stengel who said of one rookie, "He's 20 years old and in ten years, he has a great chance to be 30." His comic relief helped make a season bearable for fans who followed a team that averaged one win per week.

The other expansion team, the Houston Colt .45s, wasn't as inept as the Mets.

The Yankees' Ralph Terry led the American League in wins and also led New York to a World Series crown

The last part of Dodgers' owner Walter O'Malley's California dream was realized when the team moved into its beautiful new ballpark. Dodger Stadium cost $22 million to build, and it was a state-of-the-art facility surrounded by access roads for car-crazy Californians. The inaugural season drew 2.7 million fans, making the Dodgers a financial success as well as an artistic one.

The Dodgers' pennant hopes took a serious blow in mid-July when lefthander Sandy Koufax was forced onto the disabled list because of circulatory problems in his fingers. Koufax had a 14–5 record at the time he went out and wasn't able to return until the end of September. Don Drysdale had a breakthrough season but the Dodgers were a team constructed around starting pitching, and Koufax's long-term absence was critical. The Dodgers won just once in their last 13 games.

That created the opportunity for the Giants, who had a powerful lineup that featured Willie Mays, Felipe Alou and Willie McCovey. The Giants also upgraded their pitching. Jack Sanford, who was struggling with a 6–6 record on June 13, won 16 consecutive decisions and finished the season 24–7. Billy O'Dell won 19 games, Juan Marichal had 18 wins and Billy Pierce won 16.

The Dodgers carried a 4–2 lead into the

ninth inning of the final playoff game but couldn't hold it. Reliever Stan Williams issued a bases-loaded walk to force in the tiebreaking run as the Giants rallied for four runs in the top of the ninth. Pierce came in to close out the game and send San Francisco to the World Series.

The Yankees were led by Ralph Terry, who won 23 games. His career continued to blossom as he rebounded from allowing Bill Mazeroski's World Series-winning home run in 1960. The Yankees' pipeline continued to provide young talent as second-generation Tom Tresh won the American League's Rookie of the Year award.

The Yankees didn't miss a beat, even though Roger Maris' home run production dropped from 61 to 33 and eventual MVP Mickey Mantle missed 39 games with injuries.

The surprise team in the American League was the Minnesota Twins, who had been the Washington Senators until they were transferred to the Twin Cities a year earlier. The Twins posted 21 more wins as lefthander Jim Kaat developed into a dependable pitcher. Third baseman

SHORTS Another color line fell in 1962 when the Chicago Cubs appointed Buck O'Neill to their coaching staff on May 29. O'Neill became the first black coach in the major leagues. O'Neill, 50, had joined the Cubs' organization as a scout in December of 1955.

Rich Rollins and second baseman Bernie Allen made the infield better and the Twins pulled a steal when they acquired pitcher Dick Stigman and first baseman Vic Power from Cleveland.

The new Senators were still one of the American League's worst teams but they had the newest park, Washington's D.C. Stadium. Maverick Kansas City Athletics owner Charles Finley tried to find a new home by transferring his struggling franchise to the fertile Dallas-Fort Worth market. His request for a move was rejected by the American League, but moving would be a constant theme under Finley's ownership.

The Senators weren't a good team, but they provided one of the season's biggest individual stories when righthanded pitcher Tom Cheney struck out 21 Orioles batters in a 16-inning game.

It was a great year for managers. For the first time since 1953, no manager was fired. During the last week, Kansas City's Hank Bauer and Mel McGaha of Cleveland left after learning they were not being invited back for the 1963 season. Shortly after the season, Birdie Tebbetts resigned as Milwaukee's manager to take a three-year deal in Cleveland as McGaha's replacement.

One year after offense ruled, no-hitters abounded. In the American League, Angels' rookie Bo Belinsky threw one against Baltimore. Boston had two no-hit pitchers: Earl Wilson and Bill Monbouquette. The other American League no-hitter was turned in by Minnesota's Jack Kralick. Koufax had the National League's only no-hitter.

One of the game's most famous names returned. Branch Rickey, who had built the great Brooklyn teams, signed on as a consultant to the St. Louis Cardinals.

A bizarre story played out when Boston's team bus got caught in traffic and pitcher Gene Conley and infielder Pumpsie Green left to find a rest room. They didn't return to the team until 48 hours later, amid speculation they had tried to purchase plane tickets to Israel.

It turned out to be the final year for the dual All-Star Game format. The National League took the first game at D.C. Stadium while the American League won the second game, played at Chicago's Wrigley Field.

The Dodgers' Tommy Davis emerged as a bona fide star, winning the batting title with a .346 average and driving in a Major League-best 153 runs.

The Dodgers' Tommy Davis in action during a play-off game against the San Francisco Giants

GAME 1	
NY Yankees 6	San Francisco 2
GAME 2	
San Francisco 2	NY Yankees 0
GAME 3	
NY Yankees 3	San Francisco 2
GAME 4	
San Francisco 7	NY Yankees 3
GAME 5	
NY Yankees 5	San Francisco 3
GAME 6	
San Francisco 5	NY Yankees 2
GAME 7	
NY Yankees 1	San Francisco 0
MVP: Ralph Terry, NY Yankees	

Whitey Ford winds up for the Bronx Bombers during the 1962 World Series against the Giants

Maybe the San Francisco Giants spent too much energy and emotion just getting to the World Series.

While the New York Yankees cruised to their third consecutive American League pennant, the Giants needed to extend the regular season to break a tie with the Los Angeles Dodgers.

The Giants won the best-of-three playoff against the Dodgers and claimed their first pennant since moving west in time for the 1957 season.

After coming from behind to beat the Dodgers in the third game of their playoff series, the Giants were at least spared a cross-country trip to open the Series. Home-field advantage was meaningless against Whitey Ford in Game 1 as he pitched the Yankees to a 6–2 win. The Giants broke Ford's streak of World Series shutout innings at 33, but couldn't do much more with the Yankees' crafty lefthander.

Ford won his tenth World Series game to set a record. Clete Boyer's home run in the seventh broke a 2–2 tie, and the Yankees padded the score in the final innings.

Jack Sanford pitched brilliantly to even the Series for the Giants after two games. Sanford threw a three-hit shutout and Willie McCovey hit a solo homer as the Giants won 2–0 against Ralph Terry.

The pitchers' duel in Game 3 between San Francisco's Billy Pierce and New York's Bill Stafford was scoreless when Roger Maris singled in two runs in the seventh. The Yankees went ahead 3–0 in the inning, which provided a cushion against Ed Bailey's two-run, ninth-inning homer off Stafford.

In Game 4, infielder Chuck Hiller became the first National League player in history to hit a grand slam in the World Series. Hiller's blast came off reliever Marshall Bridges in the seventh

and broke a 2–2 tie. The winning pitcher for the Giants was Don Larsen, who exactly six years earlier had also been a Series winner in the same park. The game was played on the anniversary of Larsen's perfect game for the Yankees against the Brooklyn Dodgers.

After a day off for rain, the Series resumed in New York with Sanford facing Terry. Sanford struck out 10 in 7⅓ innings, but he also gave up the home run which changed the Series. Rookie Tom Tresh connected for a three-run homer in the eighth inning and broke a 2–2 tie.

There was even more of a wait for Game 6. A travel day was scheduled, then the teams waited three more days because of rain in San Francisco. Pierce forced a seventh game by pitching a three-hitter and beating the Yankees 5–2. Orlando Cepeda had three hits and drove in a pair of runs.

Terry and Sanford matched up in the deciding game. The Yankees scored a run in the fifth. Bill Skowron and Boyer singled. Terry drew a walk to load the bases and the run scored when Tony Kubek grounded into a double play.

Reliever Billy O'Dell worked out of a bases-loaded situation in the eighth. The Yankees got just the single run, but Terry made it stand up. He

took a two-hitter into the ninth inning, clinging to the slim lead.

Matty Alou started the inning by bunting for a single. Terry came back to strike out Hiller and Felipe Alou. Willie Mays then lined a double to right field, where Maris made a strong fielding play and relay to hold Alou at third base.

With first base open, Yankees' manager Ralph Houk let the righthanded Terry pitch to McCovey, a lefthanded batter, with the righthanded-hitting Cepeda on deck. The unconventional strategy worked when McCovey lined a 1–1 pitch to second, where Bobby Richardson leaped and made the catch that gave the Yankees their second consecutive World Series victory. It was also redemption for Terry, who had given up the home run to Bill Mazeroski that had won the 1960 Series for the Pittsburgh Pirates.

The Yankees again showed their depth by winning despite a minimal contribution from Mickey Mantle, who batted only .120. Maris hit just .174, but Tresh hit a team-best .321 and Boyer batted .318.

In his two seasons as New York Yankees' manager, Ralph Houk had now won two championships.

Chuck Hiller is mobbed by teammates after his seventh-inning Grand Slam ties the Series at 2–2

STAN MUSIAL

TEAMS
St. Louis Cardinals 1941–63

Games	3,026
At-Bats	10,972
Runs	1,949
RBI	1,951
Home runs	475
Hits	3,630
Doubles	725
Triples	166
Stolen Bases	78
Average	.331
Slugging percentage	.559

It's a familiar story: the young pitcher is such a good hitter that he's converted to the outfield to get his bat in the lineup every day.

It worked for Babe Ruth and was the career path for Stan Musial, too. Signed as a pitcher, Musial became an outfielder and forged a 22-year career with the St. Louis Cardinals that saw him play in 24 All-Star games, win seven batting titles, three Most Valuable Player awards and gain Hall of Fame election on the first ballot.

Musial lashed line drives out of a self-invented, unconventional stance that had him crouched and turned partly away from the pitcher. He'd unleash the corkscrew and make consistent, solid contact.

Preacher Roe of the Brooklyn Dodgers said he developed a foolproof method for dealing with Musial: "I'd throw him four wide ones and try to pick him off first base."

Musial learned to hit by swinging a broomstick at a ball of tape. He became an adept opposite field hitter because of a quirk in the ball field in his hometown of Donora, Pennsylvania. There was a short right field, so Musial trained himself to stroke the ball to left. If he hadn't, the ball would be lost and the game would end.

There was a method behind the unorthodox stance. Musial said he got into the crouch to cut down on the strike zone and to put himself in a position to punch the ball to left field. It was effective. Musial's talent became apparent at an early stage when he was struggling in the low minors as a pitcher. In 1940 he was sent to a farm team at Daytona Beach, where the manager played him in the outfield on the days he wasn't pitching. Musial injured his shoulder diving for a ball and became a full-time outfielder. Shortly after that, he became a major leaguer.

The Cardinals called him up in September of 1941. He settled in for a stay that would last through 1963 and set a team record for longevity. Musial answered questions about whether his odd stance would work against superior major league pitching.

"A lot of guys saw my hitting style and said I'd never hit in the big leagues," Musial said.

They couldn't have been more incorrect. In his second full season in the majors, Musial won his first batting title. He hit .300 18 times and was a .330 hitter the same year he celebrated his 42nd birthday.

Gifted with speed, he led the National League in doubles eight times and was the leader in triples five times. Musial was not thought of as a power hitter but he finished with 475 home runs, the most by a hitter who never led his league.

From 1948–57 he averaged 31 homers per season. In 1948 he hit 39 home runs, one behind co-leaders Johnny Mize and Ralph Kiner. That single home run cost him the Triple Crown.

Musial hit five home runs in a doubleheader on May 2, 1954, and ended the 1955 All-Star game with a 12th-inning home run. He finished with 1,377 extra base hits, more than Ruth. Like a lot of players of his era, Musial lost time to military service in World War II. He spent 14 months on Navy duty, beginning in 1945.

In 1958 Musial became the eighth player to reach 3,000 hits. Perhaps his consistency is best illustrated by this statistic—he collected 1,815 hits at home and 1,815 on the road.

Musial's nickname, "Stan the Man", came from Brooklyn fans, who were awed by his consistent success against their Dodgers. He belonged to St. Louis, where general manager Frank Lane, who never met a trade he wouldn't consider, designated Musial an untouchable.

"He's part of this town," Lane said. "I might as well trade the Mississippi River."

Musial spent a year as the Cardinals' general manager upon his retirement, then had a long run as a vice president with the team. In 1968 the Cardinals unveiled a statue of Musial in his familiar crouch.

It bears the words of former commissioner Ford Frick: "Here stands baseball's perfect warrior. Here stands baseball's perfect knight."

Stan Musial follows through after crashing a pinch-hit double for his 3,000th ML-hit against Chicago in May 13, 1956.

MOST VALUABLE PLAYER
AL: Elston Howard, NY Yankees
NL: Sandy Koufax, Los Angeles

CY YOUNG AWARD
AL, NL: Sandy Koufax, Los Angeles

ROOKIE OF THE YEAR
AL: Gary Peters, Chicago White Sox
NL: Pete Rose, Cincinnati

LEADERS
BATTING AVERAGE
AL: Carl Yastrzemski, Boston Red Sox, .321
NL: Tommy Davis, Los Angeles, .326

HOME RUNS
AL: Harmon Killebrew, Minnesota, 45
NL: Hank Aaron, Milwaukee; Willie McCovey, San Francisco, 44

RUNS BATTED IN
AL: Dick Stuart, Boston Red Sox, 118
NL: Hank Aaron, Milwaukee, 130

STOLEN BASES
AL: Luis Aparicio, Baltimore, 40
NL: Maury Wills, Los Angeles, 40

PITCHING VICTORIES
AL: Whitey Ford, NY Yankees, 24
NL: Sandy Koufax, Los Angeles; Juan Marichal, San Francisco, 25

EARNED RUN AVERAGE
AL: Gary Peters, Chicago White Sox, 2.33
NL: Sandy Koufax, Los Angeles, 1.88

STRIKEOUTS
AL: Camilo Pascual, Minnesota, 202
NL: Sandy Koufax, Los Angeles, 306

Baseball decided to alter the rules to make life better for the pitchers in 1963. Sandy Koufax didn't need the help. The Dodgers' lefthander had a dominating year, winning the Cy Young and Most Valuable Player awards and pitching Los Angeles to the World Series. So just how devastating was Koufax?

Pittsburgh slugger Willie Stargell once said that hitting against Koufax was, "like trying to eat soup with a fork".

After watching baseballs fly out of the park in 1961, the powers of the game decided that something needed to be done to help the pitchers. It was determined in a January meeting that the strike zone should be expanded to its pre-1950 dimensions: from the top of the batter's shoulders to the bottom of his knees. Previously, the accepted parameters had strikes crossing an area between the hitter's armpits and the tops of his knees. The bigger strike zone gave the pitchers a crucial advantage and greatly reduced offensive figures.

In that climate, it should have come as little surprise that the Dodgers would be successful. The organization traditionally placed a premium on pitching. The Dodgers had good hitters but they didn't have a devastating array of sluggers. Management knew its pitching staff would allow it to win low-scoring games, so the Dodgers had gotten into the habit of manufacturing their runs.

Koufax had missed a significant portion of

the 1962 season due to a mysterious circulatory ailment that caused numbness in his fingers. The malady went away in 1963 and Koufax was clearly the game's best pitcher. He went 25–5 and 11 of those victories were shutouts. He also pitched one of the season's three no-hitters.

Superior pitching helped the Dodgers hold off a strong challenge from the Cardinals. St. Louis benefited greatly from an off-season trade with the Pirates that brought shortstop Dick Groat to the Cardinals. Groat, an All-America basketball player at Duke University, had been one of the anchors of the Pirates' 1960 championship team.

After two seasons of disappointment, the Pirates decided to start over and traded away three-fourths of their 1960 infield. Third baseman Don Hoak went to Philadelphia and powerful first baseman Dick Stuart wound up in Boston.

None of the trades worked out as well as St. Louis' acquisition of Groat. He gave the Cardinals a reliable hitter, a solid defensive player and a clubhouse presence. The Cardinals had built an impressive collection of talent and Groat

Sandy Koufax's dominance on the mound saw him collect the MVP and Cy Young awards in 1963

Hard-throwing Jim Bouton shows the form that earned him the nickname "Bulldog"

Jan. 26: Baseball's Rules Committee expands the strike zone to area from the top of the batter's shoulders to the bottom of his knees.

April 1: Duke Snider's career-long association with the Dodgers ended when he was purchased by the Mets.

June 27: Tony Gonzalez of the Phillies mishandled a ball in Pittsburgh, his first error in 205 games. His errorless streak broke the record of 199 games set by Cincinnati's Gus Bell.

June 28: Milwaukee's Warren Spahn pitched a three-hitter to beat Don Drysdale 1–0. It was Spahn's first win on the Dodgers' home field since August 21, 1948. He had lost 14 straight decisions—nine at Ebbets Field, four at the Los Angeles Memorial Coliseum and one at Dodger Stadium.

July 9: The National League wins the All-Star Game 5–3 at Cleveland. Only 44,160 tickets were sold in Municipal Stadium, which seated 73,811.

July 13: Early Wynn of the Cleveland Indians won his 300th career game.

July 17: The Detroit Tigers dedicated a plaque to the memory of Hall of Famer Ty Cobb on the second anniversary of his death.

Aug. 21: Pittsburgh's Jerry Lynch hit his 15th career pinch home run, breaking George Crowe's major league record.

Sept. 18: The Mets closed the Polo Grounds with a 5–1 loss to the Phillies.

Sept. 27: The Colt .45s started a lineup consisting entirely of rookies, whose average age was 19. Included in the group was second baseman Joe Morgan, a future Hall of Famer.

Sept. 29: Stan Musial of the Cardinals retired at 42, the National League's career leader in hits (3,630) and runs batted in (1,951).

Nov. 7: Elston Howard of the Yankees became the first black player to win the American League's Most Valuable Player award.

was another important part of the mix.

The Dodgers appeared to have a comfortable lead until the Cardinals went on a run that saw them win 19 of 20 games. Los Angeles didn't do badly, either; the Dodgers were 13–6 in the same span. Yet the Cardinals got to within a game of the league-leading Dodgers heading into a showdown series in mid-September. Los Angeles bought some breathing space by sweeping the three-game series.

The Giants and Cubs had taken runs at the lead but the Cardinals were the only serious challenger left by the middle of August.

It wasn't just Koufax. The Dodgers also got contributions from Don Drysdale and Johnny Podres in the rotation and had Ron Perranoski in the bullpen to close games. Those four pitchers were responsible for 74 of the Dodgers' 99 wins.

Outfielder Tommy Davis won his second consecutive batting title with a .326 average. Maury Wills, who set a record by stealing 104 bases in 1962, stole only 40 in 1963 after an opening-day foot injury slowed him.

The defending National League champion Giants fell to third place after their pitching disappointed. The Phillies, doormats in previous years, jumped up to fourth place under fiery manager Gene Mauch.

A couple of long-term stars voluntarily ended their careers. Stan Musial, who spent his entire career with the Cardinals, decided to retire. On September 10, Musial's family helped him achieve a memorable milestone. That was the

SHORTS The Hall of Fame got crowded with the biggest class in history. Seven were inducted although only one, Luke Appling, was voted in by the panel. Appling needed a second ballot after falling short on the first try. The other six were chosen by the Veterans Commitee: Urban (Red) Faber, Burleigh Grimes and Tim Keefe, Heinie Manush, Miller Huggins and John Montgomery Ward. The seven new members raised the Hall's membership list to 101.

Yankees' catcher Elston Howard celebrates becoming the first black player to capture the American League MVP award

day his daughter-in-law gave birth to a son. That night, Musial homered off the Cubs' Glen Hobbie, his first at-bat since becoming a grandfather. Musial was honored with a day before a late-season game and stayed in the Cardinals organization as a vice president.

In May, the New York Mets gave Gil Hodges his release so he could join the Washington Senators as their manager. Hodges, an anchor of the Brooklyn Dodgers teams of the 1950s, had been brought back east from Los Angeles by the upstart Mets to finish his career in New York. Hodges, clearly at the end of the line as a player, jumped at the chance to start his managing career at the major league level, even it meant serving the lowly Senators. He succeeded Mickey Vernon on May 22 in the first of three managerial changes.

The continuing dominance of the Yankees led to frustration among other American League clubs. The Detroit Tigers were the next team to change managers, firing Bob Scheffing on June 17 and bringing ex-Brooklyn manager Charlie Dressen in to replace him. The Baltimore Orioles waited until the end of the year to terminate Billy Hitchcock. After Eddie Stanky turned down the job, Hank Bauer was hired.

One other managerial change was accomplished with the formality of a title switch. Bob Kennedy, who had been serving as head coach in the Cubs' system of rotating coaches, was named manager.

Despite losing Mickey Mantle and Roger Maris for a significant portion of the season, the Yankees breezed to the American League title, winning by ten games and claiming their fourth consecutive pennant. Not since 1947 had the Yankees won by that large a margin.

Their pitching staff got a boost from the emergence of righthander Jim Bouton, who was in his second major league season. Bouton earned the nickname "Bulldog" for his competitive tendencies and threw his fastball so hard that his cap fell off on most deliveries. The Yankees also got a lift from promoting lefthander Al Downing from the minor leagues.

The mainstay of the Yankees' staff was still lefthander Whitey Ford. He and Bouton were the winningest 1–2 combination in the majors. Ford went 24–7 and Bouton was 21–7 even though he didn't join the rotation until May 12. Downing contributed a 13–5 record in his first major league season.

Mantle fractured a foot, which also led to knee problems. He appeared in only 65 games and 13 of those were pinch hitting assignments. Maris was limited to 90 games by an assortment of injuries, including lingering back problems. The two players were in the starting lineup together just 30 times the entire season.

The Yankees found offense from other sources. John Blanchard and Hector Lopez combined for 30 home runs. First baseman Joe Pepitone, who succeeded Bill Showron, hit .271 with 27 home runs and 89 runs batted in. Catcher Elston Howard won the American League MVP award after hitting .287 with 28 homers and 85 RBIs.

The White Sox finished second, helped by the work of two rookies—lefthanded pitcher Gary Peters and third baseman Pete Ward. Peters went 19–8 and led the American League with a 2.33 ERA. At one point, Peters won 11 consecutive decisions and pitched ten complete games in that span. Ward hit .295 with 22 home runs and 84 RBIs.

Things were almost as interesting off the field. The Braves, who had transferred to Milwaukee in 1953, were plagued by dwindling attendance. Atlanta and San Diego both came calling with inducements to lure them away.

Charles O. Finley continued to try to move the Athletics from Kansas City, a pattern that had started from the moment Finley bought the franchise. He began the year wanting to move the team to Louisville, then focused his attention on Oakland.

The newest National League teams, the Mets and Colt .45s, were both getting ready to close old ballparks. The Mets closed the ancient Polo

San Francisco Giants' pitcher Juan Marichal finished the regular season with an impressive 25 wins

Grounds but the Colts were going to endure one more season in Colt Stadium while their domed stadium was completed. In the meantime, Houston received permission from the National League to schedule Sunday night games in an effort to avoid the oppressive afternoon Texas heat.

In Pittsburgh, the Pirates were threatening to move as efforts to get a new stadium were stalled by local government.

Finley, who was acquiring a reputation as a maverick, made some radical suggestions. He advocated opening the World Series on a Saturday so that if the Series went the full seven games, it would encompass two weekends, when more people would be available to watch it. Finley also proposed playing the midweek Series games at night in order to attract a larger television audience. His ideas were quickly rejected.

In addition to Koufax, two other pitchers threw no-hitters. Houston's Don Nottebart beat the Phillies 4–1 on May 17 (the run scored on an error). On June 15, the Giants' Juan Marichal returned the favor against Houston, beating the Colts 1–0.

The game lost one of its Hall of Famers when Rogers Hornsby died in Chicago on January 5 at 66. Hornsby had coached for the Mets in their inaugural season, 1962.

SHORTS It was better late than never for Early Wynn. Wynn labored through five innings for the Cleveland Indians on July 13 and beat the Kansas City Athletics 7–4 with relief help from Jerry Walker. The victory was his 300th and last in the major leagues.

GAME 1	
Los Angeles 5	NY Yankees 2
GAME 2	
Los Angeles 4	NY Yankees 1
GAME 3	
Los Angeles 1	NY Yankees 0
GAME 4	
Los Angeles 2	NY Yankees 1
MVP: Sandy Koufax, Los Angeles	

The New York Yankees scored two runs in the first game of the 1963 World Series. Little did they know it would be their biggest offensive outburst of the Series.

The Los Angeles Dodgers' pitching, led by Sandy Koufax, thoroughly dominated the Series, holding the Yankees to four runs and a .171 team batting average en route to a four-game sweep.

The Yankees found out quickly what National League batters had discovered over the course of the season—no pitcher could control a game the way that Koufax could. He was 25–5 in the regular season with a 1.88 earned run average and struck out 306 batters in 311 innings.

He quickly established a similar pattern in the Series, striking out the first five batters in the first game of the Series. Tony Kubek, Bobby Richardson, Tom Tresh, Mickey Mantle and Roger Maris were all strikeout victims. Mantle would wind up getting just two hits in 15 at-bats

in the Series; Maris was hitless in five at-bats before injuries forced him to the bench.

John Roseboro hit a three-run homer off Whitey Ford in the second inning, while earlier, ex-Yankee Bill Skowron had an RBI single as the Dodgers staked Koufax to a 4–0 lead.

The Yankees didn't get a baserunner through the first four innings. New York's runs came on Tresh's home run in the eighth inning. That was little more than a temporary inconvenience for Koufax, who finished the game with a flourish, striking out pinch hitter Harry Bright.

With 15 strikeouts, Koufax set a World Series record, breaking the mark Carl Erskine had set with the Brooklyn Dodgers exactly ten years earlier. Mantle had struck out four times against Erskine while Koufax got him twice.

Sandy Koufax lets it all out as his Dodgers complete a clean sweep of the New York Yankees

Johnny Podres wasn't as spectacular in Game Two, but he was just as effective. Podres held the Yankees to six hits and a run before giving way to Ron Perranoski, who got the game's last two outs. The Dodgers again took an early lead, this time on Willie Davis' two-run double in the first inning against Al Downing. Skowron homered for the Dodgers and Tommy Davis also drove in a run in the 4–1 win. Elston Howard had the Yankees' RBI.

Maris was injured in the second game, which ended his participation in the Series. He hurt his knee and elbow when he crashed into a railing chasing a ball.

The Dodgers went home to finish the Series, their first in Los Angeles since the opening of Dodger Stadium the previous season. Righthander Don Drysdale picked up where lefties Koufax and Podres had left off.

Drysdale allowed just three hits in a complete game 1–0 win. He walked one and struck out nine as he out-dueled Jim Bouton.

The Dodgers got their run in the first inning, manufacturing it with a walk, a wild pitch and Tommy Davis' RBI single.

Koufax and Whitey Ford were scoreless through four innings in Game Four until Frank Howard put the Dodgers ahead with a solo home run. Mantle, who struggled through-

out the Series, got the run back in the seventh with a homer.

Yankees' first baseman, Joe Pepitone, made an error in the bottom of the seventh and that was the opening the Dodgers needed to create the winning run. Pepitone couldn't find third baseman Clete Boyer's throw on Jim Gilliam's grounder to lead off the inning. Gilliam got to third base on the play.

Willie Davis hit a sacrifice fly and Koufax made the run stand up over the final two innings. He held the Yankees to six hits, didn't walk a batter and struck out eight.

The Dodgers used only four pitchers in the whole Series and the starters accounted for all but the two outs. Koufax had the staff's highest ERA at 1.50.

Tommy Davis, who had won the National League batting title, hit .400 in the Series. Skowron, who had extensive World Series experience with the Yankees, batted .385 and Howard hit .300.

Although the Yankees were considered the power team, the Dodgers outhomered them, 3–2.

It was a sweet reverse for the Dodgers. While in Brooklyn, they had met the Yankees seven times in the World Series with New York taking six of them.

The Mick strikes out again during the Yankees 5–2 loss in Game One. Sandy Koufax finished with 15 K's

MOST VALUABLE PLAYER
AL: Brooks Robinson, Baltimore
NL: Ken Boyer, St. Louis Cardinals

CY YOUNG AWARD
AL, NL: Dean Chance, Los Angeles

ROOKIE OF THE YEAR
AL: Tony Oliva, Minnesota
NL: Dick Allen, Philadelphia Phillies

LEADERS
BATTING AVERAGE
AL: Tony Oliva, Minnesota, .323
NL: Roberto Clemente, Pittsburgh, .339

HOME RUNS
AL: Harmon Killebrew, Minnesota, 49
NL: Willie Mays, San Francisco, 47

RUNS BATTED IN
AL: Brooks Robinson, Baltimore, 118
NL: Ken Boyer, St. Louis Cardinals, 119

STOLEN BASES
AL: Luis Aparicio, Baltimore, 57
NL: Maury Wills, Los Angeles, 53

PITCHING VICTORIES
AL: Dean Chance, Los Angeles; Gary Peters, Chicago White Sox, 20
NL: Larry Jackson, Chicago Cubs, 24

EARNED RUN AVERAGE
AL: Dean Chance, Los Angeles, 1.65
NL: Sandy Koufax, Los Angeles, 1.74

STRIKEOUTS
AL: Al Downing, NY Yankees, 217
NL: Bob Veale, Pittsburgh, 250

It was one of the most unforgettable seasons in Philadelphia Phillies' history—for all the wrong reasons. The Phillies appeared to be headed for the National League pennant when they collapsed at the same time their competitors were playing their best baseball of the season.

When it all shook out, the St. Louis Cardinals took the title to complete a bizarre season that will always be remembered as the year the Phillies lost the pennant.

In the American League, the New York Yankees didn't have the luxury of sitting back and watching their potential World Series opponents wear each other out. The Yankees were locked in their tightest pennant race since 1949 and held off the Chicago White Sox and Baltimore Orioles to take their fifth consecutive American League title.

The National League race wound up being a four-team derby involving the Phillies, Cardinals, Cincinnati Reds and San Francisco Giants. The National League office was preparing playoff contingencies for all manners of ties. San Francisco was eliminated on the next-to-last day of the season but the possibility of a three-way tie existed on the final day.

The Phillies stayed alive by beating the Reds 10–0, knocking out Cincinnati. St. Louis ended the race with an 11–5 win over the Mets that ended an 18-year pennant drought for the Cardinals. The Phillies had occupied first place for 134 days during the season; the Cardinals were in first for just six days. They didn't get into first until September 29.

What happened to the Phillies? Ask a Phillies fan of a certain age and clear several hours to listen to theories. Manager Gene Mauch has always been assigned some of the blame. Mauch had only two reliable starting pitchers—righthander Jim Bunning and lefty Chris Short. Mauch pitched each of them on two days' rest on three occasions during the last three weeks. Bunning and Short didn't win any of those games.

There were other reasons, though. Some players have said the Phillies simply weren't good enough to last the entire season. It didn't help when Frank Thomas fractured a thumb on September 8 and took a veteran presence out of the lineup.

Two players carried the Phillies offensively: right fielder Johnny Callison and third baseman Dick Allen. Despite a league-high 138 strikeouts, Allen was the National League's top rookie with a .318 average, 29 home runs and 91 RBIs.

The Phillies had a ten-game losing streak

Phillies' boss Gene Mauch sees it slip away

down the stretch. The Cardinals won eight straight and the Reds had a nine-game winning streak.

It had been a strange year for the Cardinals, who found themselves tied for seventh place and 10 games off first place on July 23. That disappointing performance led to the firing of general manager Bing Devine on August 17. There were also reports that Cardinals' ownership wanted to replace manager Johnny Keane with Leo Durocher.

Phillies' ace Jim Bunning en route to a perfect game against the Mets

Appreciation for Devine's contributions grew after he left the organization. He made a bold trade at the June 15 deadline. It was a multiple-player deal with the Cubs, but there were two key figures: the Cardinals gave up starting pitcher Ernie Broglio, a former 20-game winner, and acquired outfielder Lou Brock.

Brock, who had batted only .251 with the Cubs, hit .348 for the rest of the season with the Cardinals. He proved to be the perfect left field replacement for the retired Stan Musial, and Brock's speed made him a catalyst at the top of an order that had some solid run producers.

Third baseman Ken Boyer won the National League's Most Valuable Player award and led the league with 119 RBIs. Right fielder Mike Shannon came up from the minor leagues in early July and helped. The Cardinals' pitching improved, too. Bob Gibson started the season 10–10 but won nine of his last 11 decisions. Veteran Curt Simmons won his last six decisions.

Shortly before Devine was fired, he brought up 38-year-old knuckleballer Barney Schultz from the minor leagues. In the last ten days of the season, Schultz pitched in seven of the Cardinals' nine games and didn't allow a run.

He helped solidify a bullpen that had been a problem area for much of the season.

The Reds were playing under an emotional burden. Manager Fred Hutchinson was diagnosed with cancer and took an extended leave of absence from the team. Coach Dick Sisler managed the club while Hutchinson was away.

The defending champion Dodgers were not a factor. Sandy Koufax's season ended on August 16 when he injured an elbow in a mishap sliding into a base. Koufax had another brilliant season, winning 19 games, leading the league with a 1.74 ERA and pitching his third career no-hitter.

The American League race was still up for grabs with three days left in the season. The Yankees' pennant-winning streak continued

SHORTS The season had more than its fair share of tragedy as three active participants died during the year. Cubs' second baseman Ken Hubbs, 22, was killed in a February 15 plane crash. Houston reliever Jim Umbricht died of cancer at 33 on April 8. Cancer forced Reds' manager Fred Hutchinson to leave the club twice during the season. He died in Florida on November 12 at 45.

T I M E L I N E

Feb. 15: Cubs' second baseman Ken Hubbs, the National League's Rookie of the Year in 1962, died when the single-engine airplane he was piloting crashed in a snowstorm near Provo, Utah.

April 8: Colt .45s' relief pitcher Jim Umbricht died of cancer in Houston at the age of 33.

April 17: The Mets opened Shea Stadium with a 4–3 loss to the Pirates.

April 23: Houston's Ken Johnson pitched a no-hitter against the Reds and lost 1–0. Two errors, one by Johnson, allowed the Reds to score in the ninth inning. He became the only pitcher to lose a complete-game no-hitter.

June 4: Sandy Koufax of the Dodgers pitched his third career no-hitter and beat the Phillies 3–0.

June 15: The Cardinals traded pitchers Ernie Broglio and Bobby Shantz and outfielder Doug Clemens to the Cubs for outfielder Lou Brock and pitchers Jack Spring and Paul Toth.

June 21: The Phillies' Jim Bunning pitched a perfect game against the Mets in New York.

July 7: The Phillies' Johnny Callison won the All-Star Game for the National League with a three-run homer off Boston's Dick Radatz in the ninth inning.

July 10: Rookie Jesus Alou of the Giants went 6-for-6 against the Cubs with each hit coming off a different pitcher.

Aug. 13: Cancer-stricken manager Fred Hutchinson left the Reds. Coach Dick Sisler became interim manager.

Aug. 17: The fifth-place Cardinals fired General Manager Bing Devine, who would go on to win *The Sporting News*' Executive of the Year award.

Oct. 16: The Yankees fired manager Yogi Berra and Johnny Keane resigned as Cardinals' manager.

Nov. 2: CBS paid $11.2 million to purchase the Yankees from Dan Topping and Del Webb.

Nov. 12: Fred Hutchinson died in Bradenton, Florida at 45.

The Cardinals' Ken Boyer gets a hero's welcome after his grand slam during the World Series. Boyer won the National League MVP award

through a third different manager. Yogi Berra succeeded Ralph Houk and won in his first year as a manager.

The ride wasn't smooth. On a hot day after a loss in Chicago, Berra was annoyed to hear a harmonica being played in the back of the bus. He found infielder Phil Linz was the musician and the two argued. While some players said the incident helped galvanize the club, management didn't have the same view. It was more ammunition against Berra, who was fired after the World Series for failing to communicate well with his players.

The Yankees' offense sagged. An exception was Mickey Mantle, who hit .303 with 35 home runs and 111 RBIs despite being bothered by lingering knee problems. It was his most productive season since 1961. The Yankees made a couple of key in-season moves. Right-hander Mel Stottlemyre was promoted from the

minor leagues on August 11 and went 9–3 with a 2.06 ERA. The Yankees bolstered a spotty bullpen by acquiring Pedro Ramos late in the season from Cleveland.

Whitey Ford went 17–6 with eight shutouts despite missing time with hip and foot injuries. Ralph Terry, who had won 23 and 17 games in the previous two seasons, fell to 3–8 and was traded to Cleveland as compensation for Ramos after the season.

SHORTS Shea Stadium had a decade's worth of memorable moments in its first season. The Phillies' Jim Bunning pitched baseball's ninth perfect game there on June 21 and another Philadelphia player, Johnny Callison, ended the All-Star Game with a three-run homer on July 7. On May 31, the Mets and Giants played a doubleheader that took nearly 10 hours to complete. The second game went 23 innings. The first pitch was at 1:08 p.m.; the last out at 11:25.

The White Sox had strong pitching but fell short offensively. The Orioles held first place for 84 days, more than any other team. Brooks Robinson had a career-best year, hitting .317 with 28 home runs and 118 RBIs while winning the Most Valuable Player award. Rookie Wally Bunker, a 19-year-old who had spent only one year in professional baseball, won 19 games. The Orioles' hitting slumped at the end of the season and they faltered.

Masanori Murakami became the first Japanese-born player to pitch in the major leagues. He won his only decision with the Giants.

Off the field, the big news was the purchase of the Yankees for $11.2 million by CBS. It sparked fears that baseball games would eventually be offered on pay TV.

Baseball approved two franchise shifts, one of which was radical. The Milwaukee Braves were granted permission to move to Atlanta for the 1966 season to take advantage of an untapped regional market and benefit from a new stadium. The Braves were stuck in Milwaukee for a lame-duck 1965 season. The other shift was less dramatic. The Angels were allowed to leave Los Angeles and head slightly further south to Anaheim in time for 1966. There was another new stadium awaiting a tenant in Anaheim.

Keane had heard the rumors that the Cardinals were courting Durocher as his replacement. He got his revenge after winning the World Series, spurning the Cardinals' offer of a lucrative contract extension to hand in a letter of resignation that was dated September 28.

Other managerial changes were made. Kansas City fired Ed Lopat on June 11 and hired Mel McGaha to replace him. On September 19, Colt .45s' manager Harry Craft was succeeded by Luman Harris. On the next to last day of the season, the Red Sox fired Johnny Pesky and hired Billy Herman. The Giants handed Alvin Dark his release on the final day of the season and promoted coach Herman Franks. Pittsburgh's Danny Murtaugh resigned four years after leading the team to a World Series win, citing health concerns.

Baseball instituted an annual amateur draft, an effort to spare the owners from their own spending excesses. Clubs had gotten into the habit of handing huge signing bonuses to unproven players. With a draft, a player could only negotiate with the team that had selected him.

Athletics' owner Charles O. Finley became even more prominent, threatening again to

Yogi Berra's first year in charge of the Yankees was a rollercoaster-ride that ended in disappointment

move his franchise from Kansas City to Louisville. His fellow owners ordered Finley to either sign a new agreement with Kansas City or face expulsion. He agreed to a four-year deal.

Finley ran afoul of the league office when he created a "Pennant Porch" by shortening the distance to the right field fence to duplicate the dimensions of Yankee Stadium. Finley was ordered to restore the park to its original configuration.

National League umpires threatened to go on strike. The problem was averted when their pension benefits were increased. Umpire Jocko Conlan called it a career.

Several prominent players announced their intentions to retire—Duke Snider, Billy Pierce, Nellie Fox and Bobby Shantz.

GAME 1	
St. Louis Cardinals 9	NY Yankees 5
GAME 2	
NY Yankees 8	St. Louis Cardinals 3
GAME 3	
NY Yankees 2	St. Louis Cardinals 1
GAME 4	
St. Louis Cardinals 4	NY Yankees 3
GAME 5	
St. Louis Cardinals 5	NY Yankees 2
GAME 6	
NY Yankees 8	St. Louis Cardinals 3
GAME 7	
St. Louis Cardinals 7	NY Yankees 5
MVP: Bob Gibson, St. Louis Cardinals	

Ken Boyer and the Cards celebrate their pennant and prepare to face the might of the Yankees in the World Series

The St. Louis Cardinals caused a sensation when they fired their general manager and tried to get rid of their manager, too. It was a strange course of events for a World Series-winning team.

The Cardinals stormed to the National League pennant in the frenzied last weeks, taking advantage of the Philadelphia Phillies' collapse. It was the first Series appearance for the Cardinals since 1946. By contrast, the Yankees were in the postseason for the 14th time in 16 years.

Neither team had an easy path to the Series. The Yankees held off a strong challenge from the Chicago White Sox to win under first-year manager Yogi Berra. The Cardinals were stuck in fifth place when ownership fired general manager Bing Devine. The front office also planned to fire manager Johnny Keane when the season ended and replace him with Leo Durocher.

That plan changed when the Cardinals broke free of the pack and won the National League pennant as the Phillies flopped.

In contrast with the pitching-dominated 1963 Series, offense ruled in 1964. In the opener, the Cardinals came back from a 4–2 deficit in the sixth inning to win 9–5. Mike Shannon hit a game-tying home run, and pinch hitter Carl Warwick broke the tie with a single.

Ford left the game with arm problems. It turned out to be his last career World Series appearance.

Rookie Mel Stottlemyre pitched the Yankees into a 1–1 Series tie with an 8–3 complete game win. Bob Gibson gave up four runs in eight innings and the Yankees beat up the

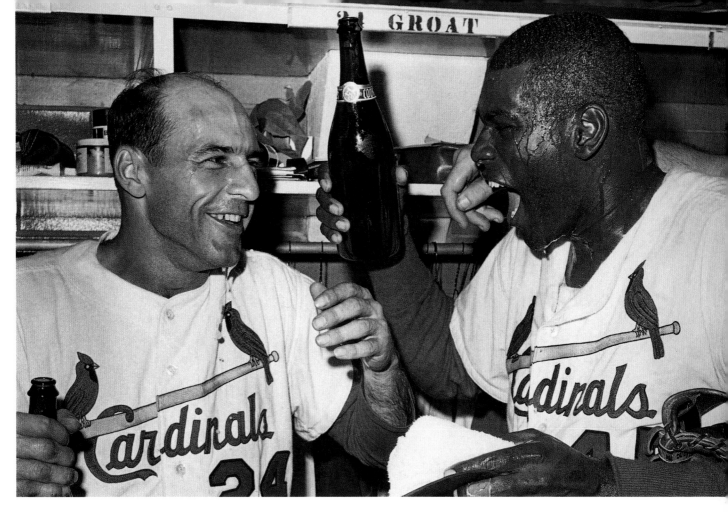

Cardinals' bullpen in the final inning.

Game Three was the only pitchers duel of the Series. Curt Simmons of the Cardinals and New York's Jim Bouton were tied at 1–1 through eight innings. The Yankees won the game in the ninth when Mickey Mantle homered off reliever Barney Schultz.

The Yankees appeared to have the momentum when they scored their runs in the first inning against Ray Sadecki in Game Four. The Series changed when Cardinals' third baseman Ken Boyer hit a grand slam off Al Downing in the sixth.

Sadecki, a 20-game winner in the regular season, lasted just one-third of an inning in his first Series start. Relievers Roger Craig and Ron Taylor saved the day for the Cardinals, holding the Yankees to just two hits over the final 8⅓ innings.

Gibson was leading 2–0 with one out to go in Game Five when Tom Tresh tied the game with a two-run homer. That sent the game to extra innings and the Cardinals won it when catcher Tim McCarver hit a three-run homer off Pete Mikkelsen.

In Game Six, Roger Maris and Mantle homered on consecutive pitches against Curt Simmons to break a 1–1 tie in the sixth inning. Joe Pepitone hit a grand slam off reliever Gordon Richardson in the eighth and the Yankees cruised to a Series-tying 8–3 win behind Bouton.

The Cardinals scored three runs in the fourth and three more in the fifth inning of Game Seven. The runs came off Stottlemyre and Downing, who had a disastrous relief appearance.

The cushion was big enough for Gibson, who was clearly wearing down in his third appearance of the Series. Mantle hit a three-run homer off him in the sixth and he allowed solo homers to Clete Boyer and Phil Linz in the ninth. Even though he was faltering, Keane stuck with Gibson, based on his belief in his ace and the doubts he had about his bullpen.

The Cardinals won the game 7–5 and took the Series, which triggered an odd series of events. The Yankees fired Berra after just one season on the job, claiming he couldn't communicate with the players. Keane had the satisfaction of rejecting the Cardinals' offer of a new contract and resigned shortly after the season ended. To add another wrinkle to the story, he was hired by the Yankees to replace Berra.

It turned out to be the last Series for both Mantle and Ford. Mantle finished with 18 World Series home runs, breaking Babe Ruth's major league record.

One of the unsung heroes of the Series was Warwick, the spare outfielder who went 3-for-4 as a pinch hitter, including the key hit in Game One. The Yankees' best pitcher was Bouton, who won both of his starts and posted a 1.50 ERA.

Gibson went 2–1 with a 3.00 ERA to take MVP honors in a Series dominated by offense.

Series MVP Bob Gibson soaks it up with Dick Groat after St Louis' dramatic triumph over New York

YOGI BERRA

TEAMS

New York Yankees 1946–63;
New York Mets 1965

Games	2,120
At-Bats	7,555
Runs	1,175
RBI	1,430
Home runs	358
Hits	2,150
Doubles	321
Triples	49
Stolen Bases	30
Average	.285
Slugging percentage	.482

Yogi Berra had a funny name, an odd physique and a knack for saying things in a convoluted way that inspired laughs.

Sometimes those things obscured just how good a ballplayer he was. For example, everyone is aware of Berra's famous quote about the danger of premature celebration ("It ain't over until it's over"), but how many know he's one of only four catchers in major league history to compile a perfect 1.000 fielding average over an entire season (1958)?

Berra is remembered for his offhand dismissal of a popular restaurant ("Nobody goes there any more, it's too crowded"), rather than being a member of 15 consecutive All-Star teams.

Baseball people remember two things about Berra—his ability to hit bad pitches and his knack for producing when the game was on the line. It was possible to get burned by throwing a pitch out of the strike zone to Berra, who often lifted pitches that were a few inches off the ground over the fence.

"Every pitch I threw to him I wanted back," said Don Newcombe, who faced Berra in the World Series as a member of the Brooklyn Dodgers.

Berra might have a quiet offensive game, only to deliver a hit when it was needed most.

Said long-time baseball man Whitey Herzog, "The best hitter from the seventh inning on was Yogi. He was the kind of guy who made a lot of easy outs in the early innings, but from the seventh inning on he was the toughest out I've ever seen."

Lawrence Peter Berra was born in St. Louis to immigrant parents who didn't understand how their son could make a living playing a game. He was known as "Lawdy" as a boy, but his friends started calling him Yogi after a character in a movie. He was signed by the Yankees, but had his career interrupted by a stint in the Navy from 1944–46.

Berra made his major league debut on September 22, 1946 and served in a part-time role until he became the Yankees' regular catcher in 1949. Berra was tutored by Bill Dickey, the Hall of Famer from whom he inherited the No. 8 with the Yankees.

From 1949–55, Berra led the Yankees in RBIs each season and won three Most Valuable Player awards. From 1957–59, he caught 148 games without making an error and handled 950 chances.

Playing with the Yankees meant plenty of World Series exposure, and Berra's unique name became known to people who didn't follow baseball. His legend grew with the advent of "Yogi-isms", the fractured observations that came from everyday experiences.

There was Yogi on the value of being a spectator ("You can observe a lot just by watching"), and Berra on the importance of originality ("If you can't imitate him, don't copy him"). Were they all legitimate? Probably not. Berra may have had some help from the competitive New York newspapermen, who knew that Yogi was great copy. His boyhood friend from St. Louis, Joe Garagiola, used Berra as a comedic foil when he launched his broadcasting career.

Toward the end of his career, Berra's defensive skills began to wane and he moved to the outfield to make room for Elston Howard. His retirement was abrupt when the Yankees shocked the baseball world by naming him manager for the 1964 season. It was an awkward position for Berra, who had no managerial experience and now had to be an authority figure for players who were teammates a day earlier. His Yankees won the American League pennant, but Berra was fired for what the team said was a lack of communication skills.

He moved cross-town to the Mets as a player-coach, but mostly the latter. He appeared in four games at the age of 40 for the 1965 Mets, his only playing experience in a uniform other than the Yankees pinstripes.

Berra managed the Mets after the death of Gil Hodges and took the 1973 team to the World Series, joining Joe McCarthy as the only manager to win pennants in both leagues. He came back to manage the Yankees in 1984–85 and coached for Houston before retiring to his New Jersey home—the one for which he once offered directions by saying, "When you come to the fork in the road, take it."

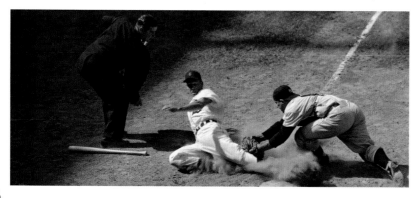

Yogi Berra stretches as he tags Detroit's Bill Tuttle from third base on Reno Bertoia's slow roller down the third-base line in the fourth inning of the New York-Detroit game on May 1, 1957

The awesome Sandy Koufax finished the season with both the pitching Triple Crown and the Cy Young award

Baseball people who argue that pitching is the most important component in baseball success have their textbook example in the performance of the 1965 Los Angeles Dodgers.

It was a season-long struggle for the Dodgers to score runs, but their pitching staff did an excellent job of preventing them and the team used that formula to win the World Series.

It was an unusually turbulent year for the game, which placed its first team indoors, jilted a once-thriving market in Milwaukee, shifted to the untapped southeastern United States and dealt with an ugly bat-attack episode involving one of the game's finest pitchers.

It was also the year the New York Yankees first started to show their age and fell to sixth place without being a significant factor in the American League pennant race all season.

First, the Dodgers, who prevailed in what was a six-team pennant race at the beginning of the season's final month. They didn't plan to do it without offense; those were the circumstances forced upon them. Tommy Davis, a two-time batting champion, fractured his ankle on the bases

Willie Mays had an awesome season, winning the National League's MVP award

TIMELINE

Jan. 20: Rocky Colavito, whose trade from the Indians to Tigers touched off a controversy in 1960, returned to Cleveland in a deal with Kansas City.

March 7: Tigers' manager Charley Dressen suffered a heart attack during spring training and left the club until May 31. Coach Bob Swift served as interim manager.

April 9: The Astrodome opened with an exhibition game between the Yankees and Astros.

June 8-9: Baseball held its first free agent draft in New York. The Athletics chose Arizona State outfielder Rick Monday first and signed him for a reported $104,000 bonus.

July 19: The Mets released Warren Spahn, 43, after he lost eight consecutive decisions. Spahn would then sign with the Giants.

July 23: Phillies' first baseman Dick Stuart homered at Shea Stadium, which gave him at least one home run in every current major league park.

Aug. 19: Jim Maloney of the Reds pitched a no-hitter against the Cubs.

Aug. 22: The Dodgers and Giants brawled after San Francisco pitcher Juan Marichal hit Los Angeles catcher John Roseboro over the head with his bat.

Aug. 29: Casey Stengel resigned as manager of the New York Mets, ending his 56-year career in professional baseball.

Aug. 29: Hall of Fame outfielder Paul Waner died at 62 in Sarasota, Florida.

Sept. 13: Willie Mays hit his 500th career home run off Houston's Don Nottebart in the Astrodome.

Sept. 16: Boston's Dave Morehead beat Cleveland 2–0 in the American League's only no-hitter.

Sept. 26: The Twins clinched their first American League pennant in their fifth season since leaving Washington D.C.

Sept. 29: Sandy Koufax pitched a perfect game against the Cubs for his fourth career no-hitter.

Dec. 9: Branch Rickey, who broke baseball's color line by signing Jackie Robinson to the Brooklyn Dodgers in 1947, died at 83 in Columbia, Missouri.

and, coupled with the loss of slugger Frank Howard in a trade with Washington, the Dodgers were consigned to a season in which they would scrap for runs.

Their team batting average of .245 was the lowest ever for a National League pennant winner. The Dodgers hit only 78 home runs, the lowest figure for a first-place team in 20 years. The Dodgers were forced to make adjustments throughout the season. When Davis was injured on May 1, Lou Johnson, a 31-year-old non-prospect was summoned from the minor leagues. When third base proved to be a problem, 38-year-old coach Jim Gilliam rejoined the active roster and wound up hitting .280

SHORTS Indoor baseball was a new concept so it's little wonder that Houston's Astrodome had some kinks to work out. It was immediately discovered that the skylight dome made the simplest fly ball a hazard. The decision was quickly made to paint the outside of the Dome, an investment of $20,000 and 700 gallons of paint. During an April visit, the Mets charged that engineers were altering air conditioning currents to favor the Astros. The commissioners' office investigated and pronounced the charges groundless. The novelty of the Dome tripled Houston's attendance to 2.1 million.

Fortunately for the Dodgers, their pitching staff didn't need much run support. Sandy Koufax continued to build on his already-established reputation as the game's most dominant pitcher. Koufax was a unanimous choice for the Cy Young award. He went 26–8 and a 2.04 earned run average allowed him to lead the league in that category. Koufax also threw eight shutouts and struck out 382 batters in 336 innings.

Koufax pitched a no-hitter for the fourth consecutive season. He improved in that area, too, making 1965's no-hitter a perfect game against the Cubs.

Right behind Koufax was the other part of the Dodgers' formidable 1–2 combination, righthander Don Drysdale. He worked 308 innings, posting a 23–12 record with a 2.78 ERA and seven shutouts. He even helped the Dodgers' offensive attack, batting .300.

Claude Osteen, who came from Washington in the Howard trade, quickly adapted to the Dodgers' formula. His 15–15 record was deceptive since he'd been given just 28 runs of support in his 15 losses. Osteen's ERA was a more-than-respectable 2.79 and he also provid-

Giants' ace Juan Marichal saw red as he hit Dodgers' catcher John Roseboro with a bat. He was later suspended for nine days

ed innings, falling just 13 short of 300.

The race narrowed to three teams down the stretch: the Dodgers, San Francisco Giants and Cincinnati Reds. The Giants got virtually nothing from Orlando Cepeda, who was limited to 33 games by injuries. Willie Mays was the League's Most Valuable Player after batting .317 with 52 home runs and 112 RBIs. Others picked up some of the slack in Cepeda's absence. Third baseman Jim Ray Hart hit .299 with 23 home runs and 99 RBIs. First baseman Willie McCovey had 39 homers and 92 RBIs to go along with a .276 average.

The Giants were betrayed by their pitching and those problems may have had their roots in an August 22 Sunday afternoon game against the Dodgers. Both sides were sensitive to close pitches. Although the Dodgers and Giants had moved across the country, they managed to preserve the rivalry that had characterized their co-existence in New York. After an exchange of words with catcher John Roseboro, Juan Marichal's anger escalated. He lifted his bat and cracked it across Roseboro's head, drawing an immediate ejection and touching off an ugly 14-minute incident that emptied the benches.

Commissioner Ford Frick fined Marichal $1,750 and, more importantly, suspended him for nine days, a time frame that included eight games. The Giants were a pitcher short for that period because they were not allowed to replace Marichal on the roster.

The episode cost Marichal two starts and

seriously disrupted the Giants' rotation.

The Reds came up short in pitching and wound up third. The Pirates overcame a 9–24 start by winning 19 of 21 and finished a surprising fourth in their first season under new manager Harry Walker. Things were so bad early in the year that eventual batting champion Roberto Clemente, who had missed spring training with malaria, asked to be traded.

The Braves had six players with at least 20 home runs (Hank Aaron, Felipe Alou, Joe Torre, Eddie Mathews, Mack Jones and Gene Oliver) but that was the extent of the good news in Milwaukee. The Braves had received permission to move to Atlanta for the 1966 season but had to play a final season in front of the jilted Milwaukee fans. Not surprisingly, the atmosphere was terrible and support was nonexistent. Season attendance was just 555,584 and the team couldn't find sponsors for its game broadcasts. The Braves drew fewer than 1,000 fans for some games. Efforts to accelerate the move by buying out the Milwaukee lease failed so the Braves finished the season as lame ducks.

SHORTS William D. "Spike" Eckert, a retired Air Force general, was selected to replace the retiring Ford Frick as commissioner. Eckert was chosen for the $65,000 a year job from a field whose 156 nominees included former Vice President Richard Nixon, Supreme Court Justice Byron "Whizzer" White, former Oklahoma University football coach Bud Wilkinson and Sargent Shriver, former Peace Corps director.

A happier story was played out in Houston, where the Colt .45s adopted a new space-age name (Astros) for their new domed home. The Astrodome opened for two exhibition games against the Yankees and Mickey Mantle hit the first indoor home run. The Astros drew 2.1 million fans anxious to see a structure billed as the "Eighth Wonder of the World." The surroundings were better than the team.

In a season where indoor baseball debuted, perhaps it was appropriate that one of the game's most venerable legends said good-bye. Mets' manager Casey Stengel fractured a hip as he exited a car following a party and was sidelined. It was the end of the line for Stengel, 75, who was replaced by coach Wes Westrum. Stengel's humor had served the Mets well through the first three years; but with New York clamoring for a real baseball team rather than a novelty, it was time for a new approach.

The defending champion Cardinals were not a factor under first-year manager Red Schoendienst. The Cardinals still had it better than the Yankees, who had hired manager Johnny Keane when he resigned after leading the Cardinals to the World Series. Keane got there at precisely the wrong time as too many of the Yankee players were fading after the team's five consecutive pennants.

Mantle hit only .255 with just 19 home runs. Catcher Elston Howard missed six weeks with an injury. The Yankees' team batting average fell to .235, second-lowest in the American League. Jim Bouton, who had won 21 and 18 games in the previous two seasons, fell to 4–15 with a 4.83 ERA.

This created an opportunity for the Minnesota Twins, who were led by shortstop Zoilo Versalles, one of the most unlikely MVP award winners. Versalles, who had been fined by manager Sam Mele for poor effort in spring training, sparked the Twins, who overcame injuries to important players. Pitcher Camilo Pascual and slugger Harmon Killebrew were among those who missed significant time with injuries.

Pitching coach Johnny Sain's switch to a four-man rotation paid dividends and righthander Jim "Mudcat" Grant led the staff with 21 wins and helped the Griffith family win its first pennant since 1933.

The Twins held off the White Sox, who had thin talent but a brilliant manager in Al Lopez and a devastating bullpen combination of Eddie Fisher and Hoyt Wilhelm.

Other managers didn't fare as well. The Cubs fired Bob Kennedy on June 15 and replaced him with Lou Klein. Haywood Sullivan,

who replaced Mel McGaha in Kansas City on May 15, quit at the end of the season for a front office position with the Red Sox.

Despite their run at the pennant, the Reds dropped Dick Sisler at the end of the season and hired Don Heffner to replace him. The Astros cleaned out their new house, firing both general manager Paul Richards and manager Luman Harris. Those jobs were taken by Tal Smith and Grady Hatton, respectively.

Roly-poly White Sox catcher Smoky Burgess raised his career total of pinch hits to 115, surpassing the major league record that had been held by Charles "Red" Lucas. Another individual superlative came on September 16 when Boston's Dave Morehead pitched a no-hitter against Cleveland.

The summer was marked by some episodes of violence before and after the Roseboro-Marichal confrontation. The American League handed Mele a $500 fine and five-day suspension for seemingly throwing a punch during an argument with umpire Bill Valentine. Late in the season, Cleveland's Pedro Gonzalez charged the mound with a bat in his hand, earning him a fine and suspension. The Phillies kept their squabble within the family. Some needling around the batting cage between Dick Allen and Frank Thomas escalated into a fight that led to Thomas' immediate release.

Mets' manager Casey Stengel with coaches Yogi Berra and Warren Spahn

GAME 1	
Minnesota 8	Los Angeles 2
GAME 2	
Minnesota 5	Los Angeles 1
GAME 3	
Los Angeles 4	Minnesota 0
GAME 4	
Los Angeles 7	Minnesota 2
GAME 5	
Los Angeles 7	Minnesota 0
GAME 6	
Minnesota 5	Los Angeles1
GAME 7	
Los Angeles 2	Minnesota 0
MVP: Sandy Koufax, Los Angeles	

Don Drysdale had a disappointing start to the World Series, but his Dodgers still proved too much for the Twins

tart a World Series by beating Don Drysdale and Sandy Koufax and the rest should be easy. The Minnesota Twins discovered it wasn't.

The Twins made their first Series appearance against the Dodgers, who had reached the postseason for the second time in three years. The Twins were surprise winners in the American League, taking the title as the New York Yankees' four-year streak ended.

The Twins must have thought they were getting a break when Koufax had to excuse himself from the first game of the Series because it fell on Yom Kippur, the Jewish holiday.

Drysdale got the start instead and was knocked out in the third inning by the powerful Twins. Don Mincher's solo homer got Minnesota on the board in the first and short-stop Zolio Versalles' three-run homer highlighted a six-run third inning. Staked to a 7–1 lead, pitcher Jim Grant pitched the complete game and won 8–2.

Koufax worked the second game but lost, despite allowing just one earned run in six innings. Third baseman Jim Gilliam made an error in the fifth that helped the Twins to a 2–0 lead. Tony Oliva doubled in a run and Harmon Killebrew contributed an RBI single. The Twins tagged reliever Ron Perranoski for three runs and won 5–1 behind lefthander Jim Kaat.

Koufax and Drysdale had gone a combined 49–20 in the regular season, but they were soon 0–2 in the Series. But the Series turned around for the Dodgers in Game Three, behind No. 3 starter Claude Osteen. The Dodgers had added Osteen a year earlier in a major trade with the Washington Senators that had sent slugger Frank Howard to the American League. Osteen, a tricky lefthander who understood the art of pitching, was the perfect complement to the 1–2

combination of Koufax and Drysdale. Osteen was largely overlooked on a starting staff dominated by two future Hall of Famers, but he won 15 games in the regular season for Los Angeles and had an earned run average of 2.79.

The Twins had faced him before in the American League, but the experience didn't help them in Game Three. Osteen pitched a five hitter to win 4–0. John Roseboro, who had shown a knack for getting key postseason hits, had a two-run single off starter Camilo Pascual.

Drysdale evened the Series with a 7–2 win in Game Four. He struck out 11 and allowed solo home runs to Oliva and Killebrew. Wes Parker and Lou Johnson homered for the Dodgers and Ron Fairly drove in three runs.

Koufax was back on top of his game and gave the Dodgers their third consecutive win in Game Five. Koufax allowed just four singles and struck out ten as he pitched a complete game. Leadoff hitter Maury Wills went 4-for-5 and scored twice while Gilliam had two RBIs.

The Dodgers missed a chance to wrap up the Series in six games. Grant, working on just two days' rest, held Los Angeles to six hits and struck out five as he pitched a complete game

and won 5–1. Bob Allison hit a two-run homer and Grant made it a memorable day with a three-run homer of his own.

Faced with a choice of Koufax or Drysdale for Game Seven, manager Walter Alston opted for Koufax, who was pitching on short rest. Koufax responded in typical fashion, throwing a three-hit, 2–0 shutout. For the second time in the Series he struck out ten.

Johnson started the fourth with a solo home run off Jim Kaat, one of several big hits Johnson had in the Series. Johnson was 32, a well-traveled player who had spent much of his career in the minor leagues. He was called up when Tommy Davis broke his ankle in May and went on to bat a solid .296 in the Series.

Fairly had the best offensive Series among the Dodgers' regulars. He batted .379, hit two homers and drove in six runs.

Killebrew led the Twins with a .286 average, but only drove in two runs in the seven games. Allison's homer was one of just two hits he had in 16 at-bats.

Despite winding up with a 2–1 record, Koufax's ERA for the Series was 0.38 and he struck out 29 batters in 24 innings.

Sandy Koufax celebrates his fourth no-hitter after tossing a perfect game against the Cubs

CY YOUNG AWARD
AL, NL: Sandy Koufax, Los Angeles

ROOKIE OF THE YEAR
AL: Tonmie Agee, Chicago White Sox
NL: Tommy Helms, Cincinnati

LEADERS
BATTING AVERAGE
AL: Frank Robinson, Baltimore, .316
NL: Matty Alou, Pittsburgh, .342

HOME RUNS
AL: Frank Robinson, Baltimore, 49
NL: Hank Aaron, Atlanta, 44

RUNS BATTED IN
AL: Frank Robinson, Baltimore, 122
NL: Hank Aaron, Atlanta, 127

STOLEN BASES
AL: Bert Campaneris, Kansas City, 52
NL: Lou Brock, St. Louis Cardinals, 74

PITCHING VICTORIES
AL: Jim Kaat, Minnesota, 25
NL: Sandy Koufax, Los Angeles, 27

EARNED RUN AVERAGE
AL: Gary Peters, Chicago White Sox, 1.98
NL: Sandy Koufax, Los Angeles, 1.73

STRIKEOUTS
AL: Sam McDowell, Cleveland, 225
NL: Sandy Koufax, Los Angeles, 317

Triple Crown winner Frank
Robinson relaxes with teammates
Moe Drabowsky (l) and Brooks
Robinson (r) in the O's locker room

The Cincinnati Reds gave Frank Robinson a new address and a fresh supply of motivation. The Reds needed pitching and closed a deal with the Baltimore Orioles, sending Robinson to the American League.

On the way out, one of the Reds' executive suggested that although Robinson was only 30, he was "an old 30", implying that his best days were probably in the past.

Stung by that evaluation, Robinson responded with the finest season of his career. He won the Triple Crown, leading the league in batting average (.316), home runs (49) and runs batted in (122). Just for good measure, he also led the league in runs scored with 122 and dispelled any notion his career was in decline.

The Orioles had a formidable offense, which made up for pitching that was sometimes spotty. Prior to the season, manager Hank Bauer boldly predicted that four of his players—Frank Robinson, Brooks Robinson, Boog Powell and Curt Blefary—would combine for 100 home runs. He was happy to be wrong when they actually hit 129. The Orioles also had three hitters with at least 100 RBIs. In addition to Frank

Robinson's 122, Powell had 109 and Brooks Robinson knocked in 100 runs. In the previous season, the entire American League only had two batters drive in at least 100 runs.

Baltimore had a relatively easy time delivering the city's first baseball championship in 70 years. It was the Orioles' best season since the St. Louis Browns transferred to Baltimore for the 1953 season.

The defending champion Minnesota Twins took a run at the Orioles but fell short. The big news in the American League was at the other end of the standings. The New York Yankees, who had won five consecutive pennants to start the decade, fell to last place for the first time since 1912. When the team started the season 4–16, manager Johnny Keane was fired and general manager Ralph Houk returned to the field to take over the club.

What happened? The Yankees' stars were

The Robinson "Twins", Frank and Brooks, helped lead the Birds to the American League pennant

getting older and the organization had not done a good job of scouting and developing replacements. The Yankees stayed out of the bonus baby chase of the late 1950s and early 1960s. Short term, it saved them from some of the expensive mistakes other teams made. Long range, though, the policy deprived them of a reliable pipeline of young talent to replace stars who were wearing out.

The National League season started with a major off-the-field development. The anchors of the Los Angeles Dodgers' rotation, Sandy Koufax and Don Drysdale, decided to unite in a contract holdout, aiming for as much as a million dollars between them. They were dealing from

a position of strength, having just won a World Series. The Dodgers were a team largely dependent on their starting pitching.

The holdout was the story of the spring. At one point, Koufax and Drysdale signed with a movie studio, threatening to give up baseball for acting. Drysdale had actually appeared on some television shows but no one believed for a minute that the reticent Koufax wanted a career in front of the cameras. The holdout was settled at the end of spring training. The pitchers got far less money than they'd sought but they both came away with six-figure deals, the status symbol of the day.

The Dodgers were locked in a torrid three-team race with the San Francisco Giants and the surprising Pittsburgh Pirates. With hitting guru Harry Walker as their manager, the Pirates boasted one of the most potent offenses in the game with Roberto Clemente putting together his finest all-around season. Clemente, always a dangerous hitter for average, took Walker's advice and tried to improve his power numbers, too. He hit a career-best 29 home runs in spacious Forbes Field and drove in 119 runs to take

SHORTS Two important things happened to the New York Mets in 1966: they escaped last place for the first time and they got Tom Seaver. The Braves had illegally signed Seaver while he was still at the University of Southern California. The Mets, Phillies and Indians had their names put in a hat and the Mets were drawn. They signed Seaver for $50,000 and acquired a pitcher who would lead their staff to two World Series appearances.

TIMELINE

March 30: Dodgers' pitchers Sandy Koufax and Don Drysdale ended their joint holdout by signing for $130,000 and $105,000, respectively.

April 11: The American League's Emmett Ashford became the first black major league umpire.

April 12: The Braves lost their first game in Atlanta, 3–2 to the Pirates.

April 24: Washington's Pete Richert struck out seven consecutive batters but lost 4–0 to the Tigers.

May 1: Sam McDowell of the Indians pitched his second consecutive one-hitter.

May 4: Willie Mays hit his 512th home run against the Dodgers to surpass Mel Ott as the National League's career leader.

May 8: The Cardinals traded pitcher Ray Sadecki to San Francisco for first baseman Orlando Cepeda.

May 12: New Busch Stadium opened in St. Louis with a 4–3 Cardinals win over the Giants in 12 innings.

May 26: Juan Marichal of the Giants pitched all 14 innings of a 1–0 win over the Phillies.

June 9: Rich Rollins, Zoilo Versalles, Tony Oliva, Don Mincher and Harmon Killebrew hit home runs in the seventh inning of a game against Kansas City.

June 10: Cleveland's Sonny Siebert pitched a no-hitter against Washington.

Aug. 10: Tigers' manager Charley Dressen died in Detroit at 67.

Aug. 17: Willie Mays became the game's second-leading career home run hitter when he hit his 535th off the Giants' Ray Sadecki.

Aug. 22: Only 431 fans at Yankee Stadium see the White Sox win 4–1.

Aug. 31: Bobby Richardson of the Yankees, the MVP of the 1960 World Series, retired.

Sept. 22: The Orioles beat Kansas City to clinch their first American League pennant.

Oct. 2: Despite pitching on two days' rest, Sandy Koufax beat the Phillies and clinched the Dodgers' second consecutive National League title.

Dec. 8: Roger Maris, who hit 61 home runs in 1961, was traded to St. Louis for third baseman Charlie Smith by the Yankees.

305

the National League's Most Valuable Player award for the first time.

Willie Stargell also had a breakthrough season and established himself as a quality major league hitter. Like the Orioles, the Pirates also made a smart off-season deal, although it didn't have the multifaceted impact that Baltimore's acquisition of Frank Robinson did. The Pirates picked up outfielder Matty Alou from the Giants at a cheap price that befit the .231 average he'd posted in 1965. Using Walker's advice to take a shorter swing and chop at the ball, Alou won the National League batting title with a .342 average.

The Pirates were ultimately doomed by a starting staff that didn't have the depth to compete with the Dodgers and Giants. Pittsburgh fell out of the race at the end by losing seven of the last 11 games, including a doubleheader sweep at the hands of the Giants.

The Dodgers made a savvy trade, too,

acquiring righthander Phil Regan from the Detroit Tigers. Regan went 14–1, saved 17 games and had an ERA of 1.62. He was a major help to a bullpen that had come to rely heavily on Ron Perranoski.

The Phillies, still trying to shake the stigma of their 1964 collapse, fell short again. Their hopes were hurt when Dick Allen went out with a shoulder injury. Outfielder Johnny Callison, who had been a major contributor, saw his production fall off so dramatically that he was fitted for glasses during the season in the hope improved vision would restore his old form.

The Phillies helped themselves by acquiring two veteran pitchers from the Cubs—Larry Jackson and Bob Buhl. Although Jackson and Buhl contributed, the Phillies would regret the deal for years to come. They traded away a young Canadian pitcher with an unusual name—Ferguson Jenkins.

The Cardinals still weren't able to repeat their

The Pirates' Roberto Clemente hit for both average and power on his way to capturing the National League MVP award

1964 success. Pitcher Larry Jaster did throw five consecutive shutouts against the Dodgers.

Interesting things were happening down south. The Braves' move to Atlanta was everything the organization hoped it would be. Major league baseball caught on instantly in a city that had been a minor league hotbed for decades. The Braves' attendance increased by nearly a million admissions over the final lame-duck season in Milwaukee. The team also showed an operating profit of nearly a million dollars. Meanwhile, the legality of the shift was an issue in the courts. It got all the way to the U.S. Supreme Court before it was determined the Braves were within their rights to move. Back in Milwaukee, local leaders plotted ways to bring a team back to that city. One of the people working on the effort was a car dealer named Bud Selig.

It was a tumultuous year for managers. Don Heffner was fired after just three months on the job with the Cincinnati Reds and replaced by young Dave Bristol, who brought a more aggressive style to the team. Birdie Tebbetts resigned in Cleveland. Coach George Strickland took over temporarily, then the team hired Joe Adcock, who had no managing experience.

The situation in Detroit was tragic. Charley Dressen suffered a second heart attack and had to leave the team. He developed complications and died during the season. His replacement, Bob Swift, was diagnosed with cancer and died shortly after the season ended. Another coach, Frank Skaff, finished the season. The Tigers signed Mayo Smith to a two-year contract when the season ended.

Bobby Bragan was fired in Atlanta and Billy Hitchcock, former manager of the Orioles, took over. In Boston, Pete Runnells was a temporary replacement when Billy Herman was released. Boston hired one of its former players, Dick Williams, after the season.

The American League opened a new park as the Angels moved to Anaheim and changed their name to the California Angels. The National League continued to try to correct flaws at one of its new parks. Artificial turf was installed in the Astrodome after efforts to grow grass indoors failed. The initial plan was to use

Emmett Ashford became the first black umpire to officiate in the major leagues on April 11

the carpet-like surface only in the infield. It was so well received that the entire field was covered in ersatz grass by July and groundskeepers no longer had to wrestle with the problem of maintaining grass under glass.

In March, the players made a move that would have a great impact on the game. They hired Marvin Miller, 48, to serve as executive director of the Players Association. Miller had been the No. 2 man in the United Steelworkers before taking the job with the players' union.

Another color line was broken when Emmett Ashford became the American League's first black umpire. He joined the staff at the start of the season.

In the second-ever June free agent draft, the New York Mets passed on Reggie Jackson of Arizona State to select catcher Steve Chilcott. The Kansas City Athletics immediately took Jackson with the second overall pick.

One of the season's most impressive hitting displays came from a pitcher. Tony Cloninger of the Braves hit a pair of grand slam home runs against the Giants on July 3 and drove in nine runs in his team's 17–3 win.

SHORTS When he took over as manager of the Chicago Cubs, Leo Durocher promised it was not an eighth-place team. To his regret, he was correct. The Cubs finished last in the 10-team National League. Both Chicago teams went for high-profile managers in 1966. The Cubs signed the loquacious Durocher and the White Sox hired Eddie Stanky.

1966 POSTSEASON

GAME 1	
Baltimore 5	Los Angeles 2
GAME 2	
Baltimore 6	Los Angeles 0
GAME 3	
Baltimore 1	Los Angeles 0
GAME 4	
Baltimore 1	Los Angeles 0

The Los Angeles Dodgers were finally defeated at their own game. No club understood better the value of top-quality pitching than the Dodgers, whose considerable success hinged on exceptional pitching and a very average offense.

The Baltimore Orioles turned the tables, outpitching the Dodgers and sweeping the 1966 World Series. The Orioles needed just four pitchers, who compiled a collective earned run average of 0.50, to hold the Dodgers to two earned runs in four games. The Dodgers scored their final run of the Series in the third inning of the first game.

Baltimore jumped out to a 3–0 lead in Game One and never trailed in the Series. The big inning came against Don Drysdale and featured consecutive home runs by Frank Robinson and Brooks Robinson. Frank Robinson continued the hot hitting that had made him a Triple Crown winner in his first American League season.

Robinson had spent his entire career in the National League with the Cincinnati Reds, so he was no stranger to the Dodgers' pitching staff. He had an especially intense and volatile rivalry with Drysdale, given Robinson's tendency to crowd the plate and Drysdale's willingness to

throw inside at batters who took a stance directly on top of the plate.

The lead should have made things comfortable for Baltimore starter Dave McNally, but that wasn't the case. McNally had a 4–0 lead in the second inning, but allowed Los Angeles to score a run in the second. When he walked the bases full in the second, manager Hank Bauer didn't waste any time pulling him.

He replaced him with journeyman reliever Moe Drabowsky, a 31 year-old who had spent much of his career pitching for bad teams. Drabowsky pitched the game of his career, working 6⅔ innings, allowing just one hit and striking out 11. He tied a World Series record for consecutive strikeouts when he struck out the side in the fourth and fifth innings. Baltimore won 5–2 and the Dodgers never recovered.

In Game Two, Jim Palmer outpitched Sandy Koufax, winning 6–0. Koufax allowed four runs, but only one was earned as center fielder Willie

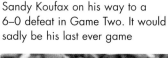

Sandy Koufax on his way to a 6–0 defeat in Game Two. It would sadly be his last ever game

Frank Robinson goes deep during the final game of the World Series. This dinger gave Baltimore the 1–0 win and the title

Davis lost consecutive fly balls in the sun. Davis also made a throwing error in the inning, giving him three errors, which was only half the total the team would amass in the sloppy game.

The 6–0 loss put the Dodgers in a 2–0 hole in the Series. They didn't know it at the time, but it was also Koufax's last game—he would announce his retirement at age 30 a little more than a month later.

Los Angeles' Claude Osteen pitched well in Game Three, but one mistake was enough to sink him. One of the three hits Osteen allowed in seven solid innings was a home run by Paul Blair, which turned out to be the difference in the 1–0 game.

Wally Bunker, just 21 years-old, held the Dodgers to six hits as he won the first World Series game ever played in Baltimore.

McNally got another chance in Game Four and he erased the bad memories of the opener. McNally held the Dodgers to four singles and won the game 1–0. Drysdale gave up a fourth-inning home run to Frank Robinson and McNally made the run stand up.

The Dodgers' weak hitting set a World Series record for the lowest batting average (.142), runs (two), hits (17) and scoreless innings (33). Among players who had more than one at-bat, the leading hitter for Los Angeles was Lou Johnson, who batted .267. The top of the Dodgers' order was especially bad: leadoff hitter Maury Wills had one hit in 13 at-bats and Willie Davis was 1-for-16.

Three of the Orioles' pitchers had ERAs of 0.00. Only McNally gave up any runs and, thanks to the shutout in the deciding game, his ERA was only 1.59. First baseman Boog Powell was Baltimore's leading hitter with a .357 average, but Frank Robinson was the Series MVP with a .286 average and two timely home runs.

It proved to be the end of an era for the Dodgers teams that competed consistently in the 1950s and '60s. They would struggle after Koufax's retirement and they had to rework their offense after Wills got into a dispute with the management and was traded to Pittsburgh for the 1967 season.

SANDY KOUFAX

TEAMS
Brooklyn Dodgers 1955–57;
Los Angeles Dodgers 1958–66

Games	.397
Games started	.314
Complete games	.137
Win–Loss	.165–87
Inning pitched	.2,324.1
Runs	.806
ERA	.2.76
Strikeouts	.2,396
Bases on balls	.817
Batting average	.097

Sandy Koufax's career had everything but longevity. At a time when he should have been entering his peak years, Koufax was working on his retirement speech. His sudden departure devastated the Los Angeles Dodgers pitching staff after a pennant-winning season and led to sighs of relief throughout the National League.

Sandy Koufax shows the strain of a perfect game in this ninth inning action shot on September 9, 1965.

For a five-year period from 1962–66, Koufax's was the game's best pitcher. He went 111–34 with a 2.02 earned run average and averaged 275 innings per season. That total would have been closer to 300 innings a year if he hadn't lost time to a finger injury in 1962 and elbow problems in 1964.

He led the National League in ERA for each of those five seasons, pitched a no-hitter for four consecutive years and won three Cy Young Awards at a time when there was one honor for both leagues. Sometimes it seemed as though the Cy Young ballots should have come preprinted with Koufax's name in the No. 1 spot.

Koufax was born in Brooklyn as Sanford Braun, but adopted the surname of his stepfather at the age of two. The 6ft 2in Koufax earned a basketball scholarship to the University of Cincinnati and spent one year there. His raw potential so intrigued Brooklyn Dodgers scouts that they offered him a contract and a $14,000 signing bonus.

Because bonus babies had to spend their first two years on the active roster of the major league club, Koufax went directly to Brooklyn and never spent a day in the minor leagues. The Dodgers were pennant contenders and had little use for a wild-throwing 19-year-old. As a rookie in 1955, he got into just 12 games and stepped up to 16 the following year.

The Dodgers kept him in the major leagues even after their roster obligation expired, but Koufax was still plagued by control problems. There were flashes of his brilliance. In 1959, he struck out 18 San Francisco Giants. He was on the losing end of a 1–0 decision in that season's World Series against the Chicago White Sox.

In his first six years, Koufax was 36–40, hardly credentials for Cooperstown. His career changed during a bus ride to a spring training game in 1961. Backup catcher, Norm Sherry, suggested that Koufax should stop trying to throw so hard. The veteran could see that Koufax's tendency to overthrow cost him control. He also knew that Koufax's natural velocity was good enough to overpower hitters.

Koufax applied the lesson and had a breakthrough of sorts, going 18–13 with a 3.52 innings. He cut his walks down to 96 in 255⅔ innings. He was better in 1962, then went 25–5 in 1963 and promptly struck out 16 New York Yankees in the first game of the World Series.

"I can see how he won 25 games," Yankees' catcher Yogi Berra said. "What I don't understand is how he lost five.

"You work on controlling nine hitters, not one," he said.

The last of his no-hitters was a 1965 perfect game that saw him strike out the last six Chicago Cubs batters. Koufax's pitching had one flaw—he tipped his pitches by altering the position of his hands. An alert batter could tell whether a fastball or curve was coming.

"A batter could guess with him easier than any other pitcher," St. Louis Cardinals' catcher Tim McCarver said. "That you still couldn't hit him was a credit to his greatness."

Koufax lived with the secret that the 1966 season would be his last. He was alarmed when doctors told him he might lose the use of his arm if he continued to pitch. He left and five years later became the sixth first-ballot Hall of Famer. His career had lasted just 12 seasons, but his dominance over the last six years was profound.

"There was such a gap between Koufax and the next best pitchers," teammate Ed Roebuck said. "It must have been like that with Babe Ruth and his peer group."

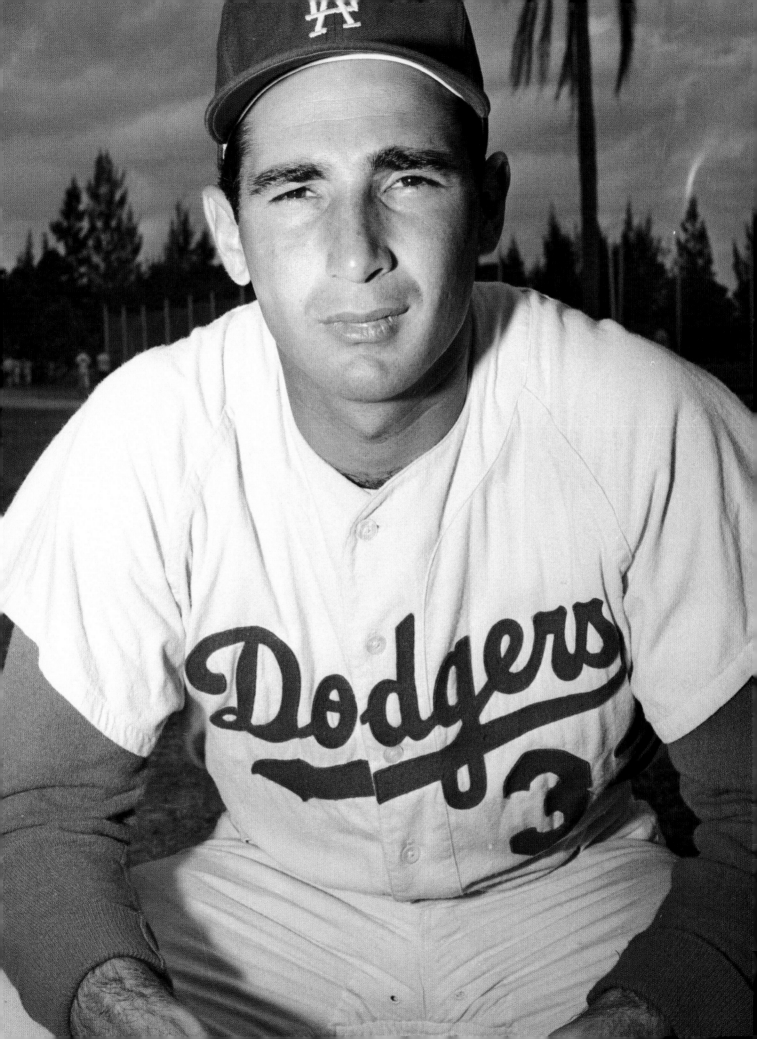

Yastrzemski. Tough to spell, tough to pronounce and, in 1967, extremely difficult to get out. Boston's Carl Yastrzemski had a dream Triple Crown season that year and he led the Red Sox to their first American League pennant since 1946.

The Red Sox outlasted the Twins, Tigers and White Sox in a four-team race that went to the final weekend of the season. In fact, the Red Sox got the news that they'd earned their berth to the World Series via the radio; they were in the clubhouse after beating Minnesota and listened to the Angels' win over the Tigers that let them celebrate.

The biggest reason for Boston's success was Yastrzemski, whose tongue-twister of a name was "Y'tzski" in the box scores and became "Yaz"—a household name throughout New England. Yastrzemski had been a good player since coming to the major leagues at the end of Ted Williams' career. There was nothing in his history to indicate he was going to have a Williams-like year in 1967.

Yastrzemski batted .326 with 44 home runs and 121 RBIs. His previous career best for home runs had been 20. He established a record for most home runs by a Boston lefthanded hitter. He finished with a flourish, getting ten hits in his last 13 at-bats to help propel the Red Sox into the postseason. The Red Sox had finished ninth in 1966, 18 games under .500 and 26 games behind the first-place Baltimore Orioles. What changed? It started at the top, with Dick Williams taking over as manager. Williams, who retired as a player following the 1964 season, paid his dues managing in the minor leagues and was ready to step in when the Red Sox decided a change was in order.

Williams was sarcastic and demanding, the kind of tough guy the Red Sox needed to shake the country club label that had been attached to the team. The Red Sox secured an important veteran when they acquired catcher Elston Howard from the fading Yankees. Howard provided leadership and brought his experience to a pitching staff that needed any edge it could get.

There were a couple of key in-season acquisitions: second baseman Jerry Adair and pitcher Gary Bell. The Red Sox were able to overcome the unexpected loss of one of their best players. Outfielder Tony Conigliaro's season ended in a horrific moment on August 18. He was struck in the face by a pitch from the Angels' Jack Hamilton and sustained eye damage.

Boston's Carl Yastrzemski launches another homer in a season that saw him capture the elusive Triple Crown

Jerry Adair was acquired in a mid-season trade by the Red Sox and made an impact

The mental toughness Williams brought may have manifested itself in one obvious way—the Red Sox were the only American League team to post a winning record on the road. That was vital in their outlasting the other contenders.

The pitching staff was led by Jim Lonborg, who won 22 games and the Cy Young award.

The defending champion Baltimore Orioles were never in the race. One season after winning the Triple Crown, Frank Robinson lost considerable time to a head injury. The Twins improved their pitching staff by getting Dean Chance from the Angels and Ron Kline from the Senators.

The White Sox proved the value of quality pitching by staying in contention all season despite a terrible offensive attack. Their leading hitter was outfielder Ken Berry, whose .241 average ranked 37th in the American League. Third baseman Pete Ward led the team in the power categories with 18

home runs and 62 RBIs.

The White Sox batted .225 as a team, the lowest average for a first-division team in the American League since the 1909 White Sox. In an effort to beef up the offense, the White Sox acquired a couple of veteran hitters for the stretch drive. Both Rocky Colavito and Ken Boyer were near the end of their careers and unable to contribute much.

The White Sox staff was led by Joel Horlen, who counted a no-hitter among his 19 wins. That pitching staff kept the White Sox in first place for much of the year under manager Eddie Stanky.

The Yankees showed that their 1966 nose-dive was no fluke. They traded Roger Maris to the Cardinals and shifted Mickey Mantle to first base because of the limited mobility he had after a series of knee and leg injuries restricted his agility. Bill Robinson, a rookie brought in to take over at third base, flopped big time and batted just .196.

After a tumultuous season in Kansas City, the Athletics got what they really wanted on October 18. The American League granted owner Charles O. Finley permission to move the franchise to Oakland. It was the third move for the Athletics, who had started in Philadelphia. The shift also gave the American League its second California franchise but created competition for the Giants, who were across the bay in San Francisco.

The National League pennant race was virtually nonexistent, thanks to the powerful St. Louis Cardinals. The Cardinals took three of four games from the Giants in mid-August to repel their main competition.

The Cardinals retooled, moving Mike Shannon to third base in order to open right field for Maris. Orlando Cepeda re-established himself as one of game's most feared power hitters and was a vocal leader. Rookie Dick Hughes joined a solid starting staff that included Bob Gibson and Nelson Briles. Despite losing Gibson to a broken leg for two months, the Cardinals won the pennant by 10½ games, the largest margin since the Brooklyn Dodgers took the 1955 title by 13½ games.

After mid-July, the Cardinals never had a losing streak longer than three games as manager Red Schoendienst won his first championship in convincing style.

The surprise team was the Cubs, who finished third. The Cubs' offense was augmented by a starting staff that included Ferguson Jenkins and Ken Holtzman.

The defending champion Dodgers lost

SHORTS

The designated hitter rule, adopted in 1975 by the American League, can trace its roots to 1967. The weak-hitting Chicago White Sox petitioned the League to experiment with a "designated pinch hitter" rule in spring training. The player would be designated before the game and would be allowed to bat twice in the game, provided he made no more than one plate appearance per inning.

The White Sox were anxious to implement the rule because they had 40-year-old Smoky Burgess, one of the game's premier pinch hitters. The rule was tested on a limited basis during exhibition games, then shelved.

The Red Sox faithful mob hero Jim Lonberg after his 5–3 win over Twins at Fenway Park

Sandy Koufax to retirement and Maury Wills to a trade and didn't adequately replace either. Koufax stepped down after an arthritic condition in his left elbow threatened to cripple him. He immediately stepped into the broadcast booth and became part of NBC's *Game of the Week* announcing team. Without their ace pitcher and offensive spark, the Dodgers tumbled to eighth place, their worst finish in 62 years.

Wills angered the Dodgers by jumping the team on a postseason trip to Japan. When they returned, the Dodgers traded Wills to the Pirates, who wanted his speed to complement the power the team already had. A lack of pitching doomed the Pirates and led to the firing of manager Harry Walker three days after Pittsburgh general manager Joe L. Brown had told reporters, "It will be a long time before we change managers."

Players were becoming more bold and willing to criticize management. Orioles' power prospect Mike Epstein refused a minor league demotion and went on a personal strike that lasted 19 days. The impasse ended when the Orioles traded him to Washington, where he could play regularly. Epstein, a first baseman, was trapped behind Boog Powell in the Baltimore organization.

The Athletics' Finley had his hands full with player insubordination and rebellion. After a rowdy commercial flight, Finley fined pitcher Lew Krausse for his conduct, which touched off a firestorm within the club. Later, Finley released first baseman Ken Harrelson after the player had criticized the owner.

If Finley thought he was punishing Harrelson, he erred badly. Harrelson had his choice of six contract offers and wound up signing with the

SHORTS Athletics' owner Charles O. Finley got his long-standing wish and was granted permission to transfer his franchise to Oakland. Finley had been trying to move the Athletics since he bought the team, using Louisville and Dallas-Fort Worth as other proposed relocation sites.

Cubs' pitcher Ken Holtzman helped his team to a surprising third place finish in the league

Red Sox for a reported $75,000. While Kansas City finished last, Harrelson was in the World Series with Boston.

Mantle and Eddie Mathews both reached the 500 home run level. There were retirements of high-profile players, headed by the Yankees' Whitey Ford, who had been doubling as the team's pitching coach. Three pitchers with outstanding track records also called it quits: Vernon Law of Pittsburgh and Curt Simmons and Lou Burdette, both of whom were with the Angels. Bill "Moose" Skowron played his last game, as did Jimmy Piersall.

Robin Roberts, released at the end of the 1966 season, signed on with a Phillies farm team at Reading, Pennsylvania. Roberts stayed there through June but no one wanted a pitcher who had once posted six consecutive 20-win seasons.

Sam Mele, who managed the Twins to the pennant in 1965, was fired in June. Mele had come to be so loathed by his players that they excluded him from getting any share of potential postseason money. Alvin Dark was fired by the Athletics during the season and the Mets' Wes Westrum resigned in late September. Billy Hitchcock of Atlanta and Joe Adcock of the Indians were fired at the end of the season.

Washington was looking for a new manager after Gil Hodges went back to New York to take the vacant Mets job.

Stan Musial stepped down as general manager in St. Louis after he became the first GM to win the World Series in his first year on the job. Musial cited the need to tend to non-baseball business interests and remained as a consultant. His replacement was Bing Devine, who had been fired while the 1964 Cardinals were on their way to a World Series title.

GAME 1	
St. Louis Cardinals 2	Boston Red Sox 1
GAME 2	
Boston Red Sox 5	St. Louis Cardinals 0
GAME 3	
St. Louis Cardinals 5	Boston Red Sox 2
GAME 4	
St. Louis Cardinals 6	Boston Red Sox 0
GAME 5	
Boston Red Sox 3	St. Louis Cardinals 0
GAME 6	
Boston Red Sox 8	St. Louis Cardinals 4
GAME 7	
St. Louis Cardinals 7	Boston Red Sox 2
MVP: Bob Gibson, St. Louis Cardinals	

They called it the "Impossible Dream" and, thanks to the powerful St. Louis Cardinals, the billing proved to be accurate—painfully so—for the downtrodden Boston Red Sox.

The Red Sox jumped from ninth to first in the American League on the strength of career-best seasons from Carl Yastrzemski and pitcher Jim Lonborg. Boston endured in a wild, four-team race to win its first pennant since 1946. The Red Sox pushed the Cardinals to a seventh game before Bob Gibson clinched St. Louis' second World Series win in four years.

Yastrzemski could have been elected Mayor of Boston in 1967 had he been willing to take a pay cut. The man New Englanders called "Yaz" had been a solid player throughout his career, but he jumped his game to another level in 1967. His .326 average led the league, his 44 homers tied Minnesota's Harmon Killebrew for the lead and his 121 RBIs were the most in the majors.

Lonborg won 22 games to lead the Red Sox staff.

The Cardinals featured a talented everyday lineup that emphasized speed and defense, tailored for their spacious home park. Leadoff man Lou Brock had quickly developed into one of the game's best base stealers and Curt Flood was the quintessential No. 2 hitter and a Gold Glove, award-winning center fielder.

The middle of the lineup featured power, thanks to a trade that sent lefthander Ray Sadecki to San Francisco for first baseman Orlando Cepeda during the 1966 season. Cepeda may have been unwanted by the Giants, but he was the perfect fit for the Cardinals. He was a legitimate home run threat and his boisterous personality added life to the clubhouse and helped galvanize the team.

Gibson was backed up by a solid corps of young starters—Dick Hughes, Nelson Briles and Steve Carlton. Gibson's misfortune turned into an opportunity for Briles. Gibson missed two months of the season after Roberto Clemente's line drive broke his leg. Briles moved into the rotation on a full-time basis and more than held his own, winning 14 games.

Because Lonborg had to pitch on the last day of the regular season, Jose Santiago started the first game for Boston against Gibson. The Cardinals won 2–1 as Gibson allowed six hits and struck out ten. Roger Maris drove in both runs and Boston's only run came on Santiago's home run.

Lonborg took a no-hitter into the eighth inning of Game Two before allowing Julian Javier's two-out double. It was the only hit Lonborg gave up in the 5–0 win. Yastrzemski took care of the offense, driving in four runs with a pair of homers.

Game Three starter Gary Bell was no Lonborg and the Cardinals roughed him up, winning 5–2. Briles pitched a complete game, holding Boston to seven hits while Mike Shannon hit a two-run homer.

Gibson ruled in Game Four, winning 6–0

while limiting the Red Sox to just five hits. Santiago didn't make it out of the first inning, allowing four runs. Maris and Tim McCarver each drove in a pair of runs as the Cardinals came within a game of winning the Series.

Lonborg kept the Red Sox alive and won 3–1 to send the Series back to Fenway Park. Lonborg was within one out of a shutout when he gave up a home run to Maris. It was one of three hits St. Louis managed against Lonborg.

The Cardinals scored two runs in the seventh inning of Game Six to tie the score at 4–4, but the bullpen allowed four runs in the bottom of the seventh and the Red Sox held on for the 8–4 win. Bell, who hadn't pitched well in Game Three,

held St. Louis scoreless over the last two innings. Hughes set a dubious Series record by allowing three home runs in one inning: Yastrzemski, Reggie Smith and Rico Petrocelli all tagged him.

Game Seven matched the teams' aces: Gibson and Lonborg. Both were 2–0 and both had pitched brilliantly. Gibson had allowed just one run in his 18 innings and Lonborg had limited the Cardinals to four hits and a run in his 18 innings.

Gibson won the game 7–2, hitting a home run of Lonborg to help the cause mightily. Second baseman Julian Javier hit a three-run homer off Lonborg, who allowed six earned runs in his six innings.

Bob Gibson and the Cards celebrate after his decisive win in Game Seven against the Red Sox

ROBERTO CLEMENTE

TEAMS	
Pittsburgh Pirates 1955–72	
Games:	2,433
At-Bats:	9,454
Runs:	1,416
RBI:	1,305
Home runs:	240
Hits:	3,000
Doubles:	440
Triples:	166
Stolen Bases:	83
Average:	317
Slugging percentage:	475

The Pittsburgh Pirates lost 101 games and finished dead last in the National League in 1954. It turned out to be one of the best things the franchise ever did.

Finishing last gave the Pirates the first pick in the minor league draft that winter. They saw through the Brooklyn Dodgers' desperate efforts to hide Roberto Clemente at their Class AAA farm team in Montreal.

Clemente spent his entire 17-year career in a Pirates' uniform, collecting exactly 3,000 hits, helping the franchise to a pair of World Series wins and becoming an almost-mythical figure when he died in a plane crash while on a mercy mission for earthquake victims.

Scouts discovered Clemente in Puerto Rico and he signed with Brooklyn for $10,000. The Dodgers had no room for him on their talent-laden major league roster and sent him to Montreal with orders to keep him out of the lineup as much as possible. Veteran Pirates scout Clyde Sukeforth was wise to the ruse and told the Dodgers, "You might as well play him because we're going to draft him."

For the $4,000 draft price, the Pirates had a player who would become the cornerstone of their team. He had no problem cracking the weak Pittsburgh lineup and started 118 games at age 20, batting .255 with five home runs and 47 RBIs. He remained a regular for the rest of his career, as much as his health permitted.

By his estimate, very few of his 2,133 games were played without some sort of malady. A national magazine ran a story on Clemente titled, "Aches and Pains and Three Batting Titles". The sole illustration was a full-length illustration of Clemente with arrows detailing various medical problems ranging from tension headaches to a strained instep.

He said he had insomnia but claimed sleeping pills kept him awake. The frequent complaints gave Clemente the tag of hypochondriac, which he resented. It was the source of friction between Clemente and the media throughout his career.

Clemente had been a good player, winning batting titles and earning his way onto All-Star teams. His breakthrough season was 1966, when he batted .317 with 29 home runs and 119 RBIs. He carried the Pirates into the last week of the season as part of a three-team race and won the Most Valuable Player award.

Disappointing seasons followed for the Pirates, and Clemente was again an exceptional player on a mediocre team.

That changed in 1970 when the rebuilt Pirates climbed back to first place and started a run of Eastern Division titles. Clemente was 36 in 1970 and limited to 101 games but he batted .352.

The following year he hit .341 in 20 more games and drove in 86 runs. It is worth noting he had a successful regular season because what he did in the postseason overshadowed that season and everything else in his career.

He batted .333 in the four-game win over San Francisco in the National League playoffs. The national spotlight had at last found him and he wouldn't disappoint. For the nine days of the World Series, he offered a capsule version of his career. He delivered clutch hits, he played exceptional defense and he led his team to a comeback win over the favored Baltimore Orioles.

In their prime, Willie Mays and Hank Aaron may have been better players. At 37, no one could touch Clemente.

When it was done, he had the World Series MVP award and the status that had eluded him. The 1972 season was a victory tour of sorts as the Pirates breezed to another divisional title. The subplot was Clemente's chase for the 3,000th hit, which he got on September 30.

Three months later, the photo of Clemente standing alone on second base and acknowledging a standing ovation would haunt. On January 1, 1973, the news arrived in horrible bursts. Clemente had boarded a plane bound for Nicaragua with relief supplies. The overloaded aircraft plunged into the ocean while trying to take off. Clemente's body was never recovered.

The Hall of Fame waived its five-year waiting period and Clemente was voted in immediately. The Pirates retired his no. 21 before the first game of the 1973 season.

In 1999, the city of Pittsburgh renamed the bridge that leads to the Pirates' ballpark the Roberto Clemente Bridge.

The 1971 World Series provided the perfect stage for Clemente's talents

MOST VALUABLE PLAYER

AL: Denny McLain, Detroit
NL: Bob Gibson, St. Louis Cardinals

CY YOUNG AWARD

AL: Denny McLain, Detroit
NL: Bob Gibson, St. Louis Cardinals

ROOKIE OF THE YEAR

AL: Stan Bahnsen, NY Yankees
NL: Johnny Bench, Cincinnati

BATTING AVERAGE

AL: Carl Yastrzemski, Boston Red Sox, .301
NL: Pete Rose, Cincinnati, .335

HOME RUNS

AL: Frank Howard, Washington, 44
NL: Willie McCovey, San Francisco, 36

RUNS BATTED IN

AL: Ken Harrelson, Boston Red Sox, 109
NL: Willie McCovey, San Francisco, 105

STOLEN BASES

AL: Bert Campaneris, Oakland, 62
NL: Lou Brock, St. Louis Cardinals, 62

PITCHING VICTORIES

AL: Denny McLain, Detroit, 31
NL: Juan Marichal, San Francisco, 26

EARNED RUN AVERAGE

AL: Luis Tiant, Cleveland, 1.60
NL: Bob Gibson, St. Louis Cardinals, 1.12

STRIKEOUTS

AL: Sam McDowell, Cleveland, 283
NL: Bob Gibson, St. Louis Cardinals, 268

It sure was a great year to be a pitcher. A decade that had started with an awesome offensive explosion and Roger Maris' stunning assault on Babe Ruth's single-season home run record, was winding down with the pitchers holding a decided upper hand. Consider if you will some of the things that happened in 1968:

—Detroit's Denny McLain became the game's first 30-game winner since Dizzy Dean in 1934.

—Bob Gibson of St. Louis led the majors with an earned run average of 1.12, the lowest figure since the Dead Ball Era ended in 1920.

—Home run production dropped by 300 in one year. It was down 700 home runs from 1966 and an amazing 1,000 from 1962.

—Carl Yastrzemski was the American League's leading hitter at .301 and went into the final weekend of the season threatening to become the first batting champion with an average under .300.

—The Yankees had a .214 team batting average, the lowest figure in the franchise's history.

—The frequency of shutouts doubled in a six-year time frame. The runs per game average of 6.84 was the game's lowest since 1908.

What happened to cause such a shift in balance in a game that had produced eight hitters with at least 40 home runs just seven seasons earlier? Plenty of theories were floated to explain the sudden dominance of the pitchers.

A popular belief held that pitchers had simply gotten better and more were using a slider as a breaking pitch. A slider looked like a fastball out

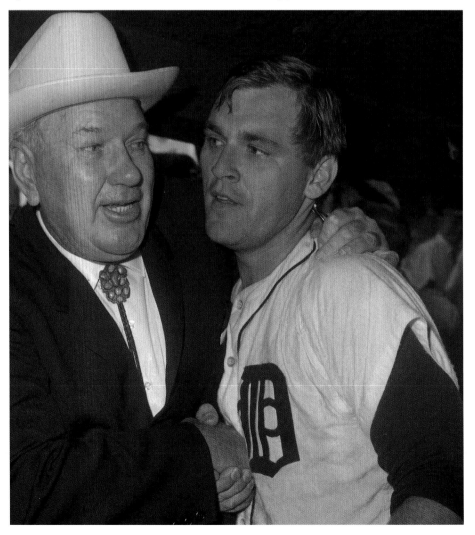

Denny McLain is embraced by Dizzy Dean, after he becomes baseball's first 30-game winner since Dean himself.

Carl Yastrzemski, Reggie Smith and Tony Conigliaro pose for the cameras

April 2: Red Sox outfielder Tony Conigliaro experienced lingering vision problems and returned to Boston for treatment.

April 14: Pittsburgh's Jim Bunning beat the Dodgers 4–0 in Los Angeles for his 40th career shutout. He also got his 1,000th major league strikeout and became the first pitcher since Cy Young to strike out 1,000 in both leagues.

April 15: The Astros and Mets played 23 scoreless innings in Houston. The Astros won the game with an unearned run.

April 17: The Athletics played their first game in Oakland and lost 4–1 to the Orioles.

April 27: Baltimore's Tom Phoebus pitched a no-hitter against the Red Sox.

May 9: Catfish Hunter of the Athletics pitched a perfect game against the Twins.

May 10: Detroit moved into first place to stay with a 12–1 win at Washington.

May 27: Montreal and San Diego were awarded franchises for 1969 by the National League.

June 2: The Cardinals swept a double-header from the Mets and took over first place, which they would not relinquish.

June 24: Detroit's Jim Northrup hit two grand slams in one game against Cleveland.

June 25: The Giants' Bobby Bonds became the second player to hit a grand slam homer in his first major league game.

July 24: Hoyt Wilhelm made his 907th appearance, breaking Cy Young's record.

Sept. 14: Denny McLain won his 30th game with a 5–4 victory over Oakland.

Sept. 17: Gaylord Perry of the Giants pitched a no-hitter against the Cardinals.

Sept. 18: St. Louis' Ray Washburn pitched a no-hitter against the Giants, the first time consecutive no-hit games were thrown in the same park.

Sept. 19: McLain got his 31st win while surrendering Mickey Mantle's 535th home run.

Sept. 22: Minnesota's Cesar Tovar played all nine positions in one game.

Dec. 6: Commissioner William Eckert resigned.

of the pitcher's hand, then had a sudden and sharp movement that darted away from hitters. Relief pitching had become more of a specialized craft; a hitter was more likely to see a fresh reliever late in the game rather than a tiring starter who had already displayed his repertoire of pitchers through three plate appearances.

Whatever the case, the pitchers were in charge. Average pitchers were better and excellent pitchers, like the Cardinals' Gibson, were virtually unhittable.

Gibson was 22–9, the best record of his ten-year major league career. He won 15 consecutive games and pitched 13 shutouts during the season with a league-leading 268 strikeouts.

As good as Gibson was, McLain had nine more wins in the American League. McLain was 31–6 in 41 starts, which included 28 complete games. In his 336 innings, he struck out 280 to set a Tigers team record.

He led the Tigers to their first pennant since

1945. The Tigers had 40 wins from the seventh inning on and spent all but 15 days of the season in first place. The Tigers weren't immune to the hitting woes. They batted only .235 as a team but they had 185 home runs to lead the major leagues.

They had a relatively easy path to the pennant. Baltimore finished second but at one point, the Orioles won 11 of 14 games and still lost a half game to the Tigers in the standings. The Orioles were one of seven teams to make a managerial change during the year, firing Hank Bauer, who led the team to the 1966 World Series victory. Bauer was replaced on July 19 by Earl Weaver, a longtime minor league manager in the organization who was in his first year as the major league team's first base coach.

Cleveland had a good pitching staff, headed up by Luis Tiant and Sam McDowell, but the Indians were doomed by poor offense. They fell out of the race in early August when they lost six of seven games to the Tigers.

Boston's hopes of repeating probably vanished on Christmas Eve 1967. That's when pitcher Jim Lonborg tore knee ligaments in a skiing accident. The 1967 American League Cy Young award winner won only six games. Yastrzemski repeated as batting champion but his other offensive totals declined drastically

SHORTS Don Drysdale's record-setting shutout streak was extended by an unusual call. Drysdale hit Giants catcher Dick Dietz with the bases loaded on May 30. However, umpire Harry Wendestedt ruled that Dietz was not entitled to a base because he didn't try to avoid the pitch. Drysdale's streak lasted until Philadelphia's Howie Bedell hit a sacrifice fly on June 8. It was Bedell's only RBI of 1968 and one of three in his career.

after a Triple Crown season. His home runs dropped to 23 from 44 and his RBI total was 74, down from 121. Tony Conigliaro, who was hit in the face by a pitch in 1967, didn't play at all in 1968. George Scott's average took a serious dip from .303 to .171.

The White Sox made a strong run at the 1967 title but never recovered from a 0–10 start in 1968. The decline cost Eddie Stanky his job. He was fired on July 12 with three years left on his contract. His replacement, Al Lopez, was promptly sidelined by an emergency appendectomy and coach Les Moss became the team's third choice.

The excitement in Washington was limited to watching Frank Howard's power displays. Howard was nicknamed "Capital Punishment" by opposing pitchers with good reason. Howard hit 44 home runs, which included a stretch in mid-May that saw him hit ten in 20 at-bats. The Senators painted some seats white at D.C. Stadium to designate where his tape-measure blasts landed. Washington had baseball's worst attendance so most of those seats were empty and visible.

The Cardinals locked up the National League title on September 15, their earliest clinching ever. The formidable pitching staff made up for a team-wide offensive decline. Gibson led the staff and Nelson Briles contributed 19 wins; Ray Washburn chipped in with 14. Rapidly-improving lefthander Steve Carlton won 13 games.

The Cardinals posted 30 shutouts, a team

record. They held opponents to one run in 31 games and limited them to two runs in 21 others. In more than half of the schedule, St. Louis' opponents scored two runs or less.

The Giants finished second for a fourth consecutive season, which set a major league record. During the season, manager Herman Franks said he'd quit if his team didn't win the pennant. The team held him to that promise and Clyde King was named manager after the season ended.

The Cubs continued to get better and finished third for the second consecutive year. Ferguson Jenkins became the first Cubs pitcher to have consecutive 20-win seasons since Lon Warneke in 1934–35. Jenkins also broke his own team record with 260 strikeouts.

The Pirates were the pre-season pick to win after acquiring Jim Bunning from the Phillies. But Bunning struggled with a variety of injuries and went 4–14 as the Pirates were the league's most disappointing team.

The Dodgers stayed in the second division but provided one of the season's best ongoing stories when Don Drysdale pitched 56⅔ consecutive shutout innings.

The Phillies were bad enough to get manager Gene Mauch fired after a team-record eight years and two months on the job. Mauch's rocky relationship with slugger Dick Allen helped hasten the switch to Bob Skinner.

Despite finishing ninth, the Mets were the surprise team, thanks to a young pitching staff. Lefthander Jerry Koosman won 19 games and Tom Seaver won 16. Koosman, who was nearly released in the minor leagues, pitched seven shutouts and 17 complete games.

The Astros finished last for the first time, which led to a managerial change. Harry Walker replaced Grady Hatton on June 18.

Off the field, the National League approved expansion at a May meeting. The American League had decided a year earlier to place new franchises in Kansas City and Seattle in 1969. The National League chose Montreal and San Diego over Milwaukee, Dallas-Fort Worth and Buffalo.

William Eckert, the retired Air Force general who was serving as commissioner, was relieved of his command just three years into a seven-year contract. The favorites to replace him were all familiar baseball names: longtime Giants executive Chub Feeney, Yankees' president Mike Burke, Yankees' general manager Lee MacPhail and John McHale, a veteran executive who had just recently signed on as president of the new Montreal club.

The Cardinals' Steve Carlton on his way to a one-hitter against the Chicago Cubs

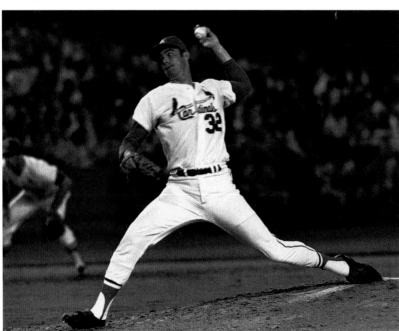

After no one on the slate could muster enough votes, a compromise candidate was chosen. National League attorney Bowie Kuhn was awarded the job based on his 18 years of experience handling the National League's legal affairs. Kuhn, 42, proved to have one trait in common with his predecessor; he was largely unknown to the general public. "Bowie Who?" headlines were commonplace on stories announcing his election.

The Players Association made noise about a possible strike over issues that included pension funding and fringe benefits. Umpires formed a union just one year after two

American League umpires, Bill Valentine and Al Salerno, were fired. The league said they were fired for incompetence but umpires suspected they were dismissed for leading the attempts to unionize.

Umpire Chris Pelekoudas made headlines when he ejected Cubs' pitcher Phil Regan for using a foreign substance on the baseball. The league office failed to back him though, charging that Pelekoudas didn't have enough physical evidence to toss Regan.

Buzzie Bavasi, the Dodgers' general manager who had confronted the Koufax–Drysdale combined holdout in 1966, left his longtime employer to head the new team in San Diego. Bavasi got an ownership stake in San Diego.

Mauch wasn't unemployed for long. The Montreal team hired him as its first manager.

Finally, the first indoor All-Star Game at the Astrodome was a 1–0 win for the National League. But what else could it be in the year of the pitcher?

Don Drysdale gets career win No. 200 against the Giants

SHORTS On August 31, Steve Blass was Pittsburgh's starting pitcher. After one batter, Blass moved to left field and Roy Face relieved. Face got his hitter and Blass completed the game. The appearance allowed Face to tie Walter Johnson's record of 802 games with one club before he was sold to Detroit.

1968 POSTSEASON

GAME 1	
St. Louis Cardinals 4	Detroit 0

GAME 2	
Detroit 8	St. Louis Cardinals 1

GAME 3	
St. Louis Cardinals 7	Detroit 3

GAME 4	
St. Louis Cardinals 10	Detroit 1

GAME 5	
Detroit 5	St. Louis Cardinals 3

GAME 6	
Detroit 13	St. Louis Cardinals 1

GAME 7	
Detroit 4	St. Louis Cardinals 1
MVP: Mickey Lolich, Detroit	

Mickey Lolich's 4–1 win in Game Seven gave the Tigers the Series and won him the MVP award

The regular season headlines belonged to Denny McLain, who became the major leagues' first 30-game winner in 34 years. The postseason belonged to another Detroit Tigers pitcher, though.

Mickey Lolich won three of the four games as the Tigers knocked off the defending World Series champion St. Louis Cardinals.

For all his regular-season success, McLain was a pitching footnote in a Series that was dominated by the irrepressible Lolich and the Cardinals' Bob Gibson.

Lolich, a portly lefthander, was a better athlete than he appeared to be. He had gone 17–9 in the regular season for Detroit, but his accomplishments were understandably overshadowed by McLain's spectacular season. McLain was 31–6 and won his 30th in a nationally televised game that was broadcast by Dizzy Dean, the majors' last 30-game winner.

McLain was great copy for sports writers. He was the son-in-law of baseball legend Lou Boudreau, he was a professional entertainer and piloted his own plane to some of his jobs as a musician. McLain was also notorious for downing as many as 24 sugar-laden bottles of Pepsi Cola every day, a training regime that certainly defied athletic tradition.

By contrast, Lolich was a guy who went out and did his job effectively with a minimum of fuss and attention.

Gibson, meanwhile, had been on the mound for two Game Seven clinchings in four years. He had a remarkable regular season, even for a year in which pitching dominated. Gibson was 22–9 with a 1.12 earned run average.

He and McLain matched up in Game One and Gibson won 4–0 in spectacular fashion. He struck out 17 batters to break the single-game World Series record that Sandy Koufax had set against the 1963 New York Yankees.

There was no hangover for the Tigers as they bounced back and won Game Two, 8–1. Lolich allowed just six singles and also hit a home run, the only one of his major league career. The

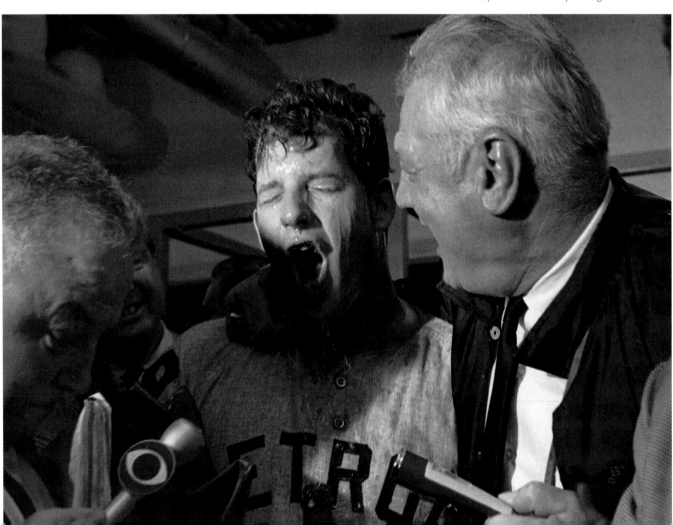

Tigers also got homers from more conventional sources—Willie Horton and Norm Cash. Detroit manager Mayo Smith made a bold gamble in the Series to get more offense in his lineup. He benched shortstop Ray Oyler, a .186 hitter and moved Mickey Stanley from center field to play short. Smith also shifted right fielder Jim Northrup to center to take Stanley's place, which also made Al Kaline the regular right fielder.

St. Louis won Game Three, 7–3, behind Ray Washburn and 3⅔ innings of scoreless relief from a confident Joe Hoerner. McCarver hit a three-run homer and Orlando Cepeda also added a two-run shot.

Gibson ran his personal World Series winning streak to seven games with a 10–1 win in Game Four that gave the Cardinals a 3–1 lead in the Series. Gibson also hit his second Series home run and Lou Brock drove in four runs as St. Louis beat up McLain. The Tigers' 31-game winner couldn't finish the third inning and was charged with three earned runs.

Cepeda slammed a two-run homer off Lolich in the first inning of Game Five, but after allowing three runs in the first inning, Lolich threw eight shutout innings and gave his team a vital chance to catch up.

Kaline had a bases-loaded single, but the pivotal play for the Tigers came on defense. Brock had a chance to score on Javier's single but surprisingly opted not to slide into the plate. Horton's accurate throw from left field nailed Brock and kept the Tigers in the hunt just one run behind at 3–2.

McLain had an easy time in Game Six, winning 10–1 as the Tigers bombed Washburn and the St. Louis bullpen. Jim Northrup hit a grand slam and the Tigers' ten-run third inning tied a Series record set by the Philadelphia Athletics in 1929.

Lolich and Gibson were scoreless through six innings of the crucial deciding game. The Cardinals again had a lot of trouble on the bases—Brock and Flood each got a hit and each was picked off by Lolich.

Flood uncharacteristically misjudged a fly ball to center in the seventh, which led to three runs. It was atypical of the fundamentally sound Cardinals to cost themselves a game with poor base running and defense.

That uncharacteristic lapse in concentration on the part of the Cardinals was all Lolich needed to win his third game of the Series and secure the Tigers' first title since 1945.

Bob Gibson gets his 16th K on his way to a 4–0 win in Game One against the Tigers

It was the year that man walked on the moon and the New York Mets won the World Series. The difference between those two monumental events? The midsummer moon landing wasn't unexpected. The Mets rose from ninth place to first on the strength of some exceptional young pitching talent and an efficient but not spectacular everyday lineup. The Mets had started as baseball's biggest joke in 1962. They finished the decade as its best team.

The transition had its roots in the mid-60s when the Mets began stockpiling young arms. Former Brooklyn Dodgers hero Gil Hodges came back to manage the club after serving an apprenticeship with the Washington Senators. Hodges' firm but low-key style was what the team needed to overcome a Chicago Cubs club that arguably had significantly more talent.

Maybe it was the total lack of expectation that kept the Mets on course in 1969. A second- or third-place finish would have been a major accomplishment for a team that had finished out of the basement just once in its existence and had averaged 100 losses in its sorry seven-year history.

It was a year of significant change for baseball. Because each league added two expansion teams, the leagues were split into East and West divisions, with a layer of playoffs added for good measure.

The season started inauspiciously for the Mets, who lost to the expansion Montreal Expos. It was a clean sweep for the new teams as the San Diego Padres, Kansas City Royals and Seattle Pilots also won their inaugural games.

The Cubs were favored to win the first National League East title with good reason. The Cubs had a solid rotation headed by Ferguson Jenkins, Ken Holtzman and Bill Hands. Their offense attack was strong with Ernie Banks, Billy Williams and Ron Santo clustered in the middle of the order in a park that favored hitters.

Maury Wills faces the Mets' Tom Seaver during the expansion Montreal Expos' first major league game

Atlanta's knuckleballer Phil Niekro finished the year with his first 20-win season

Manager Leo Durocher was the anti-Hodges, a loud, flamboyant presence who loved to be the center of attention. The Cubs spent 155 consecutive days in first place. On August 14, the Cubs were eight games in front of the second-place St. Louis Cardinals with the Mets in third, a game behind the Cardinals.

By September 7, the Cubs' lead was down to two games. On September 10, the Mets overtook the Cubs and stayed in first place the rest of the way. The Cubs lost eight straight and 11 of 12 at the same time the Mets were winning ten in a row and 12 of 15.

The Cubs' collapse was complete. The team

SHORTS The Seattle Pilots' first season was also their last. The Pilots, plagued by poor attendance at an inadequate ballpark, failed to capture the fans of the Pacific Northwest and ran up a large debt. The team was sold to a group in Milwaukee just before the 1970 season. Their final game in Seattle was a 3–1 loss to Oakland on October 2, witnessed by 5,473 fans.

hit just .219 in September. The starting pitchers were unsuccessful; after September 3, Dick Selma was 0–4, Holtzman was 1–5 and Jenkins was 2–4.

The Mets caught fire in early August and went on a 38–11 run from August 13. Tom Seaver led the way with a 25–7 record that included a near-perfect game against the Cubs. Jerry Koosman, the lefthanded complement to Seaver at the top of the rotation, was 17–9. Gary Gentry was 13–12. The Mets also got contributions from starters Jim McAndrew, Don Cardwell and Nolan Ryan.

Outfielders Cleon Jones and Tommie Agee were the best offensive players. Jerry Grote, a rough-and-tumble Texan, rode herd over the pitching staff and spindly shortstop Bud Harrelson anchored the infield.

In the West, the Atlanta Braves were a good team but not nearly as good a story as the Mets. Hank Aaron hit 44 home runs and passed a number of legendary sluggers on the career home run list. Aaron vaulted past Eddie Mathews, Ted Williams, Jimmie Foxx and Mickey Mantle when he finished the season with 554 career homers.

Knuckleball specialist Phil Niekro anchored the starting staff, which also got a tremendous lift from Ron Reed, a former professional basketball player. Reed won 18 games and took nine of 11 decisions down the stretch.

The Braves got hot when it counted most. They won 17 of 20 at one point in the stretch, which included a ten-game winning streak.

The San Francisco Giants finished in second place for the fifth consecutive year. An early season injury to Jim Ray Hart cost the Giants some power, although first baseman Willie McCovey had one of his best seasons.

The Cincinnati Reds had plenty of offense but were short on pitching.

In the American League, the Baltimore Orioles breezed to the first-ever East title under manager Earl Weaver. The Orioles won 109 games and fell two short of the American League record set by the Cleveland Indians in 1954. The Orioles led by 14 games in the middle of July.

Frank Robinson hit ten home runs in April to spark the team to a good start. Offensive improvement seemed to be contagious: sure-handed shortstop Mark Belanger increased his average from .208 to .287. Paul Blair, the best-fielding center fielder in the league, jumped from .211 to .285. Second baseman Dave Johnson upped his average to .280 from .242 despite struggling with back problems.

TIMELINE

Feb. 25: Ted Williams signed a five-year contract to manage the Washington Senators.

March 1: Mickey Mantle retired.

April 8: Kansas City, Seattle, Montreal and San Diego all won their first games.

April 8: Tony Conigliaro started for the Red Sox for the first time since 1967 and hit a two-run 10th inning home run.

April 14: The Expos beat St. Louis 8–7 in the first major league game in Canada.

April 17: Montreal's Bill Stoneman won his first game as a starter with a no-hitter against Philadelphia.

April 27: Harmon Killebrew of Minnesota hit his 400th career home run.

April 30: Cincinnati's Jim Maloney pitched a 10–0 no-hitter against Houston, striking out 13.

May 1: Houston's Don Wilson returned the favor with a no-hitter against the Reds.

May 18: Minnesota's Rod Carew stole second, third and home in an 8–2 loss to Detroit.

June 11: Maury Wills was traded back to the Dodgers by Montreal.

July 9: Jim Qualls' bloop single to center ended Tom Seaver's perfect game against the Cubs after 8 ⅔ innings.

July 16: Rod Carew stole home for the seventh time, tying Pete Reiser's major league record.

Aug. 1: Dave McNally of Baltimore had a 17-game winning streak end with a loss to the Twins.

Aug. 5: The Pirates' Willie Stargell became the first player to hit a ball completely out of Dodger Stadium.

Aug. 11: Don Drysdale retired.

Sept. 9: Phil Niekro of the Braves became a 20-game winner for the first time in his career.

Sept. 12: The Mets swept a doubleheader from the Pirates, winning both games 1–0. In each game, the pitcher (Jerry Koosman and Don Cardwell) gets the only RBI.

Sept. 15: Steve Carlton of St. Louis struck out 19 Mets but lost 4–3.

Sept. 20: Pittsburgh's Bob Moose pitched a no-hitter against the pennant-bound Mets.

327

Ed Charles, Jerry Koosman and Jerry Grote celebrate the Miracle Mets' amazing season

The strong pitching staff was led by Mike Cuellar, a lefthander who had been acquired at a modest price several seasons earlier from Houston. Cuellar won 13 of his 15 decisions in the second half of the season and shared the Cy Young award.

Jim Palmer returned from a season of inactivity and went 16–4. When Palmer's back problems recurred, he showed that he was fully recovered by throwing a no-hitter against Oakland four days after he came off the disabled list.

The defending World Series champion Detroit Tigers were no match for Baltimore, even though Denny McLain went 24–9 and Mickey Lolich won 19 games.

The Red Sox welcomed back Tony Conigliaro, who recovered from a 1967 beaning. They also saw the emergence of Rico Petrocelli as a power hitter with 40 home runs. But Boston lacked pitching and had a messy player mutiny. Manager Dick Williams was fired shortly after he fined star Carl Yastrzemski $500 for not hustling.

The Minnesota Twins won the West with Jim Perry and Dave Boswell each posting 20-win seasons. The offense was impressive: Rod Carew won the batting title and Harmon Killebrew led the league with 49 home runs and 140 RBIs. The Twins were an interesting team under first-year manager Billy Martin; he and Boswell got into a fight during one road trip.

Oakland's Reggie Jackson looked like he was headed for a challenge of the single-season home run record when he had 37 homers at the All-Star break. Jackson cooled off in the second half and wound up not even leading the league.

The offense may have been the result of some rules tweaking. After a year dominated by pitching, baseball lowered the pitchers mound and reduced the size of the strike zone.

It was a tumultuous year off the field, which made it an interesting rookie season for commissioner Bowie Kuhn. The players threatened to strike during spring training because they were unhappy with pension-related issues. The dispute was resolved without a work stoppage.

Curt Flood, traded to Philadelphia by the St. Louis Cardinals, decided he wasn't going. Flood filed a civil suit against baseball, challenging the reserve clause, a part of the standard players' contract that bound a player to a team until the club decided to dispose of the player. Flood had business interests in St. Louis and did not want to

SHORTS Pirates' righthander Steve Blass was a pretty good pitcher—when he didn't have to face Billy Williams of the Cubs. Williams hit Blass well and regularly. Williams' dominance was never more evident than it was on September 5. Blass beat the Cubs 9–2 with a four-hitter. Williams had all four of the hits.

move to Philadelphia, not even for a massive $90,000 salary.

Donn Clendenon became the property of three different clubs in short order. Clendenon, who had played for the Pirates in 1968, was selected by Montreal in the expansion draft. The Expos traded him to Houston and Clendenon refused to report, opting instead for retirement at 33. Clendenon didn't have to go and the Expos wound up trading him to the Mets in June.

Boston's Ken Harrelson was traded to Cleveland but balked at the move. He also cited outside business interests as the reason for refusing to accept the trade. Harrelson eventually went to Cleveland.

The Chicago White Sox became the first team to install artificial turf on an outdoor field.

The season began with Mickey Mantle's retirement in March. During the year, Don Drysdale, the last active player who had worn a

Brooklyn Dodgers uniform, also called it quits. Drysdale was bothered by elbow pain and called it a career just one season after he'd set a record for consecutive shutout innings.

Ten of the 24 teams endured managerial changes. The most surprising was Martin's firing in Minnesota. The Twins decided to make a change after Martin complained publicly about the quality of the organization's farm system. The Twins found a capable replacement in Bill Rigney, who had been fired after more than eight years with the Angels. Bob Skinner resigned in Philadelphia, complaining that the organization had failed to support him in a dispute with star player Dick Allen.

The most famous rookie manager was Ted Williams, who returned to baseball on a full-time basis. Williams managed the Senators and although the club showed improvement, it was not a serious contender.

Braves' slugger Hank Aaron gets hit number 2,900 against the Expos in Atlanta

329

AL CHAMPIONSHIP SERIES	
GAME 1	
Baltimore 4	Minnesota 3
GAME 2	
Baltimore 1	Minnesota 0
GAME 3	
Baltimore 11	Minnesota 2
NL CHAMPIONSHIP SERIES	
GAME 1	
NY Mets 9	Atlanta 5
GAME 2	
NY Mets 11	Atlanta 6
GAME 3	
NY Mets 7	Atlanta 4
WORLD SERIES	
GAME 1	
Baltimore 4	NY Mets 1
GAME 2	
NY Mets 2	Baltimore 1
GAME 3	
NY Mets 5	Baltimore 0
GAME 4	
NY Mets 2	Baltimore 1
GAME 5	
NY Mets 5	Baltimore 3
MVP: Donn Clendenon, NY Mets	

These weren't Casey Stengel's New York Mets anymore. That became clear in the regular season, when the Mets not only posted a winning record for the first time in the club's eight-year history, but also overtook a more talented Chicago Cubs team to win the first-ever National League East title.

The Mets breezed through the inaugural playoff series without any trouble, sweeping three games from the Atlanta Braves.

They outclassed the Baltimore Orioles in the World Series, too, playing with poise and confidence and featuring a wide array of heroes. The Mets took the Series in five games to complete their transition from a doormat expansion franchise to baseball's best team.

The Mets won 100 games in the regular season, second only to Baltimore's 109 victories. They blew past the fading Cubs in late summer and took their division by a comfortable margin of eight games.

They set a postseason tone in the first game of the playoffs when they rallied for five runs in the eighth inning to beat the Braves in Atlanta, 9–5. The Mets took the second game 11–6, then returned home and earned their berth to the Series with a 7–4 win in the third game.

Nolan Ryan saved the Mets in the clincher. He relieved Gary Gentry in the third with two runners in a scoring position, no outs and with Atlanta holding a 2–0 lead. Ryan worked out of that impossible jam without allowing a run and finished the game with seven innings of three-hit pitching.

The Orioles made short work of the West Division champion Minnesota Twins in the American League playoffs—although the Twins didn't make it easy for them. Boog Powell hit a ninth-inning home run to tie the first game and the Orioles won it 4–3 in the 12th on Paul Blair's squeeze bunt.

Dave McNally pitched a three-hit, 11-inning, 1–0 shutout for Baltimore in the second game and Baltimore wrapped up the American League title with an 11–2 blowout.

The Series began looking like the mismatch it was predicted to be. Don Buford hit a homer on Tom Seaver's second pitch of Game One and Baltimore tacked on three more runs in the fourth. Mike Cuellar sailed to the 4–1 win.

Mets lefthander Jerry Koosman pitched six no-hit innings in Game Two. Donn Clendenon's fourth-inning homer off McNally gave the Mets a 1–0 lead. The Orioles tied the score on Brooks Robinson's seventh-inning single, but the Mets found a way to win in the ninth—Ed Charles, Jerry Grote and Al Weis all singled with two out, and reliever Ron Taylor saved the game for Koosman.

In Game Three, Gentry and Ryan combined on a four-hitter to beat the Orioles 5–0. Tommie Agee hit a first-inning home run and it may have been the least of his contributions in the game. Agee saved five runs with some spectacular defensive plays.

Mets' pitcher Nolan Ryan in action during Game Three of the World Series against the O's

Tommie Agie was a human high-light reel in Game Three with both bat and ball

Speaking of defense, it was Ron Swoboda's turn in Game Four. The right fielder made a diving catch off Brooks Robinson's sinking liner to take the wind out of a possible big inning in the ninth. Seaver won the game 2–1 as Clendenon hit another home run. The Mets won in the tenth as Grote doubled and pitcher Pete Richert made a throwing error on J.C. Martin's bunt.

It appeared the Orioles were going to send the Series back to Baltimore. They jumped out to a 3–0 lead in Game Five on McNally's two-run homer and a solo shot by Frank Robinson. But Clendenon hit a two-run homer in the sixth and Weis led off the seventh with a game-tying home run.

Jones and Swoboda hit doubles in the eighth

to break the tie and the Mets tacked on another run on a Baltimore error. Koosman pitched the complete game and the 5–3 win started the party at Shea Stadium.

The key to the Series was the Mets' pitching. Among the regulars in Baltimore's formidable lineup, only Powell produced—batting .363 in the Series. Frank Robinson hit .188, Dave Johnson batted .083 and Brooks Robinson hit .063.

Koosman was the pitching standout with two wins and a 2.04 ERA, and the Mets consistently got production from unlikely sources— Clendenon led the way, winning the Series' Most Valuable Player award after batting .357 with three home runs and four RBIs.

MICKEY **MANTLE**

TEAMS
New York Yankees 1951–68

Games:	2,401
At-Bats:	8,102
Runs:	1,677
RBI:	1,509
Home runs:	536
Hits:	2,415
Doubles:	344
Triples:	72
Stolen Bases:	153
Average:	.298
Slugging percentage:	.557

Mickey Mantle: the game's best-known player on the game's most famous team

That name. That face. Those long-distance home runs. The country boy starring in the biggest city. Mickey Mantle seemed to be out of central casting, someone's idea of how a baseball story should play out.

He came from Commerce, Oklahoma, to become the biggest star on the biggest stage. His star power would outlast his playing career.

Mantle was born to play baseball. His father named him after a baseball hero of his own, catcher Mickey Cochrane. He taught him to switch hit because he knew that if his son could handle the bat from both sides of the plate, he wouldn't have to worry about riding the bench when a manager wanted to platoon. Mantle's grandfather was lefthanded and his father was righthanded. They'd take turns pitching to him to develop his switch hitting skills.

Scouts wanted to sign Mantle when he was 16. When he came of age, New York Yankees' scout Tom Greenwade was there with a contract. Greenwade would later call Mantle the finest prospect he'd ever seen.

Mantle could hit with power from both sides of the plate. He had a sprinter's speed that let him cover ground in center field.

He first came to the New York still short of his 20th birthday. Mantle struggled and the Yankees sent him back to their farm team at Kansas City. When he returned, he stayed and became part of New York's sports history.

As a rookie he batted .267 with 13 home runs and 65 runs batted in. He played alongside Joe DiMaggio, whom he would replace the following year. Mantle settled in as the Yankees' regular center fielder. His star-crossed career would be interrupted by serious injuries. The first came when he got his spikes caught in a drain cover while running in the outfield. It would cause leg problems that would linger throughout his career.

His finest season came in 1956 when he won the Triple Crown. Asked before the season if he thought he had a chance to break Babe Ruth's single-season home run of 60, Mantle replied that his focus was on leading the league in batting average, home runs and runs batted in. He did that, hitting .353 with 52 home runs and 130 RBIs.

He was the best-known player on the game's most famous team. Mantle became a national figure due to the Yankees' constant presence in the World Series. Teresa Brewer had a hit single with "I Love Mickey," on which Mantle contributed a spoken-word cameo. Mantle did commercials and he hit some of the longest home runs in baseball.

When the Yankees acquired Roger Maris, he and Mantle became the "M & M Boys" and staged a double assault on Ruth's record in 1961. Maris topped the record with 61; Mantle had to settle for 54.

By the early 1960s, Mantle's injuries were beginning to catch up with him. Teammates recall how he was wrapped up, mummy-like, in yards of tape beneath his uniform.

Mantle was slowing down and the Yankees were in decline, too. He spent the last years of his career playing at first base to ease the burden on his legs. Mantle decided to retire in the spring of 1969. He'd played on 12 American League champions and in seven World Series. He set Series records for both home runs (18) and RBIs (40).

Mantle was elected to the Hall of Fame in his first year of eligibility and remained immensely popular as an industry developed around autograph shows and fantasy camps.

Mantle liked to joke, "If I had known I was going to live this long, I would have taken better care of myself."

There was a cruel truth beneath the punch line. Convinced that he would die young, as other men in his family had, Mantle often indulged in self-destructive behavior and wound up being treated for alcoholism. The idol of millions of children sadly admitted he hadn't been much of a father for his own sons.

Mantle needed a liver transplant in 1995 and used his fame to encourage organ donations and to warn people not to live the way he had. Facing death, he became a truly heroic figure by attempting to use his dire circumstances to help others.

Shortly after receiving the transplant, Mantle was found to have rapidly-spreading cancer. He died on August 13, 1995.

1970

The most important player in the decade? That's an easy choice. It was Marvin Miller, executive director of the Players Association, who steered his membership through tumultuous times to make the organization one of the most effective labor unions in history.

At the start of the decade, $100,000 was the benchmark annual salary for star players. Within ten years, baseball had $1-million-per-year players, thanks to some court victories and Miller's deft handling of the players' newfound freedom.

Free agency changed the way the game was played forever. Pete Rose, Reggie Jackson and Catfish Hunter were among the early stars to take advantage of the system and sell their talents to the highest bidder.

The Oakland A's and Cincinnati Reds were the power teams of the decade, just a notch ahead of the Pittsburgh Pirates. The New York Yankees came back to prominence with a circus led by Jackson and Billy Martin.

Plane crashes claimed two of the game's biggest stars: Pittsburgh's Roberto Clemente and Thurman Munson of the Yankees. Baseball abandoned the nation's capital for the Dallas market and the American League grew by two with franchises in Toronto and Seattle. The National League got new stadiums in Cincinnati, Pittsburgh, Philadelphia and Montreal and defied anyone to tell them apart.

From their humble roots as the transplanted St. Louis Browns, the Baltimore Orioles built an organization that was the envy of baseball. The Orioles established both a rock-solid scouting and player-development operation, made smart trades and hired the right manager to lead a group that played fundamental baseball better than anyone.

Earl Weaver was a career minor leaguer when the Orioles promoted him to the major league staff for the relatively unimportant job of first base coach. When the time came to dismiss Hank Bauer in 1968, Weaver got the call.

Small in stature, Weaver made his presence known quickly. Just ask any American League umpire who was forced to stand stoically and watch Weaver's dirt-kicking, cap-tossing antics. A good team had the leader it needed, a baseball lifer who was always a move or two ahead of the opposition.

Weaver's managerial skill didn't prevent the Orioles from being upset by the New York Mets in 1969, but it did help him keep the team focused on getting back to the World Series in 1970. Including the postseason, Weaver's Orioles won 113 games in 1969. They bettered that by two games in 1970 with a team that didn't have a glaring weakness.

Pitching? The Orioles' rotation boasted three 20-game winners—Mike Cuellar (24 wins), Dave McNally (24) and Jim Palmer (20). Defense? They had the best infield in the American League with third baseman Brooks Robinson, shortstop Mark Belanger, second baseman Dave Johnson and first baseman Boog Powell, a surprisingly agile, big man. Powell and Frank Robinson led an offense built around the big inning, because of the manager's aversion to playing for a run at a time.

The Orioles spent all but eight days of the 1970 season in first place. When it was over, their top three starters had set a record for wins by three pitchers, topping by one the total of 67 victories posted by Bob Lemon, Early Wynn and Mike Garcia of the 1952 Cleveland Indians. Weaver's career record stood an impressive 124 games over .500 at the end of the season.

The Orioles' token opposition came from the resurgent New York Yankees, who had their best finish since they won the 1964 pennant. The Yankees had a team-wide hitting slump in July that killed their chances to seriously contend. But after five years of decline, the Yankees were improved. For the first time since 1961, they had two players with .300 averages—Rookie of the Year catcher Thurman Munson and Danny Cater. Fritz Peterson won 20 games for the first time in his career and did it the hard way. Peterson won

Orioles' manager, Earl Weaver, gets a victory bath after leading his team to a three-game sweep of the Minnesota Twins for the American League championship

The Tigers' Denny McLain had a miserable year thanks to his off-field antics

his last three decisions to finish the year 20–11.

The Yankees, in the fourth year of a five-year plan, were headed in the right direction and may have made a more serious run at first place if their opponent hadn't been as formidable as Baltimore.

The other big story in the American League East was Detroit pitcher Denny McLain. Just two years removed from a 31-win season, McLain was back in the headlines for all the wrong reasons. He was suspended three times during the season, twice by commissioner Bowie Kuhn and once by his own team. He was in uniform for just 58 games.

The most serious episode resulted in McLain's being suspended for the first half of the season. He was accused of consorting with bookmakers, which led Kuhn to ban him until July 1. McLain's season ended early when the commissioner determined that McLain had been carrying a gun while traveling with the team in mid-August.

In between, McLain got into hot water with the Tigers after he dumped buckets of ice water on two sportswriters in separate incidents—that cost him a $500 fine and a 12-day suspension. On the eve of the World Series, McLain was traded to the Washington Senators, who needed to create some sort of interest.

After showing some improvement in Ted Williams' first year as a manager, the Senators fell back into last place and saw attendance drop by almost 100,000.

Billy Martin, ousted in Minnesota after one

year and a Western Division title, signed on with the Tigers, replacing Mayo Smith at the end of the bizarre season.

The Twins were reinvented under new manager, Bill Rigney, and a thorough personnel overhaul, but the result remained the same. The Twins won the West, holding off the Oakland A's.

Tony Oliva had his finest major league season, batting .325 with 23 home runs and 107 RBIs. Cesar Tovar batted .300 for the first time in his career. Jim Perry won 24 games and the Cy Young award. Dave Boswell fell from a 20-win season to 3–7, but 19-year-old rookie, Bert Blyleven, gave the staff a boost by winning ten games.

The A's season was marred by bickering between owner, Charles O. Finley, and budding star, Reggie Jackson. Jackson's home run total dropped from 47 to 23. Shortstop Bert Campaneris won the stolen base title for the fifth time in six years. Lefthander Vida Blue was promoted to the majors in September and pitched a no-hitter and one-hitter.

Milwaukee rejoined the major leagues, thanks to an 11th-hour transfer of the Seattle Pilots. The future of the team was still in question in mid-March while the Pilots were playing exhibition games in Arizona. The fate of the team wasn't decided until April 1, six days before the opener.

The legacy of the Pilots was between hard covers. Jim Bouton, who spent much of the 1969 season with the Pilots, kept a diary of the

TIMELINE

Jan. 16: Curt Flood filed a civil suit challenging baseball's reserve clause.

Feb. 19: Denny McLain of the Tigers was suspended for three months, effective April 1, for his alleged involvement in a book-making scheme.

April 11: The Cincinnati Reds spent their only day out of first place in the National League West, trailing San Francisco by ½ game.

April 22: The Mets' Tom Seaver struck out 19 San Diego batters, the last ten in a row, in a 2–1 win.

April 30: Billy Williams played his 1,000th consecutive game for the Cubs.

May 12: Ernie Banks hit his 500th home run off the Braves' Pat Jarvis and also got his 1,600th RBI.

May 16: Atlanta's Rico Carty had his hitting streak ended at 31 games by the Reds' Jim McGlothlin.

May 30: The fans got the right to vote for All-Stars for the first time since 1958.

June 12: Pittsburgh's Dock Ellis pitched a no-hitter at San Diego.

June 21: Cesar Guttierez went 7-for-7 for the Tigers in a 12-inning game.

June 24: Cincinnati's Crosley Field closed with the Reds' 5–4 win over the Giants.

June 28: Forbes Field in Pittsburgh closed as the Pirates swept a doubleheader from the Cubs.

July 20: The Dodgers' Bill Singer pitched a no-hitter against the Phillies.

July 21: San Diego's Clay Kirby had pitched eight no-hit innings when manager Preston Gomez lifted him for a pinch hitter. The Padres lost 3–0.

Aug. 12: Curt Flood lost his lawsuit, although the judge recommends baseball voluntarily revises the reserve clause.

Aug. 29: Mickey Mantle joined the Yankees' coaching staff.

Sept. 21: Vida Blue of Oakland pitched a no-hitter in his second major league start, beating the division champion Twins, 6–0.

Nov. 3: The Phillies traded Curt Flood to Washington.

The Braves' Hank Aaron joined the 3,000-hit club adding further to his glowing reputation

season with the idea of presenting an insider's look at the world of Major League Baseball. Helped by a perceptive editor in New York sportswriter Leonard Shecter, Bouton's *Ball Four* was an instant classic. The candor and language shocked baseball and resulted in Kuhn summoning Bouton to the commissioner's office for a June 1 meeting.

The ensuing publicity only added to publicity for the book. Although it had an original projected print run of 10,000, the demand grew and the print run increased tenfold.

In the National League, Pirates' manager Danny Murtaugh proved he knew a good thing when he saw it. Murtaugh had stepped down

as the team's manager following the 1964 season, citing health concerns. He took a front office position with the Pirates. That gave him the opportunity to see the Pirates' minor league talent, and Murtaugh could see the organization had a bumper crop of young talent ready for the major leagues. When his old job opened following the firing of Larry Shepherd, Murtaugh got his doctor's approval and returned.

The Pirates already had Roberto Clemente and Willie Stargell; they were adding Al Oliver, Manny Sanguillen, Richie Hebner and Bob Robertson to the mix. Dave Giusti, picked up in a trade from St. Louis, became a reliever by default and solidified the bullpen, going 9–3 with 26 saves.

Both National League division winners opened new parks. The Pirates left Forbes Field for Three Rivers Stadium on July 16 and the Reds abandoned quirky Crosley Field for Riverfront Stadium, which appeared to be cut from the same cookie cutter as Three Rivers.

The Reds set a team record with 102 wins, and did it despite losing starter Jim Maloney to

SHORTS The Seattle Pilots' home opener was set for April 7. The question was where: Seattle, Milwaukee or Dallas? The Pilots ran up debts during their inaugural season and the other two cities were trying to get the franchise. Milwaukee succeeded on April 1 when a group headed by auto dealer Bud Selig spent $10.8 million to bring baseball back five years after the Braves left for Atlanta.

The Giants' Willie Mays hit career homer No. 607 in a season that also saw him reach 3,000 career hits

an Achilles tendon injury just ten games into the season. Like the Pirates, the Reds had an influx of rookies who were eager and ready to play.

Gary Nolan, 19 years old and a year removed from high school, helped make up for Maloney's absence. So did hard-throwing Wayne Simpson. Hal McRae and Bernie Carbo shared left field. Dave Concepcion made himself a factor at shortstop.

Johnny Bench had a monster season, batting .293 with a major league-leading 45 home runs and 148 RBIs. After several disappointing seasons, the Los Angeles Dodgers rebounded to finish second. The San Francisco Giants ended a five-year run of second-place finishes by coming in third. A slow start cost manager

Clyde King his job and coach Charlie Fox replaced him.

The defending champion Mets showed there's a short shelf life on miracles. Aside from Tom Seaver, their pitching was a disappointment. Even Seaver struggled to get results—he was 14–5 at the All-Star break, but finished 18–12. Injuries knocked Jerry Koosman out for nearly two months. The Mets' last hope of repeating ended when they lost six games to the Pirates in September.

Curt Flood spent the year in Denmark rather than accept a trade from the St. Louis Cardinals to the Philadelphia Phillies. Flood sued baseball, challenging the reserve clause. Former stars Jackie Robinson and Hank Greenberg testified against the reserve clause; player-turned-broadcaster Joe Garagiola appeared in court to support it. Flood lost the case, but the battle was far from over.

On another labor front, the umpires staged a strike that lasted one day and resulted in substitutes working the first games of the respective league playoff series.

SHORTS It was a year for milestones involving future Hall of Famers. Hank Aaron got his 3,000 hit on May 17 and Willie Mays joined him on July 18. Juan Marichal won his 200th game on August 28 and on August 11, Jim Bunning became the first pitcher since Cy Young to get 100 wins in each league.

Keeping his cool at the hot corner, Brooks Robinson continually denied the Reds with his defensive wizardry

The Cincinnati Reds kept making a fundamental mistake in the World Series—they kept hitting the ball to Brooks Robinson. The Baltimore third baseman used the five-game series to show off his defensive skills and help the Orioles to their first World Series win since 1966.

The Orioles spent the 1970 season on a mission. They had a great year in 1969, but ended on a sour note with a World Series loss to the New York Mets in five games. Baltimore won 108 games in the regular season and their 15-game margin in the American League West was the most lopsided win in the four divisions.

Just as they had done a year earlier, the Orioles swept three games from the Minnesota Twins to advance to the World Series. The 1969 playoffs had been close, with the first two games going to extra innings. There was no such intrigue this time.

The score was tied 2–2 after three innings in the first game when the Orioles exploded for seven runs en route to a 10–6 win. They won the second game 11–3 and ended the series with a 6–1 win behind Jim Palmer.

The Reds had almost as easy a time in the regular season. They outdistanced the Los Angeles Dodgers by 14½ games and advanced to the postseason for the first time since 1961. Although the Reds were best known for their offense, it was pitching that made the difference in the playoffs against the Pittsburgh Pirates.

The Pirates managed only three runs in the three games. The teams played nine scoreless innings in the opener before the Reds put up three runs in the tenth to win. The Reds took the second game 3–1 with Don Gullett contributing 3⅓ innings of hitless relief. The Reds ended the playoffs with a 3–2 victory in the third game, pushing across the winning run in the eighth inning.

Baltimore rebounded from a 3–0 deficit in Game One of the World Series and won 4–3 on home runs by Boog Powell, Elrod Hendricks and Brooks Robinson. The first game also featured the Series' most controversial play.

With one out and runners at first and third, Ty Cline hit a ball that took a high bounce in front of the plate. Hendricks fielded the ball and

lunged at Bernie Carbo, who was trying to score from third. In the confusion, Hendricks collided with umpire Ken Burkhart, who was in poor position to make a call. Burkhart called Carbo out, even though replays indicated Hendricks tagged Carbo with his empty mitt rather than with the ball.

The Reds tried the same formula in Game Two, taking a 3–0 lead, but it backfired again. A five-run fourth inning carried the Orioles to a 6–5 win. Powell hit a home run and Hendricks doubled in two runs.

Robinson made a key play early in Game Three, snaring Tony Perez's grounder and turning a certain hit into a double play to choke off a potential rally. It was the first of three outstanding plays Robinson made in the game and his fourth of the Series.

The Orioles won 9–3 as winning pitcher Dave McNally contributed a grand slam home run.

Lee May hit a three-run homer in Game Four to give the Reds a 6–5 win, their only victory

of the Series.

Sore-armed Jim Merritt started Game Five for the Reds, but didn't last two innings. Cincinnati jumped out to a 3–0 lead for the third time in five series games. For the third time, they also lost after taking a 3–0 lead.

The Orioles won the game 9–3 and took the Series, gaining their revenge for the previous year's loss to the Mets.

In addition to his stellar work in the field, Robinson batted .429 and drove in six runs. The Series was a major factor in his being elected to the Hall of Fame in 1983. Paul Blair hit .429 for the Orioles.

Cincinnati's May hit .389 and had two of his team's five home runs.

The Reds' pitching, so strong in the playoffs, failed them in the Series. Wayne Simpson, who was 14–3 in the regular season, was unavailable in the postseason because of a shoulder injury. Merritt was bothered by pain in his elbow.

Baltimore Orioles' Don Burford (l) and Paul Blair kid around with Cincinnati's Pete Rose (r) during warm-up before Game Three of the World Series

TEAMS
Chicago Cubs 1953–71

Games	.2,528
At-Bats	.9,421
Runs	.1,305
RBI	.1,636
Home runs	.512
Hits	.2,583
Doubles	.407
Triples	.90
Stolen Bases	.50
Average	.274
Slugging percentage	.500

Playing on some dismal Chicago Cubs teams couldn't wipe the smile off Ernie Banks' face.

The genial Banks is best remembered for his catch phrase—"Let's Play Two"—which summed up the joy he felt in playing baseball.

Banks spent his entire 19-year major league career with the Cubs, moving straight from the Kansas City Monarchs of the Negro Leagues without a stop in the minors. The Cubs didn't reach the postseason during his career and their best shot at a pennant fell apart in the notorious 1969 collapse that saw them overtaken by the New York Mets.

Despite playing a lot of games with little at stake, Banks was one of the game's best ambassadors and one of its most feared hitters.

"He was a beautiful person and added enthusiasm to the team," teammate Hank Sauer said.

Banks also added power, uncommon to shortstops of the era. He joined the Cubs in 1953 and became a regular the following season, replacing Roy Smalley Sr. By 1955, he had established himself as one of baseball's top power threats with 44 home runs and 117 RBIs.

Banks had a lean build and swung a relatively light bat. He got his power from wrists that were exceptionally strong and quick. He was in the All-Star game every year from 1955–62 and hit more home runs from 1955–60 than any other player. Cozy Wrigley Field helped his power production, but Banks would have been a star in any park.

He was a former softball player who got into baseball at the urging of his father. After playing for a barnstorming team, Banks was signed to the Monarchs by the legendary Cool Papa Bell. Integration would help speed the demise of the Negro Leagues and the Cubs made Banks their first black player. He was an instant fan favorite because of what he did on the field and his bubbly personality.

Banks won consecutive Most Valuable Player awards playing for a non-contending team, which stands as testimony to how productive he was. The MVP rarely goes to a player on a non-winning team, but Banks' contributions were impossible to dismiss, even if they didn't put the Cubs in the pennant race.

In 1958, he led the National League in home runs (47), RBIs (129) and slugging percentage (.614). The following year he drove in 143 runs. He was durable, too. From 1953–56 he appeared in 424 games until a broken hand knocked him out of the lineup.

Banks worked hard enough at defense to win a Gold Glove Award at shortstop, a significant turnaround for a player who had once made 34 errors in a season. The Cubs moved him to first base in 1962 and he spent the rest of his career there, continuing to pile up home runs as the Cubs accumulated losses.

Chicago literally hit rock bottom when it became the first team to finish behind the New York Mets. It was the first year for manager Leo Durocher, who promised to change the Cubs' lengthy run of losing.

Their opportunity came in 1969 when the Cubs led for most of the season, only to sputter at the same time the Mets were surging. That also turned out to be the last full season for Banks, who batted .253 with 23 home runs and 60 RBIs. While the numbers were respectable, they were far from what he used to generate and the Cubs were looking at potential replacements.

Banks played again in 1970 although his role diminished. The Cubs came up short in a three-team race the Pirates eventually won. Banks' season highlight came on May 12, 1970, when he tagged Atlanta's Pat Jarvis for his 500th career home run.

Banks would hit 12 more homers and retire after a 1971 season that saw him hit just .190 with three home runs and four RBIs at age 40. He spent some time coaching and also did some front office work for the Cubs, who were anxious to keep Banks associated with the team. His No. 14 was the first uniform number the Cubs retired and he was inducted into the Hall of Fame in 1977. In Chicago, he's still known as "Mr. Cub".

Banks' career was marked by excellence—and exuberance

The Pittsburgh newspapers were on strike for most of the summer and what a story they missed. The Pittsburgh Pirates, fresh from a National League East title in 1970, rode Roberto Clemente's brilliance and an underrated pitching staff led by Steve Blass to the team's first World Series title in 11 years.

The Pirates moved into first place to stay on June 11 and survived a midseason swoon that saw them follow an 11-game winning streak with a 12–23 stretch. The St. Louis Cardinals swept a four-game series from them in August to get four games behind, but the Pirates rebounded from that and went on to clinch the division in St. Louis the following month.

It was an odd season in some respects for the Pirates. Dock Ellis was one of the National League's best pitchers in the first half of the season, but won just five games after the All-Star break. Willie Stargell dominated the league in the first half, until aching knees caught up on him and limited his production in the second half.

The Pirates were deep enough in both areas to compensate. When Ellis faltered, rookie Bruce Kison came up from the minor leagues and helped the pitching staff. Stargell was surrounded by talented hitters who could pick up some of the slack.

General manager Joe L. Brown made a smart deal in the offseason, acquiring pitcher Nelson Briles and outfielder/first baseman Vic Davalillo from the Cardinals for outfielder Matty Alou and pitcher George Brunet. Briles proved to be a valuable swing man for the Pirates, starting and relieving. Davalillo was an ideal bench player and pinch hitter, the lefthanded complement to the efficient Jose Pagan.

In-season, Brown was able to get much-traveled reliever Bob Miller and he helped take some of the load off Dave Giusti, who was the National League's best relief pitcher.

Manager Danny Murtaugh played his cards as efficiently as anyone and coolly guided the Pirates through their tough times.

The Pirates' two main competitors fell apart in successive months. The Cardinals went 8–21 in June and the New York Mets had a 1–11 stretch in July. Both teams fell too far back to take advantage of the Pirates' slump in August.

Things were so strange in Chicago that Cubs' owner Philip Wrigley felt a need to buy full-page newspaper ads supporting manager Leo Durocher. In his sixth season with the Cubs, the hard-driving Durocher had alienated some of his players. The Cubs added former pitcher Hank Aguirre as an "information services coach." His

Dock Ellis proved an integral part of a Pirates' staff that caught many by surprise

job was to serve as a liaison between both Durocher and the Cubs' players.

Despite the vote of confidence, Durocher resigned in July and took a month off before he was hired to replace Harry Walker as Houston's manager.

In the West, the San Francisco Giants rode a hot start to their first title since 1962. The Giants opened the season 37–14, which provided the cushion they needed. After May, the Giants were 53–58 and they staggered to the finish line, going 8–16 and holding off a late charge from the surprising Dodgers.

Two rookies helped the Giants considerably—shortstop Chris Speier was a solid contributor at the age of 21 and Dave Kingman hit home runs in three of his first four major league games.

The defending champion Reds saw their hopes dashed on the basketball court. Outfielder Bobby Tolan was playing in a celebrity game in January when he ruptured his Achilles

Roberto Clemente's athleticism was evident in the field, as well as at the plate, all season

TIMELINE

Feb. 17: The Red Sox signed Carl Yastrzemski to a three-year contract worth $500,000, believed to be the richest deal in baseball.

March 1: Willie Mays signed with the Giants for two years at a reported $165,000 per season.

April 10: The Phillies opened Veterans Stadium with a 4–1 win over Montreal.

April 21: Pittsburgh's Willie Stargell had his second three-homer game in 11 days.

April 27: Hank Aaron hit his 600th career home run.

April 27: Willie Stargell set a record by hitting his 11th home run in April.

May 30: Willie Mays hit his 638th home run and the run was his 1,950th, breaking Stan Musial's National League record.

June 3: Ken Holtzman of the Cubs pitched his second career no-hitter, beating the Reds, 1–0.

July 7: Negro League players gained full admission to the Hall of Fame. Originally, they had been part of a separate display.

July 15: The Pirates beat San Diego on Roberto Clemente's 17th-inning home run after tying the game in the ninth, 13th and 16th innings.

July 18: Luke Walker of the Pirates lost his no-hitter in the ninth when the Dodgers' Joe Ferguson homered.

Aug. 7: Oakland's Vida Blue beat the White Sox 1–0 for his 20th win.

Aug. 10: Harmon Killebrew of the Twins hit his 500th and 501st home runs.

Sept. 13: Frank Robinson hit his 500th home run.

Sept. 24: The Orioles swept a doubleheader with Mike Cuellar and Pat Dobson each posting his 20th win.

Sept. 26: Jim Palmer won his 20th, giving the Orioles four pitchers with at least 20 wins.

Sept. 26: Ernie Banks of the Cubs got his final hit, no. 2,583, in his career.

Sept. 30: The Senators take a 7–5 lead over the Yankees into the ninth inning of the last game in Washington. They lose 9–0 on a forfeit when unruly fans storm the field.

tendon, an injury that knocked him out for the entire season.

Jim Merritt, a 20-game winner the year before, started the season by losing his first 11 decisions. Wayne Simpson, who was 14–3 as a rookie, was dogged by elbow problems. Johnny Bench, fresh from an MVP season that saw him hit .293 with 45 home runs and 148 RBIs, saw those figures decline drastically. He hit .238, with 27 homers and 61 RBIs.

In the American League, the Orioles won another Eastern Division title with their usual style and efficiency. After having three 20-game winners in 1970, the Orioles expanded the group to include all four starters. Mike Cuellar, Dave McNally, Jim Palmer and Pat Dobson combined

for an 81–31 record as the Orioles won at least 100 games for a third consecutive season.

When first baseman Boog Powell was out with a broken wrist, the Orioles moved Frank Robinson to first and dipped into their formidable minor league system to get Merv Rettenmund to fill the outfield spot Robinson had vacated.

The challenge in the American League East was to determine who would be runner-up to the Orioles. The Tigers took the honor behind Mickey Lolich's 25–14 season and a steal of a trade that general manager Jim Campbell made after the 1970 season. Campbell bundled up a package of unwanted players for the Washington Senators. His return was Joe

Willie Stargell rounding the bases was a familiar sight in 1971. The Pirates' slugger finished the season with 48 home runs

Coleman, who won 20 games, and a new left side of the infield—third baseman Aurelio Rodriguez and shortstop Ed Brinkman. The Tigers missed the postseason, despite having the game's fourth-best record.

One of the players the Tigers sent to Washington was the notorious Denny McLain. The righthander made headlines in 1968 with his 31-win season and was back in the news in 1970 for a series of off-the-field transgressions that resulted in three suspensions. The Senators featured great story lines and terrible baseball. McLain lost 22 games. Curt Flood tried to return after taking a season off to sue baseball over the reserve clause. The suit wasn't successful and Flood found it too difficult to return after missing so much time.

He appeared in just 13 games, batting .200, when he fled to Denmark and announced his retirement in a 22-word telegram to the team's owner, Robert Short. Flood had drawn half of his $110,000 salary when he bolted.

If Washington fans thought they were suffering with the Senators, they got a bigger jolt late in the season—they discovered the team would become Dallas' problem. The Senators were granted permission to move to Texas for the 1972 season at a league meeting on September 20. Ten days later, the Senators ended Washington's 71-year major league history with a forfeit loss when fans stormed the field in the ninth inning.

The Cleveland Indians couldn't do anything right. They loaded some of their contracts with

The Orioles were armed and dangerous as they became the first club since 1920 to include four 20-game winners: (l to r) Jim Palmer, Dave McNally, Mike Cuellar and Pat Dobson

incentive clauses that were judged illegal by the commissioner's office. Cleveland's best pitcher, Sam McDowell, left the team for ten days while the mess was sorted out. Alvin Dark was fired as manager and things didn't improve when John Lipon replaced him. After the season, the Indians dismissed Lipon, too, and brought in Ken Aspromonte.

The Oakland A's breezed to the Western Division title, finishing 16 games ahead of Kansas City. Jim "Catfish" Hunter had his first 20-win season and a managerial hunch paid off when Dick Williams decided that starter Rollie Fingers was better suited for relief pitching. The A's got 55 of their 101 wins on the road to set an American League record.

Speaking of managerial hunches, Chuck Tanner of the White Sox had the bright idea to make knuckleballer Wilbur Wood a full-time starter. Wood was 22–13 and pitched 14 times on just two days' rest, thanks to the minimal arm strain his specialty pitch created.

The second-place Royals featured speed at the top of the order with Amos Otis and Fred Patek and won 88 games.

The season's most bizarre story came from California, where Angels' outfielder Alex Johnson was involved in a series of disputes.

Johnson's problems started in spring training when he was fined by manager Lefty Phillips for not hustling. In one game, Johnson positioned himself in the shade of a light pole rather than shifting to play the individual hitters.

Johnson alleged that teammate Chico Ruiz had threatened him with a gun. When Phillips wanted to call a meeting about Johnson, he asked the troubled player to leave the room. When Johnson refused, the manager and 24 players moved to another room, leaving Johnson in the clubhouse alone.

The Players Association defended Johnson against charges that he was playing indifferently. A psychiatrist found that Johnson was emotionally disturbed and therefore not responsible for some of his erratic behavior.

At the end of the season, the Angels did their best to eradicate the season-long problem. Johnson was traded to Cleveland while Phillips and general manager Dick Walsh were both fired.

Another Angels outfielder had a troublesome season. Tony Conigliaro, who had suffered eye damage when he was hit by a pitch in 1967, announced his retirement. Conigliaro summoned reporters to a 5:15 a.m. news conference to tell them he had no depth perception in his left eye and couldn't play.

Bob Gibson pitched the first no-hitter of his brilliant career, adding to the Pirates' late-summer miseries with an 11–0 win in Pittsburgh on August 14. Philadelphia's Rick Wise had the most impressive performance of the year on June 23 at Cincinnati—he not only pitched a no-hitter against the Reds, he also supported himself with a pair of home runs.

SHORTS Charlie Williams will always be remembered as the player traded for Willie Mays. The San Francisco Giants were facing a cash crisis when Mays was shipped to the New York Mets for Williams and $50,000. Mays moved to a contender and was able to finish his career in the city where it had begun.

AL CHAMPIONSHIP SERIES

GAME 1	
Baltimore 5	Oakland 3

GAME 2	
Baltimore 5	Oakland 1

GAME 3	
Baltimore 5	Oakland 3

NL CHAMPIONSHIP SERIES

GAME 1	
San Francisco 5	Pittsburgh 4

GAME 2	
Pittsburgh 9	San Francisco 4

GAME 3	
Pittsburgh 2	San Francisco 1

GAME 4	
Pittsburgh 9	San Francisco 5

WORLD SERIES

GAME 1	
Baltimore 5	Pittsburgh 3

GAME 2	
Baltimore 11	Pittsburgh 3

GAME 3	
Pittsburgh 5	Baltimore 1

GAME 4	
Pittsburgh 4	Baltimore 3

GAME 5	
Pittsburgh 4	Baltimore 0

GAME 6	
Baltimore 3	Pittsburgh 2

GAME 7	
Pittsburgh 2	Baltimore 1

MVP: Roberto Clemente, Pittsburgh

If Pittsburgh Pirates' fans already knew how good Roberto Clemente was, the rest of the baseball world found out in the 1971 World Series.

Clemente, a supporting player in the Pirates' 1960 championship, made the 1971 Series his personal showcase, rallying his team from a 2–0 deficit in games against a team that boasted four 20-game winners.

The Pirates' opponent was—who else?—the Baltimore Orioles. The powerhouse Orioles won their third consecutive American League East title and advanced to the Series after their third consecutive three-game sweep in the American League playoffs. The only difference this time was that their opponent was the Oakland A's. The Orioles had beaten the Minnesota Twins in the previous two years.

Oakland had a 3–1 lead through six innings of the first playoff game. That mattered little to the Orioles, who overcame 3–0 deficits in three games of the 1970 World Series against Cincinnati. The Orioles scored four runs in the seventh and won 5–3, beating Vida Blue.

Mike Cuellar won the second game 5–1 as Boog Powell homered twice and the Orioles also got home runs from Brooks Robinson and Elrod Hendricks. Baltimore wrapped up the playoffs with Jim Palmer's 5–3 win.

The Pirates had a slightly more difficult path, losing the first game 5–4 to the Giants in San Francisco. It was a bad start since every previous best-of-five playoff series had ended in a three-game sweep.

Pittsburgh broke that trend by winning the second game 9–4. The series turned in the third game. Nelson Briles was unable to pitch, so the Pirates switched to Bob Johnson, who had given the club a disappointing 9–10 regular season after being traded from Kansas City. Johnson pitched his best game in a Pirates uniform, winning 2–1 with relief help from Dave Giusti. Richie Hebner's eighth-inning solo homer provided the margin of victory.

The Pirates, who had gone quickly and quietly against the Reds in the 1970 playoffs, won the fourth game 9–5 and advanced to the Series for the first time in 11 years.

Pittsburgh got a quick 3–0 lead in Game One, but Dave McNally shook that off and won 5–3. He didn't allow a hit after the third inning and was supported by home runs from Merv Rettenmund, Frank Robinson and Don Buford.

Game Two was an 11–3 blowout win for Jim Palmer as Johnson failed to repeat his playoff success.

Manager Danny Murtaugh had a simple message for his team as it headed home down 2–0—they haven't seen our real team yet, Murtaugh said.

Steve Blass pitched a three-hitter to win Game Three, 5–1, against Cuellar. Bob Robertson missed a bunt sign and wound up hitting a three-run homer, a sign that the Pirates' fortunes were changing.

Willie Stargell talks to the Pirates' coach, Danny Murtaugh

The first night game in Series history was almost a disaster for the Pirates. Starter Luke Walker was knocked out in the first inning after giving up three runs and was replaced by 21-year-old rookie, Bruce Kison. The steely Kison shut out the Orioles on one hit over 6⅓ innings, setting the stage for another 21 year-old, reserve catcher Milt May, to pinch hit a tie-breaking single. Clemente was 3-for-4 in the game. Kison also infuriated the Orioles by hitting three batters with pitches, then executing a take-out slide at second base trying to break up a double play.

Briles made up for his playoff absence by pitching a two-hit, 4–0 shutout in Game Five to give the Pirates their third consecutive win. Clemente

drove in a run and Briles had an RBI single.

The Orioles won Game Six, 3–2, in ten innings to force a Game Seven matchup between Blass and Cuellar. Blass limited the Orioles to four hits and won 2–1. Clemente homered for the first run—the second was scored when Willie Stargell singled, then lumbered around the bases on bad knees to score on Jose Pagan's single.

Clemente batted .414 in the Series and stretched his World Series hitting streak to 14 games. He also hit two of the Pirates' five home runs and was an easy choice for Series MVP. Blass was excellent, Briles' win was pivotal and Kison's emergency relief work was a major plus, but it was clear this Series belonged to Clemente.

The spotlight finally shone on Roberto Clemente as he clinched the MVP award with his awesome Game Seven display

TEAMS
Boston Red Sox 1961–83

Games	3,308
At-Bats	11,988
Runs	1,816
RBI	1,844
Home runs	452
Hits	3419
Doubles	646
Triples	59
Stolen Bases	168
Average	285
Slugging percentage	462

The Boston Red Sox were facing a dilemma that affects almost every team at some time—who replaces the resident retiring superstar?

In Boston's case the year was 1960 and the player departing was Ted Williams, arguably the best hitter in the history of the game. While the replacement couldn't be exactly the same player Williams was, Carl Yastrzemski more than held his own when he took over left field following Williams' retirement.

Yastrzemski never had a .406 season like Williams did, but he did match his mentor by winning a Triple Crown.

To replace one Hall of Famer, the Red Sox found another. It turned out to be Yastrzemski, who took a $100,000 bonus to leave Notre Dame and begin his professional career as a shortstop in 1959. Within two seasons he was the player who was trusted with Ted Williams' old spot.

Yastrzemski got a hit in his first at-bat on April 11, 1961, but it wasn't the start of a trend. Yastrzemski struggled to keep his average over .200 and sent an SOS to Ted Williams' fishing boat. Williams came back to Boston, gave his replacement some tips and a boost of confidence and Yastrzemski quickly established himself as a worthy heir.

"Ted liked both his swing and his attitude," said Frank Malzone, who was a teammate to both players.

Yastrzemski was consumed with the idea of being successful. Said former teammate Joe Lahoud, "He lived, breathed, ate and slept baseball."

Yastrzemski led the American League in batting in 1963 with an average of .321 and made the All-Star team for the first time. He also won the first of his six Gold Glove awards that season.

As it turned out, everything he'd done in his career was a mere warm-up for 1967, the Red Sox "Impossible Dream" season. Yastrzemski willed his team into the World Series, helping the Red Sox win a tight four-team race that went to the last weekend of the season.

One of the teams the Red Sox eliminated was the Chicago White Sox, who came to regret a comment their manager made about Yastrzemski in June. Eddie Stanky called Yastrzemski "an All-Star from the neck down", an insult that obviously stung.

After Stanky's words appeared in newspapers, the Red Sox and White Sox played a dou-

bleheader. Yastrzemski went 6-for-9. When he homered in his last at-bat, he tipped his cap to Stanky as he rounded third.

In the last 12 games of the 1967 season, Yastrzemski was 23-for-44 (.523) with five home runs, 14 runs and 16 RBIs. When Boston was faced with a must-win situation in the last two games, Yastrzemski was 7-for-8 with five RBIs, including a three-run homer.

He won the Triple Crown with a .326 average, 44 home runs and 121 RBIs and would have been a unanimous choice for Most Valuable Player had one Minnesota voter not inexplicably cast his vote for Cesar Tovar of the hometown Twins.

The Red Sox came up short in the World Series against St. Louis, which was no fault of Yastrzemski. He batted .400 with three home runs in the seven-game Series.

Yastrzemski would repeat as batting champion in 1968 (with an average of .301), but it was the last time he led the league in one of the major offensive categories. He continued to be a regular on the All-Star team, though, and won Gold Gloves in half of his 12 seasons as a left fielder.

In 1979, he collected his 3,000th career hit and stuck around four more seasons to increase his total to 3,419. Yastrzemski never played on a World Series winner in Boston, but batted .352 in 14 Series games and .455 in his only playoff appearance.

He will always be remembered for one of his most frustrating moments—the Red Sox lost a one-game playoff to the New York Yankees for the American League East title in 1978. Yastrzemski popped up to end the game and complete the collapse that saw the Red Sox blow a large lead.

On balance, though, no Red Sox fan could quarrel with Yastrzemski's contributions. The accomplishment that made him proudest was getting 3,000 hits and 400 home runs, something that neither Joe DiMaggio, Lou Gehrig nor even his Boston idol Ted Williams could achieve in their distinguished careers.

"They were Cadillacs," Yastrzemski said. "I'm a Chevrolet."

He retired from Major League baseball in 1983 and was elected to the Hall of Fame in 1989.

After replacing one Red Sox legend in left field, Yaz became a Red Sox hero, too

HARMON KILLEBREW

Minnesota's Metropolitan Stadium was demolished in the 1980s. The wrecking ball finished a job that Harmon Killebrew had started 20 years earlier.

Killebrew was the Minnesota Twins' squatty slugger who literally wrecked a pair of upper-deck seats with the power of one of his blasts. It was one of the 573 home runs that Killebrew had hit in a 22-year career that earned him a spot in the Hall of Fame. As a lasting tribute to Killebrew's muscle, the Twins left those seats in disrepair in an unconventional monument.

Killebrew hit at least 40 home runs eight times and led the American League in six of those seasons. He also led the league in RBIs three times en route to a career total of 1,584.

Scouts found Killebrew, even though he hailed from a rural Idaho town near the Oregon border. He spurned a football scholarship to the University of Oregon when baseball scouts came offering bonus money. He gave up his dream of playing for the Boston Red Sox when the Washington Senators made the best offer—a $4,000 signing bonus and the promise of a $6,000 salary for each of his first three years.

Killebrew couldn't play his natural position because the Senators had Eddie Yost at third base. He moved to second base, one of many position shifts he'd make in his long career. Killebrew played regularly at second, third, left field and first base before finishing his career as a designated hitter.

He became a regular in 1959 when Pete Runnels' injury cleared a spot at second base and Killebrew hit two home runs in his first game as Runnels' replacement.

Once he made his way into the lineup, Killebrew became a long-term fixture for the Senators, who moved to Minnesota in 1961 and were renamed the Twins.

"I was apprehensive about moving to Minnesota, but it all worked out," Killebrew said.

Metropolitan Stadium was hitter-friendly. He became both the Twins' biggest star and their most popular player. He hosted a pre-game television show for 12 years. The post-game show often featured highlights of Killebrew's home runs.

He cleared the left field roof at Detroit's Tiger Stadium with a shot off Jim Bunning in 1962 and broke the seats at Metropolitan Stadium five years later. From 1962–64, he led the League in home runs every year.

Killebrew hit 11 home runs in the final 12 games of 1962 to take the title. His chances of a fourth straight title vanished when he missed seven weeks of the 1965 season with a dislocated elbow. He was back in time to help the Twins stretch the Los Angeles Dodgers to seven games in the World Series.

The Twins developed a team around Killebrew and became contenders, burying the reputation for mediocrity that they had developed as the Senators.

Minnesota went to the wire in 1967, before falling short in a three-team race. Killebrew missed significant time in 1968 when he injured a hamstring during the All-Star game. He rebounded for his best season in 1969—49 home runs, 140 RBIs and an amazing 145 walks. He led the Twins to the first American League West title and was voted the American League's Most Valuable Player.

Killebrew hit 41 home runs in 1970 as the Twins repeated as division champions. His total dropped to 28 in 1971, although he still drove in 114 runs. One of those home runs was his 500th, hit off Baltimore's Mike Cuellar on August 19. At the time he was the tenth player in history to reach that level.

In 1972 Killebrew hit 26 home runs and it was becoming clear that his career was on the wane. He wound up staying with the Twins through 1974. Friction with the front office led to a mutual decision to part company and Killebrew played one final season with the Kansas City Royals.

Killebrew retired as the fifth most prolific home run hitter in history and second only to Babe Ruth among American League players. He was third in frequency of home runs, trailing Ruth and Ralph Kiner.

In 1984, 30 years after he signed that first professional contract, Killebrew became the first Twins player to be elected to the Hall of Fame.

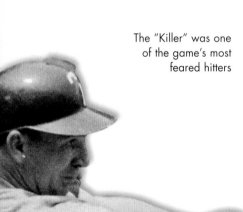

The "Killer" was one of the game's most feared hitters

MOST VALUABLE PLAYER
AL: Dick Allen, Chicago White Sox
NL: Johnny Bench, Cincinnati

CY YOUNG AWARD
AL: Gaylord Perry, Cleveland
NL: Steve Carlton, Philadelphia Phillies

ROOKIE OF THE YEAR
AL: Carlton Fisk, Boston Red Sox
NL: Jon Matlack, NY Mets

LEADERS
BATTING AVERAGE
AL: Rod Carew, Minnesota, .318
NL: Billy Williams, Chicago Cubs, .333

HOME RUNS
AL: Dick Allen, Chicago White Sox, 37
NL: Johnny Bench, Cincinnati, 40

RUNS BATTED IN
AL: Dick Allen, Chicago White Sox, 113
NL: Johnny Bench, Cincinnati, 125

STOLEN BASES
AL: Bert Campaneris, Oakland, 52
NL: Lou Brock, St. Louis Cardinals, 63

PITCHING VICTORIES
AL: Gaylord Perry, Cleveland; Wilbur Wood,
Chicago White Sox, 24
NL: Steve Carlton, Philadelphia Phillies, 27

EARNED RUN AVERAGE
AL: Luis Tiant, Boston Red Sox, 1.91
NL: Steve Carlton, Philadelphia Phillies, 1.97

STRIKEOUTS
AL: Nolan Ryan, California, 329
NL: Steve Carlton, Philadelphia Phillies, 310

SAVES
AL: Sparky Lyle, NY Yankees, 35
NL: Clay Carroll, Cincinnati, 37

Oakland A's owner Charles O. Finley was baseball's best-known maverick, a reputation that masked a big secret. Finley was also one of the game's sharpest operators. By 1972, Finley's intuitive feel for the game was obvious as he assembled a formidable team that wound up winning the World Series.

The Indians' Gaylord Perry wrapped up the Cy Young Award thanks to a 24–16 regular season

Finley had been a thorn in the side of the baseball establishment from the time he bought the struggling Kansas City Athletics in the early 1960s. In short order, Finley discarded the drab traditional uniforms the A's had been wearing and outfitted them in gaudy green and gold with white shoes. He hired a female play-by-play announcer and advocated the use of orange baseballs.

He changed managers impulsively, often calling them in the dugout from his Chicago base to question strategy. From the first moment he bought the team, he was angling for ways to move it out of Kansas City and to a more lucrative market. Finley used both Dallas and Louisville as suitors before he was finally permitted to

Johnny Bench's tenacity behind the plate epitomized his 1972 season as he won the NL MVP

TIMELINE

Jan. 19: Sandy Koufax was elected to the Hall of Fame at 36, the youngest age of any inductee.

Feb. 25: The Cardinals traded Steve Carlton to the Phillies for Rick Wise.

March 30: The players authorized a strike vote: 663 were in favor, ten were against it and two abstained.

April 2: Mets' manager, Gil Hodges, died of a heart attack two days before his 48th birthday.

April 13: The strike ended with an abbreviated season to begin in two days.

April 16: Burt Hooton of the Cubs pitched a no-hitter against the Phillies.

April 21: The Texas Rangers played their first home game and beat the Angels, 7–6.

May 11: The Giants traded Willie Mays to the Mets.

May 14: Mays hit a game-winning home run against the Giants.

June 18: The U.S. Supreme Court upheld lower court decisions and ruled against Curt Flood's suit against baseball.

July 8: Detroit pitcher John Hiller came back 18 months after suffering a heart attack.

July 21: The Dodgers released Hoyt Wilhelm just short of his 49th birthday and after 1,070 career appearances.

Aug. 1: San Diego's Nate Colbert had five home runs and 13 RBIs in a doubleheader against the Braves.

Aug. 21: Steve Carlton's 15-game winning streak ended with a 2–1 loss to the Braves in 11 innings.

Sept. 2: Milt Pappas of the Cubs pitched a no-hitter against the Padres and lost the perfect game with a two-out walk to Larry Stahl with two out in the ninth.

Sept. 30: The Pirates' Roberto Clemente got his 3,000th hit.

Oct. 4: Ted Williams managed his last game.

Oct. 24: Jackie Robinson died at 53.

Nov. 28: The Dodgers traded Frank Robinson to the Angels after a single season in Los Angeles.

Dec. 31: Roberto Clemente died in a plane crash off the coast of Puerto Rico.

invade the Bay Area and intrude on the market the San Francisco Giants had held exclusively.

Some of Finley's unconventional ideas were solid and reluctantly adopted by baseball. Finley was the first to suggest that the World Series should open on a Saturday, so that a full seven-game Series would occupy two weekends and draw a bigger television audience. Finley suggested that weekday Series games be played at night for the same reason.

Finley advocated specialization and took the designated hitter concept a step further—his rosters included track stars with no baseball background whose sole purpose was to pinch run at important junctures in games.

Finley was the brash insurance man in the loud jacket who had crashed baseball's staid party. He found the game stuffy and tried to liven it up with a mule mascot he immodestly named "Charlie O."

People who fixated on Finley's unconventional style missed his substance. Despite having the smallest front office staff in baseball (by design), he put together a team that had all the components to dominate.

Finley's A's made the postseason in 1971, but fell to Baltimore in the playoffs. They were back again, thanks mostly to a skillful pitching staff led by Jim "Catfish" Hunter, a North Carolina farm boy whose nickname came from a fib concocted by the publicity conscious Finley. Hunter was 21–7 with a 2.04 earned run average and became the first Athletics' pitcher to have consecutive 20-win seasons since Lefty Grove.

Despite a spring holdout, Vida Blue went 20–4. Another lefthander, Ken Holtzman, came in a trade from the Chicago Cubs and won 19 games. In the bullpen, Rollie Fingers won 11 games and saved 21 others.

The offense was good enough, but not spectacular. Joe Rudi hit .305, the fifth-best average in the American League.

The A's used 11 different second basemen during the season, largely because of a bizarre strategy. The A's didn't have a solid offensive player at second, so whenever that spot came up in a run-scoring situation, manager Dick Williams would use a pinch hitter—even early in games. The suggestion had come from Finley. The A's held off the rapidly improving White Sox, who flourished in Chuck Tanner's first full season as manager. Wilbur Wood led the staff with 24 wins and Stan Bahnsen, stolen in a trade from the New York Yankees, went 21–16. The bullpen got a boost from the addition of Terry Forster, a 20-year-old lefthander who went 6–5 and saved 29 games.

The biggest addition was Dick Allen, who had worn out his welcome with three other clubs. Tanner ignored that baggage though and leaned on a hometown connection—both Allen and Tanner were both from western Pennsylvania and got along famously. Allen responded with a huge season—a .308 average, 37 home runs and 113 RBIs.

The Twins' combination of good pitching and poor offense got manager Bill Rigney fired less than two years after he'd won a divisional title. Frank Quilici replaced him.

The Kansas City Royals slipped, too, and that resulted in Jack McKeon taking over from Bob Lemon.

The California Angels didn't do much, but it wasn't Nolan Ryan's fault. Energized by a fresh start after his trade from the New York Mets, Ryan had 329 strikeouts, the fourth-highest total in history. He loved his new home park, too. Ryan was 13–8 at home and opponents hit just .143 against him. He had 11 starts in which he allowed four hits or fewer.

The Washington Senators became the Texas Rangers, but a new address didn't prevent another last-place finish. Frank Howard, the biggest star in the Washington years, was sold to Detroit on waivers and manager Ted Williams threw in the towel, resigning after nearly four years. Attendance increased fewer than 8,000 over the last year in Washington.

In the East, the Tigers overcame weak offense with pitching and defense and beat out the Boston Red Sox on the season's next to last day. Mickey Lolich won 22 games and shortstop Ed Brinkman had a streak of 72 errorless games. Al Kaline's .313 average was his best since 1961.

The Red Sox could blame their shortfall on a scheduling issue that resulted from the players' strike that delayed the start of the season. The players walked after reaching an impasse on pension and benefit issues. When the season finally started, it was determined that an abbreviated schedule would be played. Because of schedule open days, that meant the teams didn't necessarily play the same number of games.

The Red Sox played one game less than the Tigers and that was a factor in their coming up short at the end. After three years on top of the Eastern Division, the Baltimore Orioles fell, mostly because of a weak offense. The Orioles had four 20-game winners in 1971, but only Jim Palmer repeated that feat. Dave McNally fell to

Willie Mays hit a game-winning home run for the Mets against his former team—San Francisco

Roberto Clemente collected his 3,000th hit, but the year would end in tragedy when Clemente died in a plane crash as he helped organize supplies for the Nicaraguan earthquake victims

13–17, but in nine games the Orioles supported him with just one run.

After making the ill-advised trade that sent Bahnsen to the White Sox, the Yankees benefited from a better deal. Sparky Lyle came over from the Red Sox and had 29 saves.

The only attraction in Cleveland was Gaylord Perry, who had been traded from the San Francisco Giants. Perry had 24 wins, or 33 percent of his team's total. He became the sixth player to have 20-win seasons in both leagues.

After a one-year hiatus the Cincinnati Reds were back on top the National League West. Johnny Bench rebounded from a poor season to post numbers that won him the Most Valuable Player award, including 40 home runs and 125 RBIs.

Pete Rose had his eighth consecutive .300 season and Joe Morgan, newly acquired from Houston, hit a career-best .292 and scored 122 runs. The strength of the pitching staff was the bullpen, where Clay Carroll, Pedro Borbon and Tom Hall combined for 56 saves.

Houston had its best season, but couldn't catch the Reds. Lee May, who went to the Astros in the Morgan trade, hit 29 homers and drove in 98 runs. Cesar Cedeno was an emerging star with a .320 average.

The Dodgers had strong pitching but bad defense, averaging more than one error per game. The defending champion Giants slumped to fifth. Willie McCovey missed time with a broken arm, McDowell was a major disappointment at 10–8 and the cash-strapped Giants traded Willie Mays to the Mets in May.

It was a familiar story in the East with the Pirates winning their third consecutive title. This time it was under Bill Virdon, who took over as manager when Danny Murtaugh retired as a World Series winner. The Pirates were last on May 11, but took over first on June 18 and stayed there. They had nine players with at least 100 hits and Steve Blass, the pitching hero of the 1971 World Series, won 19 games.

Despite starting just once in a stretch of 40 midsummer games, Roberto Clemente collected his 3,000th hit on September 28. His double into the gap off the Mets' Jon Matlack was also his last regular season hit.

The Mets' fortunes forever changed on April 2 when manager Gil Hodges collapsed and died of a heart attack after returning from a golf outing. Yogi Berra took over from Hodges.

The big story in the East was Steve Carlton, who had been traded to the Philadelphia Phillies for Rick Wise by the St. Louis Cardinals. Despite being on a terrible team, Carlton was the league's best pitcher, winning 27 games. He led the league in wins, games started, complete games, innings, strikeouts and ERA. The Phillies only won 59 games, which meant that Carlton accounted for nearly 46 percent of his team's victories.

Philadelphia was the site of one of the game's ten managerial changes as Paul Owens stepped in from his front office role after Frank Lucchesi was fired.

San Diego fired its original manager, Preston Gomez, and hired Don Zimmer. Del Crandall took over from Dave Bristol in Milwaukee, Eddie Mathews replaced Luman Harris in Atlanta and Bobby Winkles followed Del Rice with the Angels.

SHORTS Charlie Williams will always be remembered as the player traded for Willie Mays. The San Francisco Giants were facing a cash crisis when Mays was shipped to the New York Mets for Williams and $50,000. Mays moved to a contender and was able to finish his career in the city where it had begun.

AL CHAMPIONSHIP SERIES

GAME 1
Oakland 3   Detroit 2

GAME 2
Oakland 5   Detroit 0

GAME 3
Detroit 3   Oakland 0

GAME 4
Detroit 4   Oakland 3

GAME 5
Oakland 2   Detroit 1

NL CHAMPIONSHIP SERIES

GAME 1
Pittsburgh 5   Cincinnati 1

GAME 2
Cincinnati 5   Pittsburgh 3

GAME 3
Pittsburgh 3   Cincinnati 2

GAME 4
Cincinnati 7   Pittsburgh 1

GAME 5
Cincinnati 4   Pittsburgh 3

WORLD SERIES

GAME 1
Oakland 3   Cincinnati 2

GAME 2
Oakland 2   Cincinnati 1

GAME 3
Cincinnati 1   Oakland 0

GAME 4
Oakland 3   Cincinnati 2

GAME 5
Cincinnati 5   Oakland 4

GAME 6
Cincinnati 8   Oakland 1

GAME 7
Oakland 3   Cincinnati 1

MVP: Gene Tenace, Oakland

The Athletics were better known for their changes of address than their success.

The Philadelphia Athletics had been a charter franchise in the American League and won five World Series before moving to Kansas City in 1955. The proud legacy of the Athletics stayed in Philadelphia; the Kansas City Athletics were a punching bag for the best teams in the American League. They also served as a de facto farm club for the New York Yankees, thanks to a series of bad trades for over-the-hill Yankees veterans.

The Athletics had only been in Kansas City for six years when they were purchased by Charles O. Finley, a brash businessman from Chicago who had made a fortune selling insurance. Almost immediately, Finley was shopping for a new location, always without the American League's approval.

Finley tried Louisville. Then Dallas-Fort Worth. Toronto was a factor. Then Oakland became a serious suitor in the mid-1960s. Finley's A's finished the 1967 season in Kansas City, then invaded the Bay Area, infringing on the territory the San Francisco Giants had staked out on their 1958 move west.

But after decades of losing, the A's had changed more than their zip code. Finley had a knack for hiring smart baseball people and always had the smallest front office staff in baseball. He quickly amassed young talent and the A's were on the verge of breaking through as one of the game's finest teams.

They won the American League West in 1971 but lost the playoffs in three games to the Baltimore Orioles. They took the West again in 1972, this time knocking off the Detroit Tigers to participate in their first World Series since 1931.

In typical A's fashion, they couldn't do it without a controversy. The series went the limit for the first time in the short history of the playoffs and was marred by a bench-clearing fight in the sec-

A's owner Charles O. Finley (l) tried to keep the A's on the move

ond game. A's shortstop Bert Campaneris felt that Detroit pitcher Lerrin LaGrow was throwing at him. Campaneris responded by flinging his bat at the pitcher, touching off the brawl and earning Campaneris a suspension for the rest of the series.

When they weren't fighting, the A's and Tigers were playing compelling baseball. Oakland took the first game 3–2 in 11 innings, scoring twice after the Tigers had taken the lead in the top of the 11th. Blue Moon Odom pitched a three-hit, 5–0 shutout to win the rowdy second game. Joe Coleman pitched a 7–0 shutout for the Tigers in the third game and Detroit evened the series by winning the fourth game 4–3 in ten innings.

Odom won the deciding game with four solid innings of relief from Vida Blue to put the A's in the Series.

The National League playoffs were just as tense as the defending World Series champion Pirates matched up with the Cincinnati Reds. The teams split the first four games and the Pirates led the fifth game 3–2 in the ninth. But Johnny Bench homered off relief ace Dave Giusti to tie the score and a Reds rally led to Bob Moose's

wild pitch, which allowed the winning run.

Utilityman Gene Tenace was the unlikely hero in Game One, hitting homers in his first two Series at-bats and driving in all the runs in a 3–2 win. Joe Rudi keyed a 2–1 victory in Game Two, hitting a home run and making a spectacular defensive play in left field.

Jack Billingham and Clay Carroll combined on a 1–0 win for the Reds in Game Three, but Oakland bounced back to win 3–2 in the ninth inning of Game Four.

Tenace hit a three-run homer in Game Five, but the Reds won 5–4 on Pete Rose's tie-breaking single in the ninth inning. Cincinnati forced a seventh game with an 8–1 victory in Game Six.

Tenace was again a key figure in the 3–2 win in Game Seven. Tenace drove in two runs with a single and double and manager Dick Williams pulled out all the stops, using starters Catfish Hunter and Ken Holtzman in relief before Rollie Fingers closed out the win with two shutout innings.

The A's prevailed without one of their biggest weapons—Reggie Jackson missed the Series with a hamstring injury he sustained in the playoffs. He would more than make up for that absence later in his career.

The Reds' Pete Rose and the A's Gene Tenace exchange words, but Tenace would have the final say as he belted a record-tying four homers in the Series

MOST VALUABLE PLAYER
AL: Reggie Jackson, Oakland
NL: Pete Rose, Cincinnati

CY YOUNG AWARD
AL: Jim Palmer, Baltimore
NL: Tom Seaver, NY Mets

ROOKIE OF THE YEAR
AL: Al Bumbry, Baltimore
NL: Gary Matthews, San Francisco

LEADERS
BATTING AVERAGE
AL: Rod Carew, Minnesota, .350
NL: Pete Rose, Cincinnati, .338

HOME RUNS
AL: Reggie Jackson, Oakland, 32
NL: Willie Stargell, Pittsburgh, 44

RUNS BATTED IN
AL: Reggie Jackson, Oakland, 117
NL: Willie Stargell, Pittsburgh, 119

STOLEN BASES
AL: Tommy Harper, Boston Red Sox, 54
NL: Lou Brock, St. Louis Cardinals, 70

PITCHING VICTORIES
AL: Wilbur Wood, Chicago White Sox, 24
NL: Ron Bryant, San Francisco, 24

EARNED RUN AVERAGE
AL: Jim Palmer, Baltimore, 2.40
NL: Tom Seaver, NY Mets, 2.08

STRIKEOUTS
AL: Nolan Ryan, California, 383
NL: Tom Seaver, NY Mets, 251

SAVES
AL: John Hiller, Detroit, 38
NL: Mike Marshall, Montreal, 31

Baseball became a ten-man game in half of the games in 1973. The American League adopted the designated hitter rule on an experimental basis—a test period that would wind up lasting the rest of the century.

The American League was more adventurous than its sometimes-stodgy counterpart. The American League also had more franchises confronting attendance problems, so it did what baseball had traditionally done in times of crisis—it made changes to beef up the offense.

The idea was to get weak-hitting pitchers out of the batting order and replace them with slug-

gers. Technically, the DH could replace any hitter in the lineup, but the intent was to get another bat in the lineup while sparing fans the sight of pitchers flailing away helplessly.

The rule had another effect. It would provide a job for high-profile players who had gotten too old or creaky to play in the field. The DH made his four plate appearances per game and spent

Clemente's death left a gaping hole in Pittsburgh's lineup—and baseball itself

The Pirates' Willie Stargell responded in trying times

TIMELINE

Jan. 3: George Steinbrenner and a group of investors bought the Yankees from CBS for $10 million.

March 20: Roberto Clemente was elected to the Hall of Fame in a special election. The five-year waiting period was waived after Clemente died in a New Year's Eve plane crash in Puerto Rico.

March 27: Five years after he won 31 games for the Tigers, the Braves released Denny McLain, ending his career at 29.

April 6: Ron Blomberg of the Yankees became the game's first designated hitter. He was 1-for-3 in the game against Boston.

April 27: Steve Busby of the Royals pitched a no-hitter against Detroit.

May 15: Nolan Ryan of the Angels pitched his first career no-hitter, beating the Royals.

June 19: Pete Rose got his 2,000th career hit.

June 20: Bobby Bonds hit his 22nd leadoff home run to set a National League record.

June 27: David Clyde, the first player chosen in the June 7 draft, made his major league debut and pitched five innings to beat the Twins.

July 11: Jim Northrup had eight RBIs in Detroit's 14–2 win over Texas.

July 15: Nolan Ryan pitched his second no-hitter of the season, beating the Tigers 6–0 with 17 strikeouts.

July 21: Hank Aaron hit his 700th home run.

July 30: Jim Bibby of the Rangers pitched a no-hitter against Oakland.

Aug. 17: Willie Mays hit his 660th career home run.

Sept. 6: The Pirates fired manager Bill Virdon and brought back Danny Murtaugh for a fourth time.

Sept. 8: Billy Martin became manager of the Rangers, replacing Whitey Herzog.

Sept. 20: Willie Mays announced his plans to retire at the end of the season.

Dec. 7: The Giants sold pitcher Juan Marichal to the Red Sox.

the rest of the time in the dugout. For example, the rule was perfect for Tony Oliva of the Minnesota Twins, a still-dangerous hitter whose bad knees had made him a liability in the field.

While the owners were enthusiastic about the change, some of the players weren't.

Said California Angels' pitcher Clyde Wright, "It's a joke. They're taking away part of the game. Hitting is a challenge to me."

Boog Powell of the Baltimore Orioles arrived at the same conclusion for different reasons: "I'm not an old man. I want to play in the field. I don't want to see all that work go down the drain."

Two New York Yankees old-timers checked in with contrasting opinions. Joe DiMaggio said, "I think it's great. It's a change and if there's anything baseball needs, it's change." But Mickey Mantle countered, "What keeps baseball going? It's the records. They're making records easier to erase."

Designated hitters accounted for 227 home runs in 1973. That was a ratio of one in 33 at-bats. In 1972, pitchers homered at a rate of one in every 217 at-bats. The American League saw an increase of 1½ runs per game so the "experiment" was considered a success.

The National League had another concern—a six-team fight for a division title that was less of a race than a group stumble.

The National League East was nicknamed the "National League Least" because all six teams were having difficulty staying on the plus side of .500.

The division was thrown open because of the problems that afflicted the Pittsburgh Pirates, who had won the division in each of the three previous seasons. Their superstar, right fielder Roberto Clemente, had died in a New Year's Eve plane crash off the coast of Puerto Rico. Clemente was aboard a plane overloaded with relief supplies for earthquake-ravaged Nicaragua. The Pirates still had a powerful team without Clemente, but the emotional toll of his absence was incalculable.

Maybe the Pirates would have succeeded and won without Clemente if their pitching staff hadn't fallen apart. No. 1 starter Steve Blass, a 19-game winner in 1972, had some control problems in an opening day start against St. Louis. No one thought much of it, yet it proved to be a season-long issue and led to the premature end of Blass' career. Blass, who had succeeded because of his ability to pinpoint his

Vida Blue was one of three
20-game winners for the A's

going. Faced with an added burden because of Clemente's sudden loss, Stargell responded with the finest overall season of his career—a .299 average, 44 home runs and 119 RBIs. It wasn't enough as the Pirates' pitching staff stumbled and a season-long problem at shortstop hurt the defense.

The failure of any team to take control left the door open for the New York Mets, who were in last place on August 30. The Mets spent 70 days in the basement and had plenty of problems. Injuries sidelined Jerry Grote, Cleon Jones and Bud Harrelson and reliever Tug McGraw was unreliable in save situations. But the Mets got hot at the right time, winning 20 out of 28 to jump from fifth to first. Their 82–79 record would represent the lowest winning percentage of any first-place team in baseball history. They didn't clinch the division until the day after the season officially ended because they had to win a make-up game while Pittsburgh was losing a similar game that required the San Diego Padres to fly cross-country after the season ended.

The St. Louis Cardinals' chances took a dive when Bob Gibson was injured and could make just one appearance in the last two months. Alan Foster turned

pitches, suddenly couldn't throw the ball over the plate. The problem got so bad that the Pirates had to remove him from their rotation later in the season.

Blass tried visualization, hypnosis and any number of adjustments to his pitching mechanics. Nothing worked. He finished the season 3–9, a shocking turnaround for a pitcher who was counted on to win close to 20 games.

Willie Stargell did his best to keep the Pirates

into their top starter with a 13–9 record and Ted Simmons batted .310 with 91 RBIs. Lou Brock batted .297 and stole 70 bases.

The Montreal Expos contended for the first time as Ken Singleton batted .302 with 23 home runs and 103 RBIs. Bob Bailey had a solid season with a .273 average, 26 home runs and 86 RBIs. Mike Marshall was a stalwart out of the bullpen, appearing in 92 games with 14 wins and 31 saves.

The Philadelphia Phillies may have joined the crowd, but Steve Carlton dropped from 27 wins to a 13–20 record. Rookie third baseman Mike Schmidt batted .198 with 18 home runs and struck out 136 times.

In the West the Cincinnati Reds pulled away from the Los Angeles Dodgers and won their third title in four years. Gary Nolan and Roger Nelson were both sidelined with arm problems, but Don Gullett was 18–8. Pete Rose batted .338 for his third batting title.

The Dodgers held first place until September 4, when a nine-game losing streak killed their chances.

In the American League, the Oakland A's reached .500 in May and never looked back. The A's had three 20-game winners in Catfish Hunter (21–15), Ken Holtzman (21–13) and Vida Blue (20–9) and backed them up with reliever Rollie Fingers. Deron Johnson was acquired from Philadelphia to help fill the DH spot.

Kansas City finished second as first-year manager Jack McKeon didn't have enough starting pitching or a reliable DH. Paul Splittorff became the Royals' first 20-game winner at 20–11 and Steve Busby was 16–15. John Mayberry's 100 RBIs were third in the league and Amos Otis had a breakthrough season with a .300 average, 26 home runs and 93 RBIs.

After four knee operations, DH was the ideal job for Minnesota's Oliva. He hit .291 with 16 homers and 92 RBIs as the Twins finished .500 for the second consecutive year. Rod Carew won his third straight batting title as the Twins led the league in hitting but couldn't find enough pitching.

Nolan Ryan's 383 strikeouts were the highlight of the California Angels' season. Bill Singer won 20 games and Frank Robinson had his 11th career 30-homer season. The Angels lost promising prospect Bobby Valentine to a gruesome ankle injury that would wind up derailing his career.

The Chicago White Sox spent 58 days in first place, but Dick Allen injured an ankle and had just five at-bats after June 5. Ken Henderson missed the last two months with a knee injury and the White Sox couldn't replace their two best hitters. For the first time in 20 years, a team had two 20-game losers: Wilbur Wood was 24–20 but gave the White Sox 359 innings; Stan Bahnsen was 18–21.

Baltimore had 14-game winning streak at the right time and won its fourth American League East title in five years. The Orioles changed from power to speed as Al Bumbry and Rich Coggins

The New York Yankees' Thurman Munson

keyed their offense. Jim Palmer finished the year 14–3 to finish 22–9 and post his fourth straight 20-win season.

The Boston Red Sox' strong finish still came up 1½ games short of the Orioles. Luis Tiant had a comeback season to end 20–13 and Bill Lee was 17–11 with a 2.75 ERA, third best in the League.

Billy Martin was fired in Detroit where the happier story was the comeback of John Hiller from a 1971 heart attack. Hiller won ten games and saved 38 others.

The Yankees led the division for two months, but faded to a 21–38 record over the last two months. Thurman Munson added to his credentials by winning his first Gold Glove award.

Milwaukee was bad enough to get manager Del Crandall fired and a second-half push by the Cleveland Indians was too late.

AL CHAMPIONSHIP SERIES

GAME 1	
Baltimore 6	Oakland 0

GAME 2	
Oakland 6	Baltimore 3

GAME 3	
Oakland 2	Baltimore 1

GAME 4	
Baltimore 5	Oakland 4

GAME 5	
Oakland 3	Baltimore 0

NL CHAMPIONSHIP SERIES

GAME 1	
Cincinnati 2	NY Mets 1

GAME 2	
NY Mets 5	Cincinnati 0

GAME 3	
NY Mets 9	Cincinnati 2

GAME 4	
Cincinnati 2	NY Mets 1

GAME 5	
NY Mets 7	Cincinnati 2

WORLD SERIES

GAME 1	
Oakland 2	NY Mets 1

GAME 2	
NY Mets 10	Oakland 7

GAME 3	
Oakland 3	NY Mets 2

GAME 4	
NY Mets 6	Oakland 1

GAME 5	
NY Mets 2	Oakland 0

GAME 6	
Oakland 3	NY Mets 1

GAME 7	
Oakland 5	NY Mets 2

MVP: Reggie Jackson, Oakland

Mutiny in the middle of the World Series? Only the Oakland A's could stage one and still manage to win the biggest games of the season.

The A's won their third consecutive American League West title and found themselves facing the Baltimore Orioles, the team that had knocked them off in three straight to win the 1971 pennant. But these were different A's, fresh from winning a World Series. They had arguably the best talent in baseball and now they had the confidence that is the inevitable by-product of success.

For the second consecutive year, the A's went the five-game limit in the playoffs before winning. Baltimore's Jim Palmer pitched a five-hitter to win the opening game 5–0 as a four-run first knocked out starter Vida Blue.

In the second game Oakland hit four home runs—two by Sal Bando—and won 6–3. Ken Holtzman of the A's outdueled Mike Cuellar to win the third game 2–1 in 11 innings. Bert Campaneris' home run broke the tie.

Baltimore roughed up reliever Rollie Fingers to win the fourth game 5–4. Catfish Hunter threw a five-hitter in the fifth game to win 3–0 and send the A's back to the World Series.

The National League playoffs also went five games and included a brawl in the middle game that made Cincinnati's Pete Rose a marked man in New York. The Mets had prevailed in a mediocre East Division, outlasting a four-team field despite winning just 82 games and posting a winning percentage of .509, which was only the ninth best in the majors.

Rose and Johnny Bench homered in the opener to beat Tom Seaver 2–1. Jon Matlack pitched the Mets to a 2–0 win in the second game with a two-hitter. The Mets lost the fight, but won the third game 9–2. Trouble started when Rose and scrawny shortstop Bud Harrelson scrapped after a slide at second base. The crowd got so ugly that manager Sparky Anderson pulled the Reds off the field and Mets' manager Yogi Berra and some New York players took the field to plead with the fans to settle down.

Tony Perez and Rose homered in the fourth game for another 2–1 win. The Mets won the deciding game 7–2 behind Seaver and Tug McGraw and returned to the Series for the second time in five years.

The A's won Game One, 2–1, behind Ken Holtzman, who helped himself with a double. It was surprising considering American League

pitchers hadn't batted all season because the designated hitter rule was implemented.

The Mets won Game Two, 10–7, ending the game after 12 innings and a Series-record four hours and 13 minutes. But that wasn't the big story. A's second baseman Mike Andrews made two costly errors and impulsive owner Charles O. Finley decided to do something about it. Even though Series rosters are frozen before the postseason begins, Finley thought he'd found a loophole that would allow him to drop Andrews.

He attempted to put him on the disabled list, claiming Andrews was bothered by a shoulder injury. Commissioner Bowie Kuhn disallowed the move, which had created a furor among the A's. The players were offended at Finley's attempt to humiliate Andrews in the high-profile environment of the World Series and were vocal in their disdain for the owner and his methods.

The affair settled, Oakland won Game Three, 3–2, in 11 innings before losing 6–1 to Matlack

in Game Four. Rusty Staub was the Mets' hitting star, going 4-for-4 and driving in five runs.

Jerry Koosman and McGraw combined on a three-hitter to win 2–0 and put the Mets a win away from the title.

In Game Six, Catfish Hunter outpitched Seaver to win 3–1. Reggie Jackson, who had missed the 1972 Series with a hamstring injury, had three hits and drove in two of the runs.

The A's hadn't hit a homer in the first six games, but got a pair of two-run home runs in the second inning to win Game Seven, 5–2. Campaneris and Jackson hit the homers to make the A's the first repeat winners since the 1961–62 Yankees.

The Series was the end of the line for Willie Mays, who spent his final season and a half with the Mets. He had two hits in seven at-bats.

It was also the end for Mike Andrews. His pinch-hitting appearance in Game Three was his last in the major leagues.

Oakland A's owner Charles O. Finley with the World Series trophy

A's slugger Reggie Jackson was awarded MVP honors thanks to a dominating performance at the plate, including this double in Game Six

WILLIE MAYS

TEAMS
NY/SF Giants 1951–72; NY Mets 1972–73

Games	2,992
At-Bats	10,881
Runs	2,062
RBI	1,903
Home runs	660
Hits	3,283
Doubles	523
Triples	140
Stolen Bases	338
Average	302
Slugging percentage	557

The "Say-Hey" Kid

Willie Mays started his major league career by going hitless in his first 12 at-bats.

Leo Durocher, Mays' manager with the New York Giants at the time, told his rookie not to worry, and that he was going to be a fine major league player. Durocher couldn't have been more accurate.

Mays developed into one of those rare baseball players who could help his team win in so many games. He hit for a high average, he hit for power, he could run, he could throw and he could play defense. That combination of skills put him in 24 consecutive All-Star games and got him elected to the Hall of Fame the instant he was eligible.

Mays not only played well, he played with unbridled enthusiasm. Legend had the young Mays playing stickball in the streets with neighborhood kids after he got home from the Giants' games. He liked to take infield practice at shortstop because playing that position was his long-standing secret ambition. Had the Giants chosen to move him there, he probably could have handled it.

"Athletically Willie could do anything he wanted," long-time opponent Don Newcombe said.

Mays' contribution wasn't limited to his skills. His attitude was a plus, too.

Said Bill Rigney, who was a team-mate and later the Giants' manager, "The exuberance and joy of playing would just pour out of him. You could see the way he ran the bases, the way he caught the ball, the way his hat flew off—he gave a lift to everybody."

Mays caught routine fly balls with a flashy basket catch. He held his glove open at waist level and let the ball fall into it. Rumor had it that Mays selected his caps a size small so that they would come loose when he was in a full gallop chasing the ball.

Despite that full-tilt style he was a durable player. Mays played at least 150 games for 13 consecutive seasons.

Mays, who grew up in Alabama, joined the Negro Leagues' Birmingham Barons as a 17-year-old. Once Jackie Robinson broke baseball's color line, the Giants hustled to sign Mays. The Dodgers had a shot at him, but reportedly rejected him because of doubts about his ability to hit breaking pitches.

The Giants signed Mays for $6,000 and he spent part of two seasons in the minor leagues before he came to the Giants in 1951. Mays was named Rookie of the Year after batting .274 with 20 home runs and 68 RBIs in 121 games. He lost two seasons to military service, but came back in 1954 and won the Most Valuable Player award with a .345 average, 41 home runs and 110 RBIs.

In the 1954 World Series, Mays made his famous catch against Vic Wertz of the Cleveland Indians. Mays ran into the cavernous center field at the Polo Grounds to make the better-than-average catch, then topped that by alertly making a strong and accurate throw to get the ball back to the infield.

Mays won four stolen base titles from 1956–59. While his production stayed on a steady course, his career changed dramatically with the Giants' move to San Francisco in 1958. Fans there seemed to embrace players who were more identified with San Francisco, like Orlando Cepeda and Willie McCovey. Mays?

He was still considered a New York Giant.

From 1958–66, Mays had eight seasons with at least 100 runs and 100 RBIs. He led the National League in home runs in 1962, 1964 and 1965. In early 1966, he hit his 511th home run to surpass Mel Ott as the National League's career leader.

Mays' career started to slow in the late 1960s and by 1972 his contract was too expensive for the Giants. They traded him back to New York and he ended his career with the Mets, struggling to make plays he used to make easily. Despite a World Series season in 1973, Mays announced his retirement, saying, "Willie, it's time to say goodbye to America."

For six years he was banned from baseball because he held a public relations job with a casino. He was welcomed back in 1985 and has held a ceremonial front office title with the Giants.

MOST VALUABLE PLAYER
AL: Jeff Burroughs, Texas
NL: Steve Garvey, Los Angeles

CY YOUNG AWARD
AL: Jim "Catfish" Hunter, Oakland
NL: Mike Marshall, Los Angeles

ROOKIE OF THE YEAR
AL: Mike Hargrove, Texas
NL: Bake McBride, St. Louis Cardinals

LEADERS
BATTING AVERAGE
AL: Rod Carew, Minnesota, .364
NL; Ralph Garr, Atlanta, .353

HOME RUNS
AL: Dick Allen, Chicago White Sox, 32
NL: Mike Schmidt, Philadelphia Phillies, 36

RUNS BATTED IN
AL: Jeff Burroughs, Texas, 118
NL: Johnny Bench, Cincinnati, 129

STOLEN BASES
AL: Bill North, Oakland, 54
NL: Lou Brock, St. Louis Cardinals, 118

PITCHING VICTORIES
AL: Jim "Catfish" Hunter, Oakland; Ferguson Jenkins, Texas, 25
NL: Andy Messersmith, Los Angeles; Phil Niekro, Atlanta, 20

EARNED RUN AVERAGE
AL: Jim "Catfish" Hunter, Oakland, 2.49
NL: Buzz Capra, Atlanta, 2.28

STRIKEOUTS
AL: Nolan Ryan, California, 367
NL: Steve Carlton, Philadelphia Phillies, 240

SAVES
AL: Terry Forster, Chicago White Sox, 24
NL: Mike Marshall, Los Angeles, 21

The Oakland A's weren't just a great baseball team. They were a pretty compelling soap opera, too. Owner Charles O. Finley assembled an enviable roster of baseball talent and a volatile mix of personalities who often clashed and destroyed the myth that teams needed clubhouse harmony to be successful on the field.

Despite the success he'd enjoyed in Oakland, Dick Williams had enough of Finley's meddling and resigned after winning the 1973 World Series. Naturally, Finley contested Williams' right to leave and prevented the New York Yankees from hiring him.

Finley's choice to replace Williams was almost an afterthought. Alvin Dark didn't get the call until three days before spring training began. Dark hadn't had a managing job since he handled the Cleveland Indians without success from 1968 to 1971.

Dark was a religious man fond of quoting Scripture. How would he fit in with the rollicking A's? Very effectively, as it turned out. The relationship was not always smooth, though. Third baseman and acknowledged team leader, Sal Bando, loudly criticized Dark after one game, unaware that the manager was within earshot. In midseason, Dark engineered some changes on the coaching staff because he was convinced some of Williams' former aides were undermining him.

On June 5, the A's had another clubhouse fight, an event that had become standard for the team. Reggie Jackson and Bill North got into a scuffle and Jackson came away with a bruised

shoulder that affected his play. Catcher Ray Fosse, a would-be peacemaker, got the worst of it. He was injured as he tried to break up the fight and wound up missing nearly three months. But nothing could derail the A's, who had the major leagues' most-impressive combination of pitching, power and defense. Oakland moved into first place on May 20 and stayed there for the rest of the season.

The staff's 2.95 earned run average was the best in the majors. Jim "Catfish" Hunter, just 8–8 in mid-June, went 17–4 over the rest of the season. It was his fourth consecutive 20-win season and his ERA of 2.49 was the American League's best.

Hunter was backed up by Ken Holtzman (19–17) and Vida Blue (17–15). Reliever Rollie Fingers appeared in 76 games and had nine wins and 18 saves.

Despite failing to find a reliable designated hitter, the A's had a balanced offense. Bando batted only .243, but hit 22 home runs and drove in 103 runs. Joe Rudi hit .293 with 22 homers and 99 RBIs. Like Bando, Gene Tenace had a low average (.211), but impressive power totals—26 home runs and 73 RBIs.

Bill North and Bert Campaneris provided

Texas Rangers' Billy Martin starts off the new season by refreshing the memory of umpire Bill Kunkel regarding the rule on balking

The Twins' Rod Carew completed a three-peat, as he again won the American League batting crown

speed at the top of the order, combining for 88 stolen bases. One of Finley's pet projects was using a roster spot for a pinch running specialist. Herb Washington was a sprinter rather than a baseball player, but he managed 29 stolen bases in his limited role.

The A's stiffest competition came from the Texas Rangers, who caught the spark that manager Billy Martin had earlier provided in Minnesota and Detroit. The Rangers had made a beauty of a trade in December, sending infielders Bill Madlock and Vic Harris to the Chicago Cubs for Ferguson Jenkins, who went 25–12 with a 2.83 ERA in his first American League season. Jenkins pitched 328 innings and struck out 225 while walking only 45. He pitched through a leg injury that kept him 1–8 through June, or he would have had a legitimate shot at 30 wins.

Jeff Burroughs was the American League's Most Valuable Player with a .301 average and 118 RBIs. Mike Hargrove jumped from Class A and hit .323.

The highlight of the Minnesota Twins' season was Rod Carew's fourth career batting title. Carew also became the first player since Ty Cobb to lead the American League in hitting for three consecutive seasons.

The Chicago White Sox didn't follow up on their success and the good vibrations with slugger Dick Allen didn't last either. Allen announced on September 13 that he was retiring from the game, a decision that turned out not to be final.

The Kansas City Royals were unsuccessful enough to cost general manager Cedric Tallis his job. Steve Busby won 22 games, one of them a no-hitter.

The California Angels finished last for the first time, which prompted a managerial change. Bobby Winkles, who had clashed with Frank Robinson, was fired and replaced by Williams. Robinson was shipped to Cleveland on waivers in September and the Indians became his fourth team in four years. None of the turmoil seemed to bother Nolan Ryan, who had 367 strikeouts and became the first pitcher in modern history to have three consecutive 300-strikeout seasons.

In the East, the Baltimore Orioles surged to overcome the Boston Red Sox. Trailing the Red Sox by eight games on August 29, the Orioles went on a 28–6 rush to edge out Boston the day before the season ended.

The New York Yankees didn't get Dick Williams, but their second choice worked out well. Bill Virdon, fired by the Pirates the previous season, was the American League's Manager of the Year after leading the Yankees to a second-place finish. George Medich won 19 games and Sparky Lyle had nine wins, 15 saves and a 1.66 ERA.

The Braves' Hank Aaron achieved baseball immortality as he broke the Babe's home-run record

The Red Sox went 8–20 down the stretch to finish third. Their ace, Luis Tiant, lost five games in that span. Boston was short on offense all season, a problem that got worse when catcher Carlton Fisk sustained a knee injury in late June.

Gaylord Perry and his brother Jim led the Indians, combining for 38 wins. Manager Ken Aspromonte was fired and the team announced that Frank Robinson would be player-manager in 1975 and become the first black man to manage in the majors.

The Detroit Tigers finished last for just the second time in 74 years and started breaking up a veteran group. Norm Cash was released and Jim Northrup was sold to Montreal. Al Kaline stuck around long enough to get his 3,000th hit and announced his retirement when the season ended.

In the National League, the Los Angeles Dodgers built a big lead and held off the Cincinnati Reds at the end. Jim Wynn, acquired from Houston, hit 32 home runs and drove in 108 runs. Reliever Mike Marshall appeared in 106 games and finished 83 of them. From June 18 to July 3, Marshall appeared in 13 consecutive games. Andy Messersmith won 20 games and Tommy John was 13–3 before having to have elbow surgery

that would cost him a season and a half.

The Reds were the second-winningest team in the majors with 98 wins. Johnny Bench drove in 129 runs, but Pete Rose's streak of .300 seasons stopped at eight.

Hank Aaron's record-setting home run in April was the second of 20 for him in his final season with the Atlanta Braves. He appeared in 112 games, the fewest of his career in the majors. Despite having a winning record, the Braves fired manager Eddie Mathews and replaced him with Clyde King.

The Houston Astros were doomed by their 4–14 record against the Reds. The San Francisco Giants' winning percentage of .444 was their worst since 1956 and Wes Westrum replaced Charlie Fox as manager.

The San Diego Padres were still bad but they were more interesting. McDonald's baron, Ray Kroc, bought the team to prevent it from being moved to Washington D.C. and established his presence by going on the stadium public address system during a poor performance to announce that his team was guilty of "some of the most stupid ballplaying I've ever seen."

The Pittsburgh Pirates were in last place on June 15, but, galvanized by a bench-clearing

fight with Cincinnati in mid-July, rallied to win the East. Ken Brett had a big first half and Dock Ellis took over in the second half when injuries slowed Brett.

The St. Louis Cardinals chased the Pirates to the end. Philadelphia Phillies' second baseman, Dave Cash, borrowed the slogan "Yes We Can" from a popular song. No, the Phillies couldn't, despite 36 home runs and 116 RBIs from Mike Schmidt.

Tom Seaver fell to 11–11 and Tug McGraw had just three saves to doom the New York Mets. The Chicago Cubs hired Jim Marshall as manager in-season after Whitey Lockman resigned and returned to the front office.

There were three no-hitters—Busby beat Milwaukee on June 19; Cleveland's Dick Bosman defeated Oakland a month later; and the Angels' Ryan overpowered Minnesota on September 28. Ryan struck out 15 batters. Bosman was in the rotation only because of an injury to Steve Kline.

The game lost a Hall of Fame pitcher and one of its most popular characters on July 17 when Dizzy Dean died at 63 in Reno, Nevada. After retiring, Dean remained active in the game as a broadcaster, often fracturing the language.

Baseball had become more promotion-oriented and Cleveland offered a textbook example of how not to do it with "Ten-cent Beer Night". Unruly fans overran the field and the umpires forfeited the game to the Texas Rangers.

The Dodgers' Steve Garvey completed an impressive double winning both the regular season and All-Star awards

AL CHAMPIONSHIP SERIES

GAME 1

Baltimore 6	Oakland 3

GAME 2

Oakland 5	Baltimore 0

GAME 3

Oakland 1	Baltimore 0

GAME 4

Oakland 2	Baltimore 1

NL CHAMPIONSHIP SERIES

GAME 1

Los Angeles 3	Pittsburgh 0

GAME 2

Los Angeles 5	Pittsburgh 2

GAME 3

Pittsburgh 7	Los Angeles 0

GAME 4

Los Angeles 12	Pittsburgh 1

WORLD SERIES

GAME 1

Oakland 3	Los Angeles 2

GAME 2

Los Angeles 3	Oakland 2

GAME 3

Oakland 3	Los Angeles 2

GAME 4

Oakland 5	Los Angeles 2

GAME 5

Oakland 3	Los Angeles 2

MVP: Rollie Fingers, Oakland

The A's Reggie Jackson began the Series with a home run in Game One

There was no telling how long the Oakland A's dynasty might last, but that didn't matter to manager Dick Williams.

Williams, fed up with owner Charles O. Finley's meddling ways, stepped down from his job even as the celebration of the A's second World Series title was in full bloom.

If Williams thought he was finished with Finley, he was wrong. The owner successfully blocked his former manager from taking a job with the New York Yankees.

It was just one of several issues along the way as the A's continued to fight among themselves and win. Pitcher Catfish Hunter had discovered a contract technicality that he felt would free him from the A's and allow him to become a free agent. Mike Andrews, the second baseman Finley tried to fire during the 1973 World Series, filed a slander suit against the owner. Teammates Blue Moon Odom and Rollie Fingers scuffled in the clubhouse before the Series started.

In other words, it was pretty much business as usual for the A's, who seemed to accept turmoil as part of their daily routine. To replace the fiery Williams, Finley reached into the A's past and hired Alvin Dark, one of the many managers Finley had previously fired during his ownership of the franchise.

Dark was a religious man and some of the players tested him early in his tenure. Whether they liked or respected Dark wasn't an issue; the A's knew what it took to win and had the talent to do it, no matter what the issues were off the field.

Oakland held off the upstart Texas Rangers to win the American League West for a fourth consecutive year. They faced Baltimore in the playoffs for the third time in that run and needed only four games to eliminate the Orioles for the second straight year.

Baltimore's only win came in the opening game as Mike Cuellar beat Hunter 6–3. Ken Holtzman pitched a five-hit, 5–0 win in the second game and Vida Blue beat Jim Palmer 1–0 with a two-hitter in the third game. Hunter and Fingers teamed up for the 2–1 win in the clincher.

In the National League, the Los Angeles Dodgers got back to the postseason for the first time since 1966, behind a strong pitching staff headed by Andy Messersmith, Don Sutton and iron-man reliever, Mike Marshall. The Dodgers handled the Pittsburgh Pirates easily in the play-offs, holding them scoreless in 17 of the first 18 innings. Sutton pitched a four-hitter in the opener and Messersmith and Marshall combined to win the second game 5–2.

The Pirates won 7–0 before the Dodgers ended the series with a 12–1 win behind Sutton.

After going seven games in each of their first two World Series, the A's had an easier time with the Dodgers, ending the Series after just five games.

Oakland won Game One, 3–2, as Reggie Jackson hit a second-inning home run off Messersmith. Holtzman doubled and scored on Bert Campaneris' squeeze bunt, while third baseman Ron Cey's throwing error gave the A's another run.

The Dodgers won Game Two, 3–2, and Finley had an embarrassment. One of his pet projects was a designated runner and he ordered the A's to spend a roster spot on Herb Washington, a former track star who had no background in

baseball. Washington, whose sole purpose was to pinch run, was picked off by Marshall, taking the potential tying run off the bases.

The A's won Game Three, 3–2, behind Hunter and with the help of two unearned runs. The Dodgers' runs came on home runs by Bill Buckner and Willie Crawford.

Holtzman again helped himself at the plate to key the win in Game Four. Holtzman hit a solo home run and the A's went on to a 5–2 win with a four-run sixth inning.

Joe Rudi homered off Marshall in the seventh inning of Game Five to break a 2–2 tie. The Dodgers missed a chance to tie the game when Buckner tried to get to third base on a ball mishandled by center fielder Bill North. Buckner was thrown out and the Dodgers were done, even though Oakland had batted only .211 in the Series.

Celebration time for Reggie Jackson and the A's after claiming the world championship in four games

HANK AARON

TEAMS
Milwaukee Braves 1954–65; Atlanta Braves
1966–74; Milwaukee Brewers 1975–76

Games:	3,298
At-Bats:	12,364
Runs:	2,174
RBI:	2,297
Home runs:	755
Hits:	3,771
Doubles:	624
Triples:	98
Stolen Bases:	240
Average:	305
Slugging percentage:	555

When baseball created an award in the name of the game's most prolific home run hitter, Hank Aaron wanted one assurance— that the award wasn't only for home runs.

"I wasn't just a home run hitter," Aaron said. "I was able to do something else in baseball. I was able to field my position, run the bases. I batted in a lot of runs. I would like people to realize that."

So instead of celebrating home runs only, the Hank Aaron Award is based on a number of offensive achievements—batting average, runs scored, runs batted in, stolen bases and, yes, home runs. It takes a well-rounded player to win the Aaron award and that's keeping it true to the spirit of its namesake. Aaron will always be remembered for his 755 home runs, particularly No. 715 which allowed him to surpass Babe Ruth's career record early in the 1974 season.

It seemed as though Aaron was able to sneak up on the record. He was never as flamboyant a player as Willie Mays and never as famous as Mickey Mantle. For most of his career, Aaron was based in Milwaukee, which wasn't exactly a media capital.

The perception of Aaron was one of a steady player who produced consistently year after year. He said he didn't begin to think Ruth's record was in reach until the 1972 season, two years before he broke it.

Aaron was born in Mobile, Alabama, and grew up there in the segregated south. His high school didn't have a baseball team so he played fast-pitch softball. He got his baseball experience playing on semipro teams, an activity he started when he was just 15.

A scout named Ed Scott spotted Aaron and signed him for the Indianapolis Clowns of the Negro Leagues. He started as a shortstop there and eventually caught the attention of the Braves. In May of 1952, they paid $7,500 for his contract and sent him to the minor leagues.

Aaron spent just a year and a half in the minors. His chance came in 1954 when Bobby Thomson broke an ankle while sliding during spring training. That cleared a spot in the lineup and Aaron grabbed it.

He settled into the best kind of routine. He produced every year. He was one of those rare players able to combine power with a high batting average. He won the National League batting title in 1956, his third year with the Braves. In 1958, he narrowly missed the Triple Crown. He led the league in home runs (44) and RBIs (132), but was third in batting average.

He took his second batting title a year later with a .355 average. In 1963, there was another near-miss on the Triple Crown. Aaron led the league with 44 home runs and 130 RBIs, but his batting average was just seven points off the lead.

"Hank could do anything he wanted to do," long-time teammate Warren Spahn said. "If he wanted to be a pitcher, he could have been a 20-game winner. He wanted to be a complete player so he stole 40 bases. He wanted to outdo (teammate Eddie) Mathews so he became a home run hitter. Whoever thought he would be a home run hitter? He wanted to be the best and he had both the ability and desire to do it. He was so great, I thought he'd be a .400 hitter, not another Ruth."

The chase of baseball's most-cherished record ended that April night when Aaron hit a pitch from Al Downing over the fence for No. 715. He had to endure hate mail and death threats, but he did it. That 1974 season turned out to be his last with the Braves. He went back to Milwaukee to play two seasons in the American League with the Brewers—but nothing was ever quite the same after 715.

"After I passed Babe Ruth, I thought, 'What else can I accomplish?'" Aaron said. "It was a complete letdown."

Aaron's choice of his all-time favorite home run says something important about him. On his list, the record-setting homer is No. 2. The one he holds most special was No. 107. It came off Howie Pollett of the St. Louis Cardinals and won the game that clinched the 1957 National League pennant for the Braves. Why that one and not the one that bumped Ruth from the record books? "It meant so much to the team."

Hank Aaron passed the Babe to become the "Home Run King"

FRANK ROBINSON

TEAMS
Cincinnati Reds 1956–65; Baltimore Orioles
1966–71; Los Angeles Dodgers 1972;
California Angels 1973–74; Cleveland Indians
1974–76

Games: 2,808
At-Bats: .10,006
Runs: 1,829
RBI: 1,812
Home runs: 586
Hits: 2,943
Doubles: 528
Triples: 72
Stolen Bases: 204
Average: 294
Slugging percentage: 537

Frank Robinson is best remembered as baseball's first black manager and as the only person to win Most Valuable Player awards in both the National and American

Those accomplishments are certainly noteworthy, but they are mere shorthand for his career. Robinson deserves to be remembered as one of the toughest competitors to have ever played the game.

Robinson featured a hard-driving, aggressive style that both angered opponents and galvanized teammates. He crowded the plate, daring pitchers to back him off and reclaim the inside part. He ran the bases aggressively and made hard slides that often infuriated infielders.

Perhaps Robinson's biggest disappointment as a manager was having to accept that not everyone played the game with the same passion he did. He didn't make a lot of friends when he played.

Consider this assessment from Stan Williams, a former Los Angeles Dodgers pitcher, who had a reputation for knocking down hitters: "I never really cared for Robinson, but I had great respect for his talent and determination. No one was mentally tougher than him. If you knocked him on his butt three times in a row and came anywhere near the plate the fourth time, he'd hit it a country mile. You didn't want to wake him up."

Ryne Duren, who knew Robinson as both a team-mate and an opponent, called him, "the best competitor I ever saw."

Robinson debuted with the Cincinnati Reds in 1956, winning the National League's Rookie of the Year award. He tied Wally Berger's rookie home run record of 38 and led the National League with 122 runs. He was also hit by a pitch 20 times.

In 1957, Reds fans stuffed the All-Star ballot box, voting the entire Cincinnati team to the starting lineup. Commissioner Ford Frick cleaned up the mess and Robinson was the only Reds player who was allowed to play.

In 1959, a hard slide into third baseman Eddie Mathews touched off a brawl with the Milwaukee Braves.

Robinson had his first MVP season in 1961, leading Cincinnati to the National League pennant with a .323 average, 37 home runs, 134 RBIs and 117 runs. His .611 slugging percentage was the league's best and he was also the

National League's most efficient base stealer, succeeding on 22 of 25 attempts.

By 1965, though, Cincinnati management tired of Robinson and traded him to Baltimore. One Reds executive suggested that Robinson was an "old 30", meaning that his full-tilt style had taken a heavy toll on his body.

They should have known better. That was precisely the kind of challenge that brought out the best in Robinson. Duren guessed that Robinson hit "about .500" after he'd been knocked down. The correlation became so obvious that Philadelphia manager, Gene Mauch, started fining Phillies pitchers who came too far inside against Robinson.

In his first year with the Orioles, Robinson won the Triple Crown and led the team to a World Series sweep over the Dodgers. Robinson had a shot at a second Triple Crown in 1967, but injuries limited him to only 129 games.

The Orioles became consistent winners. At 36, Robinson was traded to the Dodgers shortly after Baltimore lost the 1971 World Series. He spent just one year back in the National League before moving to the California Angels.

Robinson sacrificed his offseasons to manage in winter leagues with the idea of landing a major league job. In late 1974 the Cleveland Indians acquired Robinson with the transparent goal of making him a player-manager in 1975.

He hit a home run in the historic season opener and helped the woeful Indians improve. He led them to their third winning season in 18 years. It wasn't enough, though, and he was fired in 1977.

Robinson also managed the San Francisco Giants from 1981–85 and had overachieving teams in contention twice. His last managing stop was Baltimore. Robinson took over during a season-opening, 21-game, losing streak in 1988. He had the Orioles in contention in 1989.

Robinson played in All-Star games in both leagues. He also hit at least 200 home runs in each league. He retired with the fourth-best home run total in history (586), trailing only Babe Ruth, Hank Aaron and Willie Mays and was voted into the Hall of Fame in 1982.

Robinson was a stand-out in both leagues before joining the managerial ranks

Pete Rose helped "The Big Red Machine" roll to victory

With 64 typewritten pages, arbitrator Peter Seitz changed baseball more than Babe Ruth had with 60 home runs.

Following the 1975 season, Seitz changed the major league landscape forever with his decision in favor of Andy Messersmith and Dave McNally, two pitchers who, backed by the Players Association, had challenged baseball's reserve clause.

Player dissatisfaction with the reserve clause was nothing new. As far back as the early 1900s, there were stories that players wanted the clause overturned.

Put as simply as possible, the clause bound a player to the club that held his rights in perpetuity. Only the club could dispose of a contract, either through sale, trade or unconditional release. Even if a player retired and attempted to come back two years later, his rights would still belong to his last club.

Curt Flood had challenged the reserve clause when he was traded from St. Louis, where he had business interests, to Philadelphia

following the 1969 season. Flood took his case all the way to the Supreme Court but lost.

It was clear, however, that the reserve clause was in trouble. Messersmith and McNally opted not to sign 1975 contracts, believing they were entitled to become free agents after serving out the renewal the contract mandated. The issue—was that renewal for one season or for every season?

Seitz ruled the latter. He maintained that he gave baseball management ample chance to settle without a decision from his office. He urged the owners to negotiate a compromise with the union. When it didn't happen, Seitz issued his decision and baseball was forever changed.

His ruling struck down the reserve clause and essentially made every player a free agent.

"The economic consequences to the clubs would be enormous," Commissioner Bowie Kuhn said.

He was correct. The baseball world had already gotten a sneak preview when Catfish Hunter of the Oakland A's was declared a free agent the previous offseason due to a technicality in his contract. The teams bid furiously for the services of the game's best pitcher and Hunter wound up with a groundbreaking multi-million-dollar deal from the New York Yankees.

The owners had only their own arrogance to blame for a decision that would forever change the way they had to do business and, in some cases, would drive them from baseball.

Before the decision on free agency, baseball's biggest problem was dealing with the Cincinnati Reds.

The Reds had been good throughout the 1970s but they stepped up to another level in 1975. "The Big Red Machine" set a club record with 108 wins, the third-highest total in National League history and the largest since 1909. They clinched the pennant on September 7, the earliest that any team had wrapped up any kind of title in the major leagues.

The Reds were just 20–20 on May 21 and trailing the defending champion Los Angeles Dodgers by five games. By the All-Star break in less than two months, Cincinnati was 61–29 and had a 21½- game edge on the Dodgers. They finished 20 games ahead of the Dodgers.

While it's true that the Dodgers had an uncommon run of injuries, there was also a great deal of truth in Pete Rose's statement: "The worst injury the Dodgers had was when we won 41 out of 50 games."

On May 3, Reds' manager Sparky Anderson made a lineup change that had a lasting impact. He benched light-hitting third baseman John Vukovich and moved Rose back to third. That opened left field for George Foster, who hit .300 and had 23 home runs in his first work as a regular. No starting pitcher had more than 15 wins—Don Gullett was 15–4—but the Reds had a solid four-man relief corps of Clay Carroll, Pedro Borbon, Rawly Eastwick and Will McEnaney. The pitching staff was supported by exceptional defense—four players won Gold Glove awards.

At various times the Dodgers were missing Bill Russell, Bill Buckner, Mike Marshall and Joe Ferguson. But manager Walter Alston agreed

Boston's Fred Lynn won both MVP and Rookie of the Year honors

Leading by example for Cleveland's player-manager and designated hitter, Frank Robinson

that even a full squad may have failed against the Reds. "I doubt if anyone would have beaten them the way they played," Alston said.

Steve Garvey became the first Dodger in more than 50 years to have consecutive 200-hit seasons. The Dodgers made an important move by acquiring pitcher Burt Hooton from the Cubs. He was 18–9 with a 3.06 ERA.

The biggest issue with the Giants were the rumors that the franchise would leave San Francisco. Willie Montanez came over from the Phillies and hit .302 with 101 RBIs while John "The Count" Montefusco won Rookie of the Year honors with a 15–9 record and 215 strikeouts.

The San Diego Padres escaped last place for the first time in their history, finishing fourth. Atlanta fell to fifth and Houston was last. The Astros lost pitcher Don Wilson to an offseason carbon monoxide accident.

The Pittsburgh Pirates won the East for the fifth time in six years, but it wasn't easy. Their defense was bad and pitcher Dock Ellis was disruptive, earning a suspension after yelling at manager Danny Murtaugh. Jerry Reuss won 18 games and Willie Stargell hit .295 with 22 home runs and 90 RBIs.

The Philadelphia Phillies fell behind the Pirates after injuries sidelined pitchers Steve Carlton and Jim Lonborg. Dick Allen's return to Philadelphia was a disappointment as he hit .233 with just 12 home runs.

The New York Mets released outfielder Cleon Jones after he clashed with manager Yogi Berra, then fired Berra later in the season. Dave Kingman set a team record with 36 home runs, but batted only .231 and struck out 153 times. Tom Seaver won 22 games and the Cy Young award.

Bob Gibson's St. Louis Cardinals career ended with a whimper—he was 3–10. The Chicago Cubs were nine games better but still tied for last with Montreal, where Gary Carter (.270 average, 17 home runs and 68 RBIs) and Larry Parrish (.274, 10 homers, 65 RBIs) were emerging as stars.

Rookie Fred Lynn did it all for the Red Sox to help Boston win the American League East. Lynn took both Most Valuable Player and Rookie of the Year honors as he batted .331 with 21 homers, 105 RBIs and a league-leading 103 runs. Fellow rookie Jim Rice batted .309 and drove in 109 runs before a broken arm ended his season in September.

Baltimore was stuck in last place in May before the Orioles made a charge. Their record of 49–25 after the All-Star break was the best in baseball, but the Orioles had fallen too far behind. Brooks Robinson had his worst season, batting .201. Jim Palmer won the Cy Young award as he went 23–11 with a league-best 2.09 ERA.

The New York Yankees fell out of first place in June. Injuries to Bobby Bonds and Elliot Maddox helped drop the Yankees to third place. Thurman Munson was third in hitting at .318 and Hunter was 23–14 with 30 complete games. The Yankees were no longer Bronx Bombers—they hit only 110 home runs.

Cleveland finished the year 27–15 in Frank Robinson's first year as manager. That earned Robinson a chance to come back as non-playing manager. He played his final game on September 20. The Indians traded pitchers Gaylord and Jim Perry and Dick Bosman and released outfielder Ken Berry. The moves cleared roster spots for pitcher Dennis Eckersley and center fielder Rick Manning. Robinson's former Orioles teammate, Boog Powell, came to Cleveland and batted .297 with 27 home runs and 86 RBIs.

Hank Aaron's return to Milwaukee was a disappointment as the Brewers lost 59 out of 84 to close the season. The Detroit Tigers lost 102 games, the second-worst season in their history.

The loss of Hunter didn't stop Oakland from winning the West again. Vida Blue was 22–11, his third 20-win season in five years. Bosman was 11–4 after he came over from Cleveland. The A's had a tough three-man bullpen with Rollie Fingers, Paul Lindblad and Jim Todd. Claudell Washington hit .308 and stole 40 bases, taking over in left field and bumping Joe Rudi to first base. Dick Green finally made good on his promises to retire, but Phil Garner was an adequate replacement.

The Royals had 91 wins, the best total in Kansas City history, but never seriously challenged for the title. Whitey Herzog replaced Jack McKeon as manager. George Brett's .308 average was sixth in the league and he led with 195 hits.

Texas had some sharp reversals as Ferguson Jenkins' record fell from 25–12 to 17–18 while Jeff Burroughs' average tumbled from .301 to .226.

The Minnesota Twins didn't have enough pitching, a point illustrated by a six-game stretch that saw them score 38 runs but go 0–6 because they gave up 54.

Ex-Twin Jim Kaat won 20 games for the

Chicago White Sox with a new no-windup delivery. The big story in Chicago was an on-going feud between flamboyant broadcaster Harry Caray and a pair of players, Bill Melton and Ken Henderson.

The California Angels had 220 stolen bases, the most since the 1916 Boston Braves (234). That didn't prevent them from finishing last. Nolan Ryan was 14–12 and missed the last month of the season.

Hank Aaron returned to Milwaukee but the Brewers posted a losing record

AL CHAMPIONSHIP SERIES

GAME 1
Boston Red Sox 7   Oakland 1

GAME 2
Boston Red Sox 6   Oakland 3

GAME 3
Boston Red Sox 5   Oakland 3

NL CHAMPIONSHIP SERIES

GAME 1
Cincinnati 8   Pittsburgh 3

GAME 2
Cincinnati 6   Pittsburgh 1

GAME 3
Cincinnati 5   Pittsburgh 3

WORLD SERIES

GAME 1
Boston Red Sox 6   Cincinnati 0

GAME 2
Cincinnati 3   Boston Red Sox 2

GAME 3
Cincinnati 6   Boston Red Sox 5

GAME 4
Boston Red Sox 5   Cincinnati 4

GAME 5
Cincinnati 6   Boston Red Sox 5

GAME 6
Boston Red Sox 7   Cincinnati 6

GAME 7
Cincinnati 4   Boston Red Sox 3

MVP: Pete Rose, Cincinnati

Rain delayed Game Six of the World Series by three days. It was well worth the wait. The game turned out to be a World Series classic between the Cincinnati Reds and Boston Red Sox and created an enduring video image of Boston catcher Carlton Fisk commanding his high fly to left to stay fair.

Long before Fisk unleashed his desperate body language, the Reds were threatening to storm through the Series just the way they'd dominated the regular season and the National League play-offs. Cincinnati won the National League West by 20 games over the defending champion Los Angeles Dodgers. To put that margin in perspective, the last-place team in the National League East, Montreal, finished 17½ games behind the division-winning Pittsburgh Pirates.

The Pirates were gone in three games, playing a series in which only one game was even competitive. Cincinnati swept the first two at Riverfront Stadium, winning 8–3 and 6–1. Don Gullett hit a home run, drove in three runs and held the Pirates to eight hits in the opener. The Reds ran at will against the Pirates and looked like they were headed for an easy sweep.

Rookie lefthander John Candelaria delayed the inevitable with a masterful job in the third game. Candelaria set a playoff record with 14 strikeouts and had a 2–1 lead in the eighth inning. He had allowed just one hit, Dave Concepcion's second-inning home run. Pete Rose hit a two-run homer in the eighth for a 3–2 lead. The Pirates tied the game in the ninth, but lost in the tenth.

Boston had prevailed over the Baltimore Orioles in the American League East, then ended Oakland's three-year championship run with a playoff sweep. The A's made four errors and lost the opener 7–1. Boston rallied in the late innings for a 6–3 win in the second game and Rick Wise dealt Ken Holtzman his second loss of the short series in the final game.

Luis Tiant pitched a five-hitter to win Game

The Reds' Tony Perez in action during the classic World Series encounter against the Red Sox

Cincinnati's Big Red Machine, including Johnny Bench, clashed with the Red Sox and came out on top

One of the Series, 6–0. The Reds trailed 2–1 in the eighth inning of Game Two before rallying to win 3–2. Dave Concepcion hit the game-tying single and scored on Ken Griffey's double. Rawly Eastwick pitched the last two innings and protected the lead.

The Reds scored in the tenth to win Game Three, 6–5. They survived losing a 5–1 lead that was built on home runs by Johnny Bench, Concepcion and Cesar Geronimo. The Red Sox maintained that the Series was changed by a non-call which led to the winning run. Geronimo singled to open the tenth and pinch hitter Ed Armbrister bunted. Fisk jumped out to get the ball, but his path was impeded by Armbrister. Fisk made a bad throw to second, putting runners at second and third with nobody out. Umpire Larry Arnett rejected the Red Sox's pleas for an interference call and the Reds wound up winning the game on Joe Morgan's single.

Tiant won Game Four to even the Series. He pitched a complete game despite allowing four runs. In Game Five, Tony Perez broke a 0-for-15 streak with two home runs that accounted for four of the runs in a 6–2 win.

That gave the Reds a chance to win, but the rain gave the Red Sox the chance to trot out Tiant again. Fred Lynn's home run gave the Red Sox a 3–0 lead in the first inning. The Reds tied it in the fifth when Griffey's triple drove in two runs and Bench had an RBI single.

Cincinnati went ahead 6–3 when George Foster hit a two-run double in the seventh and Geronimo homered an inning later. Bernie Carbo, who had started his career with the Reds, pinch hit a three-run homer in the eighth to tie the score. After threats from both teams were dashed, Fisk led off the 12th against Pat Darcy. The towering drive off the foul pole gave the Red Sox the 7–6 and forced the seventh game.

Boston took a quick 3–0 lead, but the Reds tied the game in the seventh. Griffey walked in the ninth and advanced on two outs. Morgan hit a tie-breaking single off Jim Burton and Will McEnaney shut down the Red Sox in the ninth for the Reds' first championship since 1940.

MOST VALUABLE PLAYER
AL: Thurman Munson, NY Yankees
NL: Joe Morgan, Cincinnati

CY YOUNG AWARD
AL: Jim Palmer, Baltimore
NL: Randy Jones, San Diego

ROOKIE OF THE YEAR
AL: Mark Fidrych, Detroit
NL: Butch Metzger, San Diego; Pat Zachry, Cincinnati

LEADERS
BATTING AVERAGE
AL: George Brett, Kansas City, .333
NL: Bill Madlock, Chicago Cubs, .339

HOME RUNS
AL: Graig Nettles, NY Yankees, 32
NL: Mike Schmidt, Philadelphia Phillies, 38

RUNS BATTED IN
AL: Lee May, Baltimore, 109
NL: George Foster, Cincinnati, 121

STOLEN BASES
AL: Bill North, Oakland, 75
NL: Davey Lopes, Los Angeles, 63

PITCHING VICTORIES
AL: Jim Palmer, Baltimore, 22
NL: Randy Jones, San Diego, 22

EARNED RUN AVERAGE
AL: Mark Fidrych, Detroit, 2.34
NL: John Denny, St. Louis Cardinals, 2.52

STRIKEOUTS
AL: Nolan Ryan, California, 327
NL: Tom Seaver, NY Mets, 235

SAVES
AL: Sparky Lyle, NY Yankees, 23
NL: Rawly Eastwick, Cincinnati, 26

America celebrated its bicentennial and major league players marked the year by gaining unprecedented freedom. A challenge of the reserve clause by pitchers Andy Messersmith of the Los Angeles Dodgers and Dave McNally of the Montreal Expos gave baseball players some of the rights Curt Flood had been seeking several years earlier.

Messersmith and McNally refused to sign contracts for the 1975 season while they continued to perform for their respective teams. The teams exercised the rights to automatically renew those contracts. The players argued that the club was entitled to just one more year. Management contended it could renew the contracts in perpetuity.

Arbitrator Peter Seitz earned his spot in baseball history by ruling in favor of the players' case. The ruling was later upheld by the courts and baseball's reserve clause was struck down. Stated as simply as possible, the reserve clause bound a player to the team that held his rights until that team decided to reassign those rights—either by trade or unconditional release.

The players had won total freedom, but their union negotiated limits in a new agreement that was struck after the owners delayed the start of spring training by closing camps. It was the beginning of changes that would shake baseball's very foundation over future decades.

It was all too new to have a widespread direct impact on the 1976 season. Status quo was good for the Cincinnati Reds, who had one of the strongest offensive lineups in baseball. The Reds made it five National League West titles in seven years by storming to an easy win over the Los Angeles Dodgers.

The Reds became the National League's first back-to-back World Series winner since the 1921–22 New York Giants. Cincinnati placed five starters among the eight position players on the National League All-Star team and five regulars hit above .300.

Joe Morgan won his second consecutive National League Most Valuable Player award. The Reds' .280 batting average was the highest in 46 years and their 857 runs set a club record. They stole 210 bases, the most by a Cincinnati team since 1914.

Seven pitchers won in double figures, led by Gary Nolan, who had 15 victories. Pete Rose had his eighth season with at least 200 hits, one short of Ty Cobb's record. The Reds were great entertainment, which is why they drew more than 2.6 million fans.

Once again it was the Dodgers' misfortune to share a division with a powerhouse. Los Angeles' 92–70 record was the majors' fourth best, but the Dodgers finished ten games behind the Reds in manager Walter Alston's final year. The Reds swept four games from the Dodgers in August to knock them 13 games behind and end any hope of contending. The Dodgers compensated for Messersmith's move to Atlanta with Don Sutton posting his first 20-win season. Rookie

Pete Rose epitomized the Reds' excellence as they again won the National League West title

Rick Rhoden went 12–3.

Houston was on the upswing with a new management team consisting of general manager Tal Smith and manager Bill Virdon. The Astros boasted a young pitching staff, headed by hard-throwing J.R. Richard, which enjoyed working in the pitcher-friendly Astrodome.

The Giants didn't have a good season, but San Francisco was relieved to still have a team. A plan to sell the Giants to a group in Toronto was scuttled when Robert Lurie stepped up to buy the team for $8 million.

San Diego had its most successful season, winning 73 games, but the Padres had a power shortage. Dave Winfield led the team in home runs with a modest total of 13. Lefthander Randy Jones was 16–3 at the All-Star break and wound up 22–14—a frequent victim of his team's poor offense.

Messersmith found pitching for the Braves much more difficult than it was with the more talented Dodgers. He was just 11–11. His signing was orchestrated by Ted Turner, a flamboyant television executive and yachtsman who had purchased the struggling franchise.

After being frustrated by the Pittsburgh Pirates' dominance of the National League East, the Philadelphia Phillies finally broke through and won the division. The Phillies had a franchise-record 101 wins and finished nine games ahead of Pittsburgh.

Steve Carlton was 20–7 and Ron Reed had eight wins and 14 saves in part of an effective bullpen that also included Tug McGraw and Gene Garber. Mike Schmidt won his third consecutive home run title with 38 and Garry

Ted Turner had plenty to smile about as he joined the ranks of Major League owners

Maddox had a breakthrough season, batting .330 and providing exceptional defense in center field.

The Pirates' run of five titles in six years ended and so did the reign of the men most responsible for that success. General manager Joe L. Brown and manager Danny Murtaugh retired, ending a partnership that had started in the minor leagues two decades earlier.

The Pirates made a late run at the Phillies, drawing within three games thanks to a 15–2 streak. Phillies cast-off, Bill Robinson, blossomed in his home town, batting .303 for the Pirates with 21 homers and 64 RBIs. Lefthander John Candelaria emerged as the team's best pitcher and threw a no-hitter at the Dodgers in August. George Medich flopped after coming over from the New York Yankees in an off-season trade and the Pirates were supplanted by the rising Phillies.

The New York Mets were counting on Mike Vail to make up for the absence of Rusty Staub, who was traded to Detroit. Vail, however, broke his ankle in an off-season basketball game and the main player acquired in the trade, Mickey Lolich, was a disappointment, going just 8–13. Tom Seaver spent much of the season locked in a contract dispute with the Mets.

Montreal changed managers after Karl Kuehl clashed with one of his players, Tim Foli. Charlie

TIMELINE

Jan. 14: Ted Turner purchased the Atlanta Braves.

March 17: After a lockout of more than two weeks, commissioner Bowie Kuhn ordered spring training camps open.

April 2: Oakland traded Reggie Jackson and Ken Holtzman to Baltimore.

April 10: The Braves signed free agent Andy Messersmith to a $1 million contract.

April 15: Refurbished Yankee Stadium opened with the Yankees' 13–4 win over the Twins.

Apsril 17: The Phillies' Mike Schmidt had four home runs and eight RBIs as his team rallied from a 12–2 deficit to beat the Cubs 18–12 in ten innings.

May 15: Mark Fidrych of the Tigers pitched a two-hitter in his first major league start and beat the Indians 2–1.

May 29: Houston's Joe Niekro hit a home run off his brother Phil of the Braves.

June 15: A game at Houston's Astrodome was postponed because of rain. The visiting Pirates made it to the park through heavy rains, but the umpires and stadium employees didn't.

June 22: Randy Jones of the Padres set a record by pitching his 68th consecutive inning without allowing a walk.

July 3: Mark Fidrych won his eighth consecutive game for the Tigers.

July 20: Hank Aaron hit the 755th and last home run of his career off Dick Drago of the Angels.

Sept. 12: Minnie Minoso, 53, got a single for the White Sox as he played in his fourth decade. Minoso was a White Sox coach who was placed on the roster for the last month, 12 years after his retirement.

Nov. 5: Expansion franchises in Seattle and Toronto drafted players.

Nov. 29: Reggie Jackson signed with the Yankees as a free agent.

Dec. 5: Danny Murtaugh, who managed the Pirates to World Series titles in 1960 and 1971, died in Chester, Pennsylvania at 59.

Mike Schmidt's hot bat helped the Phillies to a division title

Fox stepped in briefly until the Expos hired Dick Williams, who had been fired by the California Angels.

The Yankees celebrated the opening of their refurbished stadium with a divisional title, their first since 1974. Thurman Munson became the Yankees' first MVP since Elston Howard in 1963 and Graig Nettles was the team's first home run champion since Roger Maris eclipsed Babe Ruth's record in 1961.

Sending Medich to Pittsburgh worked out per-

fectly for the Yankees. Dock Ellis pitched well and second baseman Willie Randolph established himself as a major leaguer. Ed Figueroa won 19 games and manager Billy Martin furthered his reputation for improving the teams that hired him.

The Baltimore Orioles had a bad start, which they came to regret when they played the Yankees on even terms after the All-Star break. The Orioles traded for Reggie Jackson and Ken Holtzman, free agents to be who were discarded by Oakland.

The Boston Red Sox had a disappointing year from their pitching staff, 21-game winner Luis Tiant aside. The team fired Darrell Johnson and replaced him with Don Zimmer. The Red Sox tried to buy outfielder Joe Rudi and reliever Rollie Fingers from the A's, but Commissioner Bowie Kuhn rejected the sales.

A's owner Charles O. Finley's answer to free agency was to sell off players while he still had their rights. In addition to packaging Rudi and Fingers to the Red Sox for $1 million, Finley also tried to sell Vida Blue to the Yankees. That deal was also voided with Kuhn invoking his broad powers to act in the best interest of the game.

Kuhn's fear was that Finley would turn players into cash for himself, then leave the Oakland organization devoid of talent before he sold the franchise. Finley and Kuhn slugged it out in the courts and Finley shifted his focus on trades.

For the first time since 1970, Finley's A's didn't win the American League West. They were overtaken by the Kansas City Royals, who

SHORTS One of the season's most impressive managing jobs was turned in by Chuck Tanner in his only year with Oakland. Despite all the distractions and defections, Tanner kept the A's in the race. He was so impressive that the Pirates sent their starting catcher, Manny Sanguillen, and $100,000 to Oakland to acquire the right to hire Tanner as Danny Murtaugh's replacement.

brought that city its first title. The Royals won despite pitching ace Steve Busby's shoulder woes and a 12–22 finish.

Gene Mauch's Minnesota Twins batted .274 with Rod Carew posting his third 200-hit season. The Twins disposed of Bert Blyleven during the season, trading their No. 1 starter to Texas. The Rangers, however, undermined their pitching staff with poor offense. At one point, Gaylord Perry pitched 30 innings without getting a single run of support.

The Angels celebrated the unpopular Williams' departure by playing well for Norm Sherry, who replaced him in July. The Angels had an impressive right-left combination at the top of their rotation. Nolan Ryan had 327 strikeouts and Frank Tanana was 19–10 with a 2.44 earned run average and 261 strikeouts.

Bill Veeck brought customer service back to the Chicago White Sox, but couldn't offer much of a team. The White Sox were woefully short of power and they lost their No. 1 starter on May 9, when Wilbur Wood sustained a fractured kneecap.

After the season, baseball held its first free agent re-entry draft. Appropriately, it was held in the tony atmosphere of New York's Plaza Hotel as baseball executives got to the business of making the players wealthy. Minnesota reliever, Bill Campbell, became the first player to sign with a new team when he made a deal with the Red Sox.

American League MVP Thurman Munson led by example as the Yanks won their first pennant since 1964

387

AL CHAMPIONSHIP SERIES

GAME 1	
NY Yankees 4	Kansas City 1

GAME 2	
Kansas City 7	NY Yankees 3

GAME 3	
NY Yankees 5	Kansas City 3

GAME 4	
Kansas City 7	NY Yankees 4

GAME 5	
NY Yankees 7	Kansas City 6

NL CHAMPIONSHIP SERIES

GAME 1	
Cincinnati 6	Philadelphia 3

GAME 2	
Cincinnati 6	Philadelphia 2

GAME 3	
Cincinnati 7	Philadelphia 6

WORLD SERIES

GAME 1	
Cincinnati 5	NY Yankees 1

GAME 2	
Cincinnati 4	NY Yankees 3

GAME 3	
Cincinnati 6	NY Yankees 2

GAME 4	
Cincinnati 7	NY Yankees 2

MVP: Johnny Bench, Cincinnati

Whoever tagged the Cincinnati Reds "The Big Red Machine" looked like a prophet in 1976. The Reds won the championship as efficiently as possible. They led the major leagues with 102 wins in the regular season, swept the Philadelphia Phillies in the playoffs, then swept the New York Yankees in the World Series.

The Reds combined power and speed better than any club in the game. Pete Rose, Ken Griffey and Joe Morgan set the table and Tony Perez, George Foster and Johnny Bench drove in the runs. The offense let the Reds get by with a pitching staff that was less than spectacular, and manager Sparky Anderson was masterful in using his bullpen.

Little wonder that the Reds were being compared favorably with some of baseball's finest teams. The other teams in the postseason field were relative newcomers.

The Yankees were the game's most-storied franchise, but they hadn't been in the postseason since losing the 1964 World Series to the St. Louis Cardinals. That was the end of a phenomenal run that saw the Yankees dominate the American League for nearly two decades. The organization's fertile farm system dried up and when stars got old and injured there was no pipeline of replacements.

The Yankees hit rock bottom in the late 1960s before they started to get better in the early part of the 1970s. New owner George Steinbrenner would accelerate that process by whipping out his checkbook once free agency became part of the game.

New York had gotten a head start on free agency when a contract technicality allowed Catfish Hunter to escape Oakland. The bidding war was fierce for the game's best pitcher, one who was also in the prime of his career and battle-tested in the postseason. The Yankees signed Hunter and he helped them finally overcome Baltimore in the American League East.

In the West, Kansas City ended Oakland's five-year title reign as the A's slipped to second without Hunter in their rotation. The Royals used

The formidable Cincinnati Reds received favorable comparisons with baseball's greatest ever teams

pitching, speed and defense under Whitey Herzog's aggressive managing.

The Philadelphia Phillies were finally able to overtake Pittsburgh in the National League East. The Phillies were doormats in the early part of the 1970s, but they made shrewd trades and developed talent and turned their club around. The Phillies finished nine games ahead of Pittsburgh.

Philadelphia was no match for the Reds, though. Cincinnati beat Phillies ace Steve Carlton in the opening game of the playoffs and it was downhill from there for Philadelphia. The Reds won the second game 6–2 and wrapped up the series with a three-run ninth inning that gave them a 7–6 victory.

The Yankees needed the full five games and Chris Chambliss' dramatic home run to dispose of the Royals. The teams traded wins in the first four games before Chambliss connected off Mark Littell in the bottom of the ninth of the last game.

Before the World Series, Reds scout Ray Shore boldly predicted at an organizational meeting that Cincinnati would sweep the Yankees. Shore was mortified when his private

prediction became public, but the Reds got him off the hook. Shore had spent several weeks following the Yankees to formulate a scouting report and his experience told him the Yankees simply weren't as good as the Reds. He was right.

Cincinnati took the opening game of the World Series 5–1. Morgan homered in the first off Doyle Alexander, while Don Gullett and Pedro Borbon combined on a five-hitter. The Reds beat Hunter in Game Two when shortstop Fred Stanley's error led to a tie-breaking run in the ninth inning and a 4–3 win.

The first Series with the designated hitter rule helped the Reds more than the Yankees. Reds DH Dan Driessen was 3-for-3 with a home run in Game Three's 6–2 win. Driessen didn't have a regular role with the Reds, which spoke volumes about the depth of Cincinnati's offensive talent. Driessen would have been a starter on most clubs.

Bench helped end the Series when he drove in five runs with a pair of homers in Game Four. The Reds won 7–2 and became the first National League team to win consecutive World Series since the New York Giants of 1921–22.

Johnny Bench's two home runs were enough to complete the Reds' sweep

JOHNNY BENCH

A player had to be awfully good to stand out on the powerful Cincinnati Reds teams of the 1970s. Johnny Bench didn't have a problem making his presence known.

TEAMS
Cincinnati Reds 1967–83

Games:	2,158
At-Bats:	7,658
Runs:	1,091
RBI:	1,376
Home runs:	389
Hits:	2,048
Doubles:	381
Triples:	24
Stolen Bases:	68
Average:	0.267
Slugging percentage:	0.476

Bench was the steady hand behind the plate for the Cincinnati Reds, a major force in the middle of their batting order and a first-ballot Hall of Famer.

Bench came from the tiny town of Binger, Oklahoma, where his father had worked to develop his skills. Making throws to second base was no problem in the major leagues, because Bench had trained by throwing twice the distance from home to second—from a crouch.

Frequent batting practice sharpened a stroke that would produce 389 home runs, a record for catchers at the time. Just to prove that the baseball draft is an inexact science, all 20 major league teams passed over Bench when he was eligible in 1965. The Reds took him on the second round.

In short order, Bench established himself as a blue chip prospect. He was so dominant in his first year of professional baseball that his team retired his uniform number. Bench earned the honor by hitting 22 home runs in 98 games for Peninsula of the Carolina League.

He advanced to Class AAA Buffalo the next season, but Cincinnati came calling before the year was out. The Reds were so convinced that Bench was the answer that they traded veteran Johnny Edwards. The job belonged to the 20-year-old Bench.

In 1968 he became the National League's Rookie of the Year, catching 154 games, which stands as a record for a first-year catcher. He made the All-Star team that summer and the game would become a regular stop on his schedule. He was chosen to play in the All-Star game 14 times, including every game from 1968 to 1975. Bench batted .370 in All-Star games.

He helped change the way the position was played. Bench was gifted with large hands and perfected the knack of receiving the ball with one hand. He used a large hinged glove and

kept his throwing hand behind his back to protect it from foul tips. Bench was quick enough to bring his hand up if he needed to make a throw. Baseball purists criticized his methods, but Bench won ten consecutive Gold Glove awards and within a few years almost every catcher was using his style.

He was a key component on Reds teams that won six division titles and two World Series. Until then, conventional wisdom in baseball held that catchers should handle the pitching staff and perform defensively. Offense was considered a bonus.

No one provided a bigger bonus than Bench. He twice led the National League in home runs and was the RBI leader in three seasons. His first great year was 1970, when he won the Most Valuable Player award for the first time.

Bench hit 45 home runs and drove in 148 runs, both records for catchers.

A contract holdout slowed him in 1971, but he bounced back in 1972, again helping the Reds to a Western Division title. At one point in the season Bench hit a total of seven home runs in five consecutive games and wound up with 40 homers and 125 RBIs.

Bench had a bad postseason in 1975, batting .077 in the playoffs against Pittsburgh and then hitting just .207 in the World Series against Boston. He made up for it in 1976.

Despite a subpar regular season (.234 average, 16 home runs and 74 RBIs), Bench was unstoppable in the postseason. He hit .333 in the three-game playoff sweep of the Phillies. He saved the best for the World Series.

It was an intriguing matchup of two high-profile catchers—Thurman Munson of the New York Yankees against Bench. Munson was great, hitting .529 with two RBIs. Bench was even better, batting .533 with six RBIs to take Series MVP honors as the Reds won four straight games.

Bench caught at least 100 games in each of his first 13 seasons and the grind caught up with him. He moved to first base briefly, then played mostly at third base until he retired after the 1983 season. He was inducted into the Hall of Fame in 1989.

Bench redefined many catching fundamentals—but was also a huge offensive threat

It was bad news for the legions of New York Yankees haters. The Yankees were not only back on top, they had reacquired that swagger for which Yankees teams had become famous a generation earlier.

The Yankees' Reggie Jackson impacted box scores and headlines with equal regularity

The team and its daily off-field drama had become so familiar that some of the key characters were easily identified by first name only—Billy. Reggie. George.

Billy was Martin, the manager who had spent most of his playing career with the Yankees and fulfilled a dream by managing the team his mentor, Casey Stengel, had led.

Reggie was Jackson, the high-profile star who sought the spotlight and had a knack for doing dramatic things in key situations.

And George was Steinbrenner, the impulsive owner, who loved attention as much as Jackson did and seemingly always had an angle to keep the Yankees in the news.

Steinbrenner had stacks of money and baseball-savvy advisers who made sure he spent it on the right players. The Yankees had been building through their farm system, with players like catcher Thurman Munson and lefthander Ron Guidry. They made shrewd trades to get future stars like Willie Randolph and Graig Nettles.

The new free agency system was the last piece of the player procurement puzzle and the Yankees used their money and know-how to lock up Catfish Hunter and Reggie Jackson.

It all came together with the Yankees' first World Series championship in 15 years, but it was anything but a smooth ride. The unofficial count had Martin fired five different times during the season. Luckily, none of them counted and Martin stayed for the entire year.

Martin and Jackson clashed openly, but never as blatantly as they did on the afternoon of June 18 at Boston. Jackson was slow to get to a ball and Martin fumed, believing Jackson had given less than a good effort on the play. He sent a replacement in and ordered Jackson off the field in the middle of the inning, an embarrassment of the highest order to a player.

Jackson was incredulous when he reached the dugout and asked Martin why he was being removed. The manager told him and the two men tried to get at each other. Players and

New Dodger manager Tom Lasorda (l) gives some tips to outfielder Rick Monday

March 21: Mark Fidrych of the Tigers sustained a knee injury during spring training.

March 28: Texas infielder Lenny Randle physically attacked manager Frank Lucchesi.

April 5: The White Sox traded shortstop Bucky Dent to the Yankees.

April 6: Major league baseball returned to Seattle as the expansion Mariners lost 7–0 to the Angels.

April 7: The Toronto Blue Jays debuted with a 9–5 win over the White Sox as Al Woods hit a pinch homer in his first major league at bat.

April 15: The Phillies beat the Expos 7–2 in the first game at Olympic Stadium.

May 11: Braves' owner Ted Turner sent manager Dave Bristol on vacation and managed the team to a 2–1 loss in Pittsburgh.

May 14: Kansas City's Jim Colborn pitched a no-hitter against Texas.

May 17: The Cubs hit seven home runs and beat San Diego 23–6.

May 28: Alvin Dark replaced John McNamara as Padres' manager.

May 30: Cleveland's Dennis Eckersley pitched a no-hitter against the Angels.

May 31: The Mets fired Joe Frazier and named Joe Torre as player-manager.

June 10: The A's fired Jack McKeon and hired Bobby Winkles as manager.

June 15: The Mets traded Tom Seaver to Cincinnati.

June 19: Cleveland fired Frank Robinson and replaced him with Jeff Torborg.

July 25: Pete Rose got his 2,881st career hit, topping Frankie Frisch's record for career hits by a switch hitter.

Aug. 27: Toby Harrah and Bump Wills of Texas hit inside-the-park homers on consecutive pitches.

Aug. 29: Lou Brock stole his 893rd base to break Ty Cobb's career record.

Sept. 16: The Royals' 16-game winning streak ended with a 4–1 loss to Seattle.

Sept. 20: The Dodgers beat the Giants to clinch the National League West and deny the Reds a chance at a third straight championship.

coaches wrestled them apart and Jackson disappeared into the clubhouse. The game was nationally televised and kicked off a series of Yankees explosions that would be the talk of baseball for the next two decades.

When the Yankees weren't fighting they were winning, much as Jackson's Oakland A's teams had done earlier in the decade. The Yankees were strong down the stretch, due in no small part to a lineup adjustment Martin had made. On August 10, Martin installed Jackson in the cleanup spot and the Yankees responded by going 41–12 the rest of the season. Martin may not have cared for Jackson or his flamboyant style, but he recognized his talent.

Woe were the teams that managed 97 games but found themselves in the same division as the Yankees. The Baltimore Orioles and Boston Red Sox each won 97, an impressive total in most years.

The Orioles played well even though free agency had blown some major holes in their roster. In one offseason, the Orioles lost Jackson to the Yankees, infielder Bobby Grich to the California Angels and pitcher Wayne Garland to Cleveland. Doug DeCinces stepped up to replace Brooks Robinson at third base. Eddie Murray, a 21-year-old rookie, took over at first base and hit 27 home runs, the same number Jackson had hit the previous season.

Jim Palmer was 20–11, the seventh time in eight years that he won 20 games. The Orioles had the franchise's fourth-best win total, but couldn't catch the Yankees.

The Red Sox also posted the fourth-highest number of victories and had an amazing offensive season. Boston had four players hit at least 25 home runs and led the majors with 213

The Phillies' Greg Luzinski hit for both average and power as Philadelphia won the National League East title

homers, the fifth-highest total in baseball history. But the Red Sox also served up plenty of home runs with a poor pitching staff whose biggest winner was Luis Tiant with just 12 victories.

Mark Fidrych's magical rookie season was not repeated in Detroit. After 19 wins and an earned run average title in 1976, Fidrych was limited to 11 starts and went 6–4. Fidrych struggled after tearing cartilage in his knee. The Tigers got a surprising 15–7 season from Dave Rozema, whose season ended early with shoulder problems.

The big story in Cleveland was the firing of Frank Robinson two-and-a-half years after he had become the game's first black manager. Coach Jeff Torborg took over. The Indians also demonstrated how chancy the free agent game was with a ten-year, $12.3-million commitment to Garland, who went 13–19.

In the West, the Kansas City Royals had winning streaks of eight, ten and 16 games en route to their second consecutive divisional title. The 16-game streak was the majors' longest in 24 years. The Royals won 102 games, tops in the major leagues, and went 26–6 in September to easily outdistance the Texas Rangers. Righthander Dennis Leonard was just 4–8 on June 8, but finished the season 20–12.

Texas finally settled on a manager when Bill Hunter took over after a long run as one of Earl Weaver's coaches in Baltimore.

The Chicago White Sox shed their label of "punchless" by hitting a club record 192 home runs. Oscar Gamble and Richie Zisk provided

a good deal of the power with Zisk knocking in 101 runs.

The Minnesota Twins had offense but not enough pitching. Rod Carew won the batting title with a .388 average, the highest since Ted Williams hit .406 in 1941. The Twins also got a solid one-two punch from Larry Hisle and Lyman Bostock.

Grich's first year with the Angels ended in early June when he required back surgery. Another free agent, Joe Rudi, broke his hand and missed considerable time. Manager Norm Sherry was fired and replaced by Dave Garcia.

Oakland, decimated by free agency, lost 98 games and finished behind the expansion Seattle Mariners.

In the National League, the Los Angeles Dodgers started the season 17–3 and breezed to the West Division title. Ron Cey did much of the damage in April, hitting .425 in the opening month with nine home runs and a record-setting 29 RBI. The Dodgers hit 191 home runs, a high for the franchise in Los Angeles. They also

SHORTS Each league had a manager for a day under bizarre circumstances. With the Atlanta Braves struggling, owner Ted Turner told manager Dave Bristol to take some time off and suited up as Bristol's replacement. Turner's presence was strictly ceremonial as coach Vern Benson made the moves. The National League office ended Turner's managerial career after one game. The Texas Rangers fired Frank Lucchesi and hired Eddie Stanky. But Stanky quit after one game, saying he was homesick.

became the first team to have four players with at least 30 home runs—Steve Garvey, Reggie Smith, Cey and Dusty Baker.

Lefthander Tommy John had his first 20-win season and Rick Rhoden contributed 16 wins. John rebounded nicely after revolutionary surgery replaced a tendon in his arm.

The season was a satisfying debut for Tom Lasorda, who had succeeded Walter Alston as manager following a long stint in the Dodgers' minor league system. The Dodgers' success scuttled the Cincinnati Reds' chances of winning a third consecutive World Series. George Foster had an impressive season, batting .320 with 52 home runs and 149 RBIs.

The Reds also acquired Tom Seaver in-season after he clashed with the New York Mets' front office.

Seaver finished the season by winning 13 of 14 games, but that and Pete Rose's ninth 200-hit season weren't enough to overtake the Dodgers.

The San Francisco Giants reclaimed Willie McCovey after Oakland had released him and he rewarded their confidence with a comeback season that included 28 home runs and 86 RBIs.

The San Diego Padres had mixed results with former Oakland free agents—reliever Rollie Fingers had a good season, but catcher Gene Tenace didn't. Pitcher Butch Metzger didn't repeat the success that had won him a share of

the Rookie of the Year award and was traded.

The Atlanta Braves lost 101 games, their worst season since 1937. It wasn't the fault of Jeff Burroughs, who hit 41 home runs and drove in 114 runs.

The Philadelphia Phillies went 101–61 for a second consecutive year and won another East Division title. Greg Luzinski had his third straight year over .300, batting .309 with 39 home runs and 130 RBIs. Steve Carlton led the staff with a 23–10 season and free agent Richie Hebner, who had been part of five division winners with Pittsburgh, plugged a hole at first base.

Dave Parker emerged as one of the game's best players with the Pirates, putting together a pair of 22-game hitting streaks. The Pirates finally had speed to accompany their power—Frank Taveras stole 70 bases, breaking the team record Max Carey set in 1916. He became part of a running game that new manager Chuck Tanner emphasized. John Candelaria became the Pirates' best pitcher, going 20–5 with a 9–1 finish. Reliever Rich Gossage, acquired from the White Sox on Tanner's recommendation, was 11–9 with 26 saves.

The St. Louis Cardinals finished second despite getting just 96 home runs, the second-lowest total in the majors. The Chicago Cubs led the East briefly and were 25 games over .500 at midseason. They faded and finished third.

The Phillies' Steve Carlton wound up with 23 wins and the Cy Young award

1977 POSTSEASON

AL CHAMPIONSHIP SERIES

GAME 1

Kansas City 7 | NY Yankees 2

GAME 2

NY Yankees 6 | Kansas City 2

GAME 3

Kansas City 6 | NY Yankees 2

GAME 4

NY Yankees 6 | Kansas City 4

GAME 5

NY Yankees 5 | Kansas City 3

NL CHAMPIONSHIP SERIES

GAME 1

Philadelphia Phillies 7 | Los Angeles 5

GAME 2

Los Angeles 7 | Philadelphia Phillies 1

GAME 3

Los Angeles 6 | Philadelphia Phillies 5

GAME 4

Los Angeles 4 | Philadelphia Phillies 1

WORLD SERIES

GAME 1

NY Yankees 4 | Los Angeles 3

GAME 2

Los Angeles 6 | NY Yankees 1

GAME 3

NY Yankees 5 | Los Angeles 3

GAME 4

NY Yankees 4 | Los Angeles 2

GAME 5

Los Angeles 10 | NY Yankees 4

GAME 6

NY Yankees 8 | Los Angeles 4

MVP: Reggie Jackson, NY Yankees

No one enjoyed the spotlight more than Reggie Jackson. The 1977 World Series was his show, the event that gave Jackson the nickname "Mr. October."

Jackson signed with the New York Yankees because the nation's largest media market would provide him with the most attention. It wasn't always good. Jackson and manager Billy Martin were both headstrong and almost instantly distrusted each other. They were a volatile mix all season and had a nationally-televised showdown when Martin yanked Jackson off the field for what he perceived as a lack of hustle on the player's part.

Jackson also clashed with Thurman Munson, the Yankee's dumpy, no-nonsense catcher who had been the team's focal point before Jackson arrived. The two men were polar opposites and Munson resented Jackson's high-profile approach.

But Jackson learned one thing with Oakland, the organization that first brought him to the big leagues. Personalities are put aside for the bigger goal. The A's teams that Jackson played on were filled with conflict, but it never got in the way of winning. The A's may not have always liked each other, but they were committed to getting the job done on the field, no matter what differences they may have had in the clubhouse.

So it was with the Yankees, who headed into the season still disappointed by their four-game loss to the Cincinnati Reds in the previous year's World Series. The Yankees outlasted Boston and Baltimore in a three-team race to again win the American League East.

The Kansas City Royals were repeat winners in the West, so the teams matched up again after their classic 1976 playoff battle ended with Chris Chambliss' ninth-inning home run in the fifth game. This one was also destined to go the limit.

Reggie Jackson is congratulated at home plate after his Game Six heroics

The Dodgers' Don Sutton kept LA's hopes alive with a crucial victory in Game Five

The Royals won the first game 7–2 behind Paul Splittorff, with Hal McRae, John Mayberry and Al Cowens all hitting home runs. Ron Guidry pitched the Yankees to a 6–2 win in the second game. Kansas City bounced back in the third game with Dennis Leonard pitching the Royals to a 6–2 win. The Yankees won the fourth game, 6–4, to force a deciding game.

Kansas City took a 3–2 lead into the ninth, but Leonard, Larry Gura and Mark Littell couldn't hold it. Paul Blair started the three-run rally with a bloop single and the Yankees earned their ticket back to the World Series with a 5–3 win preserved by Sparky Lyle.

The Los Angeles Dodgers succeeded the two-time World Series champion Cincinnati Reds in the National League West and needed four games to eliminate the Philadelphia Phillies. The teams split the first two games before the playoffs turned in the third game.

The Phillies had a 5–3 lead in the ninth inning with nobody on base and two outs. The Dodgers came up with four consecutive hits to win the game, 6–5, and change the direction of the series. Tommy John beat Steve Carlton in the fourth game and baseball was due for its first Yankees–Dodgers World Series since 1963.

New York won Game One in 12 innings when Willie Randolph doubled and scored on Blair's single. Ron Cey, Reggie Smith and Steve Yeager homered off Catfish Hunter in Game Two and Burt Hooton won for the Dodgers, 6–1.

The Yankees won the next two games to come within a victory of winning the Series. Mike Torrez beat Tommy John 5–3 in Game Three and Ron Guidry won Game Four, 4–2.

Don Sutton helped the Dodgers stay alive by winning Game Five, 10–4, with a three-run homer from Yeager.

That set the stage for Jackson in Game Six. The Yankees trailed 3–2 in the fourth with Munson on first base after a single. Jackson blasted Hooton's first pitch into the right field stands for a 4–3 lead.

An inning later, Jackson homered again with a runner on first. His second home run in as many innings came on Elias Sosa's first pitch.

Jackson completed his hat-trick in the eighth inning against knuckleball specialist, Charlie Hough. His towering shot into the center field bleachers came on Hough's first pitch.

Three at-bats, three pitches, three home runs. It didn't take long to count the ballots for the Series' Most Valuable Player.

TEAMS

Kansas City Athletics 1967; Oakland Athletics 1968–75; Baltimore Orioles 1976; New York Yankees 1977–81; California Angels 1982–86; Oakland Athletics 1987

Games	2,820
At-Bats	9,864
Runs	1,551
RBI	1,702
Home runs	563
Hits	2,584
Doubles	463
Triples	49
Stolen Bases	228
Average	0.262
Slugging percentage	0.490

Jackson relished the added pressure of playing in New York, and responded

Reggie Jackson didn't do anything on a small scale. He spent most of his 21 major league seasons doing things that demanded the spotlight.

From 1971 to 1982, he helped three different teams to win a total of ten division championships, six league titles and five World Series.

You don't get the nickname "Mr. October" because you wilt under postseason pressure. It figures that a high-profile player would do his best work in the showcase portion of the baseball schedule. Jackson was twice voted the Most Valuable Player of the World Series. He batted .357 in Series games and his career slugging percentage of .755 is a Series record.

He won four home run titles, struck out more than anyone in baseball history, slammed 563 home runs and made enough noise off the field to keep his name constantly in the headlines.

Jackson should have been playing in New York much sooner than he did. The New York Mets had the first pick in the 1966 draft and spent it on a catcher named Steve Chilcott, who would never reach the majors. Jackson was the second pick.

Jackson broke in with the Athletics, who were still based in Kansas City, when he made his major league debut in 1967. A year later, the A's moved to Oakland and Jackson began to establish himself as one of the game's best young power hitters. He hit 29 home runs and drove in 74 runs in 1968. A year later, he led the American League with a .608 slugging percentage. His career dipped in 1970, but was revived in 1971 when he hit a towering home run that nearly cleared the roof at Detroit's Tiger Stadium during the All-Star game.

That blast helped put Jackson's name in the mainstream and the A's started winning championships. They had a five-year run of titles from 1971–75 that also included three World Series wins. Jackson was MVP of the 1973 Series win over the New York Mets.

Jackson was one of those rare players who could get hot and carry an entire team for an extended period. He showed that in 1969, when the A's went to Boston for a weekend series and Jackson drove in 15 runs in 14 at-bats.

Getting 15 RBIs would be a good month for some players—Jackson did it in four days.

By 1976, though, the baseball climate had been changed by free agency. Faced with the prospect of losing Jackson, the A's dealt him to the Baltimore Orioles. Jackson knew that his future was in New York, however, where the Yankees had rebuilt a moribund franchise. He signed a five-year contract with the Yankees that started with the 1977 season and announced, "I didn't come to New York to be a star, I brought my star with me."

Pronouncements like that were the reason Oakland teammate, Darold Knowles, said, "There isn't enough mustard in the world to cover that hot dog."

Another teammate, Catfish Hunter, had a wry summary of the conflicted emotions Jackson inspired: "He'd give you the shirt off his back. Of course, he'd call a press conference to announce it."

New York was perfect for Jackson. The tabloids abbreviated his name to "Jax" for headlines, and there were plenty of them. He clashed with manager Billy Martin. He feuded with teammate Thurman Munson. He had a candy bar named after him. He aggravated people, and, above all, he helped the Yankees to win.

He hit five home runs in the 1977 World Series, including three in one game on consecutive pitches from three different Los Angeles Dodgers pitchers—Burt Hooton, Elias Sosa and Charlie Hough. Jackson showed a nation why he deserved to be called "Mr. October".

"It was probably the greatest single-game performance by a player I've ever seen," teammate Graig Nettles said.

Jackson left the Yankees at the end of his contract and signed with the California Angels, where he had a successful first season. He won his last home run title in 1982 with 39 dingers. His career was on the decline, though, and Jackson batted just .227 over his last five seasons. He returned to Oakland for his last year at the age of 41 and hit .220 with 15 home runs. That gave him the sixth-best homer total in baseball history and a 1993 Hall of Fame induction.

Talk about cramming the ultimate high and low into the same season—Bob Lemon had the experience of being fired as manager of the Chicago White Sox, then ending the season by raising the World Series trophy as manager of the New York Yankees.

Lemon jumped on the Yankees' managing carousel just in time for one of the most amazing comebacks in baseball history.

On July 19, the Yankees were 14 games behind in the American League East, a deficit from which no team had ever rebounded to clinch first place. The Yankees were a team in turmoil with manager Billy Martin at the center of the upheaval, involved in a three-way spat with owner George Steinbrenner and star outfielder Reggie Jackson.

When Martin uttered his famous dismissive line about the pair—"One's a born liar, the other is convicted"—the wheels of change went into overdrive and Martin was pressured to resign on July 24.

The Yankees found the perfect replacement in Lemon, who had been dismissed by the White Sox at the end of June. Lemon, a former star pitcher with the Cleveland Indians, had a calm demeanor and didn't care to be in the spotlight. The volatile atmosphere around the team eased and the Yankees began to play up to their talent level.

From July 19 until the end of the season they were 52–21 for an amazing .712 winning percentage. Rich (Goose) Gossage, who signed a $2.7 million free agent contract, was an intimidating force out of the bullpen. Ed Figueroa became the game's first Puerto Rican-born, 20-game winner.

But the most important pitcher was a blade-thin lefthander nicknamed "Louisiana Lightning." Ron Guidry was 25–3 for the best winning percentage (.893) in baseball history for a 20-game winner. His 1.74 earned run average tied Sandy Koufax for the lowest ERA by a lefthander. He struck out 248 batters to break a 78-year-old

Reggie Jackson's feud with manager Billy Martin ended when Martin resigned in July

Yankees record. Guidry had nine shutouts, tying Babe Ruth's record for the most in a season by an American League lefthander.

The Yankees' hot streak coincided with a slide by the first-place Boston Red Sox. Even though the Red Sox had added ex-Yankee Mike Torrez to their rotation, they didn't have the depth to withstand a bad run of injuries. Their 14-game lead shriveled to 4½ games as they lost nine of ten in July.

The Red Sox, who had fallen behind the Yankees, rallied at the end of the season and the teams finished with 99–63 records, good enough to handily win any of the other three divisions. The one-game playoff was in Boston on October 2 and the Yankees won 5–4, with Bucky Dent hitting a decisive and unlikely homer over the left field Green Monster for the margin of victory. Gossage got Carl Yastrzemski to pop out to put another heartbreaking end to a New England baseball season.

The Milwaukee Brewers were the surprise team of the East under manager George Bamberger. Mike Caldwell stepped into the rotation to replace the injured Moose Haas and went 22–9. Larry Hisle batted .290 with 34 home runs and 115 RBIs and Gorman Thomas emerged as a power threat, hitting 32 home runs.

TIMELINE

March 15: The Oakland A's traded pitcher Vida Blue to the San Francisco Giants for seven players and nearly $400,000.

March 21: San Diego fired Alvin Dark and replaced him with Roger Craig. Dark and the Cubs' Phil Cavarretta (1954) are the only managers fired during spring training.

March 28: Dick Allen's career ended when the A's released him.

April 12: Reggie Jackson of the Yankees hit a three-run, first inning home run on the day that "Reggie" candy bars were distributed to fans.

April 16: Bob Forsch of the Cardinals pitched a 4–0 no-hitter over Montreal.

May 5: Pete Rose got his 3,000th hit against Montreal's Steve Rogers and the Cincinnati Reds won 4–3.

May 23: Despite having a first-place team, Bobby Winkles resigned as A's manager and was replaced by Jack McKeon.

June 3: Philadelphia's Dave Johnson got his second pinch hit grand slam of the season.

June 17: The Yankees' Ron Guidry improved to 11–0 with an 18-strikeout 4–0 win over the Angels.

June 30: Willie McCovey of the Giants hit his 500th career home run off Atlanta's Jamie Easterly.

July 17: Reggie Jackson defied manager Billy Martin's orders and was suspended by the Yankees for five games.

July 30: The Montreal Expos had 28 hits and eight homers in a 19–0 rout of the Braves.

Aug. 25: Major league umpires staged a one-day strike over travel-related issues.

Sept. 14: Jim Bouton, 38, completed his comeback by pitching Atlanta to a 4–1 victory over the Giants in San Francisco for his first win in the majors since 1970.

Sept. 30: Philadelphia pitcher Randy Lerch hit two home runs to help the Phillies beat the Pirates and clinch the National League East.

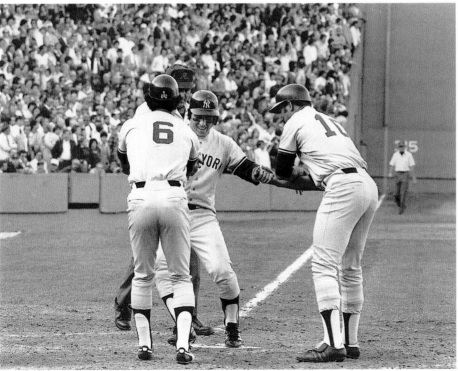

Bucky Dent's playoff homer ensured more postseason misery for the Red Sox

Hired by the White Sox, Larry Doby became the game's second black manager

The Orioles weren't a factor in the race. They wound up nine games behind the Yankees and sorely missed Al Bumbry, who sat out most of the season with a broken leg. Detroit was also a non-factor as erstwhile rookie phenom Mark Fidrych was limited to just three starts by injury.

The Kansas City Royals won the American League West for the third consecutive year, but had their most difficult race, thanks to the California Angels and Texas Rangers.

Third baseman George Brett missed 30 games with a shoulder injury, leaving a huge hole in the Royals' lineup. Kansas City owed its title to both a 20–8 July and a strong pitching staff. Dennis Leonard was 21–17 for his second consecutive 20-win season and Larry Gura went 16–4. Al Hrabosky won eight games and saved 20.

California was in first place as late as August 26. Angels' ace Frank Tanana was 11–3 in the first half of the season, but just 7–9 the rest of the way. The Angels made a managerial change on May 31, firing Dave Garcia and replacing him with Jim Fregosi, who had been one of the most popular players in franchise history.

Ferguson Jenkins went to Texas in the offseason in what was considered a minor transaction. At 34 Jenkins was thought to be finished, burned out by too many busy seasons. He went 18–6 with a 3.04 ERA and helped the Rangers to stay in the race. Al Oliver came over in a trade from Pittsburgh and showed that he needed no time to adjust to a new league. Oliver, one of the most consistent line drive hitters in the game, batted .324 and drove in 89 runs.

Minnesota's Rod Carew won his seventh batting title, but the Twins were too thin after the free agent departures of Hisle and Lyman Bostock. The White Sox replaced Lemon with Larry Doby, who became baseball's second black manager. The White Sox, though, had lost too many players to free agency to seriously compete.

To show his disgust with baseball's growing trend to big money free agents, Oakland A's owner Charles O. Finley immediately put his No.

SHORTS Tragedy visited the star-crossed California Angels again on September 22 when outfielder Lyman Bostock was shot to death while sitting in a car in Gary, Indiana. Bostock, 27, was killed by a bullet apparently intended for someone else. Bostock had impressed fans by offering to donate his first month's salary to charity after getting off to a slow start under terms of a rich free agent contract.

SHORTS

Pete Rose's 44-game hitting streak was ended by a pitcher he didn't even know. Rose's charge at Joe DiMaggio's record stopped when he went hitless against Larry McWilliams and Gene Garber of the Braves. Rose didn't realize that the person sitting next to him at a post-game press conference was McWilliams.

1 draft pick in the major leagues. Mike Morgan, fresh out of high school, started three games and lost them all until Finley mercifully let him go to the minors.

In the National League, the Los Angeles Dodgers became the first team to draw three million fans, even though there were fewer home run fireworks. The Dodgers went from four players with at least 30 home runs to none. Don Sutton and Steve Garvey had a celebrated clubhouse fight to give the Dodgers' season a Yankees-like touch. Burt Hooton won 19 games as all five starters had a double-digit win total. Terry Forster, who came over as a free agent from Pittsburgh, saved some key games down the stretch.

Pete Rose got his 3,000th hit and fashioned a 44-game hitting streak, but the Reds finished second and officially ended the "Big Red Machine" era of the 1970s. Rose was allowed to leave as a free agent after the season and manager Sparky Anderson was fired after five divisional titles, four National League pennants and two World Series championships.

Tom Seaver pitched a no-hitter for the Reds and George Foster had another big season with 40 home runs and 120 RBIs, although those totals were down from 52 and 149, respectively. Reds spark plug Joe Morgan struggled with a pulled muscle and batted just .236 and the Reds were doomed by a 10–18 August.

The San Francisco Giants were in first place at the All-Star break and even had a one-game lead on Labor Day. They faltered, going 9–16 over the last three weeks. The Giants had an emerging star in Jack Clark, 22, who had a 26-game hitting streak and hit 25 home runs with 98 RBIs.

San Diego had its first winning season, but the Houston Astros fell short because J.R. Richard was their only consistent starter. The Atlanta Braves made Bob Horner their top draft pick, paid him a $175,000 bonus and immediately installed him in their lineup. He homered against Pittsburgh's Bert Blyleven in his third major league at-bat.

The National League East had an interesting race when the Philadelphia Phillies headed into Pittsburgh with a four-game lead and a season-ending four-game series against the Pirates. When Pittsburgh swept the Friday night doubleheader, the Phillies had to win a wild Saturday afternoon game to nail down their third consecutive National League East title.

The Pirates' late charge allowed them to overcome an 11½-game deficit on August 12. They won 24 games at home and got a lift from burly rookie Don Robinson, who jumped from Class AA to go 14–6. Dave Parker won his second batting title and Omar Moreno set a team record with 71 stolen bases, but pitcher John Candelaria slumped from a 20-win season to 12–11.

Despite playing in a great hitters' park, the Chicago Cubs managed only 72 home runs. Dave Kingman hit 28 of them. Ross Grimsley became the Montreal Expos' first 20-game winner.

The St. Louis Cardinals' winning percentage of .426 was their worst since 1924 and led to Ken Boyer replacing Vern Rapp as manager. The New York Mets finished last, and one-time ace Jerry Koosman won just three of his 32 starts.

Labor and money issues continued to be important. Parker signed a ground-breaking, five-year contract with the Pirates that promised him deferred money through 2007. Rose became a free agent and shopped his services with the aid of a 25-minute promotional film. Six clubs were interested, but Rose opted for the Phillies so he could chase Stan Musial's record of 3,630 career National League hits.

Pete Rose collected his 3,000th career hit and then joined the Phillies as a free agent

AMERICAN LEAGUE CHAMPIONSHIP SERIES

GAME 1	
NY Yankees 7	Kansas City 1

GAME 2	
Kansas City 10	NY Yankees 4

GAME 3	
NY Yankees 6	Kansas City 5

GAME 4	
NY Yankees 2	Kansas City 1

NATIONAL LEAGUE CHAMPIONSHIP SERIES

GAME 1	
Los Angeles 9	Philadelphia Phillies 5

GAME 2	
Los Angeles 4	Philadelphia Phillies 0

GAME 3	
Philadelphia Phillies 9	Los Angeles 4

GAME 4	
Los Angeles 4	Philadelphia Phillies 3

WORLD SERIES

GAME 1	
Los Angeles 11	NY Yankees 5

GAME 2	
Los Angeles 4	NY Yankees 3

GAME 3	
NY Yankees 5	Los Angeles 1

GAME 4	
NY Yankees 4	Los Angeles 3

GAME 5	
NY Yankees 12	Los Angeles 2

GAME 6	
NY Yankees 7	Los Angeles 2

Nothing came easy for the New York Yankees in 1978. They spotted the Boston Red Sox's huge lead in the American League East in the regular season and needed a frenzied comeback and a one-game playoff in the season's 163rd game to win the division. Along the way, they changed managers, replacing volatile Billy Martin with sedate Bob Lemon, who had been fired by the Chicago White Sox. Lemon's cool was probably what the Yankees needed to get through the turmoil they would have to endure.

The playoffs weren't much of a problem as the Yankees continued their mastery of the Kansas City Royals. In the World Series, though, the Yankees became the first team to win a six-game Series after dropping the first two games.

For a second consecutive year, the Yankees knocked off the Los Angeles Dodgers. In doing so, they became the first Yankees teams to win consecutive World Series since 1961–62.

The Dodgers held off Cincinnati in the National League West and beat the Philadelphia Phillies in the playoffs. It was the third consecutive year the Phillies had won the National League East, but failed to get to the World Series.

Time to celebrate for the Yankees as they complete a Series victory in Game Six

Los Angeles took the first two games, winning the opener 9–5 with the help of four home runs. Steve Garvey hit two while Davey Lopes and Steve Yeager each had one. Tommy John pitched a four-hitter in the second game to win 4–0.

Philadelphia won the third game 9–4. Steve Carlton pitched a complete game and also hit a home run, but the Dodgers came up with a run in the bottom of the tenth in the fourth game to win the series.

The Phillies blew a prime opportunity in the first inning, loading the bases with no outs and still failing to score.

Garry Maddox, whose stellar play in center had earned him the nickname "Secretary of Defense" dropped a line drive in the tenth inning, which was followed by Bill Russell's game-winning single.

Shortly after Bucky Dent's home run sunk the Red Sox, the Yankees were on their way to Kansas City for the start of the playoffs the following day. They won the opener 7–1 behind Jim Beattie and Ken Clay, beating Kansas City's ace, Dennis Leonard.

The Royals pounded 16 hits and won the second game 10–4. George Brett hit three home runs off Catfish Hunter in the third game, but it wasn't enough for the Royals, who lost 6–5. Thurman Munson hit a two-run homer that put the Yankees ahead in the eighth and closer Goose Gossage got the final three outs.

Ron Guidry, a 25-game winner, combined with Gossage to win a taut 2–1 game that sent the Yankees back to the Series.

Lopes hit two homers in the Series opener and drove in five runs as the Dodgers won 11–5. Ron Cey drove in all the runs in the Dodgers' 4–3 win in Game Two. Rookie Bob Welch turned in some solid relief and struck out Jackson with two runners on base in the ninth.

The Series went back to New York and things started to go the Yankees' way. New York won 5–1 and third baseman Graig Nettles turned in a defensive performance that brought comparisons to Brooks Robinson's glovework for the Orioles in the 1970 Series. In Game Four, the Yankees tied the Series with a ten-inning, 4–3 win. Lou Piniella hit the game-winning single.

Every World Series seems to have one controversial play and it came in Game Four. Jackson was caught between bases, but prolonged the inning when first baseman Steve Garvey's throw glanced off his hip. The Dodgers argued for an interference call, but didn't get it.

Beattie pitched his first major league complete game in Game Five, winning 12–2. The Yankees got 18 hits and Munson had five RBIs.

Dent and Denny Doyle each had three hits for the second consecutive game as the Yankees ended the Series with a 7–2 win in Game Six. Dent drove in three runs and Doyle had two RBIs. Jackson also had two RBIs and homered off Welch to complete the Series by gaining personal revenge for the critical strikeout in Game Two.

A ticker-tape parade through the streets of New York for the World Champion Yankees

WILLIE McCOVEY

TEAMS
San Francisco Giants 1959–73, 1977–80;
San Diego Padres 1974–76;
Oakland Athletics 1976

Games	.2,588
At-Bats	.8,197
Runs	.1,229
RBI	.1,555
Home runs	.521
Hits	.2,211
Doubles	.353
Triples	.46
Stolen Bases	.26
Average	.270
Slugging percentage	.515

As the "other" Willie, McCovey combined with Mays to create an awesome 1–2 punch

He was the San Francisco Giants' "other" Willie in the 1960s.

Willie McCovey, the man with the powerful swing and wobbly knees, teamed up with Willie Mays to keep the Giants in contention for much of the decade. Tall and thin, McCovey was plagued by pain in his knees throughout his career, but his troublesome legs didn't prevent him from hitting 521 runs or winning election to the Hall of Fame in 1986.

McCovey led the National League in home runs three times, was tops in RBIs twice and was the National League's Most Valuable Player in 1969. He was one of the most feared sluggers in the game and offered protection for Mays in the Giants' order. The price for pitching around Mays was dealing with McCovey. They formed one of the most formidable power combinations of their era.

The Giants signed him out of Mobile, Alabama, in 1955, when the major league club was still headquartered in New York. McCovey quickly established himself as a prime prospect by leading the Georgia State League with 113 RBIs. Promoted to the Pacific Coast League, his production remained just as impressive. He hit .319 with 89 RBIs at Class AAA.

Still, the Giants had a problem finding a spot for McCovey on the major league roster. His best position was first base and the Giants were well covered there with Orlando Cepeda, the National League's Rookie of the Year in 1958. McCovey was too talented to remain in the minors, though, and the Giants promoted him. For several seasons, they shuttled McCovey and Cepeda between first base and the outfield.

McCovey made his major league debut against the Philadelphia Phillies on July 30, 1959, and made a positive first impression. He went 4-for-4 against future Hall of Famer Robin Roberts, collecting two triples and two singles.

He struggled and went back to the minor leagues for a time in 1960 before returning to stay. However, McCovey didn't establish himself as a regular player until 1963 and didn't claim first base on a full-time basis until Cepeda was traded to the St. Louis Cardinals during the 1966 season.

McCovey's most famous moment came in the 1962 World Series against the New York Yankees. He batted with runners at second and third with two out in the bottom of the ninth with the Giants trailing 1–0. McCovey ripped Ralph Terry's 1–1 pitch toward right field for what appeared to be a Series-winning hit.

It was not to be. Yankees' second baseman, Bobby Richardson, leaped and snagged the ball, ending the Giants' threat, the game and the Series. McCovey's line drive is still discussed when San Francisco baseball fans gather to commiserate. McCovey missed becoming a World Series hero by a matter of inches. "The hardest ball I ever hit," McCovey called it.

In his MVP 1969 season, McCovey batted .320 with 45 home runs and 126 RBIs.

Pitchers learned from their mistakes. The following season, McCovey drew 137 walks and set a record with 45 intentional walks. Despite not having many pitches to hit, he still managed 39 home runs and led the National League in slugging percentage.

Mays left the Giants in 1972 to finish his career in New York with the Mets. He was given away in a trade, mostly to dispose of his contract. The Giants had fallen on hard times and needed to rebuild. McCovey's departure came in 1974 when he was traded to the San Diego Padres. He played three seasons there, then spent a brief time on the other side of the Bay with the Oakland A's.

The Giants brought him back in 1977 and McCovey's return earned a standing ovation from fans at Candlestick Park. He showed there was more than sentiment involved by winning the Comeback Player of the Year award by hitting .280 with 28 home runs. McCovey played into 1980 to become a four-decade player. He retired at the age of 42, still tottering on creaky knees. McCovey finished with 521 home runs, the same total as Ted Williams, who had tutored McCovey in the minor leagues. He was elected to the Hall of Fame seven years after Mays had been inducted.

The Giants retired his No. 44, a number common to prolific home run hitters. Hank Aaron and Reggie Jackson are among the other players who wore No. 44 during their Hall of Fame careers.

MOST VALUABLE PLAYER
AL: Don Baylor, California
NL: Willie Stargell, Pittsburgh;
Keith Hernandez, St. Louis Cardinals

CY YOUNG AWARD
AL: Mike Flanagan, Baltimore
NL: Bruce Sutter, Chicago Cubs

ROOKIE OF THE YEAR
AL: John Castino, Minnesota; Alfredo Griffin,
Toronto; NL: Rick Sutcliffe, Los Angeles

LEADERS
BATTING AVERAGE
AL: Fred Lynn, Boston Red Sox, .333
NL: Keith Hernandez, St. Louis Cardinals, .344

HOME RUNS
AL: Gorman Thomas, Milwaukee, 45
NL: Dave Kingman, Chicago Cubs, 48

RUNS BATTED IN
AL: Don Baylor, California, 139
NL: Dave Winfield, San Diego, 118

STOLEN BASES
AL: Willie Wilson, Kansas City, 83
NL: Omar Moreno, Pittsburgh, 77

PITCHING VICTORIES
AL: Mike Flanagan, Baltimore, 23
NL: John Niekro, Houston;
Phil Niekro, Atlanta, 21

EARNED RUN AVERAGE
AL: Ron Guidry, NY Yankees, 2.78
NL: J.R. Richard, Houston, 2.79

STRIKEOUTS
AL: Nolan Ryan, California, 223
NL: J.R. Richard, Houston, 313

SAVES
AL: Mike Marshall, Minnesota, 32
NL: Bruce Sutter, Chicago Cubs, 37

They were "fam-a-lee." The Pittsburgh Pirates rocked their way to their first National League East title since 1975 and their first World Series win since 1971. They did it to the disco beat of a song by Sister Sledge called, "We Are Family", which blared in their clubhouse and via the Three Rivers Stadium public address system.

A couple of secrets about that: first, the record was gender-inappropriate. The semi-autobiographical song recorded by sisters Debra, Kim, Joni and Kathy Sledge of North Philadelphia repeated the line, "I've got all my sisters with me." Also, the Pirates pirated the song as their anthem. Pirates' captain Willie Stargell heard the St. Louis Cardinals using "We Are Family" and promptly stole it.

No matter, it was catchy and the title summed up the fun-loving Stargell's concept of what he wanted a ball club to be. It was a family, which meant there were sometimes arguments and jealousies and bruised feelings, all more than offset by a deep sense of loyalty and devotion to a single purpose.

Stargell had become the patriarch of the Pirates' clubhouse by his virtue of seniority and his personality. He first came to the major leagues in 1962 and became a regular the following season. Stargell developed into a power-hitting star in the late 1960s and had his best years in the early 1970s. The Pirates moved into symmetrical Three Rivers Stadium and left massive Forbes Field, which was a welcome change for a home-run hitter like Stargell.

Stargell had been the Pirates' No. 2 star to Roberto Clemente. The Pirates were jolted badly by Clemente's sudden death in a New Year's Eve 1972 plane crash, but Stargell developed into the leader Clemente had been. In 1976 it looked as though Stargell's career was on the wane, but he had been distracted by his wife's serious illness. He was back in 1977 and

The Pittsburgh Pirates' family values were based on teamwork

remained one of the game's most dangerous power hitters and best-liked players. Opposing players begged for the gold Stargell stars that adorned the caps of the Pirates.

Pirates' manager Chuck Tanner's hands-off style was perfect for this group. Tanner would smile while the throbbing beat of the music in the clubhouse caused items to shake in his office. Stargell ran the clubhouse and it was a happy place filled with confident players. Sometimes it was difficult to tell when the Pirates had lost because they were so certain they'd win the next day.

After winning the National League East in five of the six seasons between 1970–75, the Pirates were runners-up to the Philadelphia Phillies in three consecutive seasons. Pittsburgh was still good—Philadelphia was just a little better.

In 1979, though, the Pirates' main competition came from the Montreal Expos, who took the race down to the final weekend.

The Pirates had a formidable team, but general manager Pete Peterson made two in-season trades that put them over the top. In April, Peterson became fed up with Frank Taveras' erratic play at shortstop and traded him to New York

SHORTS Chicago disc jockey Steve Dahl had popularized an anti-disco movement and Mike Veeck, son of White Sox owner Bill Veeck, had taken note of Dahl's popularity with the young people the team was trying to attract. They decided to stage a Disco Demolition night in which the offending records would be blown up. The good idea went bad when fans stormed the field and forced the umpires to forfeit the second game of the scheduled doubleheader.

for Tim Foli. The scrappy Foli was a perfect fit. He made up for diminished range by playing smartly at shortstop and his penchant for bat control made him the ideal No. 2 hitter behind base stealer Omar Moreno.

Then in June, Peterson sent a bundle of pitching talent to San Francisco and got Bill Madlock. Rennie Stennett had not recovered from a broken ankle he sustained in 1978 and struggled at second base. The Giants trade enabled the Pirates to install Madlock at third, move Phil Garner to second and strengthen the lineup at two positions.

Tanner had a mix-and-match system for the late innings with righthanded set-up man Enrique Romo, lefthander Grant Jackson and closer Kent Tekulve. John Candelaria led the starting staff with 14 wins and Bruce Kison, who was 4–0 in September, was 13–7. Jim Bibby and Bert Blyleven each won a dozen games.

Dave Parker batted .310 with 24 home runs and 94 RBI. Stargell had 32 homers, drove in 82 runs and shared National League Most Valuable Player honors with Keith Hernandez of St. Louis.

Moreno, thanks to offseason tutoring from hitting guru Harry Walker, improved his average from .235 to .282 and had 69 RBIs, tops for any leadoff hitter. Moreno set a club record with a league-leading 77 stolen bases and he caught everything in center field.

The Pirates beat the Chicago Cubs on the last day of the season and, coupled with Montreal's loss to Steve Carlton and the Philadelphia Phillies, took the division title.

In the West, the Cincinnati Reds ended the Dodgers' three-year hold on the title. General manager Dick Wagner had redefined the Reds

T I M E L I N E

Feb. 3: The Twins traded Rod Carew to the Angels.

April 4: Major league umpires officially went on strike, setting up a picket line at the season opener in Cincinnati.

April 5: Orioles' manager Earl Weaver won his 1,000th game.

April 7: Ken Forsch of the Astros pitched a no-hitter against Atlanta.

April 19: Yankees' reliever Rich "Goose" Gossage injured his thumb in a locker room scuffle with teammate Cliff Johnson.

May 17: The Phillies beat the Cubs 23–22 in windy Wrigley Field. Mike Schmidt's second home run was the game winner.

May 19: Major league umpires returned to work.

June 12: Sparky Anderson became manager of the Tigers, replacing Les Moss.

June 28: The Pirates acquired Bill Madlock in a six-player deal with the Giants.

Aug. 2: Yankees' catcher Thurman Munson died in Canton, Ohio when he crashed his plane whilst practicing landings.

Aug. 3: Tony LaRussa became manager of the Chicago White Sox, replacing Don Kessinger.

Aug. 9: Dodgers' owner Walter O'Malley died at 75.

Aug. 13: Lou Brock of the Cardinals got his 3,000th career hit.

Aug. 31: Dallas Green replaced Danny Ozark as Phillies' manager.

Sept. 6: Joe Altobelli was fired as Giants manager and replaced by Dave Bristol.

Sept. 12: Carl Yastrzemski got his 3,000th hit in a game against the Yankees.

Sept. 30: The Padres fired Manager Roger Craig and Toronto dismissed Roy Hartsfield.

Oct. 28: Billy Martin was fired as Yankees' manager after a bar fight with a marshmallow salesman.

Oct. 29: Willie Mays resigned a figurehead front office job with the Mets to take a position with Bally's casino. Commissioner Bowie Kuhn ordered that Mays disassociate himself from baseball if he worked in the gambling industry.

The Astros' J.R. Richard led the league in ERA and strikeouts

The Yankees remember Thurman Munson who died mid-season piloting his own plane

by firing popular manager Sparky Anderson following the 1978 season and replacing him with John McNamara. Wagner also declined to get into a bidding war for Pete Rose, who signed with the Phillies.

The Reds had to battle the Houston Astros until the end of the season. Cincinnati got breakthrough seasons from several young pitchers. Mike LaCoss was 14–8, reliever Tom Hume was 10–9 with a 2.76 ERA and 17 saves and Frank Pastore came back from the minor leagues to go 5–2 down the stretch. Staff leader Tom Seaver was 16–6 and won 11 straight decisions in the middle of the season.

Dave Collins helped the Reds to overcome injuries to George Foster and Ken Griffey. Collins batted .318, tied for the club lead with Ray Knight, who replaced Rose at third base.

Shortstop Dave Concepcion batted .281 and had career highs for home runs (16) and RBIs (84). Johnny Bench hit .276 with 22 home runs and 80 RBIs.

The Astros came up short because of their offense. Their pitching was more than adequate with Joe Niekro leading the way with a 21–11 record. Hard-throwing J.R. Richard was 18–11, led the league with an ERA of 2.71 and had 313 strikeouts, most in either league. Reliever Joe Sambito saved 22 games.

In the American League, manager Earl

Weaver masterfully manipulated the Baltimore Orioles to the East Division title. Ken Singleton hit .295 with a career bests in home runs (35) and RBIs (111). Eddie Murray matched his .295 average and hit 25 homers with 99 RBIs. Weaver, who studied charts of past performances in making out his lineup, did his best work in getting the most out of part-time players like Terry Crowley, John Lowenstein and Benny Ayala. Weaver was at his best in picking the right spots for those players.

The Orioles had a solid pitching staff that Weaver pronounced better than the 1971 staff that featured four 20-game winners. Mike Flanagan was 23–9 and was one of six pitchers who had a double-digit win total. Reliever Don Stanhouse stressed out his manager, but collected 23 saves.

The Milwaukee Brewers finished second to Baltimore as the Boston Red Sox fell apart in the second half and wound up third.

The three-time Eastern Division champion New York Yankees were never a factor. They were unable to recover from the shock of captain Thurman Munson's death in an August 2 plane crash. Munson had gotten a pilot's license in order to spend off days with his family in Canton, Ohio. He had recently purchased a jet to make the trips home even quicker. Munson was practicing takeoffs and

SHORTS Marginal utility player Cliff Johnson dealt the Yankees' postseason hopes a severe blow on April 19 when he fought with reliever Rich (Goose) Gossage. Gossage injured his thumb in the scrap and missed nearly three months of the season. The Yankees' patience with Johnson ran out and he was traded to Cleveland, the closest thing baseball had to an exile.

landings when he missed the landing strip and died in the fiery crash.

The Yankees were having problems even before they lost Munson. Reliever Rich "Goose" Gossage and utility player Cliff Johnson got into a locker room argument that escalated into a wrestling match that wound up with Gossage injuring his thumb. He missed 83 games, just over half of the season.

The California Angels' American League West championship proved that the free agent system could get a club some important help. Don Baylor hit .296 with 36 home runs and 139 RBIs. The hulking Baylor even stole 22 bases. Bobby Grich came back from serious back surgery to hit .290 with 30 homers and 101 RBIs. The Angels had a solid everyday line-up that helped them overcome a so-so pitching

staff. Only one other first-place team in history had won with a higher staff ERA than the Angels' 4.34. Nolan Ryan led the way with a 16–14 record and 3.59 ERA while Dave Frost was 16–10 with a 3.58 ERA.

The Kansas City Royals fell to second place after winning three straight divisional titles. The Royals couldn't overcome poor pitching and wound up three games behind the Angels, who won in Jim Fregosi's first full year as manager.

The season opened with a strike by the umpires. Each league hired four full-time umpires and rounded out the crews with local umpires. The strike lasted until the regular umpires returned on May 19. Their new contract called for benefits including, for the first time, in-season vacations.

The Yankees continued to have a circus atmosphere as Billy Martin returned again as manager, succeeding Bob Lemon. Differences with Martin and owner George Steinbrenner led Al Rosen to resign as team president. Martin was fired again after the season after the news broke that he had gotten into a fight with a marshmallow salesman in a Minnesota restaurant. Martin's erratic behavior drew a warning from Commissioner Bowie Kuhn.

The Cardinals' players lend their congratulations to Lou Brock after he gets his 3,000th career hit

AL CHAMPIONSHIP SERIES

GAME 1	
Baltimore 6	California 3

GAME 2	
Baltimore 9	California 8

GAME 3	
California 4	Baltimore 3

GAME 4	
Baltimore 8	California 0

NL CHAMPIONSHIP SERIES

GAME 1	
Pittsburgh 5	Cincinnati 2

GAME 2	
Pittsburgh 3	Cincinnati 2

GAME 3	
Pittsburgh 7	Cincinnati 1

WORLD SERIES

GAME 1	
Baltimore 5	Pittsburgh 4

GAME 2	
Pittsburgh 3	Baltimore 2

GAME 3	
Baltimore 8	Pittsburgh 4

GAME 4	
Baltimore 9	Pittsburgh 6

GAME 5	
Pittsburgh 7	Baltimore 1

GAME 6	
Pittsburgh 4	Baltimore 0

GAME 7	
Pittsburgh 4	Baltimore 1

MVP: Willie Stargell, Pittsburgh

Willie Stargell carried his regular season momentum into the World Series

Willie Stargell hadn't been able to enjoy his first World Series experience.

Stargell was happy to be part of the 1971 World Champion Pittsburgh Pirates, but he hit only .208 in the Series after dominating the National League for more than half the season. Stargell was playing on bad knees and he knew he was due for surgery just as soon as the Pirates' season ended.

He wound up being one of the supporting players in a World Series dominated by Roberto Clemente and Steve Blass. The Pirates never would have gotten to the 1971 Series without Stargell, but once they arrived, he wasn't able to do much.

There was no such problem in 1979. Stargell had evolved into a genial father figure. As a sarcastic reference to his advancing age, teammate Dave Parker started calling him "Pops", but Stargell was so good-natured and suited for the name that it became a term of affection.

Stargell made the most of his second World Series by winning MVP honors as the Pirates rallied from a 3–1 deficit in games to again beat the Baltimore Orioles. In fact, Stargell nearly made a clean sweep of MVP honors. He shared the reg-

ular season award with Keith Hernandez, then won outright in the playoffs and World Series.

The Pirates went to the wire to hold off the Montreal Expos' challenge and end Philadelphia's three-year run as National League East champions. In the West, the Cincinnati Reds outlasted Houston and dethroned the Los Angeles Dodgers after two years.

Baltimore had the largest margin of the four division winners, finishing eight games ahead of Milwaukee. The California Angels reached the postseason for the first time as Kansas City's three-year run ended.

Stargell won the opening game for the Pirates with an 11th inning, three-run homer off Tom Hume. The Pirates used six pitchers to win the second game 3–2 with a run in the tenth off Doug Bair. The Reds argued that Dave Collins had made a clean catch of a Phil Garner liner in the fifth. Umpire Frank Pulli ruled Collins had trapped the ball and Garner's hit led to a run.

There was no controversy in the third game as Bert Blyleven pitched a complete game to win 7–1. Stargell had a home run and a two-run double.

The Orioles won the opener of the American League playoffs when John Lowenstein pinch hit a three-run homer in the tenth inning. Baltimore took the second game 9–8, holding off a late Angels charge.

California avoided elimination by scoring twice in the ninth to win the third game 4–3, but Baltimore ended the series with an 8–0 win

behind Scott McGregor's six-hitter.

That set up a rematch of the 1971 Series, with Stargell one of the handful of Pirates who had stayed with the team over the intervening years. The Orioles tagged 1971 hero Bruce Kison for five runs in the first inning of Game One and won 5–4.

Manny Sanguillen, another veteran of the 1971 Series, gave the Pirates a 3–2 win in Game Two with a tie-breaking pinch single in the ninth inning off reliever Don Stanhouse.

The Orioles relied on lesser names to win Game Three, 8–3. Kiko Garcia had four hits and four RBIs and Benny Ayala hit a two-run homer. Baltimore's bench made the difference in Game Four as pinch hitters Lowenstein and Terry Crowley each hit two-run doubles in the eighth. Baltimore turned a 6–3 deficit into a 9–6 win and pulled within a game of winning the Series.

Pittsburgh roughed up Orioles ace Mike Flanagan for a 7–1 win in Game Five. Jim Rooker, who had won just four games in the regular season, pitched five strong innings, holding the Orioles to a single run. Blyleven finished and the Pirates grabbed the momentum.

John Candelaria and Kent Tekulve combined on a 4–0 shutout in Game Six and the Pirates won Game 7, 4–1, thanks to a 4-for-5 game from Stargell which included a two-run homer. Relievers Grant Jackson and Tekulve held the Orioles hitless over the last 4⅓ innings as the Pirates again came from behind to end a Series against the Orioles in Baltimore.

Benny Ayala hit a two-run blast in the O's Game Three victory

1980

It was the last decade when pennants were won more with superior baseball knowledge than bankrolls.

Twenty one different teams reached the postseason during the 1980s. Teams from low-revenue markets like Oakland could get there more often than the New York Yankees—and did.

The Los Angeles Dodgers played in the postseason four times but the action was spread around, unlike other decades that had been dominated by single-team dynasties.

Two significant off-field developments came at opposite ends of the 1980s. In 1981, a strike by the Players Association shut down the season from June to August and necessitated an extra round of playoffs after the season was split into two separate pennant races. It presented the odd situation that allowed a first-half winner to coast through the second half, knowing that an October berth was secure. The system also denied a postseason spot to the Cincinnati Reds, who had the best total record but didn't win either pennant race.

In 1989, all-time hits leader Pete Rose agreed to a lifetime suspension after an extensive investigation into his gambling habits. Just days after finally resolving the messy Rose matter, Commissioner A. Bartlett Giamatti died suddenly of a heart attack.

The fans who booed Santa Claus had something to cheer about in 1980. Philadelphia fans, who relished their reputation as the country's toughest, couldn't find much fault with a team that delivered the first World Series championship in Phillies' history.

Nolan Ryan joined the ranks of the game's great pitchers, collecting his 3,000th career strikeout after switching from California to Houston

There was no doubt that the Phillies had talent. After finishing a close second to the Pittsburgh Pirates in 1975, the Phillies won the next three National League East titles. They lost in the playoffs each year, earning the wrath of those Philadelphia fans.

The Phillies were a non-factor in the 1979 race as Pittsburgh edged Montreal on the final day of the season to take the division. The Phillies' history had been long and undistinguished. Born in 1883, they had never won a championship.

Their 1950 "Whiz Kids" had a memorable season, only to fall quickly and decisively to the New York Yankees in the World Series. In 1964, the Phillies appeared to be poised for a return to the World Series, but they collapsed down the stretch and the St. Louis Cardinals took the National League pennant.

The organization endured some perfectly awful years in the early 1970s to follow a building plan. The Phillies had assembled an efficient system of player development and their minor league clubs sent some talented players to the major leagues. The Phillies hit a home run on the trade market, acquiring Steve Carlton from the St. Louis Cardinals.

When free agency became a factor, the Phillies handled that aspect of the game well, too. They spent money wisely for Pete Rose, knowing that he'd be productive and also bring an attitude that the Phillies hadn't had. Owner Bill Giles creatively structured a deal with the Phillies' TV outlet that essentially made them part-

SHORTS

J.R. Richard was one of the game's most intimidating pitchers, a giant of a man who struck fear in some of the best hitters because of his powerful fastball. Richard complained of fatigue but doctors were at a loss to diagnose any problem. Richard suffered a stroke while pitching on the sideline in July and his career was effectively ended that day, adding another sad chapter to the Astros' star-crossed history.

ners in the Rose investment.

But the final piece of the puzzle was a manager who was an intimidating presence—Dallas Green. The Phillies had gotten used to the laid-back style of Danny Ozark, a long-time Los Angeles Dodgers coach who treated the players as professionals and let them motivate themselves. The problem with that approach was a gradual erosion of some of the fire and passion that are necessary to succeed in sports. Baseball is a sport of controlled aggression, so some of the rah-rah tactics used by football coaches would be counterproductive.

But Green sensed that the Phillies were on the wrong side of that line between aggressive and passive and wanted to do something about it. A big man with a big voice, he commanded the Phillies to lose their calculated cool and play the game with more emotion.

Rose's presence helped in that regard. No matter what uniform he wore, Rose was going to play aggressively and do whatever he could to win. It was a mindset more of the Phillies needed if they were to get to another level of success.

Green's approach was not immediately embraced. Some of the Phillies players had tenure and thought the prevailing attitude was fine. When Green started talking about the concept of "We, not I," shortstop Larry Bowa sarcastically asked, "When are the pompom girls arriving?"

Green would impose his will on the team. He yelled, he cursed, he upset furniture. He demanded that the players care as much as he did. If players were snickering at his philosophies, he didn't care. He stuck with what he thought was right—and his validation came in October.

The Phillies needed an extra-inning win over Montreal on the next-to-last game of the season to clinch the title. Carlton went 24–9 and won the Cy Young award. Dick Ruthven rebounded from elbow surgery a year earlier to post a 17–10 record. Two rookies also contributed—Bob Walk was 11–7 and Marty Bystrom was 5–0 with a 1.50 earned run average when he was called up in September.

Reliever Tug McGraw was 5–4 with 20 saves, but did his best work after he came off the disabled list in mid-July—a 5–1 record, 13 saves and a 0.52 ERA.

TIMELINE

Jan. 24: Nelson Doubleday and Fred Wilpon paid a record $24 million for the Mets.

Jan. 31: Joe Morgan signed as a free agent with the Astros, his original team.

Feb. 20: The Oakland A's hired Billy Martin as manager.

April 12: Houston's Nolan Ryan returned to the NL and hit a home run off Don Sutton of the Dodgers in his first start.

May 1: Bill Madlock of the Pirates poked his glove in the face of umpire Jerry Crawford during an argument. The action earned him a $5,000 fine and 15-game suspension from the National League.

May 3: Ferguson Jenkins posted his 100th AL win and became the fourth pitcher to win 100 games in each league.

May 4: Mike Squires of the White Sox became the first lefthanded thrower to catch in the majors since Dale Long in 1958.

June 3: The Mets made outfielder Darryl Strawberry the first pick in the draft.

June 6: Willie McCovey retired.

June 6: Ken Boyer was fired as Cardinals manager after the first game of a doubleheader.

June 27: Jerry Reuss of the Dodgers pitched an 8–0 no-hitter against the Giants. Shortstop Bill Russell's throwing error cost him a perfect game.

July 4: Nolan Ryan got his 3,000th career strikeout.

July 25: Preston Gomez was fired as Cubs' manager and replaced by Joe Amalfitano.

Aug. 4: Maury Wills became the major leagues' third black manager when Seattle hired him to replace Darrell Johnson.

Aug. 20: Omar Moreno of the Pirates stole his 70th base and became the first player in the century to have three consecutive seasons with at least 70 steals.

Aug. 24: Gene Mauch resigned as Twins manager.

Sept. 30: Oakland's Rickey Henderson stole his 98th base to break the American League record set by Ty Cobb in 1915.

Mike Schmidt and Bake McBride provided much of the Phillies' offense

The Houston Astros celebrate their fourth division title in 19 years

August 10. From that point, the Phillies won 36 of 55 games. He repeated the message during a September 1 meeting.

In the West, the Houston Astros won the title with just their fourth winning season in 19 years. They won even though their most dominating pitcher, J.R. Richard, was lost for the season after he suffered a life-threatening stroke shortly after the All-Star break. Richard, whose overpowering fastball made him the most feared pitcher in the league, was 10–4 at the time he was stricken.

20-game winner Joe Niekro, Nolan Ryan and Ken Forsch formed the league's best veteran rotation and Vern Ruhle stepped in after Richard's illness and was 12–4. Joe Sambito, Frank LaCorte and rookie Dave Smith combined for 23 wins and 38 saves.

The Dodgers came up a game short to Houston when they lost a one-game playoff. It was the fourth time the Dodgers were beaten in a playoff for first place.

Los Angeles had a good season even though its investment in free agent pitchers Dave Goltz and Don Stanhouse failed to bring the expected return. Goltz was 7–11 and injuries limited Stanhouse to 22 games.

Jerry Reuss was the Dodgers' big winner at 18–6 and rookie Steve Howe posted 17 saves.

In the American League, the New York Yankees won 103 games and needed every victory because second-place Baltimore won 100. First-year manager Dick Howser brought some calm to the Yankees, but wound up resigning after the season because of differences with owner George Steinbrenner.

Freed of the ongoing Billy Martin circus, Reggie Jackson enjoyed his finest year with the Yankees, batting .300 for the first time, tying for the home run lead with 41 and driving in 111 runs. Tommy John had his second straight 20-win season, going 22–9. Reliever Rich "Goose" Gossage had 33 saves and a 2.27 ERA. Free agent Rudy May was a swing man on the staff and went 15–5, even though he didn't have a defined role.

Baltimore went 52–20 after July 21, but their 100–62 record wasn't good enough in a year the Yankees dominated.

The Kansas City Royals returned to first place in the American League West, winning the title for the fourth time in five years. First-year manager Jim Frey led the team to an 8½-game lead at the All-Star break and the Royals were in front by 20 games at the end of August—they wound up winning the division by 14 games.

George Brett batted .390 after taking a legitimate run at .400 for a good portion of the sea-

Mike Schmidt's 48 home runs set a major league record for a third baseman. He also led the league in RBIs (121) and slugging percentage (.624). Schmidt was the National League's Most Valuable Player, an honor he would also take in the World Series.

Rose hit .282, but led the league with 185 hits. Right fielder Bake McBride batted .308 and drove in 87 runs, a career best.

Green had two major explosions. The first came after a doubleheader loss in Pittsburgh on

son. Willie Wilson batted .326 and stole 79 bases. Dennis Leonard had 20 wins for the third time in four seasons. Larry Gura won 18 games and Dan Quisenberry saved 33 games.

The players threatened an in-season strike as the owners argued for a pay scale and a better system to compensate clubs losing free agents.

Even as the owners were blaming escalating salaries for financial peril, the pay scale got another upward jolt when Dave Winfield signed with the Yankees after the season for $13 million over ten years. His average salary of $1.3 million set a new standard.

The game's economics were a factor in forcing out two colorful owners. Charles O. Finley left the game after nearly two decades when he sold the Oakland A's. Bill Veeck's final run as a franchise owner ended when he decided to sell the Chicago White Sox. Both owners had struggled to stay solvent and competitive in the new environment.

On August 4, the Seattle Mariners fired Manager Darrell Johnson and replaced him with Maury Wills, who became the third black manager in major league history. Gene Mauch resigned as manager of the Minnesota Twins late in the season.

Some players feuded with their own clubs. Atlanta third baseman Bob Horner resisted a move engineered by owner Ted Turner to send him to the minor leagues. After the Players Association fielded a grievance on his behalf, Horner was reinstated and went on to hit .268 with 35 home runs and 89 RBIs in 124 games.

One year after the Pittsburgh Pirates won the World Series with the theme song, "We Are Family," a family squabble developed. Pitcher Bert Blyleven, unhappy with the way manager Chuck Tanner handled him, left the team at the end of April. He was on the disqualified list for about two weeks. The Pirates agreed to his trade request after the season, sending him to Cleveland.

Another Pirate, third baseman Bill Madlock, got into trouble with the National League when he used his glove to gesture at umpire Gerry

The Royals' George Brett had plenty to celebrate—including a .390 average and a division title

Crawford and the laces of the glove struck Crawford in the face. Madlock was suspended for 15 days and fined $5,000.

AL CHAMPIONSHIP SERIES

GAME 1

| Kansas City 7 | NY Yankees 2 |

GAME 2

| Kansas City 3 | NY Yankees 2 |

GAME 3

| Kansas City 4 | NY Yankees 2 |

NL CHAMPIONSHIP SERIES

GAME 1

| Philadelphia Phillies 3 | Houston 1 |

GAME 2

| Houston 7 | Philadelphia Phillies 4 |

GAME 3

| Houston 1 | Philadelphia Phillies 0 |

GAME 4

| Philadelphia Phillies 5 | Houston 3 |

GAME 5

| Philadelphia Phillies 8 | Houston 7 |

WORLD SERIES

GAME 1

| Philadelphia Phillies 7 | Kansas City 6 |

GAME 2

| Philadelphia Phillies 6 | Kansas City 4 |

GAME 3

| Kansas City 4 | Philadelphia Phillies 3 |

GAME 4

| Kansas City 5 | Philadelphia Phillies 3 |

GAME 5

| Philadelphia Phillies 4 | Kansas City 3 |

GAME 6

| Philadelphia Phillies 4 | Kansas City 1 |

MVP: Mike Schmidt, Philadelphia Phillies

The Philadelphia Phillies finally didn't have to wait until next year.

Since joining the National League in 1903, the Phillies hadn't won a World Series and had only been there twice. In 1915 they lost to the Boston Red Sox and the 1950 Whiz Kids had fallen to the New York Yankees.

Then there was the celebrated late-season collapse in 1964 that saw a team that had led the league for most of the year fold down the stretch and finish third.

The era of expansion had brought a different kind of heartache for long-suffering Phillies fans. The team won National League East titles for three consecutive seasons, but lost the playoffs each year—once to the Cincinnati Reds and twice to the Los Angeles Dodgers. The Phillies only won two playoff games in the three years.

That finally changed in 1980 under the leadership of demanding manager, Dallas Green. Green was a screamer in a club that prided itself on rarely showing emotion. He lit into his team after a game in Pittsburgh that season, which was something of a turning point for the Phillies.

The Kansas City Royals hadn't joined the American League until 1969, but they had managed to pack some frustration into their limited history as well. The Royals started a streak of three consecutive American League West titles in 1976 and lost all three playoff series to the New York Yankees. The Royals had come close, twice stretching the series to the full five games, only to lose in the last at-bat.

This time the Royals had no problem with the Yankees, sweeping the three games to earn their first trip to the World Series. Things started on a familiar note for the Royals—they were behind 2–0 in the first inning after back-to-back home

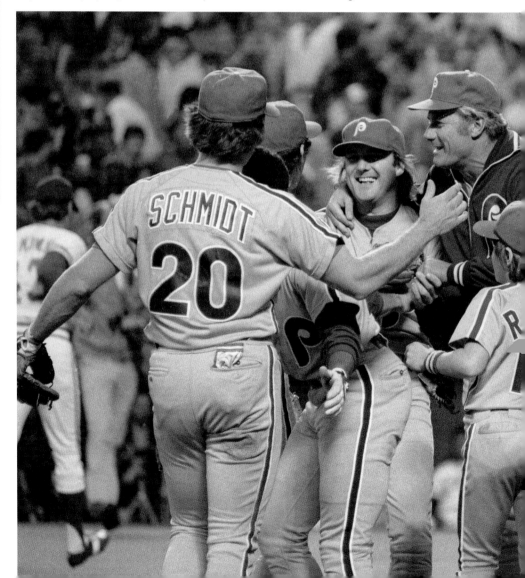

Philadelphia Phillies' pitcher Tug McGraw is hugged by his coach Dallas Green after coming on in relief to beat the Kansas City Royals 4–3 in Game Five of the World Series

runs by Rick Cerone and Lou Piniella, but Willie Mays, Aikens and Willie Wilson each drove in two runs and Kansas City won 7–2.

The Royals took the second game 3–2 and scored all their runs with four consecutive hits in the third inning. They ended the series with a 4–2 win that was sealed when George Brett hit a three-run homer off Goose Gossage in the seventh inning.

The Phillies had a tougher time with the Houston Astros, who were making their first post-season appearance. The series went the maximum of five games and the last four games went to extra innings.

The only game completed in nine innings was the opener, won 3–1 by the Phillies. Greg Luzinski hit a two-run homer. Tug McGraw couldn't hold a lead in the second game and the Astros scored four runs in the tenth to win 7–4.

Joe Morgan opened the 11th inning of the

third game with a triple and scored on a sacrifice fly as Houston won 1–0. The Phillies took the fourth game 5–3 in ten innings. The game was interrupted by a 20-minute argument over a possible triple play that led to both teams playing the game under protest.

The Astros took a 5–2 lead in the fifth game, but fell behind 7–5 before forcing an extra innings. The Phillies won 8–7 with Dick Ruthven pitching the final two innings.

Because they had used so many pitchers to win the playoffs, the Phillies had to start rookie Bob Walk in Game One of the World Series. Walk allowed six runs in seven innings, but the Phillies won 7–6 as they overcame a 4–0 deficit. Aikens hit a pair of two-run homers for the Royals.

Kansas City led 3–2 in the seventh inning of Game Two, but wound up winning 6–4. George Brett, whose hemorrhoid surgery made headlines during the Series, homered in his first at-bat in Game Three. Aikens' ninth-inning single gave the Royals a 4–3 win.

Aikens hit two more home runs in Game Four to lead the Royals to a 5–3 win.

The Phillies salvaged one game in Kansas City, winning 4–3 in Game Five with a two-run ninth inning against Dan Quisenberry. Pinch hitter Del Unser doubled in the tying run and Manny Trillo's infield single put the Phillies ahead.

Philadelphia won Game Six, 4–1, behind Steve Carlton and Tug McGraw to end the Phillies' 97 years of disappointment.

Pete Rose is all smiles as he looks at the World Champion of baseball trophy at a rally for the Phillies

GEORGE BRETT

Games	2,707
At-Bats	10,349
Runs	1,583
RBI	1,595
Home runs	317
Hits	3,154
Doubles	634
Triples	134
Stolen Bases	201
Average	0.305
Slugging percentage	0.487

George Brett came to the major leagues with a family reputation to uphold. His older brother, Ken, had pitched in the 1967 World Series at the age of 19 for the Boston Red Sox and was the winning pitcher in the 1974 All-Star game for the Pittsburgh Pirates.

At the '74 All-Star break, George was struggling with an average around .200 and giving the Kansas City Royals ample reason to wonder if they'd erred by giving him the third base position. Kansas City had traded Paul Schaal to the California Angels during the offseason to clear a spot for Brett, and it was looking like a mistake almost halfway through the season.

Brett spent the break watching his older brother on television and taking stock of his own career. It turned out to be the launching point for both a Hall of Fame career and a new identity for Ken Brett—he'd forever be known as George Brett's brother instead of the other way around.

Royals' batting coach, Charlie Lau, had some ideas on how to improve Brett's swing. He also had a very receptive pupil. "I had nothing to lose," Brett said. Suddenly, a player who had never hit .300 in the minor leagues was threatening to hit .400, thanks to Lau's theories and his own relentless work.

Lau tore down Brett's old swing and completely reinvented him as a hitter. He started with his weight shifted to his back foot and with his bat moving slightly. Then he rocked into his swing, keeping his hands back.

The results were impressive. Brett became the only player in history to win batting titles in three different decades. He had 11 seasons with an average over .300 and helped the Royals reach the American League Championship Series six times. The reworked swing, coupled with his own determination, made him one of baseball's toughest outs.

"When the game was on the line, we all wanted George up there," teammate John Wathan said.

Brett the competitor was never more in evidence than in the 1985 playoffs. The Royals trailed the Toronto Blue Jays in games, 3–1, and were on the verge of elimination. Brett hit two home runs, a double and a single and made a defensive play that prevented the tying run from scoring. The Royals went on to win both the playoffs and the World Series. Said pitcher Mark Gubicza, "It was the greatest game I ever saw. George just said climb on my back and we did."

In 1980, Brett made a run at .400 and settled for a .390 average, the game's highest since Ted Williams hit .406 in 1941. Brett had a 30-game hitting streak in 1980.

He is also remembered for two secondary issues in his career. Brett developed hemorrhoids during the 1980 World Series and experienced so much pain that he had to be removed from one of the games against the Philadelphia Phillies. He continued in the Series after undergoing surgery for 20 minutes on an off day.

Brett understood that the condition would make him the butt of jokes—something that he handled with as much grace as possible. That was largely forgotten, though, when he had the infamous pine tar incident in a 1983 game against the New York Yankees.

Brett had homered against Yankees' relief ace, Goose Gossage, and had just accepted congratulations in the dugout when Yankees manager, Billy Martin, went out to confront the plate umpire. Martin protested that Brett's bat was illegal because it had pine tar too far up the handle. By the letter of the rule, Martin was correct and the umpires disallowed the home run.

Brett came charging out of the dugout and had to be restrained by both teammates and other umpires. Sanity eventually ruled and the American League office correctly ruled that the pine tar hadn't aided Brett's home run, which was allowed to stand.

On September 30, 1992, Brett collected his 3,000th career hit, which solidified his already impressive Hall of Fame credentials. When his name appeared on the ballot, he got 98.2 percent of the vote, the fourth highest total in Hall of Fame voting history.

Brett's career was marked by a relentless work ethic and a passion for the game

MOST VALUABLE PLAYER
AL: Rollie Fingers, Milwaukee
NL: Mike Schmidt, Philadelphia Phillies

CY YOUNG AWARD
AL: Rollie Fingers, Milwaukee
NL: Feranando Valenzuela, Los Angeles

ROOKIE OF THE YEAR
AL: Dave Righetti, NY Yankees
NL: Feranando Valenzuela, Los Angeles

LEADERS
BATTING AVERAGE
AL: Carney Lansford, Boston Red Sox, .336
NL: Bill Madlock, Pittsburgh, .341

HOME RUNS
AL: Tony Armas, A's; Dwight Evans, Red Sox;
Bobby Grich, Angels; Eddie Murray, Orioles, 22
NL: Mlke Schmidt, Philadelphia Phillies, 31

RUNS BATTED IN
AL: Eddie Murray, Baltimore, 78
NL: Mlke Schmidt, Philadelphia Phillies, 91

STOLEN BASES
AL: Rickey Henderson, Oakland, 56
NL: Tim Raines, Montreal, 71

PITCHING VICTORIES
AL: Dennis Martinez, Baltimore; Steve McCatty,
Oakland; Jack Morris, Detroit; Pete Vukovich,
Milwaukee, 14; NL: Tom Seaver, Reds, 14

EARNED RUN AVERAGE
AL: Dave Righetti, NY Yankees, 2.06
NL: Nolan Ryan, Houston, 1.69

STRIKEOUTS
AL: Len Barker, Cleveland, 127
NL: Feranando Valenzuela, Los Angeles, 180

SAVES
AL: Rollie Fingers, Milwaukee, 28
NL: Bruce Sutter, St. Louis Cardinals, 25

Part of the magic of the baseball season is the endurance it requires. The team that jumps out to the fast lead in April may be at the bottom of the standings in October. The team with the big first half may not be able to sustain that success through the last three months of the season.

The Indians' Len Barker led the American League in strikeouts with 127

The season requires a team to prove itself over the long haul because it has a beginning, a middle and an end. Until 1981.

It was the season without a middle, the result of a players' strike called in June that lasted until August.

As always seems to be the case, baseball was enjoying a wonderful season when the labor problems intruded. The seeming prosperity was interrupted again when owners and players couldn't find a satisfactory way to divide revenues that were making both sides wealthy beyond any reasonable measure.

Since the late 1960s, when the Players Association first became prominent under executive director Marvin Miller, baseball had been plagued by the threat of work stoppages. They had delayed the openings of seasons, most notably in 1972 when the season had to be abbreviated after a strike wiped out some early games. But no sport had ever shut down in mid-season in the history of professional sports in North America. That changed on June 12.

Pennant races that were just beginning to

SHORTS The phenomenon known as "Fernando-mania" got its start on opening day. Jerry Reuss, who had been scheduled to start for the Dodgers, was sidelined by a muscle pull, so the Dodgers turned to rookie Fernando Valenzuela. Valenzuela shut out the Astros for the first of eight consecutive victories that helped him with the Cy Young and Rookie of the Year awards.

develop were put aside. Pete Rose's chase of the National League record for career hits went on hold. Ballparks shut down just when warmer weather was arriving.

The most incredible aspect of the strike was that the disgruntled players were earning, on average, nearly $200,000 per year, a wage ten times that of the average worker.

In all, 712 games were canceled. The cost of the stoppage was softened for owners who had purchased strike insurance and got some of the lost revenue back from their policies. But even that didn't begin to cover the losses sustained when the games had to be canceled.

The root of the issue was free agent compensation, a sticking point since players had been granted the freedom to change teams by a 1975 arbitrator's decision. The owners argued that a team losing a free agent was entitled to significant compensation. The union argued that such limits would actually impede movement and take away some of the gains the players had won.

The system that had been developed allowed teams losing free agents to collect their compensation via extra selections in the June draft. But since the draft represented a long-range, low-percentage proposition, the teams wanted the compensation to take the form of major league players. The union contended that this would quash the market because a team would be less willing to sign a free agent, knowing that it would cause the loss of another major league player and defeat the purpose of acquiring a free agent.

The owners were willing to take a hard-line stance. They took the unusual step of imposing a gag order on their members. When Milwaukee Brewers' executive Harry Dalton commented publicly on the delicate negotiations, he was fined $50,000.

One week before the strike, the union offered a compromise that would have provided compensation via a pool system. It was not accepted.

On Friday, June 12, the strike was on. Players on the road with their teams were uncertain of where to go or what to do. A game between the San Diego Padres and Chicago Cubs scheduled for Wrigley Field was the first to be affected. Then the entire slate of night games was wiped out and the parks were closed throughout the major leagues.

As the strike dragged on, media outlets looked for some baseball content other than sporadic coverage of unproductive labor negotiations. Some staged fantasy games involving teams of the past with the results determined either by computerized play or reality-based board games. Some broadcast outlets went to their archives for classic games to repeat. Others sent crews to the minor leagues to cover games involving the affiliates of the major league team. Some teams brought their minor league teams to play in the otherwise-vacant major league stadiums.

Some of the players went to work.

Dodgers' Rookie of the Year and Cy Young winner, Fernando Valenzuela

425

Astros' Nolan Ryan led the National League with a 1.69 earned run average

ing to the allotment of service time during the strike.

The teams convened again on August 1 for workouts. Several clubs found their stadiums unavailable because of football commitments and had to find suitable facilities elsewhere. The Montreal Expos were forced to reassemble at their Florida training base.

The hot issue was how to determine pennant winners. The notion of picking up the season where it left off was rejected on the grounds that teams buried in the standings had no chance to catch up in a shortened season. The decision was made to declare the June 12 standings final for the first half of the season, then start anew when the games resumed.

In the American League East, the New York Yankees won the first "half" pennant while Oakland took the West. Philadelphia won the National League East with the Los Angeles Dodgers edging the Cincinnati Reds for the West Division crown.

After a couple of exhibition games per team and the delayed All-Star game in Cleveland, the season resumed on August 10 at Wrigley Field. The attitude of fans toward the strike was reflected in the attendance. Only 7,551 turned out for the reopening day game between the Cubs and New York Mets.

In Philadelphia, more than 60,000 fans showed up to see Rose get the hit that made him the National League's all-time leader in hits. His 3,631st hit allowed him to pass Stan Musial.

In San Diego, Padres' owner Ray Kroc, who learned something about customer service in launching McDonald's, provided free admission to his team's first game and more than 52,000 people took advantage.

Eventually the baseball itself would bring fans back. Houston's Nolan Ryan pitched his fifth no-hitter, beating the Dodgers 5–0 on September 26. There had been two no-hitters before the strike—Charlie Lea of the Expos threw one against San Francisco and Cleveland's Len Barker had a perfect game against Toronto.

Manufactured though the excitement may have been, there were tight pennant races for the second half titles. Oakland came closest to repeating, but Kansas City won in the American League West despite the unbalanced schedule. The Milwaukee Brewers took the American League East, narrowly edging Detroit and Boston.

Montreal reached the postseason for the first time in franchise history by finishing on top in the National League East for the second half.

Newspapers carried photos of players dedicating themselves to less-glamorous pursuits. Detroit Tigers' infielder Richie Hebner was again digging graves, one of the jobs he'd held before striking it rich in baseball.

On July 31, the strike was settled, thanks in part to the intervention of American League president Lee MacPhail. A number of points involving free agent compensation were the centerpiece of the treaty, as were issues relat-

SHORTS It took Pete Rose 60 days to get two hits. On June 10, Rose singled off Nolan Ryan for his 3,630th career hit, tying Stan Musial's National League record. Rose broke the record on Aug. 10 in the first game after the players' strike ended. The record-setting single came off Mark Littell of the Cardinals at Veterans Stadium in Philadelphia.

Houston was a game and a half better than Cincinnati in the West.

The system was a sore point in two parts of the country. The Cincinnati Reds had the National League's best record for the season (66–42), but were shut out of the postseason because they hadn't finished first in either of the races. The St. Louis Cardinals (59–43) had the best winning percentage in the National League East, but they were also excluded from the play-offs.

The Royals made it to the postseason by winning the second half. The Royals, though, had a chance to become the first team to win a World Series championship with a losing record. Kansas City was 50–53 for the season.

Two longtime baseball families chose to get out of the game. The Carpenter family sold the Phillies to a group headed by team president Bill Giles. That ended a family own-ership that had started in 1943. Ruly Carpenter said he was getting out because of differences with other owners on how base-ball business should be conducted. Carpenter was said to have had his fill of the game in the free agent era.

The Wrigley family, facing estate tax prob-lems, sold the Cubs to the Chicago Tribune Corp. The Wrigleys had held a majority stake in the team since 1921.

Bill Veeck's ownership of the Chicago White Sox ended when he sold out to Jerry Reinsdorf and Eddie Einhorn.

Strike or no strike, managers still had little job security. Maury Wills was fired in Seattle after less than a year on the job. Rene Lachemann replaced him. Johnny Goryl was dropped by the Minnesota Twins and replaced by Billy Gardner.

The California Angels fired Jim Fregosi and named Gene Mauch to replace him. Jim Frey was out less than a year after leading Kansas City to the World Series. Dick Howser was hired to take over. Gene Michael was fired by the Yankees and Bob Lemon came back for a second turn. En route to the second-half pennant, Montreal ousted Dick Williams and brought in Jim Fanning.

The Players Association executive director Marvin Miller talks to the press during the players' strike that lasted from June to August

AL CHAMPIONSHIP SERIES

GAME 1

| NY Yankees 3 | Oakland 1 |

GAME 2

| NY Yankees 13 | Oakland 3 |

GAME 3

| NY Yankees 4 | Oakland 0 |

NL CHAMPIONSHIP SERIES

GAME 1

| Los Angeles 5 | Montreal 1 |

GAME 2

| Montreal 3 | Los Angeles 0 |

GAME 3

| Montreal 4 | Los Angeles 1 |

GAME 4

| Los Angeles 7 | Montreal 1 |

GAME 5

| Los Angeles 2 | Montreal 1 |

WORLD SERIES

GAME 1

| NY Yankees 5 | Los Angeles 3 |

GAME 2

| NY Yankees 3 | Los Angeles 0 |

GAME 3

| Los Angeles 5 | NY Yankees 4 |

GAME 4

| Los Angeles 8 | NY Yankees 7 |

GAME 5

| Los Angeles 2 | NY Yankees 1 |

GAME 6

| Los Angeles 9 | NY Yankees 2 |

MVPs: Pedro Guerrero, Steve Yeager and Ron Cey, Los Angeles

Because of a players' strike that blew a 50-day hole in the middle of the season, baseball had to add an extra tier of playoffs.

It still came down to the New York Yankees versus the Los Angeles Dodgers for the third time in five years and the 11th time in World Series history.

The players walked out in June and didn't return until August. Baseball put together a system that declared division winners for each "half" of the season and had them play each other to get to the traditional best-of-five playoff series.

The 1980 World Series teams didn't survive the preliminary round in the postseason. Montreal beat the Philadelphia Phillies and the Oakland A's beat Kansas City.

The Dodgers won their series against Houston to claim the National League West title and the Yankees survived a strong challenge from the Milwaukee Brewers to take the American League East.

Montreal was in the postseason for the first time in franchise history. Oakland, which had won three consecutive World Series from 1972–74, was back with a completely different team led by Billy Martin. Under Martin, the overachieving A's were playing a hustling brand of baseball that came to be known as "Billy Ball". It was an irresistible story—Martin, who had

been fired so many times by Yankees owner, George Steinbrenner, was now prepared to become his old team's worst enemy. But the A's ran into an experienced Yankees team and lost the playoffs in three games.

Yankees third baseman Graig Nettles had gotten just one hit in 17 at-bats against the Brewers, but picked things up in the playoffs, going 6-for-12 and setting a championship series record with nine RBIs.

Tommy John, Ron Davis and Goose Gossage held the A's to six hits in the Yankees' 3–1 win in the opener. Nettles had a three-run double in the first inning off Mike Norris.

The Yankees were trailing 3–1 in the second game when they scored seven runs in the fourth inning en route to a 13–3 win. Lou Piniella's three-run homer highlighted the inning.

The Yankees wrapped up the playoffs when Dave Righetti, Davis and Gossage combined on a 4–0 shutout. Nettles had another three-run double.

New York had extra time to rest while the Dodgers went to the last inning of the last game to beat the Expos. The Dodgers had been on a 18–1 streak at home against Montreal and that dominance continued with a 5–1 win in the opening game. The Expos broke their Dodgers Stadium jinx by winning the second game 3–0 on a five-hitter by Ray Burris.

Steve Rogers pitched nearly as well to give the Expos a 4–1 win in the third game. Jerry White hit a two-run homer. The Dodgers avoided elimination with a 7–1 win in the fourth game, scoring six runs in the last two innings to break a 1–1 tie. Steve Garvey hit a two-run homer.

That set up the dramatic ending that put Dodgers' outfielder Rick Monday's name in postseason lore. The teams were tied 1–1 in the ninth, the result of a tense duel between Burris and rookie Fernando Valenzuela. After Burris was lifted for a pinch hitter, Rogers, Montreal's biggest winner, came in to pitch the ninth. Monday hit a home run with two outs and the bases empty and the Dodgers advanced to the Series when Valenzuela and Bob Welch closed out the ninth.

The Yankees took the first two games, scoring three runs in the first inning of the Series to win Game One, 5–3. John and Gossage combined on a four-hit 3–0 win in Game Two.

Valenzuela had a messy 5–4 win in Game

Co-MVP Ron Cey, dubbed the Penguin, played a vital role in the Dodgers' triumph

Three, which was highlighted by Ron Cey's three-run homer in the first inning. The Dodgers got two runs in the seventh inning of Game Four and held on for an 8–7 win. Los Angeles overcame a 4–0 deficit and as a result the momentum shifted in their favor.

Jerry Reuss won Game Five, 2–1, as Pedro Guerrero and Steve Yeager hit back-to-back home runs off Ron Guidry in the seventh.

The Dodgers won Game Six, 9–2, to claim their first World Series title since 1963. Guerrero drove in five runs as the Dodgers broke open a game that was tied 1–1 in the fourth. The losing pitcher was reliever George Frazier, who set a Series record by losing three games.

Jubilant Dodgers celebrate their World Championship as catcher Steve Yeager hugs relief pitcher Steve Howe. Steve Garvey is left and at right is Derek Thomas

MOST VALUABLE PLAYER
AL: Robin Yount, Milwaukee
NL: Dale Murphy, Atlanta

CY YOUNG AWARD
AL: Pete Vuckovich, Milwaukee
NL: Steve Carlton, Philadelphia Phillies

ROOKIE OF THE YEAR
AL: Cal Ripken Jr., Baltimore
NL: Steve Sax, Los Angeles

LEADERS
BATTING AVERAGE
AL: Willie Wilson, Kansas City, .332
NL: Al Oliver, Montreal, .331

HOME RUNS
AL: Reggie Jackson, California; Gorman Thomas, Milwaukee, 39; NL: Dave Kingman, NY Mets, 37

RUNS BATTED IN
AL: Hal McRae, Kansas City, 133; NL: Dale Murphy, Milwaukee; Al Oliver, Montreal, 109

STOLEN BASES
AL: Rickey Henderson, Oakland, 130
NL: Tim Raines, Montreal, 78

PITCHING VICTORIES
AL: LaMarr Hoyt, Chicago White Sox, 19
NL: Steve Carlton, Philadelphia Phillies, 23

EARNED RUN AVERAGE
AL: Rick Sutcliffe, Cleveland, 2.96
NL: Steve Rogers, Montreal. 2.40

STRIKEOUTS
AL: Floyd Bannister, Seattle, 209
NL: Steve Carlton, Philadelphia Phillies, 286

SAVES
AL: Dan Quisenberry, Kansas City, 35
NL: Bruce Sutter, St. Louis Cardinals, 36

AL MVP—Robin Yount of the Milwaukee Braves

After a lengthy season strike and behind-the-scenes strife, baseball needed a great year on the field. That's exactly what it got.

There were four exciting pennant races, each decided by fewer than five games. It was the first time all four races were that close since divisional play was instituted in 1969.

The Atlanta Braves opened the season with 13 consecutive wins under new manager Joe Torre. Later, though, the Braves would endure a streak of 19 losses in 21 games. Their descent would help open the race in the National League West. In the season's final two games, the Braves, Los Angeles Dodgers and San Francisco Giants all had a chance to take the division.

On the next-to-last day, the Dodgers eliminated the Giants with a 15–2 win that coincided

SHORTS

with a 4–2 Braves win against San Diego. On the final day of the season, Atlanta missed a chance to clinch the pennant on its own by losing 5–1 to the Padres.

The Braves gathered around television sets in their clubhouse and watched the final game between the Giants and Dodgers. The long-time rivals, who had competed bitterly in New York and California, battled in a close game. If the Giants couldn't win, they did the next-best thing by guaranteeing that the Dodgers wouldn't. Joe Morgan's three-run homer in the seventh helped the Giants win 5–3, which gave the Western Divisional title to the Braves.

The National League East was the first division to be decided. The St. Louis Cardinals wrapped up the title on September 27 with a 4–2 win in Montreal. The Cardinals finished three games ahead of the Philadelphia Phillies. It was the Cardinals' first trip to the postseason in 14 years.

The Cardinals were remarkably consistent. They never had a losing streak of more than three games. Two winning streaks made the difference—the Cardinals won 12 in a row early in the season to jump out front and then took the

division with an eight-game streak in September.

The American League East was a wild scramble at the end. The Milwaukee Brewers went into Baltimore for a season-ending, four-game series, needing just one win to wrap up the franchise's first title. The Orioles, however, swept a doubleheader on Friday night. Then Baltimore won the Saturday game, turning the season into a one-game showdown on Sunday.

Robin Yount hit two home runs to support Don Sutton and the Brewers won the game 10–2 to take the title. It spoiled what could have been a storybook ending for retiring Orioles' manager Earl Weaver.

The California Angels clinched the American League West on October 2 and finished three games ahead of Kansas City.

Cardinals' manager Whitey Herzog worked three new starters into his lineup. Lonnie Smith, a part-time player for the Phillies, became the regular left fielder in St. Louis and led the league with 120 runs. His .307 average was fourth in the National League and his 68 stolen bases ranked second.

Shortstop Ozzie Smith replaced Garry Templeton, for whom he was traded, and was brilliant in the field. Willie McGee, stolen from the New York Yankees in a trade for pitcher Bob Sykes, played center and batted .296 after he was called up from the minor leagues in May. Pitcher Joaquin Andujar was 15–10, but he got better as the season went on. After August 12, Andujar had a 1.68 earned run average and the Cardinals won 13 of his 14 starts. Bob Forsch also won 15 games.

TIMELINE

Jan. 22: Reggie Jackson ended his five-year Yankees career by signing with the Angels as a free agent.

Feb. 8: The Dodgers traded Davey Lopes to Oakland, breaking up an infield that had been intact since 1974.

April 25: The Yankees fired Bob Lemon after just 14 games. His replacement was Gene Michael, who had also preceded Lemon in the job.

May 15: Gaylord Perry of Seattle beat the Yankees for his 300th win. Perry was the 15th pitcher to win 300 games.

June 2: Milwaukee replaced manager Buck Rodgers with Harvey Kuenn.

June 22: Pete Rose got his 3,772nd career hit, passing Hank Aaron for second place.

July 8: Oakland Manager Billy Martin got his 1,000th career win.

July 21: John McNamara was fired as Reds manager and replaced by Russ Nixon.

Aug. 10: Bill Virdon, Astros' manager since 1975, was fired and replaced by coach Bob Lillis.

Aug. 21: Rollie Fingers of the Brewers got his 300th career save.

Aug. 30: The Brewers acquired Don Sutton from Houston for the stretch run.

Sept. 1: The Mets beat Houston to end a 15-game losing streak.

Sept. 6: The Pirates held a day to honor retiring star Willie Stargell.

Sept. 13: Steve Carlton became the majors' first 20-game winner.

Oct. 22: Gene Mauch resigned as Angels' manager after winning the American League West title.

Nov. 11: The Orioles chose former Giants' manager Joe Altobelli to replace Earl Weaver, who retired.

Dec. 16: Tom Seaver was traded back to the Mets by the Reds.

Dec. 21: Steve Garvey ended his Dodgers career after nine seasons by signing as a free agent with San Diego.

Dale Murphy's 36 homers and 109 RBIs helped Atlanta to a division crown

Cal Ripken Jr. made a big splash in Baltimore winning Rookie of the Year honors

The Cardinals were strong in the late innings because of closer Bruce Sutter. He won nine games and had 36 saves, the most in the majors.

Torre masterfully worked around injuries to the starting rotation and came up with combinations that kept the Braves in contention. The strength of their staff was a bullpen led by Gene Garber and Steve Bedrosian. Garber had 30 saves and Bedrosian had 11 after moving out of the rotation.

Dale Murphy led the offense with 36 home runs and 109 RBIs. Bob Horner had 32 home runs and Chris Chambliss had 20, a career high. Claudell Washington also hit 16 homers and drove in 80 runs.

Milwaukee's explosive offense under new manager Harvey Kuenn earned the Brewers the nickname "Harvey's Wallbangers". They hit 216 home runs and scored 891 runs.

Robin Yount missed winning the batting title by a point. He hit .331 and was among the league leaders in most offensive categories, a season that won him the Most Valuable Player award. Gorman Thomas hit 39 home runs, Ben Oglivie had 34 and Cecil Cooper hit 32. Cooper, Thomas, Oglivie and Yount all drove in at least 100 runs and Ted Simmons had 97 RBIs.

Pete Vuckovich led the starting staff with an 18–6 record and 3.34 ERA that earned him the Cy Young award. Mike Caldwell won 17 games. Sutton, who pitched the clinching victory against Baltimore, had been obtained for the stretch run from Houston. He went 4–1 with the Brewers.

Reliever Rollie Fingers saved 29 games before an arm injury forced him out in September. Dwight Bernard got six saves and Pete Ladd picked up three in Fingers' absence.

The Orioles pulled themselves back into the race with a 27–5 streak between August 19 and September 20. After the All-Star break Baltimore was 50–30—the best record in either league.

Eddie Murray hit .316 with 32 home runs and 110 RBIs. Jim Palmer came back from the first losing season in his career to go 15–5 with a .313 ERA. The Orioles made room for prospect Cal Ripken, Jr. to take over initially at third base, then shortstop. After a .117 start, Ripken finished at .264 with 28 home runs and 93 RBIs to win Rookie of the Year honors.

The Angels reaped the benefits of an offseason overhaul that saw them add Reggie Jackson, Doug DeCinces, Bob Boone and Tim Foli. They made team history by winning 93 games and manager Gene Mauch won his first title of any kind in 22 years of managing.

DeCinces batted .301 with 30 home runs and 97 RBIs. Jackson ended his stormy career in New York for the more placid environment of southern California and flourished at the age of 36. He hit 39 homers and drove in 101 runs. Holdover Brian Downing batted .281 with 28 home runs and 84 RBIs. Fred Lynn bounced back from a bad year and batted .299 with 21 homers and 86 RBIs. Rod Carew hit .319, his 14th consecutive season over .300. Geoff Zahn led the pitching staff with 18 wins.

Several players celebrated career milestones. The biggest was Gaylord Perry's 300th career win for the Seattle Mariners on May 6, a 7–3 victory over the Yankees. Perry compiled most of his wins with San Francisco, Cleveland, San Diego and Texas. He was clearly at the end of the line at age 43 and needed a team as much as Seattle needed a gate attraction. Perry posted a 10–12 record and ended the season with 307 career wins.

Philadelphia's Pete Rose played in his 3,000th game on June 20 and got hit No. 3,772 on June 22 to take over second place on the career list. Rose passed Hank Aaron and trailed only Ty Cobb.

Steve Garvey of the Dodgers played in every game and ran his consecutive game streak to 1,107 and ended the season just ten games short of Billy Williams' National League record.

Oakland outfielder Rickey Henderson stole 130 bases to break Lou Brock's 1974 single-season record of 118.

Even by Yankees' standards it was a turbulent year in the Bronx, as owner George Steinbrenner kept making changes to shake up his club. He fired Bob Lemon as manager after just 14 games and a 6–8 record. Gene Michael was named manager and he lasted until August 3. Even though Michael had a three-year contract to manage, he was out after 86 games, replaced by Clyde King. The Yankees used five different pitching coaches and three batting instructors.

The Brewers had greater success with a managerial change. Buck Rodgers was dropped on June 2 and was replaced by Kuenn, a member of the coaching staff. Kuenn's message to the team was simple: "Have fun," he told them at the introductory meeting and the team respond-

ed to his low-key approach.

Weaver's final year wasn't without controversy. He was suspended for a week and fined $2,000 for making contact with umpire Terry Cooney during an argument.

But no one had a more stressful year than Commissioner Bowie Kuhn, who was under fire from a group of dissident owners that included Atlanta's Ted Turner. The militant owners, most of whom had only recently come to baseball, contended that Kuhn lacked the business acumen to lead the game through its radical economic changes. More owners were losing money and they blamed Kuhn for failing to provide the proper guidance. Kuhn was also assigned some of the blame for the prolonged players' strike that wiped out the middle of the 1981 season.

Moderates, like Peter O'Malley of the Los Angeles Dodgers, argued on Kuhn's behalf. Ultimately, the anti-Kuhn forces won and he was denied another term as Commissioner.

Seattle's Gaylord Perry reached the 300-win plateau and celebrated in style

AL CHAMPIONSHIP SERIES

GAME 1

California 8	Milwaukee 3

GAME 2

California 4	Milwaukee 2

GAME 3

Milwaukee 5	California 3

GAME 4

Milwaukee 9	California 5

GAME 5

Milwaukee 4	California 3

MVP: Fred Lynn, California

NL CHAMPIONSHIP SERIES

GAME 1

St. Louis Cardinals 7	Atlanta 0

GAME 2

St. Louis Cardinals 4	Atlanta 3

GAME 3

St. Louis Cardinals 6	Atlanta 2

MVP: Darrell Porter, St. Louis Cardinals

WORLD SERIES

GAME 1

Milwaukee 10	St. Louis Cardinals 0

GAME 2

St. Louis Cardinals 5	Milwaukee 4

GAME 3

St. Louis Cardinals 6	Milwaukee 2

GAME 4

Milwaukee 7	St. Louis Cardinals 5

GAME 5

Milwaukee 6	St. Louis Cardinals 4

GAME 6

St. Louis Cardinals 13	Milwaukee 1

GAME 7

St. Louis Cardinals 6	Milwaukee 3

MVP: Darrell Porter, St. Louis Cardinals

The St. Louis Cardinals went through the 1970s without reaching the postseason and they knew exactly what they needed—Whitey Herzog.

Herzog was one of the game's sharpest talent evaluators and an exceptional manager. He had worked in the New York Mets farm system when that organization was building its championship club. He managed the Kansas City Royals when that team enjoyed its first success.

After too many disappointing seasons, the Cardinals wisely put their operation into Herzog's hands. The reward came when the club he helped to build outlasted the Milwaukee Brewers in a seven-game World Series.

The Cardinals fought off Philadelphia to win the National League East, then quickly disposed of the Atlanta Braves, who rode a 13–0 start to a Western Division title. The Braves went to the last day of the season before prevailing over the defending World Series champion Los Angeles Dodgers and San Francisco Giants for their first title since 1969.

The Braves wound up making little more than a cameo appearance in the playoffs. The scheduled opener in St. Louis was wiped out by rain in the fifth inning with Atlanta leading 1–0. More importantly, the Braves wasted their best pitcher, Phil Niekro, in the non-game.

Pascual Perez started the rescheduled opener and lost 7–0 as Bob Forsch pitched a three-hitter.

Niekro pitched the second game and left with a lead. Reliever Gene Garber gave up single runs in the eighth and ninth for a 4–3 Cardinals win.

The Cardinals effectively wrapped up the playoffs with a four-run second inning against Perez in the third game. Joaquin Andujar won with relief help from Bruce Sutter and the Cardinals took the series, thanks in large part to catcher Darrell Porter. Porter was on base ten times in 14 plate appearances.

The Brewers made history, becoming the first team to win three straight playoff games after losing the first two. Milwaukee lost the first game 8–3 and Bruce Kison beat Pete Vuckovich 4–2 in the second game.

Paul Molitor had a two-run homer and Don Sutton won the third game 5–3. Substitute outfielder, Mark Brouhard, drove in three runs and scored four in a 9–5 win that tied the series after four games.

Cecil Cooper had a two-run single in the seventh to end a personal 0-for-9 streak and send the Brewers to their first World Series.

Milwaukee showed why manager Harvey Kuenn's Brewers had been nicknamed "Harvey's Wallbangers" in Game One. They collected 17 hits in a 10–0 win as Mike Caldwell pitched a three-hitter.

The Cardinals shook that off and won Game Two, 5–4, with a run in the eighth inning. The tiebreaking run came when Pete Ladd walked Steve Braun with the bases loaded. Sutter pitched the last 2⅓ innings to get the win.

St. Louis won Game Three, 6–2, thanks to a pair of home runs by Willie McGee off Vuckovich. The game turned into a showcase for the rookie outfielder, who also made two exceptional defensive plays in center to shut down Brewers rallies.

The Cardinals held a 5–1 lead in the seventh inning of Game Four when a seemingly minor error by pitcher Dave LaPoint gave the Brewers an extra opportunity. They scored six runs in the inning against four Cardinals pitchers and won the game 7–5 to tie the Series. Robin Yount and Gorman Thomas each singled in two runs in the inning.

Caldwell allowed 14 hits in 8⅔ innings of Game Five, but still won 6–4 with Bob McClure's relief help. Yount was 4-for-4 with a home run.

The Cardinals bombed Sutton and reliever George Medich to win Game Six, 13–1. Hernandez and Porter each hit two-run homers. The Cardinals benefited from the use of the designated hitter rule as Dane Iorg had two doubles and a triple.

Andujar was back on the mound for Game Seven, despite taking a Ted Simmons line drive off his kneecap in Game Three. Milwaukee led 3–1 in the sixth, but Hernandez tied the game with a bases-loaded single and George Hendrick's single put the Cardinals ahead.

Whitey Herzog's renowned savvy landed him in St. Louis

St. Louis' catcher Darrell Porter jumps into the arms of Cardinal relief pitcher Bruce Sutter after winning 6–3 to take the World Series

PETE ROSE

TEAMS
Cincinnati Reds 1963–78, 1985–86;
Philadelphia Phillies 1979–83;
Montreal Expos 1984

Games	.3,562
At-Bats	.14,053
Runs	.2,165
RBI	.1,314
Home runs	.160
Hits	.4,256
Doubles	.746
Triples	.135
Stolen Bases	.198
Average	.0.303
Slugging percentage	.0.409

Pete Rose didn't care whether or not people liked him; his goal was to make sure they noticed him.

He succeeded by playing the game with an uncommon drive that earned the grudging respect of opponents and led to victories for the teams that employed him. It continued even after his career ended when Rose refused to fade away and cannily kept his lifetime banishment from the game a hot issue for more than a decade.

Rose was groomed for baseball by his father, who was a semipro athlete in Cincinnati. The father taught the son to switch hit, believing that added versatility could help Rose reach the major leagues more quickly.

The hometown Reds signed Rose without much hope that he was a prime major league prospect. He wasn't gifted with a lot of natural ability but had an abundance of determination and a willingness to work longer and harder than anyone else.

Those qualities made Rose one of the dominant players of his time even though he wasn't a power hitter. He became baseball's all-time hits leader, played more games than anyone and played five different positions regularly in 24 seasons, which doesn't count the player-manager role he had at the end of his career. He collected more than 1,000 hits beyond the age of 38 and once had a streak of nine years with averages over .300. When that was interrupted by a .284 season, Rose hit over .300 for each of the next five seasons.

Rose finished his career with a .303 average, which led him to say, "I never said I was the best hitter, just the one with the most hits."

Rose was a surprise starter when the Reds broke camp in 1963. He played well enough to bump veteran Don Blasingame out of a job and impressed the staff with his nonstop effort. When he drew a walk, he'd cast aside his bat and run to first base. His original nickname, "Charlie Hustle", was meant as a term of derision by New York Yankees players who thought Rose's sprints to first on a walk were minor league stuff.

Rose made his first All-Star game in 1965 and won the first of his three batting titles three years later. Cincinnati loved him; the rest of the National League didn't. Rose was flashy and popularized the headfirst slide into bases.

By 1970, the Reds were contenders and Rose had his first big moment in the national spotlight. Playing in the All-Star game, he was waved home on Jim Hickman's single. Rose could see the play at the plate was going to be close and decided his only chance to be safe was to bowl over catcher Ray Fosse. Rose threw his shoulder block, the ball became dislodged and the call was safe. But Fosse also suffered a separated shoulder and was never the same player.

Rose may have been sympathetic but wasn't apologetic. That's the way he played the game, even if it was an All-Star game that most considered meaningless.

In the 1973 playoffs, Rose wound up in a scrap with New York Mets' shortstop Bud Harrelson after a tag play at second base. In the regular season, Rose had batted .338 with 230 hits to win the Most Valuable Player award.

He and the Reds won the World Series in 1975, with Rose taking Series MVP honors after compiling a .370 average. Rose had a 44-game hitting streak in 1978, his last season with the Reds. In 1980, he helped the Philadelphia Phillies win their first World Series.

Rose became the National League's all-time leader in hits in 1981 and left the Phillies after the 1983 season. He landed with Montreal and was doing poorly when the Expos sent him to the Reds, who hoped his return as player-manager would revive a moribund franchise.

On September 11, 1985, Rose completed his drive to break Ty Cobb's record and got his 4,193rd hit against San Diego's Eric Show. Within three years, the all-time leader would be a pariah in his own game.

Baseball investigated charges that Rose was involved in illegal gambling activities. The case ended when Rose signed an agreement for lifetime banishment without an admission of guilt.

It might not have been intended as a term of endearment, but "Charlie Hustle" fitted like a glove

Joe Altobelli was the right man at the right time for the Orioles

When the manager of a first-place team is summoned to the front office for a midseason meeting, he has every right to expect something good. A raise, perhaps. Maybe a contract extension. At minimum, some pats on the back for having the team where every club wants to be.

Perhaps that agenda was on Pat Corrales' mind when he met with the upper management of the Philadelphia Phillies on July 18. The Phillies were atop the National League East with a modest 43–42 record.

When Corrales walked out of the office that day, he was unemployed and the responsibility of managing the Phillies again fell to general manager Paul Owens, who was willing to take on a dual role at the age of 59.

The Phillies were in first place, but it was Owens' belief that their penchant for underachievement was dangerous. A record one game over .500 usually isn't good enough to lead a division. The National League East was weak, but how long would it stay that way?

Owens wasn't about to gamble to find out. He made the change and promised owner Bill Giles that the Phillies were still good enough to win. "I still think this is the best team we've put together," Owens told Giles.

That was saying something, considering the Phillies were just three seasons removed from the first World Series title in franchise history.

Owens was a smart baseball man and he had to recognize there was a "now or never" feel to this year's Phillies team. The newspapers had named them the "Wheeze Kids", a takeoff on the 1950 "Whiz Kids" pennant winner and a nod to the advanced ages of some key players.

The Phillies had imported parts from Cincinnati's old "Big Red Machine". Pete Rose, Joe Morgan and Tony Perez were all playing for the Phillies. Although none of the three produced the way they did in their primes with the Reds, they were still viable players with great leadership skills.

The roster was a never-ending issue. The Phillies wound up using 40 different players. Some of the players groused about the frequent changes. Third baseman Mike Schmidt went public with his concerns over the chain of command under Owens. He wasn't a hands-on manager, instead preferring to delegate responsibilities to his coaches.

Owens made changes, some of them bold. He benched Rose, who wound up hitting just .245, and inserted Len Matuszek at first base. He platooned in the outfield.

But mostly pitching let the Phillies win their division. Steve Carlton abdicated the No. 1 spot with a sub-.500 record (15–16), but John Denny was there to take over, winning 19 games with a 2.37 ERA, second-best in the league. Denny was 6–0 in September and the Phillies won 14 of 16 to finish six games ahead of Pittsburgh.

The Baltimore Orioles had their own managerial issue to confront. Earl Weaver had decided for early retirement and the team opted to replace its legend with Joe Altobelli, who had been fired by San

Long-time Dodgers' favorite Steve Garvey moved down the coast in a switch with the Padres

Feb. 19: The Dodgers' Fernando Valenzuela became the first player to receive a salary in excess of $1 million via salary arbitration.

April 16: Steve Garvey of the Padres played in his 1,118th consecutive game, breaking the National League record Billy Williams set with the Cubs.

April 27: Houston's Nolan Ryan struck out Brad Mills of Montreal. His 3,509th strikeout broke Walter Johnson's career record.

May 16: Darryl Strawberry of the Mets hit his first major league homer.

June 3: George Bamberger resigned as Mets manager and was replaced by coach Frank Howard.

June 12: For the first time in his career, Nolan Ryan pitched a complete game with no walks.

June 24: Don Sutton of Milwaukee got his 3,000th career strikeout.

June 15: Del Crandall replaced Rene Lachemann as Mariners' manager.

July 4: Dave Righetti pitched a 4–0 no-hitter against the Red Sox. It was the Yankees' first no-hitter since Don Larsen's perfect game in the 1956 World Series.

July 18: Pat Corrales was fired as Phillies' manager, even though he had the team in first place.

Aug. 22: Cubs' manager Lee Elia was fired and replaced by Charlie Fox.

Sept. 17: The Chicago White Sox clinched the American League West, their first title of any kind since 1959.

Sept. 23: Steve Carlton of the Phillies won his 300th game, beating the Cardinals.

Oct. 2: Carl Yastrzemski played his last major league game.

Dec. 8: Former Yankees' player Dr. Bobby Brown became president of the American League.

Dec. 16: The Yankees fired Billy Martin as manager for the third time. The choice to replace him was Yogi Berra, who had managed the team in 1964 but was fired after losing the World Series.

Francisco a few years earlier.

This time Altobelli was in the right place at the right time. The Orioles were a solid team, efficient and fundamentally sound. They had a farm system that seemed to consistently send up fresh prospects to replace players who had moved to other teams or were past their usefulness.

The Orioles had a stretch in which they won 34 out of 44, including a 26–6 streak. Scott McGregor led the staff with an 18–7 record and a 3.18 ERA. Mike Boddicker was 16–8 with a 2.77 ERA. Reliever Tippy Martinez appeared in 65 games and saved 21.

The hottest hitters down the stretch were Cal Ripken and Eddie Murray. In the last 37 games, Ripken batted .394 with ten home runs and 30 RBIs. Murray hit nine homers and drove in 32 runs. Their consistent production helped Baltimore to finish six games ahead of Detroit.

Baltimore won the right to compete with the surprise winner in the American League West. The Chicago White Sox overcame a bad start to post a 99–63 record that was the best in the majors.

They turned an opponent's backhanded compliment into a rallying cry. When rival manager Doug Rader of Texas complained that the White Sox were "winning ugly," the White Sox embraced the concept. Rader meant that the White Sox wouldn't get any style points for some of the ways they won.

Perhaps he was just envious of how the White Sox ran away with the West. They set a record by finishing 20 games in front of second-place Kansas City.

Outfielder Tom Paciorek explained why a team that looked so average at so many positions was able to succeed: "Individually we're not that good, but collectively we were great."

In the National League West, the Los

Pedro Guerrero led the Dodgers' batting with a .298 average

The Yankees called on closer Rich "Goose" Gossage to face Brett.

Brett sent a pitch over the right field wall to give the Royals a 5–4 lead. Or did he? On the Yankees' bench, manager Billy Martin and coach Don Zimmer played their trump card. They noticed earlier that Brett had pine tar up his bat further than the 18 inches allowed under the rules.

Martin went to the plate and made his case. Umpire Tim McClelland measured the bat against home plate and determined that Brett was in violation of Rule 1.10(b) and nullified the home run. Brett was declared out and the Yankees won the game 4–3. Or did they?

Brett came charging out of the dugout, enraged by the call. Another umpire, Joe Brinkman, was able to restrain him. The Royals filed an official protest, which was upheld ten days later. The league office determined that although Brett had violated the letter of the law, he had not given himself any advantage by using the pine tar further up the bat.

The game was to be completed on August 18, which had been an open date for the Yankees. Or was it? That morning, a judge ruled that the game should not be played. Another ruling by another judge later that afternoon reinstated completion of the game. The Yankees didn't take it seriously, playing pitcher Ron Guidry in center field and putting lefthanded-throwing Don Mattingly at second base.

The Yankees immediately appealed at first and second, charging that either Washington or Brett had failed to touch one of the bases. Their argument was that the new umpiring crew assigned to the completion of the game hadn't seen the original play. But someone brilliantly anticipated the argument and had the original umpires sign a notarized letter saying the two

Angeles Dodgers overtook the Atlanta Braves. Despite a rebuilding program, the Dodgers were able to win. Their long-standing infield was broken up when Steve Garvey went to San Diego as a free agent and third baseman Ron Cey was traded to the Chicago Cubs.

Greg Brock took over at first and Pedro Guerrero was the choice at third. Mike Marshall broke into the outfield and finished with a .284 average, second-best to Guerrero's .298.

The Dodgers did not have their traditionally strong pitching staff. Bob Welch led the team with 15 wins and a 2.65 ERA. Fernando Valenzuela had 15 wins, but was 7–8 in the second half of the season. Jerry Reuss went 11 weeks without a win, still finishing with 12 victories. Hooton pitched badly enough to be demoted to the bullpen.

It was a year marked by some bizarre incidents, none stranger than the July 24 games between the Kansas City Royals and New York Yankees that turned on George Brett's application of pine tar to his bat.

The Royals trailed 4–3 in the ninth inning when U.L. Washington singled off Dale Murray.

SHORTS If the Pine Tar Game wasn't unusual enough, how about the Sea Gull Game? The Yankees' Dave Winfield created an international incident on Aug. 5 when one of his warm-up throws struck a seagull that had landed on the field at Exhibition Stadium. Winfield was formally charged with cruelty to animals and had to post $500 bond.

players had touched all the bases.

Hal McRae struck out for the last Royals out. Dan Quisenberry retired the side in the bottom of the inning to wrap up the win and 1,245 fans who had paid $2.50 each had sat in on 12 minutes of history.

The story still wasn't over. On August 30, Commissioner Bowie Kuhn issued the largest fine of his term in office. He fined Yankees' owner George Steinbrenner $250,000 for comments made about the umpires.

Steinbrenner wasn't the only owner to get in trouble. Atlanta's Ted Turner was fined when he revealed the names of three players who would complete a trade for pitcher Len Barker. The kicker was that Barker was a disappointment, going 1–3 and failing to help the Braves win.

The game was losing some of its big names. Gaylord Perry retired in September after 314 career wins. Bobby Murcer ended his career and took a job in the Yankees' television booth. On June 10, Johnny Bench announced that he would retire at the end of the season.

Carl Yastrzemski ended his career with a victory tour around the American League. Phil Niekro was released by Atlanta, but had no interest in retiring. After the World Series, the Phillies cut ties with Rose, Morgan and Perez, all of whom sought new jobs elsewhere.

George Brett challenges the umpire over the "Pine Tar" incident

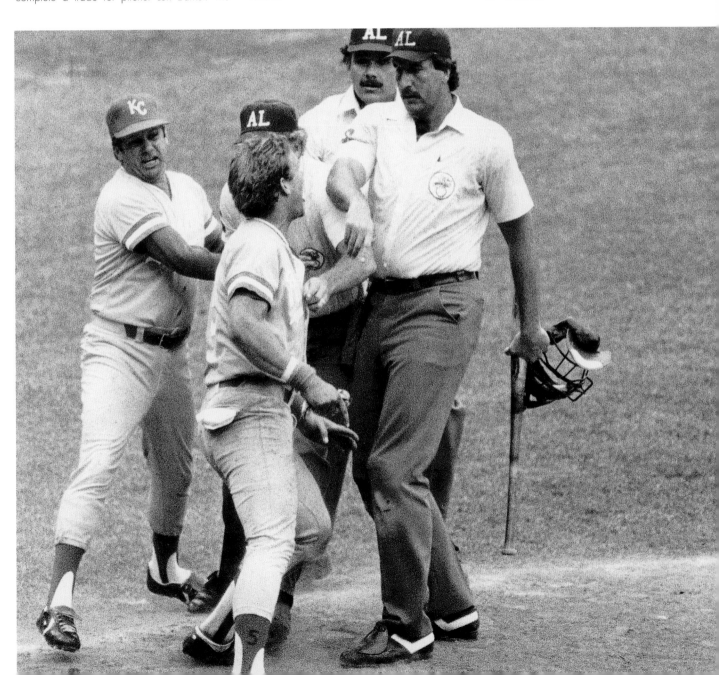

AL CHAMPIONSHIP SERIES

GAME 1

| Chicago White Sox 2 | Baltimore 1 |

GAME 2

| Baltimore 4 | Chicago White Sox 0 |

GAME 3

| Baltimore 11 | Chicago White Sox 1 |

GAME 4

| Baltimore 3 | Chicago White Sox 0 |

MVP: Mike Boddicker, Baltimore

NL CHAMPIONSHIP SERIES

GAME 1

| Philadelphia Phillies 1 | Los Angeles 0 |

GAME 2

| Los Angeles 4 | Philadelphia Phillies 1 |

GAME 3

| Philadelphia Phillies 7 | Los Angeles 2 |

GAME 4

| Philadelphia Phillies 7 | Los Angeles 2 |

MVP: Gary Matthews, Philadelphia Phillies

WORLD SERIES

GAME 1

| Philadelphia Phillies 2 | Baltimore 1 |

GAME 2

| Baltimore 4 | Philadelphia Phillies 1 |

GAME 3

| Baltimore 3 | Philadelphia Phillies 2 |

GAME 4

| Baltimore 5 | Philadelphia Phillies 4 |

GAME 5

| Baltimore 5 | Philadelphia Phillies 0 |

MVP: Rick Dempsey, Baltimore

If experience alone guaranteed success, the Philadelphia Phillies would have swept the World Series. The Phillies had four players over 40, Steve Carlton was 38 and three more players were at least 33.

But long resumes didn't help the Phillies, who lost the World Series to the Baltimore Orioles in five games.

The Phillies had been through an unusual year that saw manager Pat Corrales fired, despite having the team in first place. The feeling was that the Phillies, who were flirting with the .500 mark, should have been better.

Management had invested heavily in its veterans, including a troika who were postseason regulars with the Cincinnati Reds. Pete Rose, Joe Morgan and Tony Perez were all with the Phillies. Rose began the Series on a 1-for-8 slide and was replaced in the lineup by Perez. The move was made by interim manager Paul Owens, the 59-year-old general manager who had returned to the dugout after making the decision to fire Corrales.

The Orioles were led by first-year manager Joe Altobelli, whose previous experience managing in San Francisco hadn't been nearly as successful. Baltimore fought off the Detroit Tigers to win the American League East for the first time since 1979.

Baltimore had a fresh opponent in the playoffs. The Chicago White Sox had blown away the rest of the American League West and taken the division by a whopping 20-game margin. The White

Sox were the only team with a winning record in the division.

The Orioles lost the opening game 2–1, managing just five hits against Sox starter LaMarr Hoyt. From that point, the Orioles pitching staff took over. Baltimore's pitchers held the White Sox to just one run over the remaining 31 innings of the series.

Mike Boddicker pitched a five-hit, 4–0 shutout in the second game. Mike Flanagan and Sammy Stewart combined on an 11–1 blowout in the third game as Eddie Murray broke a 0-for-29 postseason streak with a three-run homer.

The series ended with Baltimore's 3–0 win in the fourth game. The White Sox got ten hits and three walks, but couldn't score. Tito Landrum ended the scoreless tie in the top of the tenth, when he hit a three-run homer off Salome Barojas.

The Phillies matched up against the Los Angeles Dodgers, the team that had beaten them in both the 1977 and 1978 playoffs.

Carlton and Al Holland team up to beat the Dodgers 1–0 in the opening game. The Dodgers' only win came in the second game when Fernando Valenzuela beat 19-game winner John Denny 4–1.

The turning point came in the third game when

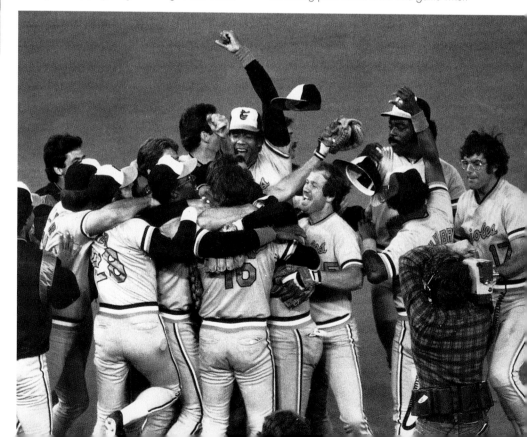

The Orioles celebrate their first championship since 1970

Gary Matthews had three hits and four RBIs in the Phillies' 7–2 win. Matthews hit his second home run of the series and Charles Hudson pitched a complete game.

Matthews was back in the fourth game, blasting a three-run homer in the first inning to help the Phillies to another 7–2 win. Carlton and two relievers shut down the Dodgers and Philadelphia prepared for its second World Series in four years.

The Phillies won Game One, 2–1, with what Baltimore considered an assist from President Ronald Reagan. The game was delayed about five minutes while television conducted a live interview with the President, a former minor league baseball, play-by-play broadcaster.

Immediately after the delay, Scott McGregor served up what proved to be the game-winning home run to Garry Maddox.

The Orioles swept the next four games. They won Game Two, 4–1, behind Mike Boddicker's complete game and John Lowenstein's homer.

Rose was on the bench for Game Three, but it didn't change things for the Phillies. Perez went 1-for-4 in Rose's place and the Orioles won 3–2, scoring twice in the seventh. Owens then made a decision that was even more controversial than benching Rose. He let Carlton bat in the sixth with two runners on base. Carlton struck out to kill the rally, then allowed the two deciding runs in the next inning.

Baltimore won Game Four, 5–4, as Rich Dauer had three hits and drove in three runs. The Orioles ended the Series in Philadelphia in Game Five, winning 5–0 behind McGregor. Murray hit two home runs and Series MVP, Rick Dempsey, also homered.

Baltimore Orioles catcher, Rick Dempsey, is hugged by teammate Scott McGregor after winning the World Series against the Phillies in five games

STEVE CARLTON

TEAMS

St. Louis Cardinals 1965–71; Philadelphia Phillies 1972–86; San Francisco Giants 1986; Chicago White Sox 1986; Cleveland Indians 1987; Minnesota Twins 1987–88

Games	.741
Games started	.709
Complete games	.254
Win–Loss	.329–244
Inning pitched	.5,217.1
Runs	.2,130
ERA	.3.22
Strikeouts	.4,136
Bases on balls	.1,833
Batting average	.0.201

For most of the 1970s Steve Carlton led major league pitchers in everything but post-game comments.

Carlton was the second-winningest lefthander in major league history and the second most prolific strikeout pitcher in the game. Yet he's probably best remembered for the long media boycott that covered some of the best years of his career. Too bad he was silent. There was plenty to discuss.

In 1972, Carlton had one of the greatest years a pitcher had ever enjoyed and he did it on a wretched, last-place Philadelphia Phillies team. Carlton went 27–10 and his victory total represented a full 45 percent of his team's win total, a major league record. With better support, Carlton surely would have won 30 games. In that season he won the pitching Triple Crown, leading in victories, earned run average (1.97) and strikeouts (310).

He had a 15-game winning streak during the season, pitched eight shutouts and completed 30 games. He was the unanimous choice for the National League's Cy Young Award and finished fifth in the Most Valuable Player voting, even though the Phillies were never in contention.

The following year Carlton lost 20 games, which spurred his media blackout. Carlton felt that some journalists had crossed a line by delving into his personal life and vowed that he was done dealing with the press. It was a promise he consistently kept and he didn't relax the policy until his career was nearly over.

Carlton had come up through the St. Louis Cardinals' organization, signing for $5,000, which was $1,000 more than the Pittsburgh Pirates had offered him. He first reached the major leagues in 1965 and pitched on the Cardinals' pennant-winning teams of 1967 and 1968. His career took an important turn during a tour of Japan following the 1968 World Series.

Carlton began to develop a slider, a breaking pitch to augment his fastball. The slider looked like a fastball out of his hand, but broke down just as it reached the plate. It was a deadly pitch to righthanded batters and helped Carlton upgrade his game.

In September 1969, he set a record by striking out 19 New York Mets batters. In 1971, he won 20 games and was promptly traded. Carlton and the Cardinals were $5,000 apart on a new contract—he wanted $60,000—and ownership wouldn't budge. Instead they traded him to Philadelphia for Rick Wise and watched him become the League's dominant pitcher over the next ten years. Carlton often reminded the Cardinals of their mistake—he was 38–14 against St. Louis. Then, he was tough against just about everyone.

Carlton's career got a boost when Tim McCarver went to the Phillies and became his personal catcher. McCarver suggested he reposition his stance on the mound and Carlton was again a consistent winner.

The Phillies won their division for three consecutive years and Carlton won 59 games in that span. He had become something of a mystical character. The silence with the media set him apart, as did his unconventional training routine. Carlton spent two hours a day working out with trainer Gus Hoefling. He incorporated isometrics and martial arts training into his workouts and plunged his arms into buckets of rice, strengthening his hands and arms by twisting and turning them against the resistance of the grain.

At some point Carlton outlined his philosophy of pitching: "I've never paced myself. I've always thrown as hard as I can for as long as I can."

In 1980, he contributed to the Phillies' first World Series championship. He was 24–9 during the season to win his third Cy Young award and he beat the Kansas City Royals twice in the Series.

Eventually, age and declining skills caught up with Carlton. By 1983, John Denny had supplanted him as the Phillies' No. 1 starter. Carlton had just one complete game in 1984. In 1985, he was 1–8 when he went on the disabled list for the first time in his career.

The Phillies tried to convince him to retire in 1986, but he declined and the team released him. Carlton pitched for the San Francisco Giants, Chicago White Sox, Cleveland Indians and Minnesota Twins before retiring in 1988, aged 43.

The Hall of Fame called in 1994 and Carlton opted against silence and made the traditional speech.

Carlton's media boycott only added to his mystique

MOST VALUABLE PLAYER

AL: Willie Hernandez, Detroit

NL: Ryne Sandberg, Chicago Cubs

CY YOUNG AWARD

AL: Willie Hernandez, Detroit

NL: Rick Sutcliffe, Chicago Cubs

ROOKIE OF THE YEAR

AL: Alvin Davis, Seattle

NL: Dwight Gooden, NY Mets

LEADERS

BATTING AVERAGE

AL: Don Mattingly, NY Yankees, .343

NL: Tony Gwynn, San Diego, .351

HOME RUNS

AL: Tony Armas, Boston Red Sox, 43

NL: Mike Schmidt, Philadelphia Phillies; Dale Murphy, Atlanta, 36

RUNS BATTED IN

AL: Tony Armas, Boston Red Sox, 123

NL: Mike Schmidt, Philadelphia Phillies; Gary Carter, Montreal, 106

STOLEN BASES

AL: Rickey Henderson, Oakland, 66

NL: Tim Raines, Montreal, 75

PITCHING VICTORIES

AL: Mike Boddicker, Baltimore, 20

NL: Joaquin Andujar, St. Louis Cardinals, 20

EARNED RUN AVERAGE

AL: Mike Boddicker, Baltimore, 2.79

NL: Alejandro Pena, Los Angeles, 2.48

STRIKEOUTS

AL: Mark Langston, Seattle, 204

NL: Dwight Gooden, NY Mets, 276

SAVES

AL: Dan Quisenberry, Kansas City, 44

NL: Bruce Sutter, St. Louis Cardinals, 45

Like any player, Willie Hernandez undoubtedly had confidence in his ability. Still, it is doubtful he could have realistically imagined the way his season would end. Fortunately for the Detroit Tigers and their manager, Sparky Anderson, it all came together for Hernandez at the same time that it came together for the club.

In one of the strongest starts in major league history, the Tigers finished the month of April with a 16–2 record. By May 24, they were 35–6. From the first day of the season to the last they held first place, clinching the American League East on September 18.

Hernandez's work out of the Detroit bullpen, including a league-leading 80 appearances, a 9–3 record, 32 saves and a 1.92 ERA earned him not only the league's Cy Young Award but Most Valuable Player honors as well. But he was just one element—albeit a major one—in the Tigers' success.

Jack Morris paced the starting rotation with a 19–11 record. Catcher Lance Parrish knocked 33 home runs and shortstop Alan Trammell hit for a .314 average. Kirk Gibson's 27 homers, coupled with a team-leading 29 stolen bases, made him a complete offensive threat.

The Toronto Blue Jays got a respectable performance from pitcher Doyle Alexander, whose 17–6 record gave him the league's best winning percentage at .739. George Bell's 26 home runs powered the team and Dave Collins, with 60 stolen bases and a .304 batting mark, provided a spark on the bases. Collins and teammate Lloyd Moseby also shared the league lead in triples with 15.

The New York Yankees finished third for manager Yogi Berra as Don Mattingly and Dave Winfield finished first and second in the battle for the American League batting crown. In the last game of the season, Mattingly got four hits in five at-bats to finish with a .343 average, while Winfield only managed one hit in four trips, finishing at .340. Don Baylor, the Yankees' designated hitter, belted 27 home runs.

The fourth-place Boston Red Sox could boast

Detroit's Willie Hernandez had a season for the ages

the league's leading home run hitter and RBI man in Jim Rice, with 43 round trippers and 123 runs batted in. Third baseman Wade Boggs finished third in the batting race with .325.

The defending World Champion Baltimore Orioles dropped to fifth place as all of the regulars suffered down years offensively. Pitcher Mike Boddicker, however, was the American League's only 20-game winner.

Andre Thornton's 33 home runs topped the Cleveland Indians, while the Milwaukee Brewers finished in the Eastern Division cellar.

In the Western Division the race was much closer, as Dick Howser's Kansas City Royals finished three games ahead of both California and Minnesota. The Royals did not clinch the title until September 28.

Steve Balboni's 28 home runs and Willie Wilson's 47 stolen bases and .301 batting average led the Kansas City offense. Pitcher Bud Black led the starting corps with a 17–12 mark, but reliever Dan Quisenberry's league-leading 44 saves represented the Royals' biggest individual accomplishment.

The California Angels and Minnesota Twins finished in a tie for second place in the American League West as Reggie Jackson slammed 25 home runs for the Angels, including the 500th of a career that also included stops in Oakland, Baltimore and New York. Mike Witt was the ace of the pitching staff with a 15–11 mark, capped by a perfect game on the last day of the season against the Texas Rangers. It was the first perfect game in the history of the Angels.

The Twins had some good offensive performances. First baseman Kent Hrbek hit .311 batting average and right fielder Tom Brunansky hit 32 home runs for Minnesota. Frank Viola topped the Twins' pitching staff with an 18–12 record.

TIMELINE

Jan. 5: Joe Niekro signed a two-year contract with the Yankees.

March 3: Peter Ueberroth was elected to a five-year term as Commissioner. His reign would begin at the end of the 1984 season.

March 17: The Cubs released pitcher Ferguson Jenkins.

April 7: Jack Morris threw a no-hitter for Detroit against the White Sox, striking out eight and walking six.

April 21: Expos' pitcher David Palmer pitched five perfect innings against St. Louis. The game was stopped because of rain after the fifth inning, making it an official game.

May 20: Rookie pitcher Roger Clemens got his first major league victory as Boston topped Minnesota 5–4.

May 31: Cincinnati pitcher Mario Soto was suspended for five days for shoving umpire Steve Rippley and threatening a vendor who had thrown ice at him.

June 13: The Chicago Cubs traded Mel Hall, Joe Carter and Daryl Banks to the Cleveland Indians for Rick Sutcliffe, George Frazier and Ron Hassey.

June 20: Dave Kingman, released by the Mets before the season, hit his third grand slam of the season for Oakland against the Royals.

June 26: Jason Thompson hit two home runs in each game of a doubleheader for the Pirates against Chicago.

July 4: Phil Niekro, pitching for the Yankees, became the ninth hurler in major league history to reach 3,000 career strikeouts.

July 19: Dodgers' pitcher Orel Hershiser pitched his third consecutive shutout, allowing the Cardinals only two hits.

Sept. 7: Rookie pitcher Dwight Gooden pitched a one-hitter for the Mets, striking out 11 Chicago Cubs.

Sept. 28: The Kansas City Royals clinched the American League Western Division championship.

Sept. 30: Don Mattingly went 4-for-5 to win the American League batting championship, edging out teammate Dave Winfield. Mattingly finished with a .343 mark while Winfield ended up at .340.

Wearing an Angels uniform Reggie Jackson hit his 500th career homer

Dwight Gooden took home Rookie of the Year honors thanks to a 17–9 record

SHORTS When New York Mets' pitcher Dwight Gooden took the mound at the All-Star Game on July 10, he was the youngest player in All-Star history at the age of just 19. His predecessor, Fernando Valenzuela, had fanned Dave Winfield, Reggie Jackson and George Brett in order. Gooden continued the string by striking out Lance Parrish, Chet Lemon and Alvin Davis.

the league. His successor, Jackie Moore, fared no better as the team finished eight games below the .500 mark.

The defending division champion Chicago White Sox got a good showing from Tom Seaver with a 15–11 record, but their 1983 ace and Cy Young Award winner Lamarr Hoyt skidded from a 24–10 mark in 1983 to a 13–18 record in 1984.

The Seattle Mariners had the Rookie of the Year in first baseman Alvin Davis, who hit 27 home runs and had 116 RBIs. Doug Rader's Texas Rangers finished last.

In the National League East it was a race between the Chicago Cubs and New York Mets. The Mets, behind the pitching of Dwight "Doc" Gooden and the power hitting of Darryl Strawberry, seemed to be on their way to supremacy in the division. On July 28, they held a 4½-game lead over the Cubs. But Chicago made two key trades earlier in the season that paid off in a big way. On May 25, they traded first baseman Bill Buckner to the Boston Red Sox for pitcher Dennis Eckersley and Mike Brumley, a minor league prospect.

Buckner was hitting a disappointing .209 with no extra base hits for Chicago and had been in a secondary role to Leon Durham for most of the season. Eckersley posted a 4–4 mark in nine starts for Boston, but would go 10–6 for the Cubs.

The other deal was even more significant as on June 13 Chicago sent outfielders Mel Hall and Joe Carter along with farm prospect Daryl Banks to Cleveland for pitchers Rick Sutcliffe and George Frazier and catcher Ron Hassey. Sutcliffe was 4–5 for the Indians, while Frazier had a 3–2 record in a relief role. He was outstanding for the Cubs, however, posting a 16–1 record for them and earning the Cy Young Award in the National League.

Ryne Sandberg's .314 batting average and league-leading 19 triples led the offensive attack for Chicago, while Ron Cey provided power with 25 home runs.

Sutcliffe's two-hitter against the Pirates on September 24th gave him his 14th straight victory and clinched the National League East for

Dave Kingman, released by the New York Mets in the off-season, signed on with the Oakland Athletics as their designated hitter and hit 35 home runs while driving in 118 runs. Speedy Rickey Henderson led the league with 66 stolen bases, but Oakland skipper Steve Boros became the first managerial casualty in

Chicago. For the first time since 1945 the Cubs went into postseason play.

Gooden won the Rookie of the Year award and turned in a 17–9 record for the Mets, striking out a league-best 276 batters. Strawberry's 26 home runs and Keith Hernandez's .311 batting mark paced the New York offense.

The third-place St. Louis Cardinals had the National League's only 20-game winner in Joaquin Andujar (20–14) and the league's leading reliever as Bruce Sutter posted 45 saves, setting a National League record. They also had a budding star in third baseman Terry Pendleton, who came up from the minor leagues in late summer and posted a .324 batting average.

Mike Schmidt continued to provide most of the Philadelphia Phillies' offensive power with 36 home runs, tying him with Atlanta's Dale Murphy for the league lead, and 106 runs batted in, tying him with Montreal's Gary Carter for the lead in that department. Montreal's Tim Raines continued to shine at the plate and on the bases with 75 steals to lead the league. Raines also hit .309 in his leadoff role for the Expos and was a catalyst.

Chuck Tanner's Pittsburgh Pirates finished in the Eastern Division cellar.

The Western Division battle proved to be no contest as the San Diego Padres went to postseason play for the first time in their history, clinching the title on September 20. Right fielder Tony Gwynn, in his first full year in the major leagues, took the National League batting title with a .351 average. Eric Show was the ace of the San Diego pitching staff with a 15–9 mark.

Dale Murphy's league-tying 36 home runs and 100 RBIs keyed the Atlanta Braves' offense. Pascual Perez at 14–9 was tops on a Braves' pitching staff plagued by injuries and suspensions.

A major area of controversy in the 1984 season was the discovery of cocaine use among several players. The problems began to surface when Atlanta pitcher Pascual Perez was arrested for possession in the Dominican Republic. Although Perez proclaimed his innocence, he spent the start of the season awaiting trial from his jail cell.

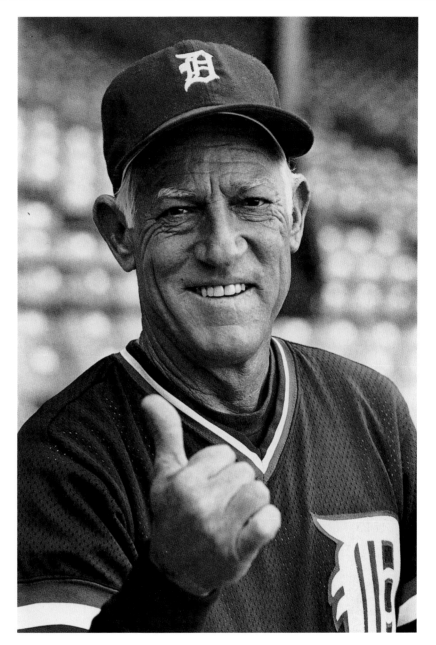

Detroit Tigers' manager Sparky Anderson

SHORTS In a season that was full of milestones, Detroit Tigers manager Sparky Anderson accomplished something that no manager had done before. He became the first to win 100 games in a season for two different major league teams. As manager of the Cincinnati Reds he had done so on three occasions—in 1970, 1975 and 1976, all league championship seasons for Cincinnati.

Pittsburgh relief pitcher Rod Scurry checked himself into a drug rehab program in early April, but returned to the Pirates on May 13.

In July, Commissioner Bowie Kuhn suspended pitcher Vida Blue, a free agent, because of his conviction in late 1983 on charges of cocaine possession. The suspension was for the rest of the season.

The most serious injury of the season occurred when Houston shortstop Dickie Thon was struck in the face by a Mike Torrez fastball in a game against the Mets on April 8. Thon's vision was blurred and he was forced to miss the remainder of the season.

AL CHAMPIONSHIP SERIES

GAME 1

Detroit 8	Kansas City 1

GAME 2

Detroit 5	Kansas City 3

GAME 3

Detroit 1	Kansas City 0

MVP: Kirk Gibson, Detroit

NL CHAMPIONSHIP SERIES

GAME 1

Chicago Cubs 13	San Diego 0

GAME 2

Chicago Cubs 4	San Diego 2

GAME 3

San Diego 7	Chicago Cubs 1

GAME 4

San Diego 7	Chicago Cubs 5

GAME 5

San Diego 6	Chicago Cubs 3

MVP: Steve Garvey, San Diego

WORLD SERIES

GAME 1

Detroit 3	San Diego 2

GAME 2

San Diego 5	Detroit 3

GAME 3

Detroit 5	San Diego 2

GAME 4

Detroit 4	San Diego 2

GAME 5

Detroit 8	San Diego 4

MVP: Alan Trammell, Detroit

No one in the American League could handle the Detroit Tigers, and the National League representative didn't do any better in the World Series.

The Tigers, wire-to-wire winners of the American League East, swept the Kansas City Royals in the playoffs, then blitzed the overmatched Padres in five games to win the Series.

Everything went right for Sparky Anderson, who knew something about managing powerhouse clubs from his days with the Cincinnati Reds in the 1970s. The Tigers had one of those magical years, winning 104 games and taking the usually competitive American League East by 15 games over second-place Toronto.

The Tigers had great balance—they didn't have a single league leader, a 20-game winner or a 100-RBI hitter. Detroit started the season with a 35–5 record and cruised the rest of the way.

Their playoff opponent was involved in the only close race among the four divisions. Kansas City finished three games ahead of the California Angels in the American League West.

Both National League teams won by fairly comfortable margins. The Padres won the West by 12 games over Atlanta. The Chicago Cubs finished 6½ games ahead of the New York Mets and ended a streak of 39 years without a postseason game.

The Cubs were clearly the sentimental pick and their legion of fans loved the first two games of the series. They won the opener 13–0, with five home runs among their 16 hits. All three figures set National League playoff records. Winning pitcher, Rick Sutcliffe, was among those who hit a home run. The Cubs won the second game 4–2, as Steve Trout and Lee Smith held San Diego to five hits.

The Cubs went west needing just one win to go to the Series. They took a 1–0 lead in the third game, but lost 7–1, as Kevin McReynolds hit a three-run homer. Steve Garvey helped the Padres tie the series with a 7–5 win in the fourth game. Garvey had four hits and five RBIs, including a game-winning, two-run homer off Lee Smith in the ninth inning.

Chicago had a 3–2 lead after six innings of the fifth game and hadn't done much against Sutcliffe. Tim Flannery's grounder went through Cubs' first baseman Leon Durham's legs to score the tying run. Tony Gwynn's grounder took a bad

Detroit Tigers manager Sparky Anderson relaxes with his pipe

hop over second baseman Ryne Sandberg's shoulder and Garvey delivered an RBI single as the Padres won 6–3.

There was far less drama in the American League playoffs. Detroit got home runs from Larry Herndon, Alan Trammell and Lance Parrish to win the first game 8–1. John Grubb hit a two-run double in the 11th inning of the second game for a 5–3 win. Milt Wilcox and Willie Hernandez pitched a three-hitter for a 1–0 victory that ended the series.

Detroit won Game One of the World Series 3–2, as Jack Morris made a 3–2 lead hold up for five innings. Herndon's two-run homer in the fifth put the Tigers ahead to stay.

San Diego's only win came with Game Two. Detroit scored three runs in the first inning to knock out Ed Whitson, but the Padres got excellent relief work from Andy Hawkins and Craig Lefferts. Kurt Bevacqua tagged Dan Petry for a three-run homer.

The Padres pitchers provided plenty of help in Game Three, walking 11 batters in the first five innings. Two of the runs were easy: Herndon walked to force in a run and Kirk Gibson was hit by a pitch with the bases full. Marty Castillo hit a two-run homer for the Tigers and Wilcox got the victory.

The Tigers took full control of the Series in Game Four, with a 4–2 win. Trammell hit a pair of two-run homers to account for all of Detroit's scoring. Morris pitched a complete game for his second win of the Series.

Gibson put an exclamation point on Detroit's championship with two home runs in the deciding game. Both reached the upper deck in right field at Tiger Stadium. Gibson had broken a 3–3 tie with aggressive base running in the fifth. He dashed home on a fly ball to short right field that was caught by the second baseman. Parrish also homered for the Tigers in the 8–4 win.

Anderson had become the first man to manage a World Series champion in both leagues. He also earned rings while managing the Reds in 1975 and 1976.

Alan Trammell drove in all of the Tigers' runs as Detroit took control in Game Four

As more reports of substance abuse among some major league players began to surface late in the 1985 season, the patience of baseball fans who had already been subjected to a two-day strike the previous month was put to the supreme test. But followers of the game proved forgiving once again as attendance records were set throughout the nation.

The Angels' Rod Carew joined the 3,000-hit club, but just failed to reach the postseason

Several individuals reached key plateaus during the season. Houston Astros' pitcher Joe Niekro got his 200th career win on July 2. He and brother Phil thus joined Gaylord and Jim Perry as the only brother duos in major league history to post 200 wins each.

Nine days later another Houston pitcher, Nolan Ryan, struck out New York's Danny Heep for his 4,000th career strikeout making him the first pitcher to reach that level.

Detroit's Darrell Evans belted his 300th career home run on July 28. Two milestones were reached on August 4 as Tom Seaver, pitching in the unfamiliar uniform of the Chicago White Sox, gained his 300th victory and Rod Carew got his 3,000th hit for California against his old club, the Minnesota Twins. And on September 11, Pete Rose became the all-time leader in career hits as he singled for his 4,192nd, breaking the record

held by the legendary Ty Cobb for more than 50 years.

The race for the American League Eastern Division title came down to two teams in short order as the Toronto Blue Jays and New York Yankees battled until mid-September for the right to go to the postseason.

George Bell's 28 home runs and clutch pitching from veteran Doyle Alexander, who ended with a 17–10 mark for the Blue Jays, proved to be the key for Toronto. The momentum seemed to be in the Yankees' favor when they began a crucial four game series against the Jays in Yankee Stadium. Taking the first game, New York moved to within 1½ games of Toronto. But the Blue Jays swept the remaining three and the Yankees lost their next five as well.

The turmoil-plagued Yankees still managed to finish two games behind Toronto, thanks to outstanding hitting by Don Mattingly who hit 35 home runs, drove in a league-leading 145 runs and slugged 48 doubles to lead the circuit in that department as well. Those numbers, along with his .324 batting average, made Mattingly the overwhelming choice for Most Valuable Player in the American League. Ron Guidry continued to be one of the premier pitchers in the league with a 22–8 record. Rickey Henderson, acquired from Oakland in the off-season, continued to fuel his reputation as baseball's best leadoff hitter with a .314 batting mark and a league-leading 80 stolen bases.

The Detroit Tigers, last year's division winners, dropped to third. Evans, moved to first base to replace the injured Dave Bergman, hit 40 home runs to lead the league, but his primary replacement in the designated hitter role, Nelson Simmons, produced only 21 extra base hits.

With 105 games remaining in the season, Earl Weaver returned to manage the Baltimore Orioles. But despite solid power hitting from Eddie Murray and Cal Ripken Jr., the Orioles managed only a fourth-place finish.

Boston's Wade Boggs took the batting title with a .368 mark. At one point in the season, Boggs had a 28-game hitting streak.

The American League West was even more of a race as the Kansas City Royals and California Angels battled to the very end of the season. On September 30, California had a one game lead over the Royals as the two teams prepared to face off in a four-game set in Kansas City. The Royals won three of the four games, and went on to clinch the crown against Oakland.

Bret Saberhagen anchored the Royals' pitching staff with a 20–6 record while George Brett's .335 batting average and 30 home runs topped the Kansas City offense, along with 36 home runs by Steve Balboni.

The Angels had two future Hall of Famers in their lineup—Reggie Jackson and Rod Carew. Jackson still had some power as he slugged 27 home runs. Mike Witt topped the California pitching staff with a 15–9 record.

The Chicago White Sox, under manager

Pete Rose passed Ty Cobb as baseball's all-time hit king

Tony LaRussa, were competitive as well, finishing third just six games behind the Royals. Chicago shortstop Ozzie Guillen took Rookie of the Year honors. Catcher Carlton Fisk hit 37 home runs and drove in 107.

Frank Viola's 18–14 record was the best on the Minnesota pitching staff, while Tom Brunansky continued to lead the offense with 27 home runs.

Few experts considered the St. Louis Cardinals a serious threat to win the National League East flag, but several factors contributed to the Redbirds' success in 1985. On February 1, St. Louis traded four players to the San Francisco Giants for hard-hitting first baseman Jack Clark. Clark, despite missing nearly 40 games with a broken rib, still managed to hit 22 home runs. But the real hitting star for the Cardinals was center fielder Willie McGee who hit a league-leading .353 with 26 doubles, 18 triples (also a league-leading mark) and ten home runs. McGee's numbers earned him Most Valuable Player honors.

The Cardinals also had another award winner in Vince Coleman, whose 110 stolen bases

The Cards' Willie McGee proved that practice makes perfect in winning the NL MVP honors

not only led the league by a wide margin, but also gave him Rookie of the Year honors. Finally in one of the greatest turnarounds in pitching history, John Tudor, after going 1–7 in the beginning of the season, won 20 of his final 21 games, including ten shutouts, to top the league.

Dwight Gooden, however, was 24–4 for the second-place New York Mets and took the Cy Young Award. First baseman Keith Hernandez hit .309, but his accomplishments were clouded when he admitted to having used cocaine during a federal trial in Pittsburgh. Hernandez was one of several players granted immunity from prosecution in exchange for testimony before a federal grand jury. Injuries to Darryl Strawberry and Mookie Wilson certainly hurt the Mets' offense, but catcher Gary Carter, obtained from Montreal in the off-season, hit 32 home runs and drove in 100 runs.

SHORTS Often mentioned in the same breath because of their accomplishments on the field, the names of Willie Mays and Mickey Mantle were linked again in 1985, but for different reasons. Commissioner Bowie Kuhn barred both from associating with baseball because they accepted employment as "greeters" for some Atlantic City casinos. New Commissioner Peter Ueberroth rescinded the ban, which proved to be a popular decision.

The Mets took over first place in mid-August and held it until September 11 when the Cardinals, behind John Tudor, shut them out in ten innings. Recent acquisition Cesar Cedeno provided the game winner with a home run for the Cardinals.

Shortstop Hubie Brooks, one of the players traded by the Mets to Montreal for Carter, drove in 100 runs for the Expos and Andre Dawson topped Montreal in home runs with 23.

The defending division champion Chicago

SHORTS In a bizarre story, writer George Plimpton published a piece in the April issue of *Sports Illustrated* on a pitcher for the New York Mets named Sidd Finch. Player quotes hailed Finch's fastball, reportedly clocked at 168 miles per hour. Trouble was—it wasn't true. The story, the pitcher and quotes were all fictional. P.T. Barnum would have been proud.

Cubs started well, gaining first place early in the season before suffering a 13-game losing streak in June. They got good offensive numbers from second baseman Ryne Sandberg with a .305 average and 26 home runs, but a shoulder injury to 1984 Cy Young winner Rick Sutcliffe dropped his record to 8–8. Dennis Eckerlsey had shoulder problems as well, but led the staff with an 11–7 record.

Mike Schmidt's 33 home runs stood out for the Philadelphia Phillies and Joe Orsulak managed a .300 mark for the Pittsburgh Pirates, who finished in the cellar as the proximity of the drug trials cast a shadow on their season. The Galbreath family put the franchise up for sale and the Pirates finished the season wondering if they had played their last game in Pittsburgh.

In the Western Division, the defending champion San Diego Padres got off to a good start but faded in early July, while the Los Angeles Dodgers, led by Orel Hershiser's 19–3 record and Pedro Guerrero's .320 batting average and 33 home runs, moved into the top spot and never left.

Pete Rose's Cincinnati Reds finished second, 5½ games behind the Dodgers thanks in part to a 20–9 performance by Tom Browning and Dave Parker's 34 home runs and league-leading 125 RBIs. Parker also led the league in doubles with 42.

But Parker was also one of the major players in the cocaine scandal and he, like Hernandez, Lonnie Smith, Jeffrey Leonard and Tim Raines accepted immunity from prosecution in exchange for testimony before the federal jury.

The Houston Astros finished third, despite solid hitting from Jose Cruz (.300) and Glenn Davis (20 home runs). Mike Scott's 18–6 record was best on their staff.

Tony Gwynn posted a .317 mark for the Padres, but speedy Alan Wiggins, who had stolen 70 bases in 1984, entered drug rehab after nine games and was traded to Baltimore after he had completed his program. Andy Hawkins topped the San Diego pitching staff with an 18–8 record after starting the season 11–0.

Dale Murphy was the league's home run leader with 37 for the Atlanta Braves. Rick Mahler posted a 17–15 record for the Braves as well.

San Francisco Giants outfielder Jeffrey Leonard distinguished himself on June 27 by becoming the first Giant since Dave Kingman to hit for the cycle.

In the All-Star Game played at the Metrodome in Minnesota, the National League took the win 6–1 over the American League, behind the nearly flawless pitching of the Padres' Lamarr Hoyt who took the game's Most Valuable Player honors.

The Mets' Dwight Gooden went 24-4 in capturing the Cy Young Award

AL CHAMPIONSHIP SERIES

GAME 1	
Toronto 6	Kansas City 1

GAME 2	
Toronto 6	Kansas City 5

GAME 3	
Kansas City 6	Toronto 5

GAME 4	
Toronto 3	Kansas City 1

GAME 5	
Kansas City 2	Toronto 0

GAME 6	
Kansas City 5	Toronto 3

GAME 7	
Kansas City 6	Toronto 2

MVP: George Brett, Kansas City

NL CHAMPIONSHIP SERIES

GAME 1	
Los Angeles 4	St. Louis Cardinals 1

GAME 2	
Los Angeles 8	St. Louis Cardinals 2

GAME 3	
St. Louis Cardinals 4	Los Angeles 2

GAME 4	
St. Louis Cardinals 12	Los Angeles 2

GAME 5	
St. Louis Cardinals 3	Los Angeles 2

GAME 6	
St. Louis Cardinals 7	Los Angeles 5

MVP: Ozzie Smith, St. Louis Cardinals

WORLD SERIES

GAME 1	
St. Louis Cardinals 3	Kansas City 1

GAME 2	
St. Louis Cardinals 4	Kansas City 2

GAME 3	
Kansas City 6	St. Louis Cardinals 1

GAME 4	
St. Louis Cardinals 3	Kansas City 0

GAME 5	
Kansas City 6	St. Louis Cardinals 1

GAME 6	
Kansas City 2	St. Louis Cardinals 1

GAME 7	
Kansas City 11	St. Louis Cardinals 0

MVP: Bret Saberhagen, Kansas City

The St. Louis Cardinals had lost one of their best players to a freak accident with a tarp and lost a pivotal World Series game on a horrible call by an umpire.

After a dramatic victory over the Los Angeles Dodgers in the National League playoffs, the World Series turned into a huge disappointment for the Cardinals.

They lost to intrastate rival Kansas City as the Royals claimed their first World Series trophy in their sixth trip to the postseason.

Kansas City overcame 3–1 deficits in both the playoffs and Series and won by holding the Cardinals to a composite .185 batting average.

Dick Howser's Royals won their division by the slimmest of margins—they finished one game ahead of the California Angels. Baseball expand-ed its playoffs to a best-of-seven series in 1985 and the Royals needed the full term to eliminate the Toronto Blue Jays.

Toronto had prevailed over the New York Yankees to win its first American League East title. Dave Stieb pitched the Blue Jays to a 6–1 win in the first game. The Royals dropped the second game 6–5 in ten innings, which extended their postseason losing streak to 11 games. Kansas City couldn't hold a 3–0 lead. The Royals scored a run in the top of the tenth when Al Oliver hit a tie-breaking single off Dan Quisenberry.

George Brett got the Royals back in the series with a 6–5 win in the third game that saw him go 4-for-4 with two home runs. The Blue Jays rallied for three runs in the top of the ninth in the fourth game. Oliver had another game-winning hit.

Danny Jackson won the fifth game 2–0 to buy the Royals the trip back to Toronto. Kansas City took the sixth game 5–3 as Brett broke a 2–2 tie

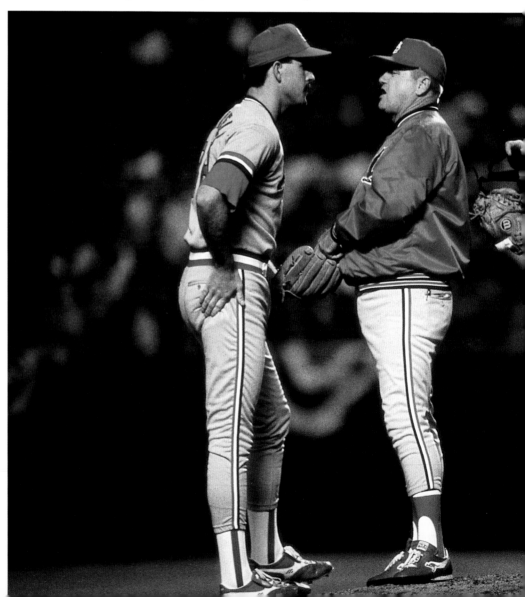

Cardinals manager Whitey Herzog watched it all fall apart as the Royals won in seven games

in the fifth with his third home run of the series.

Royals starter Bret Saberhagen lasted just three innings in the deciding game when he was struck in the hand by a line drive. Charlie Leibrandt worked 5⅓ innings of relief and Jim Sundberg was the offensive star with four RBIs.

The Cardinals, best known for an attack based on speed, relied on home runs to put away the Dodgers. The Dodgers took the first two games, winning 4–1 behind Fernando Valenzuela, then roughing up Cardinals ace, Joaquin Andujar, for an 8–2 win.

St. Louis came home and won the third game 4–2. Tito Landrum went 4-for-5 with three RBIs to key a 12–2 blowout in the fourth game.

The series swung in the Cardinals' favor with a 3–2 win in the fifth game. Dodgers' closer Tom Niedenfuer was pitching in the ninth inning of the 2–2 game when light-hitting Ozzie Smith lined a home run down the right field line.

Bret Saberhagen celebrates the Royals' World Series victory and his MVP award

In the sixth game, Niedenfuer was trying to preserve a 5–4 lead in the ninth. With two runners on base, Dodgers' manager Tom Lasorda chose to pitch to dangerous Jack Clark rather than Andy Van Slyke, who was just 1-for-11 in the series. Clark blasted a home run and Ken Dayley breezed through the ninth to send the Cardinals to the World Series.

The Cardinals had already lost a big part of their attack when base-stealing leader Vince Coleman was struck by an automatic tarp.

St. Louis showed no sign of missing Coleman, winning the first two games of the Series in Kansas City. John Tudor and Todd Worrell combined on a 3–1 win in the opener and Terry Pendleton had the game-winning RBI in Game Two's 4–2 victory. No team had ever lost the first two games at home and won the Series.

Saberhagen won Game Three, 6–1, but Tudor was excellent in a 3–0 win in Game Four. Game Five was a 6–1 Royals win behind Jackson. Game Six made Denkinger a household name. He was umpiring at first base when he blatantly missed a call on a ball hit by Jorge Orta. The Cardinals compounded the mistake with a passed ball and a foul pop that wasn't caught by Clark and lost 2–1.

The Royals took Game Seven, 11–1, behind Saberhagen. It was a mess of a game that saw both Andujar and manager Whitey Herzog ejected for arguing on pitches, a holdover from the previous game's beef with Denkinger.

TOM SEAVER

TEAMS
New York Mets 1967–77, 1983; Cincinnati
Reds 1977–82; Chicago White Sox 1984–86;
Boston Red Sox 1986

Games	.656
Games started	.647
Complete games	.231
Win–Loss	.311–205
Inning pitched	.4,782.2
Runs	.1,674
ERA	.2.86
Strikeouts	.3,640
Bases on balls	.1,390
Batting average	.0.154

Seaver's talents helped the Mets
evolve into World Champions

It's always been difficult to find first-rate major league pitchers, yet the New York Mets got theirs in a lottery.

The Mets were the winners of a three-way drawing for the services of Tom Seaver, who anchored their staff for ten years and helped take them to the World Series twice.

The unusual circumstances came about when the Atlanta Braves signed Seaver, then at the University of Southern California, to a $40,000 bonus contract in 1966. Baseball commissioner, William Eckert, determined that the Braves' signing had been in violation of established rules.

Eckert ruled that his office would have a drawing for Seaver's services. Any team that was willing to match the Braves' $40,000 bonus figure was welcome to enter. The Cleveland Indians, Philadelphia Phillies and Mets all expressed their interest. Their names were literally put in a hat and the Mets were the winners.

Seaver was in the major leagues by 1967 to start a career that would find him on the All-Star team 11 times. He had five 20-win seasons, won three Cy Young awards and struck out at least 200 batters in a season ten times, including nine years in a row.

One of his greatest accomplishments was mostly intangible—he changed the perception of the Mets. They had come into the National League in 1962 as a comedy show, a collection of cast-offs that provided one-liners for septuagenarian manager, Casey Stengel. Stengel faded away, but the Mets remained losers.

The addition of Seaver helped serve notice that the Mets were about to change. He went 16–13 with a 2.76 earned run average and won the Rookie of the Year award, the first significant league-wide honor for any Mets player.

By 1969, Seaver was the No. 1 starter on a team that would shock the baseball world by winning the World Series. On July 9 of that season, Seaver came within two outs of a perfect game against the Chicago Cubs. He lost it when an obscure player, Jim Qualls, singled.

Seaver still won the game and 24 others as he helped the Mets to pull away from the Cubs and win the National League East.

The Mets didn't win over the next several seasons, but Seaver was still a consistent force. On April 22, 1970, he struck out 19 San Diego Padres batters and finished the game with ten consecutive strikeouts.

Seaver may have had his finest season in 1971, leading the National League with a 1.76 earned run average and 289 strikeouts. His record was only 20–10 because of the Mets' frequently poor offensive support.

The Mets were back to the World Series in 1973 with Seaver's 19–10 season and a 2.08 ERA. In 1974, his record was 11–11 and his ERA was 3.20, the first time it had been over 3.00. Seaver had his last big season with the Mets in 1975, going 22–9 en route to another Cy Young Award.

By 1976, the relationship between Seaver and the Mets began to unravel. He was unhappy with the team's direction and commitment to winning and wound up at odds with M. Donald Grant, the Mets' previously anonymous chairman of the board. The nasty feud expanded to include New York columnist Dick Young and by 1977, Seaver was demanding a trade.

On June 15, 1977, the Mets dealt him to the Cincinnati Reds for a package of four players, headed by outfielder Steve Henderson and pitcher Pat Zachry. Seaver went on to have five winning seasons with the Reds while the Mets sank.

Seaver had a disappointing 5–13 season in 1982, which prompted a trade back to the Mets, who were under new ownership. His stay lasted just a year in which he went 9–14. The Mets left him unprotected in the compensation draft and the Chicago White Sox chose him. He stayed there three seasons, long enough to become the game's 17th 300-game winner on August 4, 1985. The White Sox traded Seaver to Boston in 1986 and he wound up his career with the Red Sox. The Mets invited him back for a third stay but Seaver scuttled the comeback after determining he couldn't meet the standard he'd set for himself.

He was elected to the Hall of Fame with 98.84 per cent of the vote, the closest the Hall has come to a unanimous choice.

MOST VALUABLE PLAYER
AL: Roger Clemens, Boston Red Sox
NL: Mike Schmidt, Philadelphia Phillies

CY YOUNG AWARD
AL: Roger Clemens, Boston Red Sox
NL: Mike Scott, Houston

ROOKIE OF THE YEAR
AL: Jose Canseco, Oakland
NL: Todd Worrell, St. Louis Cardinals

LEADERS

BATTING AVERAGE
AL: Wade Boggs, Boston Red Sox, .357
NL: Tim Raines, Montreal, .334

HOME RUNS
AL: Jesse Barfield, Toronto, 40
NL: Mike Schmidt, Philadelphia, 37

RUNS BATTED IN
AL: Joe Carter, Cleveland, 121
NL: Mike Schmidt, Philadelphia Phillies, 119

STOLEN BASES
AL: Rickey Henderson, NY Yankees, 87
NL: Vince Coleman, St. Louis Cardinals, 107

PITCHING VICTORIES
AL: Roger Clemens, Boston Red Sox, 24
NL: Fernando Valenzuela, Los Angeles, 21

EARNED RUN AVERAGE
AL: Roger Clemens, Boston Red Sox, 2.48
NL: Mike Scott, Houston, 2.22

STRIKEOUTS
AL: Mark Langston, Seattle, 245
NL: Mike Scott, Houston, 306

SAVES
AL: Dave Righetti, NY Yankees, 46
NL: Todd Worrell, St. Louis Cardinals, 36

Baseball's 1986 regular season had plenty of dramatic individual performances, which helped make up for a lack of compelling pennant races. There were four new division winners in 1986 and each earned its postseason berth with a minimum of stress. The New York Mets ran away with the National League East, posting a major league-best record of 108–54. The Mets finished 21½ games ahead of runner-up Philadelphia.

In the West, the Houston Astros pulled ahead of the San Francisco Giants on July 21 and stayed there all season under rookie manager Hal Lanier. The Astros had the most stylish clinching—righthander Mike Scott threw a no-hitter on September 25 to beat the Giants and wrap up the division title. Houston was 96–66 and had a ten-game lead over Cincinnati at season's end.

In the American League the races were slightly closer. Boosted by Roger Clemens' 14–0 start, the Boston Red Sox jumped out to an early lead in the East Division. Boston took over first place on May 15 and had a seven-game lead at the All-Star break.

The Western Division champion California Angels outlasted the Texas Rangers down the stretch. Despite the blemish of the previous season's drug scandal, baseball set an attendance record by drawing 47,506,203 fans. One of the first orders of 1986 business for commissioner Peter Ueberroth was to hand out penalties for those who had admitted to past drug use in a federal trial that took place in Pittsburgh during the 1985 season.

The after-effects of that scandal didn't linger, largely because there were so many interesting storylines being played out on the field. The hard-throwing Clemens was dominant, even though he'd had surgery on his pitching arm just eight months prior to the season. On April 29, he struck out 20 Seattle Mariners in a win at Fenway Park to establish a major league record. It was another milestone in Clemens' phenomenal start, which would get him a 24–4 record and earn him both his league's Most Valuable Player and Cy Young Awards.

A pitcher of a more dubious pedigree had a

A change of Sox for Tom Seaver—from White to Red

special achievement on September 19. Joe Cowley of the Chicago White Sox threw a sloppy no-hitter against the Angels in California, a game that saw him issue seven walks in nine innings. Cowley made it difficult on himself by walking the first three batters he faced in the sixth inning, but he survived the crisis and completed the game.

Don Sutton won his 300th game while pitching for the Angels on June 18. Sutton pitched a three-hitter to beat the Rangers in a home game. With the win Sutton, who broke into the majors in 1966, became the fourth active member of the 300-win club. Sutton's career was a testament to endurance and consistency—he had been a 20-game winner just once in his 21 major league seasons.

Pitchers who, like Sutton, were bound for the Hall of Fame, were having difficulty holding jobs in their twilight years. Steve Carlton, the ace of the Philadelphia staff for more than a decade, was released by the Phillies on June 24 after the organization failed to persuade him to retire. Carlton signed with the San Francisco Giants, but lost three of four decisions and was released by them on August 7. Carlton finished the season with the Chicago White Sox and managed to go 4–3 even though his devastating slider was a shadow of the pitch that made him one of baseball's most feared pitchers.

Phil Niekro, unwanted by Atlanta after nearly 14 years, found a spot on the New York Yankees' staff, joining his brother and fellow knuckleball pitcher Joe. That storybook tale was scuttled at the end of spring training when the Yankees decided to cut Phil at the age of 47. Phil Niekro was then signed by the Cleveland Indians, for whom he was 11–11 and the second biggest winner on the staff.

Tom Seaver decided he wanted to leave the Chicago White Sox in the interest of pitching for a club closer to his Connecticut home. Seaver changed Sox and went to Boston in a June 29 trade that sent outfielder Steve Lyons to Chicago. Seaver had many of the injuries that often plague 41-year-old athletes and finished

Twenty-four wins helped Boston's Roger Clemens to the Cy Young Award and his teammates to the division title

with a 7–13 record.

There were three 20-game winners in addition to Clemens. Two of them came from Mexico—Fernando Valenzuela of the Los Angeles Dodgers and Teddy Higuera of the Milwaukee Brewers—and that led many teams to dispatch scouts to that country to search for pitching talent. Mike Krukow of the Giants also won 20, reaching that level on the season's final day.

In the bullpen, Dave Righetti saved 46 games for the New York Yankees, topping the major league record that had been shared by Dan Quisenberry and Bruce Sutter. Toronto's Jesse Barfield led the American League with 40 home runs and Joe Carter of Cleveland was the league's RBI champion with 121. In the National League, Philadelphia's Mike Schmidt led the league with 37 home runs and 119 RBIs.

Boston's Wade Boggs won his third American League batting title in four seasons, posting a .357 average and surviving a bizarre injury—Boggs missed time with a

TIMELINE

Jan. 2: Bill Veeck, fan-oriented franchise owner with three clubs, died of a cardiac arrest at 71.

April 7: President Ronald Reagan officially opened the season by throwing the first pitch in Baltimore.

April 29: Boston's Roger Clemens struck out 20 batters in a 3–1 win over Seattle.

May 27: Fog ends a game between the Red Sox and Indians in Cleveland after six innings.

June 18: California's Don Sutton pitched a three-hitter to beat Texas 5–1 and win his 300th career game.

June 24: Steve Carlton was released by Philadelphia.

June 29: Tom Seaver was traded to Boston by the Chicago White Sox.

July 6: Atlanta's Bob Horner hit four home runs against Montreal, becoming the first player in 25 years to accomplish that feat in a nine-inning game.

Sept. 4: Hall of Fame outfielder Hank Greenberg died of cancer at 75.

Sept. 19: Despite walking seven, Joe Cowley of the Chicago White Sox pitches a no-hitter against the California Angels.

Sept. 25: Houston's Mike Scott pitches a no-hitter against San Francisco to clinch the National League West title for the Astros.

Oct. 12: Dave Henderson of Boston homered off California reliever Donnie Moore to avoid elimination in Game Five of the American League Championship Series.

Oct. 15: New York Mets won a classic 15-inning Game Six in the National League championship series to oust Houston and advance to the World Series.

Oct. 15: Boston Red Sox completed a comeback from a 3–1 deficit in games to beat the California Angels and move to the World Series.

Oct. 25: A routine ground ball got through the legs of Boston first baseman Bill Buckner's legs, allowing the Mets to force a seventh game in the World Series.

Oct. 27: After a one-day delay because of weather, the Mets came back from a 3–0 deficit to win Game Seven of the World Series.

Steve Carlton was released by the Phillies in June after more than a decade's service

cracked rib sustained when he was removing his cowboy boots.

Atlanta's Bob Horner became the first player since Willie Mays in 1961 to hit four home runs in a nine-inning game. Horner hit four against the Montreal Expos on July 6, becoming the 11th player in major league history to accomplish that feat. Befitting the Braves' miserable season, they lost the game 11–8 despite Horner's power show.

Baseball scored a coup when Bo Jackson spurned the National Football League and signed with the Kansas City Royals in midsummer. Jackson won the Heisman Trophy, symbolic of college football's best player, but couldn't come to terms with the Tampa Bay Buccaneers. He was assigned to a Kansas City farm team in June and made his major league debut in September.

Three teams changed ownership—

SHORTS Baseball fans lost their strongest advocate when Bill Veeck died on January 2 at 71. Veeck owned three major league franchises— the St. Louis Browns, Cleveland Indians and Chicago White Sox— during a lifelong association with baseball. He made customer service a way of life and often sunned himself in the bleachers on warm days to stay in touch with the fans.

Cleveland, Philadelphia and the Mets. National League president Charles Feeney retired and was replaced by A. Bartlett Giamatti, the former president of Yale.

The front offices were uncommonly busy with a steady stream of managerial changes. The San Diego Padres found Dick Williams' hard-driving style too tough and replaced him with nice-guy Steve Boros. After a disappointing season, the Padres deemed Boros too soft and replaced him with Larry Bowa, who was even more intense and demanding than Williams had been.

Williams wasn't out of work long. The Seattle Mariners hired him in May to replace Chuck Cottier. The Mariners were Williams' sixth team, which allowed him to tie Jimmy Dykes' major league record for most clubs managed.

Both Chicago teams made changes, dropping managers who had led their teams to the postseason in previous years. The Cubs fired Jim Frey and hired Gene Michael to replace him. The White Sox dismissed Tony La Russa and brought in Jim Fregosi.

La Russa was hired in Oakland after Jackie Moore was fired. Two veteran managers chose to retire—Earl Weaver stepped down in Baltimore and his former pitching coach, George Bamberger, left the Milwaukee Brewers. Weaver's replacement was long-time organizational fixture Cal Ripken Sr., while Tom Trebelhorn took over the Brewers. In Minnesota, Tom Kelly took over for Ray Miller.

One change was made of tragic necessity. Dick Howser was forced to leave the Kansas City Royals in the season after he led them to a World Series championship. Howser, 50, was diagnosed with a brain tumor and required surgery after he took a leave of absence on July 18. Coach Mike Ferraro, himself a cancer survivor, became the interim manager.

In postseason awards, Clemens narrowly edged the Yankees' Don Mattingly for the MVP, but he won the Cy Young handily over Higuera. John McNamara of Boston was a close winner over Texas' Bobby Valentine for manager of the year and Oakland slugger Jose Canseco was chosen as the top rookie.

In the National League, Schmidt was the MVP and Scott edged Valenzuela for the Cy Young Award. Houston's Lanier was the top manager and reliever Todd Worrell of the St. Louis Cardinals was the Rookie of the Year.

Billy Williams and Jim "Catfish" Hunter were voted into the Hall of Fame. Williams starred with the Cubs before finishing with Oakland while Hunter won World Series rings with Oakland and the Yankees. Thanks to a contract irregularity, Hunter also became baseball's first

high-profile free agent in 1975, one year before players won the right to shop their services.

The year opened on a sad note with the death of Bill Veeck on January 2. Veeck was the innovative owner of the St. Louis Browns, Cleveland Indians and Chicago White Sox who had a love for unpredictable stunts and ideas that made coming to the ballpark fun. His best-known escapade came in 1951 when he sent midget Eddie Gaedel up to pinch hit for the Browns.

Hall of Famers Hank Greenberg, Red Ruffing and Ted Lyons also died in 1986.

Houston's Mike Scott threw a no-hitter against the Giants on September 25 to wrap up the division title

The New York Mets and Boston Red Sox were not enjoying a classic World Series through five games. But what happened in the last two games more than made up for that.

When it was over Ray Knight was a hero, Bill Buckner was a goat and Red Sox fans were convinced more than ever that their favorite team was cursed.

The Red Sox were on the verge of losing the playoffs in five games to the California Angels. They came back to win that game and the series.

Despite having the best record in baseball, the Mets struggled in their playoff series against the Houston Astros.

It looked like Angels' manager, Gene Mauch, had finally buried the ghost of the late-season collapse of his 1964 Philadelphia Phillies. California won the first game 8–1, tagging Roger Clemens for all the runs. The Red Sox won the second game 9–2 behind Bruce Hurst.

Dick Schofield and Gary Pettis homered to give California a 5–3 win in the third game. California fell behind 3–0 in the fourth game, but won 4–3 in 11 innings.

In the fifth game, the Angels were a strike away from ending the series. Dave Henderson hit Donnie Moore's 1–2 pitch for a home run that put the Red Sox ahead 6–5. Even then the Angels tied the game to force extra innings.

Henderson won another matchup with Moore, delivering a sacrifice fly in the 11th that gave Boston a 7–6 victory. The Angels were never the same, losing the next two games 10–4 and 8–1 and giving Mauch another albatross.

Mike Scott outdueled Dwight Gooden to give Houston a 1–0 win in the first game. Bob Ojeda beat Nolan Ryan in the second game, 5–1. Lenny Dykstra hit a two–run homer in the bottom of the ninth to give the Mets the third game, 6–5. Scott tied the series with a 3–1 win in the fourth game. A tense duel between Gooden and Ryan was 1–1 and in the hands of the bullpens in the 12th when New York's Gary Carter broke a 1-for-21 slump with a game-winning single.

The sixth game was agony for the managers and great theater for the fans. The Astros scored three runs in the first and the Mets matched that in the ninth. New York got a run in the 14th, but Houston's Billy Hatcher homered to tie the game again.

The Mets used three hits, a walk and two wild pitches to score three times in the top of the 16th. Houston got two runs in the bottom of the

Bob Ojeda cut Boston's lead with a crucial win in Game Three

inning and had the tying and winning runs on base when Jesse Orosco ended the series by striking out Kevin Bass.

The Mets had two days to regroup before they opened the Series at home with a 1–0 loss. Hurst and Calvin Schiraldi combined on a four-hitter. Boston won Game Two, 9–3, despite a shaky start by Clemens. Ojeda got the Mets back in the Series with a 7–1 win in Game Three. Ron Darling, the hard-luck loser in the opener, won Game Four, 6–2.

Hurst beat Gooden 4–2 in Game Five, which set up the memorable Game Six. The Red Sox had taken a 5–3 lead in the tenth against Rick Aguilera and Schiraldi was one out away from closing out the Series for Boston.

Carter and pinch hitter Kevin Mitchell hit sin-

gles. Knight blooped a single that scored Carter and moved Mitchell to third. Bob Stanley came in to face Mookie Wilson and Stanley's wild pitch tied the game and advanced Knight to second.

Wilson's roller to first got through Buckner's legs and let Knight score the winning run. The Red Sox got extra time to forget about the game—Game Seven was delayed a day by rain.

Boston took a 3–0 lead against Darling in the second, but the Mets scored three in the sixth. Knight broke the tie with a home run off Schiraldi in the seventh and the Mets added two more for a 6–3 lead. Boston scored twice in the eighth before Orosco closed out the inning. New York got two more in the bottom of the eighth and Orosco retired the side to give the Mets their second title.

The Mets' Gary Carter and Ray Knight embrace after victory over Boston in the World Series

465

MIKE SCHMIDT

TEAMS

Teams: Philadelphia Phillies 1972–89

Games:	2,404
At-Bats:	8,352
Runs:	1,506
RBI:	1,595
Home runs:	548
Hits:	2,234
Doubles:	408
Triples:	59
Stolen Bases:	174
Average:	267
Slugging percentage:	527

Mike Schmidt regularly led the National League in home runs, RBIs and self-doubt.

Schmidt was a Hall of Famer with the Philadelphia Phillies who never quite believed he was as good as everyone else thought he was. When his career ended in its 17th season, Schmidt admitted that he didn't enjoy it as much as he should have because he was often consumed by the pressure to produce.

Maybe that's part of what made him so good. Schmidt combined power, run production and defense to become the premier third baseman of his generation.

The Phillies suspected he had that kind of ability when they made him their second pick in the 1971 draft. Schmidt had played at Ohio University and the only drawback was chronically bad knees. His knees had been troublesome enough to end his collegiate basketball career and would be a concern throughout his baseball career.

Schmidt was on the fast track to the majors. The Phillies of the early 1970s were bad and needed help as quickly as possible. When Schmidt came to Philadelphia, though, it was difficult to see how he was going to improve things.

His rookie season of 1973 was a disaster. He shared third base with veteran Cesar Tovar, but spot duty didn't help. Schmidt batted a woeful .196 and struck out 136 times in 367 at-bats. He spent that winter playing in Puerto Rico and turned around his career. Schmidt discovered a new swing and was a completely different player in his second season with the Phillies.

In 1974, Schmidt hit 36 home runs to lead the National League. It was the first of three consecutive home run titles for him. He also had the first of his nine seasons with at least 100 RBIs and led the league in slugging percentage, which he would do five times in his career.

Schmidt also played superbly at third base. His quick reactions and strong arm made him a natural for the position and he would go on to win ten Gold Glove awards, second only to Brooks Robinson among third basemen.

Schmidt didn't have the bulky build of some power hitters. He was tall and lean and generated power from his wrists and forearms. His credentials as a power hitter grew with his performance against the Chicago Cubs at Wrigley Field on April 17, 1976. He hit home runs in four consecutive at-bats and helped the Phillies overcome a 13–2 deficit to beat the Cubs 18–16. In the game, Schmidt also drove in eight runs and had 17 total bases, one short of a record. His last home run proved to be the game-winning hit.

As Schmidt got better, so did the Phillies. They started a run of three consecutive National League East titles in 1976. The Phillies didn't win any of the playoff series and Schmidt took a good deal of the heat for those failures.

His game continued to advance, though. In 1978, Schmidt revamped his approach to hitting. He concentrated on hitting the ball to all fields rather than being a predictable dead pull hitter. The change didn't cost him any power because he had the strength to drive the ball in any direction.

In 1979, the Phillies signed Pete Rose as a free agent and that took some of the leadership burden from the softly-spoken Schmidt. Rose thrived in the spotlight and Schmidt was happy to let him have it. Schmidt hit 45 home runs in 1979, even though pitchers did their best to avoid him by walking him 120 times.

His vindication for postseason failures came in 1980 when the Phillies won their first World Series. Schmidt was the regular season Most Valuable Player and took the same honor in the Series after he batted .381 with six runs and seven RBIs.

Schmidt produced consistently for seven more seasons. He moved to first base in 1985 to clear a spot for rookie Rick Schu, but that experiment ended after a season. Schmidt sustained a torn rotator cuff in 1988 and retired abruptly in May of the following season. Teammates and friends urged him to stay, but Schmidt called it quits at the age of 39 with a tearful press conference.

In 1995, he became the 26th player elected to the Hall of Fame on the first ballot.

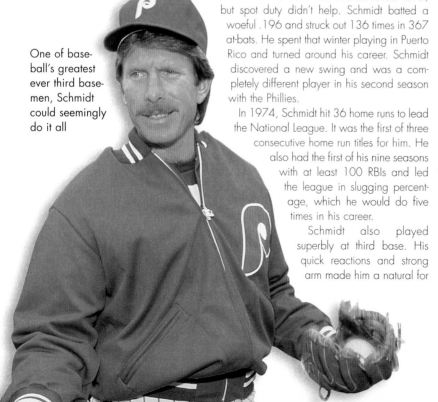

One of baseball's greatest ever third basemen, Schmidt could seemingly do it all

MOST VALUABLE PLAYER
AL: George Bell, Toronto
NL: Andre Dawson, Chicago Cubs

CY YOUNG AWARD
AL: Roger Clemens, Boston Red Sox
NL: Steve Bedrosian, Philadelphia Phillies

ROOKIE OF THE YEAR
AL: Mark McGwire, Oakland
NL: Benito Santiago, San Diego

LEADERS

BATTING AVERAGE
AL: Wade Boggs, Boston Red Sox, .363
NL: Tony Gwynn, San Diego, .370

HOME RUNS
AL: Mark McGwire, Oakland, 49
NL: Andre Dawson, Chicago Cubs, 49

RUNS BATTED IN
AL: George Bell, Toronto, 134
NL: Andre Dawson, Chicago Cubs, 137

STOLEN BASES
AL: Harold Reynolds, Seattle, 60
NL: Vince Coleman, St. Louis Cardinals, 109

PITCHING VICTORIES
AL: Dave Stewart, Oakland; Roger Clemens, Boston Red Sox, 20
NL: Rick Sutcliffe, Chicago Cubs, 18

EARNED RUN AVERAGE
AL: Jimmy Key, Toronto, 2.76
NL: Nolan Ryan, Houston, 2.76

STRIKEOUTS
AL: Mark Langston, Seattle, 262
NL: Nolan Ryan, Houston, 270

SAVES
AL: Tom Henke, Toronto, 34
NL: Steve Bedrosian, Philadelphia Phillies, 40

It seemed as though the 1987 baseball menu had something for every taste.

For those who liked home runs, Oakland A's rookie Mark McGwire and a slugger steeped in the Yankee tradition named Don Mattingly provided plenty of thrills.

If the preference was for pure hitting, the Milwaukee Brewers' Paul Molitor more than filled the bill.

Blazing fastballs your idea of excitement? Then Boston's Roger Clemens was your man.

The race for the American League Eastern Division title was exciting from beginning to end as the Detroit Tigers and Toronto Blue Jays battled into the last series of the season. Trailing by one game as they prepared to face Toronto in a three-game set to end the season, Detroit swept the series and captured the division championship.

Jack Morris anchored the Detroit pitching staff, posting an 18–11 record. Darrell Evans' 34 home runs and Alan Trammell's 105 runs batted in and .343 batting average topped the Tigers' offense.

Another key factor in Detroit's success was an August trade that brought Doyle Alexander to the team in exchange for John Smoltz, then a minor league pitching prospect. Alexander posted a perfect 9–0 record after joining his new club.

The Blue Jays, meanwhile, continued to get big power numbers from George Bell, who hit 47 home runs and drove in a league-leading 134 runs. Jimmy Key led the league with a 2.76 earned run average and finished with a 17–8 mark. But an elbow injury to shortstop Tony Fernandez in the first game of their crucial season-ending series against Detroit certainly didn't help their chances for a postseason berth.

The Milwaukee Brewers began their season with an 11-game winning streak, but their biggest story proved to be designated hitter Molitor's 39-game hitting stretch. Molitor's .353 batting average and 45 stolen bases showed he was a complete player.

New York Yankee first baseman Mattingly not only homered in eight consecutive games during one stretch, but belted six grand slam home runs for the season, setting a new record. His 115 runs batted in led the team, but the Yankees' home run leader was third baseman Mike Pagliarulo with 32.

Injuries to Jim Rice and Rich Gedman hurt the defending league champion Boston Red Sox, but Wade Boggs' .363 average led the American League. Clemens' 20–9 record was also the best in the League and led him to his second straight Cy Young Award.

Oakland A's Mark McGwire hit a rookie-record 49 home runs

The Twins' Gary Gaetti drove in 109 runs as Minnesota won the American League West title

The American League West race was also tight, with the Minnesota Twins emerging from the pack in late September, thanks in part to Kent Hrbek's 34 home runs, Tom Brunansky's 32 homers and Gary Gaetti's 109 RBIs and 31 home runs. Frank Viola's 17–10 record led the Minnesota pitching staff.

The Kansas City Royals, emotionally shaken by the pre-season resignation of manager Dick Howser due to illness and his subsequent death later in the season, still managed a second-place finish in the division. Danny Tartabull's 34 home runs, 101 runs batted in and .309 batting average made him the undisputed hitting star of the club, while Bret Saberhagen's 18–10 mark led the Kansas City pitching staff.

Probably the biggest individual story of the season, however, centered around McGwire, Oakland's rookie first baseman. McGwire, up with the team briefly as a third baseman in the previous season, was the talk of the media—not only because of the number of home runs he hit,

but the distance of some of the shots. At several points during the season, McGwire was on pace to topple the single-season record held by Roger Maris. When it was all over, the man who would be known as "Big Mac" not only won the American League home run crown, but set a new rookie record in the process with 49.

The Seattle Mariners had the league's best base-stealer in Howard Reynolds with 60, as well as the No. 1 strikeout pitcher. Mark Langston had 262 strikeouts and a 19–13 record.

Floyd Bannister's 16–11 record was tops for the Chicago White Sox. The makeup of the defending Western Division champion California Angels was very different in 1987. Reggie Jackson had gone back to Oakland to end his career where it had started. Dick Schofield and Bob Boone both suffered injuries that kept them out of action for part of the season. Wally Joyner's 34 home runs and 117 runs batted in led the Angels' offense.

The rivalry between the St. Louis Cardinals and New York Mets that first developed during their division race in 1985, resumed in 1987 as Whitey Herzog's Redbirds fought for their third Eastern Division title of the decade.

Injuries plagued the club. Especially costly were the absences of pitcher John Tudor and first baseman Jack Clark, who still managed to hit a club-leading 35 home runs. Vince Coleman's

SHORTS Andre Dawson's main desire at the beginning of 1987 was to play on real grass, which was better for his knees. As a result, the Chicago Cubs signed him for $650,000, which was below market value for a player of Dawson's experience and accomplishment. Dawson got to play at Wrigley Field and the Cubs got a Most Valuable Player who hit 49 home runs for them.

Pitcher Frank Viola's 17 wins were an integral part of the Twins' success

109 stolen bases and Ozzie Smith's sparkling defensive play at shortstop, along with a .303 batting average, were the high points of the Cardinals' attack. Tudor's leg was broken on April 19 when Mets' catcher Barry Lyons crashed into him in the Cardinal dugout while going after a foul ball. He did not pitch again until August 1.

Eleven victories were the most any Cardinal could manage, but three different pitchers reached that mark—Bob Forsch, Danny Cox and Greg Matthews.

Meanwhile the Mets, hurt early in the season by the absence of their ace Dwight Gooden, were in the hunt all the way. Gooden had failed a pre-season drug test. Threatened with suspension, he agreed to enter a rehabilitation program and missed the first two months of the season. He still managed to post a 15–7 record for New York. Darryl Strawberry's 39 home runs and 104 RBIs led the offensive attack.

The Montreal Expos were also very much in the running as third baseman Tim Wallach sparked their attack with 26 home runs and 123 runs batted in, but by September it was primarily a two-team race.

Mike Schmidt continued to lead the Philadelphia Phillies' offense with 35 home runs and 113 runs batted in while Shane Rawley topped the starting staff with a 17–11 record. But it was relief pitcher Steve Bedrosian's league-leading 40 saves, 5–3 record and 2.63 earned run average who took center stage on the Philadelphia pitching staff and earned Bedrosian the Cy Young Award.

Schmidt got his 500th career home run early in the season against Don Robinson in Pittsburgh.

Barry Bonds was the offensive standout for Jim Leyland's Pittsburgh Pirates with 25 home runs.

But it was Andre Dawson, signed by the Cubs as a free agent in March, who took the National League's Most Valuable Player award, hitting a league-leading 49 home runs and 137 runs batted in for Chicago. Dawson signed at a bargain price with the Cubs because he was anxious to play his home games on a grass field after years of having his bad knees aggravated by Montreal's artificial turf.

First baseman Will Clark proved to be a total offensive package for the San Francisco Giants. His 35 home runs and .308 batting average helped to carry them to the Western

Division crown. A mid-season trade bolstered both the pitching staff and the offense as the Giants obtained lefthanded pitchers Dave Dravecky and Craig Lefferts and outfielder Kevin Mitchell from the San Diego Padres. Mitchell hit 15 home runs after joining his new club, while Dravecky posted a 7–5 record with the Giants.

The second-place Cincinnati Reds, under manager Pete Rose, could boast a total package of their own in outfielder Eric Davis. Davis hit 37 home runs, drove in 100 runs and stole 50 bases while narrowly missing the .300 mark, finishing at .293.

Houston's legendary pitcher Nolan Ryan appeared to be living proof of the theory among some baseball experts who say that a pitcher's won-lost record is not a fair indicator of a pitcher's value to his team. Ryan finished the season with an 8–16 mark, but his 270 strikeouts and 2.76 earned run average led the National League. Ryan's strikeout total also marked the 11th season that he had topped the 200 strikeout mark, a major league record. The Astros, the 1986 division champions, suffered from Dickie Thon's lingering eye problems and poor seasons from some of their regulars.

Outfielder Pedro Guerrero continued to spark the Dodgers' offense with a .336 average and 27 home runs. Orel Hershiser, for the second season in a row, finished with a .500 record at 16–16.

Atlanta's Dale Murphy belted 44 home runs and 105 RBIs, while Zane Smith posted a respectable 15–10 record. One of Murphy's home runs was his 300th.

Tony Gwynn continued to set the standard for major league batters with a .370 mark to take the title, his second in four seasons. At one point in June, Gwynn's average was .387. He also swiped 56 bases. Rookie catcher Benito Santiago also distinguished himself by hitting safely in 27 consecutive games, a new record for a first-year player.

Sparking talk that the baseball may be "juiced" or easier to drive longer distances, major league players hit a record 4,458 home runs in 1987.

Will Clark's huge season helped the Giants to a division title

AL CHAMPIONSHIP SERIES

GAME 1	
Minnesota 8	Detroit 5
GAME 2	
Minnesota 6	Detroit 3
GAME 3	
Detroit 7	Twins 6
GAME 4	
Minnesota 5	Detroit 3
GAME 5	
Minnesota 9	Detroit 5
MVP: Gary Gaetti, Minnesota	

NL CHAMPIONSHIP SERIES

GAME 1	
St. Louis Cardinals 5	San Francisco 3
GAME 2	
San Francisco 5	St. Louis Cardinals 0
GAME 3	
St. Louis Cardinals 6	San Francisco 5
GAME 4	
San Francisco 4	St. Louis Cardinals 2
GAME 5	
San Francisco 6	St. Louis Cardinals 3
GAME 5	
St. Louis Cardinals 1	San Francisco 0
GAME 7	
St. Louis Cardinals 6	San Francisco 0
MVP: Jeffrey Leonard, San Francisco	

WORLD SERIES

GAME 1	
Minnesota 10	St. Louis Cardinals 1
GAME 2	
Minnesota 8	St. Louis Cardinals 4
GAME 3	
St. Louis Cardinals 3	Minnesota 1
GAME 4	
St. Louis Cardinals 7	Minnesota 2
GAME 5	
St. Louis Cardinals 4	Minnesota 2
GAME 6	
Minnesota 11	St. Louis Cardinals 5
GAME 7	
Minnesota 4	St. Louis Cardinals 2
MVP: Frank Viola, Minnesota	

It was the year "Dome Field Advantage" became part of baseball's lexicon.

The World Series had moved indoors for the first time in history, much to the delight of the Minnesota Twins, who thrived in the nontraditional environment of the Hubert H. Humphrey Metrodome all season—and carried that over to the postseason. The Twins shocked the Detroit Tigers in the playoffs, then scored another upset by beating the St. Louis Cardinals in seven games to take the first World Series championship in franchise history.

Minnesota didn't command much respect. The Twins had only won 85 games in the regular season, but the total was good enough to win the weakest division in the majors. They were back in the postseason for the first time since they lost the first two American League playoff series in 1969 and 1970.

Much of their success came at home, where they were 56–25. The hitter-friendly environment favored the Twins and a large crowd could generate as much noise as an airport runway in the enclosed stadium.

The Twins had home field advantage in both the playoffs and Series and were 6–0 in games played in the Metrodome.

They opened the playoffs with an 8–5 come-from-behind win over the Tigers. Don Baylor, a stretch-drive addition, hit a tie-breaking single. The Twins made it two straight with a 6–3 win over Tigers ace Jack Morris.

Minnesota came back from a 5–0 deficit in the third game and led 6–5 in the eighth before Pat Sheridan's two-run homer gave the Tigers a 7–6 win. The Twins won the fourth game, 5–3, behind Frank Viola as Darrell Evans misplayed a couple of balls for the Tigers. Minnesota then ended the series with a 9–5 win as Tom Brunansky sealed the game with a three-run homer.

The Cardinals couldn't handle Jeffrey Leonard, who batted .417 with four home runs. Minus Leonard, though, the rest of the San Francisco Giants hit just .218 and didn't score

The Twins' starting rotation for the World Series: (r to l) Frank Viola, Bert Blyleven and Les Straker

at all in the last two games.

Greg Mathews won the opener as he replaced the injured Danny Cox in style. Mathews pitched into the eighth and had a two-run single in the 5–3 win. Will Clark and Leonard hit home runs in the second game and Dave Dravecky pitched a two-hitter for a 5–0 win.

Veteran Bob Forsch provided quality relief in the third game and St. Louis held on to win 6–5. Leonard, Robby Thompson and Bob Brenly all homered as the Giants won the fourth game, 4–2.

San Francisco won the fifth game, 6–3, as Joe Price pitched five innings of one-hit relief. John Tudor and two relievers beat Dravecky, 1–0, in the sixth game. The Giants were held scoreless again in the final game, losing 6–0 to Danny Cox.

The home team won every game in the Series and the Twins had the advantage of playing four games at the Metrodome. Because Jack Clark was out with an ankle injury, St. Louis was without an important part of its offense .

Minnesota won the opener 10–1 behind Viola

with a grand slam from Dan Gladden. Bert Blyleven won Game Two as the Twins scored six runs in the fourth. Gary Gaetti and Tim Laudner hit home runs.

The shift to St. Louis had the expected effect on scoring. The Cardinals got their first win in Game Three, 3–1, as Tudor pitched a strong game with relief from Todd Worrell.

Tom Lawless hit a three-run homer off Viola in Game Four to help the Cardinals to a 7–2 win that tied the Series at two games each. St. Louis won Game Five, 4–2, as Cox beat Blyleven. Curt Ford had a two-run single for the Cardinals.

St. Louis took a 5–2 lead into the fifth inning of Game Six, but Tudor couldn't hold it. Baylor's two-run homer capped a three-run fifth that tied the score and Ombardozzi had an RBI single to give the Twins the lead. Kent Hrbek hit a grand slam off lefthander Ken Dayley in the sixth and Minnesota wound up winning 11–5.

Greg Gagne hit a two-out single to break a 2–2 tie in the fifth and the Twins went on to win 4–2. Jeff Reardon, who was acquired in a February trade, pitched the last inning, his fourth scoreless appearance in the Series.

Minnesota's players greet Steve Gladden after his grand slam home run in Game One of the World Series

MOST VALUABLE PLAYER
AL: Jose Canseco, Oakland
NL: Kirk Gibson, Los Angeles

CY YOUNG AWARD
AL: Frank Viola, Minnesota
NL: Orel Hershiser, Los Angeles

ROOKIE OF THE YEAR
AL: Walt Weiss, Oakland
NL: Chris Sabo, Cincinnati

LEADERS
BATTING AVERAGE
AL: Wade Boggs, Boston Red Sox, .366
NL: Tony Gwynn, San Diego, .313

HOME RUNS
AL: Jose Canseco, Oakland, 42
NL: Darryl Strawberry, NY Mets, 39

RUNS BATTED IN
AL: Jose Canseco, Oakland, 124
NL: Will Clark, NY Giants, 109

STOLEN BASES
AL: Rickey Henderson, NY Yankees, 93
NL: Vince Coleman, St. Louis Cardinals, 81

PITCHING VICTORIES
AL: Frank Viola, Minnesota, 24
NL: Danny Jackson, Cincinnati; Orel Hershiser,
Los Angeles, 23

EARNED RUN AVERAGE
AL: Allan Anderson, Minnesota; Teddy Higuera,
Milwaukee, 2.45
NL: Joe Magrane, St. Louis Cardinals, 2.18

STRIKEOUTS
AL: Roger Clemens, Boston Red Sox, 291
NL: Nolan Ryan, Houston, 228

SAVES
AL: Dennis Eckersley, Oakland, 45
NL: John Franco, Cincinnati, 39

The managerial situation of the New York Yankees had already begun to take on comical proportions, but when Billy Martin was fired by Yankees' owner George Steinbrenner for the fifth time and replaced once again by Lou Piniella, the joke began to wear a little thin.

Meanwhile, the Yankees were one of five teams in the American League Eastern Division who were in contention for the title. The eventual champions, the Boston Red Sox, were just one game over .500 in mid-July when their manager, John McNamara, was fired and replaced by third base coach Joe Morgan (not to be confused with Hall of Famer Joe Morgan).

Morgan led the Red Sox to a 46–31 record the rest of the way. The Red Sox continued to get their usual solid hitting from league leader Wade Boggs (.366). Mike Greenwell contributed 22 home runs and 119 RBIs. Roger Clemens was 18–12 and Bruce Hurst went 18–6. Reliever Lee Smith's 29 saves and 2.80 ERA also contributed to the Red Sox success.

The defending division champion Detroit Tigers made a strong effort to repeat. They were in first place at the end of August, but by late September Boston was able to clinch the title.

No doubt hurt by the loss of free agent Kirk Gibson to the Los Angeles Dodgers, the Tigers continued to get solid pitching from Jack Morris (15–13) and reliever Mike Henneman (22 saves and a 1.87 ERA). Darrell Evans led the club in home runs and Alan Trammell continued to stand out at the plate with a .311 batting average.

The Milwaukee Brewers finished two games behind Boston. Paul Molitor's .312 average topped the team and Rob Deer hit 23 home runs. Teddy Higuera posted a 16–9 record with a 2.45 earned run average and Dan Plesac's 30 saves made him the team's relief ace.

Toronto joined the Brewers in a tie for third

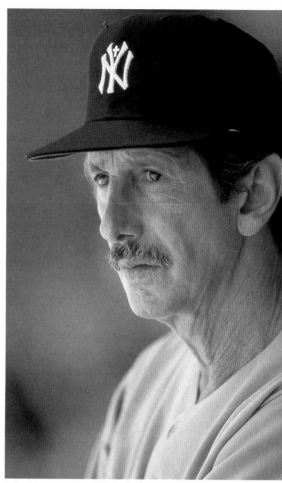

Billy Martin again fell foul of the Yankees' ever-revolving managerial door

place as first baseman Fred McGriff belted 34 home runs and Dave Stieb topped the starting staff with a 16–8 mark along with a 3.04 ERA. The 1987 American League save leader, Tom Henke, posted 25 saves.

Under Martin, the Yankees had a 40–28 record. With Piniella, their record was 45–48. New York finished 3½ games out of first place. Dave Winfield proved to be a triple threat, hitting .322, driving in 107 runs and belting 25 home runs. Pre-season acquisition Jack Clark was used as a designated hitter and hit a team-high 27 home runs in that role.

In the American League West it was no contest at all as the Oakland Athletics coasted to a 104–88 record and a 13-game advantage at the end of the season. Mark McGwire hit 32 home runs in his second full season, but it was his "Bash Brother" Jose Canseco who provided the most home run excitement with a league-leading 42 home runs and 132 RBIs, as well as posting a .307 average. Dave Stewart continued as the

SHORTS Popular singing group The Statler Brothers had a country hit in the 1970s called "Don't Wait On Me" in which they named several events that would never happen. One of the lines was "When the lights go on at Wrigley Field." They continued to perform the song in 1988, but their disclaimer at the beginning drew laughter from their audiences.

The A's sprinted to their division title, helped by the dominating performances of Jose Canseco

TIMELINE

Jan. 13: Steve Garvey, a star for the Dodgers and Padres, announced his retirement from baseball.

Jan. 14: After a year in Japan, Bob Horner signed with the St. Louis Cardinals.

Feb. 12: The Chicago Cubs traded Keith Moreland and two minor league prospects to the San Diego Padres for relief pitcher Rich "Goose" Gossage.

April 4: The New York Mets hit six home runs, including two each by Kevin McReynolds and Darryl Strawberry, to set a record for an Opening Day game.

April 12: The Baltimore Orioles fired Cal Ripken Sr. as manager and hired Frank Robinson as his replacement.

May 4: The Minnesota Twins released pitcher Joe Niekro.

May 9: White Sox' pitcher Jerry Reuss beat Baltimore and won the 200th game of his career.

May 20: Philadelphia's Mike Schmidt surpassed Jimmie Foxx on the all-time home run list with his 535th.

June 3: The Cleveland Indians traded infielder Pat Tabler to Kansas City for pitcher Bud Black.

June 12: The Brewers' Robin Yount hit for the cycle against Chicago.

July 9: San Francisco shortstop Chris Speier hit for the cycle against St. Louis.

July 10: The Dodgers released Don Sutton, their all-time leader in victories.

Sept. 4: Cincinnati Reds' pitcher Danny Jackson won his 20th game, the first pitcher to reach that milestone for the season.

Sept. 9: Bruce Sutter of the Braves recorded his 300th career save.

Sept. 23: Jose Canseco of the Athletics became the first player in history to hit 40 home runs and steal 40 bases.

Sept. 26: Los Angeles clinched the National League Western Division championship with a 3–2 win over San Diego.

Oct. 24: The Minnesota Twins traded Tommy Herr, Eric Bullock and Tom Nieto to the Philadelphia Phillies for pitcher Shane Rawley.

ace of the pitching staff with a 21–12 record.

Dennis Eckersley, one of the game's top starting pitchers for most of his career, had begun to settle into his new role as a reliever in 1987. In 1988 he was established in the job. Eckersley led the league with 45 saves and also posted a 4–2 record with a 2.35 ERA.

The defending American League champion Minnesota Twins finished a distant second as Bert Blyleven's record plummeted to a dismal 10–17 and Tom Brunansky was gone from their lineup after being traded to the St. Louis Cardinals for second baseman Tommy Herr. While Blyleven's record was down, the Twins got a Cy Young Award season from Frank Viola with a 24–7 record. Kirby Puckett's .356 average and 121 runs batted in put him among the league leaders in those departments and Gary Gaetti hit 28 home runs as well.

Minnesota also had the league's top ERA man in Allan Anderson with 2.45.

Mark Gubicza's 20–8 record stood out for the Kansas City Royals as George Brett hit .306 while hitting 24 home runs and driving in 103 runs. Danny Tartabull's 26 home runs, however, topped the club in that department.

Second baseman Johnny Ray's .306 batting average and Brian Downing's 25 home runs as a designated hitter topped the California Angels' offense.

Oakland catcher Terry Steinbach drove in both American League runs in the All-Star Game with a home run and a sacrifice fly to lead them to a 2–1 win at Riverfront Stadium. Steinbach

was named the game's Most Valuable Player.

In the National League, the New York Mets ran away with the Eastern Division crown behind the outstanding pitching of David Cone, who posted a 20–3 mark with a 2.22 ERA. Darryl Strawberry led the league with 39 home runs and also drove in 101 runs, while second baseman Wally Backman hit .303. The Mets clinched the division crown on September 22.

Andy Van Slyke and Bobby Bonilla each drove in 100 runs for the Pittsburgh Pirates. Van Slyke also led the club with 25 home runs. Bonilla and outfielder Barry Bonds also hit 24 home runs each for the Bucs. Doug Drabek anchored the pitching staff with a 15–7 record and Jim Gott had 34 saves out of the Pittsburgh bullpen.

First baseman Andres Galarraga hit 29 home runs and batted .302 to lead the Montreal Expos. Dennis Martinez led the pitching staff with a 15–13 record.

History was made in Chicago as the lights went on in Wrigley Field for the first time on August 8 in a rain-shortened game between the Cubs and Mets. The teams managed to play an official game the following night under the lights. Andre Dawson hit 24 home runs, while pitcher Greg Maddux posted a record of 18–8.

Defending National League champion St. Louis Cardinals tried to make up for the loss of hard-hitting Clark at first base by trading for Brunansky from the Twins. Brunansky did hit a club-leading 22 home runs, but Clark's replacement, Bob Horner, was a disappointment in light of all the anticipation created by his signing.

Horner was plagued by injuries and hit just three home runs. Joe Magrane pitched well, posting a league-leading 2.18 ERA, but his 5–9 record was indicative of the lack of run support by the Cardinals.

Mike Schmidt surpassed Mickey Mantle on the all-time home run list with his 537th career blast, but injuries kept his home run total for the season to a mere 12. Chris James led the Philadelphia club in home runs with 19. Phillies' manager Lee Elia was fired in late September and coach John Vukovich finished the season as interim skipper before Nick Leyva was hired in October to take over next season.

The signing of free agent Gibson proved to be just the shot in the arm that the Los Angeles Dodgers needed as they won the Western Division title. Gibson's 25 home runs led him to the National League Most Valuable Player

A study in concentration, the New York Mets' Darryl Strawberry

award. The Dodgers had another award winner in Orel Hershiser, whose 23–8 record not only tied Cincinnati's Danny Jackson for league best, it also enabled him to win the Cy Young Award. Hershiser also posted a 2.26 ERA.

Cincinnati finished second in the division, seven games behind the Dodgers, but their fiery manager Pete Rose was suspended for the entire month of May after a confrontation with umpire Dave Pallone. Rose shoved Pallone in the ninth inning of a game against the New York Mets and National League president A. Bartlett Giamatti imposed the suspension.

Aside from Danny Jackson's 23–8 record, the Reds also had the league's save leader in John Franco, who had 39. Their offense was led by Eric Davis with 26 home runs. Reds' third baseman Chris Sabo took Rookie of the Year honors for the National League with a .271 batting average and 11 home runs.

San Diego's Tony Gwynn won his second straight batting title with a .313 average while Eric Show's 16–11 mark topped the Padres' pitching staff. On May 28, the Padres fired Larry Bowa as manager and gave the job to Jack McKeon, who was serving as vice-president of operations for the club.

Veteran pitcher Rick Reuschel posted a 19–11 record for the defending Western Division champion San Francisco Giants. First baseman Will Clark drove in a league-leading 109 runs while hitting 29 home runs, but the Giants were unable to muster a sufficient assault on the division crown.

Glenn Davis hit 30 home runs for the Houston Astros and Mike Scott's 14–8 record was the best on their pitching staff. Scott also narrowly missed a no-hitter against Atlanta when Ken Oberkfell hit a single with two outs in the ninth inning.

The Atlanta Braves dropped their first ten games of the season and lingered in the cellar throughout. Dale Murphy's 24 home runs topped the Atlanta offense. Manager Chuck Tanner was fired on May 23 and Russ Nixon took over for the remainder of the season.

The Phillies' Mike Schmidt passed Mickey Mantle on the all-time home run list

AL CHAMPIONSHIP SERIES

GAME 1
| Oakland 2 | Boston Red Sox 1 |

GAME 2
| Oakland 4 | Boston Red Sox 3 |

GAME 3
| Oakland 10 | Boston Red Sox 6 |

GAME 4
| Oakland 4 | Boston Red Sox 1 |

MVP: Dennis Eckersley, Oakland

NL CHAMPIONSHIP SERIES

GAME 1
| NY Mets 3 | Los Angeles 2 |

GAME 2
| Los Angeles 6 | NY Mets 3 |

GAME 3
| NY Mets 8 | Los Angeles 4 |

GAME 4
| Los Angeles 5 | NY Mets 4 |

GAME 5
| Los Angeles 7 | NY Mets 4 |

GAME 6
| NY Mets 5 | Los Angeles 1 |

GAME 7
| Los Angeles 6 | NY Mets 0 |

MVP: Orel Hershiser, Los Angeles

WORLD SERIES

GAME 1
| Los Angeles 5 | Oakland 4 |

GAME 2
| Los Angeles 6 | Oakland 0 |

GAME 3
| Oakland 2 | Los Angeles 1 |

GAME 4
| Los Angeles 4 | Oakland 3 |

GAME 5
| Los Angeles 5 | Oakland 2 |

MVP: Orel Hershiser, Los Angeles

Certain World Series moments become frozen in time: Yogi Berra leaping into Don Larsen's arms after their perfect game win in 1956. Bill Mazeroski's euphoric helmet-waving tour around the bases in 1960. Carlton Fisk pleading with the baseball to stay fair in 1975. Kirk Gibson put his name on that short list in 1988.

Hobbled by a leg injury and presumed to be unavailable for the World Series, Gibson crashed a game-winning home run off the game's best relief pitcher and limped around the bases, pumping his fists.

Gibson's homer didn't win the World Series for the Los Angeles, but it set a tone that carried them through their five-game win over the Oakland A's.

The Dodgers had a clear path to the postseason, winning 94 games to take the National League West. They then upset the New York Mets in the playoffs to take the National League pennant.

The Mets were the National League's power franchise, winning 100 games in the regular season. David Cone was a 20-game winner and Darryl Strawberry's 101 RBIs were second in the National League.

The Mets had been a come-from-behind team all season and that was the method they used to win the first game of the playoffs. The Mets were behind 2–0 going into the ninth inning against Dodgers closer Jay Howell. The Mets rally produced the tie-breaking run when Kevin McReynolds upended catcher Mike Scioscia at the plate.

The Dodgers took a quick 5–0 lead in the second game and held it, winning 6–3. They scored five runs in two innings against Cone, who may have inadvertently supplied some extra motivation. Cone agreed to provide some insights to a newspaper, which would then produce a column under Cone's byline.

True to New York tabloid style, it was lively reading. It was probably too lively for Cone's own good. His slights of the Dodgers and Howell became a rallying point for manager Tom Lasorda and his team. Cone was rocked in his first start and Los Angeles rookie Tim Belcher struck out ten.

It was another Mets comeback in the third game. Trailing by a run, they scored five in the eighth and beat the Dodgers 8–4. Howell quickly discovered he had bigger problems than Cone's opinion of his work. He was found to have pine tar on his glove and was promptly ejected from the game. Without their best reliever the Dodgers struggled and the Mets feasted.

It looked as though the Mets had built momentum. They overcame an early 2–0 deficit to go ahead 4–2 through eight innings. The Dodgers, though, borrowed the Mets game plan and tied the game in the ninth with Scioscia's two-run homer. Gibson broke the tie with a home run off Roger McDowell in the 12th and the Dodgers used three pitchers, including No. 1 starter Orel Hershiser, to close the game.

Gibson homered again in the fifth game, a 7–4 Dodgers win. Cone pitched a five-hit 5–1 in to tie the series before Hershiser wrapped it up for the Dodgers with a 6–0 win, holding the Mets to five hits.

Oakland swept Boston in the American League playoffs as Dennis Eckersley set a playoff record by saving all four games.

Eckersley was the central figure in Gibson's Series moment. He was called upon to preserve a one-run lead in Game One. Mike Davis drew a walk and desperate Dodgers manager, Tom Lasorda, called upon the injured Gibson. He worked the count 3–2 before he drove Eckersley's pitch into the seats to cement his place in postseason history.

Hershiser pitched a three-hitter to win Game Two, 6-0. Mark McGwire gave the A's their only win with a ninth-inning homer off Howell in Game Three. But Howell saved Game Four's 4–3 win for Tim Belcher, a rookie who had come to the Dodgers in a trade from Oakland.

Journeyman utility player Mickey Hatcher helped the Dodgers close out the Series with a 5–2 win behind Hershiser. Hatcher hit a two-run homer in the first off Storm Davis and Mike Davis added a two-run homer later. Hershiser pitched the complete game for his second win of the short Series and took MVP honors, just as he had in the playoffs.

Orel Hershiser won two games on his way to the Series MVP

Kirk Gibson is congratulated by his teammates after hitting a two-run homer in the ninth-inning to give the Dodgers a 5–4 victory in Game One of the World Series

Throughout his career, Pete Rose's hard-nosed, relentlessly aggressive style made him stand out among modern players.

The eventful career of Pete Rose took its most dramatic turn in August

He was baseball's all-time hit leader, having bested the immortal Ty Cobb. He was considered old school—a throwback player who made the inevitable move into managing. But in August of 1989, the sure-shot Hall of Famer was out of baseball completely. After a long investigation by the Commissioner's office into his gambling habits, Rose signed an agreement that ended the probe by agreeing to a lifetime banishment—with the possibility of reinstatement.

Even as the sordid Rose story played out, the on-field activity in major league baseball continued to thrill fans.

In the American League Eastern Division the Baltimore Orioles, coming from last place in 1988, held the division lead for most of the season. But the Toronto Blue Jays battled and, on September 30, they clinched the division with a victory over Frank Robinson's Orioles.

Heading the Toronto attack was first baseman Fred McGriff, whose 36 home runs led the league. George Bell drove in 104 runs and hit 18 home runs. Dave Steib anchored the pitching staff with a 17-8 mark, while Tom Henke posted 20 saves, compiling a 1.92 ERA.

Baltimore's rise from the Eastern Division cellar in 1988 could be attributed in part to the pitching of Jeff Ballard (18–8) and Gregg Olson (27 saves, a 1.89 ERA and a 5–2 record) as well as 26 home runs from Mickey Tettleton.

The Boston Red Sox were also contenders as hard-throwing Roger Clemens posted a 17–11 record. Wade Boggs hit .330 and Dwight Evans belted 20 home runs and drove in 100 runs to lead the offense. Reliever Lee Smith had a 6–1 record with 25 saves.

The Milwaukee Brewers finished fourth at an even .500 mark behind the power of Rob Deer, who hit 26 home runs, and the all-around hitting of Robin Yount with a .318 average, 21 home runs and 103 runs batted in. Chris Bosio led the pitching staff with a 15–10 record.

Don Mattingly did some all-around hitting of his own for the New York Yankees with 23 home runs and 113 runs batted in. Second baseman Steve Sax, signed as a free agent in the off-season, led his new club in batting with a .315 mark.

Dave Stewart continued to demonstrate why he was nicknamed "Smoke" as his fastball carried him to a 21–9 record for the Oakland Athletics, who repeated as Western Division champions. It was Stewart's third consecutive 20-win season. Dennis Eckersley's 4–0 record, 33 saves and 1.56 earned run average continued

The Royals' Bret Saberhagen was a no-brainer for the American League Cy Young Award

Jan. 17: Claudell Washington, a free agent, signed a three-year contract with the California Angels.

Feb. 21: Pete Rose met with the Commissioner's office to discuss his alleged gambling problem.

March 9: Plagued by shoulder problems, Bob Horner retired at the age of 31. Horner was the first player chosen in the 1978 draft.

April 19: Kevin Elster, playing for the New York Mets, set a new major league record for shortstops by playing his 73rd straight game without an error.

May 12: Rick Reuschel, pitching for the Giants, won the 200th game of his career.

May 25: The Expos traded three pitchers—Randy Johnson, Gene Harris and Brian Holman—to Seattle for Mark Langston.

June 21: The New York Yankees traded Rickey Henderson to Oakland for Greg Cadaret, Eric Plunk and Luis Polonia.

July 11: The American League All-Stars defeated the National League 5–3.

July 18: Former major league pitcher Donnie Moore shot and wounded his wife, then committed suicide.

July 28: Vince Coleman's string of 50 straight successful stolen base attempts was broken by Expos' catcher Nelson Santovenia.

Aug. 8: Toronto pitcher Mauro Gozzo made his major league debut and tossed eight scoreless innings against Texas.

Aug. 10: Rangers' pitcher Nolan Ryan carried a no-hitter into the ninth inning against Detroit, but Dave Bergman singled with one out.

Aug. 18: New York Yankees' manager Dallas Green was fired and replaced by Bucky Dent.

Sept. 1: Baseball Commissioner A. Bartlett Giamatti died of a heart attack at 51.

Sept. 22: Pitcher Dave Stewart of the Oakland Athletics won his 20th game, his third consecutive season with at least 20 wins.

Sept. 30: The Toronto Blue Jays clinched the American League Eastern Division title with a win over the Orioles.

Dec. 25: Former player and manager Billy Martin died in an automobile accident. Martin was 61.

to help define the role of the modern-day relief pitcher in baseball. Mark McGwire's 33 home runs led the team's power production and Carney Lansford's .336 batting average placed him second to Minnesota's Kirby Puckett among the league leaders in that department.

Bret Saberhagen's 23 wins against six losses, along with his league-leading 2.16 earned run average left little room for debate as he earned his second Cy Young Award pitching for the Kansas City Royals. The Royals also had a bona fide slugger in Bo Jackson, whose 32 home runs and 105 RBIs led the Kansas City offense.

Veteran Bert Blyleven topped the California Angels' pitchers with a 17–5 record, but another California pitcher captured headlines for a different reason. Jim Abbott, who came to the major leagues directly from college without playing minor league baseball first, pitched despite having only one hand. Abbott posted a 12–12 record for the Angels.

Bobby Valentine's Texas Rangers could boast two league leaders—relief pitcher Jeff Russell with 38 saves and outfielder Ruben Sierra with 119 runs batted in. Russell also posted an impressive 1.98 ERA with a 6–4 record and Sierra hit 29 home runs. Nolan Ryan showed he was still a winner with a 16–10 mark as he posted his 5,000th career strikeout on August 22, the most in major league history.

Minnesota's Kirby Puckett won the American League batting championship with a .339 average and Allan Anderson posted a 17–10

AL Batting champ, Minnesota's Kirby Puckett

SHORTS When Tommy John took the pitcher's mound to start for the New York Yankees on Opening Day of 1989, he was beginning his 26th season in the major leagues—a record for the modern era. The 45-year-old John notched his 287th career victory, beating the Minnesota Twins 4–2.

record to lead the Twins' pitching staff, but 1988's Cy Young Award winner, Frank Viola, dropped to an 8–12 mark before being traded to the New York Mets on July 31. Reliever Jeff Reardon's 31 saves put him among the league leaders in that department.

On July 11 in Anaheim, the American League All-Stars topped the National League 5–3 as Bo Jackson and Wade Boggs belted back-to-back home runs in the first inning. Jackson was named the game's Most Valuable Player.

The Chicago Cubs captured the National League's Eastern Division crown behind the pitching of Greg Maddux (19–12) and reliever Mitch Williams (36 saves) and a lineup packed with solid hitters like Ryne Sandberg (30 home runs) and Mark Grace (.314 batting average). The Cubs also got good production from rookie outfielder Jerome Walton, who had a 30-game hitting streak at one point during the season. Walton finished with a .293 batting average to earn National League Rookie of the Year honors.

Howard Johnson's 36 home runs and 101 runs batted in topped the second-place New York Mets regulars. Darryl Strawberry was second on the club with 29 homers, including the 200th of his career. In an effort to bolster their troubled pitching staff, they traded for Viola, the 1988 American League Cy Young Award winner. Viola joined the team on August 1 and posted a disappointing 5–5 record for the remainder of the season.

Joe Magrane posted another good season for the St. Louis Cardinals with an 18–9 record and a 2.91 ERA. Tom Brunansky led the Redbirds in home runs with 20, but it was first baseman Pedro Guerrero who paced their hitting attack with a .311 batting average, 117 runs batted in and 17 home runs.

The Montreal Expos finished at the .500 mark in fourth place. Dennis Martinez led the pitching staff with a 16–7 record and Andres Galarraga continued to shine at first base with 23 home runs.

Bobby Bonilla's 24 home runs were the high mark for Jim Leyland's Pittsburgh Pirates, but outfielder Barry Bonds' 19 homers helped make history. Barry and his father Bobby became the all-time father and son home run leaders, surpassing two other combinations with ties to the Pirates—Yogi and Dale Berra and Gus and Buddy Bell.

The Philadelphia Phillies finished in the cellar, but the big news came on May 29 when their venerable third baseman Mike Schmidt announced his retirement at the age of 39, effective immediately. Schmidt finished with 548 career home runs, seventh on the all time list. Despite his retirement, he was elected by the fans to start at third base in the All-Star Game, but elected not to play. Charlie Hayes, obtained in a June trade from the Giants, took over the regular duties at third.

Kevin Mitchell led the league in home runs (47) and runs batted in (122) and helped the San Francisco Giants to the Western Division title. Will Clark batted .333 and hit 23 home runs with 111 RBIs. Pitcher Scott Garrelts' 2.28 earned run average was also the league's best and veteran Rick Reuschel finished with a 17–8 record.

The San Diego Padres finished second as Tony Gwynn captured his third consecutive batting title with a .336 average. First baseman Jack Clark hit 26 home runs. The Padres also had the league's best relief pitcher in Mark Davis with 44 saves, a 4–3 record and a 1.85 ERA. Ed Whitson's 16–11 mark topped the San Diego starting corps.

Houston's pitching staff was headed by Mike Scott with a 20–10 record. First baseman Glenn Davis led the club in home runs with 34.

The defending World Champion Los Angeles Dodgers skidded to a fourth place finish in 1989 as Orel Hershiser finished with an even 15–15 record while posting an impressive 2.31 earned run average. Kirk Gibson, the 1988 Most Valuable Player, was bothered by injuries. Veteran Eddie Murray, obtained from Baltimore in the off-season, provided 20 home runs in his first National League experience.

Eric Davis hit 34 home runs and drove in 101 runs to provide Cincinnati fans something to cheer about in an otherwise bleak season at Riverfront Stadium. Rose began the season as the Reds' manager and led the club for 125 games while rumblings of an investigation by the office of Commissioner A. Bartlett Giamatti floated throughout baseball.

On August 24, it all came to a head when Giamatti and Rose came to the agreement that barred the all-time hit leader. Without denial or apology, Rose signed the agreement and Tommy Helms took over as manager of the club to the end of the season.

To add genuine tragedy to an already sad story, Giamatti died of a heart attack on September 1, just eight days after imposing the ban on Rose.

Another significant retirement occurred on July 17 when "submarine-style" relief pitcher Kent Tekulve ended his career after appearing in 37 games for the Reds. Tekulve needed just 21 games to surpass Hoyt Wilhelm as the all-time leader in career game appearances, but decided his 5.02 earned run average was unacceptable.

Commissioner Giamatti's death bought tragedy to an already tumultuous season

SHORTS Players who wished to extend or resurrect their professional baseball careers were given the opportunity to do so when the Senior Professional Baseball Association was formed in May. Eight cities in Florida would host the teams. Play would begin in November. Minimum age for eligibility—35. Several retired major league players, as well as a host of hopefuls, expressed interest in the venture.

AL CHAMPIONSHIP SERIES

GAME 1	
Oakland 7	Toronto 3

GAME 2	
Oakland 6	Toronto 3

GAME 3	
Toronto 7	Oakland 3

GAME 4	
Oakland 6	Toronto 5

GAME 5	
Oakland 4	Toronto 3

MVP: Rickey Henderson, Oakland

NATIONAL LEAGUE CHAMPIONSHIP SERIES

GAME 1	
San Francisco 11	Chicago Cubs 3

GAME 2	
San Francisco 9	Chicago Cubs 5

GAME 3	
Chicago Cubs 5	San Francisco 4

GAME 4	
San Francisco 6	Chicago Cubs 4

GAME 5	
San Francisco 3	Chicago Cubs 2

MVP: Will Clark, San Francisco

WORLD SERIES

GAME 1	
Oakland 5	San Francisco 0

GAME 2	
Oakland 5	San Francisco 1

GAME 3	
Oakland 13	San Francisco 7

GAME 4	
Oakland 9	San Francisco 6

MVP: Dave Stewart, Oakland

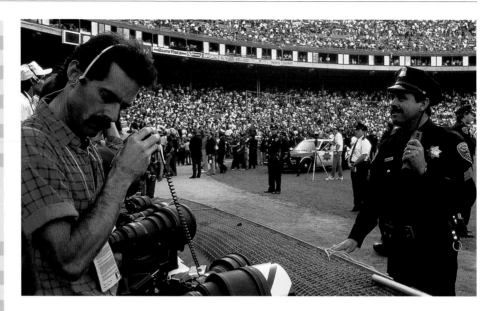

The fans in Candlestick Park (top right) had a lucky escape when the earthquake struck

The damage caused by the earthquake meant that baseball was put on the backburner for a while

It was the World Series that will always be remembered for something other than baseball.

The 1989 Series had a built-in story angle, matching the San Francisco Giants and Oakland A's, who had been sharing the same market since the A's moved from Kansas City in time for the 1968 season. If it didn't have the luster of a genuine New York subway series, it was one in which the proximity of both venues made it interesting.

Having all the games in the same general area turned out to be a curse when a devastating earthquake rocked northern California shortly before Game 3 started. Given the destruction outside of Candlestick Park, it was a miracle that there were no serious injuries inside a stadium packed with more than 50,000 people.

The disaster consigned the Series to insignificance in the Bay Area. Baseball waited out a ten-day delay, to give the area a chance to recover and to make sure it was safe to play again and to fill the stands.

It had been a magical season in the Bay, with the Giants holding off San Diego to take the National League West and Oakland comfortably winning its second American League West title.

The Chicago Cubs provided the opposition in the National League playoffs and fell in five games. The game opened under the lights at Wrigley Field and the spotlight was on Giants first baseman, Will Clark. He had four hits and six RBIs, including a grand slam as the Giants won 11–3. The Cubs used a six-run first inning to win the second game, 9–6. Chicago roughed up long-time Cubs ace, Rick Reuschel, in the first.

The Giants were back in the third game, one that changed the series. Second baseman, Robby Thompson, hit a two-run homer in the seventh inning off Les Lancaster to put the Giants ahead 5–4.

San Francisco won the final two games to advance to the World Series for the first time since 1962. Steve Bedrosian saved both games, a 6–4 win in the fourth game and a 3–2 Reuschel win in the clincher.

Oakland's combination of speed and power was too much for Toronto as the A's won the American League playoffs in five games. Henderson, the most prolific base stealer in baseball history, dominated the first two games with his abilities on the bases. Oakland won the

opening game 7–3 and expanded its lead with a 6–3 win in the second game.

The American League series mirrored the Giants–Cubs series with the loser coming up with its only win in the third game. Toronto beat the A's 7–3 behind a strong effort from Jimmy Key and two relievers. But Henderson returned to vex the Blue Jays in the fourth game.

This time he used power rather than speed and hit a pair of home runs to lead Oakland to a 6–5 win. Jose Canseco also homered for the A's as Bob Welch got the win with relief help from Eckersley.

Dave Stewart and Eckersley then teamed up for the 4–3 win that sent the A's back to the Series for a second consecutive year. Eckersley saved three of the four games for Oakland, and Henderson led the offense with a .400 average, eight stolen bases, eight runs, two homers and five RBIs.

The Giants were no match for the A's in the Series. Oakland engineered the first sweep since the 1976 Cincinnati Reds took four straight from the New York Yankees.

Dave Stewart and Mike Moore each won two games for the A's. Stewart beat Scott Garrelts 5–0 in Game One with a five-hitter. Walt Weiss and Dave Parker both hit home runs for the A's.

Moore beat Reuschel 5–1 in the second game and the teams prepared to move to San Francisco. The festive atmosphere vanished with the area's worst earthquake since 1906.

When the Series resumed after the ten-day delay, the A's picked up where they had left off. Stewart won Game Three, 13–7, beating Garrelts again. The A's then ended the Series on October 28, winning 9–6 behind Moore.

Stewart was named the Series MVP, winning out over catcher Terry Steinbach, who had a Series-best seven RBIs.

Oakland A's Mike Moore finished the Series with two wins and a 2.08 ERA

1990

The decade saw the season without a World Series and the first $10 million per year player.

To say it was an historic decade for baseball would be a massive understatement.

By the end of the decade, it was apparent that, except for the rare fluke, the wealthiest teams were also destined to be the most successful ones. Competitive balance was seriously threatened as major-revenue teams like the New York Yankees, Atlanta Braves and Cleveland Indians had become automatic for the postseason. Sure, the Florida Marlins had grabbed a World Series title, but they'd done it by temporarily raising their payroll to a Yankees-like level.

Acrimony between the owners and the Players Association resulted in the 1994 World Series being canceled by a strike that started in August. Owners were prepared to dilute their product with replacement teams until a Federal court struck down their plans.

The other trend in the 1990s was the retro ballpark. It started with Camden Yards in Baltimore and continued with Cleveland's Jacobs Field and others. The idea was to combine old-time charm and all the money-generating extras needed to survive in the new climate.

The look may have been classic, but the game had changed drastically.

The players were locked out to start the season, the game's all-time hits leader was locked up and the team he once led had a lock on first place all season long. Just another tumultuous year in the history of baseball in the modern era.

Labor strife had become as much a part of the landscape as sore arms and rain delays—and about as welcome. The 1990 version was an owner-engineered spring training lockout that kept the camps closed for four weeks.

By the time the settlement was hammered out, the start of the season had been pushed back a week and teams were scrambling to make up some games on what had been scheduled off days. Commissioner Fay Vincent stepped in to help the process move forward, a move that would draw the ire of some hard-line owners and eventually lead to Vincent's forced resignation in the future.

Pete Rose, baseball's all-time hit leader, began serving a prison sentence for filing false tax returns on August 8. Rose reported to a minimum security facility in Illinois, where he spent his five-month sentence working in the machine shop.

That's where Rose was when the Cincinnati Reds completed a season that saw them in first place wire-to-wire by winning their first World Series since 1976, when Rose was part of the

Manager Lou Piniella steered his Reds to a wire-to-wire victory in the National League West

SHORTS

Is it proper to call for a fly ball by saying, "I got it ... Dad?" The Griffeys had to confront that issue on August 31 when Ken Griffey, Sr., 40, and Ken, Jr., 20, became the first father and son combination to play in a major league game. Ken, Sr. signed with the Mariners a few days after his release from the Reds.

"Big Red Machine." The 1990 Reds became the first National League team to spend the entire year in first place since the 162-game schedule was adopted in 1962.

The Reds were 33–12 on June 3, a record-setting start for Cincinnati. Manager Lou Piniella fashioned a three-man bullpen crew that came to be known as the "Nasty Boys." Hard-throwing righthander Rob Dibble was 8–3 with a 1.74 earned run average and 11 saves. His lefthanded counterpart was Randy Myers, who posted 31 saves. There was also lefty Norm Charlton.

The bullpen was especially important because of the truncated spring training. Starters began the season pitching only five or six innings because they didn't have the luxury of following a normal program. A superior group of relievers helped the Reds.

Charlton stepped into the starting rotation when injuries sidelined Jose Rijo, Tom Browning, Danny Jackson and Jack Armstrong. Browning led the staff with a 15–9 record and Rijo was 14–8. Third baseman Chris Sabo surprised the Reds by hitting 25 home runs, one more than Eric Davis. They had a solid attack, but didn't have anyone with overwhelming numbers.

The Los Angeles Dodgers used 21 pitchers trying to find a formula to replace Orel Hershiser, who was out for the season because of shoulder surgery. Ramon Martinez, 22, became the Dodgers' youngest 20-game winner since Ralph Branca in 1947. Second-year pitcher John Wetteland was assigned to the bullpen where his overpowering fastball helped him to become a closer.

The defending National League champion San Francisco Giants slipped to third place and went through 51 players, 26 of them pitchers. Third baseman Matt Williams hit 33 home runs and drove in 122 runs.

In San Diego 30 front office employees were fired, including general manager Jack McKeon.

Cincinnati's Jose Rijo posted a 14–8 record, but it was the Reds' dominating bullpen that would make all the headlines as the season unfolded

TIMELINE

March 18: Players and owners agreed on a four-year labor contract. The consensus ended a 32-day lockout and opened spring camps.

April 27: Orel Hershiser of the Dodgers had his season end when he had to undergo shoulder surgery.

May 29: Oakland's Rickey Henderson got his 893rd career stolen base, beating Ty Cobb's American League record.

June 11: Nolan Ryan of the Rangers pitched his sixth no-hitter, beating Oakland 5–0.

June 14: The National League announced plans to add two expansion teams for the 1993 season.

June 29: Oakland's Dave Stewart and Fernando Valenzuela of the Dodgers pitched no-hitters. Stewart defeated Toronto 5–0 and Valenzuela beat St. Louis 6–0.

July 30: Yankees' owner George Steinbrenner was banned from running the team by Commissioner Fay Vincent for conduct "not in the best interests of baseball."

July 31: Nolan Ryan won his 300th game, beating Milwaukee 11–3. He became the 20th pitcher to win 300 games.

Aug. 8: Baseball's all-time career hits leader, Pete Rose, began a five-month sentence for income tax evasion at a work camp in Marion, Illinois.

Aug. 15: Mark McGwire of Oakland hit his 30th homer, making him the first major league player to have at least 30 home runs in each of his first four seasons.

Sept. 8: Dave Stieb of the Toronto Blue Jays pitched a no-hitter against the Cleveland Indians. It was the first in Toronto history, but was also the ninth of the season, a major league record.

Sept. 30: The Pirates beat the Cardinals to clinch the National League East, their first title since 1979.

Oct. 3: Cecil Fielder of the Tigers hit home runs Nos. 50 and 51 against the Yankees. He became the first player in 13 years to hit at least 50.

The Houston Astros couldn't get any hitting and the Atlanta Braves couldn't do anything right, losing 97 games for the worst record in the majors.

After failing to reach the postseason throughout the 1980s, the Pittsburgh Pirates opened a new decade with their first National League East title since 1979. The Pirates had tried to trade Barry Bonds over the winter, but couldn't find a deal that made sense. They kept Bonds and were glad they did as he wound up the National League's Most Valuable Player. He hit .301 with 33 home runs, 114 RBIs, 104 runs and 52 stolen bases. Doug Drabek won the Cy Young award with a 22–6 record and 2.76 ERA. The Pirates' in-season acquisition of Zane Smith from Montreal was the last element they needed to move past the New York Mets. Randy Tomlin came up from Class AA after free agent Walt Terrell was a bust.

The Mets underachieved and were nearly overtaken by a rookie-laden Montreal Expos team. The failure cost Mets' manager Davey Johnson his job as he was replaced by coach Bud Harrelson.

Larry Walker, Marquis Grissom and Delino DeShields all broke in with Montreal and contributed to an 85-win season. The Cubs failed to repeat as division champions because their pitching failed. The St. Louis Cardinals were bad enough to make manager Whitey Herzog resign in July.

The Oakland A's took the American League West, leading the majors in wins for the third straight season. Pitching and defense carried the A's in a season that saw them tested by both injuries and the upstart Chicago White Sox. Bob Welch led the staff with 27 wins, the most in the league since Detroit's Denny McLain won 31 in 1968. Dave Stewart also won a career-best 22 games and posted his fourth straight 20-win season. Their combined total of 49 wins was the most by two teammates since Sandy Koufax and Don Drysdale won 49 for the 1965 Dodgers. Dennis Eckersley saved 48 games in 50 tries.

The White Sox ended 80 years at Comiskey Park by making a run at the title with the league's second-best record, 94–68. The White Sox had

an amazing crop of young talent—third baseman Robin Ventura, first baseman Frank Thomas, right fielder Sammy Sosa and pitcher Alex Fernandez.

The Texas Rangers couldn't overcome a poor start and finished third, 20 games behind Oakland.

The Boston Red Sox won the American League East with an 88–74 record that put them two games ahead of Toronto. Roger Clemens was 21–6 before a sore shoulder sidelined him for most of September. Mike Boddicker was 17–8. Greg Harris, whose chance came because of injuries, won 13 games. Wade Boggs led the team with a .302 average that was 50 points below his career average. He also failed to get 200 hits for the first time in nine seasons. Free agent catcher Tony Pena was an important addition and Ellis Burks had an exceptional year for the Red Sox.

The Blue Jays finished two games out for the third time in four years. All aspects of their game were inconsistent. Despite a second-half slump, Kelly Gruber had a career year with 31 home runs, 118 RBIs and a Gold Glove award. Fred McGriff led Toronto with 35 home runs.

Massive Cecil Fielder was the biggest story in Detroit. He returned from Japan to hit 51 home runs and drive in 132 runs. He was the first American League player to top 50 home runs since Roger Maris hit 61 for the 1961 New York Yankees.

The Cleveland Indians' offense was good enough, but their pitching wasn't. Sandy Alomar, acquired in a trade from San Diego, won the American League Rookie of the Year award.

After staging one of the biggest improvements in 1989, the Baltimore Orioles regressed, falling into fifth place. The Milwaukee Brewers saw their win total decline for a third straight year.

The Yankees lost 95 games, their largest total since 1912. The Yankees–Red Sox rivalry was one-sided as New York lost every game in Fenway Park. In typical Yankee fashion, there was a managerial change (Stump Merrill replaced Bucky Dent) and a change in general

Boston's Roger Clemens continued to overpower hitters finishing with a 21–6 record

A .302 average was good enough for Wade Boggs to lead the AL East champion Red Sox

managers (Gene Michael took over for Pete Peterson). The biggest development was the suspension Vincent imposed on owner George Steinbrenner for his involvement with a gambler. Technically, entertainment mogul Robert Nederlander became the Yankees' "Boss."

The root of the labor problems was economics. The owners called for a partnership with the Players Association that would earmark a prescribed percentage of revenues for player salaries. In exchange, the union would agree to a payroll cap. The owners also wanted a salary scale to be set for arbitration purposes.

The union, which had always rejected any limits on its members' earning power, wanted no part of the proposals. The Players Association charged that the owners had not presented evidence of a competitive imbalance brought on by differences in revenue.

For proof, the union could offer the 1990 season, as three small-revenue teams—Cincinnati, Pittsburgh and Oakland—were division winners while both New York teams failed miserably because of poor management of their resources.

The owners sustained another labor-related loss during the summer when more collusion cases were resolved in favor of players. The union charged that the owners conspired to quash the free agent market after the 1985, 1986 and 1987 seasons. The owners agreed to pay $280 million to the players who were free agents during those years. Fifteen players were also granted "new look" free agency. Among them were Jack Morris, Gary Gaetti, Jack Clark, Dave Henderson and Chili Davis.

The average salary of a major league player rose to $582,256.70 and that figure continued to rise. The pay scale got another jolt when Oakland broke new ground on a deal with Jose Canseco. He got a five-year extension worth $23.5 million.

The long, sad Tony Conigliaro story came to a tragic end on February 24 when the star-crossed outfielder died at 45 in a Boston hospital. Conigliaro had hit 24 home runs as a 19-year-old rookie with the Red Sox in 1964. His career was never the same after a pitch struck him in the face in 1967 and affected his vision.

1990 POSTSEASON

AL CHAMPIONSHIP SERIES

GAME 1	
Oakland 9	Boston Red Sox 1

GAME 2	
Oakland 4	Boston Red Sox 1

GAME 3	
Oakland 4	Boston Red Sox 1

GAME 4	
Oakland 3	Boston Red Sox 1

MVP: Dave Stewart, Oakland

NL CHAMPIONSHIP SERIES

GAME 1	
Pittsburgh 4	Cincinnati 3

GAME 2	
Cincinnati 2	Pittsburgh 1

GAME 3	
Cincinnati 6	Pittsburgh 3

GAME 4	
Cincinnati 5	Pittsburgh 3

GAME 5	
Pittsburgh 3	Cincinnati 2

GAME 6	
Cincinnati 2	Pittsburgh 1

MVP: Rob Dibble, Randy Myers, Cincinnati

WORLD SERIES

GAME 1	
Cincinnati 7	Oakland 0

GAME 2	
Cincinnati 5	Oakland 4

GAME 3	
Cincinnati 8	Oakland 3

GAME 4	
Cincinnati 2	Oakland 1

MVP: Jose Rijo, Cincinnati

The Cincinnati Reds' "Nasty Boys" were at their nastiest when it mattered most. Just when it appeared the Oakland Athletics were on the verge of repeating their 1970s dynasty, the Reds came along and eliminated them in a four-game sweep.

Oakland was fresh from its four-game sweep of San Francisco in the earthquake-interrupted 1989 World Series that took two weeks to complete.

The Reds were coming off a 1989 season that saw them finish next-to-last in the National League West, 12 games below .500 and 17 games out of first place.

Cincinnati had its first division-winning season since 1976, finishing five games in front of the Los Angeles Dodgers. Manager Lou Piniella developed a multiple-choice bullpen around a pair of hard-throwing young pitchers—Rob Dibble and Randy Myers. With Norm Charlton, who also spent time as a starter, they called themselves the "Nasty Boys," a tag that Myers seemed to particularly enjoy.

Cincinnati's playoff opponent was familiar. The Pittsburgh Pirates were back on top for the first time since they'd taken the 1979 World Series. After falling into the basement with consecutive 100-loss seasons, the Pirates had rebuilt and returned to prominence under manager Jim Leyland. Pittsburgh outlasted the New York Mets and posted a National League-leading 95 wins to get back to the playoffs.

Oakland had the widest margin of victory among the four division winners. The A's won the American League West by nine games over the Chicago White Sox and had the best record in the majors at 103–59.

The Boston Red Sox won the American League East by two games over the Toronto Blue Jays. Their .543 winning percentage was the lowest among the four division winners.

The Athletics didn't hit a home run in the playoffs but still knocked off the Red Sox in a four-game sweep. Boston's Roger Clemens left the opening game after six innings with a one-run lead. Oakland jumped on five relievers for nine runs in the last three innings and set a tone.

In the second game, Oakland scored three runs in the last three innings to win 4–1 and take a 2–0 lead in the series. The Athletics won the third game 4–1 and wrapped up the series with a 3–1 win behind Dave Stewart, who won his second game.

The National League playoffs were more competitive. Bob Walk pitched the Pirates to a 4–3 win in the opener but Cincinnati came back to beat Doug Drabek 2–1 to even the series. The Reds got home runs from unlikely sources—Billy Hatcher and Mariano Duncan—to win the third game 6–3. Dibble saved Jose Rijo's 5–3 win in the fifth game to put the Reds a game away from clinching. Drabek kept the Pirates alive by winning the fifth game 2–1.

Piniella's use of Glenn Braggs as

Hot pitching from Randy Myers in Game Four helped the Reds to a Series sweep

Billy Hatcher set a World Series record by making his debut with seven consecutive hits

a defensive replacement proved to be precisely the right move in the late innings of the sixth game. Braggs leaped up over the fence and robbed Carmelo Martinez of a two-run homer to save the Reds' 2–1 win. Myers nailed down the win for Charlton to send Cincinnati to the World Series.

After playing close games in the playoffs, the Reds broke loose for seven runs in the first five innings of Game One and Rijo beat Stewart 7–0. Eric Davis hit a two-run homer in the first inning and drove in three runs.

Oakland led Game Two 4–2 after three innings, roughing up starter Danny Jackson. It was 4–3 when A's right fielder Jose Canseco got a bad jump on a ball hit by Billy Hatcher that fell for a triple in the eighth. The Reds beat Dennis Eckersley in the 10th when Joe Oliver's grounder down the third-base line went for an RBI single. Pinch hitter Billy Bates and Chris

Sabo had opened the inning with singles off Eckersley.

The Series moved to Oakland and the Reds kept rolling. They scored seven runs in the third inning of Game Three against Scott Sanderson and won 8–3. Sabo hit two homers for the Reds.

Rijo and Myers combined on a two-hitter in Game Four and the Reds ended the Series with a 2-1 win. They swept Oakland the way their 1976 "Big Red Machine" had rolled through the New York Yankees in four games.

Heroes abounded for the Reds. Hatcher, who was acquired from Pittsburgh in a trade, batted .750 and set a record by making his Series debut with seven consecutive hits in the first two games. Rijo took Most Valuable Player honors with two wins and a 0.59 ERA. Neither Myers nor Dibble allowed a run in the postseason.

MOST VALUABLE PLAYER
AL: Cal Ripken Jr., Baltimore
NL: Terry Pendleton, Atlanta

CY YOUNG AWARD
AL: Roger Clemens, Boston Red Sox
NL: Tom Glavine, Atlanta

ROOKIE OF THE YEAR
AL: Chuck Knoblauch, Minnesota
NL: Jeff Bagwell, Houston

LEADERS
BATTING AVERAGE
AL: Julio Franco, Texas, .341
NL: Terry Pendleton, Atlanta, .319

HOME RUNS
AL: Jose Canseco, Oakland; Cecil Fielder, Detroit, 44; NL: Howard Johnson, NY Mets, 38

RUNS BATTED IN
AL: Cecil Fielder, Detroit, 133
NL: Howard Johnson, NY Mets, 117

STOLEN BASES
AL: Rickey Henderson, Oakland, 58
NL: Marquis Grisson, Montreal, 76

PITCHING VICTORIES
AL: Scott Erickson, Minnesota; Bill Gullickson, Detroit, 20; NL: Tom Glavine, Atlanta; John Smiley, Pittsburgh, 20

EARNED RUN AVERAGE
AL: Roger Clemens, Boston Red Sox, 2.62
NL: Dennis Martinez, Montreal, 2.39

STRIKEOUTS
AL: Roger Clemens, Boston Red Sox, 241
NL: David Cone, NY Mets, 241

SAVES
AL: Bryan Harvey, California, 46
NL: Lee Smith, St. Louis Cardinals, 47

It's unusual enough for a team to go from last to first in a single season, and even more unlikely to have two clubs do it in the same year. Yet that's exactly what happened in 1991, as both the Minnesota Twins and Atlanta Braves executed the "worst-to-first" scenario and advanced to the World Series.

Minnesota won the American League West with a league-best 95 wins. They needed them because the division was exceptionally tough. No team in the West finished with a record below .500. The Chicago White Sox were within one game of the Twins on August 10, but Minnesota wound up taking the division by 11 games over Oakland.

The Twins had an interesting mix. They brought pitcher Jack Morris back to his native state as a free agent. Chili Davis, another free agent signing, gave the lineup an experienced hitter. The Twins also signed Mike Pagliarulo. They were also able to work young players into their lineup, like pitcher Scott Erickson and second baseman Chuck Knoblauch.

The new faces combined with holdovers like Kent Hrbek and Kirby Puckett and the Twins had another successful season, thanks in part to the tremendous home-field advantage the Metrodome provided.

Tom Kelly was named Manager of the Year for his skill in bringing the elements together. The Twins had a team-record 15-game winning streak in June to help pull away from the pack.

Elsewhere in the West, the White Sox opened Comiskey Park and signed Bo Jackson, who had been cut loose by Kansas City after a hip injury jeopardized his two-sport career. The Royals, meanwhile, were disappointed by free agent Kirk Gibson, who batted just .236.

In Oakland, Mark McGwire hit 22 home runs and drove in 75 runs, but his average was a paltry .201. Seattle had its first winning record and Texas marked its third consecutive year over

Jack Morris helped his hometown Twins to an unlikely division crown

.500, thanks in large part to Ruben Sierra, who batted .307 with 25 homers and 116 RBIs.

The California Angels had a strong pitching staff led by a trio of lefthanders—Mark Langston was 19–8, Jim Abbott had an 18–11 record and Chuck Finley went 18–9.

Atlanta's rise could be traced to the improvement in its pitching staff. The Braves had been wisely stockpiling pitchers and enduring the tough seasons as those young pitchers took their lumps and got experience. They got better in 1991 and helped to carry the Braves into first place for the first time since 1982.

The Braves actually trailed by 9½ games at

SHORTS The Expos could have put their home uniforms in storage in early September. They were forced to play their final 26 games on the road after a 55-ton cement beam fell from Olympic Stadium. No one was injured and the Expos went 13–13 on the trip that started September 9 and continued through October 6.

Kirby Puckett and the Twins had a fairytale season going from worst to first in the West

the All-Star break, but charged to the top and resisted the challenge of the Los Angeles Dodgers down the stretch. An eight-game winning streak that ran from September 27 to October 5 allowed the Braves to eliminate the Dodgers one day before the season ended.

Four of the Braves' starters accounted for 67 of the team's 94 wins as Atlanta became the first National League team to follow a last-place season with a championship. Tom Glavine, who had been drafted by hockey's Los Angeles Kings, showed that he made the correct career choice by winning 20 games and taking the National League Cy Young award.

The other two division winners were more familiar with the postseason scene. The Toronto Blue Jays took the American League East for the second time in three years and the Pittsburgh Pirates claimed their second consecutive National League East title.

Toronto won 15 of 18 just before the All-Star break and succeeded in holding off both Detroit and Boston in September. Injuries to No. 1 starter Dave Stieb and reliever Tom Henke caused some problems. Third baseman Kelly Gruber also lost time to an injury.

The Blue Jays' front office made an excellent trade, getting outfielder Joe Carter and second baseman Roberto Alomar from the San Diego Padres. Carter batted .273 with 33 home runs and 108 RBIs while Alomar hit .295 and stole 53 bases. Devon White came over from the California Angels and batted .282 with 111 runs and 33 steals.

With Stieb limited to nine games, Jimmy Key went 16–12 while Todd Stottlemyre and David Wells each won 15 games. Duane Ward had 23 saves to go with Henke's 32. The Blue Jays wound up seven games ahead of Boston.

The Pirates became the first National League team to repeat since both the Philadelphia Phillies and Los Angeles Dodgers in 1977–78. Pitcher Doug Drabek and left fielder Barry Bonds both got off to slow starts but played key roles.

Bonds had a .292 average with 25 home runs, 116 RBIs and 43 stolen bases. Drabek wound up 15–14, but his 3.07 ERA was the staff's best, even though John Smiley (20–8) and Zane Smith (20–10) had more wins. The Pirates lacked the dominant closer most championship teams have, but manager Jim Leyland split the duties between Bill Landrum (17 saves) and Stan Belinda (16). When third baseman Jeff King was sidelined with a back injury, Pittsburgh acquired Steve Buechele from Texas. The Pirates were the National League's best road team with a record

The Braves' Tom Glavine was a 20-game winner as Atlanta triumphed in a tight division race

the lowest figure for a Cardinals' leader since 1920. No St. Louis pitcher won more than 12 games.

The Chicago Cubs couldn't close games—their 27 blown saves were a National League high. The Cubs also suffered with a couple of free agent pitching busts—starter Danny Jackson and reliever Dave Smith.

Howard Johnson was a positive force for the New York Mets with 38 home runs and 30 stolen bases. Mostly, though, the Mets suffered under the weak leadership of manager Bud Harrelson, who did nothing when Vince Coleman challenged the authority of coach Mike Cubbage on July 26. Later, Harrelson admitted he sent pitching coach Mel Stottlemyre to make a pitching change because he knew the crowd would boo him if he stepped onto the field.

Montreal finished last, but had the league ERA leader in Dennis Martinez (2.39).

Houston's chances to compete in the West were severely limited after former 20-game winner Mike Scott failed to come back from rotator cuff surgery. Scott appeared in just two games and announced his retirement before the end of the season.

There were eight no-hitters during a season in which new guidelines were issued for defining an official no-hit game. The decision was that a game had to have ended with the pitcher allowing no hits. That eliminated a game like the one Montreal's Mark Gardner pitched against Los Angeles on July 26.

Gardner didn't allow a hit through nine innings, but gave up one in the tenth and lost 1–0. Not only was it not a victory, it also wasn't a no-hitter. The ruling also wiped off the books the 12 perfect innings Pittsburgh's Harvey Haddix pitched against Milwaukee in 1959.

Nolan Ryan pitched his seventh no-hitter, Montreal's Martinez pitched the 15th perfect game in major league history and three Atlanta pitchers had the National League's first combined nine-inning no-hitter.

The only thing more frequent than no-hitters in 1991 was managerial changes. Twelve clubs decided to make a change, beginning on April 23, when the Philadelphia Phillies dumped Nick Leyva in favor of Jim Fregosi. It was the second-

of 46–32.

The Pirates didn't have much competition in the East aside from the Cardinals and they finished 14 games ahead of second-place St. Louis. The Cardinals didn't have much offensive firepower, a deficiency demonstrated by this fact—Todd Zeile's 11 home runs led the team,

SHORTS The Kansas City Royals decided Bo Jackson's baseball career was over. Bo knew better. Despite a devastating hip injury he sustained while playing football for the Oakland Raiders, Jackson was able to return to baseball on Sept. 2 for the Chicago White Sox, who signed him in January after the Royals released him.

The Expos' Dennis Martinez threw a perfect game in July, retiring the Dodgers in order

fastest change in major league history.

There were three changes in three days in May as the Cubs dropped Don Zimmer, the Kansas City Royals axed John Wathan and the Baltimore Orioles released Frank Robinson. That was topped at the end of the season when four changes were made in four days as the New York Yankees canned Stump Merrill, the Red Sox fired Joe Morgan, the Milwaukee Brewers said goodbye to Tom Treblehorn and the Seattle Mariners fired Jim Lefebvre.

In another statistical ruling, Commissioner Fay Vincent decided that the game should only have one single-season home run record. So Babe Ruth's mark of 60 home runs in a 154-game schedule in 1927 disappeared and the official record was the 61 Roger Maris hit in the first 162-game schedule in 1961.

Denver and Miami each paid $95 million to join the National League in 1993 and began scouting operations to assemble their first teams.

Jim Palmer tried to return to the Baltimore Orioles' pitching staff just one year after his first work in that role earned him a spot in the Hall of Fame. Palmer, left unfulfilled because his career had ended with an injury, decided to try a comeback. He gave up after one spring appearance, but the effort landed him plenty of publicity, which helped his second career as a television personality and product pitchman.

Real-life tragedy played out on September 2 when American League umpire Steve Palermo was shot and wounded. Palermo and some friends were at a restaurant when they tried to thwart a robbery. Shots were fired and Palermo was struck in the spinal cord, partially paralyzing him and bringing an instant end to his umpiring career.

AL CHAMPIONSHIP SERIES:

GAME 1	
Minnesota 5	Toronto 4

GAME 2	
Toronto 5	Minnesota 2

GAME 3	
Minnesota 3	Toronto 2

GAME 4	
Minnesota 9	Toronto 3

GAME 5	
Minnesota 8	Toronto 5

MVP: Kirby Puckett, Minnesota.

NL CHAMPIONSHIP SERIES

GAME 1	
Pittsburgh 5	Atlanta 1

GAME 2	
Atlanta 1	Pittsburgh 0

GAME 3	
Atlanta 10	Pittsburgh 3

GAME 4	
Pittsburgh 3	Atlanta 2

GAME 5	
Pittsburgh 1	Atlanta 0

GAME 6	
Atlanta 1	Pittsburgh 0

GAME 7	
Atlanta 4	Pittsburgh 0

MVP: Steve Avery, Atlanta.

WORLD SERIES:

GAME 1	
Minnesota 5	Atlanta 2

GAME 2	
Minnesota 3	Atlanta 2

GAME 3	
Atlanta 5	Minnesota 4

GAME 4	
Atlanta 3	Minnesota 2

GAME 5	
Atlanta 14	Minnesota 5

GAME 6	
Minnesota 4	Atlanta 3

GAME 7	
Minnesota 1	Atlanta 0

MVP: Jack Morris, Minnesota.

Worst to first. The Minnesota Twins made the stunning transition by winning the American League West, knocking off the Toronto Blue Jays in the playoffs, then defeating the favored Atlanta Braves in the World Series.

The Twins prevailed in a surprisingly tough division, where no team had a losing record. Even the last-place California Angels finished at .500. Minnesota ended the Oakland Athletics' three-year run of division titles and did it with an interesting mix.

At the core of the team were homegrown stars like Kirby Puckett and Kent Hrbek. Young players like Scott Erickson and Chuck Knoblauch were added and the Twins pursued several free agents, including native son Jack Morris. When the season ended, the Twins had an American League-best 95 wins and had become the first team in league history to vault from last place to first in consecutive seasons.

Toronto was challenged by several key injuries, but prevailed to take their second American League East title in three years. The Blue Jays reaped the benefits of a shrewd trade that saw them acquire Joe Carter and Roberto

Kirby Puckett's dramatic game-winning dinger kept the Twins' dream alive

Alomar from the San Diego Padres.

The Atlanta Braves had a Twins-like rise, moving from bottom to top in a single season. Led by a formidable young starting staff, the Braves took the National League West, edging the Los Angeles Dodgers by a game. The Braves came back from a 9½-game midseason deficit to overtake the Dodgers.

The Pittsburgh Pirates won their second consecutive National League East title. They took over first place on April 20 and became the first National League team to repeat since the Philadelphia Phillies and Dodgers in 1978.

Minnesota needed only five games to win the championship series against the Blue Jays. The teams split the first two games before the Twins won three straight in Toronto.

Morris won the opener 5–4 with relief from Rick Aguilera. Toronto bounced back to take the second game 5–2 behind Juan Guzman. Mike Pagliarulo swung the series in the Twins' favor with a game-winning homer off Mike Timlin in the tenth inning of the third game. Aguilera closed out the 3–2 win for his second save.

Morris won the fourth game 9–3 and Hrbek's two-run single keyed a three-run eighth inning and an 8–5 win in the fifth game.

The National League series went to the limit before the Braves' dominating pitching gave Atlanta its first World Series. The Pirates won the opener 5–1 behind Doug Drabek. Steve Avery and Alejandro Pena combined on a six-hit, 1–0 shutout in the second game, making ex-Brave Zane Smith a hard-luck loser.

The Braves beat up 20-game winner John Smiley for a 10–3 win in the third game as Ron Gant, Greg Olson and Sid Bream homered. Pittsburgh tied the series with a 3–2 win in ten innings in the fourth game.

The teams traded 1–0 games with the Pirates winning the fifth behind Smith and Roger Mason and losing the sixth to Avery and Pena. Brian Hunter hit a three-run homer off Smiley in the first inning of the seventh game and the Braves won 4–0 behind Smoltz. Atlanta held the Pirates to one run over the last 27 innings.

Greg Gagne's three-run homer helped Morris to a 5–2 win in Game One. The Twins took a 2–0 lead in games when Scott Leius hit a tiebreaking home run off Tom Glavine in the eighth for a 3–2 win preserved by Aguilera.

Aguilera lost Game Three when he surrendered a two-out single to Mark Lemke in the 12th inning. Lemke was the central figure in Game Four when he tripled in the ninth and scored the winning run on Jerry Willard's fly ball.

After three tight games, Atlanta broke out with 17 hits and a 14–5 win in Game Five.

The Series shifted back to Minnesota for the final two games and it was back to the familiar format of close games. The Twins stayed alive, winning Game Six 4–3 in the 11th inning when Puckett homered off Charlie Leibrandt.

Morris and Smoltz had a scoreless duel in Game Seven. Smoltz left in the eighth, but Morris stayed and became the winning pitcher when Gene Larkin singled in the game's only run in the tenth inning.

MOST VALUABLE PLAYER
AL: Dennis Eckersley, Oakland
NL: Barry Bonds, Pittsburgh

CY YOUNG AWARD
AL: Dennis Eckersley, Oakland
NL: Greg Maddux, Chicago Cubs

ROOKIE OF THE YEAR
AL: Pat Listach, Milwaukee
NL: Eric Karros, Los Angeles

LEADERS

BATTING AVERAGE
AL: Edgar Martinez, Seattle, .343
NL: Gary Sheffield, San Diego, .330

HOME RUNS
AL: Juan Gonzalez, Texas, 43
NL: Fred McGriff, San Diego, 35

RUNS BATTED IN
AL: Cecil Fielder, Detroit, 124
NL: Darren Daulton, Philadelphia Phillies, 109

STOLEN BASES
AL: Kenny Lofton, Cleveland, 66
NL: Marquis Grisson, Montreal, 78

PITCHING VICTORIES
AL: Kevin Brown, Texas; Jack Morris, Toronto, 21
NL: Tom Glavine, Atlanta; Greg Maddux, Chicago Cubs, 20

ERA
AL: Roger Clemens, Boston Red Sox, 2.41
NL: Bill Swift, San Francisco, 2.08

STRIKEOUTS
AL: Randy Johnson, Seattle, 241
NL: John Smoltz, Atlanta, 215

SAVES
AL: Dennis Eckersley, Oakland, 51
NL: Lee Smith, St. Louis Cardinals, 43

The World Series moved north of the border and the game moved forward without a Commissioner.

After winning their third American League East title in four years, the Toronto Blue Jays finally made it to the World Series. But the space reserved for the facsimile signature of the Commissioner on the official World Series baseball was blank. Fay Vincent, who had stepped in following the sudden death of A. Bartlett Giamatti in 1989, was forced to resign from the job as a season-long soap opera played out behind the scenes.

First, the Blue Jays. To overcome their past postseason failures, they invested in experience. They added pitcher Jack Morris and outfielder-designated hitter Dave Winfield, hoping that players with experience would help take them to the next level.

Toronto won six games at the start of the season to reestablish a winning attitude. When the Blue Jays weren't leading the East, they were never more than half a game from first place. A key trade with San Diego helped as Toronto was able to acquire outfielder Joe Carter and second baseman Roberto Alomar. Late in the season, when Milwaukee was charging toward the top, the Blue Jays traded for New York Mets' starter David Cone, another experienced arm.

The acquisitions couldn't have worked out better. Carter hit 34 home runs and drove in 119 runs. Alomar batted .310 with 76 RBIs and provided exceptional defense. Winfield batted .290 with 26 home runs and 108 RBIs, becoming the first player in baseball history to

drive in at least 100 runs past the age of 40. The team went 23–11 after Cone joined the pitching staff.

Tom Henke was solid in the bullpen, converting 34 of his 37 save opportunities. The whole of Toronto loved the Blue Jays as the team set a record with attendance over four million, including 68 sellouts out of the 81 home dates.

Milwaukee's late rush fell short as the Brewers went 21–7 from September 1 to October 1 to get within one. The Brewers caught a spark when Cal Eldred came up from the minor leagues and went 11–2 with a 1.79 earned run average.

Elsewhere in the East, Baltimore was a half game behind the Blue Jays on September 5, but the Orioles couldn't inaugurate Camden Yards with any postseason games. Mike Devereaux hit 24 home runs and drove in 107 runs. Mike Mussina was 18–5 to lead the league with a .783 winning percentage and had a 2.54 ERA. Brady Anderson stepped up with 21 home runs, 75 RBIs and 50 stolen bases. Reliever Alan Mills was 10–4 with a 2.61 ERA. The Orioles opened their new retro park with a 10–1 record, the best record any club had posted in a new venue. Overall, the Orioles' 89–73 record represented a 22-game improvement.

The Boston Red Sox had their first last-place finish in 60 years. The Red Sox lost 13 of 17 in September. The bright spot, though, was Roger Clemens, who won 18 games and had a 15–4 record when he pitched after a Boston loss.

The New York Yankees ran into trouble when reliever Steve Howe was suspended for the seventh time for violating substance abuse policies.

The Detroit Tigers made sweeping changes, which included the firing of general manager Jim Campbell, who had worked for the team since 1949. The Cleveland Indians managed a 19-game improvement as Carlos Baerga topped .300 in average, the 20-home run mark and had more than 100 RBIs and runs scored. Baerga collected 205 hits. Kenny Lofton led the league with 66 stolen bases and became the

Faye Vincent's unpopularity forced his resignation—leaving baseball without a commissioner

SHORTS The Pirates were ready to release minor league first baseman Tim Wakefield because of his weak bat. But minor league manager Woody Huyke remembered that Wakefield threw a knuckleball and suggested they try him as a pitcher. Smart call. Wakefield helped the Pirates win their division and had two wins in the playoffs.

The Orioles' new ballpark, Camden Yards, provided a stunning canvas for its resurgent team

T I M E L I N E

March 17: The Pirates, struggling financially despite consecutive National League East titles, traded 20-game winner John Smiley to Minnesota for two prospects.

April 6: The first retro-styled new ballpark opened. The Orioles beat Cleveland 2–0 in the first game at Camden Yards.

April 12: Matt Young of the Red Sox pitched a no-hitter against Cleveland and lost 2–1. He became the third pitcher in major league history to pitch a complete game no-hitter and lose.

May 21: Angels' manager Buck Rodgers was seriously injured when the team's bus crashed on the New Jersey Turnpike while making a trip from New York to Baltimore.

May 22: Felipe Alou became the first Dominican to manage in the majors when Montreal hired him to replace Tom Runnells.

May 27: The Braves started a stretch of 41 wins in 56 games that would carry Atlanta to a second consecutive National League West title.

July 31: The Pirates called up rookie Tim Wakefield from the minor leagues and the knuckleball specialist went 8–1 in his first major league experience.

Aug. 31: Oakland traded Jose Canseco to Texas in a four-player deal.

Sept. 7: Fay Vincent resigned as baseball commissioner after a vote of no-confidence from the owners.

Sept. 9: Robin Yount of the Brewers got his 3,000th career hit.

Sept. 27: Phillies second baseman Mickey Morandini was credited with the ninth unassisted triple play in major league history. It was the National League's first since 1927.

Sept. 30: Kansas City's George Brett collected his 3,000th career hit.

Oct. 6: Lou Piniella resigned as Reds' manager.

Oct. 22: Legendary announcer Red Barber died at 84 in Tallahassee, Florida.

Nov. 17: The expansion draft was conducted to stock the Florida Marlins and Colorado Rockies.

first rookie to lead the league since 1956.

The Oakland A's claimed their fourth American League West title in five years, but had to overcome a run of injuries to win 96 games. The A's took over first place on August 5 and stayed there the rest of the season. Minnesota had led by two games at the All-Star break with a 53–34 record, but the Twins went just 37–38 after the break and wound up six games behind Oakland.

The A's wound up using 45 different players, including 22 pitchers and 15 outfielders. Some of the changes were voluntary, like the big trade with Texas that happened after Jose Canseco wore out his welcome with the A's. Oakland got Ruben Sierra, Bobby Witt and Jeff Russell in return for Canseco, who had been half of the A's "Bash Brothers."

The A's had to deal with extended injury absences to Dave Henderson, Rickey Henderson, Walt Weiss, Bob Welch, Dave Stewart and Mark McGwire. McGwire missed time with a muscle strain and finished with 42 homers, second to league-leader Juan Gonzalez. In all, Oakland placed 16 players on the disabled list for a total of 22 assignments.

Mike Moore won 17 games and Ron Darling pitched three two-hitters. The workhorse of the staff was closer Dennis Eckersley, who had 51 saves and didn't fail on a save opportunity until August 8. Pitchers usually don't win the Most Valuable Player award and relievers hardly ever win the Cy Young award. Eckersley took both honors.

The Twins had the best record in the majors at 60–38 near the end of July. They led the West by three games. From August 4 to 20, though, they lost five straight games to last-place teams. Kirby Puckett led Minnesota with a .329 average, 110 RBIs and 109 runs. John Smiley, picked up in a spring training trade from Pittsburgh, eased the loss of Morris by winning 16 games.

Seattle lost 14 straight games at the end of the season to tumble into last place.

The California Angels were just happy to be alive after a frightening bus crash on their way from New York to Baltimore in April. Manager Buck Rodgers missed 100 games to recover from his injuries and coach John Wathan filled in. Frank Thomas had a big year for the Chicago White Sox, becoming the first player to top .300, 20 home runs, 100 RBIs, 100 runs and 100 walks.

The Kansas City Royals started the season 1–16 and were 10½ games out before the end of April.

The Pirates won the National League East again, despite the free agent departure of Bobby Bonilla and the financially-motivated trade of Smiley, who had been a 20-game winner the previous season. The Pirates won their third straight title, matching the streak they'd had from 1970–72. They were out of first place for eight days in May, otherwise they had a comfortable ride. Barry Bonds won the MVP award for the second time in three years

Dennis Eckersley's 51-save season was rewarded with both MVP and Cy Young honors

with a .311 average, 34 home runs and 103 RBIs. Andy Van Slyke hit .324 and led the league with 45 doubles.

The big story for Pittsburgh was the emergence of knuckleball specialist Tim Wakefield, a converted first baseman who came up and went 8–1 with a 2.15 ERA.

The New York Mets took a run at the Pirates that ended in August when they went to Pittsburgh trailing by 5½ games. They lost 12 out of 13 and fell 14½ back. Dwight Gooden had his first losing record at 10–13. St. Louis lost eight games to Pittsburgh in back-to-back weekends and fell from 4½ behind to 12 behind.

The Philadelphia Phillies acquired Curt Schilling from Houston, hoping he'd help in middle relief. He won 14 games, had a 2.35 ERA and became their No. 1 starter.

Atlanta's strong pitching helped the Braves to both a franchise-record 98 wins and a second straight Western Division title. Tom Glavine won 13 straight en route to his second 20-win season. Terry Pendleton hit .311 with 21 home runs and 105 RBIs. The Braves went 41–15 from May 27 to August 2 to move from last to first.

The National League expansion teams chose managers as they prepared to debut in 1993. Florida hired Rene Lachemann and Colorado picked Don Baylor.

Cincinnati Reds' owner Marge Schott got into trouble for allegedly making racist comments. Lou Piniella had his fill of the Reds and resigned as manager at the end of the season. The Giants threatened to move to St. Petersburg once San Francisco didn't seem interested in building them a new stadium.

Robin Yount and George Brett each got their 3,000th career hit. Bonilla's new contract with the Mets was a record-setter—five years and $29 million. Overall, the average salary topped $1 million.

Everyone, it seemed, had a better year than the beleaguered Vincent. He opened the season by sizing up the game thus: "We need about five major miracles in baseball."

The owners were already angry with Vincent because some of them believed he overstepped his authority in bringing an end to the 1990 spring training lockout. Vincent also backed a proposed realignment of the National League that earned him more enemies.

He upheld a geographically-logical move that would have put St. Louis in Chicago in the West while moving Atlanta and Cincinnati to the East. Pressure on Vincent increased, prompting him to say on August 20, "I will not resign—ever."

On September 7, Vincent submitted his resignation.

The Pirates' Barry Bonds led the Bucs to their third straight division title

AL CHAMPIONSHIP SERIES	
GAME 1	
Oakland 4	Toronto 3
GAME 2	
Toronto 3	Oakland 1
GAME 3	
Toronto 7	Oakland 5
GAME 4	
Toronto 7	Oakland 6
GAME 5	
Oakland 6	Toronto 2
GAME 6	
Toronto 9	Oakland 2

NL CHAMPIONSHIP SERIES	
GAME 1	
Atlanta 5	Pittsburgh 1
GAME 2	
Atlanta 13	Pittsburgh 5
GAME 3	
Pittsburgh 13	Atlanta 2
GAME 4	
Atlanta 6	Pittsburgh 4
GAME 5	
Pittsburgh 7	Atlanta 1
GAME 6	
Pittsburgh 13	Atlanta 4
GAME 7	
Atlanta 3	Pittsburgh 2

WORLD SERIES	
GAME 1	
Atlanta 3	Toronto 1
GAME 2	
Toronto 5	Atlanta 4
GAME 3	
Toronto 3	Atlanta 2
GAME 4	
Toronto 2	Atlanta 1
GAME 5	
Atlanta 7	Toronto 2
GAME 6	
Toronto 4	Atlanta 3

The Toronto Blue Jays were no strangers to postseason play but the World Series remained uncharted territory for them.

The Blue Jays had first won the American League East in 1985, the franchise's ninth season. They lost the playoffs to the eventual World Series champion, Kansas City. The Blue Jays followed the same pattern two more times: they lost the 1989 playoffs to Oakland and fell to Minnesota in 1991. In both cases, the team that beat the Blue Jays would win the World Series.

This time Toronto had won the division by the slimmest margin of the four postseason teams. The Blue Jays finished four games ahead of Milwaukee. After a one-year hiatus, Oakland was back on top of the American League West, winning the division by six games over Minnesota. The Blue Jays and Oakland had identical 96–66 records.

The National League featured a return matchup of its 1991 postseason teams. Atlanta won the West by eight games over Cincinnati. The Braves' 98–64 record was the best in baseball. In the East, the Pittsburgh Pirates took their third straight title despite losing Bobby Bonilla as a free agent and trading 20-game winner John Smiley for financial reasons.

The series between Oakland and Toronto went six games and turned in the Blue Jays' favor in the fourth game. Trailing 2–1 in games and 6–1 in this particular game, the Blue Jays rallied for five runs in the last two innings to force extra innings.

The tying rally came against Oakland closer Dennis Eckersley and was capped by Roberto Alomar's game-tying two-run homer in the ninth inning. The series that appeared to be headed

Pat Borders was the home run hero in Game Four to give the Blue Jays the edge

to a 2–2 tie instead was a 3–1 advantage for the Blue Jays and Toronto caught a spark from the stirring comeback.

The Athletics won the fifth game 6–2 as Dave Stewart beat David Cone. Toronto scored six runs in the first three innings of the sixth game and turned that early lead into a series-clinching 9-2 win behind Juan Guzman.

Alomar hit .423 with two home runs and Candy Maldonado also had two homers with six RBIs. Guzman won two games with a 2.08 earned run average.

The National League series went the limit before the Braves staged a ninth-inning comeback that would be long remembered in both cities.

John Smoltz pitched Atlanta to a 5–1 win in the opener and the Braves got 14 hits against seven Pirates pitchers to take the second game 13-5. Rookie knuckleball specialist Tim Wakefield saved the Pirates in the third game with a 3-2 complete game win.

Atlanta took a commanding 3–1 lead in the series by winning the fourth game 6–4. Smoltz beat Doug Drabek for the second time with relief help from Jeff Reardon.

Bob Walk kept Pittsburgh in the series by defeating Steve Avery 7–1 in the fifth game. The series went back to Atlanta and Wakefield forced a seventh game with a 13–4 win that featured home runs by Barry Bonds, Jay Bell and Lloyd McClendon.

The Braves were trailing 2–0 entering the ninth inning of the seventh game when they staged one of the most memorable comebacks in postseason history. The game ended when pinch hitter Francisco Cabrera lined a two-run single to left to give the Braves a 3–2 win.

In the World Series, Game Two would prove to be pivotal.

Atlanta won Game One 3–1 behind Glavine and Damon Berryhill's three-run homer. The Blue Jays scored twice in the ninth inning for a 5–4 win in Game Two. Braves closer Reardon was protecting a 4–3 lead when he walked pinch hitter Derek Bell. He then served up a home run to Ed Sprague. Tom Henke pitched the bottom of the ninth for the save. The Series was even but had turned in Toronto's favor.

Kelly Gruber's eighth-inning homer tied the score in Game Three and the Blue Jays went on to win 3–2 with a run in the ninth. Toronto took a 3–1 lead in the Series with a 2–1 win in Game Four. Jimmy Key, Duane Ward and Tom Henke combined on a five-hitter and Pat Borders hit a home run.

John Smoltz pitched well, but it wasn't enough for the Braves

The Braves postponed their demise with a 7–2 win in Game Five. John Smoltz beat Jack Morris and the Braves got home runs from David Justice and Lonnie Smith.

Dave Winfield hit a two-run double in the 11th inning of Game Six and Mike Timlin closed down a Braves' rally in the bottom of the inning for a 4–3 win.

Key won two games and had a 1.00 ERA. Borders batted .450 and Joe Carter had two home runs. Deion Sanders batted .533 for the Braves.

NOLAN RYAN

It always seemed like Nolan Ryan had more up his sleeve than a powerful right arm.

Buy a ticket for a game when Ryan pitched and there might be a special bonus: one of the seven no-hitters or another of his record-setting strikeout performances.

Said Pete Rose, "He's the only guy in baseball who is capable of a no-hitter every time he takes the mound."

Ryan was capable of games that made bats mere props for hitters who had no chance to catch up his fastball. He faced 22,575 batters in his career and got a third strike on more than a fourth of them. Detroit's Norm Cash strode to the plate with a table leg instead of a bat, his commentary on the futility of trying to hit Ryan.

Ryan came to the major leagues from tiny Alvin, Texas as part of an arms stockpile by the New York Mets in the mid-1960s. The Mets decided to build with pitching and their scouts had a knack for finding talent.

Like a lot of young pitchers, Ryan struggled with his control. But his arsenal was so impressive that the Mets brought him to the major leagues as a 19-year-old in 1966.

He went to the mound with a wicked fastball and a ranch hand's work ethic: "I went out with the intention of completing every game I started and was disappointed in myself when I didn't."

Ryan was there when the 1969 Miracle Mets upset the Baltimore Orioles in the World Series. He considers the last pitch of Game Three the single most memorable pitch in his long career. Within two years, both Ryan and the Mets had soured on the relationship.

Country boy Ryan disliked New York and reportedly Mets manager Gil Hodges had decided that Ryan would never be a consistent winner. The Mets packaged Ryan and three other players to the California Angels to get third baseman Jim Fregosi.

Ryan won 19 games in his first season with the Angels and his career blossomed in California. He easily surpassed his modest goal of lasting four years in the major leagues to qualify for the players' pension fund.

He took advantage when free agency came to baseball and moved closer to home. The Houston Astros signed Ryan in 1979 and made him the first player to break the barrier of $1 million per season in salary.

The attention distracted him and Ryan's start with the Astros was rocky.

"I felt more pressure and I felt that was counterproductive," Ryan said.

Ryan got even better in Houston, developing a change-up to augment the overpowering fastball and average curve that had already made him a elite pitcher. Ryan was something of a marvel, a power pitcher who didn't have to make compromises to advancing age.

"He has bone chips that are older than some of his teammates," said Todd Jones, another Houston pitcher.

Ryan's career strikeout list included father and son combinations. That's what happens when a pitcher is able to stick around for 27 years.

After a messy breakup with the Astros, Ryan signed with the Texas Rangers and achieved some important milestones in their uniform. He won his 300th game and pitched his final no-hitter for Texas. He retired in 1993 after a farewell tour through the American League that included regular autograph requests from opposing players.

When he pitched the sixth of his seven no-hitters at age 43, Oakland pitcher Dave Stewart said, "We had an old-timers' day here last weekend and some of the players there were younger than Nolan."

Ryan retired after the 1993 season and was elected to the Hall of Fame on the first ballot.

His Hall of Fame plaque doesn't have room for his pragmatic summation of a career notable for its excellence and longevity: "I always wanted my teammates to feel that on the night I pitched, we had a chance to win and I was going to give my best effort. I wanted the fans to feel when they walked out of the park on the night I pitched that they were glad they came and felt like it was worth their effort and expense to come to the game."

From Alvin, Texas to Cooperstown, New York

MOST VALUABLE PLAYER
AL: Frank Thomas, Chicago White Sox
NL: Barry Bonds, San Francisco

CY YOUNG AWARD
AL: Jack McDowell, Chicago White Sox
NL: Greg Maddux, Atlanta

ROOKIE OF THE YEAR
AL: Tim Salmon, California
NL: Mike Piazza, Los Angeles

LEADERS
BATTING AVERAGE
AL: John Olerud, Toronto, .363
NL: Andres Galarraga, Colorado, .370

HOME RUNS
AL: Juan Gonzalez, Texas, 46
NL: Barry Bonds, San Francisco, 46

RUNS BATTED IN
AL: Albert Belle, Cleveland, 129
NL: Barry Bonds, San Francisco, 123

STOLEN BASES
AL: Kenny Lofton, Cleveland, 70
NL: Chuck Carr, Florida, 58

PITCHING VICTORIES
AL: Jack McDowell, Chicago White Sox, 22
NL: Tom Glavine, Atlanta; John Burkett, San Francisco, 22

EARNED RUN AVERAGE
AL: Kevin Appier, Kansas City, 2.76
NL: Greg Maddux, Atlanta, 2.36

STRIKEOUTS
AL: Randy Johnson, Seattle, 308
NL: Jose Rijo, Cincinnati, 227

SAVES
AL: Jeff Montgomery, Kansas City; Duane Ward, Toronto, 45; NL: Randy Myers, Chicago Cubs, 53

There's nothing like first love and it was in full bloom in the two newest National League cities.

Southern Florida embraced the Marlins and Colorado was high on its Rockies as the league had its first expansion since 1969.

Both teams won their home openers and both avoided finishing in last place, which is a significant accomplishment for a first-year team cobbled together from other clubs' castoffs.

The Marlins drew 3,064,847 fans. Colorado was even better. The one million mark, once a season goal for most teams, was topped after just 17 home dates. The Rockies drew a major league record 4,483,350 fans, becoming the first team in major league history to break four million. Miami and Denver had everything except a pennant race.

The Toronto Blue Jays took the American League East title overcoming a slow start. Toronto was a game below .500 and 4½ games behind Detroit on May 1. Part of that could be traced to the absence of pitcher Dave Stewart, who spent the first month on the disabled list. Stewart had been one of the Blue Jays' most important offseason acquisitions.

Toronto finally reached first place on June 26. The Blue Jays were either in first place or tied for it consistently from July 20. The New York Yankees were able to tie the Blue Jays on September 9. Toronto won 17 of 21 at the end and finished seven games in front.

John Olerud led the league with a .363 average and had a .400 average until August 2. Joe Carter drove in 121 runs, Paul Molitor had 111 RBIs and Olerud knocked in 107. For the first time in major league history the top three hitters in a league batting race were all from the same team. Molitor (.332) and Roberto Alomar (.326) followed Olerud. Pat Hentgen led the pitching staff with 19 wins and Duane Ward had 45 saves.

The Yankees managed an 88–74 record, which ended a streak of four consecutive losing seasons. The Baltimore Orioles went 3–6 on their last trip to fall out of the race. Catcher Chris Hoiles had a big season with a .310 average, 29 home runs and 82 RBIs.

The Boston Red Sox enjoyed a 25–5 streak

The Blue Jays' John Olerud won the AL batting title with an impressive .363 average

from June 21 to July 25 and moved into a tie for first. A 3–9 homestand in mid-August was costly. Mo Vaughn led the Red Sox with a .297 average, 29 home runs and 101 RBIs even though the weak Boston offense offered him very little protection.

Roger Clemens' worst season was also a factor in the Red Sox slide. He was 11–14 with a 4.46 ERA. A bright spot was the return of Mike Greenwell from elbow surgery.

Cleveland never seemed to recover from the spring training boating accident that killed pitchers Steve Olin and Tim Crews and seriously injured Bob Ojeda.

The Indians played their final season in massive Municipal Stadium on Lake Erie. Albert Belle hit .290 with 38 home runs and a league-leading 129 RBIs. Kenny Lofton batted .325 and stole 70 bases while scoring 116 runs.

The Chicago White Sox won the American League West, their first title since 1983. The

SHORTS A rare day off in spring training turned into tragedy for the Indians on March 22. Pitchers Steve Olin and Tim Crews were killed and another pitcher, Bob Ojeda, was seriously injured in a boating accident. The incident devastated the team. Ojeda was able to return in August but was never the same pitcher.

Albert Belle hit 38 home runs as the Cleveland Indians waved goodbye to Municipal Stadium

TIMELINE

Feb. 3: Reds owner Marge Schott was suspended and fined $25,000 for making racially insensitive remarks.

Feb. 11: Nolan Ryan announced his retirement, to become effective at the end of the season.

April 15: Sparky Anderson of the Tigers recorded his 2,000th career win as a manager.

April 27: Two-time Most Valuable Player Dale Murphy announced his retirement after less than a month with the Colorado Rockies.

April 28: Chris Bosio of Seattle pitched a no-hitter against the Red Sox.

May 13: George Brett hit his 300th career home run.

May 19: Jeff Torborg was fired as Mets manager and replaced by Dallas Green.

May 24: The Reds fired Tony Perez as manager.

June 19: Ted Simmons resigned as general manager of the Pirates and was replaced by assistant Cam Bonifay.

June 26: Roy Campanella died in Woodland Hills, Cal. at 71. Campanella, a Hall of Fame catcher, had been paralyzed since an automobile accident in January of 1958.

June 28: Carlton Fisk was released by the White Sox. He appeared in a record 2,226 games as a catcher.

July 3: Hall of Famer Don Drysdale, 56, died in Montreal while on the road with the Dodgers as a member of their broadcast team.

July 18: Atlanta acquired first baseman Fred McGriff from San Diego.

July 24: Vince Coleman of the Mets was charged with a felony after a firecracker he tossed injured three people.

July 29: George Brett got his 200th career stolen base. He joined Willie Mays and Hank Aaron as the only players with 3,000 hits, 300 home runs and 200 stolen bases.

Sept. 4: Jim Abbott of the Yankees pitched a 4–0 no-hitter against the Indians.

Sept. 9: Houston's Darryl Kile pitched the season's third no-hitter, beating the Mets 7–1.

Sept. 16: Dave Winfield got his 3,000th career hit while playing for the Twins, his fifth major league team.

White Sox were eight games better than Texas. They moved into first place on July 7 and clinched the title on September 27.

Frank Thomas lived up to his nickname "The Big Hurt" by doing damage all over the American League. He hit .317, had 41 home runs and drove in 128 runs. Thomas reached base in 138 of his 153 games.

The White Sox built a rotation as talented as it was young. The starters' average age was just 24 and their 3.70 ERA led the league. The starting staff accounted for 76 wins and a 3.72 ERA.

Jack McDowell won the Cy Young Award with his 22-win season. McDowell was at his best at the end of the season, winning 10 of his last 15 starts. Alex Fernandez won 18 games and Wilson Alvarez had 15 wins. Jason Bere won 12 games.

Gene Lamont was named American League Manager of the Year.

Juan Gonzalez led the Texas Rangers with 46 home runs. Rafael Palmiero hit 37. Tom Henke had 40 saves and Kenny Rogers won 16 games.

Oakland had a miserable season and became the first team to fall from first place to undisputed possession of last place since the Philadelphia Athletics had the same drop in 1914–15. That was a long time and three home cities ago for the Athletics. Their fate was sealed by a 4–11 trip right after the All-Star break that put them 12½ games off the lead.

It was Oakland's first losing record since 1986. Dennis Eckersley became the first pitcher to have six consecutive seasons with at least 30 saves.

Seattle was 82–80 as the Mariners had their second winning record in franchise history.

Tim Salmon became the first California Angels player to take the Rookie of the Year award. Salmon batted .283 with 31 home runs and 95 RBIs. The Minnesota Twins endured three losing streaks of at least eight games.

Frank Thomas' outstanding offensive numbers helped the White Sox to its first title in ten years

The Philadelphia Phillies became the third National League team to go from last to first. The Phillies got off to a good start at 28–12 and were already seven games ahead of Montreal at the end of May.

The East Division opened up when Pittsburgh lost four of its best players in two years. The Pirates still won the East in 1992 after Bobby Bonilla left as a free agent and 20-game winner John Smiley was traded to cut payroll. But the Pirates couldn't make up for the losses of two-time Most Valuable Player Barry Bonds and former Cy Young award winner Doug Drabek.

St. Louis took a run at the Phillies in August, but Philadelphia had a nicely balanced team. Leadoff man Lenny Dykstra led the league in both at bats (637) and walks (129), the first time that had happened. Darren Daulton and Pete Incaviglia each hit 24 home runs. Those two,

along with Dave Hollins and John Kruk, also gave the Phillies four hitters with at least 85 RBIs.

Curt Schilling and Tommy Greene each won 16 games and Mitch Williams set a team record with 43 saves. The often-critical Philadelphia fans liked what they saw as the Phillies topped three million in attendance for the first time.

The Montreal Expos won 94 games, the second-best total in the club's history. John Wetteland emerged as a closer, saving 43 games.

The mixed results of the Cardinals were best illustrated by two statistics. Their 118 home runs were their highest total in 30 years, but their 159 errors represented a one-year increase of 65.

Pittsburgh had three rookies in its opening day lineup for the first time since 1952. Al Martin and Carlos Garcia held their own, but Kevin Young didn't. The staff ERA of 4.77 was Pittsburgh's worst in 40 years. One of the few

SHORTS Nolan Ryan said farewell to baseball with a whimper after 27 seasons. Ryan had four major injuries and was on the disabled list three separate times. He was limited to 13 starts. In his last major league game, he faced six Seattle batters without getting anyone out. He left the game when he tore ligaments in his elbow.

holdovers, Jeff King, did well. He batted .295 and drove in 98 runs. After just 18 months on the job, Ted Simmons resigned as general manager after suffering a heart attack and clashing with manager Jim Leyland. Simmons was replaced by his assistant, Cam Bonifay.

The Chicago Cubs had a 20–8 finish and wound up with their third winning record in the last 20 years. Randy Myers saved 53 games and had two wins, which meant that he figured in 65 percent of the Cubs' victories. Sammy Sosa became the first Cubs' player to have 30 home runs and 30 stolen bases.

The New York Mets were 59–103, the worst season by an established team in an expansion year. The Mets finished behind the Marlins.

The Atlanta Braves won their third straight National League West title but couldn't shake the San Francisco Giants until the last day of the season. The Braves came on strong at the end and only lost 15 games after July 15. Atlanta was 9½ games behind the Giants on August 7.

The key to the season was the acquisition of Fred McGriff from the San Diego Padres' fire sale. San Diego was chopping its payroll and the Braves were happy to acquire McGriff to replace the injured Sid Bream at first base. Before McGriff, the Braves were 53–41; after he joined the team, Atlanta was 51–17. In 68 games, McGriff batted .310 with 19 home runs and 55 RBIs with the Braves.

David Justice hit 40 homers and drove in 120 runs. Ron Gant had 36 home runs and 117 RBIs. Tom Glavine had his third straight 20-win season and free agent Greg Maddux fitted in perfectly, winning 20 games and leading the league in both ERA and complete games to win the Cy Young award.

San Francisco's Dusty Baker set a record for a rookie manager by winning 103 games. Four players won Gold Gloves, including Bonds, who batted .336 with 46 home runs and 123 RBIs.

John Burkett was 22–7, Bill Swift went 21–8 and Rod Beck had 48 saves.

Barry Bonds proved to be a perfect fit in San Francisco, as the Giants won 103 games

AL CHAMPIONSHIP SERIES

GAME 1	
Blue Jays 7	White Sox 3

GAME 2	
Blue Jays 3	White Sox 1

GAME 3	
White Sox 6	Blue Jays 1

GAME 4	
White Sox 7	Blue Jays 4

GAME 5	
Blue Jays 5	White Sox 2

GAME 6	
Blue Jays 6, White Sox 3	
MVP: Dave Stewart, Blue Jays	

NL CHAMPIONSHIP SERIES

GAME 1	
Phillies 4	Braves 3

GAME 2	
Braves 14	Phillies 3

GAME 3	
Braves 9	Phillies 4

GAME 4	
Phillies 2	Braves 1

GAME 5	
Phillies 4	Braves 3

GAME 6	
Phillies 6	Braves 3
MVP: Curt Schilling, Phillies	

WORLD SERIES

GAME 1	
Blue Jays 8	Phillies 5

GAME 2	
Phillies 6	Blue Jays 4

GAME 3	
Blue Jays 10	Phillies 3

GAME 4	
Blue Jays 15	Phillies 14

GAME 5	
Phillies 2	Blue Jays 0

GAME 6	
Blue Jays 8	Phillies 6
MVP: Paul Molitor, Blue Jays	

Carter, the Toronto Blue Jays' outfielder, added his name to the short list of baseball players famous for game-ending October home runs.

Thomson's moment had come in the 1951 National League pennant playoff when he blasted a Ralph Branca pitch for the home run that gave the New York Giants the pennant over the Brooklyn Dodgers.

Mazeroski was responsible for the only World Series Game Seven that ended with a home run. Mazeroski hit Ralph Terry's 1–0 pitch over the left field wall at Forbes Field to win the 1960 World Series for the Pittsburgh Pirates over the New York Yankees.

Carter's moment came in Game Six of the 1993 World Series when he hit a home run off reliever Mitch (Wild Thing) Williams to give the Blue Jays their second straight Series title. They became the first repeat Series winners since the 1977–78 New York Yankees.

The Blue Jays had undergone an amazing overhaul to win the American League East for a second consecutive year. Toronto lost 11 players off the roster of the 1992 club but was able to add quality personnel, including designated hitter Paul Molitor and shortstop Tony Fernandez.

The Blue Jays won 95 games and took the division by seven games over the Yankees. In the West, the Oakland Athletics dropped to last

Celebration time for the Blue Jays

place and the Chicago White Sox took the title with 94 wins. The White Sox had a comfortable eight-game margin over Texas.

The Atlanta Braves won 104 games and needed every one of them to hold off the San Francisco Giants, who had 103 wins. The Pittsburgh Pirates' string of National League East titles ended after the free agent defections of Barry Bonds and Doug Drabek.

The surprise winner in the East was the Philadelphia Phillies, who won 97 games and finished three games in front of Montreal. The Phillies went from last to first, becoming the third team in three years to make that turnaround.

Both playoff series went six games.

Molitor had a home run in the series opener as Toronto won 7–3 behind Juan Guzman. The Blue Jays took the second game 3–1 as Dave Stewart beat Alex Fernandez with relief help from Duane Ward.

The White Sox finally got going in the third game with a 6–1 win on Wilson Alvarez's seven-hitter. Chicago evened the series by winning the fourth game 7–4.

Ward shut down a White Sox rally in the ninth by striking out Bo Jackson with the bases loaded. That nailed down Toronto's 5–3 win in the fifth game. The Blue Jays sealed their second straight trip to the World Series by winning 6–3 in the sixth game. Dave Stewart improved his playoff record to 8–0 and won a pennant-clinching game for the fourth time in six years.

The Braves and Phillies split the first two games of the National League playoffs. The Phillies won the opener 4–3 in 10 innings but the Braves came back to take the second game 14–3 with four home runs. Atlanta won the third game 9–4 behind Tom Glavine but Danny Jackson got the Phillies even with a 2–1 win over John Smoltz in the fourth game.

Lenny Dykstra hit a game-winning homer in the 10th inning of the fifth game to give Williams the win over Mark Wohlers. The Phillies then ended the series with a 6–3 win over Greg Maddux in the sixth game.

Home runs by Devon White and John Olerud helped Al Leiter win Game One of the Series 8–5. The Phillies tied the Series when Terry Mulholland beat Stewart 6–4 in Game Two.

Toronto won Game Three 10–3 as Pat Hentgen beat Jackson. Game Four turned into one the sloppiest Series games in history as the Blue Jays scored six runs in the eighth inning and won 15–14.

Curt Schilling pitched a five-hitter and won

Game Five 2–0 to keep the Phillies from being eliminated. That set up Game Six at Toronto's Skydome.

Toronto took a 3–0 lead in the first and the Phillies scored their first run in the fourth. The Blue Jays scored in the bottom of the inning and had a 4–1 lead after six innings. Philadelphia scored five runs in the seventh and led 6-4 with Williams on the mound for the ninth inning.

Rickey Henderson walked and Molitor singled. Williams had a 2–2 count when Carter took the swing that put his name in the history book alongside Thomson and Mazeroski.

Molitor took Most Valuable Player honors with a .500 average, two home runs and eight RBIs. Roberto Alomar hit .480 and Fernandez batted .333 with eight RBIs. Dykstra and John Kruk each had .348 averages for the Phillies and Dykstra drove in eight runs and hit four homers.

Lenny Dykstra batted .348 in the Series, but the Phillies still fell short

1994

MOST VALUABLE PLAYER

AL: Frank Thomas, Chicago White Sox
NL: Jeff Bagwell, Houston

CY YOUNG AWARD

AL: David Cone, Kansas City
NL: Greg Maddux, Atlanta

ROOKIE OF THE YEAR

AL: Bob Hamelin, Kansas City
NL: Raul Mondesi, Los Angeles

LEADERS

BATTING AVERAGE

AL: Paul O'Neill, NY Yankees, .359
NL: Tony Gwynn, San Diego, .394

HOME RUNS

AL: Ken Griffey Jr., Seattle 40
NL: Matt Williams, San Francisco, 43

RUNS BATTED IN

AL: Kirby Puckett, Minnesota, 112
NL: Jeff Bagwell, Houston, 116

STOLEN BASES

AL: Kenny Lofton, Cleveland, 60
NL: Craig Biggio, Houston, 39

PITCHING VICTORIES

AL: Jimmy Key, NY Yankees, 22; NL: Ken Hill, Montreal; Greg Maddux, Atlanta, 16

EARNED RUN AVERAGE

AL: Steve Ontiveros, Oakland, 2.65
NL: Greg Maddux, Atlanta, 1.56

STRIKEOUTS

AL: Randy Johnson, Seattle, 204
NL: Andy Benes, San Diego, 189

SAVES

AL: Lee Smith, Baltimore, 33
NL: John Franco, NY Mets

"Whereas, the 26 Major League Baseball Clubs ("the Clubs") and the Major League Baseball Players Association (the "MLBPA") have been engaged in collective bargaining over an extended period; and

"Whereas, the MLBPA has been consistently unwilling to respond in any meaningful way to the Clubs' need to contain costs and has consistently refused to bargain with the Clubs concerning a division of industry revenues with the players or any other method of establishing aggregate player compensation; and:

"Whereas, the MLBPA's 33-days' strike has caused the cancellation of all games since August 12, 1994, and has made it impossible for the players to resume play at a championship level without a substantial training period.

"Now, therefore, be it resolved that:

"In order to protect the integrity of the Championship Season, the Division Series, the League Championship Series and the World Series, the 28 clubs have concluded with enormous regret that the remainder of the 1994 season, the Division Series, the League Championship Series and the World Series must be canceled and that the Clubs will explore all avenues to achieve a meaningful, structural reform of Baseball's player compensation system in an effort to ensure that the 1995 and future Championship Seasons can occur as scheduled and uninterrupted."

Those five paragraphs of legalese did what two World Wars and an earthquake couldn't do—they wiped out the World Series.

Baseball was enjoying one of its most memorable seasons when the players went on strike on August 12. With both ownership and the union determined to play hardball, the season was canceled when neither side would budge from its position.

The ending was no surprise to anyone who had followed the labor negotiations over the last 15 years and understood the climate of mistrust that poisoned the process. Baseball had reached a Basic Agreement in 1990 after a spring training lockout. The contract was due to expire at the end of the 1995 calendar year, but management exercised an option to reopen it one year early.

The clubs maintained that the escalation of player salaries had caused a crisis in baseball that had as many as 19 of the 28 teams showing an annual operating loss. The Players Association countered by arguing that the only thing that had risen more dramatically than player salaries was the revenues being realized by the franchise owners.

The owners proposed that the answer was a salary cap. The union said that the owners needed to do a better job of dividing their revenues among the member clubs. Although salary caps had been negotiated in other sports, the MLBPA was adamant that it would not voluntarily accept limits on how much its members could make.

The union set the strike date in the second week of August for two reasons. The MLBPA believed that if a strike were called, there would be enough time to salvage the postseason if a settlement were reached. It also knew that deferring the decision until after the season would simply let the owners conclude the season, then organize camps for next season with non-union players.

Baseball had more pennant races than ever thanks to a realignment that split each league into three divisions. The playoffs had been expanded by a round because of the inclusion of

New York's Paul O'Neill was one of the many players whose hot streaks were doused by the strike

What might have been—Ken Griffey Jr. had reached 40 homers before the strike action

a wild-card team, an idea borrowed from the National Football League.

The cancellation of the season was a cruel blow to the Montreal Expos, who appeared to be headed for the National League East title. They had baseball's best record at 74–40 and the Expos were on pace for 105 wins.

Moises Alou batted .339 with 22 home runs and 78 RBIs, making a full comeback from a serious leg injury. Larry Walker had 19 home runs and 86 RBIs and had a cannon of a throwing arm that kept opposing base runners honest. Marquis Grissom stole 36 bases and provided exceptional defense in center field.

Ken Hill led the pitching staff with a 16–5 record and Pedro Martinez was emerging as a starter with an 11–5 record and a reputation for throwing inside to keep hitters off the plate. John Wetteland had 25 saves and Mel Rojas had 16.

Despite a 13–1 start, the Atlanta Braves couldn't catch Montreal. Fred McGriff had 34 home runs, giving him seven consecutive seasons with at least 30. He led the team that had a league-best 137 homers.

The Cincinnati Reds led the new Central Division with the league's most potent offense. The Reds led the league in both batting average and runs scored. The Los Angeles Dodgers topped the West. Raul Mondesi batted .306 and drove in 56 runs. Tim Wallach had 23 home runs and 78 RBIs and catcher Mike Piazza had a .319 average with 92 RBIs. Ramon Martinez led the pitching staff with 12 wins.

The New York Yankees had a comfortable 6½-game lead in the American League East. Buck Showalter became the first manager to last three

consecutive seasons with the Yankees since Ralph Houk had a seven-year run from 1967–73.

The defending champion Toronto Blue Jays were in the midst of their first losing season since 1982, due mostly to a ten-game losing streak in early June and a 13–22 record in their division.

The Chicago White Sox were leading the Central on the broad shoulders of first baseman Frank Thomas. He hit .353 with 38 home runs and 101 RBIs. He led the league with a .729 slugging average and .486 on-base percentage, helped by a league-high 109 walks.

The Cleveland Indians were celebrating the opening of Jacobs Field with their best season in decades. The Indians were poised to take the first wild card spot. Their .584 winning percentage was their best since 1955.

Despite a 52–62 record, the Texas Rangers led the weak Western Division. Texas had a staff ERA of 5.45, second worst in the majors, but were able to outslug a lot of opponents.

Several players were left to wonder what might have been had the season continued. San Diego's Tony Gwynn was making a serious run at a .400 average and wound up at .394. Three players seemed to be poised to challenge the single-season home run records of Roger Maris and Babe Ruth. Matt Williams of the Giants had 43 homers, Ken Griffey, Jr. of Seattle had 40 and the White Sox' Thomas had 38.

Milwaukee's Robin Yount retired before the season, Ryne Sandberg of the Chicago Cubs quit in June and Kent Hrbek ended his career with Minnesota after the season.

Despite the shortened season, seven clubs made managerial changes. The Angels fired Bob Rodgers and replaced him with coach Marcel Lachemann. Kansas City dropped Hal McRae and hired Bob Boone. Kevin Kennedy was fired in Texas, Johnny Oates was ousted in Baltimore and Jim Riggleman resigned in San Diego. All took new jobs—Kennedy in Boston, replacing Butch Hobson, Oates in Texas and Riggleman with the Cubs, where Tom Trebelhorn was axed. Phil Regan took over in Baltimore and Bruce Bochy was hired in San Diego.

The All-Star game in Pittsburgh was a classic. The National League roughed up David Cone early but saw the American League come back. Montreal's Grissom homered in the sixth and McGriff of the Braves sent the game to extra innings when he hit a two-run homer off Lee Smith in the ninth. The National League won the game in the tenth when Gwynn scored from first on Alou's double. It turned out to be Montreal's only interleague highlight in the only season without a World Series.

Do clothes make the man? If a player puts on a major league uniform, does that make him a major league player?

The owners were prepared to answer those questions as they staged spring training with replacement players. It was their radical response to the labor deadlock that had started on August 12, 1994 when the players went on strike. For the first time in history the World Series was canceled, an indication of how serious the owners were about winning the latest and most bitter war against the Players Association.

Clubs spent the winter making two sets of plans. They made moves for the major league roster in the event that the strike would be settled and that the season could start with the regular players. But the teams also spent time digging deep in their files to find former minor league players who might be willing to cross the picket line and play on replacement teams.

Spring training camps were conducted with

The Braves' Greg Maddux etched his name in history winning four consecutive Cy Young Awards

The Dodgers' Hideo Nomo made a memorable start to his major league career by winning seven of his first eight decisions

March 9: Owners agreed to put expansion teams in Tampa Bay and Arizona in time for the 1998 season.

April 2: Striking players were allowed to return to work after a court injuction barred the new work rules that the owners had tried to impose.

April 25: The regular season opened, although it was shortened to 144 games because of the delay in starting.

April 30: A lockout of umpires ended with a new labor agreement.

June 3: Pedro Martinez of the Expos pitched nine perfect innings against the San Diego Padres. He lost the no-hitter when Bip Roberts doubled in the bottom of the tenth. Montreal won 1–0 but Martinez did not finish the game.

July 28: A number of procedural changes were implemented to speed up games. Most of them involved minimizing delays between plays and pitches.

July 30: Eddie Murray of the Indians got his 3,000th hit.

Aug. 10: The Los Angeles Dodgers forfeited a home game against the St. Louis Cardinals after fans threw promotional baseballs onto the field on three occasions. It was the National League's first forfeit since July 18, 1954.

Aug. 13: Yankees' Hall of Famer Mickey Mantle died in Dallas at 63.

Sept. 8: Baltimore's Cal Ripken, Jr. broke Lou Gehrig's record for consecutive games played with his 2,131st.

Oct. 2: Sparky Anderson retired as manager of the Tigers. He finished his career with 2,194 wins, third behind Connie Mack and John McGraw.

Oct. 23: Tony LaRussa became manager of the Cardinals after leaving the Athletics with two years left on his contract.

Nov. 2: Joe Torre was named manager of the Yankees.

Nov. 15: Buck Showalter, who left the Yankees on October 26, signed on as manager of the expansion Arizona Diamondbacks.

replacement players, much to the chagrin of most managers, who knew that real major league status came from more than a uniform. The owners had unilaterally imposed new labor rules, including a salary cap or payroll tax, restrictions on free agency and the abolishment of salary arbitration. In essence, the owners gave themselves everything they ever wanted without negotiating with the union.

It was pure fantasy. The owners didn't even have solidarity within their own ranks. Baltimore owner Peter Angelos refused to go along with the concept of replacement baseball—Angelos was a lawyer who had represented workers in his practice. There was another consideration, too. Cal Ripken Jr. was on pace to beat Lou Gehrig's record for consecutive games. That 13-year trek could have been derailed had the Orioles fielded a replacement team in the regular season. Laws in Toronto prevented the use of replacement workers, which meant that the Blue Jays would have had to play home games at their Florida spring training base.

Finally, at the end of March, U.S. District Judge Sonia Sotomayor put her name in baseball history by granting a preliminary injunction against management's imposition of the new work rules. The union players agreed to come back under the terms of their old Basic Agreement. Baseball hastily assembled a new schedule that called for 144 games, 18 less than usual, to begin on April 25.

Following a shortened spring training, the season got underway to a fan backlash. A number of protests were staged at ballparks and attendance was down as some fans swore off major league games after the most destructive

SHORTS Whether Montreal manager Felipe Alou needed a righthanded pitcher or a lefthander, Greg Harris was his man. Harris became the first player in more than a century to pitch with both hands in the same game. A natural righthander, he faced two batters righthanded and two lefthanded on September 28.

work stoppage. Some clubs reduced certain ticket prices or made some other concessions to win back fans.

Baseball had another inducement to offer—the first season of expanded playoffs, which would now include a wild card team to bring the field of qualifiers to four in each league. The best-of-five Division Series would now precede the traditional League Championship Series.

Once business got back to normal, the Atlanta Braves got busy winning their division. The Braves overcame Philadelphia at midseason and won 20 of 27 games in July to finish 21 games ahead of the Phillies. As usual, the Braves relied on the league's best pitching staff. Atlanta's pitchers allowed the fewest hits, had the best earned run average and the most complete games.

Greg Maddux won his fourth consecutive Cy Young award with a 19–2 season and 1.63 ERA. He was the first pitcher to post consecutive seasons with an ERA under 1.80 since Hall of Famer Walter Johnson in 1918–19. Mark Wohlers had 25 saves.

Chipper Jones returned from knee surgery and his first season as a regular was good, with a .265 average, 23 home runs and 86 RBIs.

Seattle fireballer Randy Johnson

SHORTS The Indians ended the frustration of fans in 1995. The Indians finished in first place for the first time in 41 years, winning the AL Central. After years of playing before sparse crowds in Municipal Stadium, the Indians had a packed house every night at Jacobs Field. The Cleveland plan became the model for franchises looking to rebuild.

known that Davey Johnson would not be invited back as manager, the Reds managed to win. Barry Larkin batted .319 with 15 home runs, 66 RBIs and 51 stolen bases.

Lefthander Pete Schourek was a pleasant surprise with an 18–7 record and 3.22 ERA. The Reds overcame a 1–7 start, but went into the postseason on a 10–17 slide.

Houston first baseman Jeff Bagwell broke his hand on July 30 and the Astros went 9–20 in August.

The Los Angeles Dodgers found themselves in a tight race with the Colorado Rockies. The Dodgers went 17–8 down the stretch to edge the Rockies by one game. Mike Piazza hit .346 with 32 homers and 93 RBIs. Eric Karros had a .298 average with 32 home runs and 105 RBIs. Ramon Martinez was 17–7 and Hideo Nomo started his major league career by winning seven of his first eight decisions.

Colorado led the division for 109 games, a significant accomplishment for a franchise in just its third season. The Rockies moved to Coors Field, which proved to be hitter friendly—and they had the bats to take advantage of the new surroundings. They had four players with at least 30 home runs. Dante Bichette led the group with a .340 average, 40 home runs and 128 RBIs. Larry Walker hit 36 homers, Vinny Castilla had 32 and Andres Galarraga added 31.

Fan dissatisfaction with baseball wasn't evident in Cleveland, where the city enjoyed its first first-place finish in 41 years. The Indians took the American League Central by 30 games over Kansas City, the largest margin in modern history. Their five-man rotation of Orel Hershiser, Charles Nagy, Dennis Martinez, Chad Ogea and Ken Hill went 56–21. Jose Mesa had 46 saves. The Indians blew away the Central Division pack with a 28–7 streak that started in late April.

Albert Belle hit 31 home runs in the last two months to finish with 50. Manny Ramirez had 31 homers and 107 RBIs. Jim Thome and Paul Sorrento each hit 25 home runs.

The Boston Red Sox settled into first place on May 19 and stayed there to take the American League East. Mo Vaughn batted .300 with 39

The Phillies used 26 pitchers and their hopes of staying in contention diminished when Curt Schilling needed shoulder surgery.

The Cincinnati Reds took the first National League Central title by finishing nine games ahead of Houston. Even though it was well

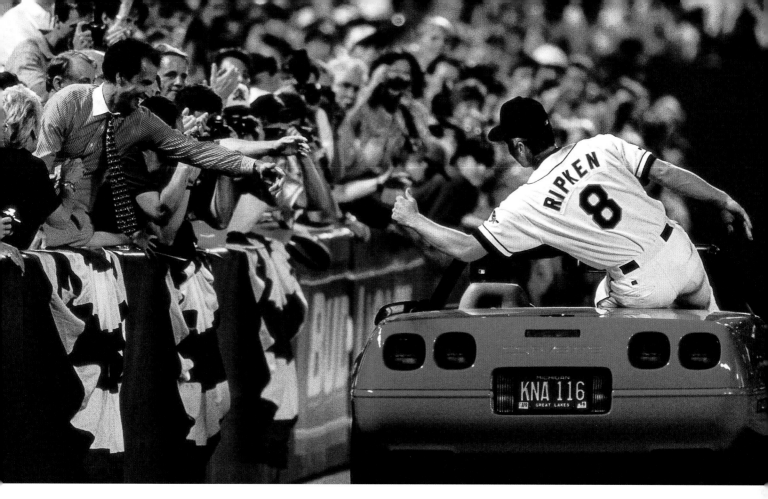

home runs and 126 RBIs and John Valentin contributed 27 homers and 102 RBIs. Knuckleball specialist Tim Wakefield was 16–8 with a 2.95 ERA and was 14–1 at one point. Wakefield was a bargain pickup for the Red Sox, who signed him after he'd been released by the Pittsburgh Pirates in spring training. Boston made an important trade, acquiring Rick Aguilera, who converted 20 of 21 save opportunities.

The New York Yankees went 21–6 in September to claim the wild card spot. On July 28, the Yankees got David Cone as a free agent, which helped them compensate for the loss of Jimmy Key to rotator cuff surgery.

The American League West had the closest race and needed a one-game playoff to break the tie between the California Angels and Seattle Mariners. Seattle won the game behind Randy Johnson to take the title. Johnson was 18–2 and the Mariners were 27–3 in the games he started. He struck out 294 with only 65 walks. The Mariners endured even though Ken Griffey Jr. missed 73 games with a broken left wrist. Edgar Martinez won the batting title with a .356 average and didn't go more than eight at-bats without getting a hit.

California had an 11-game lead over the Mariners on August 9, but fell three games behind after winning just six games in a month. When they failed to win the division, they also lost the wild card spot to the Yankees.

Baseball restored some of the good feelings on September 6 when Ripken played in his 2,131st consecutive game, breaking Lou Gehrig's record. The game was stopped when it became official and Ripken took a victory lap around the field at Camden Yards to celebrate a streak that had started on May 30, 1982. Ripken batted .262 with 17 home runs and 88 RBIs. He kept playing and his streak was 2,153 games when the season ended.

Detroit manager Sparky Anderson announced his resignation to take effect at season's end. Because Anderson had been an especially vocal critic of the replacement ball, there was no effort to talk him into staying. Anderson finished with 2,194 wins, third on the career list. He trailed only Connie Mack and John McGraw. Anderson managed the Reds for nine seasons, then spent 17 years with the Tigers.

Two long-time owners decided to sell their teams. Gene Autry, who had founded the Angels in 1961, sold the team to the Walt Disney Corp. In May, Anheuser Busch, which had owned the Cardinals since 1953, sold out to a new group in October.

Some high-profile managers were on the move. Tony LaRussa left Oakland for St. Louis, replacing Joe Torre, who went to the Yankees.

Baseball lost one of its most beloved players on August 13 when Mickey Mantle died in a Dallas hospital at 63. Mantle had battled a series of major health problems, including liver failure. He underwent transplant surgery on June 8, but cancer was discovered in Mantle's right lung on August 1.

The healing process begins as Cal Ripken Jr. celebrates his record with the fans

1995 POSTSEASON

NL DIVISION SERIES

GAME 1

Cincinnati 7	Los Angeles 2

GAME 2

Cincinnati 5	Los Angeles 4

GAME 3

Cincinnati 10	Los Angeles 1

GAME 1

Atlanta 5	Colorado 4

GAME 2

Atlanta 7	Colorado 4

GAME 3

Colorado 7	Atlanta 5

GAME 4

Atlanta 10	Colorado 4

AL DIVISION SERIES

GAME 1

Cleveland 5	Boston Red Sox 4

GAME 2

Cleveland 4	Boston Red Sox 0

GAME 3

Cleveland 8	Boston Red Sox 2

GAME 1

NY Yankees 9	Seattle 6

GAME 2

NY Yankees 7	Seattle 5

GAME 3

Seattle 7	NY Yankees 4

GAME 4

Seattle 11	NY Yankees 8

GAME 5

Seattle 6	NY Yankees 5

NL CHAMPIONSHIP SERIES

GAME 1

Atlanta 2	Cincinnati 1

GAME 2

Atlanta 6	Cincinnati 2

GAME 3

Atlanta 5	Cincinnati 2

GAME 4

Atlanta 6	Cincinnati 0

AL CHAMPIONSHIP SERIES

GAME 1

Seattle 3	Cleveland 2

GAME 2

Cleveland 5	Seattle 2

GAME 3

Seattle 5	Cleveland 2

GAME 4

Cleveland 7	Seattle 0

The fact that the 1995 postseason actually occurred was a victory as baseball had deprived fans of the playoffs the previous year.

The '95 postseason featured a new format. Baseball went to three divisions the previous year, meaning that the three first-place finishers and a wild-card team qualified for the playoffs. The new format meant that each league champion had to survive two rounds of playoffs before reaching the World Series. The Division Series would be a best-of-five series, while the League Championship Series and the World Series would both be best-of-seven.

In the Division Series in the National League, the Atlanta Braves, winners of the East, defeated the Colorado Rockies, the wild card team, in four games, while the Cincinnati Reds, the Central champs, swept the Los Angeles Dodgers, the West winners, in three games.

Thanks to their strong pitching, the Braves swept the Reds in the NLCS. Atlanta held Cincinnati to five runs in the four games. The Braves won Game One, 2–1, on Mike Devereaux's 11th-inning single. Javy Lopez's three-run homer in the tenth inning of Game Two helped the Braves to a 6–2 win. Atlanta closed out the series with 5–2 and 6–0 wins.

The American League playoffs featured the first postseason visit by the Cleveland Indians

Greg Maddux allowed just two hits as Atlanta won Game One of the World Series

since 1954. The Indians, sparked by a high-scoring offense, won the Central title with a 100–44 record and swept Boston, the East champs, in three games in the Division Series. Game One lasted five hours and one minute, the longest postseason game in history time-wise, and finally ended on Tony Pena's home run in the 13th inning. The Seattle Mariners, who won the West with a late-season charge, made their first postseason appearance and beat the wild-card New York Yankees in a memorable five-game series. The Yankees won the first two games of the series, including a 15-inning victory in Game Two, but Seattle rallied to win the final three in Seattle. The Mariners won Game Five, 6–5, on Edgar Martinez's two-run single in the 11th inning.

The Indians defeated the Mariners in six games in a hard-fought ALCS. Seattle won Game One, 3–2, while the Indians won Game Two, 5–2. Jay Buhner's 11th-inning homer gave the Mariners a 5–2 win in Game Three, but the Indians won the next three games, 7–0 in Game Four, 3–2 in Game Five and 4–0 in Game Six.

The matchup in the World Series featured a battle between the team with the best pitching (the Braves) and the team with the best hitting (the Indians). In the end, the pitching won out as the Braves took the Series in six games.

Atlanta's pitching staff, which included Greg Maddux, Tom Glavine and John Smoltz, limited the Indians to a .179 batting average. Maddux held the Indians to two hits and a pair of unearned runs in Game One while the Braves

scored twice in the seventh for a 3–2 win. The Braves also took Game Two by a 4–3 score. Glavine held the Indians to three hits in six innings and Mark Wohlers picked up the save. Javy Lopez's two-run homer in the sixth put the Braves ahead for good.

The Indians, playing their first World Series home game in 41 years, pulled out a 7–6 win in 11 innings in Game Three on Eddie Murray's single.

The Braves responded with a 5–3 win in Game Four to take a commanding 3–1 Series lead. Steve Avery allowed three hits in six innings while the Braves' bullpen finished it off. David Justice added a two-run single in a three-run Atlanta seventh. Facing elimination against Maddux in Game Five, the Indians scored four runs in seven innings against the Atlanta ace. Albert Belle hit a two-run homer in the first while Manny Ramirez and Jim Thome both had RBI singles in the sixth to spark a 5–4 win.

The Series returned to Atlanta where the Braves wrapped it up with a 1–0 win. The only run came when Justice, who criticized the Atlanta fans for not supporting their team enough, homered off Jim Poole in the sixth inning. Glavine, named the Most Valuable Player in the Series, held the Indians to one hit in eight innings, while Wohlers pitched a perfect ninth for the save.

The Braves won their first championship since 1957 and became the first franchise to win three titles in three different cities (Boston, Milwaukee, Atlanta). The title also ended the frustration the Braves had felt after losing the Series in 1991 and 1992.

World Series MVP Tom Glavine won two games as the Braves triumphed

(continued)	
GAME 5	
Cleveland 3	Seattle 2
GAME 6	
Cleveland 4	Seattle 0
WORLD SERIES	
GAME 1	
Atlanta 3	Cleveland 2
GAME 2	
Atlanta 4	Cleveland 3
GAME 3	
Cleveland 7	Atlanta 6
GAME 4	
Atlanta 5	Cleveland 2
GAME 5	
Cleveland 5	Atlanta 4
GAME 6	
Atlanta 1	Cleveland 0
MVP: Tom Glavine, Atlanta	

CAL RIPKEN JR.

TEAMS
Baltimore Orioles 1981–

Games	.2,790
At-Bats	.10,765
Runs	.1,561
RBI	.1,571
Home runs	.402
Hits	.2,991
Doubles	.571
Triples	.44
Stolen Bases	.36
Average	.278
Slugging percentage	.451

Babe Ruth became famous for home runs. Nolan Ryan became known for strikeouts. Cal Ripken, Jr?

He became one of baseball's biggest names by going to work every day. He did it more often than anyone, breaking the record that many thought would never even be approached: Lou Gehrig's 2,130 consecutive games.

From May 30, 1982 until September 21, 1998, Ripken's name was in the Baltimore Orioles' starting lineup for 2,632 consecutive games, creating another record that a lot of people don't

The Orioles' Iron Man is a certainty to enter the Hall of Fame when he becomes eligible

think will ever be threatened. Even as he surpassed Gehrig's record, Ripken took pains to mention he didn't think he measured up to the New York Yankees Hall of Fame first baseman in any other way. "I consider (Gehrig) a great player," Ripken said. "I don't consider myself a great player." How, then, would he describe himself? "I'm a grinder," Ripken said. "I go out there and grind it out every game."

He learned the game at the professional level. Cal Ripken, Sr. was a baseball lifer who managed in the minor leagues and took his family to his assigned post for the summer. Young Cal got to go to the ballpark to help out in the clubhouse or serve as batboy. When there was spare time, he could work on his own game.

Being around the players and his father didn't just teach him baseball skills. It also showed him what it means to be a professional and how to merge the fun of the game with the responsibilities that come with playing it for a living. Ripken had talent, although most scouts seemed to think his future was as a pitcher. The Orioles chose him on the second round of the 1978 draft and his four-year trek through the minor league system started

after his graduation from high school.

Ripken reached the majors in 1981 and settled in the following year. Earl Weaver was the first of seven managers to write his name in the lineup during the streak. Ripken had a streak of 8,243 consecutive innings until his father ended that when he managed the Orioles in 1987. Cal Sr. used the last innings of a blowout loss to end that streak, believing his son needed a break from media articles speculating that full-time duty was hindering his play. Remarkably, Ripken had only two close calls during his streak. He injured an ankle in 1985 but a scheduled open date the following day gave him a chance to recover. In 1993, the Orioles and Seattle Mariners got into a brawl and Ripken twisted his right knee in the confusion. Otherwise, his durability wasn't threatened in a game of bad hops, trying travel and energy-sapping hot weather.

Said Ripken, "I've always felt that if you play the game the right way, play full speed and keep your concentration up, that insulates you from some injuries." Ripken reached 2,000 games on August 1, 1994, shortly before a player's strike ended the season prematurely. Gehrig's record was broken midway through a home game against the California Angels on September 6, 1995. The game became official in the middle of the fifth inning and the celebration started at 9:20 p.m. An ovation lasted more than 22 minutes as Ripken accepted congratulations from teammates, took a lap around the field and even shook hands with the Angels.

More than four years later, the streak ended when Ripken told manager Ray Miller to leave him out of the starting lineup on September 21, 1998. Ripken was 38 years old, had gone more than 500 games past Gehrig's record and wanted to end it. "I guess I just want to say it was time," Ripken said. He got a standing ovation for not playing when Baltimore fans realized they had walked in on another historic occasion. The streak over, Ripken could concentrate on a more realistic schedule for a player entering the final years of his career.

Occasional days off helped Ripken. Early in the 2000 season, he got his 3,000th hit and further cemented his Hall of Fame credentials. His streak was a combination of good fortune, preparation, determination and, above all, an unrelenting enthusiasm for baseball. O's coach Elrod Hendricks summed up Ripken's devotion to the game thusly: "He's still like a little kid who just got his first uniform."

MOST VALUABLE PLAYER
AL: Juan Gonzalez, Texas
NL: Ken Caminiti, Houston

CY YOUNG AWARD
AL: Pat Hentgen, Toronto
NL: John Smoltz, Atlanta

ROOKIE OF THE YEAR
AL: Derek Jeter, NY Yankees
NL: Todd Hollandsworth, Los Angeles

LEADERS

BATTING AVERAGE
AL: Alex Rodriguez, Seattle, .358
NL: Tony Gwynn, San Diego, .353

HOME RUNS
AL: Mark McGwire, Oakland, 52
NL: Andres Galarraga, Colorado, 47

RUNS BATTED IN
AL: Albert Belle, Cleveland, 148
NL: Andres Galarraga, Colorado, 150

STOLEN BASES
AL: Kenny Lofton, Cleveland, 75
NL: Eric Young, Colorado, 53

PITCHING VICTORIES
AL: Andy Pettitte, NY Yankees, 21
NL: John Smoltz, Atlanta, 24

EARNED RUN AVERAGE
AL: Juan Guzman, Toronto, 2.93
NL: Kevin Brown, Florida, 1.89

STRIKEOUTS
AL: Roger Clemens, Boston Red Sox, 257
NL: John Smoltz, Atlanta, 276

SAVES
AL: John Wetteland, NY Yankees, 43; NL: Jeff Brantley, Cincinnati, Todd Worrell, Los Angeles, 44

Joe Torre played in 2,209 major league games and managed 2,059 others without ever participating in a World Series.

That changed in 1996 as Torre moved back to his hometown for what was likely to be the final stop in his long baseball career. Torre was hired to succeed Buck Showalter as the manager of the New York Yankees in November 1995.

He was not a popular choice. The back page of one New York tabloid newspaper bannered a headline, "Clueless Joe" to announce Torre's hiring. The sentiment was understandable. The Yankees were the fourth team Torre had managed. He had just been fired by the St. Louis Cardinals after an undistinguished stay there. Torre had been in New York before, serving the New York Mets as manager during some lean years.

Torre's only managerial success had come with the Atlanta Braves and that had been in 1982, when his team won a divisional title but lost in the playoffs.

It didn't appear that Torre was much more than another temporary hire for the Yankees' ever-turbulent situation. Front office executive Arthur Richman had pitched owner George Steinbrenner on the idea of hiring Torre, with whom he'd worked at the Mets.

Richman had a suspicion that Torre's calm might be a perfect fit in the volatile atmosphere that had overwhelmed other managers.

Richman was exactly right and, like the rest of the Yankees' staff, his reward came in the form of a World Series ring. Torre led the Yankees to their first divisional title since 1981 as they surprised the American League by winning the Eastern Division, then rolling through the playoffs and World Series.

Perhaps Torre's most important contribution was his ability to head off trouble before it happened. Steinbrenner, a compulsive meddler, seemed to stay at arm's length as Torre and his coaching staff created an atmosphere that allowed the players to relax and perform.

SHORTS Jim Leyland was there when the Pirates were the worst team in baseball. He didn't want to see it happen again and announced on Sept. 17 that he was leaving them after 11 seasons. He was a hot item on the free agent market and signed with the Marlins on Oct. 4.·

The O's lead-off man Brady Anderson hit an incredible 50 home runs

Mariners shortstop Alex Rodriguez posted some heady numbers

TIMELINE

April 1: Umpire John McSherry collapsed and died on the field while working the Expos–Reds season opener.

May 2: A game between the Indians and Mariners was postponed after an earthquake shook Seattle.

May 11: Al Leiter pitched the first no-hitter in Marlins' history, beating the Rockies 11–0.

May 14: Dwight Gooden of the Yankees pitched a no-hitter against the Mariners.

July 9: The NL won its third consecutive All-Star game, 6–0 at Philadelphia. Nine pitchers combined on the seven-hit shutout.

July 29: After suffering a heart attack in late June, Tommy Lasorda announced his retirement as Dodgers' manager.

Aug. 11: Kirk Gibson announced his retirement from the Tigers.

Aug. 16: The Mets and Padres opened a three-game series in Mexico.

Aug. 26: Dallas Green was fired as Mets' manager and replaced by Bobby Valentine.

Sept. 6: Eddie Murray hit his 500th career home run.

Sept. 16: Paul Molitor of the Twins tripled for his 3,000th career hit. He became the 21st player to reach 3,000 hits.

Sept. 17: After failing to finish first for 41 years, the Indians won their second consecutive divisional title.

Sept. 17: Hideo Nomo of the Dodgers pitched a no-hitter in one of the NL's most notoriously hitter-friendly parks, Colorado's Coors Field.

Sept. 18: Roger Clemens of the Red Sox struck out 20 Tigers batters.

Sept. 27: Orioles' second baseman Roberto Alomar spit in the face of umpire John Hirschbeck during an argument.

Oct. 4: The Astros hired broadcaster Larry Dierker to replace Terry Collins as manager.

Nov. 19: Free agent Albert Belle signed the most lucrative contract in baseball history. The White Sox agreed to pay him $50 million over five years to leave the Indians.

The Yankees took over first place at the end of April and finished 92–70, four games ahead of Baltimore. Derek Jeter batted .314 and drove in 78 runs. He also played exceptional defense at shortstop, settling down an important position.

Tino Martinez hit 25 home runs and drove in 117 runs. Bernie Williams had 29 homers and 102 RBIs.

Andy Pettitte led the pitching staff with 21 wins and a 3.87 earned run average. Jimmy Key and Kenny Rogers each had 12 wins. An unsung hero was reliever Mariano Rivera, who emerged as a set-up man who could get the Yankees to the ninth inning and closer John Wetteland, who had 43 saves.

The Orioles got within 2½ games of the Yankees at one point in September but had to settle for a wild card playoff spot. Baltimore almost held a fire sale of veterans in late July but owner Peter Angelos ordered his staff to keep the club intact. Starting over looked like a good idea when the Orioles were 12 games out of first

The Padres' hit king Tony Gwynn

White Sox.

Cleveland rode a powerful offense to its second straight title. Albert Belle led the way with a .311 average, 48 home runs and a League-leading 148 RBIs. Jim Thome batted .311 with 38 homers and 116 RBIs. Manny Ramirez had 33 homers and 112 RBIs while Kenny Lofton stole 75 bases to lead the League for the fifth consecutive season.

The Indians had the League's best ERA at 4.34. Charles Nagy won 17 games and Orel Hershiser had 15. Jack McDowell won 13 games. Jose Mesa had 39 saves.

Cleveland became the first team to lead the League in batting average and earned run average for consecutive seasons since the New York Yankees did it in 1957–58. Mike Hargrove became the first Indians manager to take his team to the postseason in consecutive years.

The White Sox had three players with at least 100 RBIs for the first time in team history. Frank Thomas had 134 RBIs, Robin Ventura had 105 and Danny Tartabull drove in 101 runs. Thomas also batted .349 with 40 home runs.

Milwaukee did trade off veterans in a rebuilding effort. Greg Vaughn, Pat Listach, Ricky Bones and Kevin Seitzer were among those leaving in trades for prospects.

Kansas City couldn't overcome a 6–16 start and Minnesota hit only 118 home runs, the majors' lowest total.

In the West, the Texas Rangers won the franchise's first title. The team was in first place for all but four of 182 days. Juan Gonzalez batted .310 with 47 home runs and 144 RBIs. Kevin Elster returned to playing regularly and drove in 99 runs. He also hit 24 home runs.

Seattle finished 4½ games behind Texas and hung in the race thanks to an offense that featured Alex Rodriguez and Ken Griffey, Jr. and in spite of a staff that ran though 25 pitchers. Rodriguez batted .358 with 36 home runs and 123 RBIs. Griffey missed time with a broken wrist but still managed to hit 49 homers and drive in 140 runs.

Mark McGwire was the story in Oakland with 52 home runs to go with a .312 average and 113 RBIs.

place. The team got hot, made its run at the Yankees and wound up in the postseason. Brady Anderson led the Orioles with 50 home runs.

Despite a 38–18 finish, the Boston Red Sox fell short. The Red Sox got off to a 2–12 start, the worst in franchise history. After 25 games, Boston was just 6–19. Mo Vaughn led the Red Sox with a .326 average, 44 home runs and 143 RBIs.

Pat Hentgen went 20–10 with a 3.22 ERA for Toronto and won the Cy Young award. The Detroit Tigers set a franchise record by losing 109 games. Their 6.38 ERA was the worst in American League history. The Tigers ended the season by losing their last 17 home games. One of the few bright spots was Bobby Higginson's season: .320 average, 20 home runs and 81 RBIs.

The Cleveland Indians pulled away in the American League Central after the All-Star break and finished 14½ games ahead of the Chicago

SHORTS Kirby Puckett woke up one morning in March with blurry vision. It turned out to be glaucoma and wound up abruptly ending the 12-year career of the popular Twins outfielder. Puckett batted .318 with 207 home runs and 1,085 runs batted in. Other stars who called it quits were Dave Winfield, Andre Dawson, Alan Trammell and Ozzie Smith.

Manager Tony LaRussa transferred his success from Oakland to St. Louis as the Cardinals won the National League Central. Brian Jordan batted .310 and drove in 104 runs. Jordan batted an amazing .422 with runners in scoring position. Ron Gant hit 30 home runs.

Houston finished second and manager Terry Collins was dismissed after the season. Jeff Bagwell hit .315 with 31 home runs and 120 RBIs and Shane Reynolds won 16 games. Billy Wagner established himself as a closer.

Sammy Sosa had 40 home runs and 100 RBIs for the Cubs when a broken hand ended his season on August 20. Steve Trachsel was 13–9 with a 3.03 ERA.

Jim Leyland resigned as manager in Pittsburgh rather than wait out another rebuilding plan. The Pirates traded their best pitcher, Denny Neagle, to Atlanta during the season and then traded Jeff King after he'd hit 30 home runs and driven in 111 runs.

The Atlanta Braves won the East by eight games over Montreal. The Braves hit .302 as a team in May. John Smoltz took the Cy Young award with 24 wins and 276 strikeouts. Smoltz won 14 straight decisions at one point.

In the West, the San Diego Padres swept a season-ending three-game series against Los Angeles to take the division and send the Dodgers to the wild-card berth. Ken Caminiti became the first Padres player to win the Most Valuable Player award by batting .326 with 40 home runs and 130 RBIs. Tony Gwynn won his seventh batting title.

Tommy Lasorda retired as Dodgers' manager after suffering a heart attack and was succeeded by Bill Russell. Mike Piazza batted .336 for the Dodgers with 36 home runs and 105 RBIs. Todd Worrell saved 44 games.

There were two high-profile incidents involving umpires, one tragic and one tasteless. On opening day, John McSherry collapsed and died on the field at Cincinnati's Riverfront Stadium. McSherry, 51, was felled by a massive heart attack as he tried to walk off the field after signaling for a crew mate to take over.

On September 27, umpire John Hirschbeck called Roberto Alomar of the Orioles out on strikes and an argument ensued. Alomar was ejected and was being led away by manager Davey Johnson when Alomar spat at Hirschbeck.

American League president Gene Budig suspended Alomar for five regular season games, a decision that angered Hirschbeck and the umpire's union. The lenient decision by Budig allowed Alomar to participate in the postseason.

Five high-profile players worthy of Hall of Fame consideration retired: Kirby Puckett, Dave Winfield, Andre Dawson, Alan Trammell and Ozzie Smith.

After the season, management and the Players Association finally hammered out a labor agreement, nearly two years after the World Series had to be canceled when the players went on strike.

Baseball lost two colorful figures from its past. Former Athletics owner Charles O. Finley died at 77 and longtime announcer Mel Allen died at 83.

NL MVP—San Diego's Ken Caminiti

The 1996 postseason featured an occurrence that baseball hadn't seen since 1978—the New York Yankees won the World Series.

The Yankees, winners of the American League East, rolled to their 23rd world championship in impressive fashion. New York defeated Texas in four games in the Division Series before beating Baltimore in five games in the American League Championship Series. The Yankees, making their first World Series appearance since 1981, then beat the Atlanta Braves in six games.

The other round of the Division Series featured an upset when the wild-card Baltimore Orioles defeated the Cleveland Indians, who won the AL Central with a major-league leading 99 victories. That didn't matter in the playoffs as the Orioles eliminated the Indians in four games. Baltimore won the series on Roberto Alomar's home run in the 12th inning of Game Four. Alomar was the subject of controversy throughout the series after he spat in the face of umpire John Hirschbeck during a series on the last weekend of the season.

The National League had a pair of easy wins in the Division Series. The Braves, the NL East winners, swept the wild-card Los Angeles Dodgers while the St. Louis Cardinals, the Central champs, defeated the NL West champion San Diego Padres in three games.

Both League Championship Series had compelling moments. With the Orioles leading the Yankees 4–3 in the eighth inning of Game One at Yankee Stadium, New York got a big assist from 12-year-old Jeffrey Maier, a fan sitting in the right field stands. As Derek Jeter hit a fly ball to the fence, Orioles' right fielder Tony Tarasco moved back and was in position to make the catch. Maier stuck his glove over the fence and pulled the ball into the stands.

Despite the Orioles' vehement protests, umpire Richie Garcia ruled the play a home run and the game was tied. Bernie Williams' home run in the 11th inning gave the Yankees a 5–4 win. The Orioles recovered to win Game Two by a 5–3 score and the series returned to Baltimore. The home field did nothing to help the Orioles as the Yankees won the next three games by scores of 5–2, 8–4 and 6–4.

The NLCS nearly featured a monumental upset. After the Braves took a 4–2 win in Game One in Atlanta, the Cardinals rolled to an 8–3 win in Game Two. The series returned to St. Louis, where the Cardinals eked out a 3–2 win in Game Three and rallied for a 4–3 win in Game Four.

The Braves, one game from elimination, showed why they were the defending world champs. They pounded out 22 hits in a 14–0 win in Game Five, which sent the series back to Atlanta. Behind the pitching of Greg Maddux and Mark Wohlers, Atlanta won Game Six, 3–1 before blasting St. Louis, 15–0 in Game Seven.

The Braves carried that momentum into the World Series. In Game One, the Braves hammered Yankees' starter Andy Pettitte in a 12–1 win. Braves' rookie outfielder Andruw Jones, only 19-years-old, hit two homers with five RBIs in becoming only the second player to

NL DIVISION SERIES

GAME 1	
St. Louis Cardinals 3	San Diego 1

GAME 2	
St. Louis Cardinals 5	San Diego 4

GAME 3	
St. Louis Cardinals 7	San Diego 5

GAME 1	
Atlanta 2	Los Angeles 1

GAME 2	
Atlanta 3	Los Angeles 2

GAME 3	
Atlanta 5	Los Angeles 2

AL DIVISION SERIES

GAME 1	
Baltimore 10	Cleveland 4

GAME 2	
Baltimore 7	Cleveland 4

GAME 3	
Cleveland 9	Baltimore 4

GAME 4	
Baltimore 4	Cleveland 3

GAME 1	
Texas 6	NY Yankees 2

GAME 2	
NY Yankees 5	Texas 4

GAME 3	
NY Yankees 3	Texas 2

GAME 4	
NY Yankees 6	Texas 4

NL CHAMPIONSHIP SERIES

GAME 1	
Atlanta 4	St. Louis Cardinals 2

GAME 2	
St. Louis Cardinals 8	Atlanta 3

GAME 3	
St. Louis Cardinals 3	Atlanta 2

GAME 4	
St. Louis Cardinals 4	Atlanta 3

GAME 5	
Atlanta 3	St. Louis Cardinals 0

GAME 6	
Atlanta 3	St. Louis Cardinals 1

GAME 7	
Atlanta 15	St. Louis Cardinals 0

New York's Derek Jeter benefited from an unlikely source in the ALCS

AL CHAMPIONSHIP SERIES	
GAME 1	
NY Yankees 5	Baltimore 4
GAME 2	
Baltimore 5	NY Yankees 3
GAME 3	
NY Yankees 5	Baltimore 2
GAME 4	
NY Yankees 8	Baltimore 4
GAME 5	
NY Yankees 6	Baltimore 4

WORLD SERIES	
GAME 1	
Atlanta 12	NY Yankees 1
GAME 2	
Atlanta 4	NY Yankees 0
GAME 3	
NY Yankees 5	Atlanta 2
GAME 4	
NY Yankees 8	Atlanta 6
GAME 5	
NY Yankees 1	Atlanta 0
GAME 6	
NY Yankees 3	Atlanta 2

MVP: John Wetteland, NY Yankees

John Wetteland's World Series heroics left the Yankees as number one

homer in his first two World Series at-bats. The Braves took a 4–0 decision in Game Two.

With the Series returning to Atlanta, it looked like the Yankees were in big trouble, but New York won Game Three by a 5–2 score. The turning point of the Series came in Game Four. The Braves rolled to a 6–0 lead in the fifth inning, but the Yankees got close with three runs in the sixth and tied it in the eighth on Jim Leyritz's three-run homer off Braves' closer Mark Wohlers. The Yankees took the lead in the tenth when Wade Boggs walked with the bases loaded. New York added another run and tied the Series with an 8–6 win.

The stunned Braves never recovered.

Pettitte, rebounding from his horrid performance in Game One, was magnificent in Game Five. He pitched five-hit ball in 8⅓ shutout innings before closer John Wetteland wrapped it

up. Right fielder Paul O'Neill ended the game with an over-the-shoulder catch off Luis Polonia's drive with runners on first and third. Cecil Fielder's double scored Charlie Hayes for the game's only run in the fourth and the Yankees won, 1–0.

As the Series returned to New York, the Yankees suddenly had all the momentum and they ended it with a 3–2 win in Game Six. The Yanks scored three runs in the third off Maddux. Jimmy Key and three relievers held the Braves to one run in eight innings. Wetteland allowed a run in the ninth, but became the first pitcher to save four games in a Series and was named the Most Valuable Player.

New York became only the third team to lose the first two games at home and go on to win the Series. The Yankees also went 8–0 on the road in the playoffs.

TEAMS
Chicago White Sox 1986–92, Atlanta Braves 1993

Games	.436
Games started	.432
Complete games	.93
Win–Loss	.221–126
Inning pitched	.3,068.2
Runs	.1,104
ERA	.2.81
Strikeouts	.2,160
Bases on balls	.691
Batting average	.178

Maddox's ability to locate his pitches have made him a model of consistency

There are pitchers who are more physically imposing than Greg Maddux. There are pitchers who throw harder. So why was Maddux one of the most dominant pitchers of the 1990s?

Mostly because of his ability to throw the ball exactly to the spot he wants to hit. Maddux has a good repertoire of pitches and makes them even tougher to hit by placing them precisely where he wants them to go. Other pitchers dream of the pinpoint control Maddux has developed.

"He paints the corners the way Andy Warhol paints soup cans," is the way former teammate Rich "Goose" Gossage put it. Indeed, the key to Maddux's success is the ability to spot his pitches. He does it well enough to have won four consecutive Cy Young awards. To put that feat in perspective, no pitcher had ever won more than two Cy Young awards in a row.

Maddux was drafted by the Chicago Cubs on the second round in 1984. He arrived in the major leagues four years later and began to refine the craft of pitching. He took some lumps at the beginning of his career, starting 8–18 in his first two major league seasons.

The first indication of his true potential came in 1988 when he posted an 18–8 record with a 3.19 earned run average. He was even better the next season, helping the Cubs to a divisional title with a 19–12 record and a 2.95 ERA.

Maddux was then stuck on 15 wins for two seasons as the Cubs regressed a bit. He was 15–15 in 1990 and 15–12 the following season with ERAs of 3.46 and 3.35. Considering he was often working in a hitter's park like Wrigley Field, Maddux's statistics were probably even better than they might appear. Then the Cubs made a decision that would haunt them for a decade. They opted not to re-sign Maddux as a free agent, instead letting him go to the Atlanta Braves.

The move allowed the Braves to become one of the game's most powerful teams in the 1990s and helped keep the Cubs out of the World Series for yet another decade. Maddux learned more about pitching and stepped up his career with the Braves. When the 1990s ended, his ERA for the 10-year period was 2.54. Only one other starting pitcher, Sandy Koufax of the Los Angeles Dodgers, had compiled a better ERA in a decade. Koufax had a 2.36 ERA in the 1960s and didn't pitch for the last four years following a premature retirement brought on by arm problems.

Maddux was 20–11 with a 2.18 ERA in his last year with the Cubs. In his debut with the Braves, he was 20–10 with a National League-leading 2.36 ERA. It was the first of four ERA titles he would win.

The Braves started dominating, reaching the postseason on a regular basis. Maddux anchored an exceptionally talented starting staff that was built around him, lefthander Tom Glavine and fellow righthander John Smoltz. The other members changed—Steve Avery and Denny Neagle had runs as the fourth starter—but the rotation revolved around Maddux, Glavine and Smoltz, a threesome good enough to stifle any team.

Maddux's arsenal includes a cut fastball, a superb change-up, a good slider and the occasional curveball. Despite an average physique, Maddux is an excellent athlete. He fields his position well enough to have won every Gold Glove award for pitchers in the 1990s. He hits well enough to have been used as a pinch hitter on occasion.

For 12 consecutive years, he won at least 15 games per season. His pinpoint control allowed him to pitch more than 30 consecutive innings without allowing a walk in 1999. In 1994 and 1995, his ERAs were 1.56 and 1.63, the first pitcher since Walter Johnson in 1918–19 to register ERAs under 1.80 in consecutive seasons. Those seasons were part of his four-year run as the Cy Young award winner.

Maddux looked like he might be faltering in 1999. He began the year 4–0, then went 0–3 in May with a 6.10 ERA, a streak that included a game in which he surrendered a career-high eight earned runs. In his last 21 starts, though, Maddux went 14–5 and again helped the Braves reach the postseason.

MOST VALUABLE PLAYER
AL: Ken Griffey Jr., Seattle
NL: Larry Walker, Colorado

CY YOUNG AWARD
AL: Roger Clemens, Toronto
NL: Pedro Martinez, Montreal

ROOKIE OF THE YEAR
AL: Nomar Garciaparra, Boston Red Sox
NL: Scott Rolen, Philadelphia Phillies

LEADERS

BATTING AVERAGE
AL: Frank Thomas, Chicago White Sox, .347
NL: Tony Gwynn, San Diego, .372

HOME RUNS
AL: Ken Griffey Jr., Seattle, 56
NL: Larry Walker, Colorado, 49

RUNS BATTED IN
AL: Ken Griffey Jr., Seattle, 147
NL: Larry Walker, Colorado, 140

STOLEN BASES
AL: Brian Hunter, Detroit, 74
NL: Tony Womack, Pittsburgh, 60

PITCHING VICTORIES
AL: Roger Clemens, Toronto, 21
NL: Denny Neagle, Atlanta, 20

EARNED RUN AVERAGE
AL: Roger Clemens, Toronto, 2.05
NL: Pedro Martinez, Boston Red Sox, 1.90

STRIKEOUTS
AL: Roger Clemens, Toronto, 292
NL: Curt Schilling, Philadelphia Phillies, 319

SAVES
AL: Randy Myers, Baltimore, 45
NL: Jeff Shaw, Cincinnati, 42

Baseball purists insisted that there was something fishy about the Florida Marlins' big season. Florida proved beyond any doubt the correlation between a large payroll and on-field success when it captured the wild-card spot and parlayed that berth into a World Series win.

How did they go from two games under .500 to a World Series parade? They spent. Owner Wayne Huizenga decided that the Marlins would try to accelerate their progress and authorized $89 million in contract commitments. The Marlins signed free agents and they traded for players who had gotten too expensive for other clubs.

Leading the show was manager Jim Leyland, a hot free agent in his own right. Leyland had resigned in Pittsburgh after 11 seasons when he saw that the new ownership was going to strip the Pirates and start from scratch with young players. Having endured one building program in Pittsburgh, Leyland decided he didn't want to take on another.

The Marlins grafted together a team for Leyland. Moises Alou, late of Montreal, was the

Manager Jim Leyland was one of the many big catches landed by the Marlins

Mark McGwire joined the Cardinals in July and remained hot

most consistent offensive player with a .292 average, 23 home runs and 115 RBIs. Gary Sheffield had a disappointing season, but still provided 21 home runs.

Catcher Charles Johnson, one of the few players who had been grown by the Marlins, provided excellent defense and hit 19 homers. Bobby Bonilla may have worn out his welcome elsewhere, but the Marlins loved his 96 RBIs. Free agent Alex Fernandez celebrated a return to his south Florida roots with 17 wins. Kevin Brown, who had become a hired pitching gun, won 16 games and closer Robb Nen had 35 saves.

None of it was enough to overcome the mighty Atlanta Braves, even though the Marlins won the season series from Atlanta, 8–4. The Braves moved to Turner Field and brought the winning tradition with them, taking their sixth consecutive division title.

They won 19 games in April and took over first place for good on April 14. As always, their strength was a deep and talented pitching staff that led the league in earned run average.

Denny Neagle had a league-best 20 wins, including seven straight to open the season, and his ERA was 2.97. Greg Maddux was right behind him with 19 wins, including a streak of ten straight. John Smoltz won 15 games and Tom Glavine had 14 victories. Out of the bullpen, Mark Wohlers rode a 100-mile-per-hour fastball to 33 saves.

Kenny Lofton, acquired from Cleveland,

batted .333. For the second time in franchise history, the Braves had four players with at least 20 home runs—Ryan Klesko (24), Javy Lopez (23), Fred McGriff (22) and Chipper Jones (21).

Atlanta's 101–61 record was the best in the majors.

The best pitcher who didn't wear a Braves uniform was Montreal's Pedro Martinez, a rail-thin righthander with a penchant for throwing hard and inside. Martinez won the Cy Young award with a 17–8 record, a league-leading 1.90 ERA and 305 strikeouts.

The New York Mets were too busy fighting among themselves to compete. The most serious spat was between catcher Todd Hundley and manager Bobby Valentine after Valentine suggested that Hundley needed to curtail his night life, a hissing contest perfectly tailored for the city's tabloids. The Mets' best pitcher wound up being former replacement player Rick Reed.

The Philadelphia Phillies may have been terrible, but third baseman Scott Rolen wasn't. He batted .283 with 21 home runs and 92 RBIs to win the National League Rookie of the Year award. He was the first Phillies player to take the award since Dick Allen in 1964 and he broke a five-year streak of Los Angeles Dodgers winners.

Houston prevailed in a weak Central Division, beating out the surprising Pirates by five games.

The Astros had made the bold move of moving former pitcher Larry Dierker from the broadcast booth to the manager's office. Dierker had never managed before, but Houston took over first place on July 18 and held it for the rest of the way.

Craig Biggio batted .309 and his 146 runs led the league. Jeff Bagwell hit 43 home runs and drove in 135 runs. Darryl Kile went 19–7 with a 2.57 ERA and struck out 205 batters. He had a ten-game winning streak over two months. Lefthander Mike Hampton won 15 games and Billy Wagner emerged as a closer with 23 saves.

The Pirates trimmed their payroll to an absolute minimum by taking the anti-Marlins approach. They jettisoned just about all their veterans and replaced them with prospects and low-salaried role players. And they stayed in

SHORTS Mark McGwire changed teams and leagues but it didn't seem to affect him. McGwire was traded from Oakland to St. Louis in July 31 but still became the second player to have back-to-back 50-homer seasons. He hit 58 and matched the record for a righthanded hitter held by Jimmie Foxx and Hank Greenberg.

TIMELINE

Jan. 6: The Dodgers went up for sale, ending 47 years of ownership by the O'Malley family.

Jan. 16: The decision is made to put the Arizona expansion team in the American League and the Tampa Bay franchise in the National League.

April 2: Gary Sheffield signed a record-breaking contract with Florida for six years and $72 million.

April 4: The Braves came from behind to beat the Cubs 5–4 in the first game at Turner Field.

April 19: The Cardinals and Padres played in Hawaii.

June 5: Cleveland took possession of first place in the American League Central for good.

June 10: Kevin Brown of the Marlins pitched a no-hitter against the Giants. He lost a perfect game with two out in the ninth when he hit Marvin Benard with a pitch.

June 12: The first interleague games were played.

June 13: Orioles' outfielder Eric Davis had surgery for colon cancer.

July 9: Bob Boone was fired as Royals' manager and replaced by Tony Muser.

July 12: Francisco Cordova and Ricardo Rincon of the Pirates combined on a ten-inning no-hitter against Houston. Mark Smith's three-run homer off John Hudek won the game.

July 25: Ray Knight was fired as manager of the Reds and replaced by Jack McKeon.

July 31: Oakland traded Mark McGwire to the Cardinals.

July 31: The White Sox conceded the American League Central race to Cleveland by trading three pitchers to San Francisco for six prospects.

Sept. 30: The White Sox fired manager Terry Bevington and replaced him with Jerry Manuel.

Nov. 18: The expansion draft was held to stock the two new teams. Tampa Bay chose Florida pitcher Tony Saunders with the first selection and Arizona picked Cleveland pitcher Brian Anderson.

The New York Yankees' Tino Martinez

SHORTS Mets vs. Yankees. White Sox vs. Cubs. Interleague play brought some dream match-ups and some clunkers too, but the new system helped in renewing interest in baseball. It led to some interesting developments, like having AL pitchers bat. Bobby Witt of Texas hit a home run on June 30, the first by an AL pitcher since 1972.

contention until the last week of the season and played .500 through August.

Kevin Young, who had once been released by the Pirates, came back and batted .300 with 18 homers and 74 RBIs. Jose Guillen made the jump from Class A and hit .267 with 14 homers and 70 RBIs as the regular right fielder. Rich Loiselle became the closer, converting 29 of 34 save opportunities. Tony Womack was successful on 32 consecutive stolen base attempts over four months, breaking Max Carey's team record that had stood since 1922.

The Cincinnati Reds set club records for both stolen bases (190) and errors (106). The Chicago Cubs thought Mel Rojas was the answer for their bullpen. He went 0–4 and blew six of 19 save chances before they admitted their mistake and shipped him to the Mets.

The St. Louis Cardinals, heretofore a speed-oriented team, abruptly shifted gears by acquiring Mark McGwire from Oakland. The A's were anxious to get a return for McGwire before his contract expired and dealt him on July 31. Between the two teams and two leagues, he wound up with 58 home runs.

McGwire, Seattle's Ken Griffey Jr. and Tino Martinez of the New York Yankees all took a run at Roger Maris' single-season record of 61 home runs. McGwire came the closest.

The San Francisco Giants went from worst to first to win the National League West. They spent 105 days in first place, but couldn't clinch until the season had one day left.

Barry Bonds batted .291 with 40 home runs and 101 RBIs despite being walked 145 times. Jeff Kent hit 29 home runs and drove in 121 runs, the best offensive season by a Giants' second baseman since Rogers Hornsby. Shawn Estes won 19 games and was 9–0 when he pitched following a Giants loss. Rod Beck had 37 saves.

In San Diego, Tony Gwynn tied Honus Wagner's National League record with his eighth batting title. Gwynn won four straight batting crowns and enjoyed his 15th season over .500.

Baltimore became the third American League

Tony Gwynn tied a National League record with his eighth batting title

team to lead wire to wire. The Orioles finished two games ahead of the New York Yankees. Rafael Palmiero had 38 homers and 110 RBIs in spite of an ordinary .254 average. The Orioles had a balanced offensive attack and a superior pitching staff, headed by Jimmy Key and Scott Erickson, who each won 16 games. Mike Mussina had 15 wins and Randy Myers led the league with 45 saves.

The Yankees could never get closer to first than two games, but they easily won the wild card spot.

Cleveland had an easy time winning the Central once the Chicago White Sox conceded on July 31. The White Sox traded three pitchers to San Francisco for six prospects, with owner Jerry Reinsdorf saying, "Anyone who thinks this White Sox team can catch Cleveland is crazy." The White Sox were 3½ games out with two full months left in the season.

The Indians set a club record with 220 home runs and became the first American League team to top 200 in three consecutive years. Jim Thome led with 40 homers. David Justice had 33 to go with a .329 average and 101 RBIs in his comeback season. Matt Williams hit 32. Sandy Alomar had a 30-game hitting streak, the league's longest since 1906, and wound up with a .324 average, 21 home runs and 83 RBIs.

Cleveland's pitching declined with Charles

Nagy's 15 wins leading the staff. Jose Mesa's save total dropped from 39 to 16.

Seattle won the West with a franchise-record 90 victories. In 20 years the Mariners had occupied first place for just 104 days. They logged 140 days at the top in 1997. They had a major league-record 264 home runs. Ken Griffey Jr. was able to stay free of injuries and batted .304 with 56 home runs and 147 RBIs. Randy Johnson led the pitching staff with a 20–4 record that included a 16-game winning streak. Opponents batted just .194 against Johnson.

National League fans got to see Griffey thanks to the first season of interleague play. There were three interleague periods with teams playing opponents from the corresponding division to highlight intracity rivalries like Yankees–Mets and White Sox–Cubs. The National League held a 117–97 edge in the games with Florida and Montreal both posting a 12–3 record against the American League. Fans seemed to like the idea—attendance was up 20 percent for interleague games.

The Marlins were a one-year wonder. Less than two weeks after the end of the World Series, Huizenga abruptly reversed his course and ordered the payroll slashed. Among those departing quickly were Alou, Nen, Devon White, Jeff Conine, Brown and Dennis Cook, with more subtractions ordered during the 1998 season.

NL DIVISION SERIES	
GAME 1	
Florida 2	San Francisco 1
GAME 2	
Florida 7	San Francisco 6
GAME 3	
Florida 6	San Francisco 2
GAME 1	
Atlanta 2	Houston 1
GAME 2	
Atlanta 13	Houston 3
GAME 3	
Atlanta 4	Houston 1

AL DIVISION SERIES	
GAME 1	
Baltimore 9	Seattle 3
GAME 2	
Baltimore 9	Seattle 3
GAME 3	
Seattle 4	Baltimore 2
GAME 4	
Baltimore 3	Seattle 1
GAME 1	
NY Yankees 8	Cleveland 6
GAME 2	
Cleveland 7	NY Yankees 5
GAME 3	
NY Yankees 6	Cleveland 1
GAME 4	
Cleveland 3	NY Yankees 2
GAME 5	
Cleveland 4	NY Yankees 3

NL CHAMPIONSHIP SERIES	
GAME 1	
Florida 4	Atlanta 2
GAME 2	
Atlanta 7	Florida 1
GAME 3	
Florida 5	Atlanta 2
GAME 4	
Atlanta 4	Florida 0
GAME 5	
Florida 2	Atlanta 1
GAME 6	
Florida 7	Atlanta 4

Baseball purists shuddered over the prospect of adding a wild-card team to the playoffs in each league. Most traditionalists opposed the wild card because they thought it would eliminate pennant races and dilute the playoffs.

The Florida Marlins didn't listen. In only their fifth year of existence, not only did the Marlins qualify for the playoffs, but they also became the first wild-card team to win the World Series with a victory in seven games over the Cleveland Indians.

Despite the fact that they didn't start playing until 1993, the Marlins weren't your everyday fifth-year team. Thanks to some big spending in the free-agent market, their roster consisted of such stars as pitchers Kevin Brown and Alex Fernandez, third basemen Bobby Bonilla and outfielders Moises Alou and Gary Sheffield.

The Marlins made the playoffs by finishing second in the National League East. Florida

swept NL West champ San Francisco in three games in the Division Series. In the other Division Series in the NL, Atlanta swept Houston, which won the Central, in three games.

Although the Marlins had won eight of 12 from the Braves during the regular season, Atlanta won the East by nine games, finishing 101–61 while Florida was 92–70. The Marlins won the opener in Atlanta by a 5–3 score behind Brown, but the Braves took Game Two, 7–1. The Marlins won Game Three in Miami, 5–2 before the Braves evened it again with a 4–0 win in Game Four. Florida righthander Livan Hernandez was the start of Game Five. He was allowed only three hits and set an LCS record with 15 strikeouts in the Marlins' 2–1 win.

The series returned to Atlanta, where the Marlins ended it with a 7–4 win to send manager Jim Leyland to his first World Series.

Despite finishing with the worst record of the four American League playoff teams at 86–75, the Indians won the Central and advanced to the World Series. Thanks to two wins by rookie pitcher Jaret Wright, they beat the defending World Series champion Yankees, who won the AL wild card, in five games in the Division Series. Meanwhile, the Baltimore Orioles, who won the East with a league-best 98–64 record, eliminated West champ Seattle in four games.

The Orioles were the favorites in the ALCS and looked the part with a 3–0 win in Game One at Baltimore. The Indians evened the series in Game Two when Marquis Grissom's three-run homer in the eighth gave them a 5–4 win.

The series moved to Cleveland, where the Indians took two out of three. Cleveland won Game Three, 2–1, in 11 innings before taking Game Four by an 8–7 score. The Orioles staved off elimination in Game Five with a 4–2 win.

Game Six, which was back in Baltimore, featured a classic pitching duel between the Orioles' Mike Mussina and the Indians' Charles Nagy. The game was scoreless until the 11th when Tony Fernandez's home run off

World Series MVP—Florida's Livan Hernandez

The Florida Marlins celebrate their extra-innings victory in Game Seven

Armando Benitez gave the Indians a 1–0 win and their second World Series trip in three years.

The Series began in Miami and the Marlins won Game One, 7–4, behind the pitching of Hernandez and home runs by Alou and Charles Johnson. Strong pitching by Chad Ogea and two relievers gave the Indians a 6–1 win in Game Two.

The Series moved to Cleveland for the next three games, where wind-chill readings sent the temperatures into the 20s. The Indians jumped to a 7–3 lead after five innings, but the Marlins rallied to tie it by the seventh. Florida scored seven runs in the ninth, only to see the Indians score four before the Marlins hung on for a 14–11 win. Sheffield had three hits and five RBIs for Florida.

Snow fell during Game Four, but Wright pitched well again while Manny Ramirez and Matt Williams hit two-run homers in the Indians' 10–3 win. The Indians held a 3–2 lead in Game Five, but Alou's home run off Orel Hershiser in the sixth keyed a four-run rally in the Marlins' 8–7 victory.

Back in Florida, Ogea and three relievers stopped the Marlins for a 4–1 win in Game Six, which evened the Series. That set up a classic Game Seven. Fernandez's third-inning single gave the Indians a 2–0 lead. Wright held the Marlins scoreless until Bonilla's seventh-inning home run made it 2–1. Three outs away from winning their first World Series since 1948, the Indians carried that one-run lead into the ninth, but closer Jose Mesa couldn't get the job done. Craig Counsell's sacrifice fly tied the game and the teams dueled until the 11th when Edgar Renteria's single gave Florida a 3–2 win.

MOST VALUABLE PLAYER
AL: Juan Gonzalez, Texas
NL: Sammy Sosa, Chicago Cubs

CY YOUNG AWARD
AL: Roger Clemens, Toronto
NL: Tom Glavine, Atlanta

ROOKIE OF THE YEAR
AL: Ben Grieve, Oakland
NL: Kerry Wood, Chicago Cubs

LEADERS
BATTING AVERAGE
AL: Bernie Williams, NY Yankees, .329
NL: Larry Walker, Colorado, .363

HOME RUNS
AL: Ken Griffey Jr., Seattle, 56
NL: Mark McGwire, St. Louis Cardinals, 70

RUNS BATTED IN
AL: Juan Gonzalez, Texas, 157
NL: Sammy Sosa, Chicago Cubs, 158

STOLEN BASES
AL: Rickey Henderson, Oakland, 66
NL: Tony Womack, Pittsburgh, 58

PITCHING VICTORIES
AL: Roger Clemens, Toronto; David Cone, NY Yankees, Rick Helling, Texas, 20
NL: Tom Glavine, Atlanta, 20

EARNED RUN AVERAGE
AL: Roger Clemens, Toronto, 2.65
NL: Greg Maddux, Atlanta, 2.22

STRIKEOUTS
AL: Roger Clemens, Toronto, 271
NL: Curt Schilling, Philadelphia Phillies, 300

SAVES
AL: Tom Gordon, Boston Red Sox, 46
NL: Trevor Hoffman, San Diego, 53

In 97 years, only two men had ever hit as many as 60 home runs in a major league season. In 1998, two men did it in the same month. The Mark McGwire–Sammy Sosa home run derby was one of two season-long stories that made the year special.

The other was the unprecedented excellence of the New York Yankees, who had a record-breaking year, even by their lofty standards.

It was obvious the Yankees were having a special year and would make the postseason. The only mystery was how many games they'd win and what they would do in the postseason.

McGwire–Sosa was a daily headline that even captivated casual fans.

The climate was ripe for a serious challenge to the long-standing single season home run records. Babe Ruth hit 60 in a 154-game season in 1927. That mark stood until Roger Maris slugged 61 during a 162-game schedule in 1962.

Pitching had been further diluted by expansion. Two more teams were added in 1998 and there were 22 more pitchers who would otherwise be pitching in the minor leagues. The strike zone had gotten smaller, forcing pitchers to stay away from the corners. New ballparks were designed to be hitter-friendly. Hitters were bigger than ever, including McGwire and Sosa. And although it hadn't been scientifically substantiated, there was a suspicion that the baseballs were as lively as they'd ever been.

McGwire had a football linebacker's physique and Sosa has also bulked up considerably from the early days of his career.

McGwire had come to the St. Louis Cardinals a year earlier when it became apparent the Oakland Athletics wouldn't be able to afford him. Between Oakland and St. Louis, he hit 58 home runs but didn't win the home run title in either League.

Sosa had a reputation as a free-swinging hitter who struck out too much. He had never hit more than 40 home runs in a season and had reached that level just once. Most handicappers figured that if anyone other than McGwire was likely to challenge the record, it would be Seattle's Ken Griffey, Jr. Griffey was coming off a 56-homer season.

McGwire started with an opening day grand slam and followed that with three more home runs in three games. By the end of April, he'd hit 11 and was on pace for 66. At the end of May, McGwire had 27 homers, which advanced the pace to 83. By the end of June, he'd hit 37 and was on track for 74.

Sosa started in typical fashion, hitting six home runs in April and seven in May, which put him on pace for 39. He broke a major league record with 20 home runs in June and brought his season total to 33.

Both cooled off in July; McGwire hit eight and Sosa had nine. Although Sosa occasionally passed McGwire, those moments were temporary, usually lasting a few hours. At the close of play each day, McGwire never trailed Sosa.

At the end of August, McGwire and Sosa each had 55 home runs, one away from Hack Wilson's 1930 National League record. McGwire broke Wilson's record with a two-homer game on September 1. He got No. 60 on September 5 to tie Ruth's record in the Cardinals' 142nd game. No. 61 came on September 7 and McGwire broke the record

Nobody would have thought that 66 homers would end up as second best for Sammy Sosa

Mark McGwire kept a nation on the edge of their seats in his pursuit of the home run record

March 31: The Arizona Diamondbacks debuted with 9–2 loss to Colorado, the first of five straight losses for the expansion franchise.

March 31: Pokey Reese, filling in for the injured Barry Larkin at shortstop for the Cincinnati Reds, made four errors in the season opener against the San Diego Padres. Reese made three of the errors in the first inning.

April 1: The Tampa Bay Devils Rays beat Detroit 11–8 to win the first game in franchise history. Fred McGriff drove in four runs.

May 6: Chicago Cubs' rookie Kerry Wood tied a major league record with 20 strikeouts in a 1–0, one-hit win over the Houston Astros.

May 17: David Wells of the Yankees pitched a perfect game against the Twins at Yankee Stadium. Seven of the Twins' nine starters came into the game with batting averages of .250 or lower.

July 5: Toronto's Roger Clemens got his 3,000th career strikeout.

Aug. 7: Newly-acquired Randy Johnson made his first Houston start, beating Philadelphia 9–0 on a five-hitter.

Aug. 9: Dennis Martinez of the Braves got his 244th career victory, making him the winningest Latin pitcher in major league history.

Aug. 14: Baltimore's Chris Hoiles became the first catcher in major league history to hit two grand slams in one game. Hoiles hit the home runs in the third and eighth innings of a 15–3 win at Cleveland.

Sept. 8: Mark McGwire set the single-season home run record when he hit his 62nd of the season off Steve Trachsel of the Cubs.

Sept. 13: Andy Benes of Arizona came within an out of a no-hitter against Cincinnati but lost it when Sean Casey singled.

Sept. 20: Cal Ripken Jr. voluntarily missed the game against the Yankees, ending his consecutive game streak at 2,632.

Sept. 27: The Yankees beat Tampa Bay for their 114th win, ending the most successful regular season in 92 years.

against the Cubs' Steve Trachsel on September 8.

Sosa passed both Ruth and Maris in the same game on September 13 against Milwaukee. He hit his 61st off Bronswell Patrick, then got No. 62 off Eric Plunk.

Sosa had a 45-minute lead on McGwire when he hit his 66th on September 25. McGwire got one that night and four more during the season's last weekend, beating up an inexperienced Montreal Expos pitching staff.

McGwire hit 70, four more than Sosa. But McGwire expressed many times during the season the envy he felt for Sosa because the

Cubs were in the wild-card race while the Cardinals had no chance at postseason play.

In that regard, it was a dream season for the Yankees, who set a record by going 61–20 in the first half of the season. They played 24 consecutive series without losing one. When they won their 100th game on September 4, they had lost only 38 times. Their final record of 114–48 set American League records for most wins in a season and the major league record for most wins in a 162-game schedule.

How did the Yankees do it? They had incredible balance throughout their lineup and a sense of professionalism established by veteran players and reinforced by manager Joe Torre. Shortstop Derek Jeter was the Yankees' most indispensable player and third baseman Scott Brosius emerged as a major contributor after his career had bottomed out in Oakland. Bernie Williams, Tino Martinez and Paul O'Neill were solid hitters. David Cone won 20 games and David Wells had an exceptional season that included a perfect game against Minnesota.

SHORTS There were two new major league teams with the addition of expansion franchises in Arizona and Tampa Bay. The two leagues expanded from 16 teams to 30 in less than 40 years. But the bigger news was the unprecedented switch of the Milwaukee Brewers to the National League. No team had ever changed leagues before.

David Wells celebrates perfection

Atlanta won a franchise-record 106 games en route to its seventh consecutive division title. The Braves pulled away from the New York Mets in May and had an easy ride to the postseason. The Braves hit a team-record 215 home runs and Andres Galarraga's 44 were the most ever by a Braves first baseman. Catcher Javy Lopez had 34 home runs and 106 RBIs and was the League's best at nabbing base stealers. John Smoltz came back from elbow surgery to win 17 games. Tom Glavine won 20 games for the fourth time and his 2.47 ERA was a career best.

Houston took the National League Central title, finishing 12 ½ games in front of the Cubs. The Astros set a franchise record by winning 102 games and their July 31 trade of prospects for Randy Johnson paid off when the big lefthander went 10-1. Craig Biggio batted .325 with 20 home runs, 88 RBIs and 50 stolen bases. Shane Reynolds was 19–8 and Jose Lima won 16 games.

The San Diego Padres jumped from last place to first to claim their second National League West title in three years. They led the division from June 12. Greg Vaughn batted .272 with 50 home runs and 119 RBIs. Ken Caminiti had 29 homers and 82 RBIs. Kevin Brown won 18 games and Andy Ashby added 17 wins. Trevor Hoffman's 53 saves tied a National League record.

The Cubs beat the San Francisco Giants in a one-game playoff to grab the wild-card spot. Aside from Sosa, the big story with the Cubs was rookie pitcher Kerry Wood, who won 13 games and had a 20-strikeout game before arm trouble shortened his season.

The defending champion Florida Marlins fell to 54–108 as they stripped their roster in a cost-cutting mode. Gary Sheffield, Bobby Bonilla, Charles Johnson and Jim Eisenreich were all traded to Los Angeles for Mike Piazza and Todd Zeile, who used Florida as a stopover on their way to other clubs.

The Cleveland Indians took their fourth consecutive American League Central title and became the seventh team to spend the entire season in first place. Manny Ramirez led the Indians with a .294 average, 45 home runs and 145 RBIs. Dave Burba and Charles Nagy each won 15 games.

The Texas Rangers won the American League West for the second time in three years. Juan Gonzalez batted .318 with 45 home runs and a League-leading 145 RBIs. Rick Helling was a 20-game winner on a pitching staff that ranked near the bottom of the League in most categories. John Wetteland had 42 saves.

The Boston Red Sox won 92 games in a season when that didn't even get them within shouting distance of the Yankees. The Red Sox outlasted four other teams to claim the American League wild card spot. Nomar Garciaparra batted .323 with 35 home runs and 122 RBIs. Mo Vaughn batted .337 and Tom Gordon had 46 saves.

Baseball established franchises in two traditional spring training cities, Phoenix and Tampa. The Arizona Diamondbacks joined the National League and the Tampa Bay Devil Rays became the American League's first new franchise since 1977. The additions caused some shifting, with the most significant change involving the Milwaukee Brewers.

The team that had started life as the Seattle Pilots in 1969, moved to the National League. It reestablished Milwaukee as a National League city. Its best baseball years came when the Braves won a World Series and two National League pennants during their 1953–65 tenure.

The Detroit Tigers were transferred from the American League East to the Central.

The Los Angeles Dodgers, who had long been associated with management stability, fired General Manager Fred Claire and Manager Bill Russell on June 21. Glenn Hoffman came up from the minor leagues to serve as interim

manager.

Buddy Bell was replaced in Detroit by coach Larry Parrish. Don Baylor was fired in Colorado and replaced by Jim Leyland, who resigned as Florida's manager. John Boles, Leyland's predecessor, reclaimed the Marlins job.

Chicago's Kerry Wood

NL DIVISION SERIES	
GAME 1	
Atlanta 7	Chicago Cubs 1
GAME 2	
Atlanta 2	Chicago Cubs 1
GAME 3	
Atlanta 6	Chicago Cubs 2
GAME 1	
San Diego 2	Houston 1
GAME 2	
Houston 5	San Diego 4
GAME 3	
San Diego 2	Houston 1
GAME 4	
San Diego 6	Houston 1

AL DIVISION SERIES	
GAME 1	
NY Yankees 2	Texas 0
GAME 2	
NY Yankees 3	Texas 1
GAME 3	
NY Yankees 4	Texas 0
GAME 1	
Boston 11	Cleveland 3
GAME 2	
Cleveland 9	Boston 5
GAME 3	
Cleveland 4	Boston 3
GAME 4	
Cleveland 2	Boston 1

NL CHAMPIONSHIP SERIES	
GAME 1	
San Diego 3	Atlanta 2
GAME 2	
San Diego 3	Atlanta 0
GAME 3	
San Diego 4	Atlanta 1
GAME 4	
Atlanta 8	San Diego 3
GAME 5	
Atlanta 7	San Diego 6
GAME 6	
San Diego 5	Atlanta 0

AL CHAMPIONSHIP SERIES	
GAME 1	
NY Yankees 7	Cleveland 2
GAME 2	
Cleveland 4	NY Yankees 1
GAME 3	
Cleveland 6	NY Yankees 1

The New York Yankees won their 24th World Series title with a professionalism and efficiency that had to impress even the most ardent Yankee hater.

World Series MVP Scott Brosius tries to break up an Indians double-play during the ALCS

The Yankees needed only three games to eliminate the Texas Rangers in the Division Series. Texas scored just one run in the sweep. New York got a scare in the American League Championship Series against Cleveland, losing consecutive games after winning the opener. The Indians had played their way to the ALCS by beating the Boston Red Sox in four games. The Red Sox won the opener behind Pedro Martinez, then dropped three consecutive games. Boston manager Jimy Williams resisted the temptation to start Martinez on three days' rest in the fourth game. Martinez was ready for the fifth game, which never came.

New York got its toughest challenge from the Indians. The Yankees were pushed to six games and had their only two losses in the postseason against Cleveland. The Yankees won the first game handily, scoring five runs in the first inning en route to a 7–2 win over Jaret Wright. If the Yankees needed any extra incentive in the Series, Wright's presence in the opening game provided it. The Yankees had issues with Wright going all the way back to spring training. Wright broke shortstop Luis Sojo's hand with a pitch in an exhibition game and had also hit Paul O'Neill during the regular season.

The Indians won the second game 4–1 in 12 innings as the Yankees' bullpen had one of its rare failures. The key play wasn't a home run but

a ball that traveled only about 30 feet. Travis Fryman pushed a bunt down the line and first baseman Tino Martinez threw the ball into Fryman's back for an error. Yankees' second baseman Chuck Knoblauch, who was covering first on the play, had a terrible lapse in judgment and stood at the base arguing the call while Enrique Wilson scored all the way from first.

Cleveland's Bartolo Colon outpitched Andy Pettite in the third game, won 6–1 by the Indians. Colon pitched a four-hitter to get his first postseason win.

The Yankees-Indians series turned in Game Four when Orlando "El Duque" Hernandez combined with two other pitchers on a 4–0 shutout to even the series at two games each.

David Wells won Game Five and the Yankees ended the series in Game Six, taking advantage of some poor Cleveland defense to score five unearned runs in a 9–5 victory.

In the National League playoffs, the Chicago Cubs had to beat the San Francisco Giants in a one-game showdown to claim the wild card spot. The Cubs, who had an emotional stretch run, accomplished that goal, but were spent and promptly fell in a three-game sweep by the Atlanta Braves.

Sammy Sosa, who carried the Cubs with his 66 regular season home runs to win the

National League's Most Valuable Player award, had a poor series. Sosa batted .182 without a home run or RBI. He wasn't alone—first baseman Mark Grace batted .083 and outfielder Henry Rodriguez hit .143 as the Cubs scored just four runs in 28 innings against Atlanta's superb pitching staff.

The Houston Astros won the National League Central with ease, but acquired pitcher Randy Johnson in a midsummer trade with the postseason in mind. The Astros were convinced that the overpowering lefthander would be their ticket to playoff success because of his ability to neutralize lefthanded hitters. When Johnson was acquired Houston players spoke of how valuable he'd be in a series against San Diego and Tony Gwynn.

Johnson pitched well against the Padres, but that didn't prevent him from losing twice in the four-game series. The Astros batted just .182 as a team against San Diego's less-heralded pitching staff. Houston's "Killer B's"—Craig Biggio, Jeff Bagwell and Derek Bell—all hit under .200 without a homer. Moises Alou batted .182 for Houston.

Meanwhile, Padres' utilityman Jim Leyritz kept up his amazing postseason success by hitting three home runs, including a pivotal, tie-breaking shot in Game Three. Kevin Brown, acquired by the Padres for one year before his free agency, pitched two stong games, allowing one earned run in 14⅔ innings. In some ways, getting Brown was as much a go-for-broke gesture as the Astros' trade for Johnson.

The Padres acquired Brown in the Florida Marlins' fire sale. They knew it was doubtful he'd stay for more than one year with free agency looming, but they felt that the rest of the team was good enough to compete for a championship. Brown was the kind of proven No. 1 starter every winning team needs. He also had a fresh track record of postseason success. The gamble paid off when Brown's solid work helped the Padres advance.

Dan Miceli pitched out a jam to preserve the lead in Game Four and send the Padres to the second round of the playoffs against Atlanta.

The Braves were heavily favored, but the Padres had the unmistakable look of a team with destiny on its side. So many things had fallen into place for San Diego in the regular season and that run continued in the playoffs.

The Padres won the opening game even though reliable closer Trevor Hoffman failed to hold a one-run lead. San Diego rode Brown's three-hitter in Game Two to a 2–0 lead in the series. Brown had 11 strikeouts and outpitched

Tom Glavine, a 20-game winner.

San Diego put itself on the brink of the World Series with a win in Game Three behind Sterling Hitchcock. The Braves beat Greg Maddux to take a commanding lead in the series.

Atlanta avoided a sweep by winning Game Four. Andres Galarraga's grand slam was the big blow. In Game Five, the Braves became the first team in baseball to come back from a 3–0 deficit and force a sixth game. Michael Tucker's eighth-inning home run gave Atlanta the 7–6 win.

The Braves' comeback faltered in Game Six, thanks to a strong effort from Hitchcock, who worked on short rest. Hitchcock and four relievers combined on a two-hitter in the 5–0 win.

San Diego's Cinderella story soured in the Series, though. The Yankees swept the four games.

New York had a seven-run seventh inning in the first game. Brown had to leave the game in the seventh because of the lingering effects of a line drive that hit his left shin in the second inning. The big blow in the inning was Tino Martinez's grand slam, which came a pitch after the Padres thought he had looked at a third strike.

The Padres wasted a scoring opportunity in the first inning of Game Two, only to see the Yankees come back and score three runs in the bottom of the inning. Andy Ashby, the Padres' second most effective starter, was gone in the third inning after allowing seven runs. Hernandez worked seven solid innings for the Yankees and New York got a balanced offensive attack.

Only the venue changed in Game Three and the home field was no advantage for the Padres. Scott Brosius hit a pair of home runs, including the game-winner in the eighth off San Diego closer Trevor Hoffman. The desperate Padres called on Hoffman an inning early and saw the strategy backfire in the 5–4 loss. Mariano Rivera got the last five outs for the Yankees.

No team has won a World Series after falling behind 3–0 in games and the Padres went quietly in the fourth game, losing 3–0. Andy Pettite, who had proven to be a quality postseason pitcher, outpitched Brown. Leyritz, a hero in the Championship Series, was hitless in ten World Series at-bats and lined out with the bases loaded in Game Four to end a threat.

How did this Yankee team compare to some of the championship clubs of the past?

"I'll let people smarter than me argue about that," pitcher David Cone said. "It's tough to compare yourself with ghosts of the past, but we've made our mark."

(continued)	
GAME 4	
NY Yankees 4	Cleveland 0
GAME 5	
NY Yankees 5	Cleveland 3
GAME 6	
NY Yankees 9	Cleveland 5

WORLD SERIES

GAME 1	
NY Yankees 9	San Diego 6
GAME 2	
NY Yankees 9	San Diego 3
GAME 3	
NY Yankees 5	San Diego 4
GAME 4	
NY Yankees 3	San Diego 0

MVP: Scott Brosius, NY Yankees

New York closer Mariano Rivera lets it all out as the Yankees complete a Series sweep to end their record-breaking season

MARK MCGWIRE

Games	1,688
At-Bats	5,652
Runs	1,059
RBI	1,227
Home runs	522
Hits	1,498
Doubles	240
Triples	6
Stolen Bases	11
Average	.265
Slugging percentage	.587

McGwire's assault on the record books helped rejuvenate the ailing game in 1998

Anyone who didn't enjoy Mark McGwire's pursuit of the single-season home run record in 1998 was probably either a pitcher or an Oakland Athletics fan.

Pitchers didn't like it for obvious reasons. Oakland fans, who watched McGwire's heroics from afar, were left to wonder what might have been had baseball's lopsided economic system not forced McGwire's trade to the St. Louis Cardinals for three pitchers during the 1997 season.

McGwire's 70 home run season in 1998 didn't just set a record. It provided baseball with a compelling storyline and helped bring the battered sport back to the forefront after a destructive labor stoppage in 1994. Even casual fans were mesmerized by the drama.

He didn't just draw crowds for games, he drew them for batting practice. Fans showed up 90 minutes early solely to see how far McGwire could blast the lobs of Cardinals coach Dave McKay. That McGwire would be the one to overtake Babe Ruth and Roger Maris should have come as no surprise. In college, McGwire set a PAC-10 conference record with 32 home runs. In his first major league season, he blasted 49 to set a rookie record.

At 6-foot-5 and 250 pounds, the red-haired McGwire was built for power. With Oakland, his biggest problem was staying healthy enough to be consistent. He spent eight different stretches on the disabled list. In the 1997 season he split between Oakland and St. Louis, he wound up with 58 home runs over the two leagues. That made him an obvious candidate to challenge the cherished record of 61 that Maris set for the New York Yankees in 1961.

Legend has it that Ruth once predicted he'd hit a home run as he stepped into the batter's box. McGwire maintained that he not only didn't know when he'd hit one, he didn't try to hit the ball over the fence. "Never," he said. "You cannot try to hit a home run. It just happens."

Baseball was in a home run frenzy in 1998. Players were bigger and stronger and there wasn't enough pitching to go around. Very few pitchers could successfully deal with a smaller strike zone. McGwire opened the season with a grand slam off Los Angeles' Ramon Martinez. Through April, he was part of a pack of power hitters. By the end of May, he had 27 home runs. He had 37 by June 30 and tied Reggie Jackson's record for most homers by the all-star break.

Most of the competitors were well behind McGwire's pace with the exception of Sammy Sosa of the Chicago Cubs. One of the enjoyable sidebars of the home run story was the friendly competition that existed between McGwire and Sosa, who had genuine fondness and respect for each other.

McGwire's biggest controversy came when it was revealed that he took androstendione, an over-the-counter dietary supplement. The substance was legal under baseball policy but McGwire had to defend its use. The issue didn't connect with the public, which was demanding curtain calls after home runs against the home team. Media attention increased but the Cardinals and McGwire set up sensible guidelines to handle the crush. California cool McGwire had a simple message: "Just ride the wave, enjoy it while it's happening because we don't know if this will ever happen again."

McGwire hit No. 61 on his father's 61st birthday. After he crossed the plate, he scooped up his 10-year-old son, Matthew, who was the Cardinals' batboy for the game. No. 62 came off Steve Trachsel of the Chicago Cubs and was an un-McGwire-like line drive that just cleared the fence. He didn't stop there, finishing the season with 70, a number that established a new standard. He hit 65 more in 1999, giving him a record 135 home runs in two seasons. McGwire became the first player to his 400th and 500th home runs in consecutive seasons.

The magic of the 1998 seasons was seeing McGwire launch his high, arcing rockets as camera flashes popped throughout the stadium. "I don't think I will ever let go of the moment," McGwire said. "I don't know if I ever will be here again. So how can I let go?"

SAMMY SOSA

TEAMS
Texas 1989; White Sox 1989–91; Cubs 1992–

Games	.1,409
At-Bats	.5,289
Runs	.841
RBI	.941
Home runs	.336
Hits	.1,413
Doubles	.206
Triples	.35
Stolen Bases	.224
Average	.267
Slugging percentage	.510

The climate was ripe for the single-season home run record to fall: pitching had been diluted by expansion, the strike zone had gotten progressively smaller and hitters were stronger. It was likely that someone was going to take a run at Roger Maris' record of 61 home runs in 1961.

Sosa's infectious enthusiasm and awesome power have made him a huge hit with the fans

But the list of candidates, topped by Mark McGwire and Ken Griffey, Jr. didn't even include Sammy Sosa. Sosa was on the list of good-but-not-great players, a free-swinging 30-year-old whose best home run season had produced 36.

Sosa had become something of a controversial figure in Chicago after the Cubs had lavished a long-term big money contract on him. Detractors pointed to Sosa's deal as further evidence of the Cubs' tradition of mismanagement. The argument against Sosa was that he was an undisciplined hitter who was especially poor in clutch situations. There were numbers to back up the belief. The Cubs were Sosa's third major league organization. The Texas Rangers, who originally signed him, quickly traded him to the White Sox. After just two seasons, they passed him to the Cubs.

Sosa came to baseball late. The fifth of seven children, he grew up in poverty in the Dominican Republic. Sosa's father died when he was seven and the children took jobs to help the family survive. Sammy shined shoes, sold oranges on the street and washed cars to earn money. His sports dream was to become a boxer. At 14, he took up baseball at the urging of his older brother, Jose. The children improvised and played ball with makeshift equipment. Hitting rag balls with a thin stick helped Sosa learn to hit a baseball. He could run well enough to interest scouts, who figured he could learn baseball skills.

In July, 1985, scout Omar Minaya spotted the 16-year-old Sosa at a tryout camp and signed him for the Rangers at the age of 16. The $3,500 bonus helped the Sosa family and Sammy headed north to begin his professional career. He reached the big leagues for the first time in 1989, where Julio Franco became his mentor. After just 25 games with Texas, Sosa was traded to the White Sox.

Sosa was an impatient hitter, which is why the Rangers and White Sox ran out of patience with him. Pitchers came to learn that Sosa would chase bad pitches and they didn't bother to throw him strikes. "Sometimes I go up there and try to hit two home runs in one at bat," Sosa admitted.

At the end of 1992's spring training, the White Sox sent pitcher Ken Patterson and Sosa to the Cubs for George Bell. Sosa spent a good part of his first Cubs season on the disabled list, appearing in just 67 games. In 1993, he batted .261 with 33 home runs, 93 RBIs and 36 stolen bases. He continued to combine power, speed and strikeouts through 1997. His breakthrough 1998 season was overshadowed to some degree by Mark McGwire but Sosa had an advantage McGwire didn't—Sosa's team was in the pennant race. He not only hit 66 home runs, he hit them at opportune times.

On 21 occasions, a Sosa homer put the Cubs ahead. Six times his home run tied a game. Ten of them came with a one-run lead and eight others got the Cubs within one. Sosa led the race just twice during the season and those two occasions didn't last long. On August 19, he went ahead 48–47 but McGwire caught him in the eighth and passed him in the 10th. Sosa was ahead 66–65 on September 25 before McGwire tied him within an hour.

Sosa got numbers 61 and 62 in the same game against Milwaukee. He joined McGwire, Babe Ruth and Maris as the only players to hit more than 60. His home run routine became familiar to TV viewers. Sosa would hop out of the box, touch his heart and blow kisses to the nearest camera. The latter, he said, was a dual signal to his mother and to the fans. "I try to make them happy," he said. He did 66 times in 1998.

REGULAR SEASON

The team of the decade was crowned, the umpires called themselves out and the former "Eighth Wonder of the World" was just another obsolete ball park.

Oh, by the way ... Two players topped 60 home runs, but it didn't seem nearly as special the second time around.

The New York Yankees established their credentials as the team of the 1990s by winning another World Series. The Yankees dominated the ten-year period with an efficient machine that ran smoothly under Joe Torre's cool hand.

The Yankees settled into first place on June 9 and held the Boston Red Sox at arm's length the rest of the way. Their balance was unbeatable. Shortstop Derek Jeter hit .349 with 24 home runs and 102 RBIs. Tino Martinez had 28 home runs and drove in 105 runs. Bernie Williams hit 25 home runs and added 115 RBIs. Paul O'Neill drove in 110 runs. The Yankees didn't have a Mark McGwire or Sammy Sosa, who could dominate a game. They had a solid lineup of professional, productive hitters.

Much of the same could be said for their pitching staff, which didn't have a Randy Johnson-styled dominator. Orlando "El Duque" Hernandez won 17 games. Roger Clemens and Andy Pettitte each won 14. The Yankees were solid through middle relief, up to closer Mariano Rivera, who saved 45 games. David Cone had 12 wins, one of which was a perfect game against Montreal in July.

The wild card was the consolation prize for the Red Sox, who won 94 games. They got the last playoff berth by holding off a surprising challenge from the Oakland Athletics.

Pedro Martinez won the pitching Triple Crown with 23 wins, a 2.07 ERA and 313 strikeouts. He became the second pitcher to have more than 300 strikeouts in each league. Shortstop Nomar Garciaparra was Boston's Jeter with a league-leading .357 average, 27 home runs and 104 RBIs. Jimmy Williams handled it all well enough to be chosen as Manager of the Year. The Red Sox reached the postseason in consecutive seasons for the first time since 1917–18.

Toronto's Shawn Green had a 28-game hitting streak and ex-Yankee David Wells won 17 games, tops among American League lefthanders.

It was another disappointing season in Baltimore, where the Orioles got the worst return on their dollars. Cal Ripken, his Ironman streak long over, was knocked out three times by back spasms during the season.

The Cleveland Indians could almost be penciled into the postseason brackets in April.

The Indians were that good and the rest of the American League Central was either too weak or too inexperienced to make any kind of challenge. The Indians spent all but two days in first place and finished 21½ games in front of the Chicago White Sox. They clinched the pennant on September 8.

The Indians set a franchise record by scoring 1,009 runs. They were the first team to score more than 1,000 since 1950. Five players scored at least 100 and four players drove in at

Yankees' manager Joe Torre led his team to another pennant

MOST VALUABLE PLAYER
AL: Ivan Rodriguez, Texas
NL: Chipper Jones, Atlanta

CY YOUNG AWARD
AL: Pedro Martinez, Boston Red Sox
NL: Randy Johnson, Arizona

ROOKIE OF THE YEAR
AL: Carlos Beltran, Kansas City
NL: Scott Williamson, Cincinnati

LEADERS

BATTING AVERAGE
AL: Nomar Garciaparra, Boston Red Sox, .357
NL: Larry Walker, Colorado, .379

HOME RUNS
AL: Ken Griffey Jr., Seattle, 48
NL: Mark McGwire, St. Louis Cardinals, 65

RUNS BATTED IN
AL: Manny Ramirez, Cleveland, 165
NL: Mark McGwire, St. Louis Cardinals, 147

STOLEN BASES
AL: Brian Hunter, Detroit/Seattle, 44
NL: Tony Womack, Arizona, 72

PITCHING VICTORIES
AL: Pedro Martinez, Boston Red Sox, 23
NL: Mike Hampton, Houston, 22

EARNED RUN AVERAGE
AL: Pedro Martinez, Boston Red Sox, 2.07
NL: Randy Johnson, Arizona, 2.48

STRIKEOUTS
AL: Pedro Martinez, Boston Red Sox, 313
NL: Randy Johnson, Arizona, 364

SAVES
AL: Mariano Rivera, NY Yankees, 45
NL: Ugueth Urbina, Montreal, 41

SHORTS It was a season that had its share of tragedy for the Yankees. Two of the team's all-time greats, Joe DiMaggio and Jim (Catfish) Hunter, died during the year. Manager Joe Torre was diagnosed with prostate cancer and three players—Scott Brosius, Luis Sojo and Paul O'Neill—endured the deaths of their fathers during the season.

548

least 100, to set a pair of team records.

Manny Ramirez led the way with a .333 average, 44 home runs and 165 runs batted in. Jim Thome had 33 home runs and 108 RBIs. Richie Sexson added 31 homers and 116 RBIs. Roberto Alomar batted .323 and scored a league-leading 138 runs. Omar Vizquel hit .333 and stole 42 bases.

Bartolo Colon led the staff with 18 wins. Charles Nagy had 17, Dave Burba won 15 games and Mike Jackson had 39 saves.

The Indians won their fifth straight title and the White Sox were the runner-up for the fourth consecutive season. Chicago's Frank Thomas was limited to 135 games and failed to hit at least 20 home runs and drove in 100 for the first time in his career. Thomas wound up with 15 homers and 77 RBIs.

The Detroit Tigers had their sixth consecutive losing season and the Kansas City Royals had the worst winning percentage (.398) in their history. The lone bright spot for the Royals was Carlos Beltran, who became the first rookie in 24 years to have 100 runs and 100 RBIs.

The Western Division champion Texas Rangers had enough offense to overcome shaky pitching. The Rangers' team ERA was 5.07,

which ranked 11th in the league. It was the second-highest mark ever recorded by a team that reached the postseason.

Texas won its third title in four years mainly on the strength of their offense. Their .293 team average was the league's best. Rafael Palmiero hit .324 with 47 home runs and 148 RBIs. Juan Gonzalez batted .326 with 39 homers and 128 RBIs. Ivan Rodriguez batted .332, hit 35 home runs and drove in 113 runs. Lee Stevens hit 24 home runs and Rusty Greer drove in 101 runs. The Rangers had four 100–RBI men and Todd Zeile missed by just two.

Aaron Sele won 18 games while Rick Helling and Mike Morgan each had 13 victories. John Wetteland saved 43 games.

Oakland had its first winning season since 1992 and the Athletics' 13-game improvement was the biggest in the American League. Jason Giambi emerged as a star, batting .315 with 33 home runs and 133 RBIs.

Atlanta won its fifth consecutive National League East title, overcoming its most serious challenge during that streak. The Braves outlasted the New York Mets and clinched on September 26.

Chipper Jones keyed the offense with a .319

TIMELINE

March 10: Yankees' manager Joe Torre was diagnosed with prostate cancer. Medical treatments caused him to miss the last three weeks of spring training and the first 36 games of the regular season.

March 12: Yankees' Hall of Famer Joe DiMaggio died in Florida at the age of 84.

June 9: Astros' first baseman Jeff Bagwell hit home runs in three consecutive at-bats against the White Sox.

June 25: Jose Jiminez of the Cardinals pitched a no-hitter against Arizona as he beat Randy Johnson.

June 27: Ken Griffey Jr. hit a three-run homer in the final game at the Kingdome.

July 4: Pittsburgh Pirates' catcher Jason Kendall suffered a season-ending ankle dislocation when he stumbled over first base in a game against the Milwaukee Brewers.

July 15: Safeco Field opened in Seattle. After years in the prime home run environment of the Kingdome, the new park favored the pitchers.

July 18: David Cone of the New York Yankees pitched a perfect game against the Montreal Expos in an interleague game.

Aug. 6: Tony Gwynn of the Padres got his 3,000th career hit, a single off Dan Smith in Montreal. It was the first of Gwynn's four hits in the game.

Aug. 7: Wade Boggs of Tampa Bay became the first player to hit a home run for his 3,000th career hit. It came off Cleveland's Chris Haney. Boggs retired at the end of the season with 3,010 hits.

Sept. 10: Boston Red Sox's Pedro Martinez struck out 17 in a 3–1 win over the New York Yankees. It was his 21st win of the season.

Sept. 11: Eric Milton of the Twins pitched a no-hitter against Anaheim to improve his record to 7–11.

Oct. 27: The last out of the century was Keith Lockhart's fly ball to Chad Curtis that gave the New York Yankees their 25th World Series title.

Mark McGwire continued where he left off, hitting a remarkable 65 home runs for the Cards

The Cubs' Sammy Sosa again hit over 60 home runs—and was again second best

average, 45 home runs and 110 RBIs. Brian Jordan contributed 23 homers and 115 RBIs. Andruw Jones hit 26 home runs and the Braves won despite the season-long absence of first baseman Andres Galarraga, who was diagnosed with lymphoma.

The strength of the Braves, as usual, was the pitching staff. Atlanta led the league with a 3.63 ERA. Greg Maddux won 19 games and Kevin Millwood had 18 victories and an ERA of 2.68 that was second-best in the league. John Rocker emerged as the closer and saved 38 games.

The Mets wound up making the postseason after winning a one-game playoff against Cincinnati. The Mets lost seven in a row in September, but were able to sweep a season-ending series from Pittsburgh while the Reds were losing two of three in Milwaukee. The Mets won the playoff game 5–0 to claim the wild card berth.

Mike Piazza batted .303 with 40 home runs and 124 RBIs. The infield defense was superb. From third to first, it was Robin Ventura, Rey

SHORTS Never abandon your major league dream. That was the lesson taken from the story of Jim Morris, a high school teacher who wound up pitching for the Devils Rays at age 35. He was encouraged to attend a tryout camp by members of the high school team, who were impressed with how hard their coach threw batting practice to them.

Ordonez, Edgardo Alfonzo and John Olerud, a group that made only 27 errors. They could hit, too. Olerud batted .298 with 19 homers and 96 RBIs. Alfonzo hit .304 with 27 homers and 108 RBIs. Ventura had a .301 average, hit 32 home runs and knocked in 120 runs.

Rickey Henderson came back from a slow start and batted .315 with 37 stolen bases. Roger Cedeno was a pleasant surprise with a .313 average and 66 steals, second in the league.

The Houston Astros lost Randy Johnson as a free agent, but still won the Central Division, edging the Reds at the wire. With four games remaining, the Astros were a game behind the Reds, but Houston beat Cincinnati head-to-head,

Boston's Pedro Martinez dominated the American League as the Red Sox grabbed the wild card

then won two of three from Los Angeles while the Reds were losing to Milwaukee. Mike Hampton had a 22–4 record and 2.90 ERA and Billy Wagner had 39 saves.

Arizona proved that a good plan and plenty of cash can accelerate baseball success. The Diamondbacks went from 65 wins to 100 and set a new standard for swiftness of success by an expansion team. Matt Williams batted .303 with 35 home runs and 142 RBIs. Jay Bell hit 38 homers with 112 RBIs and Tony Womack stole 72 bases.

Randy Johnson was everything he was supposed to be, winning 17 games while leading the league with 364 strikeouts and a 2.48 ERA.

The most bizarre story of the season was a mass resignation by umpires that backfired badly. They submitted resignations, effective September 2, as part of a misguided labor strategy. The plan was rendered useless when some umpires rescinded their resignations while others never officially filed the paperwork. Baseball chose to keep some and said farewell to 22 others, getting what it wanted thanks to the blunder on the part of the union.

McGwire and Sosa scaled back their home run show slightly for an encore. McGwire hit 65 and Sosa had 63, becoming the first two players to top 60 twice.

Several parks closed, including Seattle's Kingdome, which had just hosted its first major league game in 1977. Detroit got more use out of Tiger Stadium, which opened in 1912. No one was sorry to see the San Francisco Giants say farewell to Candlestick Park, whose chilly winds had been bedeviling players and fans alike since 1960.

The original indoor stadium was one of those being abandoned. The Astrodome, a tourist attraction when it opened in 1965, was finally closing for baseball as the Astros prepared to move downtown to a new facility with a retractable roof.

Since the New York Yankees dominated most of the 20th century, it only seemed appropriate that they should end the 1990s with yet another world championship.

NL DIVISION SERIES	
GAME 1	
NY Mets 8	Arizona 4
GAME 2	
Arizona 7	NY Mets 1
GAME 3	
NY Mets 9	Arizona 2
GAME 4	
NY Mets 4	Arizona 3
GAME 1	
Houston 6	Atlanta 1
GAME 2	
Atlanta 4	Houston 1
GAME 3	
Atlanta 5	Houston 3
GAME 4	
Atlanta 7	Houston 5

AL DIVISION SERIES	
GAME 1	
Cleveland 3	Boston Red Sox 2
GAME 2	
Cleveland 11	Boston Red Sox 1
GAME 3	
Boston Red Sox 9	Cleveland 3
GAME 4	
Boston Red Sox 23	Cleveland 7
GAME 5	
Boston Red Sox 12	Cleveland 8
GAME 1	
NY Yankees 8	Texas 0
GAME 2	
NY Yankees 3	Texas 1
GAME 3	
NY Yankees 3	Texas 0

The Yankees, winning their third World Series in four years, wrapped up their record 25th title by sweeping the Atlanta Braves.

Thanks to the 1998 Yankees, who won 125 games counting the regular season and the playoffs, these Yanks had a tough act to follow. The 1999 Yankees weren't quite as powerful, but they still had an impressive season. New York won the American League East with a 98–64 record and advanced to the Division Series against Texas, which won the AL West. The matchup was strictly no-contest as the Yankees rolled to a three-game sweep. The Yankees held the Rangers, who averaged almost six runs a game during the season, to one run in the series.

The Yankees then waited for the results of the other Division Series between Boston, the wild

Roger Clemens finally got his ring winning Game Four in Yankee Stadium

card team and Cleveland, which won the AL Central. Boston ace Pedro Martinez was injured in Game One and the Indians won the first two games in Cleveland. The Red Sox won Game Three in Boston and hammered the Indians, 23–7 in Game Four to tie the series. Martinez made a surprise relief appearance in Game Five and pitched six hitless innings as the Red Sox wrapped up the series with a 12–8 win.

That set up another matchup between the Yankees and Red Sox in the American League Championship Series. The Yankees rallied late to win the first two games in New York. Bernie Williams' tenth-inning home run gave the Yankees a 4–3 win in Game One. The Yankees then rallied for two runs in the seventh to win Game Two, 3–2.

The series moved to Boston. Behind Martinez, who pitched seven shutout innings, the Red Sox rolled to a 13–1 win. The Yankees won Game Four by a 9–2 score before ending the series with a 6–1 victory in Game Five to wrap up their 35th pennant.

The National League playoffs featured the annual presence of the Atlanta Braves, who had won the East title again. Despite losing the first game of the Division Series to Houston, which won the Central, the Braves took the next three games. The other Division Series featured a battle between the Arizona Diamondbacks, who won the NL West, and the New York Mets, the wild-card team. The Mets advanced by winning the series in four games.

It looked like the NLCS would end quickly. The first two games were in Atlanta and the Braves emerged with 4–2 and 4–3 wins. Tom Glavine and two relievers combined on a shutout for a 1–0 win in Game Three in New York. It looked like the Mets were finished, but they rallied for two eighth-inning runs to win Game Four, 3–2. Game Five was another tight duel. The teams took a 2–2 tie into the 15th

Baseball's Team of the Century celebrated their 25th World Championship in style

inning when the Braves scored a run to take the lead. The Mets tied the game on Todd Pratt's bases-loaded walk. The game ended when Robin Ventura hit what appeared to be a grand slam, but he couldn't run around the bases because he was mobbed by his teammates. The hit was ruled a single and the Mets won, 4–3.

Game Six was another good one. Both teams rallied from deficits before the Braves won it, 10–9 in 11 innings when Kenny Rogers walked Andruw Jones with the bases loaded.

The World Series belonged to the Yankees. The first two games were in Atlanta, but that didn't matter to the Yankees. Trailing 1–0 in Game One, they scored four times in the eighth while Orlando Hernandez and three relievers stopped the Braves on two hits for a 4–1 win.

In Game Two, the Yankees scored three times in the first and two in the second. David Cone and two relievers held the Braves to five hits in a 7–2 win.

With the Series in New York, the Braves jumped to a 5–1 lead in Game Three, but couldn't hold it. The Yankees scored a run in the fifth and another in the seventh before Chuck Knoblauch's two-run homer tied the game in the eighth. Chad Curtis' leadoff homer in the tenth gave the Yankees a 6–5 win and the Braves were finished. The Yankees scored three runs in third and Roger Clemens allowed one run in 7⅔ innings for his first World Series win in a 4–1 victory.

The win gave the New York Yankees a title no one could argue with—the Team of the Century.

WORLD SERIES RESULTS

Year	Result
1999	NY Yankees 4, Atlanta 0
1998	NY Yankees 4, San Diego 0
1997	Florida 4, Cleveland 3
1996	NY Yankees 4, Atlanta 2
1995	Atlanta 4, Cleveland 2
1994	Not held
1993	Toronto 4, Philadelphia 2
1992	Toronto 4, Atlanta 2
1991	Minnesota 4, Atlanta 3
1990	Cincinnati 4, Oakland 0
1989	Oakland 4, San Francisco 0
1988	Los Angeles 4, Oakland 1
1987	Minnesota 4, St. Louis 3
1986	NY Mets 4, Boston 3
1985	Kansas City 4, St. Louis 3
1984	Detroit 4, San Diego 1
1983	Baltimore 4, Philadelphia 1
1982	St. Louis 4, Milwaukee 3
1981	Los Angeles 4, NY Yankees 2
1980	Philadelphia 4, Kansas City 2
1979	Pittsburgh 4, Baltimore 3
1978	NY Yankees 4, Los Angeles 2
1977	NY Yankees 4, Los Angeles 2
1976	Cincinnati 4, NY Yankees 0
1975	Cincinnati 4, Boston 3
1974	Oakland 4, Los Angeles 1
1973	Oakland 4, NY Mets 3
1972	Oakland 4, Cincinnati 3
1971	Pittsburgh 4, Baltimore 3
1970	Baltimore 4, Cincinnati 1
1969	NY Mets 4, Baltimore 1
1968	Detroit 4, St. Louis 3
1967	St. Louis 4, Boston 3
1966	Baltimore 4, Los Angeles 0
1965	Los Angeles 4, Minnesota 3
1964	St. Louis 4, NY Yankees 3
1963	Los Angeles 4, NY Yankees 0
1962	NY Yankees 4, San Francisco 3
1961	NY Yankees 4, Cincinnati 1
1960	Pittsburgh 4, NY Yankees 3
1959	Los Angeles 4, Chicago White Sox 2
1958	NY Yankees 4, Milwaukee Braves 3
1957	Milw. Braves 4, N.Y. Yankees 3
1956	NY Yankees 4, Brooklyn 3
1955	Brooklyn 4, NY Yankees 3
1954	NY Giants 4, Cleveland 0
1953	NY Yankees 4, Brooklyn 2
1952	NY Yankees 4, Brooklyn 3
1951	NY Yankees 4, NY Giants 2
1950	NY Yankees 4, Philadelphia 0
1949	NY Yankees 4, Brooklyn 1
1948	Cleveland 4, Boston Braves 2
1947	NY Yankees 4, Brooklyn 3
1946	St. Louis Cardinals 4, Boston Red Sox 3
1945	Detroit 4, Chicago Cubs 3
1944	St. Louis Cardinals 4, St. Louis Browns 2
1943	NY Yankees 4, St. Louis Cardinals 1
1942	St. Louis Cardinals 4, NY Yankees 1
1941	NY Yankees 4, Brooklyn 1
1940	Cincinnati 4, Detroit 3
1939	NY Yankees 4, Cincinnati 0
1938	NY Yankees 4, Chicago Cubs 0
1937	NY Yankees 4, N.Y. Giants 1
1936	NY Yankees 4, N.Y. Giants 2
1935	Detroit 4, Chicago Cubs 2
1934	St. Louis Cardinals 4, Detroit 3
1933	NY Giants 4, Washington 1
1932	NY Yankees 4, Chicago Cubs 0
1931	St. Louis Cardinals 4, Philadelphia A's 3
1930	Philadelphia A's 4, St. Louis Cardinals 2
1929	Philadelphia A's 4, Chicago Cubs 1
1928	NY Yankees 4, St. Louis Cardinals 0
1927	NY Yankees 4, Pittsburgh 0
1926	St. Louis Cardinals 4, NY Yankees 3
1925	Pittsburgh 4, Washington 3
1924	Washington 4, NY Giants 3
1923	NY Yankees 4, NY Giants 2
1922	NY Giants 4, NY Yankees 0 (one tie)
1921	NY Giants 5, NY Yankees 3
1920	Cleveland 5, Brooklyn 2
1919	Cincinnati 5, Chicago White Sox 3
1918	Boston Red Sox 4, Chicago Cubs 2
1917	Chicago White Sox 4, NY Giants 2
1916	Boston Red Sox 4, Brooklyn 1
1915	Boston Red Sox 4, Philadelphia Phillies 1
1914	Boston Braves 4, Philadelphia A's 0
1913	Philadelphia A's 4, NY Giants 1
1912	Boston Red Sox 4, NY Giants 3 (one tie)
1911	Philadelphia A's 4, NY Giants 2
1910	Philadelphia A's 4, Chicago Cubs 1
1909	Pittsburgh 4, Detroit 3
1908	Chicago Cubs 4, Detroit 1
1907	Chicago Cubs 4, Detroit 0 (one tie)
1906	Chicago White Sox 4, Chicago Cubs 2
1905	NY Giants 4, Philadelphia A's 1
1904	Not held
1903	Boston Red Sox 5, Pittsburgh 3

WORLD SERIES MOST VALUABLE PLAYER AWARD

Year	Player	Team
1999	Mariano Rivera	NY Yankees
1998	Scott Brosius	NY Yankees
1997	Livan Hernandez	Florida
1996	John Wetteland	NY Yankees
1995	Tom Glavine	Atlanta
1994	No World Series Played	
1993	Paul Molitor	Toronto
1992	Pat Borders	Toronto
1991	Jack Morris	Minnesota
1990	Jose Rijo	Cincinnati
1989	Dave Stewart	Oakland
1988	Orel Hershiser	Los Angeles
1987	Frank Viola	Minnesota
1986	Ray Knight	NY Mets
1985	Bret Saberhagen	Kansas City
1984	Alan Trammell	Detroit
1983	Rick Dempsey	Baltimore
1982	Darrell Porter	St. Louis
1981	Ron Cey	Los Angeles
1981	Pedro Guerrero	Los Angeles
1981	Steve Yeager	Los Angeles
1980	Mike Schmidt	Philadelphia
1979	Willie Stargell	Pittsburgh
1978	Bucky Dent	NY Yankees
1977	Reggie Jackson	NY Yankees
1976	Johnny Bench	Cincinnati
1975	Pete Rose	Cincinnati
1974	Rollie Fingers	Oakland
1973	Reggie Jackson	Oakland
1972	Gene Tenace	Oakland
1971	Roberto Clemente	Pittsburgh
1970	Brooks Robinson	Baltimore
1969	Donn Clendenon	NY Mets
1968	Mickey Lolich	Detroit
1967	Bob Gibson	St. Louis
1966	Frank Robinson	Baltimore
1965	Sandy Koufax	Los Angeles
1964	Bob Gibson	St. Louis
1963	Sandy Koufax	Los Angeles
1962	Ralph Terry	NY Yankees
1961	Whitey Ford	NY Yankees
1960	Bobby Richardson	NY Yankees
1959	Larry Sherry	Los Angeles
1958	Bob Turley	NY Yankees
1957	Lew Burdette	Milwaukee
1956	Don Larsen	NY Yankees
1955	Johnny Podres	Brooklyn

WORLD SERIES ALL-TIME LEADERS

BATTING

Batting Average

1	Bobby Brown	.439
2	Paul Molitor	.418
	Pepper Martin	.418
3	Hal McRae	.400
4	Lou Brock	.391
5	Marquis Grissom	.390
6	George Brett	.373
	Thurman Munson	.373
7	Pat Borders	.372
8	Hank Aaron	.364
9	Frank Baker	.363
10	Roberto Clemente	.362

Games

1	Yogi Berra	75
2	Mickey Mantle	65
3	Elston Howard	54

4	Hank Bauer	53
	Gil McDougald	53
6	Phil Rizzuto	52
7	Joe DiMaggio	51
8	Frankie Frisch	50
9	Pee Wee Reese	44
10	Babe Ruth	41
	Roger Maris	41

At Bats

1	Yogi Berra	259
2	Mickey Mantle	230
3	Joe DiMaggio	199
4	Frankie Frisch	197
5	Gil McDougald	190
6	Hank Bauer	188
7	Phil Rizzuto	183
8	Elston Howard	171
9	Pee Wee Reese	169
10	Roger Maris	152

Hits

1	Yogi Berra	71
2	Mickey Mantle	59
3	Frankie Frisch	58
4	Joe DiMaggio	54
5	Hank Bauer	46
	Pee Wee Reese	46
7	Phil Rizzuto	45
	Gil McDougald	45
9	Lou Gehrig	43
10	Elston Howard	42
	Babe Ruth	42
	Eddie Collins	42

Home Runs

1	Mickey Mantle	18
2	Babe Ruth	15
3	Yogi Berra	12
4	Duke Snider	11
5	Reggie Jackson	10
	Lou Gehrig	10
7	Joe DiMaggio	8
	Bill Skowron	8
	Frank Robinson	8
10	Hank Bauer	7
	Gil McDougald	7
	Goose Goslin	7

Runs Batted In

1	Mickey Mantle	40
2	Yogi Berra	39
3	Lou Gehrig	35
4	Babe Ruth	33
5	Joe DiMaggio	30
6	Bill Skowron	29
7	Duke Snider	26
8	Reggie Jackson	24
	Hank Bauer	24
	Bill Dickey	24
	Gil McDougald	24

Stolen Bases

1	Lou Brock	14
	Eddie Collins	14
3	Frank Chance	10
	Dave Lopes	10
	Phil Rizzuto	10
6	Frank Frisch	9
	Honus Wagner	9
8	Johnny Evers	8
9	Roberto Alomar	7
	Rickey Henderson	7
	Pepper Martin	7
	Joe Morgan	7
	Joe Tinker	7

WORLD SERIES ALL-TIME LEADERS

PITCHING

Wins

1	Whitey Ford	10
2	Bob Gibson	7
	Allie Reynolds	7
	Red Ruffing	7
5	Chief Bender	6
	Lefty Gomez	6
	Waite Hoyt	6
8	Three Finger Brown	5
	Jack Coombs	5
	Jim Hunter	5
	Herb Pennock	5
	Vic Raschi	5
	Christy Mathewson	5

Innings Pitched

1	Whitey Ford	146.0
2	Christy Mathewson	101.2
3	Red Ruffing	85.2
4	Chief Bender	85.0
5	Waite Hoyt	83.2
6	Bob Gibson	81.0
7	Art Nehf	79.0
8	Allie Reynolds	77.1
9	Jim Palmer	64.2
10	Jim Hunter	63.0

Losses

1	Whitey Ford	8
2	Joe Bush	5
	Rube Marquard	5
	Christy Mathewson	5
	Eddie Plank	5
	Schoolboy Rowe	5
7	14 players with	4

Saves

1	Rollie Fingers	6
2	Johnny Murphy	4
	Allie Reynolds	4
	John Wetteland	4
5	Elroy Face	3

	Firpo Marberry	3
	Herb Pennock	3
	Will McEnaney	3
	Tug McGraw	3
	Kent Tekulve	3
	Todd Worrell	3
	Mariano Rivera	3

Strikeouts

1	Whitey Ford	94
2	Bob Gibson	92
3	Allie Reynolds	62
4	Sandy Koufax	61
	Red Ruffing	61
6	Chief Bender	59
7	George Earnshaw	56
8	Waite Hoyt	49
9	Christy Mathewson	48
10	Bob Turley	46

Walks

1	Whitey Ford	34
2	Art Nehf	32
	Allie Reynolds	32

Babe Ruth

Roger Maris

4	Jim Palmer	31
5	Bob Turley	29
6	Paul Derringer	27
	Red Ruffing	27
8.	Burleigh Grimes	26
	Don Gullet	26
10	Vic Raschi	25

Complete Games

1	Christy Mathewson	10
2	Chief Bender	9
3	Bob Gibson	8
	Red Ruffing	8
5	Whitey Ford	7
6	Waite Hoyt	6
	George Mullin	6
8	Art Nehf	6
	Eddie Plank	6
10	Three Finger Brown	5
	Joe Bush	5
	Bill Donovan	5
	George Earnshaw	5

Shutouts

1	Christy Mathewson	4
2	Three Finger Brown	3
	Whitey Ford	3
4	Lew Burdette	2
	Bill Dinneen	2
	Bob Gibson	2
	Bill Hallahan	2
	Sandy Koufax	2
	Art Nehf	2
	Allie Reynolds	2

LEAGUE CHAMPIONSHIP SERIES RESULTS

AMERICAN LEAGUE

Date	Result
1999	NY Yankees 4, Boston Red Sox 1
1998	NY Yankees 4, Cleveland 2
1997	Cleveland 4, Baltimore 2
1996	NY Yankees 4, Baltimore 1
1995	Cleveland 4, Seattle 2
1994	Not held
1993	Toronto 4, Chicago 2
1992	Toronto 4, Oakland 2
1991	Minnesota 4, Toronto 1
1990	Oakland 4, NY Yankees 0
1989	Oakland 4, Toronto 1
1988	Oakland 4, NY Yankees 0
1987	Minnesota 4, Detroit 1
1986	NY Yankees 4, California 3
1985	Kansas City 4, Toronto 3
1984	Detroit 3, Kansas City 0
1983	Baltimore 3, Chicago 1
1982	Milwaukee 3, California 2
1981	NY Yankees 3, Oakland 0
1980	Kansas City 3, New York 0
1979	Baltimore 3, California 1
1978	NY Yankees 3, Kansas City 1
1977	NY Yankees 3, Kansas City 2
1976	NY Yankees 3, Kansas City 2
1975	NY Yankees 3, Oakland 0
1974	Oakland 3, Baltimore 1
1973	Oakland 3, Baltimore 2
1972	Oakland 3, Detroit 2
1971	Baltimore 3, Oakland 0
1970	Baltimore 3, Minnesota 0
1969	Baltimore 3, Minnesota 0

NATIONAL LEAGUE

Year	Result
1999	Atlanta 4, NY Mets 2
1998	San Diego 4, Atlanta 2
1997	Florida 4, Atlanta 2
1996	Atlanta 4, St. Louis Cardinals 3
1995	Atlanta 4, Cincinnati 0
1994	Not held
1993	Philadelphia 4, Atlanta 2
1992	Atlanta 4, Pittsburgh 3
1991	Atlanta 4, Pittsburgh 3
1990	Cincinnati 4, Pittsburgh 2
1989	San Francisco 4, Chicago Cubs 1
1988	Los Angeles 4, New York 3
1987	St. Louis Cardinals 4, San Francisco 3
1986	NY Mets 4, Houston 2
1985	St. Louis Cardinals 4, Los Angeles 2
1984	San Diego 3, Chicago Cubs 2
1983	Philadelphia 3, Los Angeles
1982	St. Louis Cardinals 3, Atlanta 0
1981	Los Angeles 3, Montreal 2
1980	Philadelphia 3, Houston 2
1979	Pittsburgh 3, Cincinnati
1978	Los Angeles 3, Philadelphia 1
1977	Los Angeles 3, Philadelphia 1
1976	Cincinnati 3, Philadelphia 0
1975	Cincinnati 3, Pittsburgh 0
1974	Los Angeles 3, Pittsburgh 1
1973	NY Mets 3, Cincinnati 2
1972	Cincinnati 3, Pittsburgh 2
1971	Pittsburgh 3, San Francisco 1
1970	Cincinnati 3, Pittsburgh 0
1969	NY Mets 3, Atlanta 0

DIVISION SERIES RESULTS

AMERICAN LEAGUE

Year	Result
1999	Boston Red Sox 3, Cleveland 2
1999	NY Yankees 3, Texas 0
1998	Cleveland 3, Boston Red Sox 1
1998	NY Yankees 3, Texas 0
1997	Cleveland 3, NY Yankees 2
1997	Baltimore 3, Seattle 1
1996	NY Yankees 3, Texas 1
1996	Baltimore 3, Cleveland 1
1995	Seattle 3, NY Yankees 2
1995	Cleveland 3, Boston Red Sox 0

NATIONAL LEAGUE

Year	Result
1999	NY Mets 3, Arizona 1
1999	Atlanta 3, Houston 1
1998	San Diego 3, Houston 1

1998   Atlanta 3 , Chicago Cubs 0
1997   Florida 3, San Francisco 0
1997   Atlanta 3, Houston 0
1996   St. Louis Cardinals 3, San Diego 0
1996   Atlanta 3, Los Angeles 0
1995   Cincinnati 3, Los Angeles 0
1995   Atlanta 3, Colorado 1

ALL-STAR GAME RESULTS

Date	Host	Result
1999 July 13	Fenway Park, Boston	AL 4–1
1998 July 7	Coors Field, Colorado	AL 13–8
1997 July 8	Jacobs Field, Cleveland	AL 3–1
1996 July 9	Veterans Stadium, Philadelphia	NL 6–0
1995 July 11	The Ballpark in Arlington	NL 3–2
1994 July 12	Three Rivers Stadium, Pittsburgh	NL 8–7
1993 July 13	Camden Yards, Baltimore	AL 9–3
1992 July 14	Jack Murphy Stadium, San Diego	AL 13–6
1991 July 9	SkyDome, Toronto	AL 4–2
1990 July 10	Wrigley Field, Chicago	AL 2–0
1989 July 11	Anaheim Stadium, Anaheim	AL 5–3
1988 July 12	Riverfront Stadium, Cincinnati	AL 2–1
1987 July 14	Oakland Coliseum, Oakland	NL 2–0
1986 July 15	Astrodome, Houston	AL 3–2
1985 July 16	Metrodome, Minneapolis	NL 6–1
1984 July 10	Candlestick Park, San Francisco	NL 3–1
1983 July 6	Comiskey Park, Chicago	AL 13–3
1982 July 13	Olympic Stadium, Montreal	NL 4–1
1981 Aug. 9	Cleveland Stadium, Cleveland	NL 5–4
1980 July 8	Dodger Stadium, Los Angeles	NL 4–2
1979 July 17	Kingdome, Seattle	NL 7–6
1978 July 11	San Diego Stadium, San Diego	NL 7–3
1977 July 19	Yankee Stadium, New York	NL 7–5
1976 July 13	Veterans Stadium, Philadelphia	NL 7–1
1975 July 15	County Stadium, Milwaukee	NL 6–3
1974 July 23	Three Rivers Stad., Pittsburgh	NL 7–2
1973 July 24	Royals Stadium, Kansas City	NL 7–1
1972 July 25	Atlanta Stadium, Atlanta	NL 4–3
1971 July 13	Tiger Stadium, Detroit	AL 6–4
1970 July 14	Riverfront Stadium, Cincinnati	NL 5–4
1969 July 23	RFK Memorial Stad., Washington	NL 9–3
1968 July 9	Astrodome, Houston	NL 1–0
1967 July 11	Anaheim Stadium, Anaheim	NL 2–1
1966 July 12	Busch Memorial Stad., St. Louis	NL 2–1
1965 July 13	Metropolitan Stad., Bloomington	NL 6–5
1964 July 7	Shea Stadium, New York	NL 7–4
1963 July 9	Cleveland Stadium, Cleveland	NL 5–3
1962 July 30	Wrigley Field, Chicago	AL 9–4
1962 July 10	D.C. Stadium, Washington	NL 3–1
1961 July 31	Fenway Park, Boston	1–1 tie
1961 July 11	Candlestick Park, San Francisco	NL 5–4
1960 July 13	Yankee Stadium, New York	AL 6–0
1960 July 11	Municipal Stadium, Kansas City	AL 5–3
1959 Aug. 3	Memorial Coliseum, Los Angeles	AL 5–3
1959 July 7	Forbes Field, Pittsburgh	NL 5–4
1958 July 8	Memorial Stadium, Baltimore	AL 4–3
1957 July 9	Busch Stadium, St. Louis	AL 6–5
1956 July 10	Griffith Stadium, Washington	NL 7–3
1955 July 12	County Stadium, Milwaukee	NL 6–5
1954 July 13	Cleveland Stadium, Cleveland	AL 11–9
1953 July 14	Crosley Field, Cincinnati	NL 5–1
1952 July 8	Shibe Park, Philadelphia	NL 3–2
1951 July 10	Briggs Stadium, Detroit	NL 8–3
1950 July 11	Comiskey Park, Chicago	NL 4–3
1949 July 12	Ebbets Field, Brooklyn	AL 11–7
1948 July 13	Sportsman's Park, St. Louis	AL 5–2
1947 July 8	Wrigley Field, Chicago	AL 2–1
1946 July 9	Fenway Park, Boston	AL 12–0
1945	Game canceled	
1944 July 11	Forbes Field, Pittsburgh	NL 7–1
1943 July 13	Shibe Park, Philadelphia	AL 5–3
1942 July 6	Polo Grounds, New York	AL 3–1
1941 July 8	Briggs Stadium, Detroit	AL 7–5
1940 July 9	Sportsman's Park, St. Louis	NL 4–0
1939 July 11	Yankee Stadium, New York	AL 3–1
1938 July 6	Crosley Field, Cincinnati	NL 4–1
1937 July 7	Griffith Stadium, Washington	AL 8–3
1936 July 7	Braves Field, Boston	NL 4–3
1935 July 8	Cleveland Stadium, Cleveland	AL 4–1
1934 July 10	Polo Grounds, New York	AL 9–7
1933 July 6	Comiskey Park, Chicago	AL 4–2

* The 1952 game was shortened to five innings because of rain.

ALL-STAR GAME MOST VALUABLE PLAYER

Date	
1999	Pedro Martinez, Boston Red Sox (AL)
1998	Roberto Alomar, Baltimore (AL)
1997	Sandy Alomar Jr., Cleveland (AL)
1996	Mike Piazza, Los Angeles (NL)
1995	Jeff Conine, Florida (NL)
1994	Fred McGriff, Atlanta (NL)
1993	Kirby Puckett, Minnesota (AL)
1992	Ken Griffey Jr., Seattle (AL)
1991	Cal Ripken Jr., Baltimore (AL)
1990	Julio Franco, Texas (AL)
1989	Bo Jackson, Kansas City (AL)
1988	Terry Steinbach, Oakland A's (AL)
1987	Tim Raines, Montreal (NL)
1986	Roger Clemens, Boston Red Sox (AL)
1985	Lamarr Hoyt, San Diego (NL)
1984	Gary Carter, Montreal (NL)
1983	Fred Lynn, California (AL)
1982	Dave Concepcion, Cincinnati (NL)
1981	Gary Carter, Montreal (NL)
1980	Ken Griffey Sr., Cincinnati (NL)
1979	Dave Parker, Pittsburgh (NL)
1978	Steve Garvey, Los Angeles (NL)
1977	Don Sutton, Los Angeles (NL)
1976	George Foster, Cincinnati (NL)
1975	Bill Madlock, Chicago (NL)
	Jon Matlack, NY Mets (NL)
1974	Steve Garvey, Los Angeles (NL)
1973	Bobby Bonds, San Francisco (NL)
1972	Joe Morgan, Cincinnati (NL)
1971	Frank Robinson, Baltimore (AL)
1970	Carl Yastrzemski, Boston Red Sox (AL)
1969	Willie McCovey, San Francisco (NL)
1968	Willie Mays, San Francisco (NL)
1967	Tony Perez, Cincinnati (NL)
1966	Brooks Robinson, Baltimore (AL)
1965	Juan Marichal, San Francisco (NL)
1964	Johnny Callison, Philadelphia Phillies (NL)
1963	Willie Mays, San Francisco (NL)
1962	Maury Wills, Los Angeles (NL)
1962	Leon Wagner, Los Angeles (AL)

ALL-TIME LEADERS

CAREER BATTING

Batting Average

1	Ty Cobb	.367
2	Rogers Hornsby	.358
3	Dan Brouthers	.349
4	Ed Delahanty	.346
5	Willie Keeler	.345
	Tris Speaker	.345
7	Billy Hamilton	.344
	Ted Williams	.344
9	Jesse Burkett	.342
	Harry Heilmann	.342
	Babe Ruth	.342

At bats

1	Pete Rose	14,053
2	Hank Aaron	12,364
3	Carl Yastrzemski	11,988
4	Ty Cobb	11,429
5	Eddie Murray	11,336
6	Robin Yount	11,008
7	Dave Winfield	11,003
8	Stan Musial	10,972
9	Willie Mays	10,881
10	Paul Molitor	10,835

Hits

1	Pete Rose	4,256
2	Ty Cobb	4,191
3	Hank Aaron	3,771
4	Stan Musial	3,630
5	Tris Speaker	3,515
6	Honus Wagner	3,430
7	Carl Yastrzemski	3,419
8	Paul Molitor	3,319
9	Eddie Collins	3,313
10	Willie Mays	3,283

Home Runs

1	Hank Aaron	755
2	Babe Ruth	714
3	Willie Mays	660
4	Frank Robinson	586
5	Harmon Killebrew	573
6	Reggie Jackson	563
7	Mike Schmidt	548

8	Mickey Mantle	536
9	Jimmie Foxx	534
10	Mark McGwire	522

Runs Batted In

1	Hank Aaron	2,297
2	Babe Ruth	2,212
3	Lou Gehrig	1,995
4	Ty Cobb	1,961
5	Stan Musial	1,951
6	Jimmie Foxx	1,921
7	Eddie Murray	1,917
8	Willie Mays	1,903
9	Mel Ott	1,860
10	Carl Yastrzemski	1,844

Runs

1	Ty Cobb	2,245
2	Hank Aaron	2,174
	Babe Ruth	2,174
4	Pete Rose	2,165
5	Rickey Henderson	2,103
6	Willie Mays	2,062
7	Stan Musial	1,949
8	Lou Gehrig	1,888
9	Tris Speaker	1,881
10	Mel Ott	1,859

Stolen Bases

1	Rickey Henderson	1,334
2	Lou Brock	938
3	Billy Hamilton	937
4	Ty Cobb	892
5	Tim Raines	807
6	Vince Coleman	752
7	Eddie Collins	743
8	Max Carey	738
9	Honus Wagner	722
10	Joe Morgan	689

Games played

1	Pete Rose	3,562
2	Carl Yastrzemski	3,308
3	Hank Aaron	3,298
4	Ty Cobb	3,034
5	Eddie Murray	3,026
	Stan Musial	3,026
7	Willie Mays	2,992
8	Dave Winfield	2,973
9	Rusty Staub	2,951
10	Brooks Robinson	2,896

ALL-TIME LEADERS

CAREER PITCHING

Wins

1	Cy Young	511
2	Walter Johnson	416
3	Christy Mathewson	373
	Pete Alexander	373
5	Warren Spahn	363
6	Kid Nichols	361

	Pud Galvin	361

Innings Pitched

1	Cy Young	7356.0
2	Pud Galvin	5941.1
3	Walter Johnson	5923.0
4	Phil Niekro	5403.2
5	Nolan Ryan	5387.0
6	Gaylord Perry	5352.0
7	Don Sutton	5281.2
8	Warren Spahn	5246.0
9	Steve Carlton	5216.0
10	Pete Alexander	5189.0

ERA

1	Ed Walsh	1.82
2	Addie Joss	1.88
3	Three Finger Brown	2.06
4	Monte Ward	2.10
5	Christy Mathewson	2.13
6	Rube Waddell	2.16
7	Walter Johnson	2.17
8	Orval Overall	2.24
9	Tommy Bond	2.25
10	Will White	2.28
	Ed Reulbach	2.28

Shutouts

1	Walter Johnson	110
2	Pete Alexander	90
3	Christy Mathewson	79
4	Cy Young	76
5	Eddie Plank	69
6	Warren Spahn	63
7	Nolan Ryan	61
	Tom Seaver	61
9	Bert Blyleven	60
10	Don Sutton	58

Strikeouts

1	Nolan Ryan	5,714
2	Steve Carlton	4,136
3	Bert Blyleven	3,701
4	Tom Seaver	3,640
5	Don Sutton	3,574
6	Gaylord Perry	3,534
7	Walter Johnson	3,508
8	Phil Niekro	3,342
9	Roger Clemens	3,316
10	Ferguson Jenkins	3,192

Games pitched

1	Jesse Orosco	1,090
2	Dennis Eckersley	1,071
3	Hoyt Wilhelm	1,070
4	Kent Tekulve	1,050
5	Lee Smith	1,022
6	Rich Gossage	1,002
7	Lindy McDaniel	987
8	Rollie Fingers	944
9	Gene Garber	931
10	Cy Young	906

Games Started

1	Cy Young	818
2	Nolan Ryan	773
3	Don Sutton	756
4	Phil Niekro	716
5	Steve Carlton	709
6	Tommy John	700
7	Gaylord Perry	690
8	Bert Blyleven	685
9	Pud Galvin	682
10	Walter Johnson	666

Complete Games

1	Cy Young	751
2	Pud Galvin	641
3	Tim Keefe	554
4	Walter Johnson	531
	Kid Nichols	531
6	Mickey Welch	525
7	John Clarkson	487
8	Hoss Radbourn	479
9	Tony Mullane	464
10	Jim McCormick	462

Saves (Since 1969)

1	Lee Smith	478
2	John Franco	416
3	Dennis Eckersley	390
4	Jeff Reardon	367
5	Randy Myers	347
6	Rollie Fingers	341
7	Tom Henke	311
8	Rich Gossage	310
9	Jeff Montgomery	304
10	Doug Jones	301

ALL-TIME LEADERS

SINGLE-SEASON BATTING

Hits

1	George Sisler	257	1920
2	Lefty O'Doul	254	1929
	Bill Terry	254	1930
4	Al Simmons	253	1925
5	Rogers Hornsby	250	1922
	Chuck Klein	250	1930
7	Ty Cobb	248	1911
8	George Sisler	246	1922
9	Heinie Manush	241	1928
	Babe Herman	241	1930

Batting Average

1	Nap Lajoie	.426	1901
2	Rogers Hornsby	.424	1924
3	George Sisler	.420	1922
	Ty Cobb	.420	1911
5	Ty Cobb	.410	1912
6	Joe Jackson	.408	1911
7	George Sisler	.407	1920
8	Ted Williams	.406	1941
9	Rogers Hornsby	.403	1925

Harry Heilmann	.403	1923	

Runs

1	Babe Ruth	177	1921
2	Lou Gehrig	167	1936
3	Babe Ruth	163	1928
	Lou Gehrig	163	1931
5	Babe Ruth	158	1920
	Babe Ruth	158	1927
	Chuck Klein	158	1930
8	Rogers Hornsby	156	1929
9	Kiki Cuyler	155	1930
10	Lefty O'Doul	152	1929
	Woody English	152	1930
	Al Simmons	152	1930
	Chuck Klein	152	1932

Home Runs

1	Mark McGwire	70	1998
2	Sammy Sosa	66	1998
3	Mark McGwire	65	1999
4	Sammy Sosa	63	1999
5	Roger Maris	61	1961
6	Babe Ruth	60	1927
7	Babe Ruth	59	1921
8	Jimmie Foxx	58	1932
	Hank Greenberg	58	1938
	Mark McGwire	58	1997

Runs Batted In

1	Hack Wilson	191	1930
2	Lou Gehrig	184	1931
3	Hank Greenberg	183	1937
4	Lou Gehrig	175	1927
	Jimmie Foxx	175	1938
6	Lou Gehrig	174	1930
7	Babe Ruth	171	1921
8	Chuck Klein	170	1930
	Hank Greenberg	170	1935
10	Jimmie Foxx	169	1932

Stolen Bases

1	Rickey Henderson	130	1982
2	Lou Brock	118	1974
3	Vince Coleman	110	1985
4	Vince Coleman	109	1987
5	Rickey Henderson	108	1983
6	Vince Coleman	107	1986
7	Maury Wills	104	1962
8	Rickey Henderson	100	1980
9	Ron LeFlore	97	1980
10	Ty Cobb	96	1915
	Omar Moreno	96	1980

Walks

1	Babe Ruth	170	1923
2	Mark McGwire	162	1998
	Ted Williams	162	1949
	Ted Williams	162	1947
5.	Ted Williams	156	1946
6	Barry Bonds	151	1996
	Eddie Yost	151	1956

8	Eddie Joost	149	1949
	Jeff Bagwell	149	1999
10	Babe Ruth	148	1920
	Eddie Stanky	148	1945
	Jimmy Wynn	148	1969

ALL-TIME SINGLE-SEASON

PITCHING

Wins

1	Jack Chesbro	41	1904
2	Ed Walsh	40	1908
3	Christy Mathewson	37	1908
4	Walter Johnson	36	1913
5	Joe McGinnity	35	1904
6	Smokey Joe Wood	34	1912
7	Cy Young	33	1901
	Pete Alexander	33	1916
	Christy Mathewson	33	1904
10	Cy Young	31	1902

Innings Pitched

1	Ed Walsh	464.0	1908
2	Jack Chesbro	454.2	1904
3	Joe McGinnity	434.0	1903
4	Ed Walsh	422.1	1907
5	Vic Willis	410.0	1902

ERA

1	Dutch Leonard	0.96	1914
2	Three Finger Brown	1.04	1906
3	Bob Gibson	1.12	1968
4	Christy Mathewson	1.14	1909
	Walter Johnson	1.14	1913
6	Jack Pfiester	1.15	1907
7	Addie Joss	1.16	1908

8	Carl Lundgren	1.17	1907
9	Pete Alexander	1.22	1915
10	Cy Young	1.26	1910

Strikeouts

1	Nolan Ryan	383	1973
2	Sandy Koufax	382	1965
3	Nolan Ryan	367	1974
4	Randy Johnson	364	1999
5	Rube Waddell	349	1904
6	Bob Feller	348	1946
7	Nolan Ryan	341	1977
8	Nolan Ryan	329	1972
	Randy Johnson	329	1998
10	Nolan Ryan	327	1976

Shutouts

1	Pete Alexander	16	1916
2	Jack Coombs	13	1910
	Bob Gibson	13	1968
4	Christy Mathewson	12	1908
	Pete Alexander	12	1915

Saves

1	Bobby Thigpen	57	1990
2	Trevor Hoffman	53	1998
	Randy Myers	53	1993
4	Rod Beck	51	1998
	Dennie Eckersley	51	1992
6	Dennis Eckersley	48	1990
	Jeff Shaw	48	1998
	Rod Beck	48	1993
9	Lee Smith	47	1991
10	5 players with	46	

(left to right) Ty Cobb, Joe Jackson and Sam Crawford

MOST VALUABLE PLAYER AWARD

AMERICAN LEAGUE

1999	Ivan Rodriguez, Texas, c	
1998	Juan Gonzalez, Texas, of	
1996	Juan Gonzalez, Texas, of	
1995	Mo Vaughn, Boston Red Sox, 1b	
1994	Frank Thomas, Chicago White Sox, 1b	
1992	Dennis Eckersley, Oakland, p	
1991	Cal Ripken Jr., Baltimore, ss	
1990	Rickey Henderson, Oakland, of	
1989	Robin Yount, Milwaukee, of	
1987	George Bell, Toronto, of	
1986	Roger Clemens, Boston Red Sox, p	
1985	Don Mattingly, NY Yankees, 1b	
1984	Willie Hernandez, Detroit, p	
1983	Cal Ripken Jr., Baltimore, ss	
1982	Robin Yount, Milwaukee, ss	
1981	Rollie Fingers, Milwaukee, p	
1980	George Brett, Kansas City, 3b	
1979	Don Baylor, California, of	
1978	Jim Rice, Boston Red Sox, of	
1977	Rod Carew, Minnesota, 1b	
1976	Thurman Munson, NY Yankees, c	
1975	Fred Lynn, Boston Red Sox, of	
1974	Jeff Burroughs, Texas, of	
1972	Richie Allen, Chicago White Sox, 1b	
1971	Vida Blue, Oakland, p	
1970	Boog Powell, Baltimore, 1b	
1969	Harmon Killebrew, Minnesota 1b/3b	
1967	Carl Yastrzemski, Boston Red Sox, of	
1965	Zoilo Versalles, Minnesota, ss	

1964	Brooks Robinson, Baltimore, 3b
1963	Elston Howard, NY Yankees, c
1962	Mickey Mantle, NY Yankees, of
1961	Roger Maris, NY Yankees, of
1960	Roger Maris, NY Yankees, of
1959	Nellie Fox, Chicago White Sox, 2b
1958	Jackie Jensen, Boston Red Sox, of
1957	Mickey Mantle, NY Yankees, of
1955	Yogi Berra, NY Yankees, c
1954	Yogi Berra, NY Yankees, c
1952	Bobby Shantz, Philadelphia, p
1951	Yogi Berra, NY Yankees, c
1950	Phil Rizzuto, NY Yankees, ss
1949	Ted Williams, Boston Red Sox, of
1948	Lou Boudreau, Cleveland, ss
1947	Joe DiMaggio, NY Yankees, of
1946	Ted Williams, Boston Red Sox, of
1945	Hal Newhouser, Detroit, p
1944	Hal Newhouser, Detroit, p
1943	Spud Chandler, NY Yankees, p
1942	Joe Gordon, NY Yankees, 2b
1941	Joe DiMaggio, NY Yankees, of
1940	Hank Greenberg, Detoit, of
1939	Joe DiMaggio, NY Yankees, of
1938	Jimmie Foxx, Boston Red Sox, 1b
1937	Charlie Gehringer, Detroit, 2b
1936	Lou Gehrig, NY Yankees, 1b
1934	Mickey Cochrane, Detroit, c
1933	Jimmie Foxx, Philadelphia, 1b
1932	Jimmie Foxx, Philadelphia, 1b
1931	Lefty Grove, Philadelphia, p

NATIONAL LEAGUE

1999	Chipper Jones, Atlanta, 3B
1998	Sammy Sosa, Chicago Cubs, of
1997	Larry Walker, Colorado, of
1995	Barry Larkin, Cincinnati, ss
1993	Barry Bonds, San Francisco, of
1992	Barry Bonds, Pittsburgh, of
1991	Terry Pendleton, Atlanta, 3b
1990	Barry Bonds, Pittsburgh, of
1989	Kevin Mitchell, San Francisco, of
1988	Kirk Gibson, Los Angeles, of
1987	Andre Dawson, Chicago Cubs, of
1986	Mike Schmidt, Philadelphia, 3b
1985	Willie McGee, St. Louis Cardinals, of
1984	Ryne Sandberg, Chicago Cubs, 2b
1983	Dale Murphy, Atlanta, of
1982	Dale Murphy, Atlanta, of
1981	Mike Schmidt, Philadelphia, 3b
1980	Mike Schmidt, Philadelphia, 3b
1979	(tie) Keith Hernandez, St. Louis Cardinals, 1b; Willie Stargell, Pittsburgh, 1b
1978	Dave Parker, Pittsburgh, of
1977	George Foster, Cincinnati, of
1976	Joe Morgan, Cincinnati, 2b
1975	Joe Morgan, Cincinnati, 2b
1974	Steve Garvey, Los Angeles, 1b
1973	Pete Rose, Cincinnati, of
1972	Johnny Bench, Cincinnati, c
1971	Joe Torre, St. Louis Cardinals, 3b
1970	Johnny Bench, Cincinnati, c
1969	Willie McCovey, San Francisco, 1b
1968	Bob Gibson, St. Louis Cardinals, p
1966	Roberto Clemente, Pittsburgh, of
1965	Willie Mays, San Francisco, of
1964	Ken Boyer, St. Louis Cardinals, 3b
1963	Sandy Koufax, Los Angeles, p
1962	Maury Wills, Los Angeles, ss
1961	Frank Robinson, Cincinnati, of
1960	Dick Groat, Pittsburgh, ss
1959	Ernie Banks, Chicago Cubs, ss
1958	Ernie Banks, Chicago Cubs, ss
1957	Hank Aaron, Milwaukee, of
1956	Don Newcombe, Brooklyn, p
1955	Roy Campanella, Brooklyn, c
1954	Willie Mays, NY Giants, of
1953	Roy Campanella, Brooklyn, c
1952	Hank Sauer, Chicago Cubs, of
1951	Roy Campanella, Brooklyn, c
1950	Jim Konstanty, Philadelphia, p
1949	Jackie Robinson, Brooklyn, 2b
1948	Stan Musial, St. Louis Cardinals, of
1947	Bob Elliott, Boston Braves, 3b
1946	Stan Musial, St. Louis Cardinals,
1945	Phil Cavarretta, Chicago Cubs, 1b
1944	Marty Marion, St. Louis Cardinals, ss
1943	Stan Musial, St. Louis Cardinals, of
1942	Mort Cooper, St. Louis Cardinals, p

Willie Mays

1941	Dolph Camilli, Brooklyn, 1b
1940	Frank McCormick, Cincinnati, 1b
1939	Bucky Walters, Cincinnati, p
1938	Ernie Lombardi, Cincinnati, c
1937	Joe Medwick, St. Louis Cardinals, of
1936	Carl Hubbell, NY Giants, p
1935	Gabby Hartnett, Chicago Cubs, c
1934	Dizzy Dean, St. Louis Cardinals, p
1933	Carl Hubbell, NY Giants, p
1932	Chuck Klein, Philadelphia, of
1931	Frankie Frisch, St.Louis Cardinals, 2b

CY YOUNG AWARD WINNERS

AMERICAN LEAGUE

Year	Result
1999	Pedro Martinez, Boston Red Sox
1997	Roger Clemens, Toronto
1996	Pat Hentgen, Toronto
1995	Randy Johnson, Seattle
1994	David Cone, Kansas City
1993	Jack McDowell, Chicago White Sox
1992	Dennis Eckersley, Oakland
1991	Roger Clemens, Boston Red Sox
1990	Bob Welch, Oakland
1989	Bret Saberhagen, Kansas City
1988	Frank Viola, Minnesota
1987	Roger Clemens, Boston Red Sox
1985	Bret Saberhagen, Kansas City
1984	Willie Hernandez, Detroit
1983	LaMarr Hoyt, Chicago White Sox
1982	Pete Vuckovich, Milwaukee
1981	Rollie Fingers, Milwaukee
1980	Steve Stone, Baltimore
1979	Mike Flanagan, Baltimore
1977	Sparky Lyle, NY Yankees
1976	Jim Palmer, Baltimore
1975	Jim Palmer, Baltimore
1974	Jim Hunter, Oakland
1973	Jim Palmer, Baltimore
1972	Gaylord Perry, Cleveland
1971	Vida Blue, Oakland
1970	Jim Perry, Minnesota
1969	Mike Cuellar, Baltimore; Denny McLain, Detroit
1967	Jim Lonborg, Boston Red Sox

NATIONAL LEAGUE

Year	Result
1999	Randy Johnson, Arizona
1998	Tom Glavine, Atlanta
1997	Pedro Martinez, Montreal
1996	John Smoltz, Atlanta
1993	Greg Maddux, Atlanta
1992	Greg Maddux, Chicago Cubs
1991	Tom Glavine, Atlanta
1990	Doug Drabek, Pittsburgh
1989	Mark Davis, San Diego
1987	Steve Bedrosian, Philadelphia

1986	Mike Scott, Houston
1985	Dwight Gooden, NY Mets
1983	John Denny, Philadelphia
1982	Steve Carlton, Philadelphia
1981	Fernando Valenzuela, Los Angeles
1980	Steve Carlton, Philadelphia
1979	Bruce Sutter, Chicago Cubs
1978	Gaylord Perry, San Diego
1976	Randy Jones, San Diego
1975	Tom Seaver, NY Mets
1974	Mike Marshall, Los Angeles
1973	Tom Seaver, NY Mets
1971	Ferguson Jenkins, Chicago Cubs
1970	Bob Gibson, St. Louis Cardinals
1969	Tom Seaver, NY Mets
1967	Mike McCormick, San Francisco

(NOTE: Only one winner was selected in the major leagues from 1956 to 1966)

1965	Sandy Koufax, Los Angeles
1964	Dean Chance, Los Angeles
1962	Don Drysdale, Los Angeles
1961	Whitey Ford, NY Yankees
1960	Vernon Law, Pittsburgh
1959	Early Wynn, Chicago White Sox
1958	Bob Turley, NY Yankees
1957	Warren Spahn, Milwaukee (NL)
1956	Don Newcombe, Brooklyn (NL)

ROOKIE OF THE YEAR AWARD

AMERICAN LEAGUE

Year	Result
1999	Carlos Beltran, Kansas City
1998	Ben Grieve, Oakland
1995	Marty Cordova, Minnesota
1994	Bob Hamelin, Kansas City
1992	Pat Listach, Milwaukee
1991	Chuck Knoblauch, Minnesota
1989	Gregg Olson, Baltimore
1988	Walt Weiss, Oakland
1986	Jose Canseco, Oakland
1985	Ozzie Guillen, Chicago White Sox
1984	Alvin Davis, Seattle
1983	Ron Kittle, Chicago White Sox
1982	Cal Ripken Jr., Baltimore
1981	Dave Righetti, NY Yankees
1980	Joe Charboneau, Cleveland
1979	(tie) John Castino, Minnesota; Alfredo Griffin, Toronto
1978	Lou Whitaker, Detroit
1977	Eddie Murray, Baltimore
1976	Mark Fidrych, Detroit
1975	Fred Lynn, Boston Red Sox
1974	Mike Hargrove, Texas
1973	Al Bumbry, Baltimore
1971	Chris Chambliss, Cleveland
1970	Thurman Munson, NY Yankees
1969	Lou Piniella, Kansas City

1968	Stan Bahnsen, NY Yankees
1967	Rod Carew, Minnesota
1966	Tommie Agee, Chicago White Sox
1965	Curt Blefary, Baltimore
1964	Tony Oliva, Minnesota
1963	Gary Peters, Chicago White Sox
1962	Tom Tresh, NY Yankees
1961	Don Schwall, Boston Red Sox
1960	Ron Hansen, Baltimore
1959	Bob Allison, Washington
1958	Albie Pearson, Washington
1956	Luis Aparicio, Chicago White Sox
1955	Herb Score, Cleveland
1954	Bob Grim, NY Yankees
1953	Harvey Kuenn, Detroit
1952	Harry Byrd, Philadelphia A's
1951	Gil McDougald, NY Yankees
1950	Walt Dropo, Boston Red Sox
1949	Roy Sievers, St. Louis Browns

NATIONAL LEAGUE

Year	Result
1999	Scott Williamson, Cincinnati
1998	Kerry Wood, Chicago Cubs
1996	Todd Hollandsworth, Los Angeles
1995	Hideo Nomo, Los Angeles
1992	Eric Karros, Los Angeles
1991	Jeff Bagwell, Houston
1990	Dave Justice, Atlanta
1989	Jerome Walton, Chicago Cubs
1988	Chris Sabo, Cincinnati
1986	Todd Worrell, St. Louis Cardinals
1984	Dwight Gooden, NY Mets
1983	Darryl Strawberry, NY Mets
1982	Steve Sax, Los Angeles
1981	Fernando Valenzuela, Los Angeles
1980	Steve Howe, Los Angeles
1979	Rick Sutcliffe, Los Angeles
1978	Bob Horner, Atlanta
1977	Andre Dawson, Montreal
1976	(tie) Butch Metzger, San Diego; Pat Zachry, Cincinnati
1975	John Montefusco, San Francisco
1974	Bake McBride, St. Louis Cardinals
1973	Gary Matthews, San Francisco
1972	Jon Matlack, NY Mets
1971	Earl Williams, Atlanta
1970	Carl Morton, Montreal
1969	Ted Sizemore, Los Angeles
1968	Johnny Bench, Cincinnati
1967	Tom Seaver, NY Mets
1966	Tommy Helms, Cincinnati
1965	Jim Lefebvre, Los Angeles
1964	Richie Allen, Philadelphia
1963	Pete Rose, Cincinnati
1962	Ken Hubbs, Chicago Cubs
1961	Billy Williams, Chicago Cubs

1960   Frank Howard, Los Angeles
1959   Willie McCovey, San Francisco
1958   Orlando Cepeda, San Francisco
1957   Jack Sanford, Philadelphia
1955   Bill Virdon, St. Louis Cardinals
1954   Wally Moon, St. Louis Cardinals
1953   Jim Gilliam, Brooklyn
1952   Joe Black, Brooklyn
1951   Willie Mays, NY Giants
1950   Sam Jethroe, Boston Braves
1949   Don Newcombe, Brooklyn
(NOTE: Only one winner was selected in the major leagues from 1947 to 1948)
1948   Alvin Dark, Boston Braves
1947   Jackie Robinson, Brooklyn

SPECIAL ACHIEVEMNTS

PERFECT GAMES (20TH CENTURY)

Name	Host	Date
David Cone	New York vs. Montreal 6-0	July 18, 1999
David Wells	New York vs. Minnesota 4-0	May 17,1998
Kenny Rogers	Texas vs. California 4-0	July 28, 1994
Dennis Martinez	Montreal vs. Los Angeles 2-0	July 28, 1991
Tom Browning	Cincinnati vs. Los Angeles 1-0	Sept.16,1988
Mike Witt	California vs.Texas 1-0	Sept.30,1984
Len Barker	Cleveland vs.Toronto3-0	May 15,1981
Catfish Hunter	Oakland vs. Minnesota 4-0	May 8, 1968
Sandy Koufax	Los Angeles vs.Chicago 1-0	Sept. 9, 1965
Jim Bunning	Philadelphia vs.New York 6-0	June 21,1964
x-Don Larsen	New York (AL) vs.Brooklyn (NL) 2-0	Oct. 8, 1956
Charles Robertson	Chicago vs.Detroit 2-0	April 30,1922
Addie Joss	Cleveland vs.Chicago1-0	Oct. 2, 1908
Cy Young	Boston vs.Philadelphia 3-0	May 5, 1904

x-denotes World Series

TRIPLE CROWN WINNERS

AMERICAN LEAGUE

	Year	Avg	RBI	HR
Nap Lajoie, Philadelphia A's	1901	.426	14	125
Ty Cobb, Detroit	1909	.377	9	115
Jimmie Foxx, Philadelphia A's	1933	.356	48	163
Lou Gehrig, NY Yankees	1934	.363	49	165
Ted Williams, Boston Red Sox	1942	.356	36	137
Ted Williams, Boston Red Sox	1947	.343	32	114
Mickey Mantle, NY Yankees	1956	.353	52	130
Frank Robinson, Baltimore	1966	.316	49	122
Carl Yastrzemski, Boston Red Sox	1967	.326	44	121

NATIONAL LEAGUE

	Year	Avg	RBI	HR
Rogers Hornsby, St. Louis Cardinals	1922	.401	152	42
Rogers Hornsby, St. Louis Cardinals	1925	.403	143	39
Chuck Klien, Philadelphia Phillies	1933	.368	120	28
Joe Medwick, St. Louis Cardinals	1937	.347	154	31

TRIPLE CROWN - PITCHING

NATIONAL LEAGUE	Year	Win	ERA	K
Christy Mathewson, NY Giants	1905	31	1.27	206
Christy Mathewson, NY Giants	1908	37	1.43	259
Pete Alexander, Philadelphia Phillies	1915	31	1.22	241
Pete Alexander, Philadelphia Phillies	1916	33	1.55	167
Pete Alexander, Philadelphia Phillies	1917	30	1.86	201
Hippo Vaughn, Chicago Cubs	1918	22	1.74	148
Pete Alexander, Chicago Cubs	1920	27	1.91	173
Dazzy Vance, Brooklyn	1924	28	2.16	262
Bucky Walters, Cincinnati	1939	27	2.29	137
Sandy Koufax, Los Angeles	1963	25	1.88	306
Sandy Koufax, Los Angeles	1965	26	2.04	382
Sandy Koufax, Los Angeles	1966	27	1.73	317
Steve Carlton, Philadelphia Phillies	1972	27	1.97	310

AMERICAN LEAGUE	Year	Win	ERA	K
Dwight Gooden, MY Mets	1985	24	1.53	268
Cy Young, Boston Red Sox	1901	33	1.62	158
Rube Waddell, Philadelphia A's	1905	26	1.48	287
Walter Johnson, Washington Senators	1913	36	1.09	243
Walter Johnson, Washington Senators	1918	23	1.27	162
Walter Johnson, Washington Senators	1924	23	2.72	158
Lefty Grove, Philadelphia A's	1930	28	2.54	209
Lefty Grove, Philadelphia A's	1931	31	2.06	175
Lefty Gomez, New York Yankees	1934	26	2.33	158
Lefty Gomez, New York Yankees	1937	21	2.33	194
Hal Newhouser, Detroit Tigers	1945	25	1.81	212
Roger Clemens, Toronto	1997	21	2.05	292
Roger Clemens, Toronto	1998	20	2.65	271
Pedro Martinez, Boston Red Sox	1999	23	2.07	313

ALL-TIME WINNINGEST MANAGERS

Top 20 Major League career victories through the 1999 season.

		Career			Regular Season			Postseason			
		Yrs	W	L	Pct	W	L	Pct	W	L	Pct	Titles
1	Connie Mack	53	3755	3967	.486	3731	3948	.486	24	19	.558	9AL, 5WS
2	John McGraw	33	2866	2012	.588	2840	1984	.589	26	28	.482	10NL, 3WS
3	Sparky Anderson	26	2228	1855	.547	2194	1834	.545	34	21	.618	4NL, 1AL, 3WS
4	Bucky Harris	29	2168	2228	.493	2157	2218	.493	11	10	.524	3AL, 2WS
5	Joe McCarthy	24	2155	1346	.616	2125	1333	.615	30	13	.698	1NL, 8AL, 7WS
6	Walter Alston	23	2063	1634	.558	2040	1613	.558	23	21	.523	7NL, 4WS
7	Leo Durocher	24	2015	1717	.540	2008	1709	.540	7	8	.467	3NL, 1WS
8	Casey Stengel	25	1942	1868	.510	1905	1842	.508	37	26	.587	10AL, 7WS
9	Gene Mauch	26	1907	2044	.483	1902	2037	.483	5	7	.417	—None—
10	Bill McKechnie	25	1904	1737	.523	1896	1723	.524	8	14	.364	4NL, 2WS
11	Tony La Russa	21	1665	1531	.521	1639	1511	.520	26	20	.565	3AL, 1WS
12	Tommy Lasorda	21	1630	1469	.526	1599	1439	.526	31	30	.508	4NL, 2WS
13	Ralph Houk	20	1627	1539	.514	1619	1531	.514	8	8	.500	3AL, 2WS
14	Fred Clarke	19	1609	1189	.575	1602	1181	.576	7	8	.467	4NL, 1WS
15	Dick Williams	21	1592	1474	.519	1571	1451	.520	21	23	.477	3AL, 1NL, 2WS
16	Bobby Cox	18	1571	1247	.557	1521	1204	.558	50	43	.538	5NL, 1WS
17	Earl Weaver	17	1506	1080	.582	1480	1060	.583	26	20	.565	4AL, 1WS
18	Clark Griffith	20	1491	1367	.522	1491	1367	.522	0	0	.000	1AL(1901)
19	Miller Huggins	17	1431	1149	.555	1413	1134	.555	18	15	.545	6AL, 3WS
20	Al Lopez	17	1412	1012	.583	1410	1004	.584	2	8	.200	2AL

Notes: John McGraw's postseason record also includes two World Series tie games (1912, '22); Miller Huggins postseason record also includes one World Series tie game (1922).

WHERE THEY MANAGED

Alston—Brooklyn/Los Angeles NL(1954-76); Anderson—Cincinnati NL (1970-78), Detroit AL(1979-95); Clarke—Louisville NL (1897-99), Pittsburgh NL (1900-15); Cox—Atlanta (1978-81, 1990–), Toronto (1982-85); Durocher—Brooklyn NL (1939-46, 48), New York NL(1948-55), Chicago NL (1966-72), Houston NL (1972-73); Griffith—Chicago AL (1901-02), New York AL (1903-08), Cincinnati NL (1909-11), Washington AL (1912-20); Harris—Washington AL (1924-28, 35-42, 50-54), Detroit AL (1929-33, 55-56), Boston AL (1934), Philadelphia NL (1943), NewYork AL (1947-48); Houk—New York AL(1961-63, 66-73), Detroit AL (1974-78), Boston AL (1981-84); Huggins—St. Louis NL (1913-17), New York AL(1918-29); LaRussa—Chicago AL (1979-86), Oakland (1986-95); St.Louis (1996–)

Lasorda—Los Angeles NL (1976-96); Lopez—Cleveland AL (1951-56), Chicago AL (1957-65, 68-69).

Mack—Pittsburgh NL (1894-96), Philadelphia AL (1901-50); Mauch—Philadelphia NL (1960-68), Montreal NL (1969-75), Minnesota AL (1976-80), California AL (1981-82, 85-87); McCarthy—Chicago NL (1926-30), New York AL (1931-46), Boston AL (1948-50); McGraw—Baltimore NL (1899), Baltimore AL (1901-02), New York NL (1902-32); McKechnie—Newark FL (1915), Pittsburgh NL (1922-26), St. Louis NL (1928-29), Boston NL (1930-37), Cincinnati NL (1938-46); Stengel—Brooklyn NL (1934-36), Boston NL (1938-43), New York AL (1949-60), New York NL (1962-65); Weaver—Baltimore AL (1968-82, 85-86); Williams—Boston AL (1967-69), Oakland AL (1971-73), California AL (1974-76), Montreal NL (1977-81), San Diego NL (1982-85), Seattle AL(1986-88).

MANAGERS - WORLD SERIES VICTORIES

	App	W	L	T	Pct	WS
1 Casey Stengel	10	37	26	0	.587	7
2 Joe McCarthy	9	30	13	0	.698	7
3 John McGraw	9	26	28	2	.482	3
4 Connie Mack	8	24	19	0	.558	5
5 Walter Alston	7	20	20	0	.500	4
6 Miller Huggins	6	18	15	1	.544	3
7 Sparky Anderson	5	16	12	0	.571	3
8 Joe Torre	3	12	2	0	.857	3
9 Tommy Lasorda	4	12	11	0	.522	2
10 Dick Williams	4	12	14	0	.462	2
11 Frank Chance	4	11	9	1	.548	2
12 Bucky Harris	3	11	10	0	.524	2
13 Billy Southworth	4	11	11	0	.500	2
14 Earl Weaver	4	11	13	0	.458	1
15 Bobby Cox	5	11	18	0	.379	1
16 Whitey Herzog	3	10	11	0	.476	1
17 Bill Carrigan	2	8	2	0	.800	2
18 Danny Murtaugh	2	8	6	0	.571	2
19 Ralph Houk	3	8	8	0	.500	2
20 Bill McKechnie	4	8	14	0	.364	2

New York Yankees' Yogi Berra

BASEBALL HALL OF FAME INDUCTEES

HALL OF FAME MEMBERS

Name	Des.	* Elec. Year	Votes Rec.†	Votes cast‡	% of vote	Teams as player
Aaron, Hank	P	1982	406	415	97.8	Milwaukee NL, Atlanta NL, Milwaukee AL
Alexander, Grover C.	P	1938	212	262	80.9	Philadelphia NL, Chicago NL, St.Louis NL
Alston, Walter	M	1983	CV	—	—	St. Louis NL
Anson, Cap	P	1939	C1	—	—	Chicago NL
Aparicio, Luis	P	1984	341	403	84.6	Chicago AL, Baltimore AL, Boston AL
Appling, Luke	P	1964	189	225	84	Chicago AL
Ashburn, Richie	P	1995	CV	—	—	Philadelphia NL, Chicago NL, New York NL
Averill, Earl	P	1975	CV	—	—	Cleveland AL, Detroit AL, Boston AL
Baker, Home Run	P	1955	CV	—	—	Philadelphia AL, New York AL
Bancroft, Dave	P	1971	CV	—	—	Philadelphia NL, New York NL, Boston NL, Brooklyn NL
Banks, Ernie	P	1977	321	383	83.8	Chicago NL
Barlick, Al	U	1989	CV	—	—	
Barrow, Ed	E	1953	CV	—	—	
Beckley, Jake	P	1971	CV	—	—	Pittsburgh NL, Pittsburgh PL, New York NL, Cincinnati NL, St. Louis NL
Bell, Cool Papa	P	1974	SCNL	—	—	Negro Leagues
Bench, Johnny	P	1989	431	447	96.4	Cincinnati NL
Bender, Chief	P	1953	CV	—	—	Philadelphia AL, Philadelphia NL, Chicago AL
Berra, Yogi	P	1972	339	396	85.6	NewYork AL, NewYork NL
Bottomley, Jim	P	1974	CV	—	—	St.Louis NL, CincinnatiNL, St. Louis AL
Boudreau, Lou	P	1970	232	300	77.3	Cleveland AL, Boston AL
Bresnahan, Roger	P	1945	C2	—	—	Washington NL, Chicago NL, Baltimore AL, New York NL, St. Louis NL
Brett, George	P	1999	488	498	98.2	Kansas City, AL
Brock, Lou	P	1985	315	395	79.7	Chicago NL, St. Louis NL
Brouthers, Dan	P	1945	C2	—	—	Troy NL, Buffalo NL, Detroit NL, Boston NL, Boston PL, Boston
Brown, Three Finger	P	1949	C2	—	—	St. Louis NL, Chicago NL, Cincinnati NL
Bulkeley, Morgan	E	1937	CC	—	—	
Bunning, Jim	P	1996	CV	—	—	Detroit AL, Philadelphia NL, Pittsburgh NL, Los Angeles NL
Burkett, Jesse	P	1946	C2	—	—	New York NL, Cleveland NL, St. Louis NL, St. Louis AL, Boston

Name	Des. *	Elec. Year	Votes Rec.†	Votes cast‡	% of vote	Teams as player
Campanella, Roy	P	1969	70	340	79.4	Brooklyn NL
Carew, Rod	P	1991	401	447	89.7	Minnesota AL, California AL
Carey, Max	P	1961	CV	—	—	Pittsburgh NL, Brooklyn NL
Carlton, Steve	P	1994	436	455	95.8	St.Louis NL, Philadelphia NL, SanFrancisco NL, Chicago AL, Cleveland AL, Minnesota AL
Cartwright, Alexander	O	1938	CC	—	—	
Cepeda, Orlando	P	1999	CV	—	—	San Francisco NL, St.Louis NL, Atlanta NL, Oakland AL, Boston AL, Kansas City AL
Chadwick, Henry	O	1938	CC	—	—	
Chance, Frank	P	1946	C2	—	—	Chicago NL, New York AL
Chandler, Happy	E	1982	CV	—	—	
Charleston, Oscar	P	1976	SCNL	—	—	Negro Leagues
Chesbro, Jack	P	1946	C2	—	—	Pittsburgh NL, New York AL, Boston AL
Chylak, Nestor	U	1999	CV	—	—	
Clarke, Fred	P	1945	C2	—	—	LouisvilleNL, PittsburghNL
Clarkson, John	P	1963	CV	—	—	Worcester NL, Chicago NL, Boston NL, Cleveland NL
Clemente, Roberto	P	1973	393	424	92.7	Pittsburgh NL
Cobb, Ty	P	1936	222	226	98.2	Detroit AL, Philadelphia AL
Cochrane, Mickey	P	1947	128	161	79.5	Philadelphia AL, Detroit AL
Collins, Eddie	P	1939	213	274	77.7	Philadelphia AL, Chicago AL
Collins, Jimmy	P	1945	C2	—	—	Boston NL, Louisville NL, Boston AL, Philadelphia AL
Combs, Earle	P	1970	CV	—	—	New York AL
Comiskey, Charley	F/P	1939	C1	—	—	St. Louis AA, Chicago PL, Cincinnati NL
Conlan, Jocko	U	1974	CV	—	—	Chicago AL
Connolly, Tommy	U	1953	CV	—	—	
Connor, Roger	P	1976	CV	—	—	TroyNL, New York NL, New York PL, Philadelphia NL, St.Louis
Coveleski, Stan	P	1969	CV	—	—	Philadelphia AL, Cleveland AL, Washington AL, New York AL
Crawford, Sam	P	1957	CV	—	—	Cincinnati NL, Detroit AL
Cronin, Joe	P	1956	52	193	78.8	Pittsburgh NL, Washington AL, Boston AL
Cummings, Candy	P	1939	C1	—	—	Hartford NL, Cincinnati NL
Cuyler, Kiki	P	1968	CV	—	—	Pittsburgh NL, Chicago NL, Cincinnati NL, Brooklyn NL
Dandridge, Ray	P	1987	CV	—	—	Negro Leagues
Davis, GeorgeS.	P	1998	CV	—	—	Cleveland NL, New York NL, Chicago AL
Day, Leon	P	1995	CV	—	—	Negro Leagues
Dean, Dizzy	P	1953	209	264	79.2	St. Louis NL, Chicago NL, St.Louis AL
Delahanty, Ed	P	1945	C2	—	—	Philadelphia NL, Cleveland PL, Washington AL
Dickey, Bill	P	1954	202	252	80.2	New York AL
Dihigo, Martin	P	1977	SCNL	—	—	Negro Leagues
DiMaggio, Joe	P	1955	223	251	88.8	New York AL
Doby, Larry	P	1998	CV	.	.	Cleveland AL, Chicago AL, Detroit AL
Doerr, Bobby	P	1986	CV	—	—	Boston AL
Drysdale, Don	P	1984	316	403	78.4	Brooklyn NL, Los Angeles NL
Duffy, Hugh	P	1945	C2	—	—	Chicago NL, Chicago PL, Boston AA, Boston NL, Milwaukee AL, Philadelphia NL
Durocher, Leo	M	1994	CV	—	—	New York AL, Cincinnati NL, St.Louis NL, Brooklyn NL
Evans, Billy	U	1973	CV	—	—	
Evers, Johnny	P	1946	C2	—	—	Chicago NL, Boston NL, Philadelphia NL, Chicago AL
Ewing, Buck	P	1939	C1	—	—	Troy NL, New York NL, New York PL, Cleveland NL, Cincinnati
Faber, Red	P	1964	CV	—	—	Chicago AL
Feller, Bob	P	1962	150	160	93.8	Cleveland AL
Ferrell, Rick	P	1984	CV	—	—	St. Louis AL, Boston AL, Washington AL
Fingers, Rollie	P	1992	349	430	81.2	Oakland AL, San Diego NL, Milwaukee AL
Fisk, Carlton	P	2000	397	499	79.6	Boston AL, Chicago AL
Flick, Elmer	P	1963	CV	—	—	Philadelphia NL, Philadelphia AL, Cleveland AL
Ford, Whitey	P	1974	284	365	77.8	New York AL
Foster, Bill	P	1996	CV	—	—	Negro Leagues
Foster, Rube	P	1981	CV	—	—	Negro Leagues
Fox, Nellie	P	1997	CV	—	—	Philadelphia AL, Chicago AL, Houston NL
Foxx, Jimmie	P	1951	179	226	79.2	Philadelphia AL, Boston AL, Chicago NL, Philadelphia NL

Name	Des.	* Elec. Year	Votes Rec.†	Votes cast‡	% of vote	Teams as player
Frick, Ford	E	1970	CV	—	—	
Frisch, Frank	P	1947	136	161	84.5	New York NL, St.Louis NL
Galvin, Pud	P	1965	CV	—	—	Buffalo NL, Pittsburgh AA, Pittsburgh NL, Pittsburgh PL, St. Louis
Gehrig, Lou	P	1939	SE	—	—	New York AL
Gehringer, Charley	P	949	159	187	85.0	Detroit AL
Gibson, Bob	P	1981	337	401	84.0	St. Louis NL
Gibson, Josh	P	1972	SCNL	—	—	Negro Leagues
Giles, Warren	E	1979	CV	—	—	
Gomez, Lefty	P	1972	CV	—	—	New York AL, Washington AL
Goslin, Goose	P	1968	CV	—	—	Washington AL, St.Louis AL, Detroit AL
Greenberg, Hank	P	1956	164	193	85.0	Detroit AL, Pittsburgh NL
Griffith, Clark	M	1946	2	—	—	St. Louis AA, Boston AA, Chicago NL, Chicago AL, New York AL, Cincinnati NL, Washington AL
Grimes, Burleigh	P	1964	CV	—	—	Pittsburgh NL, Brooklyn NL, New York NL, Boston NL, St. Louis
Grove, Lefty	P	1947	123	161	76.4	Philadelphia AL, Boston AL
Hafey, Chick	P	1971	CV	—	—	St.Louis NL, Cincinnati NL
Haines, Jesse	P	1970	CV	—	—	Cincinnati NL, St. Louis NL
Hamilton, Billy	P	1961	CV	—	—	Kansas City AA, Philadelphia NL, Boston NL
Hanlon, Ned	M	1996	CV	—	—	Cleveland NL, Detroit NL, Pittsburgh NL, Pittsburgh PL, Baltimore NL
Harridge, Will	E	1972	CV	—	—	
Harris, Bucky	M	1975	CV	—	—	Washington AL, Detroit AL
Hartnett, Gabby	P	1955	195	251	77.7	Chicago NL, New York NL
Heilmann, Harry	P	1952	203	234	86.8	Detroit AL, Cincinnati NL
Herman, Billy	P	1975	CV	—	—	Chicago NL, Brooklyn NL, Boston NL, Pittsburgh NL
Hooper, Harry	P	1971	CV	—	—	Boston AL, Chicago AL
Horsby, Rogers	P	1942	182	233	78.1	St. Louis NL, New York NL, Boston NL, Chicago NL, St. Louis AL
Hoyt, Waite	P	1969	CV	—	—	New York NL, Boston AL, New York AL, Detroit AL, Philadelphia
Hubbard, Cal	U	1976	CV	—	—	
Hubbell, Carl	P	1947	140	161	87.0	New York NL
Huggins, Miller	M	1964	CV	—	—	Cincinnati NL, St. Louis NL
Hulbert, William		1995	CV	—	—	
Hunter, Catfish	P	1987	315	413	76.3	Kansas City AL, Oakland AL, New York AL
Irvin, Monte	P	1973	SCNL	—	—	New York NL, Chicago NL, Negro Leagues
Jackson, Reggie	P	1993	396	423	93.6	Kansas City AL, Oakland AL, Baltimore AL, New York AL, California AL
Jackson, Travis	P	1982	CV	—	—	New York NL
Jenkins, Ferguson	P	1991	334	447	74.7	Philadelphia NL, Chicago NL, Texas AL, Boston AL
Jennings, Hugh	P	1945	C2	—	—	Louisville AA, Louisville NL Baltimore NL, Brooklyn NL, Philadelphia NL, Detroit AL
Johnson, Ban	E	1937	CC	—	—	
Johnson, Judy	P	1975	SCNL	—	—	Negro Leagues
Johnson, Walter	P	1936	189	226	83.6	Washington AL
Joss, Addie	P	1978	CV	—	—	Cleveland AL
Kaline, Al	P	1980	340	385	88.3	Detroit AL
Keefe, Tim	P	1964	CV	—	—	Troy NL, New York AA, New York NL, New York PL, Philadelphia NL
Keeler, Willie	P	1939	207	274	75.5	New York NL, Brooklyn, NL, Baltimore NL, New York AL
Kell, George	P	1983	CV	—	—	Philadelphia AL, Detroit AL, Boston AL, Chicago AL, Baltimore
Kelley, Joe	P	1971	CV	—	—	Boston NL, Pittsburgh NL, Baltimore NL, Brooklyn NL, Baltimore
Kelly, George	P	1973	CV	—	—	New York NL, Pittsburgh NL, Cincinnati NL, Chicago NL, Brooklyn NL
Kelly, Mike	P	1945	C2	—	—	Cincinnati NL, Chicago NL, Boston NL, Boston PL, Cincinnati AA, Boston AA, New York NL
Killebrew, Harmon	P	1984	335	403	83.1	Washington AL, Minnesota AL, Kansas City AL
Kiner, Ralph	P	1975	273	362	75.4	Pittsburgh NL, Chicago NL, Cleveland AL
Klein, Chuck	P	1980	CV	—	—	Philadelphia NL, Chicago NL, Pittsburgh NL
Klem, Bill	U	1953	CV	—	—	
Koufax, Sandy	P	1972	344	396	86.9	Brooklyn NL, Los Angeles NL
Lajoie, Nap	P	1937	168	201	83.6	Philadelphia NL, Philadelphia AL, Cleveland AL
Landis, Kenesaw M.	E	1944	C2	—	—	
Lasorda, Tom	M	1997	CV	—	—	Brooklyn NL, Kansas City AL
Lazzeri, Tony	P	1991	CV	—	—	New York AL, Chicago NL, Brooklyn NL, New York NL

Name	Des.	* Elec. Year	Votes Rec.†	Votes cast‡	% of vote	Teams as player
Lemon, Bob	P	1976	305	388	78.6	Cleveland
Leonard, Buck	P	1972	SCNL	—	—	Negro Leagues
Lindstrom, Fred	P	1976	CV	—		New York NL, Pittsburgh NL, Chicago NL, Brooklyn NL
Lloyd, JohnHenry	P	1977	SCNL	—	—	Negro Leagues
Lombardi, Ernie	P	1986	CV	—	—	Brooklyn NL, Cincinnati NL, Boston NL, New York NL
Lopez, Al	M	1977	CV	—	—	Brooklyn NL, Boston NL, Pittsburgh NL, Cleveland AL
Lyons, Ted	P	1955	217	251	86.5	Chicago AL
Mack, Connie	M	1937	CC	—	—	Washington NL, Buffalo PL, Pittsburgh NL
MacPhail, Larry	E	1978	CV	—	—	
Mantle, Mickey	P	1974	322	365	88.2	New York AL
Manush, Heinie	P	1964	CV	—	—	Detroit AL, St. Louis AL, Washington AL, Boston AL, Brooklyn
Maranville, Rabbit	P	1954	209	252	82.9	Boston NL, Pittsburgh NL, Chicago NL, Brooklyn NL, St. Louis NL
Marichal, Juan	P	1983	313	374	83.7	San Francisco NL, Boston AL, Los Angeles NL
Marquard, Rube	P	1971	CV	—	—	New York NL, Brooklyn NL, Cincinnati NL, Boston NL
Mathews, Eddie	P	1978	301	379	79.4	Boston NL, Milwaukee NL, Atlanta NL, Houston NL, Detroit AL
Mathewson, Christy	P	1936	205	226	90.7	New York NL, Cincinnati NL
Mays, Willie	P	1979	409	432	94.7	New York (Giants) NL, San Francisco NL, New York (Mets) NL
McCarthy, Joe	M	1957	CV	—	—	
McCarthy, Tommy	P	1946	C2	—	—	Boston UA, Boston NL, Philadelphia NL, St. Louis AA, Brooklyn
McCovey, Willie	P	1986	346	425	81.4	San Francisco NL, San Diego NL, Oakland AL
McGinnity, Joe	P	1946	C2	—	—	Baltimore NL, Brooklyn NL, Baltimore AL, New York NL
McGowan, Bill	U	1992	CV	—	—	
McGraw, John	M	1937	CC	—	—	Baltimore AA, Baltimore NL, St. Louis NL, Baltimore AL, New
McKechnie, Bill	M	1962	CV	—	—	Pittsburgh NL, Boston NL, New York AL, New York NL, Cincinnati
McPhail, Lee	E	1998	CV			
Medwick, Joe	P	1968	240	283	84.8	St .Louis NL, Brooklyn NL, New York NL, Boston NL
Mize, Johnny	P	1981	CV	—	—	St. Louis NL, New York NL, New York AL
Morgan, Joe	P	1990	363	444	81.8	Houston NL, Cincinnati NL, San Francisco NL, Philadelphia NL, Oakland AL
Musial, Stan	P	1969	317	340	93.2	St.Louis NL
Newhouser, Hal	P	1992	CV	—	—	Detroit AL, Cleveland AL
Nichols, Kid	P	1949	C2	—	—	Boston NL, St. Louis NL, Philadelphia NL
Niekro, Phil	P	1997	380	473	80.3	Milwaukee NL, Atlanta NL, New York AL, Cleveland AL, Toronto
O'Rourke, Jim	P	1945	C2	—	—	Boston NL, Providence NL, Buffalo NL, New York NL, Washington NL, New York PL
Ott, Mel	P	1951	97	226	87.2	New York NL
Paige, Satchel	P	1971	SCNL	—	—	Cleveland AL, St. Louis AL, Kansas City AL, Negro Leagues
Palmer, Jim	P	1990	411	444	92.6	Baltimore AL
Pennock, Herb	P	1948	94	121	· 77.7	Philadelphia AL, Boston AL, New York AL
Perez, Tony	P	2000	385	499	77.2	Cincinnati NL, Montreal NL, Boston AL, Philadelphia NL
Perry, Gaylord	P	1991	342	44	76.5	San Francisco NL, Cleveland AL, Texas AL, San Diego NL, New York AL, Atlanta NL, Seattle AL, Kansas City AL
Plank, Eddie	P	1946	C2	—	—	Philadelphia AL, St. Louis AL
Radbourn, Hoss	P	1939	C1	—	—	Buffalo NL, Providence NL, Boston NL, Boston PL, Cincinnati NL
Reese, PeeWee	P	1984	CV	—	—	Brooklyn NL, Los Angeles NL
Rice, Sam	P	1963	CV	—	—	Washington AL, Cleveland AL
Rickey, Branch	E	1967	CV	—	—	St. Louis AL, New York AL
Rixey, Eppa	P	1963	CV	—	—	Philadelphia NL, Cincinnati NL
Rizzuto, Phil	P	1994	CV	—	—	New York AL
Roberts, Robin	P	1976	337	388	86.9	Philadelphia NL, Baltimore AL, Houston NL, Chicago NL
Robinson, Brooks	P	1983	344	374	92.0	Baltimore AL
Robinson, Frank	P	1982	370	415	89.2	Cincinnati NL, Baltimore AL, Los Angeles NL, California AL, Cleveland AL
Robinson, Jackie	P	1962	124	160	77.5	Brooklyn NL
Robinson, Wilbert	M	1945	C2	—	—	Philadelphia AA, Baltimore AA, Baltimore NL, St. Louis NL, Baltimore AL
Rogan, Joe Bullet	P	1998	CV	—	—	
Roush, Edd	P	1962	CV	—	—	Chicago AL, New York NL, Cincinnati NL
Ruffing, Red	P	1967	266	306	86.9	Boston AL, New York AL, Chicago AL
Rusie, Amos	P	1977	CV	—	—	Indianapolis NL, New York NL, Cincinnati NL

Name	Des. *	Elec. Year	Votes Rec.†	Votes cast‡	% of vote	Teams as player
Ruth, Babe	P	1936	215	26	95.1	Boston AL, New York AL, Boston NL
Ryan, Nolan	P	1999	491	497	98.8	New York NL, California AL, Houston NL, Texas AL
Schalk, Ray	P	1955	CV	—	—	Chicago AL, New York NL
Schmidt, Mike	P	1995	444	460	96.5	Philadelphia NL
Schoendienst, Red	P	1989	CV	—	—	St. Louis NL, NewYork (Giants)NL, Milwaukee NL
Seaver, Tom	P	1992	425	430	98.8	New York NL, Cincinnati NL, Chicago AL, Boston AL
Selee, Frank	M	1999	CV	—	—	
Sewell, ƒJoe	P	1977	CV	—	—	Cleveland AL, New York AL
Simmons, Al	P	1953	199	264	75.4	Philadelphia AL, Chicago AL, Detroit AL, Washington AL, Boston
Sisler, George	P	1939	235	274	85.8	St. Louis AL, Washington AL, Boston NL
Slaughter, Enos	P	1985	CV	—	—	St. Louis NL, New York AL, Kansas City AL, Milwaukee NL
Snider, Duke	P	1980	333	385	86.5	Brooklyn NL, LosAngeles NL, New York NL, San Francisco NL
Spahn, Warren	P	1973	316	380	83.2	Boston NL, Milwaukee NL, New York NL, San Francisco NL
Spalding, Al	P	1939	C1	—	—	Chicago NL
Speaker, Tris	P	1937	165	201	82.1	Boston AL, Cleveland AL, Washington AL, Philadelphia AL
Stargell, Willie	P	1988	352	427	82.4	Pittsburgh NL
Stengel, Casey	M	1966	CV	—	—	Brooklyn NL, Pittsburgh NL, Philadelphia NL, New York NL, Boston NL
Sutton, Don	P	1998	386	473	81.6	Los Angeles NL, Houston NL, Milwaukee AL, Oakland AL, California AL
Terry, Bill	P	1954	195	252	77.4	New York NL
Thompson, Sam	P	1974	CV	—	—	Detroit NL, Philadelphia NL, Detroit AL
Tinker, Joe	P	1946	C2	—	—	Chicago NL, Cincinnati NL
Traynor, Pie	P	1948	93	121	76.9	Pittsburgh NL
Vance, Dazzy	P	1955	205	251	81.7	Pittsburgh NL, New York AL, Brooklyn NL, St. Louis NL, Cincinnati NL
Vaughan, Arky	P	1985	CV	—	—	Pittsburgh NL, Brooklyn NL
Veeck, Bill	E	1991	CV	—	—	
Waddell, Rube	P	1946	C2	—	—	Louisville NL, Pittsburgh NL, Chicago NL, Philadelphia AL, St. Louis AL
Wagner, Honus	P	1936	215	226	95.1	Louisville NL, Pittsburgh NL
Wallace, Bobby	P	1953	CV	—	—	Cleveland NL, St. Louis NL, St. Louis AL
Walsh, Ed	P	1946	C2	—	—	Chicago AL, Boston NL
Waner, Lloyd	P	1967	CV	—	—	Pittsburgh NL, Boston NL, Cincinnati NL, Philadelphia NL, Brooklyn NL
Waner, Paul	P	1952	195	234	83.3	Pittsburgh NL, Brooklyn NL, Boston NL, New York AL
Ward, John Montgomery	P	1964	CV	—	—	Providence NL, New York NL, Brooklyn PL, Brooklyn NL
Weaver, Earl	M	1996	CV	—	—	
Weiss, George	E	1971	CV	—	—	
Welch, Mickey	P	1973	CV	—	—	Troy NL, New York NL
Wells, Willie	P	1997	CV	—	—	
Wheat, Zack	P	1959	CV	—	—	Brooklyn NL, Philadelphia AL
Wilhelm, Hoyt	P	1985	331	395	83.8	New York NL, St. Louis NL, Cleveland AL, Baltimore AL, Chicago
Williams, Billy	P	1987	354	413	85.7	Chicago NL, Oakland AL
Williams, Smokey Joe	P	1999	CV	—	—	Negro Leagues
Williams, Ted	P	1966	282	302	93.4	Boston AL
Willis, Vic	P	1995	CV	—	—	Boston NL, Pittsburgh NL, St. Louis NL
Wilson, Hack	P	1979	CV	—	—	New York NL, Chicago NL, Brooklyn NL, Philadelphia NL
Wright, George	M	1937	CC	—	—	Boston NL, Providence NL
Wright, Harry	M	1953	CV	—	—	Boston NL
Wynn, Early	P	1972	301	396	76.0	Washington AL, Cleveland AL, Chicago A
Yastrzemski, Carl	P	1989	423	447	94.6	Boston AL
Yawkey, Tom	E	1980	CV	—	—	
Young, Cy	P	1937	153	201	76.1	Cleveland NL, St.Louis NL, Boston AL, Cleveland AL, Boston NL
Youngs, Ross	P	1972	CV	—	—	New York NL
Yount, Robin	P	1999	385	497	77.5	Milwaukee AL

*Designation for which he was honored. Abbreviations: E—executive; F—founder; M—manager; O—organizer; P—player; U—umpire.
†Where an abbreviation is listed rather than a vote total, the enshrinee was selected by one of the following groups: Centennial Commission (CC),
committee of old-time player sand writers (C1), committee on old-timers (C2), Committee on Veterans(CV), special election by Baseball Writers'
Association of America (SE) or Special Committee on Negro Leagues (SCNL). ‡Votes cast by eligible members of the Baseball Writers' Association of America.
League abbreviations: AA—AmericanAssociation; AL—American League; NL—National League; PL—Players League; UA—Union Association.

INDEX

Entries are listed on a word by word basis.

Location references **for pictures** are in bold and italics.

Entries for **titles of books or songs** are in bold and italics.

INDEX

Picture credits

Carlton Books Ltd. would like to thank the following sources for their kind permission to reproduce the pictures in this book:

**Allsport UK Ltd
Corbis-Bettmann/UPI
George Gojkovich
TranscendentalGraphics**

Every effort has been made to acknowledge correctly and contact the source and/or copyright holder of each picture, and Carlton Books Limited apologises for any unintentional errors or omissions which will be corrected in future editions of this book.

The Publishers wish to express their sincere gratitude to Mark Rucker at TranscendentalGraphics for the time and assistance he has contributed to this project.